DATE DUE

DE 13 '99		
JE 5 '00		
DE 15 '00		
NY 21 '01		
NY 29 '02		
DE 21 '02		
DE 15 '03		
JE		
DE 14 '05		

DEMCO 38-296

Gender and Alcohol

Gender and Alcohol

INDIVIDUAL AND SOCIAL PERSPECTIVES

EDITED BY

Richard W. Wilsnack
and
Sharon C. Wilsnack

Publications Division
Rutgers Center of Alcohol Studies
New Brunswick, New Jersey USA

This book is the third in the Alcohol, Culture, and Social Control Monograph Series, funded in part by the Wine Institute. Editors of the series are David J. Pittman and Helene Raskin White.

To V. Maxine Allen Carlson (1914-1995) and Lloyd W. Carlson,
and to
Halina Zaikowski Wilsnack and William H. Wilsnack (1915-1993)

Contents

Acknowledgments

THIS BOOK was undertaken at the invitation of Helene Raskin White and other faculty of the Rutgers Center of Alcohol Studies, who envisioned a book on gender and alcohol as part of the Center's Alcohol, Culture, and Social Control Monograph Series. We appreciate their awareness of the importance of gender in any consideration of alcohol use in a societal context, and their confidence in our ability to edit such a volume.

We are enormously grateful to our editor at Rutgers, Alex Fundock III, for his expert editorial management, his patience and good humor throughout the publication process, and his inspiring ability to maintain high levels of professional productivity and personal "grit" despite demanding personal circumstances.

Authors of the book's 19 chapters deserve special thanks, because our requests to them went well beyond the demands of writing "yet another" review chapter in their particular areas of expertise. For a number of authors whose previous research had dealt primarily with individuals of one sex (usually women), the invitation to take a "gender" perspective added a new dimension to their conceptualization and analysis. The authors' willingness to include, in most chapters, new empirical analyses of their own research data—as well as critical overviews of major theoretical issues and research questions—has, we believe, substantially enhanced the value of the book for students, researchers, and practitioners.

Our own major research project, a national longitudinal study of women's drinking, has been supported since 1980 by the National Institute on Alcohol Abuse and Alcoholism, National Institutes of Health (grant no. R37-AA04610). This long-term support has allowed us to gather unique longitudinal data on women's drinking behavior and drinking problems over a 15-year period (see chapter 10). It has also offered us the chance to observe and participate in the evolution of gender-relevant research on alcohol use and abuse over the past two decades, thus contributing directly to the preparation of this book.

Our colleagues at the University of North Dakota School of Medicine and Health Sciences have provided invaluable professional consultation, practical assistance, and personal support throughout the preparation of this volume. They include our administrative and educational assistants Loraine Olson and Louise Diers; computer specialist Perry Benson; research colleagues Nancy Vogeltanz, T. Robert Harris, and Arlinda Kristjanson; and our supportive and inspirational former department chair, the late Richard P. Stadter. We are also grateful to University of North Dakota colleagues Kathleen Tiemann and Denise Twohey for helpful comments on early drafts of the book's Introduction.

We have dedicated this book to our parents, from whom we have learned a great deal about balanced and flexible gender roles. We also dedicate the book to our children—Joel, Brian, Peter, Kirsten, and Jonathan—with hope that they and their generation can find ways of reducing and eventually eliminating restrictive gender-role stereotypes and their wide-ranging deleterious effects.

RWW
SCW

Introduction

RICHARD W. WILSNACK AND SHARON C. WILSNACK

W hy is it important to read, and to write, a book about gender and alcohol? There are at least five reasons, which are simple to state but which deserve careful explanation. A book that tries to explain relationships between gender and alcohol should prove valuable due to the following:

1. Gender differences in alcohol use occur everywhere. Across cultures and at different times in history, men have consistently consumed more alcohol than women and have caused more problems by doing so.
2. Gender differences in alcohol use are important ways that each culture distinguishes between male and female roles. As a result, gender differences in drinking vary as cultural differences in gender roles vary.
3. Gender differences in alcohol use remain largely unexplained. No one has yet produced a theory or set of variables that adequately explains why gender differences in drinking occur so consistently yet are so variable in size.
4. Gender differences in alcohol use reveal broader differences between women's and men's behavior. Understanding how and why women and men drink differently can give insight into more fundamental characteristics of gender roles, and how gender roles may change or resist change.
5. Gender differences in alcohol use encourage costly biases in how societies try to control or reduce alcohol-related problems. Women's alcohol problems have often been neglected by others as though such problems neither needed nor deserved help, or resulted in punishment instead of treatment. Men have often learned to regard their own alcohol abuse as "normal" until after it has severely damaged their behavior and social relations.

In this Introduction, we try to explain briefly these five reasons for writing this book. In this way readers may gain some sense of the value and context of the findings and ideas provided by the many authors of the chapters that follow.

Gender Differences in Drinking Behavior

A fundamental reason for studying the influence of gender on alcohol use is that the same kind of gender imbalance in drinking behavior occurs everywhere. Men drink more frequently and more heavily than women do, and

1

men's drinking leads to more problems than women's drinking. At a time when research has challenged many supposed gender differences (Caplan & Caplan, 1994; Lorber, 1994), the persistence of this almost universal pattern is a striking exception. It has been confirmed in every major quantitative study of alcohol use or abuse in different societies and cultures (see, e.g., Fillmore et al., 1991, 1995; Helzer et al., 1990; Hupkens et al., 1993; Jaervinen & Olafsdottir, 1989). Although most research on gender and alcohol has studied North Atlantic societies, reports that heavy and problem drinking are predominantly of male origin have come from many parts of Africa (Ambler, 1991; Ikuesan, 1994; Mphi, 1994), Asia and the Pacific (Cheng & Chen, 1995; Higuchi et al., 1994; Kua, 1994; Lee et al., 1990; Toren, 1994), and Latin America (Araya, 1994; Medina-Mora, 1994; Yamamoto et al., 1993). The recurrent pattern of gender differences is typically rooted in cultural traditions (see, e.g., Gefou-Madianou, 1992a; Gotoh, 1994; McDonald, 1994b). When Child and associates (1965) examined descriptions of men's and women's drinking in historical ethnographic accounts of non-European societies, they found many societies where men's alcohol consumption exceeded women's, but none where women's use of alcohol exceeded men's. (They also found many accounts with no clear evidence of gender differences, as would be expected in qualitative ethnographies that did not focus specifically on women's and men's drinking.)

Interest in gender influences on alcohol use might decline if recent social changes (such as in women's education and employment) are giving women the same opportunities and incentives to drink that men have, and as a result are leading to a disappearance of gender differences in drinking behavior. Such a hypothesized convergence of men's and women's drinking patterns has received partial support from trends in some European countries (Hammer & Vaglum, 1989; Saelan et al., 1992). However, in most North American surveys, large gender differences have persisted over time in measures of frequent or heavy drinking in the general adult population (Bell et al., 1984; Ferrence, 1980; Midanik & Clark, 1994) and in collegiate and young adult samples (Johnston et al., 1994; Perkins, 1992; Temple, 1987); any observed declines in the size of gender differences have resulted mainly from declines in men's drinking rather than from increases in women's drinking (Johnson et al., 1994; Midanik & Clark, 1994). In general and internationally, gender differences in alcohol use have failed to disappear as hypothesized (Plant, 1990), increasing the challenge to explain their persistence.

Drinking Patterns as Gender Symbols

Some of the persistent differences in how women and men use alcohol may have a biological basis, if drinking patterns are influenced by observed or hypothesized differences in how women's and men's bodies absorb, distribute, and metabolize alcohol (Frezza et al., 1990; Thomasson, 1995; York & Welte, 1994). However, the *size* of gender differences in drinking behavior varies considerably from one cultural or historical setting to another, and that variation suggests a second important reason for writing this book. Rules and constraints of drinking behavior are important tools for the cultural construction of gender. Differences in how men and women are allowed or encouraged to drink, and to behave when drinking, help define and symbolize the cultural and social-structural distinctions between being a man and being a woman. Ethnography indicates that where gender roles are most clearly divided, so are women's and men's drinking patterns (Child et al., 1965; Gefou-Madianou, 1992a; McDonald, 1994b). Understanding how (and to what extent) women and men drink differently should help us understand better how societies divide the sexes.

For example, ethnographic studies show that drinking has often served men as a masculinity test: by their behavior when drinking heavily, men can (or may be obligated to) demonstrate their stamina, self-control, nonconformity, and willingness to take risks (Driessen, 1992; Gotoh, 1994; McDonald, 1994a). Drinking by male groups, typically in all-male settings, has often been an essential way for men to escape control by others, ignore social differences, gain social support, and form strong personal ties with one another (Gefou-Madianou, 1992b; Hendry, 1994; MacDonald, 1994; Salmore, 1989). Men may also use drinking to try to show their superiority over women, by using alcohol in ways that women are unable to or not allowed to (Ambler, 1991; MacDonald, 1994).

In contrast to men's drinking, women's drinking is more often discouraged or inhibited for fear that it will adversely affect their behavior. It has often been feared that women's intoxication will reduce social control of their sexuality, by making women either more sexually disinhibited or more vulnerable to sexual advances (Gomberg, 1982; McLaughlin, 1991; Purcell, 1994; Snare, 1989; Stewart, 1992). Women's drinking has also been restricted or concealed because intoxication was thought to signal a dangerous failure of social control over women's family relationships and public behavior, threatening the social order (McLaughlin, 1991; Mphi, 1994; Purcell, 1994). Sometimes societies have been tolerant of women using alcohol for medicinal purposes (see, e.g., Kua, 1994; Salmore, 1989), perhaps because self-medication has seemed consistent with social expectations about what women need to perform their roles adequately. However, unnecessary or unrestrained drinking, which might be allowed or even encouraged in men, has often led to condemnation, punishment, and ostracism for women (see, e.g., Driessen, 1992; Ikeusan, 1994; McLaughlin, 1991), perhaps as a reminder of the social power imbalance between men and women.

Gender roles may help create different rules and opportunities for women's and men's drinking. However, the processes by which gender roles and other social or biological factors produce actual (and varying) differences in women's and men's drinking behavior and its consequences remain largely unexplained and uncharted. The need for better explanation is a third important reason for this book, and a reason for the diversity of its contents and contributors.

Explaining Gender Differences in Drinking Behavior

The lack of adequate theories or models to explain gender differences in drinking behavior has at least two causes: (1) the slow and delayed development of research that made it possible to compare women's and men's drinking and its consequences, and (2) the complexity of the drinking behavior to be explained and the ways that gender may influence that behavior.

Gender-Specific Research

Prior to the 1970s, most alcohol research used only male subjects (e.g., McClelland et al., 1972; McCord & McCord, 1960; Tähka, 1966) or, occasionally, included smaller numbers of women but failed to analyze or report gender differences (see Sandmaier, 1980; Vannicelli, 1984). Research was able to neglect the study of women's drinking because heavy and problem drinking were more prevalent among men than among women, men's problems with alcohol (e.g., alcohol-related crime, accidents, or work problems) tended to be more visible and appeared more socially disruptive than women's problems, and male alcoholics were more accessible than female alcoholics as research subjects (e.g., in predominantly male populations at state hospitals and Veterans Administration hospitals) (Curlee, 1967; Keller, 1962; Lisansky, 1958).

Public, political, and scientific interest in women's drinking grew dramatically during the 1970s, specifically spurred by the identification of the fetal alcohol syndrome in 1973 as a distinctive alcohol problem of women (Jones & Smith, 1973), and more generally stimulated by heightened awareness of women's health issues resulting from the women's movement of the 1960s. In a single year in the early 1980s, a leading alcohol journal published abstracts of nearly twice as many research articles on women as the total that had been published between 1929 and 1970 (Wilsnack & Beckman, 1984, p. x). Studies of women have continued to proliferate, many of which have not included comparison groups of men. Such studies have helped to correct the earlier gender imbalance in research attention, and have generated important findings about how drinking patterns and risks of alcohol abuse vary among different subgroups of women (see Galanter, 1995; Gomberg & Nirenberg, 1993; S. Wilsnack, 1995). However, studies of exclusively female samples, like studies of exclusively male samples, cannot compare physiological, psychological, and sociocultural influences on women's versus men's alcohol use, and thus cannot directly reveal how gender differences in drinking behavior and its effects are created and perpetuated.

Complex Relationships

Even when adequate comparative data from women and men become available, it will still be very difficult to construct a unified model of gender influences on alcohol use and its consequences. To begin with, explanations of gender effects must be multidimensional. On the one hand, research on biological differences in how women and men absorb and metabolize alcohol may help to explain some of the consistency of how women and men drink differently, but cannot by itself explain the societal, cultural, and historical variations in gender differences. On the other hand, analyses of cultural and social-structural differences in gender roles can explain some of the variability in gender differences, but cannot adequately explain why men's drinking and drinking problems so consistently exceed women's. Some combination or interaction of many biological, personal, and social characteristics will probably be necessary in any theoretical model that would explain a large part of the gender differences in drinking behavior.

A second complication is that there are many different ways of using alcohol and experiencing consequences, and these outcomes are only loosely connected and may have different causes or predictors (see, e.g., Wilsnack et al., 1987). Even the diagnosis of "alcoholism" or psychiatric alcohol disorders is multidimensional and is likely to have different subtypes (American Psychiatric Association, 1994; Hesselbrock & Hesselbrock, 1993). Furthermore, men and women differ to varying degrees on different measures of alcohol use and effects (e.g., abstention/nonabstention, typical drinking frequencies and quantities, frequency of intoxication, adverse social consequences), even within the same society or cultural subgroup. Therefore, it is likely that any one theory of gender differences in drinking behavior could explain some but not all types of drinking differences.

Finally, it is unlikely that gender differences can be explained adequately by simply adding together causal variables in a linear combination. That level of simplicity would be analogous to believing that one can explain how to bake a cake simply by listing the amounts of ingredients. In reality, the development of patterns of drinking behavior is likely to depend on the timing, contingencies, and nonlinear interactions of many causal influences (see, e.g., Wilsnack & Wilsnack, 1992). Causal models in the social sciences rarely incorporate such complexity.

Contributions of this Book

The difficult task of explaining gender differences in drinking behavior cannot be completed in this book. Instead, the chapters here make three more modest but very important contributions to the pursuit of better explanation. First, the authors of the 19 chapters that follow analyze the links between gender and drinking behavior from many perspectives (epidemiological, genetic, physiological, psychiatric, psychological, sociological, and cultural). The intent is to provide in one place most of the many different dimensions and perspectives that will ultimately be needed for understanding gender influences on alcohol use and effects.

Second, some of the chapters identify factors that may help to explain gender differences, such as effects of metabolism (Lieber, chapter 3), family socialization (Barnes et al., chapter 6), and internalized gender roles (White & Huselid, chapter 7). Other chapters, however, find that some factors do *not* differentiate men and women as much as expected, such as spousal influences (Roberts & Leonard, chapter 11), stresses and coping styles (Cooper et al., chapter 8), and some types of sexual experience (Wilsnack et al., chapter 10). Thus, the book may help to distinguish influences that make women's and men's drinking behavior different, from influences more likely to create differences within genders than between genders.

Third, every chapter tries to help readers think about the same central question: *Why does* gender influence alcohol use and its consequences, and *why should* gender be influential? Many chapters accomplish this by reporting the results of research on both women and men. Some chapters focus specifically on women, because (a) the issue addressed has primary importance among women (e.g., drinking in pregnancy), (b) there is a lack of parallel studies or theory for men (e.g., in applying relational models of women's development to drinking behavior), or (c) a focus on women is necessary to counterbalance the continuing predominance of male-based research and conceptualization on certain issues (e.g., social policies for dealing with problem drinking). However, these chapters are also fundamentally concerned about whether and why women's drinking should be different or treated differently from men's drinking.

Implications for Gender Differentiation

Although this book focuses primarily on how gender influences alcohol use and its effects, a fourth reason for writing the book is that alcohol research may help us understand more pervasive patterns in how societies divide women and men. The chapters that follow may stimulate readers to think about questions such as these:

How Much Can Gender Differences Vary?

Gender differences in observable biological effects of alcohol (such as rapidity of intoxication or effects on pregnancy) (Lieber, chapter 3; Passaro & Little, chapter 4) are always available to societies as a substantive or symbolic basis for enforcing different rules for women's and men's social behavior. However, the great variability of gender differences in drinking norms, from one culture or era to another (Fillmore et al., chapter 1; Gilbert & Collins, chapter 14), is a powerful illustration of how flexible the social construction of gender rules and roles can be. And the fact that alcohol research reported here often did not find the gender differences the investigators looked for (Cooper et al., chapter 8; Heath et al., chapter 5; Roberts & Leonard, chapter 11; Wilsnack et al., chapter 10) suggests how culture may often lead people to expect greater differences between men's and women's behavior than actually occur.

Why Do Women and Men Sometimes Behave Differently?

General explanations of gender differences in behavior may be supported or challenged by the evidence from alcohol research. One possible explanation is that women and men are compelled to act differently by the ways that power and responsibilities are divided and organized in family life and in work (e.g., Eagly, 1987; Geis, 1993). This is consistent with patterns of how alcohol consumption is linked to violence: social structures that obligate women to stay at home while men go elsewhere make alcohol-related violence between men more likely to occur in public, while such violence against (and by) women is more likely to occur at home (see Streifel, chapter 16; Kaufman Kantor & Asdigian, chapter 12). On the other hand, historical changes in how and where women work are not necessarily associated with comparable changes in women's drinking behavior (e.g., Fillmore, 1984), indicating that gender differences in social behavior are not always tightly connected.

A second possible explanation is that women and men act differently because they learn to do so (e.g., Lott & Maluso, 1993). This theory gains support from ethnic variation in gender differentiation of drinking behavior, and from the ways that acculturation of immigrant groups modifies traditional differences in how women and men drink (Gilbert & Collins, chapter 14). However, studies of adolescent drinking indicate that social-learning explanations are incomplete: gender differences in learning explain only some of the differences between how young women and men drink, and effects of learned gender roles on drinking may depend on individual differences (see Barnes et al., chapter 6; White & Huselid, chapter 7).

A third possible explanation is that many gender differences in behavior have evolved in response to differences in environmental demands on women and men (e.g., Buss, 1995; Kenrick & Trost, 1993). The implication is that behavior differences have been adaptive, and may still be. Biological effects of alcohol may lend support to such a theory, if women's lower levels of alcohol consumption are an adaptation to the hazards of heavy alcohol use for pregnancy outcomes (Passaro & Little, chapter 4), and the greater hazards of such use for women's health (Lieber, chapter 3). However, it is hard to find evolutionary benefits of gender-specific behavior in *non*biological effects of drinking, such as the social damage resulting from men's heavier alcohol consumption (including violence toward partners), and findings that greater spousal differences in drinking patterns are associated with greater marital discord (Fillmore et al., chapter 1; Kaufman Kantor & Asdigian, chapter 12; Roberts & Leonard, chapter 11). What alcohol research can do for the various theories of gender differentiation (e.g., social-structural, socializational, and evolutionary) is to show how these theories may not be simply right or wrong, but in need of further specification.

How Does Gender Affect Social Responses to Behavior Problems?

Research on the dissimilar social reactions to women's and men's drinking problems may reveal general patterns of gender differences in how societies deal with harmful or undesirable behavior. For example, women's alcohol-related problems in the United States have often been ignored or women have been punished rather than treated (Blume, chapter 19; Walitzer & Connors, chapter 18), which may indicate the effects of androcentric cultural perspectives that regard women's behavior problems as important only to the extent that they interfere with men's activities and interests. Alcohol research has also shown ways that gender may influence how other people intervene in behavior problems (e.g., by informal versus formal procedures; Blum & Roman, chapter 15) and how other people categorize behavior problems (e.g., using different psychiatric diagnoses for some similar behaviors of women and men; Hesselbrock & Hesselbrock, chapter 2). By studying how men and women drink, we may learn not just about gender standards for normal behavior, but also about gender differences in how behavior is defined as abnormal and socially controlled.

Implications for Efforts to Reduce Alcohol-Related Problems

To some readers, contrasts between how women and men use alcohol may seem like interesting cultural phenomena or puzzles, but not much more. However, gender influences on people's ideas about drinking behavior are not only commonplace but also costly. That is the fifth reason for writing this book. Cultural stereotypes about women's and men's alcohol consumption can make drinking problems worse, by distorting how people react when drinking has harmful or hazardous effects.

Because heavy drinking is frequently associated with displays of masculinity and male camaraderie, this connection may encourage many heavy-drinking men to deny or minimize problems caused by their own drinking. Gender stereotypes make it easier for an alcohol-abusing or alcohol-dependent man to persuade himself that he does not need help controlling his drinking behavior (Davis & Morse, 1987; Nol, 1991; Thom, 1986). Such denial may make men more dependent than women on adverse social consequences (Weisner, 1993) or social encouragement (Beckman & Amaro, 1986) as incentives to seek treatment for drinking problems.

Recidivism by drivers who have been cited for driving under the influence of alcohol (DUI) is another possible sign that men may learn to ignore or minimize bad outcomes of drinking. Among drivers who are convicted of DUI, research has repeatedly found that men are more likely to be convicted of repeating the offense than are women (Peck et al., 1994; Waller & Blow, 1995; Wells-Parker et al., 1991; Yu & Williford, 1995). If repeated alcohol-impaired driving indicates that men are more likely to disregard evidence of drinking problems, that tendency would be encouraged by cultural views that it is all right for men to drink heavily when they want to. However, lower rates of recidivism among women may also reflect a tendency of law enforcement officials (often male) to ignore or disregard evidence of women's drinking problems (Wells-Parker et al., in press).

A negative effect of the stereotyped assumption that women do not drink heavily (relative to men) is that other people often resist perceiving or believing that a woman has developed alcohol-related problems. This may bias law enforcement, but it is even more likely to impede women's treatment for alcohol problems. U.S. physicians have failed to inquire about or identify alcohol problems in female patients to an even greater extent than they have overlooked alcohol problems in male patients (Buchsbaum et al., 1992; Dawson et al., 1992; Moore et al., 1989). And men recognize only a small fraction of their spouses' problems with alcohol that women themselves report (Wilsnack et al., 1986). If women's drinking behavior deviates from feminine stereotypes, this may be ignored or denied by men as long as possible.

However, when women's alcohol abuse or dependence becomes too conspicuous or interferes too much with their role responsibilities, the attitude of society is likely to shift from indifference to outrage and an attempt to punish rather than treat the woman's drinking problems. Too flagrant a deviation from gender roles and stereotypes cannot be tolerated. Women who drink too much during pregnancy may be jailed to protect the unborn, and mothers of small children whose drinking interferes with childcare may be separated from their children (Blume, chapter 19; Chavkin, 1990; Ewing, 1993; Madden, 1993). These may seem like reasonable protective precautions, but male drunk drivers who endanger lives are rarely imprisoned, and children are not taken away from alcoholic fathers as readily.

How This Book is Organized

Chapters

To serve the many purposes described above, the chapters of this book are organized in six sections to help readers find and synthesize different types of information. The first section, on gender differences in the *epidemiology* of alcohol use and related problems, introduces many of the issues discussed in subsequent chapters. This first section shows that contrasts between women's and men's experiences with alcohol are neither simple nor absolute. Instead, gender differences in alcohol use and abuse are complex and variable, influenced by age, mental health, social roles, and social contexts.

The second section of the book deals with possible gender-differentiated causes and/or consequences of alcohol use that lie within individuals and that may be largely *biogenic,* including alcohol metabolism, genetic influences, and pregnancy outcomes. The third section also analyzes influences with individuals, but focuses on possible gender-differentiated *experiential* effects on alcohol use and abuse (from socialization, stress, and aging). The fourth section considers how gender differences in *interpersonal relationships* (including sexual relationships and marriage) may affect alcohol consumption and its consequences. The fifth section examines how *social settings and contexts* (of ethnicity, work, and criminal activity) may differentiate women's and men's drinking and its effects on behavior. The final set of chapters discusses how gender influences, or should influence, *social intervention* to reduce adverse effects of drinking (by identification, treatment, and social policy).

Terms

There continues to be great variation in how scholars use terms to describe what distinguishes women from men, and what distinguishes drinking that is harmful from drinking that is not. In this book, the term "gender" is generally used to refer to differences between women's and men's personality characteristics and social behavior, differences that are assumed to result in large part from social influences. In general, the term "sex" is used more narrowly to refer to biological femaleness and maleness (Beall & Sternberg, 1993; Hare-Mustin & Marecek, 1988).

Authors here typically use the terms "alcohol-related problem" and "drinking-related problem" to refer to specific adverse physical, behavioral, or social consequences of alcohol use (e.g., drinking-related health problems, job absenteeism, or violence). The undesirability of such consequences is assumed to be consensual. "Problem drinking" or "alcohol abuse" refers to patterns of alcohol use that create such consensually negative consequences for the drinker's health, relationships, work, or other life domains. "Alcohol dependence," or the earlier term "alcoholism," describes seriously maladaptive patterns of drinking in which drinkers have become physically and/or psychologically dependent on alcohol use. When findings about "alcohol abuse" or "alcohol dependence" are based on the use of clinical diagnostic criteria (e.g., from recent editions of the American Psychiatric Association's *Diagnostic and Statistical Manual* [APA, 1987, 1994]), this use is specified.

Aims

The authors who contributed to this book were encouraged not only to provide critical overviews of published knowledge in their areas, but also to use their own most recent work to inform their discussion of major findings, problems, and questions about the links between gender and alcohol. Most chapters therefore include both reviews of available research and new empirical analyses of relevant data. This synthesis is meant to make the book more useful, for readers who hope to apply the findings the authors present or to investigate the questions the authors raise.

Although the chapters are organized in terms of different levels of analysis, the book is not designed for readers who want to learn about only one set of variables, or who want to focus only on the "normal" or on the "problem" aspects of drinking. The difficulty of reading narrowly is intended. A fragmented understanding of how men and women drink is inadequate. We hope that the authors repeatedly convince readers that it is necessary to use many different perspectives to understand how alcohol and gender are connected, and that what is considered "normal" or "problem" drinking depends to an important degree on what it means to be a woman or a man.

References

Ambler, C.H. (1991). Drunks, brewers, and chiefs: Alcohol regulation in colonial Kenya, 1900-1939. In S. Barrows & R. Rooms (Eds.), *Drinking: Behavior and belief in modern history* (pp. 165-183). Berkeley: University of California Press.

American Psychiatric Association (1987). *Diagnostic and statistical manual of mental disorders (3rd ed., rev)*. Washington, DC: Author.

American Psychiatric Association (1994). *Diagnostic and statistical manual of mental disorders (4th ed.)*. Washington, DC: Author.

Araya, R. (1994). Women's drinking and society. *Addiction, 89,* 954-956.

Beall, A.E., & Sternberg, R.J. (1993). *The psychology of gender.* New York: Guilford.

Beckman, L.J., & Amaro, H. (1986). Personal and social difficulties faced by women and men entering alcoholism treatment. *Journal of Studies on Alcohol, 47,* 135-145.

Bell, R., Havlicek, P.L., & Roncek, D.W. (1984). Sex differences in the use of alcohol and tranquilizers: Testing a role convergence hypothesis. *American Journal of Drug and Alcohol Abuse, 10,* 551-561.

Buchsbaum, D.G., Buchanan, R.G., Poses, R.M., Schnoll, S.H., & Lawton, M.J. (1992). Physician detection of drinking problems in patients attending a general medicine practice. *Journal of General Internal Medicine, 7,* 517-521.

Buss, D.M. (1995). Psychological sex differences: Origins through sexual selection. *American Psychologist, 50,* 164-168.

Caplan, P.J., & Caplan, J.P. (1994). *Thinking critically about research on sex and gender.* New York: HarperCollins.

Chavkin, W. (1990). Drug addiction and pregnancy: Policy crossroads. *American Journal of Public Health, 80,* 483-487.

Cheng, A.T.A., & Cheng W.J. (1995). Alcoholism among four aboriginal groups in Taiwan: High prevalences and their implications. *Alcoholism: Clinical and Experimental Research, 19,* 81-91.

Child, I.L., Barry, H., & Bacon, M.K. (1965). A cross-cultural study of drinking: III. Sex differences. *Quarterly Journal of Studies on Alcohol, Supplement 3,* 49-61.

Curlee, J. (1967). Alcoholic women: Some considerations for further research. *Bulletin of the Menninger Clinic, 31,* 154-163.

Davis, L.J., & Morse, R.M. (1987). Age and sex differences in the responses of alcoholics to the Self-Administered Alcoholism Screening Test. *Journal of Clinical Psychology, 43,* 423-430.

Dawson, N.V., Dadheech, G., Speroff, T., Smith, R.L., & Schubert, D.S. (1992). The effect of patient gender on the prevalence and recognition of alcoholism on a general medicine inpatient service. *Journal of General Internal Medicine, 7,* 38-45.

Driessen, H. (1992). Drinking on masculinity: Alcohol and gender in Andalusia. In D. Gefou-Madianou (Ed.), *Alcohol, gender and culture* (pp. 71-79). New York: Routledge.

Eagly, A.H. (1987). *Sex differences in social behavior: A social-role interpretation.* Hillsdale, NJ: Erlbaum.

Ewing, H. (1993). Women, addiction, and the childbearing family: Social context and recovery support. In R.P. Barth, J. Peitrzak, & M. Ramler (Eds.), *Families living with drugs and HIV: Intervention and treatment strategies* (pp. 18-36). New York: Guilford.

Ferrence, R.G. (1980). Sex differences in the prevalence of problem drinking. In O.K. Kalant (Ed.), *Research advances in alcohol and drug problems:Volume 5.Alcohol and drug problems in women* (pp. 69-124). New York: Plenum.

Fillmore, K.M. (1984). "When angels fall": Women's drinking as cultural preoccupation and as reality. In S.C. Wilsnack & L.J. Beckman (Eds.), *Alcohol problems in women: Antecedents, consequences, and intervention* (pp. 7-36). New York: Guilford.

Fillmore, K.M., Golding, J.M., Kniep, S., Leino, E.V., Shoemaker, C., Ager, C.R., & Ferrer, H.P. (1995). Gender differences for the risk of alcohol-related problems in multiple national contexts. In M. Galanter (Ed.), *Recent developments in alcoholism: Volume 12.Alcoholism and women* (pp. 409-439). New York: Plenum.

Fillmore, K.M., Hartka, E., Johnstone, B.M., Leino, E.V., Motoyoshi, M., & Temple, M.T. (1991). A meta-analysis of life course variation in drinking. *British Journal of Addiction, 86,* 1221-1268.

Frezza, M., Di Padova, C., Pozzato, G., Terpin, M., Baraona, E., & Lieber, C.S. (1990). High blood alcohol levels in women: The role of decreased gastric alcohol dehydrogenase activity and first-pass metabolism. *New England Journal of Medicine, 322,* 95-99.

Galanter, M. (Ed.) (1995). *Recent developments in alcoholism:Volume 12.Alcoholism and women.* New York: Plenum.

Gefou-Madianou, D. (Ed.). (1992a). *Alcohol, gender and culture.* New York: Routledge.

Gefou-Madianou, D. (1992b). Introduction: Alcohol commensality, identity transformations and transcendence. In D. Gefou-Madianou (Ed.), *Alcohol, gender and culture* (pp. 1-34). New York: Routledge.

Geis, F.L. (1993). Self-fulfilling prophecies: A social psychological view of gender. In A.E. Beall & R.J. Sternberg (Eds.), *The psychology of gender* (pp. 9-54). New York: Guilford.

Gomberg, E.S. (1982). Historical and political perspective: Women and drug use. *Journal of Social Issues, 38,* 9-23.

Gomberg, E.S.L., & Nirenberg, T.D. (Eds.). (1993). *Women and substance abuse.* Norwood, NJ: Ablex.

Gotoh, M. (1994). Alcohol dependence of women in Japan. *Addiction, 89,* 953-954.

Hammer, T., & Vaglum, P. (1989). The increase in alcohol consumption among women: A phenomenon related to accessibility or stress? A general population study. *British Journal of Addiction, 84,* 767-775.

Hare-Mustin, R.T., & Marecek, J. (Eds.). (1988). *Making a difference: Psychology and the construction of gender.* New Haven: Yale University Press.

Helzer, J.E., Canino, G.J., Yeh, E.-K., Bland, R.X., Lee, C.K., Hwu, H.G., & Newman, S. (1990). Alcoholism: North America and Asia. *Archives of General Psychiatry, 47,* 313-319.

Hendry, J. (1994). Drinking and gender in Japan. In M. McDonald (Ed.), *Gender, drink and drugs* (pp. 175-190). Providence, RI: Berg.

Hesselbrock, M.N., & Hesselbrock, V.M. (1993). Depression and antisocial personality disorder in alcoholism: Gender comparison. In E.S.L. Gomberg & T.D. Nirenberg (Eds.), *Women and substance abuse* (pp. 142-161). Norwood, NJ: Ablex.

Higuchi, S., Parrish, K.M., Dufour, M.C., Towle, L.H., & Harford, T.C. (1994). Relationship between age and drinking patterns and drinking problems among Japanese, Japanese-Americans, and Caucasians. *Alcoholism: Clinical and Experimental Research, 18,* 305-310.

Hupkens, C.L.H., Knibbe, R.A., & Drop, M.J. (1993). Alcohol consumption in the European Community: Uniformity and diversity in drinking patterns. *Addiction, 88,* 1391-1404.

Ikuesan, B.A. (1994). Drinking problems and the position of women in Nigeria. *Addiction, 89,* 941-944.

Jaervinen, M., & Olafsdottir, H. (1989). Drinking patterns among women in the Nordic countries. In E. Haavio-Mannila (Ed.), *Women, alcohol, and drugs in the Nordic countries* (pp. 47-75). Helsinki: Nordic Council for Alcohol and Drug Research.

Johnston, L.D., O'Malley, P.M., & Bachman, J.G. (1994). *National survey results on drug use from the Monitoring the Future Study, 1975-1993:Volume II. College students and young adults* (National Institute on Drug Abuse, NIH Publication No. 94-3810). Washington, DC: U.S. Government Printing Office.

Jones, K.L., & Smith, D.W. (1973). Recognition of the fetal alcohol syndrome in early infancy. *Lancet, ii,* 999-1001.

Keller, M. (1962). The definition of alcoholism and the estimation of its prevalence. In D.J. Pittman & C.R. Snyder (Eds.), *Society, culture, and drinking patterns* (pp. 310-329). New York: Wiley.

Kenrick, D.T., & Trost, M.R. (1993). The evolutionary perspective. In A.E. Beall & R.J. Sternberg (Eds.), *The psychology of gender* (pp. 148-172). New York: Guilford.

Kua, E.H. (1994). Chinese women who drink. *Addiction, 89,* 956-958.

Lee, C.K., Kwak, Y.S., Yamamoto, J., Rhee, H., Kim, Y.S., Han, J.H., Choi, J.O., & Lee, Y.H. (1990). Psychiatric epidemiology in Korea: Part I: Gender and age differences in Seoul. *Journal of Nervous and Mental Disease, 178,* 242-246.

Lisansky, E.S. (1958). The woman alcoholic. *Annals of the American Academy of Political and Social Science, 315,* 73-81.

Lorber, J. (1994). *Paradoxes of gender.* New Haven: Yale University Press.

Lott, B., & Maluso, D. (1993). The social learning of gender. In A.E. Beall & R.J. Sternberg (Eds.), *The psychology of gender* (pp. 99-123). New York: Guilford.

MacDonald, S. (1994). Whisky, women, and the Scottish drink problem: A view from the Highlands. In M. McDonald (Ed.), *Gender, drink and drugs* (pp. 125-143). Providence, RI: Berg.

Madden, R.G. (1993). State actions to control fetal abuse: Ramifications for child welfare practice. *Child Welfare, 72,* 129-140.

McClelland, D.C., Davis, W.N., Kalin, R., & Wanner, E. (1972). *The drinking man: Alcohol and human motivation.* New York: Free Press.

McCord, W., & McCord, J. (1960). *Origins of alcoholism.* Stanford, CA: Stanford University Press.

McDonald, M. (1994a). Drinking and social identity in the West of France. In M. McDonald (Ed.), *Gender, drink and drugs* (pp. 99-124). Providence, RI: Berg.

McDonald, M. (Ed.)(1994b). *Gender, drink and drugs.* Providence, RI: Berg.

McLaughlin, P.M. (1991). Inebriate reformatories in Scotland: An institutional history. In S. Barrows & R. Room (Eds.), *Drinking: Behavior and belief in modern history* (pp. 287-314). Berkeley: University of California Press.

Medina-Mora, E. (1994). Drinking and the oppression of women: The Mexican experience. *Addiction, 89,* 958-960

Midanik, L.T., & Clark, W.B. (1994). The demographic distribution of US drinking patterns in 1990: Description and trends from 1984. *American Journal of Public Health, 84,* 1218-1222.

Moore, R.D., Bone, L.R., Geller, G., Mamon, J.A., Stokes, E.J., & Levine, D.M. (1989). Prevalence, detection, and treatment of alcoholism in hospitalized patients. *Journal of the American Medical Association, 261,* 403-407.

Mphi, M. (1994). Female alcoholism problems in Lesotho. *Addiction, 89,* 945-949.

Nol, J. (1991). Self-object search: The role of the addictions in a patriarchal culture. In N. Van Den Bergh (Ed.), *Feminist perspectives on addictions* (pp. 31-44). New York: Springer.

Peck, R.C., Arstein-Kerslake, G.W., & Helander, C.J. (1994). Psychometric and biographical correlates of drunk-driving recidivism and treatment program compliance. *Journal of Studies on Alcohol, 55,* 667-678.

Perkins, H.W. (1992). Gender patterns in consequences of collegiate alcohol abuse: A 10-year study of trends in an undergraduate population. *Journal of Studies on Alcohol, 53,* 458-462.

Plant, M. (1990). *Women and alcohol: A review of international literature on the use of alcohol by females*. Geneva: World Health Organization Publications. (Cited in Thom, 1994)

Purcell, N. (1994). Women and wine in ancient Rome. In M. McDonald (Ed.), *Gender, drinking and drugs* (pp. 191-208). Providence, RI: Berg.

Saelen, H., Moller, L., & Koster, A. (1992). Alcohol consumption in a Danish cohort during 11 years. *Scandinavian Journal of Social Medicine, 20,* 87-93.

Salmore, K. (1989). Women's use of alcohol in a historical perspective. In E. Haavio-Mannila (Ed.), *Women, alcohol, and drugs in the Nordic countries* (pp. 21-46). Helsinki: Nordic Council for Alcohol and Drug Research.

Sandmaier, M. (1980). *The invisible alcoholics: Women and alcohol abuse in America*. New York: McGraw-Hill.

Snare, A. (1989). Women and control. In E. Haavio-Mannila (Ed.), *Women, alcohol, and drugs in the Nordic Countries* (pp. 133-152). Helsinki: Nordic Council for Alcohol and Drug Research.

Stewart, M. (1992). "I can't drink beer, I've just drunk water": Alcohol, bodily substance and commensality among Hungarian Rom. In D. Gefou-Madianou (Ed.), *Alcohol, gender and culture* (pp. 137-156). New York: Routledge.

Tähka, V. (1966). *The alcoholic personality*. Helsinki: Finnish Foundation for Alcohol Studies.

Temple, M. (1987). Alcohol use among male and female college students: Has there been a convergence? *Youth and Society, 19,* 44-72.

Thom, B. (1986). Sex differences in help-seeking for alcohol problems: 1. The barriers to help-seeking. *British Journal of Addiction, 81,* 777-788.

Thom, B. (1994). Women and alcohol: The emergence of a risk group. In M. McDonald (Ed.), *Gender, drink and drugs* (pp. 33-54). Providence, RI: Berg.

Thomasson, H.R. (1995). Gender differences in alcohol metabolism: Physiological responses to ethanol. In M. Galanter (Ed.), *Recent developments in alcoholism: Volume 12. Alcoholism and women* (pp. 163-179). New York: Plenum.

Toren, C. (1994). The drinker as chief or rebel: Kava and alcohol in Fiji. In M. McDonald (Ed.), *Gender, drink and drugs* (pp. 153-173). Providence, RI: Berg.

Vannicelli, M. (1984). Treatment outcome of alcoholic women: The state of the art in relation to sex bias and expectancy effects. In S.C. Wilsnack & L.J. Beckman (Eds.), *Alcohol problems in women: Antecedents, consequences, and intervention* (pp. 369-412). New York: Guilford.

Waller, P.F., & Blow, F.C. (1995). Women, alcohol, and driving. In M. Galanter (Ed.), *Recent developments in alcoholism: Volume 12. Alcoholism and women* (pp. 103-123). New York: Plenum.

Weisner, C. (1993). Toward an alcohol treatment entry model: A comparison of problem drinkers in the general population and in treatment. *Alcoholism: Clinical and Experimental Research, 17,* 746-752.

Wells-Parker, E., Pang, M.G., Anderson, B.J., McMillen, D.L., & Miller, D.I. (1991). Female DUI offenders: A comparison to male counterparts and an examination of the effects of intervention on women's recidivism rates. *Journal of Studies on Alcohol, 52,* 142-147.

Wells-Parker, E., Popkin, C.L., & Ashley, M. (in press). Alcohol issues for prevention research among women: Drinking and driving. In E. Taylor, J. Howard, P. Mail, & M. Hilton (Eds.), *Prevention research on women and alcohol*. Washington, DC: U.S. Government Printing Office.

Wilsnack, R.W., & Wilsnack, S.C. (1992). Women, work, and alcohol: Failures of simple theories. *Alcoholism: Clinical and Experimental Research, 16,* 172-179.

Wilsnack, R.W., Wilsnack, S.C., & Klassen, A.D. (1987). Antecedents and consequences of drinking and drinking problems in women: Patterns from a U.S. national survey. In P.C. Rivers (Ed.), *Nebraska Symposium on Motivation:Vol. 34. Alcohol and addictive behavior* (pp. 85-158). Lincoln: University of Nebraska Press.

Wilsnack, S.C. (1995). Alcohol use and alcohol problems in women. In A.L. Stanton & S.J. Gallant (Eds.), *Psychology of women's health: Progress and challenges in research and application* (pp. 381-443). Washington, DC: American Psychological Association.

Wilsnack, S.C., & Beckman, L.J. (Eds.) (1984). *Alcohol problems in women: Antecedents, consequences, and intervention.* New York: Guilford.

Wilsnack, S.C., Wilsnack, R.W., & Klassen, A.D. (1986). Epidemiological research on women's drinking, 1978-1984. In National Institute on Alcohol Abuse and Alcoholism, *Women and alcohol: Health-related issues* (NIAAA Research Monograph No. 16; Department of Health and Human Services Publication No. ADM 86-1139) (pp. 1-68). Washington, DC: U.S. Government Printing Office.

Yamamoto, J., Silva, J.A., Sasao, T., Wang, C., & Nguyen, L. (1993). Alcoholism in Peru. *American Journal of Psychiatry, 150,* 1059-1062.

York, J.L., & Welte, J.W. (1994). Gender comparisons of alcohol consumption in alcoholic and nonalcoholic populations. *Journal of Studies on Alcohol, 55,* 743-750.

Yu, J., & Williford, W.R. (1995). Drunk-driving recidivism: Predicting factors from arrest context and case disposition. *Journal of Studies on Alcohol, 56,* 60-66.

SECTION I

Gender Differences in the Epidemiology of Alcohol Use and Related Problems

Introductory Note

The first two chapters of this book describe how women and men differ in their drinking behavior, and in their alcohol-related problems and disorders, in ways more complex than just the greater use and abuse of alcohol by men. Men and women differ in their timing and sequences of alcohol use and alcohol-related problems across the lifespan and in relation to other life experiences. There are gender differences not only in how drinking patterns and problems begin, but also in how these patterns and problems persist. The prevalence of harmful drinking consequences may differ by gender also because of differences in how societies recognize and respond to the effects of women's and men's drinking. The complexity of differences between men's and women's alcohol use and abuse underscores the need for gender-comparative and gender-specific research, not only to clarify how gender influences drinking and its consequences, but also to discover how gender may modify individual differences in alcohol effects among women and men.

The chapter by Fillmore and colleagues investigates to what extent differences between men's and women's drinking behavior are consistent across societies, and to what extent gender differences in drinking behavior vary from one society to another. The authors use 38 longitudinal studies from 15 countries to compare men's and women's drinking frequencies, quantities of alcohol consumed, and problems related to drinking. Across the societies studied, men use alcohol more frequently, in larger quantities, and with higher rates of alcohol-related problems compared to women, but the rates of use and problems vary considerably. Alcohol use across the lifespan rises and falls similarly for men and women from the same society, but differently in different societies. Drinking behavior is consistently associated with marital status and depressive symptoms, but the associations are gender-specific (and often age-specific) and vary in size across the countries studied. From the patterns in the combined longitudinal datasets, the authors suggest that drinking problems are more likely to become self-perpetuating for women than for men, if women with these problems continue to drink. However, the risk may be counterbalanced by women drinkers' greater tendency to stop drinking altogether, a gender difference as yet poorly studied or understood.

The chapter by Michie Hesselbrock and Victor Hesselbrock shows how women's and men's alcoholism may differ because of gender differences in the prevalence of other psychiatric disorders that often occur with alcoholism (comorbidity). Women's alcoholism is more likely to be linked to prior depression and eating disorders, whereas men's alcoholism is more likely to be linked to antisocial personality disorder. What complicates this simple contrast is that these disorders are not homogeneous, their diagnoses vary

19

and may be gender-biased, and it is often hard to determine to what degree comorbid conditions contribute to rather than result from alcoholism and its social consequences. Furthermore, both depression and antisocial personality disorder can occur among both male and female alcoholics, and both types of comorbidity have been associated with more severe alcoholism in both sexes. Because the research on alcoholism comorbidity has been predominantly male-centered and inattentive to gender influences, it remains uncertain how gender-specific the diagnosis and treatment of such comorbidity should be.

for instance, that high school seniors in 1993 were less likely to use alcohol than high school seniors in 1979 (76% vs. 88%) (Johnstone et al., 1996). However, such analyses cannot provide an understanding of what happens in individuals' lives as they age, because the different cross-sectional surveys do not study the same people.

The second strategy is longitudinal research, which measures the same individuals at two or more different times in their lives. Longitudinal research sometimes seeks to learn whether people's drinking does or does not remain the same over the life course, and to learn what factors might "predispose" some people to drink heavily, lightly, or not at all at a later time. Longitudinal research measuring youthful behavior might help to predict heavy or problem drinking later in adulthood. It would be enormously important to learn what predicts alcohol problems later in life, because we might be able to intervene to prevent such problems from developing.

However, longitudinal research also has its disadvantages. Any one longitudinal study is likely to be slow and costly to complete, and will still cover only a limited period in the lives of only one group of people. A longitudinal record of U.S. residents begun many decades ago might not look the same as studies of other societies or of more recent U.S. cohorts. For example, U.S. residents who became adults during Prohibition may have very different patterns of lifetime drinking and related behavior from contemporaries in Europe or from U.S. adults who grew up in times of increased alcohol and other substance use in the 1960s and 1970s. If patterns in the prediction and histories of how people drink over time cannot be replicated at different times and in different societies, it may be unwise to seek any universal strategy for preventing drinking problems that depend on historical and cultural contexts. The use of research to understand, predict, and modify women's and men's drinking behavior depends not only on the ability to measure personal and social history, but also on the ability to generalize from comparisons of multiple independent studies.

The Collaborative Alcohol-Related Longitudinal Project: Rationale and Design

To overcome the limitations of single longitudinal studies, a group of scientists studying drinking behavior in 15 countries have pooled their data in the Collaborative Alcohol-Related Longitudinal Project. This project has incorporated 38 longitudinal studies of general population samples. The studies cover not only different nations but also different periods of history; for example, one study first measured individuals in 1928, while another began in 1984. The studies differ also in the ages of the individuals studied and the time intervals between measurements. Some studies began when respondents were children, while others began in adulthood; some studies have measured individuals for only a few years, while other studies have gaps of a decade or more between measurements. Finally, there are major variations across studies in the methods used. Some have sampled national populations, while others have studied local communities or school districts; some have relied on self-reports while others have used psychiatric interviews.

Despite the many differences between studies, the project has been able to synthesize their findings systematically. It is possible to determine whether women's and men's patterns of drinking practices and problems recur (are replicated) across different samples, societies, and epochs, measured with different instruments. The statistical method used for this purpose is meta-analysis (Hedges & Olkin, 1985), a procedure for statistically evaluating the similarity of results from many studies. The ability to replicate patterns or predictors of drinking behavior, regardless of the cultural or historical context, implies that these findings can be generalized (i.e., that the results should occur similarly in almost any setting or group of people).

If drinking patterns or predictors are not replicated (are dissimilar) in different studies, meta-analytic techniques can help determine whether patterns of differences between studies (e.g., in location, timing, or methods of measurement) can explain why the studies produced different results. For example, if the percentage of women with drinking problems varies greatly across studies, there is an opportunity to determine whether women's risks of drinking problems have been consistently higher or lower in certain eras and/or in certain parts of the world.

Thus far the Collaborative Project has concentrated on two general tasks. One task has been to describe drinking patterns and drinking problems in terms of their prevalence (how common a behavior pattern is), incidence (how rapidly new cases of the behavior pattern develop), and chronicity (how long a behavior pattern persists). It is important to make these descriptions age and gender specific, and to determine whether cross-study differences in the descriptive findings might be explained by the national setting, the period of history in which the study took place, or the birth cohort to which the individuals belonged.

A second task of the project has been to try to understand how biological, psychological, and sociological factors may influence the development of drinking patterns and problems across nations, eras, and birth cohorts. The research has searched specifically for factors that strongly influence the direction of people's drinking careers over the entire life course. One objective has been to determine whether certain factors, measured at one point in time, consistently predict individual or group drinking practices and problems at a later time point.

The research and methodology of the Collaborative Project, and descriptions of the studies, are outlined in Fillmore et al. (1991a) and in Johnstone et al. (1991). The steps involved in the use of meta-analysis are described in Hedges and Olkin (1985). The Collaborative Project has made a major effort to minimize the risks of error in the analyses of the multiple datasets, (1) by centralizing the data analysis in one location, and (2) by including the expertise of the original investigators of the individual studies in the development of the research plan and in the interpretation of results.

Some Findings from the Collaborative Project

Mean Quantity and Frequency of Drinking at One Point in Time

We first examined measurements at one point in time of the quantity of alcohol people drank per occasion (a comparison of 20 studies) and their frequency of drinking in a month's time (a comparison of 27 studies). Figures 1 and 2 compare the mean quantities and frequencies from the multiple studies, for men and women in the same age groups. Age groups have 5-year intervals up to age 40 and 10-year intervals after age 40 (Fillmore et al., 1991b).

FIGURE 1
Mean Quantity of Drinking per Occasion at Time 1 among Males and Females (Time 1 Abstainers Excluded)

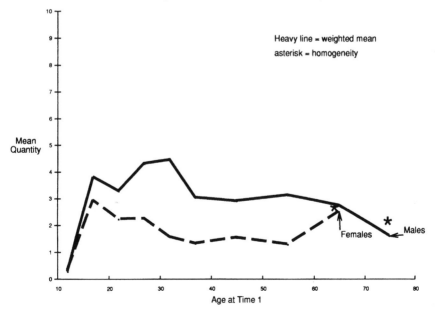

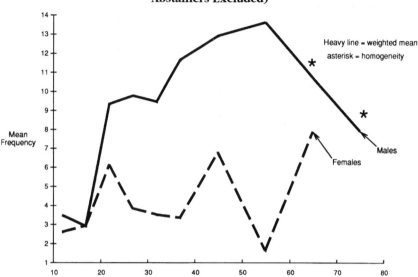

FIGURE 2
Mean Frequency of Drinking at Time 1 among Males and Females (Time 1 Abstainers Excluded)

We asked two basic questions: First, are the study findings about these two measures homogeneous for any of the age/sex groups (i.e., without major variation between studies)? Second, were men and women of the same ages similar or different with respect to these measures? We examined these questions using responses from people who were drinkers at the time that they were measured.

The quantity consumed per occasion gives a sense of what happens on typical drinking occasions, whether people genteelly sip small amounts of alcoholic beverages or consume copious amounts to the point of becoming drunk. Heavy drinking per occasion is associated with higher risks of certain alcohol-related problems (Room, 1989), such as alcohol-related accidents, alcohol-related violence, and acute alcohol poisoning. On the other hand, the frequency of drinking gives a sense of "whether drinking is a part of a person's everyday life, or a regularly recurring activity, or a special or infrequent event" (Room, 1977, p. 64). Very frequent drinking is often associated with other adverse consequences such as chronic health problems.

Each point on the lines in Figures 1 and 2 represents the weighted mean of the drinking quantity or frequency for all studies having data on that age/sex group. An asterisk at a certain point indicates that the cross-study results for that age/sex group are homogeneous. That is, the mean quantity or frequency for persons of that age and sex is consistent across all the studies.

As expected, the weighted means show that men consume larger quantities of alcohol per occasion than women at every age above 15, and men drink more frequently than women at every age after the early 20s. However, in almost all age groups the quantities and frequencies are not the same in different studies (not homogeneous), either for women's or men's drinking. The only exceptions are in the oldest age groups, where female drinkers over 60 and male drinkers over 70 drink about 8 times a month and average 2-3 drinks per occasion in all studies.

Examining the data for each country separately led to two important observations (data not shown). First, the shapes of the distributions of drinking behavior across the lifespan are similar for men and women *within* each country, but differ *between* countries. This suggests that national origin and culture influence how much and how often men and women drink at different ages. Second, for each study in which both sexes were sampled, men drank more frequently and in larger quantities than women in each age group (with only three exceptions). This suggests that while the national setting influences the age-related *patterns* of how much and how frequently men and women drink, within age groups the quantity and frequency of alcohol consumption is "universally" influenced by *gender.*

If women tend to drink less frequently and in smaller quantities than men, regardless of the social context, why would this be the case? What could account for this "universal" gender difference? Many answers to this question have been proposed, but none have fully accounted for the size and consistency of the gender gap across cultures. Biologically based hypotheses suggest than gender differences in body weight, body fluid, or alcohol metabolism lead women to drink less because a given amount of alcohol affects them more (Frezza et al., 1990; Hill, 1984; Jones & Jones, 1976; Morgan & Sherlock, 1977). Sociocultural hypotheses suggest that women have traditionally been assigned roles that discourage intoxication or reduce access to alcohol (such as roles that keep them at home and/or make them responsible for childcare) (Gefou-Madianou, 1992; McDonald, 1994). It is not yet known how well biological or sociocultural hypotheses about gender differences in drinking patterns within societies would help explain variations in men's and women's quantity and frequency of drinking between societies.

Changes over Time in Alcohol Quantity and Frequency

Figures 1 and 2 indicate that drinking patterns change over the life course. Cross-sectional surveys also suggest that aging leads some drinkers to become abstainers (Clark & Hilton, 1991), a pattern that Figures 1 and 2 cannot show. Therefore, it is important to know whether women and men change their

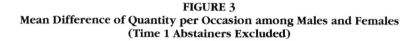

FIGURE 3
Mean Difference of Quantity per Occasion among Males and Females
(Time 1 Abstainers Excluded)

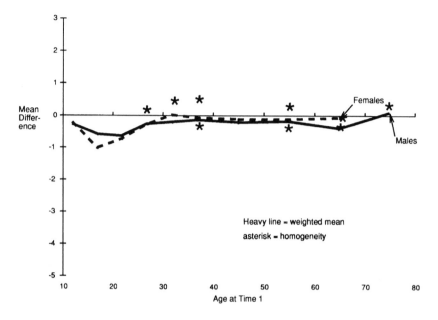

drinking patterns in similar ways as they age. Even though women and men tend to drink different quantities of alcohol with different frequency, the biological or social effects of aging may be so powerful that men's and women's drinking will follow similar trajectories over the life course.

If men and women change their drinking in similar ways over their lives, regardless of national context, this would suggest direct effects of aging, perhaps biological, that are common to all human groups. If men and women show different changes in their drinking over time, but the difference is consistent across different societies, this would suggest that aging has some gender-specific effects on alcohol consumption (based on social roles and/or biology) that transcend cultural differences. However, if different nationalities show different changes in drinking patterns as women and men age, then any effects of aging depend at least partly on cultural factors.

To evaluate how drinking patterns may change over time, we use the standardized mean difference between two longitudinal measurements: the mean for each age/sex group at the last measurement point minus the mean at the first measurement point, for those who were drinkers at the first measurement point. This measure shows the degree to which groups of people (not individuals) stabilize or change their drinking patterns, and the direction of

FIGURE 4
**Mean Difference of Frequency of Drinking per Month among Males and
Females (Time 1 Abstainers Excluded)**

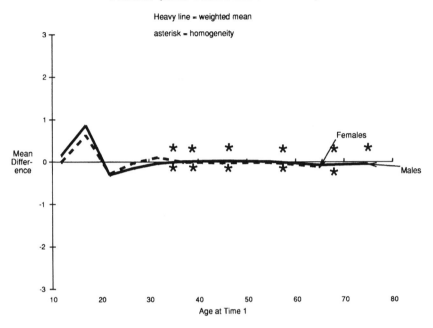

any change. It is important to distinguish group change from individual change: if influences on drinking affected individuals quite differently, with some increasing and some reducing consumption over time, the mean level for the group as a whole might remain stable.

Figures 3 and 4 display the standardized mean differences between initial and subsequent drinking quantities and frequencies for each age/sex group. The figures show how similar men and women are in how their drinking changes across the life course. When men and women are young, their mean quantity consumed per occasion decreases significantly over time, and their mean frequency of drinking rises and then falls, but neither of these patterns are homogeneous across studies. After age 30 those who were drinkers at the time of the first survey showed, on the average, relatively little change in their drinking patterns by the time of the next survey, and this pattern of minimal change was often homogeneous across studies.

Four important observations can be made from these findings: First, the patterns of drinking changes are similar for women and men across the life course. Men tend to report greater declines in quantity than women do from their 30s on, perhaps in part because their initial quantities per occasion are much higher than women's. Second, women's average changes in drinking quantities over time tend to be more homogeneous than men's, i.e., less influenced by particular social and cultural contexts. Third, youth is the time of greatest change in men's and women's drinking patterns, and the time of greatest variation in how drinking patterns change in different nations and eras. Because change apparently diminishes later in life, and drinking patterns stabilize, what happens in youth may profoundly influence drinking patterns for the rest of life. Finally, the changes in quantity per drinking occasion are consistently negative across most of the life course, indicating that aging typically leads people to drink smaller amounts or to abstain from alcohol altogether, perhaps because of a declining biological tolerance to the effects of alcohol.

The Consistency of Individual Drinking Patterns over Time

Figures 3 and 4 show the average changes in drinking quantities (per drinking occasion) and frequencies (per month) for *groups* of people who were of the same age and gender. Would the early drinking habits of *individual* drinkers tend to continue as they age? How well do an individual's drinking patterns predict how that individual will drink later in life? We evaluated the degree to which an individual's drinking at the beginning of a longitudinal survey predicted how much that person drank at the next follow-up survey. The operational measure of consistency in drinking patterns was an unstandardized regression coefficient in models in which initial drinking measure was the independent variable predicting later drinking (Fillmore et al., 1991b).

There are at least two reasons why it is important to know about consistency in individual drinking behavior over time. First, if a person drinks chronically at high levels of intake or every day (or both) for long periods of time, that person has a higher risk of developing serious alcohol-related health problems (e.g., cirrhosis of the liver). Furthermore, the crux of public concern about alcoholism is the concern that very heavy and/or very frequent drinking over a long period will lead people to become addicted to alcohol. Second, if individual drinking patterns are relatively unstable or unpredictable across the lifespan, periods of heavy drinking may not last long enough in many cases to produce health problems or alcohol dependence. However, low predictability would mean that "bouts" of heavy drinking, and related risks of accidents and injury, could arise rather suddenly, without warning, and not at any particular place in the life course.

Figures 5 and 6 show the size of the weighted unstandardized regression coefficients for drinking patterns of individual men and women at different ages. Among women drinkers, typical quantities become more stable from youth to the 60s, except for a period of lower stability in the 40s. The stability of drinking quantities among male drinkers rises until the early 30s, but then declines until male drinkers are in their 70s. Drinking frequencies among both male and female drinkers become more stable as age increases. Although the majority of

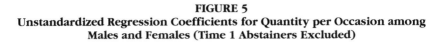

FIGURE 5
Unstandardized Regression Coefficients for Quantity per Occasion among Males and Females (Time 1 Abstainers Excluded)

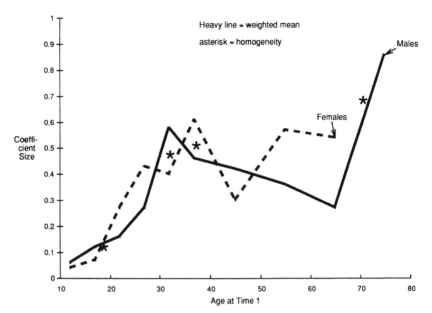

coefficients are not homogeneous across samples, the stabilization of drinking over time is a more homogeneous process among women than among men. That is, the predictability of women's drinking quantities and frequencies is more similar across studies than is the predictability of men's drinking.

Where the predictability of women's and men's drinking is lowest (during the teens and early 20s), drinkers are most likely to modify their drinking habits rapidly or to start and stop drinking altogether. These are the years of experimenting with how much to consume and how frequently to drink. It is only as people age that they develop consistency in their drinking patterns. However, the *degree* of consistency differs from one culture or population to another, particularly among men.

It is important to remember that consistency was assessed only for people who said they were drinkers when first measured. What about those who were not drinkers when first measured, or drinkers who became abstainers by the next time they were measured (Golding et al., 1993)? Women are clearly much more likely than men to abstain; over all the samples studied, 36% of women and 11% of men were abstainers. Furthermore, among those who were drinkers when first measured, more women (14%) than men (8%) became abstainers over time. This suggests that something about gender roles

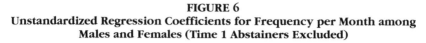

FIGURE 6
Unstandardized Regression Coefficients for Frequency per Month among
Males and Females (Time 1 Abstainers Excluded)

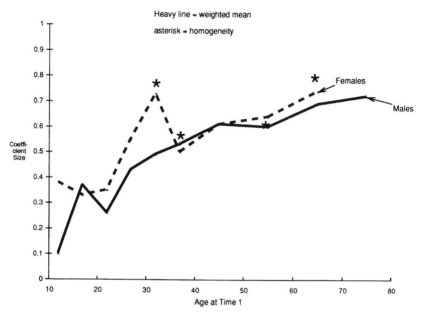

may give men a license to drink that is denied to women, or that common experiences in women's lives (e.g., childbearing, child rearing, or biological effects of aging) may give them more powerful incentives than men to stop drinking altogether. However, because relatively little is known about abstinence as a choice or change, and even less is known about what underlies gender differences in abstinence, this area is ripe for further inquiry.

A Contextual Model in a Cross-Study Design

The results described above challenge us to integrate what we have learned about group-level changes in drinking with what we have learned about the consistency of individual drinking patterns over time. Public health initiatives may try to moderate group drinking patterns or to curtail problem drinking behavior by individuals, but separate approaches may neglect the ways that changes at the group level may influence the behavior choices of individuals. We need to understand how group behavior patterns create a context for what the individual chooses to do.

It is particularly important to try to understand the connections between two patterns in the findings thus far: (1) the unpredictable and heterogeneous individual quantities and frequencies of alcohol consumption among young people, and (2) how the group-level drinking patterns in youth can set the stage for how that group will drink later in life, even though the drinking trajectories of different social and cultural groups are heterogeneous. The essential question is, are there ways that changes in group patterns of youthful alcohol use influence individual drinking then and afterwards? The sociological assumption behind this question is that agemates are a reference group that influences the drinking of individuals over time (Skog, 1980).

To answer this question, we developed contextual models in a cross-study design. These are models in which *both* the individual's drinking and the group's drinking are included among the variables that are used to predict how the individual will drink at a later time (Fillmore et al., 1993). The analyses using these models focused on two age groups (those aged 15-20 and aged 21-30 at Time 1), and used 13 general population longitudinal studies with intervals between measurements of five years or less. To predict an individual's Time 2 drinking behavior (quantity, frequency, or total volume) in separate models for each gender by age-cohort subgroup, the independent variables were the individual's Time 1 drinking behavior and the mean difference of the subgroup's change in that drinking behavior between Time 1 and Time 2.

The results of a majority of analyses were similar for young women and young men. After controlling for the effects of the individual's own drinking (quantity, frequency, volume) at Time 1, the individual's drinking (quantity, frequency, volume) at Time 2 was predicted by how his/her subgroup had changed its group drinking pattern between Time 1 and Time 2. The majority of these cross-study findings were homogeneous. Thus, drinking behavior of both young men and young women was apparently subject to the influences of their same-sex peers, in a way that was consistent across the social environments of the different studies. Future research should try to determine whether young women and men are most influenced by the drinking of same-sex peers, opposite-sex peers, or male and female peers combined.

The significant influences on individual young drinkers from trends in their same-sex peer groups suggest how social programs might be targeted to reduce high-risk drinking patterns. Strategies designed to alter the drinking norms or patterns of young people as a whole (e.g., by increasing the cost or reducing the availability of alcohol) may increase the probability that individuals in those cohorts will curtail their own heavy drinking and thereby reduce their risks of alcohol-related problems later on.

Depression and Alcohol Consumption per Occasion

We examined the relationships between consumption per occasion and symptoms of depression in longitudinal studies from the United States, Canada, and Great Britain (Hartka et al., 1991). It is important to assess these relationships in the general population, because depression is often found in clinical samples of people being treated for alcohol-related problems (e.g., Klerman, 1987). In these clinical samples, it is often hard to determine to what extent depression leads people to drink more heavily, and to what extent depression is a consequence of heavy drinking. To the extent that symptoms of depression lead people to increase their alcohol consumption, then treating them for alcohol abuse but not for depression would neglect an important source of their drinking problems. To the extent that problem drinking makes people more depressed, then treating their alcohol problems could reduce their depression.

The analyses reported here evaluated only how drinking was related to *symptoms* of depression; identification of depression in clinical samples is usually based on more rigorous diagnostic criteria. Nonetheless, any evidence of time-ordered connections between drinking and depressive symptoms may suggest paths for future clinical research. Two other characteristics of the analyses here should also be kept in mind: (1) relationships between depressive symptoms and drinking were evaluated only for individuals who were already drinkers at the first measurement point; and (2) it has already been established that men generally have higher risks of engaging in heavy drinking and developing alcohol problems, while women generally have higher risks of developing symptoms of depression.

We used three variables at the first measurement point of each longitudinal study (respondent's age, quantity of alcohol consumed per occasion, and symptoms of depression) to predict two outcome variables at the final measurement point: symptoms of depression and quantity of alcohol consumed per occasion. These analyses produced two major findings that distinguished women from men. First, both symptoms of depression and alcohol consumption (quantities per occasion) at the first measurement point generally predicted symptoms of depression at the final measurement point, but the relationships were stronger for women than for men. The predictions for women were homogeneous (consistent) across studies. Second, among women but not men, higher levels of depressive symptoms at the first measurement point were associated with high levels of consumption per occasion at the final measurement point, and this gender-specific finding was also homogeneous (consistent) across studies.

These findings substantiate the close relationships between women's drinking and depression reported in other studies (e.g., Midanik, 1983; Wilsnack et al., 1984, 1991). The question we must ask ourselves is, why is the connection between drinking and symptoms of depression consistently stronger among women than among men? One possible answer may be that women and men have different ways of coping with life problems. It may be that when women encounter life problems, they are more likely than men to try to endure or outlast such problems rather than to confront them directly and conquer them. If this is true, alcohol may seem a greater aid to women who are depressed than to men. However, this explanation is only speculative until it has been investigated more thoroughly (see the Cooper et al. chapter in this book, and Wilsnack, 1992, for differing perspectives).

Marital Changes and Alcohol Consumption

We assessed how changes in an individual's marital status were related to increases or decreases in the quantity of alcohol consumed per typical drinking occasion (Temple et al., 1991). It is widely assumed that major life changes may have powerful effects on people's drinking, either by stabilizing life circumstances or by disrupting them. For instance, it is thought that when people get married, their life circumstances tend to become more stable, and this change will lead them to reduce their alcohol consumption. On the other hand, when people become divorced, it is often assumed that the disruption of their life routines and their loss of attachments to a partner and to related role obligations may lead them to engage in heavier drinking.

Such assumptions are buttressed by data from cross-sectional studies showing that people who are married are less likely to drink heavily than those who are divorced or separated or who have never married (e.g., Clark & Hilton, 1991; Midanik & Clark, 1994). However, cross-sectional analyses cannot tell us whether drinking patterns develop before changes in marital status (e.g., people who do not drink heavily may be more likely to get married), or whether changes in marital status influence how people drink (e.g., getting married may lead people to moderate their drinking). The longitudinal analyses reported here were able to examine the time order of changes in marital status relative to drinking patterns, and were able to evaluate how consistent time-ordered patterns were across studies from different social contexts.

Relationships between drinking patterns and change or stability in marital status depended on the age and gender of the drinkers. For example, separation or divorce that occurred between the first and final measurement points of the longitudinal studies was significantly related to increases in the quantity of alcohol consumed per drinking occasion by young women (aged 18-39 at Time 1). No significant relationship was observed among young men or older drinkers. The "effects" of separation or divorce on young female drinkers were not homogeneous across studies, but they suggest that in some circumstances divorce or separation may have a stronger impact on young women's drinking than on young men's drinking. Why the effects of marital disruption on drinking are gender-specific is at this point a matter of speculation. Perhaps the emotional consequences of ending a marital relationship (such as depression) may lead women more than men to use alcohol as self-medication. A different hypothesis would be that young women may become

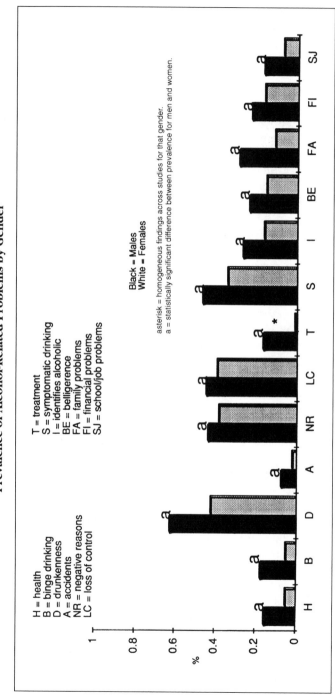

FIGURE 7

Prevalence of Alcohol-Related Problems by Gender

less constrained about how much they drink on a drinking occasion if there is no longer a marital partner to react to their drinking then or afterwards.

Young men (under 40) significantly increased their alcohol consumption per drinking occasion if they remained unmarried throughout the longitudinal studies. This homogeneous finding did not occur among young women or older drinkers, suggesting that remaining single has a special relationship to young men's drinking. Remaining unmarried may make it easier or more comforting for young men to engage in heavy drinking bouts, or episodes of heavy consumption may damage young men's chances to get married, or both.

Getting married during the period between survey measurements was associated with a decline in consumption per drinking occasion in the majority of studies for each age by gender group. However, the effect was both statistically significant and homogeneous only for female drinkers under age 40. If losing a marriage leads to less constrained drinking by young women, then becoming married apparently increases constraints on how much young women drink. Again, how much these relationships result from drinking motivations, opportunities, or consequences needs to be determined by future research.

The Prevalence of Alcohol-Related Problems

Men not only drink more frequently and in greater quantities than women, they also are more likely to report alcohol-related problems, according to the research literature (Dawson & Grant, 1993; Ferrence, 1980; Wilsnack et al., 1995). However, do women and men experience the same types of drinking problems, at the same times in life? And are women's and men's drinking problems the same across cultures and time periods? To answer these questions, we examined the prevalence of a variety of alcohol-related problems for each gender (Motoyoshi et al., 1992) and evaluated how consistent the prevalences were across social contexts (Figure 7).

The data in Figure 7, on prevalences of a large variety of alcohol-related problems, allow three immediate conclusions: First, men had significantly higher rates of every problem measured than did women. Second, the rates of every problem were heterogeneous across studies for both men and women; the prevalence of each drinking problem depended on where and when it was measured. Third, some problems (e.g., drunkenness) had larger gender differences in prevalence than other problems (e.g., loss of control over alcohol use).

One gender difference was particularly striking: the rates at which men and women had obtained treatment for alcohol problems. While the estimated percentage of men who had obtained treatment was 16% (but varied from study to study), only 1% of women had been treated for alcohol-related problems, and that was a homogeneous estimate across studies. Women may be less likely to have alcohol problems than do men, but they are very unlikely to receive treatment for the problems they do have. One possible explanation for this pattern is that women fear a more severe social reaction to their alcohol problems than men would experience, and so women are more likely to hide their deviant drinking and to avoid treatment, which would stigmatize them. An alternative hypothesis is that spouses and treatment personnel are more likely to fail or refuse to recognize alcohol problems in women than in men, preventing women from being treated appropriately. A third possibility is that women experience alcohol problems for briefer periods than do men, and so have a shorter time frame in which to seek and receive treatment. The net effect of these or other factors is to make treatment of women's alcohol problems a rarity in all the nations studied.

Associations among Alcohol-Related Problems

Clinical and epidemiological research has had a major interest in how alcohol-related problems may be linked together. In other words, if a person has one alcohol-related problem, is he or she likely to have others? The concept of alcoholism as a disease assumes that a number of alcohol-related problems will tend to occur together. Therefore, to the extent that it is valid to think of alcoholism as a disease, an individual experiencing certain alcohol-related problems should have a higher probability of experiencing others. Furthermore, one would expect the linked set of alcohol problems associated with the disease concept of alcoholism to be homogeneous across studies in different social contexts. And if connections among alcohol problems are dissimilar for men and women, this would suggest that gender differences in biology or roles alter the manifestation of alcoholism.

Our analytic approach was to try to predict two sets of problems that are thought to be consequences of alcohol dependence or abuse. The adverse consequences were (1) alcohol-related health problems (reports of any alcohol-related health problems, or advice from a physician to reduce or stop drinking); and (2) alcohol-related social role/demeanor problems (such as belligerence, conflicts at home or on the job, and role impairment, or failures in the family, school, job, or in managing finances).

The research question was how well these two sets of adverse consequences could be predicted at one point in time by a variety of other problems of alcohol use. The predictors included (1) personal concerns about drinking (e.g., self-reports of "loss of control" over drinking, identification of oneself as an alcoholic, drinking "symptomatic" of alcoholism, and receiving treatment for alcoholism); (2) alcohol-related accidents; (3) negative personal reasons for drinking (e.g., drinking to forget, drinking because of feeling tense or nervous, drinking because of feeling lonesome, drinking to improve self-confidence; (4) drunkenness; and (5) binge drinking. These problems have all been thought of as part of the development or effects of alcoholism.

We used each of the problem drinking predictor variables to determine the relative risk of (1) health problems and (2) social role/demeanor problems (Figure 8). Relative risk is a statistic indicating how the odds of one event occurring change if another event has occurred. For example, if we found that the odds ratio for health problems for those reporting binge drinking was 1.28, that would mean that the odds of having health problems increased 28% if respondents reported having engaged in binge drinking.

The odds of alcohol-related health problems and social role-demeanor problems are consistently increased by the presence of other alcohol-related problems, suggesting that such problems do interlock. For example, the odds of reporting health problems for those reporting drunkenness or binge drinking are more than four times the odds of reporting health problems among individuals who do not report drunkenness or binge drinking. However, many effects of alcohol problems on relative risks of health and behavior consequences are heterogeneous across studies. This helps explain why the apparently larger impact of binge drinking on the odds of women's health than on men's odds is not a statistically significant difference.

Men and women do differ significantly in some of the ways that alcohol-related problems affect risks of harm to health or behavior. Alcohol-related accidents are significantly more closely linked to failures in social roles or demeanor among women than among men; they make the odds of such failures in women 25 times greater. Social role/demeanor problems and existential alcohol problems (e.g., perceiving oneself as an alcoholic or out-of-control drinker) are significantly more closely linked to adverse health consequences of drinking in women than in men. These homogeneous linkages among women's alcohol problems lend credence to the idea that although women are less likely to develop alcohol problems than men, for women who do develop drinking problems everything tends to go wrong at once. An alternative hypothesis is that when women develop alcohol-related problems, they are less able than men to prevent such problems from spreading to other domains of their lives.

However, some linkages among alcohol problems are more likely among men than among women. Uncontrollable and self-medicative uses of alcohol are linked to damaged roles and demeanor, but the connection is significantly stronger for men than for women. Perhaps male problem drinkers are more likely to engage in kinds of social misbehavior that make them become aware of how they are using alcohol, or perhaps men are more likely to resist acknowledging their drinking problems until they suffer adverse social consequences. Whatever the explanation, it is important to understand better how men's and women's constellations of alcohol problems are likely to differ.

FIGURE 8

Relative Risk of Alcohol-Related Health Problems (*top*) and Social Role/Demeanor Problems (*bottom*) as Predicted by Other Alcohol-Related Problems by Gender

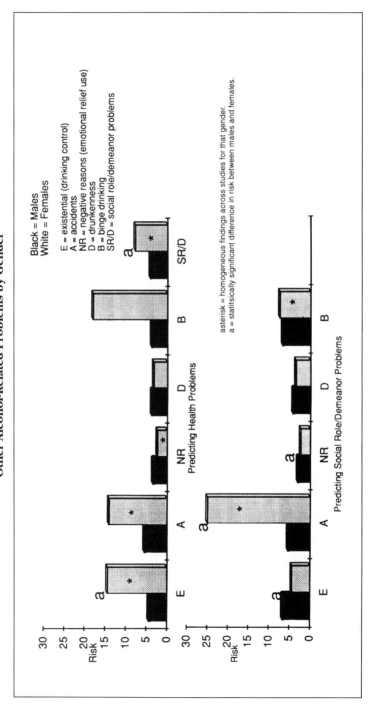

FIGURE 9
**Mean Difference Change in Alcohol-Related Problems for Those Problems
in Which Men and Women Differ Significantly**

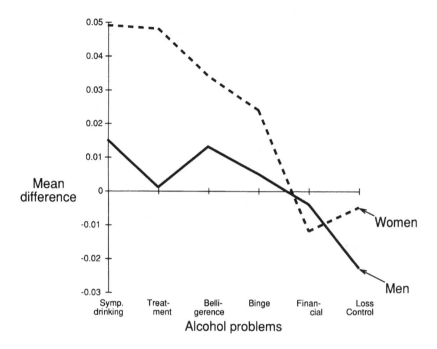

Changes over Time in Alcohol-Related Problems

The data tell us that at any given time, women are less likely to experience alcohol problems than men are, but that women's alcohol problems are interconnected to a greater extent and in different ways than men's are. However, these cross-sectional findings do not tell us how women's and men's alcohol abuse and its adverse consequences change over time. Are women's and men's alcohol problems likely to persist to the same degree, or does one sex recover more readily from these problems than the other does? Do men and women differ in their rates of recovery from different problems related to alcohol use? Clinicians and public health officials need to know whether treatments and interventions for persistent alcohol-related problems should have different goals or targets for women and men.

To begin to answer the questions above, we assessed changes over time in the percentages of specific age/gender groups that reported specific alcohol-related problems. We wanted to know whether alcohol-related problems tended to increase or decrease in all the age/gender groups in the same way, regardless of their prevalence or their societal context (Fillmore et al., 1992).

We examined standardized mean differences over time for each age/sex group, that is, the mean prevalence of a problem at the last measurement point minus the mean prevalence of that problem at the first measurement point.

Among women and men who were drinkers at both measurement points, women more than men showed increases over time in binge drinking, belligerence when drinking, symptoms of alcohol dependence, and treatment for alcoholism (see Figure 9). Furthermore, loss of control over drinking did not improve among female drinkers over time as much as it improved among men. It is possible that such gender differences may reflect a development of alcohol-related problems later in women's lives than in men's. It is also possible that women's drinking problems are more influenced and perpetuated by cumulative drinking experience than are men's.

The patterns of changes in drinking problems over time are not homogeneous across studies. That implies that predictions about increases or decreases in these problem areas cannot be readily generalized from one social context and age group to another. Gender differences in how drinking is related to the changes in drinking problems over time are further complicated by social-environmental and cultural influences. The complex ways in which age, gender, social contexts, and drinking histories influence the trajectories of drinking problems are virtually uncharted, and badly in need of further investigation.

Discussion

In the data from multinational longitudinal studies, both the similarities and differences between genders give us much to ponder.

There is no doubt that within the same nation and age group, women are generally less likely than men to drink heavily, frequently, or with problems. While biology may contribute to these differences, so does culture. In each society, women do not drink as men do. Furthermore, the men's and women's age distributions of drinking behaviors are similar *within* national settings but differ *across* national settings, meaning that culture probably influences the pattern of ages when women and men can drink heavily or frequently.

Men and women drink less per drinking occasion as they age, a trend that is more homogeneous for women. The greater decline in men's drinking quantities than women's as they age may occur partly because men are more likely than women to drink in extreme and high-risk ways when young, a pattern that may then be reduced more by the responsibilities of marriage, stable employment, and raising a family.

From the 20s on, most drinkers continue to drink at roughly the same frequency, at least during the few years between most of the first and last survey measurements. That is, drinking frequency is a relatively stable pattern in life, for those who do not quit drinking altogether. It should be remembered however, that some people shift from regular drinking to abstaining from alcohol: roughly 14% of the women and 8% of the men in all age groups and studies combined.

There is a general pattern in both genders of very heterogeneous changes in drinking frequencies and quantities in youth, followed by greater and more homogeneous stability of drinking behavior later in life. This suggests that drinking behavior "tried out" in youth may lead to habits of alcohol use sustained throughout the rest of a drinking career. Alternatively, the accumulating roles and responsibilities of adult life in all societies may compel drinkers to regularize their drinking patterns. However, the idea that drinking tends to become stabilized over adult life leaves many questions unanswered. Why do men drink more heavily and more frequently than women from youth onward? And why does youthful drinking vary so much, both culturally and historically? Attention to these questions about alcohol consumption could be a lens for examining how biology, culture, and history interact to affect larger patterns of social behavior.

One factor affecting the drinking behavior of young people in particular is the behavior of their age peers. In studies that measured drinking in youth and young adulthood, the quantity, frequency, and volume of alcohol consumption among individual men and women were, for the most part, homogeneously influenced by preceding changes in the drinking of same-sex, same-age peers, even after controlling for the individual's own earlier drinking patterns. Thus, the norms of how an age/sex category of young people drink modify how individuals in that category drink. This finding lends weight to campaigns to reduce drinking in large demographic categories, as a way to moderate individual drinking practices, at least of young drinkers.

What consistently reduces the alcohol consumption of both young women and men is getting married. Across all studies this life event resulted in homogeneous and significant declines in amounts of alcohol consumed per drinking occasion. However, young men's and women's risks of alcohol abuse from *not* being married differ. Having never married was homogeneously associated with increased alcohol consumption per occasion among young men but not among young women. In contrast, leaving or ending a marriage (by separation or divorce) increased young women's consumption per occasion more than young men's, although the effects were not homogeneous across studies.

The effects of divorce or separation on women's drinking may reflect in part the stronger relationships of women's drinking with feelings and symptoms of depression. Among women (but not men), higher levels of depressive symptoms homogeneously predicted higher levels of alcohol consumption per drinking occasion at a later measurement. One speculation is that this pattern reflects a greater inclination of women to use methods to help them endure or outlast life problems rather than to confront and conquer such problems. However, any such self-medicative drinking is apparently likely to backfire for women, because heavier drinking at the first measurement point of the surveys evaluated here was more consistently and strongly related to later depression in women than in men. For women, depression and drinking may be a vicious circle (Wilsnack et al., 1991).

Although women were significantly less likely than men to report any of the alcohol-related problems measured, the stronger links between women's drinking and depression indicate that patterns of drinking problems differ by gender. Indeed, women's alcohol problems tended to be more interconnected than men's. Women's drinking-related health problems had significantly stronger, homogeneous connections with mental/existential alcohol problems (e.g., loss of control over drinking, treatment for alcoholism, and drinking "symptomatic" of alcoholism) and with social role or demeanor problems (e.g., belligerence, family problems, school and job problems, financial problems). Women's drinking-related health problems were also more strongly (nonsignificantly) linked to accidents and binge drinking patterns. And alcohol-related social role or demeanor problems among women had a significantly stronger, homogeneous connection with alcohol-related accidents. The problem connections significantly stronger among men than women (linking social role demeanor problems to mental/existential alcohol problems and self-medicative reasons for drinking) were relatively small and not consistent across studies. If women's drinking problems are likely to perpetuate one another, this might partially explain why many drinking problems measured longitudinally increased more over time (or declined less) among women than among men. However, women's and men's changes in drinking problems over time varied across studies, indicating that such changes depend on the social and cultural contexts in which women's and men's drinking problems develop.

This chapter began by asking why anyone would be interested in describing differences between men's and women's drinking. Historical intolerance of women's drinking may sometimes increase such interest, but there are more profound reasons for research on gender and drinking. One reason is that men's and women's drinking patterns depend so much on cultural and historical contexts. We cannot adequately understand how alcohol use influences and is influenced by women's and men's behavior unless we understand the particular social environments in which they drink. In this sense the study of gender differences in drinking can be a lens for examining fundamental ways that culture and history shape women's and men's behavior.

A second reason is that there are some basic patterns of men's and women's drinking that social environments either cannot or do not change. At all ages, men consistently drink more than women do and have more problems because of drinking. And as both men and women age, they drink smaller quantities and tend to stabilize their drinking patterns (if they do not quit drinking altogether). Discerning such patterns may help us recognize possible constraints on cultural influence and social change, effects of gender, and aging that societies may accentuate or moderate but cannot eliminate.

A third reason to study gender and drinking is that gender influences but does not entirely determine how we drink or how alcohol affects us. It would be hard to find an age and gender group in any society where there are no abstainers at all or no drinkers at all. It would probably be difficult to find an age and gender group of drinkers in any society where all or none of the individuals have drinking problems. Some women or men who drink very little or very infrequently will nevertheless report problem consequences, and some women or men who drink without problems in their youth will stop drinking in middle age even though most drinkers their age do not. In almost all subgroups of the societies surveyed here there are minorities of women or men who do not conform to the majority pattern of drinking behavior, and some of the women or men who fit the predominant drinking patterns at one point in time will not do so later on. When we can begin to construct theories and models to predict not only the patterns of drinking and drinking problems for female and male age groups in specific societies, but also how individuals will conform to or deviate from those patterns, we will have made major progress toward understanding not only alcohol use but also some of the implications of being a woman or man.

Acknowledgments

This work was supported by a National Institute on Alcohol Abuse and Alcoholism (NIAAA) grant (R01-AA07034) and by a NIAAA Research Scientist Development Award (K01-AA00073) to the first author. The Collaborative Project is included in the plan of work of NIAAA as a World Health Organization (WHO) Collaborating Center on Research and Training in Alcohol-Related Problems, and is also affiliated with the WHO Global Program on Prevention and Control of Alcohol and Drug Abuse. Order of authorship in the Collaborative Alcohol-Related Longitudinal Project is designated by the following criteria: (1) the first author has taken principal responsibility for organizing and writing the research paper, (2) persons making substantial contributions follow the first author in alphabetical order, (3) collaborators, having reviewed the paper and its findings in accordance with accuracy and representation of their data and project goals, are listed as "with."

References

Bales, R.F. (1946). Cultural differences in rates of alcoholism. *Quarterly Journal of Studies on Alcohol, 6*, 480–499.

Clark, W.B. (1964). Sex roles and alcoholic beverage usage. Working paper No. F 16. Berkeley, CA: Social Research Group, School of Public Health, University of California.

Clark, W.B., & Hilton, M.E. (Eds.) (1991). *Alcohol in America: Drinking practices and problems.* Albany: SUNY Press.

Dawson, D.A., & Grant, B.F. (1993). Gender effects in diagnosing alcohol abuse and dependence. *Journal of Clinical Psychology, 49(2)*, 298–307.

Ferrence, R.G. (1980). Sex differences in the prevalence of problem drinking. In O.J. Kalant (Ed.), *Alcohol and drug problems in women: Vol. 5. Recent Advances in Alcohol and Drug Problems* (pp. 69–124). New York: Plenum.

Fillmore, K.M. (1984). "When angels fall": Women's drinking as cultural preoccupation and as reality. In S.C. Wilsnack & L.J. Beckman (Eds.), *Alcohol problems in women: Antecedents, consequences, and intervention* (pp. 7–36). New York: Guilford.

Fillmore, K.M., Golding, J.M., Leino, E.V., Motoyoshi, M., Ager, C.R., Ferrer, H., et al. (1992). *The stability of the percentage of groups reporting drinking problems over time and aggregate-level predictors of selected percentage differences: A research synthesis from the Collaborative Alcohol-Related Longitudinal Study.* Paper presented at the 36th International Congress on Alcohol and Drug Dependence, August 16–21, 1992, Glasgow, Scotland.

Fillmore, K.M., Hartka, E., Johnstone, B.M., Leino, E.V., Motoyoshi, M., & Temple, M.T. (1991a). Preliminary results from a meta-analysis of drinking behavior in multiple longitudinal studies. *British Journal of Addiction, 86,* 1203–1210.

Fillmore, K.M., Hartka, E., Johnstone, B.M., Leino, E.V., Motoyoshi, M., & Temple, M.T. (1991b). A meta-analysis of life course variation in drinking. *British Journal of Addiction, 86,* 1221–1268.

Fillmore, K.M., Johnstone, B.M., Leino, E.V., & Ager, C.R. (1993). A cross-study contextual analysis of effects from individual-level drinking and group-level drinking factors: A meta-analysis of multiple longitudinal studies from the Collaborative Alcohol-Related Longitudinal Project. *Journal of Studies on Alcohol, 54,* 37–47.

Frezza, M., DiPadova, C., Pozzato, G., Terpin, M., Baraona, E., & Lieber, C.S. (1990). High blood alcohol levels in women: The role of decreased gastric alcohol dehydrogenase activity and first-pass metabolism. *New England Journal of Medicine 322,* 95–99.

Gefou-Madianou, D. (1992). Introduction: Alcohol commensality, identity transformations and transcendence. In D. Gefou-Madianou (Ed.), *Alcohol, Gender and Culture* (pp. 1–34). London: Routledge.

Golding, J.M., Leino, E.V., Ager, C.R., Ferrer, H., & Fillmore, K.M. (1993). *Abstaining from alcohol use: A meta-analysis from the Collaborative Alcohol-Related Longitudinal Project.* Unpublished manuscript.

Gomberg, E.S. (1976). Alcoholism in women. In B. Kissin & H. Begleiter (Eds.), *Social aspects of alcoholism* (pp. 117–166). New York: Plenum.

Haas, R.M. (1975). Some details of female alcoholism. In L. Graz & E.J. Tongue (Eds.), papers presented at the 21st International Institute on the Prevention and Treatment of Alcoholism, Helsinki, June 9–15, 1975 (pp. 24–29). Lausanne: International Council on Alcohol and Addictions.

Hartka, E., Johnstone, B., Leino, E.V., Motoyoshi, M., Temple, M.T., & Fillmore, K.M. (1991). A meta-analysis of depressive symptomatology and alcohol consumption over time. *British Journal of Addiction, 86,* 1283–1298.

Hedges, L.V., & Olkin, L. (1985). *Statistical methods for meta-analysis.* New York: Academic Press.

Hill, S.Y. (1984). Vulnerability to the biomedical consequences of alcoholism and alcohol-related problems among women. In S.C. Wilsnack & L.J. Beckman (Eds.), *Alcohol problems in women* (pp. 121–154). New York: Guilford.

Johnstone, B.M., Leino, E.V., Ager, C.R., Ferrer, H., Fillmore, K.M., et al. (1996). Determinants of life-course variation in the frequency of alcohol consumption: Meta-analysis of studies from the Collaborative Alcohol-Related Longitudinal Project. *Journal of Studies on Alcohol,* in press.

Johnstone, B.M., Leino, E.V., Motoyoshi, M.M., Temple, M.T., Fillmore, K.M., & Hartka, E. (1991). An integrated approach to meta-analysis in alcohol studies. *British Journal of Addiction, 86,* 1211–1220.

Jones, B.M., & Jones M.K. (1976). Women and alcohol: Intoxication, metabolism, and the menstrual cycle. In M. Greenblatt & M.A. Schuckit (Eds.), *Alcoholism problems in women and children* (pp. 103-136). New York: Grune & Stratton.

Klerman, G. (1987). Depression associated with medical and neurological disease, drugs, and alcohol. In A.J. Marsella, R.M.A. Hirschfield, & M.M. Katz (Eds.), *The Measurement of Depression.* New York: Guilford Press.

Knupfer, G. (1964). Female drinking patterns. *Selected papers presented at the fifteenth annual meeting of the North American Association of Alcoholism Programs* (pp. 140-160). Washington, DC: North American Association of Alcoholism Programs.

Knupfer, G. (1991). Abstaining for foetal health: The fiction that even light drinking is dangerous. *British Journal of Addiction, 86,* 1063-1073.

Ledermann, S. (1956). *Alcool, alcoolisme, alcoolisation.* Institut National d'Études Démographiques. Paris: Presses Universitaires de France.

Lisansky, E.S. (1957). Alcoholism in women: Social and psychological concomitants. I. Social history data. *Quarterly Journal of Studies on Alcohol, 18,* 588-623.

McDonald, M. (Ed.)(1994). *Gender, drink and drugs.* Providence, RI: Berg.

Midanik, L.T. (1983). Alcohol problems and depressive symptoms in a national survey. *Advances in Alcohol and Substance Abuse, 2,* 9-28.

Midanik, L.T., & Clark, W.B. (1994). The demographic distribution of U.S. drinking patterns in 1990: Description and trends from 1984. *American Journal of Public Health, 84 (8),* 1218-1222.

Morgan, M.Y., & Sherlock, S. (1977). Sex-related differences among 100 patients with alcoholic liver disease. *British Medical Journal, 1,* 939-941.

Motoyoshi, M., Ager, C.R., Ferrer, H., Fillmore, K.M., Golding, J.M., Leino, E.V., et al. (1992). *The prevalence of alcohol-related problems: A research synthesis from the Collaborative Alcohol-Related Longitudinal Project.* Paper presented at the 36th International Congress on Alcohol and Drug Dependence, Glasgow, Scotland.

Room, R. (1977). Measurement and distribution of drinking patterns and problems in general populations. In G. Edwards, M.M. Gross, M. Keller, J. Moser, & R. Room, (Eds.), *Alcohol-related disabilities* (pp. 61-87), WHO Offset Publication No. 32. Geneva: World Health Organization.

Room, R. (1989). Responses to alcohol-related problems in an international perspective: Characterizing and explaining cultural wetness and dryness. Paper presented at the International Conference, "La ricerca Italiana sulle bevande alcoliche nel confronto internazionale," Santo Stefano Belbo (CN), Italy, September 22-23, 1989. Berkeley, CA: Alcohol Research Group.

Skog, O.-J. (1980). Social interaction and the distribution of alcohol consumption. *Journal of Drug Issues, 10,* 71-92.

Temple, M.T., Fillmore, K.M., Hartka, E., Johnstone, B., Leino, E.V. & Motoyoshi, M. (1991). A meta-analysis of change in marital and employment status as predictors of alcohol consumption on a typical occasion. *British Journal of Addiction, 86,* 1269-1281.

Wilsnack, R.W. (1992). Unwanted statuses and women's drinking. *Journal of Employee Assistance Research, 1(2),* 239-270.

Wilsnack, R.W., Vogeltanz, N., & Wilsnack, S.C. (1995). Alcohol consumption and adverse drinking consequences: Descriptive findings from the International Research Group on Gender and Alcohol. Presented at the 21st Annual Alcohol Epidemiology Symposium, Kettil Bruun Society for Social and Epidemiological Research on Alcohol, Porto, Portugal.

Wilsnack, R.W., Wilsnack, S.C., & Klassen, A.D. (1984). Women's drinking and drinking problems: Patterns from a 1981 national survey. *American Journal of Public Health, 74,* 1231-1238.
Wilsnack, S.C., Klassen, A.D., Schur, B.E., & Wilsnack, R.W. (1991, March). Predicting onset and chronicity of women's problem drinking: A five-year longitudinal analysis. *American Journal of Public Health, 81* (3), 305-318.

CHAPTER 2

Gender, Alcoholism, and Psychiatric Comorbidity

MICHIE N. HESSELBROCK AND VICTOR M. HESSELBROCK

Individuals diagnosed as having "alcoholism" often have additional comorbid psychiatric disorders, and this association between alcoholism and other psychiatric disorders has been documented in both community and clinical samples. In the National Institute of Mental Health's Epidemiological Catchment Area (ECA) study of five U.S. communities, 37% of the sample with an alcohol-related disorder had at least one comorbid mental disorder (Regier et al., 1990). Published results of the National Comorbidity Survey (Kessler et al., 1994) do not specify the comorbidity of alcohol disorders, but show that in the general population, 79% of lifetime mental disorders diagnosed from the survey were comorbid. Among hospitalized alcoholics, as many as 75% have one or more coexisting psychiatric disorders (Hesselbrock et al., 1985; Penick et al., 1988). Studies of comorbid psychiatric disorders among persons with alcoholism have found that the severity of psychiatric symptoms is often predictive of poor treatment outcome for substance abusers (La Porte et al., 1981; McLellan et al., 1983). However, relatively little is known about the problems and treatment needs of dually diagnosed persons.

It is difficult to assess accurately the extent of additional psychiatric disorders among persons with alcoholism, since rates vary with differences in samples (i.e., clinical vs. community samples) and methods used to assess psychiatric problems (diagnostic schedules vs. psychometric scales). Furthermore, many alcoholics experience psychiatric symptoms as a consequence of consuming alcoholic beverages, i.e., from pharmacologic and/or toxic effects of ethanol. The overlapping symptoms of alcoholism and other psychiatric disorders can be difficult to distinguish. Family and genetic studies of affective disorder and alcoholism, for example, have found that the two disorders are independent disorders with some overlap in their clinical picture and symptoms (Cadoret & Winokur, 1974; Schuckit, 1986). To make appropriate treatment decisions, it is important to differentiate affective symptoms that directly result from chronic heavy consumption of alcohol, from symptoms that are part of the major affective disorder. Alcoholism and antisocial personality disorder also often occur together. Distinguishing alcoholism from antisocial personality disorder can be difficult and may also lead to diagnostic confusion (Hesselbrock et al., 1984; Schuckit, 1973). To make appropriate diagnoses, it is necessary to differentiate the sources of different types of symptoms in terms of the time of their occurrence, persistence, and severity.

Alcoholic persons with an additional psychiatric disorder are difficult to treat because the philosophy and the focus of alcohol treatment programs often differ across inpatient and outpatient psychiatry programs. The primary goal of alcoholism treatment is to help the client cease drinking and remain sober, while an assumption sometimes made in psychiatric settings is that the psychiatric disorder causes the co-occurring alcoholism. These assumptions may lead to an incomplete intervention in both instances. Alcohol treatment programs often treat only the alcoholism and ignore the coexisting psychiatric disorders of their alcoholic clients. On the other hand, clinicians in psychiatric settings may mistakenly presume that the treatment of the psychiatric disturbance will ameliorate the alcohol-related problem (Mulinski, 1989). Hesselbrock et al. (1985) suggest the importance of considering psychiatric symptoms that exist apart from alcoholism as indicative of a true coexisting psychiatric disorder that should be considered in the development of individualized treatment plans. These findings indicate the further need to systematically review existing studies to clarify the treatment implications for those individuals with alcoholism and additional comorbid psychiatric disorders.

While alcoholism has been present throughout recorded history, most studies of alcoholism have focused on the problem as being limited to men. For the past several decades, epidemiological studies have found that men typically consume more alcohol than do women, both in clinical samples as well as in younger nonalcoholic samples. However, gender differences in the prevalence of alcoholism and the level of alcohol consumption may have decreased in recent years. Recent surveys of Caucasians in California found that similar proportions of men and women were current drinkers (85% vs. 81%, respectively) and frequent (3 or more times a week) drinkers (44% vs. 32%, respectively) (Clark & Hesselbrock, 1988). A similar pattern of use was found in the National Household Survey of drug abuse (National Institute on Drug Abuse, 1991). While the proportion of those who had used any alcohol or were heavy alcohol users was higher among men than in women, the gender differences were smaller among younger adults. The survey estimated that 70% of men and 58% of women between the ages of 18 and 25 reported alcohol use during the previous month, while 71% of men and 53% of women who were between 26 to 34 used alcohol. While the proportion of women who regularly consume alcohol appears to be approaching that for men, the rate of alcohol abuse and alcohol dependence is still higher among men than among women in community samples (Kessler et al., 1994; Regier et al., 1990). Any decline in gender differences in the rates of drinking versus abstinence does not necessarily signal a similar decline in gender differences in problem drinking and alcoholism, and there is little evidence for gender convergence of extreme drinking patterns (Clark & Hilton, 1991). Men and women still differ in the etiology, course, and associated characteristics of alcoholism. Consequently, findings from studies based on men's alcoholism may not generalize to women. If more women are entering treatment for alcoholism, this is not necessarily due to an increase in female alcoholism. The change may result from an increased willingness and financial ability to enter treatment. Thus, it is important to understand how the assessment and treatment needs for alcohol-related problems among women may differ from those of men (Wilsnack et al., 1991).

Recent studies comparing men and women with alcoholism have found that types and rates of coexisting DSM-III (American Psychiatric Association, 1980) psychiatric disorders vary according to gender. For example, antisocial personality disorder (ASPD) is very prevalent among male alcoholics, while major depressive disorder is a frequent comorbid psychiatric disorder among female alcoholics (Gomberg, 1974; Hesselbrock, M.N., et al., 1985; Ross et al., 1988). Hesselbrock, M.N., et al. (1985) found that ASPD (49%) and other substance use disorders (45%) were the most common additional lifetime psychopathologies for hospitalized men, while diagnoses of depression (in 52% of the women vs. 32% of the men) and phobia were the most common comorbid disorders for women. Ross et al. (1988) also found that women were more likely to suffer from anxiety, psychosexual disorder, and eating disorders. Furthermore, the age of onset of alcoholism and other coexisting disorders differs for men and women. Except for antisocial personality disorder (which usually begins in childhood), men tend to experience additional psychiatric disorders after being diagnosed as having alcohol dependence, while the onset of other co-occurring psychiatric disorders tends to precede alcohol dependence in women. The above studies indicate the need for further attention to gender-specific patterns of psychiatric comorbidity with alcoholism. To that end, this chapter reviews the literature on gender differences in alcoholism and other comorbid psychiatric conditions (particularly the diagnoses of eating disorder, antisocial personality disorder, and major depression).

Alcoholism and Eating Disorders

Relationships between eating disorders and alcoholism began to receive attention only when the incidence of eating disorders increased among more affluent families during the 1960s and 1970s. Also, eating disorders occur more frequently among women than among men, and studies of alcoholism did not look at eating disorders because these disorders are rare among men. However, recent clinical research suggests that there is a high prevalence rate of alcoholism or other substance abuse among women seeking treatment for eating disorders. Hatsukami et al. (1984) found a history of alcohol abuse among 14% of normal weight adults who had been referred to an eating disorders clinic in Minnesota. Because the average age of the women in their study was only 23.6 years, more of the subjects may develop alcohol-related problems as they mature through the age of risk for the development of alcoholism. Thus, the final rate of alcohol abuse found in the study sample is likely to be much higher than that typically found in the general female population. Mitchell et al. (1985) reported a higher prevalence of alcohol abuse and other substance abuse among patients who met DSM-III criteria for bulimia. Twenty-three percent acknowledged a history of alcohol abuse, while 34% reported alcohol and other substance abuse problems. In addition to abuse of alcohol and other drugs, Mitchell and colleagues found high rates of abusing laxatives (61%) and diuretics (33%). Even higher rates of alcohol abuse were reported in a small study by Beary et al. (1986). Of the women under 40 years of age who were diagnosed with bulimia, 40% had abused alcohol and 10% admitted to drinking to excess.

High rates of substance abuse have also been reported in studies of nonclinical samples of people experiencing problems with bulimia (Herzog et al., 1987; Pyle et al., 1983). Pyle et al. (1983), for example, found higher rates of alcohol abuse or dependence among college students considered to be bulimic (13.3%) than among nonbulimic students (3.6%). The rate of alcohol abuse among those treated for bulimia was even higher (27%).

High rates of eating disorders have been found among treated clinical samples of alcoholic women. Beary et al. (1986) found 35% of women ($n = 20$) in treatment for alcoholism had a history of eating disorders, while Peveler and Fairburn (1990) found that 25% of women aged 17–40 years admitted to an alcohol treatment center met criteria for a current diagnosis of an eating disorder. However, Ross et al. (1988) reported somewhat lower rates of bulimia (7.9%) and anorexia nervosa (0.4%) among patients seeking treatment for alcohol and drug abuse problems.

It is difficult to compare different studies due to variations in the samples and in the diagnostic criteria used to define eating disorders and alcohol abuse. Studies of eating disorders among alcohol abusers or alcoholics have used both clinical and nonclinical samples, with students and nonstudents. Some studies have included both alcohol abusing and alcohol dependent women, while others have studied only women diagnosed as alcohol dependent by DSM-III/III-R criteria or other formal criteria for alcoholism. Although specific rates of eating disorders among alcoholic women are difficult to establish from the existing studies, an association between alcoholism and eating disorders is a consistent finding.

Among most women who experience both eating disorders and substance abuse, the onset of eating disorders often precedes the onset of alcohol or other substance abuse. Since the onset of eating disorders is usually during the teenage years or the early twenties, with alcohol abuse or alcoholism occurring at a later age, it is likely that the onset of alcoholism is secondary to the onset of eating disorders among women with eating disorders. It is also possible that since most studies of eating disorders have examined samples in their early twenties, many of these women could later develop alcohol and other drug abuse problems.

Etiology of Alcoholism and Eating Disorders

Comparisons of the factors associated with eating disorders and alcoholism have attempted to identify phenomenological and etiological factors common to both conditions. Psychoanalytic approaches, for example, typically characterize both eating disorders and alcoholism in terms of developmental deficits and underdeveloped ego functioning. Brisman and Siegel (1984) described alcohol abuse as an "expression of ego deficits," a condition similar to food abuse among bulimic patients. Deficits in ego structure could impair the self-regulatory functioning that recognizes danger signs and provokes self-protective responses. Zweben (1987) suggests that clinicians consider the possibility of symptom substitution among patients with coexisting conditions of eating disorders and alcohol/substance abuse problems.

Others have described phenomenological commonalities between eating disorders and alcohol abuse. Yeary and Heck (1989) note that both eating disorders and alcohol/other substance abuse are characterized by impaired behavioral control. Substance abusers are unable to stop alcohol or drug consumption, while bulimics are unable to control binge eating and purging. While anorexics cannot stop their restriction of food intake, the condition may be induced by a fear that food may trigger uncontrolled eating. This loss of behavioral control persists despite the psychological and physical adverse consequences of both conditions.

Other similarities between persons with eating disorders and with alcoholism include the denial and secrecy of their behaviors. Anorexics have a distorted body image and deny that they are dangerously thin, while bulimics maintain a secrecy about their binges and purging. Unlike anorexia, it can be difficult for family members to detect bulimia, because many bulimics maintain normal weight. Alcoholic women often drink unobserved, and several years may elapse before they recognize their alcohol problems and seek treatment. Often they are forced to admit their alcohol problem due to family pressures and other social problems. Most treatment programs for both disorders consider the client's recognition of problems a major step toward recovery.

Alcoholism and eating disorders also both involve preoccupation with the substance of abuse. Persons dependent on alcohol are preoccupied with it and often hide alcohol in order to ensure its availability. Similarly, persons with eating disorders constantly think about food. Anorexics often prepare elaborate meals that they do not consume. A frequent focus of the treatment of both disorders is an attempt to control the preoccupation and/or craving. However, similarities in behavior among persons with alcohol-related problems and eating disorders do not explain why the two disorders may be associated.

Mechanisms of Association between Alcoholism and Eating Disorders

The relationship between eating disorders and alcohol abuse may have a physiological basis. Krahn (1991) reviewed animal studies indicating an increase in self-administration of drugs associated with food deprivation in laboratory animals. If a generalization to humans can be made, these data suggest that food deprivation may be a potent environmental stimulant for the desire to consume alcohol. Krahn hypothesized that food deprivation leads to binge eating and abuse of alcohol and other substances. His hypothesis is based on the observation that the relationship between dieting or food restriction and craving for drugs could be seen among bulimics. Food deprivation antedates binge eating, and food deprivation is often accompanied by a preference for sweet, high-fat foods as well as for drugs during binges.

The propensity for alcohol and other substance abuse could also be related to the tendency toward use and abuse of prescription drugs and cigarette smoking among women with eating disorders. Women with eating disorders abuse many different substances. The abuse of diet pills and diuretics is quite common (Krahn, 1993). It has been suggested that cigarette smoking among young women may be motivated by appetite suppression. Smoking and pill-taking could act as gateway drug experiences leading to more severe drug and alcohol use (Gritz, 1986).

Krahn (1993) suggests that the vulnerability for both eating disorders and chemical dependency may be inherited and that the expression of pathologic alcohol consumption may be triggered by self-imposed deprivation of food or other types of substances. However, the evidence for an association between eating disorders and alcohol abuse based on a family history of alcoholism is equivocal. High rates of both alcoholism and affective disorders have been reported among the biological relatives of persons with eating disorders (Hudson et al., 1983; Kog & Vandereyken, 1985). On the other hand, Winokur et al. (1980) found lower rates of alcoholism among the relatives of anorexic patients compared to the relatives of normal control patients, whereas higher rates of alcoholism were found among relatives of bulimia patients (Herzog, 1982; Strober et al., 1982). Interestingly, when the study of the relationship begins with alcoholic patients rather than eating disordered patients, a different picture emerges. A recent large-scale family study of alcoholism found little association between eating disorders and alcoholism in either male or female alcoholics or their biological relatives (Schuckit et al., 1996). The lifetime rates of both anorexia nervosa and bulimia among the alcoholics and the unaffected relatives were quite small. Further, much of the association that was found between alcoholism and the eating disorders occurred in the context of additional preexisting or secondary disorders.

Although the evidence associating alcoholism with eating disorders appears strong, the nature of the relationship between the two types of disorders is uncertain, and future studies must address several issues. Because most of such studies examine alcohol-related problems only in subjects with eating disorders, more studies of eating disorders among alcoholic women are needed. For example, how do alcoholic women with eating disorders differ from female alcoholics without an eating disorder? If the association of alcohol abuse and eating disorder has a physiological base, what are the factors that protect alcoholic men from developing eating disorders?

Alcoholism and Affective Disorders

Affective disorder is the psychiatric disorder probably most frequently observed to coexist with alcoholism. The rate of depression among different samples of alcoholics varies depending on the source of subjects studied, the method of assessment utilized, and the operational definition of depression employed, with prevalence rates of depressive disorder in alcoholism ranging from 30% to 70% (Schuckit & Monteiro, 1988). Studies comparing male and female alcoholics consistently have found higher rates of depression among female than among male alcoholics. One study of hospitalized alcoholics found that more than half of the women (52%) and one-third of the men (32%) in the sample met lifetime criteria for DSM-III major depressive disorder (Hesselbrock, M.N., et al., 1985). A majority of patients with a lifetime diagnosis of depression reported symptoms of depression at the time of hospitalization for the treatment of their alcoholism.

Epidemiological Studies of Alcoholics in the General Population

Gender differences in the comorbid diagnosis of depression and alcoholism have also been reported in both community samples. Helzer and Pryzbeck (1988), using the Epidemiological Catchment Area (ECA) general population database, found that female alcoholics were more likely to have a lifetime diagnosis of depression than were nonalcoholic women, whereas alcoholic and nonalcoholic men had similar rates of depression.

While more recent studies of U.S. samples generally indicate that depression is more common among alcoholic women than among alcoholic men, the literature is not entirely consistent on this issue. Rates of reported depression were similar for men and women in Toronto, Canada, who sought help for substance abuse problems (Ross et al., 1988). Based on the National

Institute of Mental Health Diagnostic Interview Schedule (NIMH-DIS) (Robins et al., 1981), 29% of the men and 30% of the women met criteria for a lifetime diagnosis of major depression. A study of a nonclinical sample of driving-while-intoxicated (DWI) offenders found no significant gender differences in rates of global depression, depressive mood, or depressive features (Windle & Miller, 1989). Weissman and associates (1980), in a New Haven, Connecticut, household survey, also detected similar rates of major depression among community dwelling men and women diagnosed as having alcoholism.

Gender differences in the comorbidity of affective and alcohol disorders may be related to the specificity and severity of diagnosed alcoholism. For example, Hesselbrock, M.N., et al. (1985) studied only hospitalized alcoholics who met DSM-III criteria for alcohol abuse/dependence, whereas Ross et al.'s (1988) sample included both inpatients and outpatients who sought assistance for a wide range of alcohol and drug problems, not just those who met criteria for abuse/dependence. The high rates of depression often observed among clinical samples of alcoholics may reflect the help-seeking behavior among alcoholics with depression in general (Vaglum et al., 1987). The higher rates of depression observed among hospitalized female alcoholics may also result from the higher rates of treatment utilization per se (including psychiatric services) among women compared to men. The combination of alcoholism and depression may increase the risk of suicidal behavior, a common reason for entering treatment (Weissman et al., 1980).

Distinguishing Affective and Alcohol-Related Symptoms

It may be hard to distinguish affective symptoms attributable to an affective disorder from those precipitated by the pharmacological effects of chronic alcohol use. The pharmacological/toxicological effects of ethanol alone may produce depressive-like symptoms. Dysphoric mood from prolonged periods of heavy drinking may result even among persons who are not alcohol abusers. This sadness can be potentiated by a combination of the pharmacological effects of ethanol and the social/psychological problems resulting from heavy alcohol use.

The ingestion of alcohol, a central nervous system depressant, can produce sadness in both alcoholics and nonalcoholics. Birnbaum and colleagues (1983) found that female social drinkers who consumed relatively low levels of ethanol reported increased depression and anger, while other investigators have reported an association between alcohol consumption and low mood in samples of alcoholics (Nathan and Lisman, 1976; Tamerin et al., 1970). The severity of the depressive symptoms reported appears to be positively associated with increased blood alcohol concentrations, longer periods of heavy drinking (Schuckit and Monteiro, 1988), the affective state prior to alcohol consumption, and the drinking circumstances (Schuckit, 1979).

Furthermore, the social and psychological problems experienced by persons drinking heavily may produce sadness. Many depressive symptoms (e.g., feeling guilty or worthless, sleep disturbance, loss of appetite, lack of concentration, irritability) are reported by alcoholics as occurring in the context of alcohol consumption. Furthermore, repetitive patterns of relapse, abstinence, and brief periods of controlled drinking by an alcoholic often require adjustments by role partners, leading to family difficulties, job problems, and financial difficulties for the alcoholic and his/her family. Treatment is often sought when the alcohol-related problems become overwhelming and the ability to cope with these problems is diminished (Schuckit & Monteiro, 1988). Persons seeking alcohol treatment frequently report difficulties coping with their life situations and demonstrate an affective state consistent with these difficulties (Schuckit & Monteiro, 1988). Fowler et al. (1980) found that male veterans with depression secondary to alcoholism reported more undesirable life events within one year of admission than those alcoholics without depression. The undesirable life events reported included divorce, legal difficulties, sexual difficulties, and personal injury or illness (Gomberg & Turnbull, 1990). Such life problems and difficulties in coping are often experienced by alcoholics seeking treatment.

Recovering alcoholics often report dysphoric mood and symptoms during alcohol withdrawal. Hershon (1977) examined various "subclinical" withdrawal symptoms that might be experienced between bouts of drinking, including physical and affective disturbances. The affective disturbances (e.g., depression, irritability, anxiety, paranoia, anger, inability to face the day, and guilt) associated with "subclinical" withdrawal symptoms were greater among female than among male alcoholics in the month prior to hospitalization (Hershon, 1977; Hesselbrock et al., 1985). These depressive symptoms, however, seemed to be transient. Other studies have noted that the presence of depressive symptoms sharply diminishes as patients move from active drinking to abstinence (Dackis et al., 1986; Dorus et al., 1987).

The phenomenology and treatment outcomes of substance use disorders may depend on whether these disorders are primary or secondary diagnoses (Schuckit, 1983a,b, 1986). Schuckit and Monteiro (1988) were able to distinguish primary and secondary alcoholism in terms of the age of onset of alcoholism in relation to other psychiatric disorders. The presence of an alcohol use disorder in the absence of any other psychiatric disorder defined "primary alcoholism," while "secondary alcoholism" developed following the onset of one or more psychiatric disorder(s).

There is evidence of gender differences in the sequence of alcoholism and affective disorder. While depressive affective disorder tends to develop prior to the onset of alcoholism among women, it tends to follow the onset of alcoholism in men. Schuckit and associates (1969) found that 44% of female alcoholics had primary depression. Other studies also have noted that depressed female alcoholics are more likely to have a diagnosis of primary affective disorder than are male alcoholics (Winokur et al., 1970, 1971). Among hospitalized alcoholics, Hesselbrock, M.N., et al. (1985) found that primary alcoholism was more common among males, while primary depression was more common among females. It is possible that alcoholism *in women* may be more "reactive" or secondary to other psychiatric problems in clinical (Jacobson, 1987; Schmidt et al., 1990) and nonclinical samples (Helzer & Pryzbeck, 1988).

Several explanations have been suggested for the high prevalence of primary affective disorder among female alcoholics. Winokur et al. (1971) hypothesized that alcoholism might be a variation of unipolar, primary affective disorder, with alcohol abuse a manifestation of depressive symptoms. However, the exact nature of such a relationship between alcoholism and depression has not been adequately explained (Berner et al., 1986).

The "self-medication" hypothesis is that people experiencing depressive symptoms may increase their drinking to medicate their own symptoms. However, Schuckit and Monteiro (1988) found that most patients with major depressive disorder either did not change their alcohol consumption or reduced their drinking after beginning to experience depressive symptoms. Also, Vaglum et al. (1987) found no dose-response relationship between the severity of depression experienced and the quantity of alcohol consumed among alcoholic women, but among nonalcoholic subjects depression scores and the amount of alcohol consumed were inversely related. Other studies suggest that depression precedes the onset of alcoholism among females because alcoholism often develops at a later age among women, giving them more time to develop clinical depression (Goodwin et al., 1977; Solomon, 1983). However, Gomberg (1986) found no differences in depression scores of young and older alcoholic women. Thus, the relationship between the onsets of affective disorder and alcoholism in women has not yet been adequately explained.

Several studies have found that depression in male alcoholics is associated with a longer, more severe course of alcoholism, a higher number of alcohol-related problems, and increased frequency of suicide attempts (Hesselbrock et al., 1986; McMahon & Davidson, 1986; O'Sullivan et al., 1983; Schuckit, 1983a,b; Yates et al., 1988). The relationship of depression to the course of women's alcoholism has been less studied. However, Turnbull and Gomberg (1988) found that alcoholic women with more depressed mood reported earlier onsets of drinking, loss of control of drinking, and binge drinking, suggesting that depressive symptoms were linked with a more severe, chronic course of alcoholism. They also found that higher levels of depressive symptoms were linked with more negative consequences of alcoholism, including social withdrawal, problems with sexuality, accidents, work problems, illness, and relationship conflicts.

Alcoholism and Suicide

Increased frequency of suicide attempts and suicide completion are often reported among persons with coexisting diagnoses of alcoholism and affective disorder (Lippmann et al., 1987; Pitts & Winokur, 1966; Solomon, 1983; Yates et al., 1988). High rates of completed suicide have been found among persons with both alcoholism and affective disorder (Pitts & Winokur, 1966), and 45% of male alcoholics with secondary depression reported a previous suicide attempt, compared with 8% of those not depressed (Yates et al., 1988). In a study comparing hospitalized alcoholics with and without a history of suicide attempts, Hesselbrock et al. (1988) reported an association between suicide attempts and a lifetime diagnosis of major depressive disorder in both male and female alcoholics. Lifetime prevalence of major depression was higher among the women than among the men in both alcoholics who had attempted suicide and those who had not.

In a study of alcoholic women under age 40, Gomberg (1989) reported that alcoholic women were nearly five times more likely to attempt suicide than were nonalcoholic women. The alcoholic women who reported suicide attempts also reported more tension, indecisiveness, anxiety, and nervousness than did the women who had not attempted suicide (Gomberg, 1989).

Affective Disorder, Alcoholism, and the Outcome of Treatment

Research has been equivocal about how depression affects alcoholism treatment outcomes, particularly for women. Some studies have noted improved treatment outcomes for female alcoholics with a coexisting affective disorder, while other studies have been less conclusive. MacDonald (1987) reported that poor treatment outcome was associated with a combination of life problems, not with depression or emotional problems alone. One year after treatment, alcoholic women reported a high level of major life problems. Emotional or nervous difficulty was most often cited as a predictor of poor treatment outcomes, while depression was not a separate predictor. Schuckit and Winokur (1972) compared 21 primary alcoholic women who had secondary affective disorder with 21 alcoholic women who had primary affective disorder. Three years after treatment, the women with primary affective disorder reported improved treatment outcomes compared to the women with primary alcoholism.

Male and female alcoholics with a history of affective disorder apparently have different treatment outcomes. A one-year post-treatment follow-up of male alcoholics with a lifetime diagnosis of depression found that they tended to relapse to drinking (Rounsaville et al., 1987). In contrast, alcoholic women with a lifetime diagnosis of depression tended to have lower rates of relapse than alcoholic women with no history of depression. However, the depressed female alcoholics also reported higher rates of affective disturbance one year after treatment than did those without depression. Furthermore, a diagnosis of depression remained more prevalent among female alcoholics than among male alcoholics one year after hospital discharge (Hesselbrock, 1991a). The continuation of depression long after the completion of treatment for alcoholism has frequently been reported (cf., Bander et al., 1983; Behar et al., 1984; Pottenger et al., 1978). Interestingly, however, concurrent alcoholism does not seem to affect the treatment outcome of persons with primary depression. Time to recovery, time to relapse, and cross-sectional clinical ratings over two years post-treatment did not vary between the primary depressives with and those without concurrent alcoholism (Hirschfeld et al., 1989).

Alcoholism and Antisocial Personality Disorder

Antisocial personality disorder is commonly reported in clinical populations with alcoholism. As with affective disorder, there can be considerable phenomenological overlap between alcoholism and antisocial personality disorder, making a differential diagnosis of ASPD and alcoholism difficult (Hesselbrock, V.M., et al., 1985; Meyer, 1986; Schuckit, 1973). Alcohol abusing individuals often display symptoms suggestive of sociopathy (e.g., fights, lying, employment problems, difficulty in interpersonal relationships, and neglect of family obligations). Furthermore, alcohol abuse among persons with ASPD is quite common (Cadoret et al., 1984; Hesselbrock, V.M., et al., 1985; Penick et al., 1984).

ASPD and early onset alcoholism may be hard to separate also because early onset of alcohol abuse is a criterion for ASPD, while behavior problems among youth may result from heavy alcohol consumption (Gerstley et al., 1990; Meyer, 1986). A proper psychiatric assessment to distinguish the two disorders should consider a person's life history of psychiatric problems (including childhood behavior problems and alcohol abuse/addiction) and the presence of a family history of ASPD and/or alcoholism, and should not focus only on the time period immediately prior to entering treatment (Hesselbrock, V.M., et al., 1985).

In alcoholics, ASPD has generally been more frequently reported among men than among women in clinical and community samples (Helzer & Pryzbeck, 1988; Hesselbrock, M.N., et al., 1985; Lewis et al., 1983). Helzer and Pryzbeck found prevalence rates of ASPD in 15% of men and 10% of women in the ECA study sample. The more recent National Comorbidity Survey found lower lifetime rates of ASPD among men (4.8%) and women (1.0%) (Kessler et al., 1994), but separate rates of ASPD were not reported for men and women who were also dependent on alcohol. In terms of clinical samples, Hesselbrock, M.N., et al. (1985) found rates of ASPD of 49% among men and 20% among women hospitalized for alcoholism. Similar rates (47.9% of men and 23.8% of women) were reported by Ross et al. (1988) in Canadian medical and surgical patients seeking assistance for alcohol and drug problems. Indicators of more extreme ASPD behaviors were also higher among male than female alcoholics as indicated by the higher rates of arrests for criminal offenses, DWI, and drunk and disorderly conduct (Blankenfield, 1990).

However, gender differences in the rates of ASPD may also be related to the age of the patients. While prevalence rates of ASPD appear to decrease for both men and women as they age, the gender difference is greater among older subjects. Among Ross et al.'s (1988) Canadian patients, ASPD was diagnosed in nearly two-thirds of the men (61%) and half of the women (50%) under age 25, but among patients 45 or older ASPD was found in 40% of the men and 4% of the women. Similar age and gender related trends were found in the rates of fights while drinking, alcohol-related arrests, and arrests for a criminal offense, in a sample of alcohol dependent men and women in treatment (Blankenfield, 1991).

Childhood behavior problems indicative of conduct disorder have also been more frequently reported among alcoholic men who are depressed than among nondepressed male alcoholics. In a study of alcoholic men, Fowler et al. (1980) reported more fights and nontraffic arrests among the depressed compared to the nondepressed men. A similar increase in sociopathic symptoms was reported among depressed males by Woodruff and colleagues (1973).

Consequences of Alcoholism: ASPD and Gender

A number of studies have shown the importance of co-occurring ASPD for the etiology of alcoholism and the outcome of alcoholism treatment. Compared with non-ASPD alcoholics, both male and female ASPD alcoholics report earlier onsets of regular drinking, of regular drinking to intoxication, and of problem drinking characteristics (Hesselbrock et al., 1984, 1985, 1986). Furthermore, ASPD alcoholics of both genders have a more severe course of the disorder, relapse sooner following treatment, and have a higher relapse rate following treatment than do non-ASPD alcoholics (Hesselbrock, 1991a,b).

It is likely, however, that ASPD, like alcoholism, is not a homogeneous disorder. For example, Loeber and Schmaling (1985) identified four types of antisocial behaviors based on the presence or absence of two factors: fighting and stealing. Differences were found between groups of boys in terms of disobedience, hyperactivity, irritability, negativism, alcohol/drug use, police contacts, and multiple offender status. The more severe types of conduct disorder are reported to persist from childhood into adulthood (Farrington, 1991), including in a sample of aggressive/nonaggressive ASPD alcoholics (Jaffe et al., 1988). Violent behavior by alcoholics in the Jaffe et al. (1988) study was greatest among those alcoholics with a history of childhood aggressive behavior.

Most studies of ASPD and alcoholism have focused only on samples of men. Few studies of alcoholism and ASPD have included female subjects.

However, ASPD has been documented among female problem drinkers, particularly in penal institutions and in delinquent samples (Gomberg, 1974). Lewis and associates (1983) studied 412 (281 women and 131 men) medical and surgical inpatients referred for psychiatric consultation, who were evaluated by psychiatric residents using a structured psychiatric screening interview. The 47 women and 34 men who met criteria for ASPD were compared with those diagnosed as not having ASPD. Antisocial men and women both had greater risks of alcoholism, with the risk greater among the ASPD men than among the ASPD women. Among those diagnosed as having alcoholism, the ASPD men and women reported an earlier age of onset of heavy drinking, with a shorter duration of heavy drinking, indicative of a faster progression to alcoholism than for non-ASPD alcoholic subjects. The age of onset of heavy drinking and duration of heavy drinking were similar for both sexes within the ASPD and non-ASPD groups. However, more males than females (both ASPD and non-ASPD) reported loss of control of drinking and problems limiting ethanol intake. Among the male alcoholic subjects, those with ASPD had a higher prevalence of loss of control and of trying to limit alcohol intake, but had rates of alcohol-related job difficulties, arrests, and fighting similar to non-ASPD alcoholic men.

Hesselbrock et al. (1984) compared hospitalized alcoholic men and women with and without ASPD, in terms of etiology and alcohol-related consequences. Persons with ASPD, regardless of gender, had an early onset of alcoholism followed by a more chronic and severe course of alcoholism. ASPD alcoholics also took their first drink and began regular drinking and drunkenness at much younger ages than their non-ASPD counterparts. ASPD alcoholics on average were 10 years younger than the non-ASPD alcoholics when assessed at the current hospitalization, but the duration of drinking problems was similar for the younger ASPD and older non-ASPD alcoholics. Furthermore, the frequency of physical, psychological, and social problems was similar for the ASPD and non-ASPD alcoholics. ASPD women, however, tended to progress more quickly from regular drinking to problem drinking than did ASPD men. Progression from regular drinking to problem drinking was similar for non-ASPD men and women. A further analysis of these data found that alcoholics who report a history of childhood conduct disorder or adult onset ASPD (i.e., subtypes of ASPD) have a form and course of alcoholism that is similar to that found among other ASPD alcoholics (Hesselbrock & Hesselbrock, 1994).

Expression of ASPD by Gender

Studies of familial relationships between ASPD and alcoholism suggest that phenotypic expression of ASPD may differ by gender (Cadoret et al., 1985; Cloninger & Reich, 1983; Cloninger et al., 1978a,b). These family study data suggest that ASPD may be a spectrum disorder expressed as sociopathy in males and expressed as somatization/Briquet's disorder in females. Consistent with this idea, a more recent longitudinal study (Windle, 1990) of boys and girls with conduct disorder found that antisocial behavior in early adolescence predicted later adolescent alcohol/substance abuse better among boys than among girls. The hypothesis that internalizing symptoms (e.g., somatic complaints, depression) rather than externalizing symptoms (e.g., conduct disorder, delinquency) may be more predictive of alcohol/drug use in girls is also consistent with data reported by Ensminger et al. (1982).

The phenomenological expression of ASPD, then, may vary both within and across gender. There appears to be at least two types of ASPD among males: aggressive and nonaggressive. For females, the severity of ASPD may influence its expression. Females with severe ASPD may closely resemble the male type of ASPD, while less severe cases may show more internalizing patterns (e.g., a histrionic, borderline, or somatoform disorder). However, there may be a gender bias in the diagnosis of ASPD. Ford and Widiger (1989) examined how the diagnosis of ASPD and histrionic disorder (another member of DSM-III-R Cluster B personality disorders) (American Psychiatric Association, 1987) was related to the gender of the patient. For an example case with symptoms meeting DSM-III-R criteria for antisocial personality disorder, clinicians diagnosed ASPD more frequently when the patient was identified as male, but diagnosed histrionic disorder more frequently when the patient was identified as female.

The Effect of ASPD and Gender on the Transmission of Alcoholism

The relationship of antisocial behavior to the genetic transmission of alcoholism may differ in men and women. Data from a sample of Swedish adoptees (Cloninger, 1987; Cloninger et al., 1981) have indicated that two distinct types of alcoholism and associated personality traits may be transmissible. Type 1 alcoholism was found to be associated with recurrent alcohol abuse in the proband, but without criminality in the biological parents. The personality features identified in Type 1 alcoholics included high levels of reward dependence (social approval) and harm avoidance (caution), but low levels of novelty seeking (preference for non-risk taking situations). Type 1 or "milieu-limited" alcoholism resembles the non-ASPD type of alcoholism often found in clinical samples in the United States. Type 2 or "male-limited" alcoholism, thought to be transmitted from father to son, was typically associated with criminality and severe alcohol use in the biological fathers. Personality traits identified in Type 2 alcoholics included low levels of reward dependence and harm avoidance, but high levels of novelty seeking. Type 2 alcoholism has many similarities to the behavior of ASPD alcoholics. Type 1 alcoholism was characterized by an age of onset after age 25, psychological dependence, and guilt and fear about alcohol dependence. Spontaneous alcohol-seeking behavior and fights and arrests when drinking were infrequent in Type 1 alcoholics. Type 2 alcoholism, however, was characterized by an onset of alcoholism before age 25, frequent alcohol-seeking behavior, and alcohol-related fighting and arrests. Psychological dependence, guilt, and fear about alcohol dependence were infrequent among persons with Type 2 alcoholism.

Examination of possible subtypes among female Swedish adoptees found only the Type 1 or "milieu-limited" form of alcoholism. Bohman et al. (1981) found that among women who were adopted away at an early age, the daughters inherited alcoholism from their biological mothers. Bohman et al. (1981) concluded that the type of alcoholism found in women was relatively homogeneous. However, the study design and the classifications of alcoholism in Cloninger et al. (1981) and Bohman et al. (1981) have been criticized for the relatively small sample size ($n = 31$ for female alcohol abusers), the sample selection methods, and the indirect measurement of the proband and father variables (i.e., use of archival record data vs. direct interview) (Vanclay & Raphael, 1990).

The presence of Type 2 or "male-limited" alcoholism has been studied in U.S. women by Glenn and Nixon (1991). They divided a sample of 51 female alcoholics according to early versus late onset of alcoholism. While Type 1 and Type 2 alcoholism could not be distinguished in terms of alcohol-related symptoms, the women with early onset more closely resembled male Type 2 alcoholics, including having a high rate of paternal and familial alcoholism. These data suggest that Type 2 alcoholism may not be limited to alcoholic males in the United States. A sample of alcoholic women and men analyzed in terms of the presence/absence of ASPD produced a similar finding (Hesselbrock, 1991). Although the number of ASPD women was small, alcoholic ASPD women had characteristics resembling Type 2 alcoholism. Babor et al. (1992), using an empirical clustering technique, found two subgroups resembling the Type 1 and Type 2 alcoholism in both male and female hospitalized alcoholics. The failure of the U.S. studies to confirm the gender differences in the Swedish adoptee study could be due to differences in the samples, methodology, culture, and other variables (Hesselbrock, 1995). Further research efforts are needed to resolve the discrepant findings noted above.

Summary and Implications

This chapter has reviewed relationships of eating disorders, affective disorder (depression), and antisocial personality disorder with alcoholism in terms of gender differences. Studies of how eating disorders are related to alcohol disorders are difficult to compare, because of variation in samples and in how both eating and alcohol disorders are defined and measured. Nevertheless, an association between alcoholism and eating disorders is a consistent finding among persons with a primary eating disorder.

Alcoholism can be hard to distinguish from depression or antisocial personality disorder using clinical phenomenology alone. The pharmacological effects of chronic ethanol consumption can produce depressive-like symptoms, and persons who chronically abuse alcohol often display a variety of conduct problems. High prevalences of depression among alcoholic women, and of antisocial personality disorder among alcoholic men, have been found in both treated and untreated samples of alcoholics. When antisocial personality disorder or its subtypes and alcoholism co-occur, they are associated with an earlier onset and a more severe course of alcoholism in both males and females. Effects of depression on the development of alcoholism are not as clear; some but not all studies have found that depressive symptoms are associated with more severe alcoholism.

Implications for Future Research

At least two methodological concerns identified here should be addressed in future studies. First, the diagnostic criteria used to identify eating disorder, affective disorder, ASPD, and alcoholism have not been consistent across studies, making direct comparisons difficult. For example, the diagnosis of depressive disorder made utilizing a standardized diagnostic interview and criteria may not agree with "depression" identified using rating scales that assess only the occurrence of symptoms (e.g., the Beck Scale) (Hesselbrock et al., 1983). The presence of a psychiatric disorder should be distinguished from the sporadic occurrence of psychiatric symptoms occurring over an extended period of time.

Second, since the majority of published studies of alcoholism have employed only samples of men, more studies of women with dual diagnoses are needed. In those studies in which women are included in the sample, gender comparisons are not always presented. With an apparent increase in the prevalence of alcoholism among women, more knowledge of possible dual diagnoses/comorbid conditions in female patients would assist clinicians in providing more appropriate and timely interventions.

References

American Psychiatric Association. (1980). *Diagnostic and statistical manual of mental disorders* (3rd ed.). Washington, DC: Author.

American Psychiatric Association. (1987). *Diagnostic and statistical manual of mental disorders* (3rd ed., rev.). Washington, DC: Author.

Babor, T.F., Hofmann, M., DelBoca, F.K., Hesselbrock, V.M., & Meyer, R.E. (1992). Types of alcoholics II: Evidence for an empirically derived typology based on indicators of vulnerability and severity. *Archives of General Psychiatry, 49,* 599-608.

Bander, K.W., Rabinowitz, E., Turner, S., & Grunberg, H. (1983). Patterns of depression in women alcoholics. *Alcoholism: Clinical and Experimental Research, 7,* 105.

Beary, M.D., Lacey, J.H., & Merry, J. (1986). Alcoholism and eating disorders in women of fertile age. *British Journal of Addiction, 81,* 685-689.

Behar, D., Winokur, G., & Berg, C.J. (1984). Depression in the abstinent alcoholic. *American Journal of Psychiatry, 141,* 1105-1107.

Berner, P., Lesch, O.M., & Walter, H. (1986). Alcohol and depression. *Psychopathology, 19* (Suppl. 2), 177-186.

Birnbaum, I.M., Taylor, T.H., & Parker, E.S. (1983). Alcohol and sober mood state in female social drinkers. *Alcoholism: Clinical and Experimental Research, 7,* 362-368.

Blankfield, A. (1990). Female alcoholics II. The expression of alcoholism in relation to gender and age. *Acta Psychiatrica Scandinavica, 81,* 448-452.

Blankfield, A. (1991). Women, alcohol dependence and crime. *Drug and Alcohol Dependence, 27,* 185-190.

Bohman, M., Sigvardsson, S., & Cloninger, C.R. (1981). Maternal inheritance of alcohol abuse: Cross-fostering analysis of adopted women. *Archives of General Psychiatry, 38,* 965-969.

Boothroyd, W.E. (1980). Nature and development of alcoholism in women. In O.J. Kalant, (Ed.), *Alcohol and Drug Problems in Women* (pp. 299-330). New York: Plenum.

Brisman, J. & Siegel, M. (1984). Bulimia and alcoholism: Two sides of the same coin? *Journal of Substance Abuse Treatment, 1,* 113-118.

Cadoret, R., & Winokur, G. (1974). Depression in alcoholism. *Annals of New York Academy of Science, 233,* 34-39

Cadoret, R.J., O'Gorman, T.W., Troughton, E., & Heywood, E. (1985). Alcoholism and antisocial personality: Interrelationships, genetic and environmental factors. *Archives of General Psychiatry, 42,* 161-167.

Cadoret, R., Troughton, E., & Widmer, R. (1984). Clinical differences between antisocial and primary alcoholics. *Comprehensive Psychiatry, 25,* 1-8.

Clark, W.B., & Hesselbrock, M. (1988). A comparative analysis of U.S. and Japanese drinking patterns. In L.H. Towle and T.D. Harford (Eds.), *Cultural influences and drinking patterns: A focus on Hispanic and Japanese populations* (pp. 79-98) (NIAAA Research Monograph No. 19; DHHS Publication No. ADM 88-1563). Washington, DC: U.S. Government Printing Office.

Clark, W.B., & Hilton, M.E. (Eds.). (1991). *Alcohol in America: Drinking practices and problems.* Albany, NY: State University of New York Press.

Cloninger, C.R. (1987). Neurogenetic adaptive mechanisms in alcoholism. *Science, 236,* 410-416.

Cloninger, C.R., Bohman, M., & Sigvardsson, S. (1981). Inheritance of alcohol abuse: Cross-fostering analysis of adopted men. *Archives of General Psychiatry, 38,* 861-868.

Cloninger, C.R., Christiansen, K.O., Reich, T., & Gottesman, I.I. (1978a). Implications of sex differences in the prevalences of antisocial personality, alcoholism, and criminality of familial transmission. *Archives of General Psychiatry, 35,* 941-951.

Cloninger, C.R., & Reich, T. (1983). Genetic heterogeneity in alcoholism and sociopathy. *Research Publications-Association for Research in Nervous and Mental Disease, 60,* 145-166.

Cloninger, C.R., Reich, T., & Guze, S.B. (1978b). Genetic-environmental interactions and antisocial behavior. In R.D. Hare, & D. Schalling (Eds.), *Psychopathic behavior: Approaches to research* (pp. 225-237). New York: Wiley.

Dackis, C.A., Gold, M.S., Pottash, A.L.C., & Sweeney, D.R. (1986). Evaluating depression in alcoholics. *Psychiatry Research, 17,* 105-109.

Dorus, W., Kennedy, J., Gibbons, R.D., & Ravi, S.D. (1987). Symptoms and diagnosis of depression in alcoholics. *Alcoholism: Clinical and Experimental Research, 11,* 150-154.

Ensminger, M., Brown, C.H., & Kellam, S. (1982). Sex differences in antecedents of substance use among adolescents. *Journal of Social Issues, 38,* 25-42.

Farrington, D.P. (1991). Antisocial personality from childhood to adulthood. *Psychologist, 4,* 389-394.

Ford, M.R., & Widiger, T.A. (1989). Sex bias in the diagnosis of histrionic and antisocial personality disorders. *Journal of Consulting and Clinical Psychology, 57,* 301-305.

Fowler, R.C., Liskow, B.I., & Tanna, V.L. (1980). Alcoholism, depression, and life events. *Journal of Affective Disorders, 2,* 125-135.

Gerstley, L.J., Alterman, A.I., McLellan, A.T., & Woody, G.E. (1990). Antisocial personality disorder in patients with substance abuse disorders: a problematic diagnosis? *American Journal of Psychiatry, 147,* 173-178.

Glenn, S.W., & Nixon, S.J. (1991). Applications of Cloninger's subtypes in a female alcoholic sample. *Alcoholism: Clinical and Experimental Research, 15,* 851-857.

Gomberg, E.S. (1974). Women and alcoholism. In V. Franks & V. Burtle (Eds.), *Women in therapy: New psychotherapies for a changing society* (pp. 169-190). New York: Brunner/Mazel.

Gomberg, E.S.L. (1986). Women and alcoholism: Psychosocial issues. In *Women and alcohol:Health related issues* (pp. 78-120) (NIAAA Research Monograph No. 16; DHHS Publication No. ADM 86-1139). Washington, DC: U.S. Government Printing Office.

Gomberg, E.S.L. (1989). Suicide risk among women with alcohol problems. *American Journal of Public Health, 79,* 1363-1365.

Gomberg, E.S.L. & Turnbull, J.E. (1990). Alcoholism in women: Pathways to treatment. *Alcoholism: Clinical and Experimental Research, 14,* 312 (Abstract).

Goodwin, D.W., Schulsinger, F., Knop, J., Mednick, S., & Guze, S.B. (1977). Alcoholism and depression in adopted-out daughter of alcoholics. *Archives of General Psychiatry, 34,* 751-755.

Gritz, E.R. (1986). Gender and the teenage smoker. In B.A. Ray & M.C. Braude (Eds.), *Women and drugs: A new era for research* (pp. 70-79) (NIDA Research Monograph No. 65; DHHS Publication No. ADM 86-1447). Washington, DC: U.S. Government Printing Office.

Hatsukami, D., Eckert, J., Mitchell, J.E., & Pyle, R. (1984). Affective disorder and substance abuse in women with bulimia. *Psychological Medicine, 14,* 701-704.

Helzer, J.E., & Pryzbeck, T.R. (1988). The co-occurrence of alcoholism with other psychiatric disorders in the general population and its impact on treatment. *Journal of Studies on Alcohol, 49,* 219-224.

Herzog, D.B. (1982). Bulimia in the adolescent. *American Journal of Diseases of Children, 136,* 985-989.

Herzog, D.B., Burus, J.F., Hamburg, P., Ott, I.L., & Concus, A. (1987). Substance use, eating behaviors, and social impairment of medical students. *Journal of Medical Education, 62,* 651-657.

Hershon, H.I. (1977). Alcohol withdrawal symptoms and drinking behavior. *Journal of Studies on Alcohol, 38,* 953-971.

Hesselbrock, M.N. (1991a). Gender comparison of antisocial personality disorder and depression in alcoholism. *Journal of Substance Abuse, 3,* 205-219.

Hesselbrock, M.N. (1991b). *Dual diagnosis in alcoholism: Gender comparison.* Paper presented at the annual meeting of the Research Society on Alcoholism.

Hesselbrock, M.N. (1995). Genetic determinants of alcoholic subtypes. In H. Begleiter & B. Kissin (Eds.), *The genetics of alcoholism* (pp. 40–69). New York: Oxford.

Hesselbrock, M.N., Meyer, R.E., & Keener J.J. (1985). Psychopathology in hospitalized alcoholics. *Archives of General Psychiatry, 42,* 1050–1055.

Hesselbrock, M.N., Hesselbrock, V.M., Babor, T.F., Stabenau, J.R., Meyer, R.E., & Weidenman, M. (1984). Antisocial behavior, psychopathology and problem drinking in the natural history of alcoholism. In D.W. Goodwin, K.T. Van Dusen, & S.A. Mednick (Eds.), *Longitudinal research in alcoholism* (pp. 197–214). Boston: Kluwer-Nijhoff.

Hesselbrock, M.N., Hesselbrock, V.M., Syzmanski, K., & Weidenman, M. (1988). Suicide attempts and alcoholism. *Journal of Studies on Alcohol, 49,* 436–442.

Hesselbrock, M.N., Hesselbrock, V.M., Tennen, H., Meyer, R.E., & Workman, K.L. (1983). Methodological considerations in the assessment of depression of alcoholics. *Journal of Consulting and Clinical Psychology, 51,* 399–405.

Hesselbrock, V.M., & Hesselbrock, M.N. (1994). Alcoholism and subtypes of antisocial personality disorder. *Alcoholic & Alcoholism, 29* (Suppl. 2), 479–484.

Hesselbrock, V.M., Hesselbrock, M.N., & Workman-Daniels, K.L. (1986). Effect of major depression and antisocial personality on alcoholism: Course and motivational patterns. *Journal of Studies on Alcohol, 47,* 207–212.

Hesselbrock, V.M., Hesselbrock, M.N. & Stabenau, J.R. (1985). Alcoholism in men patients subtyped by family history and antisocial personality. *Journal of Studies on Alcohol, 46,* 59–64.

Hirshfeld, R.M.A., Kosier, T., Keller, M.B., Lavori, P.W., & Endicott, J. (1989). The influence of alcoholism on the course of depression. *Journal of Affective Disorders, 16,* 151–158.

Hudson, J.I., Pope, H.G., Jonas, J.M., & Yurgelun-Todd, D. (1983). Family history study of anorexia nervosa and bulimia. *British Journal of Psychiatry, 142,* 428–429.

Jacobson, G. (1987). Alcohol and drug dependency problems in special populations: women. In R.E. Herrington, G.R. Jacobson, & D.G. Benzer (Eds.), *Alcohol and drug abuse handbook* (pp. 385–404). St. Louis: Warren H. Green.

Jaffe, J.H., Babor, T.F., & Fishbein, D.H. (1988). Alcoholics, aggression, and antisocial personality. *Journal of Studies on Alcohol, 49,* 211–218.

Keeler, M.H., Taylor, C.I. & Miller, W.C. (1979). Are all recently detoxified alcoholics depressed? *American Journal of Psychiatry, 136,* 586–588.

Kessler, R.C., McGonagle, K.A., Zhao, S., Nelson, C.B., Hughes, M., Eshleman, S., Wittchen, H., & Kendler, K. (1994). Lifetime and 12-month prevalence of DSM-III-R psychiatric disorders in the United States: Results from the National Comorbidity Study. *Archives of General Psychiatry, 51,* 8–19.

Kog, E., & Vandereycken, W. (1985). Family characteristics of anorexia nervosa and bulimia: A review of the research literature. *Clinical Psychology Review, 5,* 159–180.

Krahn, D.D. (1991). The relationship of eating disorders and substance abuse. *Journal of Substance Abuse, 3,* 239–253.

Krahn, D.D. (1993). The relationship of eating disorders and substance abuse. In E.S.L. Gomberg & T.D. Nirenberg (Eds.), *Women and substance abuse* (pp. 286–313). Norwood, NJ: Ablex.

LaPorte, D.J., McLellan, A.T., O'Brien, C.P., & Marshall, J.R. (1981). Treatment response in psychiatrically impaired drug abusers. *Comprehensive Psychiatry, 22,* 411–419.

Lewis, C.E., Rice, J., & Helzer, J.E. (1983). Diagnostic interactions: Alcoholism and antisocial personality. *Journal of Nervous and Mental Disease, 171,* 105–113.

Lippmann, S., Manshadi, M., Christie, S., & Gultekin, A. (1987). Depression in alcoholics by the NIMH Diagnostic Interview Schedule and Zung Self-Rating Depression Scale. *International Journal of the Addictions, 22,* 273-281.

Loeber, R., & Schmaling, K.B. (1985). The utility of differentiating between mixed and pure forms of antisocial child behavior. *Journal of Abnormal Child Psychology, 13,* 315-335.

MacDonald, J.G. (1987). Predictors of treatment outcome for alcoholic women. *International Journal of the Addictions, 22,* 235-248.

McLellan, A.T., Luborsky, L., Woody, G.E., O'Brien, C.P., & Druley, K.A. (1983). Predicting response to alcohol and drug abuse treatments: Role of psychiatric severity. *Archives of General Psychiatry, 40,* 620-625.

McMahon, R.C., & Davidson, R.S. (1986). An examination of depressed vs. nondepressed alcoholics in inpatient treatment. *Journal of Clinical Psychology, 42,* 177-184.

Meyer, R.E. (1986). How to understand the relationship between psychopathology and addictive disorders: Another example of the chicken and the egg. In R.E. Meyer (Ed.), *Psychopathology and addictive disorders* (pp. 3-16). New York: Guilford.

Mitchell, J.E., Hatsukami, D., Eckert, E.D., & Pyle, R.L. (1985). Characteristics of 275 patients with bulimia. *American Journal of Psychiatry, 142,* 482-485.

Mulinski, P. (1989). Dual diagnosis in alcoholic clients: Clinical implications. *Social Casework, 70,* 333-339.

National Institute on Drug Abuse (1991). *National Household Survey on Drug Abuse: Population estimate, 1991* (DHHS Publication No. ADM 92-1887). Washington, DC: U.S. Government Printing Office.

Nathan, P.E., & Lisman, S.A. (1976). Behavioral and motivational patterns of chronic alcoholics. In R.E. Tarter, & A.A. Sugerman (Eds.), *Alcoholism: Interdisciplinary approaches to an enduring problem* (pp. 479-522). Reading, Mass.: Addison-Wesley.

O'Sullivan, K., Whillans, P., Daly, M., Carroll, B., Clare, A., & Cooney, J. (1983). A comparison of alcoholics with and without coexisting affective disorder. *British Journal of Psychiatry, 143,* 133-138.

Penick, E.C., Powell, B.J., Othmer, E., Bingham, S.F., Rice, A.S., & Liese, B.S. (1984) Subtyping alcoholics by coexisting psychiatric syndromes: Course, family history and outcome. In D.W. Goodwin, K.T. Van-Dusen, & S.A. Mednick (Eds.), *Longitudinal Research in Alcoholism.* Boston: Kluwer-Nijhoff, pp. 167-196.

Penick, E.C., Powell, B.J., Liskow, B.I., Jackson, J.O., & Nickel, E.J. (1988). The stability of coexisting psychiatric syndromes in alcoholic men after one year. *Journal of Studies on Alcohol, 49,* 395-405.

Peveler, R., & Fairburn, C. (1990). Eating disorders in women who abuse alcohol. *British Journal of Addiction, 85,* 1633-1638.

Pitts, F.N., Jr., & Winokur, G. (1966). Affective disorder: VII. Alcoholism and affective disorder. *Journal of Psychiatric Research, 4,* 37-50.

Pottenger, M., McKernon, J., Patrie, L.E., Weissman, M.M., Ruben, H.L., & Newberry, P. (1978). The frequency of persistence of depressive symptoms in the alcohol abuser. *Journal of Nervous and Mental Disease, 166,* 562-570.

Pyle, R.L., Mitchell, J.E., Eckert, E.D., Halvorson, P.A., Neuman, P.A., & Goff, G.M. (1983). The incidence of bulimia in freshman college students. *International Journal of Eating Disorders, 2,* 75-85.

Regier, D.A., Farmer, M.E., Rae, D.S., Locke, B.Z., Keith, S.J., Judd, L.L., & Goodwin, F.K. (1990). Comorbidity of mental disorders with alcohol and other drug abuse: Results from the Epidemiologic Catchment Area (ECA) Study. *Journal of the American Medical Association, 264,* 2511-2518.

Robins, L.N., Helzer, J.E., Croughan, J. & Ratcliff, K. (1981). National Institute of Mental Health Diagnostic Interview Schedule: Its history, characteristics, and validity. *Archives of General Psychiatry, 38,* 381-389.

Ross, H.E., Glaser, F.B., & Stiasny, S. (1988). Sex differences in the prevalence of psychiatric disorders in patients with alcohol and other drug problems. *British Journal of Addiction, 83,* 1179-1192.

Rounsaville, B.J., Dolinsky, Z.S., Babor, T.F., & Meyer, R.E. (1987). Psychopathology as a predictor of treatment outcome in alcoholics. *Archives of General Psychiatry, 44,* 505-513.

Schmidt, C., Klee, L., & Ames, G. (1990). Review and analysis of literature on indicators of women's drinking problems. *British Journal of Addiction, 85,* 179-192.

Schuckit, M.A. (1973). Alcoholism and sociopathy-diagnostic confusion. *Quarterly Journal of Studies on Alcohol, 34,* 157-164.

Schuckit, M.A. (1979). Alcoholism and affective disorder: Diagnostic confusion. In D.W. Goodwin & C.K. Erickson (Eds.), *Alcoholism and affective disorders: Clinical, genetic, and biochemical studies* (pp. 9-19). New York: SP Medical and Scientific Books.

Schuckit, M.A. (1983a). Alcoholic patients with secondary depression. *American Journal of Psychiatry, 140,* 711-714.

Schuckit, M.A. (1983b). Alcoholism and other psychiatric disorders. *Hospital and Community Psychiatry, 34,* 1022-1027.

Schuckit, M.A. (1986). Genetic and clinical implications of alcoholism and affective disorder. *American Journal of Psychiatry, 143,* 140-147.

Schuckit, M.A., & Monteiro, M.G. (1988). Alcoholism, anxiety and depression. *British Journal of Addiction, 83,* 1373-1380.

Schuckit, M., Pitts, F.N., Jr., Reich, T., King, L.J., & Winokur, G. (1969). Alcoholism: I. Two types of alcoholism in women. *Archives of General Psychiatry, 20,* 301-306.

Schuckit, M.A., Rimmer, J., Reich, T., & Winokur, G. (1971). The bender alcoholic. *British Journal of Psychiatry, 119,* 183-184.

Schuckit, M.A., Tipp, J.E., Anthenelli, R.M., Bucholz, K.K., Hesselbrock, V.M., & Nurnberger, J.I. (1996). Anorexia nervosa and bulimia nervosa in alcohol dependent men and women and their relatives. *American Journal of Psychiatry, 153,* 74-82.

Schuckit, M.A., & Winokur, G. (1972). A short-term follow-up of women alcoholics. *Diseases of the Nervous System, 33,* 672-678.

Solomon, J. (1983). Psychiatric characteristics of alcoholics. In B. Kissin & H. Begleiter (Eds.), *The Pathogenesis of Alcoholism: Psychosocial Factors* (pp. 67-112). New York: Plenum.

Strober, M., Salkin, B., Burroughs, M., & Morrell, W. (1982). Validity of the bulimia-restricter distinction in anorexia nervosa: Parental personality characteristics and family psychiatric morbidity. *Journal of Nervous and Mental Disease, 170,* 345-351.

Tamerin, J.S., Weiner, S., & Mendelson, J.H. (1970). Alcoholics' expectancies and recall of experiences during intoxication. *American Journal of Psychiatry, 126,* 1697-1704.

Turnbull, J.E., & Gomberg, E.S.L. (1988). Impact of depressive symptomatology on alcohol problems in women. *Alcoholism: Clinical and Experimental Research, 12,* 374-381.

Vaglum, S., Vaglum, P., & Larsen, O. (1987). Depression and alcohol consumption in non-alcoholic and alcoholic women: A clinical study. *Acta Psychiatrica Scandinavica, 75,* 577-584.

Vanclay, F.M. & Raphael, B. (1990). Type 1 and Type 2 alcoholics: Schuckit and Irwin's negative findings. *British Journal of Addiction, 85,* 683-684 (Letter to the editor).

Weissman, M.M., Myers, J.K., & Harding, P.S. (1980). Prevalence and psychiatric heterogeneity of alcoholism in a United States urban community. *Journal of Studies on Alcohol, 41,* 672-681.

Wilsnack, S.C., Klassen, A.D., Schur, B.E., & Wilsnack, R.W. (1991). Predicting onset and chronicity of women's problem drinking: A five-year longitudinal analysis. *American Journal of Public Health, 81,* 305-318.

Windle, M. (1990). A longitudinal study of antisocial behaviors in early adolescence as predictors of late adolescent substance use: Gender and ethnic group differences. *Journal of Abnormal Psychology, 99,* 86-91.

Windle, M. & Miller, B.A. (1989). Alcoholism and depressive symptomatology among convicted DWI men and women. *Journal of Studies on Alcohol, 50,* 406-413.

Winokur, G., Reich, T., Rimmer, J., & Pitts, F.N., Jr. (1970). Alcoholism: III. Diagnosis and familial psychiatric illness in 259 alcoholic probands. *Archives of General Psychiatry, 23,* 104-111.

Winokur, G., Rimmer, J., & Reich, T. (1971). Alcoholism: IV. Is there more than one type of alcoholism? *British Journal of Psychiatry, 118,* 525-531.

Winokur, A., March, V., & Mendels, J. (1980). Primary affective disorder in relatives of patients with anorexia nervosa. *American Journal of Psychiatry, 137,* 695-698.

Woodruff, R.A., Jr., Guze, S.B., Clayton, P.J., & Carr, D. (1973). Alcoholism and depression. *Archives of General Psychiatry, 28,* 97-100.

Yates, W.R., Petty, F., & Brown, K. (1988). Factors associated with depression among primary alcoholics. *Comprehensive Psychiatry, 29,* 28-33.

Yeary, J.R., & Heck, C.L. (1989). Dual diagnosis: Eating disorders and psychoactive substance dependence. *Journal of Psychoactive Drugs, 21,* 239-249.

Zweben, J.E. (1987). Eating disorders and substance abuse. *Journal of Psychoactive Drugs, 19,* 181-192.

SECTION II

Biology and Gender Differences in Alcohol Use and Effects

Introductory Note

The authors of the chapters in this section all try to answer this question: Are there biological differences between women and men that contribute to differences in their drinking behavior and its effects? The authors find that answers to that question are more complex or more difficult than one might assume.

The first two chapters deal with well-recognized sex differences in alcohol effects. Lieber's chapter builds on two basic findings: women develop higher blood alcohol levels than do men from the same oral intake of alcohol, and women are more vulnerable than men to liver damage from alcohol use. Interpreting these findings is not easy because it is uncertain how biological differences can cause these effects and how large the effects are. Lieber relates the higher blood alcohol levels in women to sex differences in body water levels, in gastric metabolism of alcohol, and in effects of sex hormones on alcohol metabolism. Causes of women's susceptibility to liver damage are at least as complex, but identification of these causes has been much more tentative. These findings should simulate some hard thinking about an important policy issue: how women and men should be warned about alcohol use when women are known to have higher risks from drinking, but the sizes and sources of women's and men's risks are still unclear.

The same policy issue is relevant when reading Passaro and Little's chapter on alcohol effects on pregnancy. There are obvious sex differences in the ways that use of alcohol could affect pregnancy outcomes. It is also clear that some pattern of heavy alcohol consumption during pregnancy increases the likelihood that children will be born with fetal alcohol syndrome (FAS). However, the relationship between levels of alcohol use and levels of FAS risks is not yet well defined. There is even greater uncertainty about whether or to what degree moderate alcohol consumption during pregnancy adversely affects miscarriage and stillbirth risks, birth weight, and postnatal development. Passaro and Little suggest that findings vary because research has not yet adequately specified the effects of drinking *patterns* during pregnancy (rather than average levels of consumption) and the effects of the timing of consumption (before, during, and after pregnancy). They also emphasize the need for research on effects of paternal drinking (e.g., on sperm and seminal fluid), and the need to evaluate whether effects of maternal drinking may be curvilinear.

Although there are well-established differences in biological effects of alcohol on women and men, there may not be such clear differences in biological influences on how women and men use alcohol. Heath and colleagues argue that while evidence for genetic influences on alcoholism may currently

75

be more convincing for men than for women (in terms of numbers of studies and sample sizes), the evidence at present does *not* support a conclusion that genetic influences are more powerful for one sex than for the other. Comparisons of genetic influences on women's versus men's alcoholism are complicated by variations in the methods of data collection (including the use of clinical versus general population samples) and variations in the analytic models used to search for genetic effects. There are several possible behavioral pathways by which genes could affect the risks of developing alcoholism, but research has not yet determined whether these pathways differ for women and men. Again, any effort to use what is known about the biology of gender and alcohol—in prevention, treatment, or policy—must be restrained by what is not yet known.

CHAPTER 3

Gender Differences in Alcohol Metabolism and Susceptibility

CHARLES S. LIEBER

Until recently, most studies concerning the adverse effects of alcohol focused mainly on men because, on the average, men drink much more than women and therefore bear the brunt of the adverse effects. However, evidence is accumulating that women may be more affected than men by the same dosage of alcohol (Hill, 1995), and that women may be more susceptible than men to the development of somatic complications of alcoholism, such as liver disease (Van Thiel, 1991). Such gender differences will become more important if women's drinking increases (Mercer & Khavari, 1990), particularly in more recent generations (Corti & Ibrahim, 1990; Gomberg, 1993). Therefore, this chapter reviews current knowledge about gender differences in alcohol metabolism and in susceptibility to liver damage from alcohol consumption.

Gender Differences in Ethanol Distribution and Metabolism

Women have higher blood ethanol concentrations than do men after an equivalent oral dose (Jones & Jones, 1976). One explanation has been based on the observation that per kilogram of body weight, women's body water content (water insoluble in fat) is smaller than men's. A dose of ethanol will be distributed in a smaller volume of water in women than in men (a smaller *volume of distribution*), and so should produce higher concentrations of ethanol in women's blood (Arthur et al., 1984; Marshall et al., 1983). We have confirmed that the volume of distribution for ethanol is smaller in women than in men (Frezza et al., 1990). However, the volume of distribution, calculated from intravenous curves, was apparently only 12% larger in normal men than in normal women (767 ± 4 ml per kilogram in the men and 686 ± 6 in women; $p < .05$) (Frezza et al., 1990).

We wondered, therefore, whether other factors might contribute to the higher blood alcohol levels in women. We focused on how alcohol is metabolized during its "first pass" through the stomach, in a process involving the enzyme gastric alcohol dehydrogenase. Through first-pass metabolism with gastric alcohol dehydrogenase, the stomach acts as a kind of "protective" barrier against the penetration of alcohol into the body, by retaining and breaking down part of the alcohol consumed orally.

Although it is generally recognized that the liver is the main site of ethanol metabolism (Lieber, 1992), extrahepatic metabolism occurs. Ethanol oxidation in the digestive tract of the rat has been previously reported (Lamboeuf et al., 1981, 1983) and has been related to the alcohol dehydrogenase (ADH) present in this tissue (Hempel & Pietruszko, 1979; Pestalozzi et al., 1983). In the rat, the ability of the stomach to oxidize ethanol has been demonstrated *in vitro* (in tissue isolated in the laboratory) (Carter & Isselbacher, 1971) and *in vivo* (in the living organism) (Lamboeuf et al., 1983). However, the magnitude of gastrointestinal ethanol metabolism was assumed to be small (Lamboeuf et al., 1981, 1983). Some authors (Lin & Lester, 1980) could not demonstrate any significant gastrointestinal ethanol oxidation when they gave an acute high dose to rats, so they (and more recently Wagner, 1986) concluded that this process was of negligible quantitative significance. The issue was reopened when it was shown that when rats ingest alcohol in doses comparable to human "social" drinking, a significant fraction of the alcohol does not enter the systemic circulation and is oxidized mainly in the stomach (Julkunen et al., 1985a,b; Lim et al., 1993). This process also was shown to occur in man with small (0.15 g/kg) as well as moderate (0.3 g/kg) doses of alcohol (see Figures 1 and 2) (DiPadova et al., 1987; Julkunen et al., 1985a). Moreover, gastrectomy (removal of the stomach) was associated with an abolition of the first pass metabolism (Caballeria et al., 1989).

In the rat stomach, an ADH isoenzyme has been described (Cederbaum et al., 1975; Julia et al., 1987), which, contrary to the main isoenzymes of the liver, is not inhibited by high ethanol concentrations. This gastric ADH is not very effective when ethanol levels are low; it requires a large amount of the alcohol substrate, a high Km, to be most active. However, it is effective in the oxidation of ethanol at the high concentrations prevailing in the gastric lumen during alcohol consumption (Halsted et al., 1973). A similar isoenzyme has been identified in the baboon stomach (Holmes et al., 1986). Previously, only isoenzymes active at low levels of ethanol have been reported in the human stomach (Hempel & Pietruszko, 1979). However, the latter studies were done in autopsy material and at low ethanol concentrations. When we reassessed gastric ADH activity in fresh surgical specimens of human stomach tissue, using ethanol concentrations similar to those prevailing in the stomach during the drinking of alcoholic beverages, we identified several ADH isoenzymes differing in their affinity for ethanol. At the high concentrations prevailing in the gastric lumen during alcohol consumption, the combined activity of these enzymes could account for substantial oxidation of ethanol (Hernández-Muñoz et al., 1990). The magnitude of this process was assessed to amount to about 20% of the ethanol administered when given at a low dose

FIGURE 1

Bioavailability of ethanol in five normal subjects after a small dose of ethanol (0.15 g/kg body weight). Ethanol was administered in a 5% dextrose solution (5 g/100 ml) perorally or intravenously 1 hour after a standard breakfast. Drinking time was 10 minutes and that of the intravenous infusion was 20 minutes. The black area in the figure reflects the amount of ingested alcohol that did not enter the systemic circulation and gives an indication of the magnitude of the first-pass metabolism of ethanol. (From DiPadova et al., 1987. Reprinted by permission of *Gastroenterology*, vol. 92, pp. 1169–1173, 1987. Copyright 1987 by W.B. Saunders Co.)

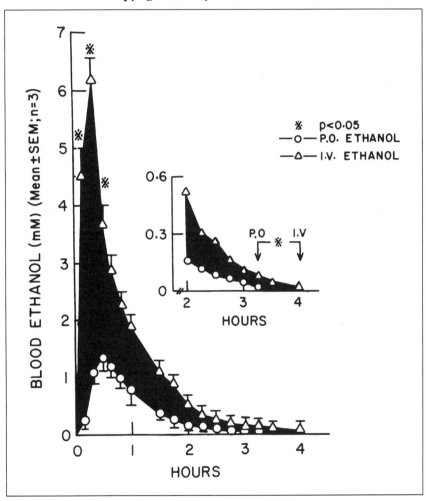

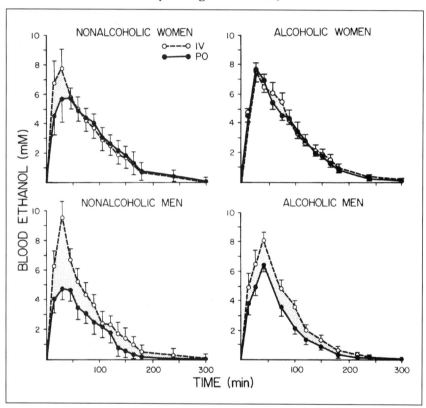

to rats (Caballeria et al., 1987; Roine et al., 1991) or to human males (Di-Padova et al., 1992).

Gastric alcohol dehydrogenase activities correlated significantly with the magnitude of the first-pass metabolism and, since the activities were lower in women than in men, as expected, first-pass metabolism also was decreased. For a given alcohol dose, men's ADH levels were two times higher than women's, and blood alcohol levels of women were higher than those in men (Figure 2). Alcoholism further decreased the ADH activity and first-pass metabolism, with a corresponding rise in blood levels of alcohol. Those effects were more striking in alcoholic women (Figure 2). In alcoholic women, blood levels of alcohol were virtually the same whether the alcohol was given orally or intravenously, and thus alcoholic women have lost the "gastric protective mechanism."

Supportive evidence was obtained in animals by Lee at al. (1992). Gastric ADH kinetic activity in female rats was significantly less than that observed in male counterparts of similar weight ($p < .04$), and ethanol damage to the gastric mucosa in female rats was more severe than in corresponding males, damage which may be linked to the lower ADH kinetic activity in the female gastric mucosa.

Thus, it is understandable that for a given dose of alcohol, blood levels achieved are higher in women than in men. This effect is particularly striking in alcoholic women, but it is also of great significance for social drinking in normal women. Indeed, for a given dose of alcohol, normal women develop higher blood levels than men for at least three reasons. First, women are usually smaller than men, but the amounts of alcohol offered to them in social settings does not take this gender difference into account. Second, the alcohol consumed is distributed in a smaller water space (*vide supra*). Finally, less of the alcohol will be broken down in the stomach and more will reach the peripheral blood. These differences are obvious at levels of social drinking (Figure 2). It is therefore clear that what is considered a moderate dose for men is not necessarily moderate for women. These gender differences are now being taken into account in recently published guidelines for moderate drinking, which define moderate consumption as not more than two drinks per day in men, but only one drink per day in women (Dietary Guidelines, 1995), with a drink considered to be 12 ounces of regular beer, 5 ounces of wine, or 1.5 ounces of distilled spirits (80 proof).

In Figure 2 (Frezza et al., 1990), the largest sex-related differences in blood ethanol concentrations appear after oral administration. These results are consistent with those of Marshall et al. (1983), who found that the area under the blood alcohol concentration (BAC) time curve was greater in women than in men, indicating that after oral administration of the same dose of alcohol, women's BACs were higher than men's and remained high for a longer time. We found a much smaller sex-related difference after intravenous administration (Frezza et al., 1990). Could sex differences in ADH activity in the gastric mucosa explain the relatively striking difference in blood ethanol levels after oral intake (Figure 2)? Lower rates of first-pass metabolism in normal women compared with normal men (Frezza et al., 1990) and in alcoholics compared with nonalcoholics of each sex (Di Padova et al., 1987; Frezza et al., 1990) all parallelled changes in gastric ADH activities that were consistent with the role of gastric ethanol oxidation. Because peripheral blood levels of alcohol represent the difference between the amount of alcohol that reaches the circulation and the amount metabolized, even a modest excess of alcohol intake over the metabolic capacity can produce relatively large changes in blood levels of alcohol, with consequently substantial effects on the brain and other tissues.

In contemporary social settings, younger women are commonly served amounts of alcohol comparable to those given to men. Making women aware of their increased vulnerability may strengthen their resolve to resist the social pressures that may lead to inappropriate levels of consumption, possibly resulting in impairment of the ability to drive an automobile and to perform other similar tasks. In addition, the increased bioavailability also may influence the severity of medical problems related to drinking (as discussed later with regard to liver disease).

Women and men differ in other aspects of ethanol metabolism. Some studies have found that women eliminate ethanol more rapidly than do men (Cole-Harding & Wilson, 1987; Mishra et al., 1989), particularly when comparing natural siblings (with less genetic variability). Furthermore, women have higher ethanol-induced acetaldehyde levels than do men (Fukunaga et al., 1993). Individual differences may be great enough, however, that comparisons of randomly chosen subjects may not find gender differences (Marshall et al., 1983). One explanation for any slower elimination of ethanol by men is that hepatic ADH activity is suppressed by testosterone and its derivatives, both *in vivo* (Teschke & Wiese, 1982) and at high concentrations *in vitro* (Mezey et al., 1986). ADH activity in the liver is significantly higher in women than in men until they reach their early 50s (Maly & Sasse, 1991), suggesting that the difference may be premenopausal.

The menstrual cycle is important for women's metabolism of alcohol particularly through its effects on gastric emptying (Cripps & Williams, 1975; Datta et al., 1974; Scott et al., 1983; Van Thiel et al., 1976, 1977, 1979; Wald et al., 1982). Gastric emptying is delayed during the luteal phase of the menstrual cycle, which is characterized by high estradiol and progesterone. As discussed before, gastric emptying is one of the factors which determines the rate of first-pass metabolism of ethanol in the stomach and the speed of intestinal absorption. Other research on women has found faster elimination and disappearance of ethanol from the bloodstream, and reduced areas under the BAC time curve, during the midluteal phase (Sutker et al., 1987). Therefore, blood alcohol levels and related effects of alcohol intake should vary for women over the menstrual cycle, with somewhat less alcohol in the bloodstream during the luteal phase. Other studies on the pharmacokinetics of ethanol administration during different phases of the menstrual cycle were discussed recently in detail by Van Thiel (1991) and Parrish and associates (1991).

One confounding variable, not always fully taken into account in the gender studies, is the superimposed effect of age, affecting both the response to ethanol (Engel, 1985) and possibly its metabolism. In experimental animals, it was observed that the ethanol metabolic rates decreased linearly with advancing age,

TABLE 1
Effect of Age and Sex on Gastric Alcohol Dehydrogenase Activity (from Seitz et al., 1990)

Site Value	ALCOHOL DEHYDROGENASE ACTIVITY				
	Age 17–49 (nmol/mg of protein min)	No. of Subjects	Age 50–83 (nmol/mg of protein min)	No. of Subjects	p
Antrum					
Women	6.0 ± 1.3*	9	7.1 ± 0.6*	14	NS
Men	9.5 ± 1.3	11	3.7 ± 0.4	9	< .001
Corpus					
Women	6.4 ± 0.7*	14	6.2 ± 0.7*	19	NS
Men	8.8 ± 0.6	15	4.7 ± 0.6	14	< .001

*$p < .001$ for the comparison with men in the same group.

associated with a linear decrease in hepatic ADH activity (Hahn & Burch, 1983), whereas no such effect was seen in human males (Vestal et al., 1977). The latter study revealed, however, that age-related decrease in body fluids resulted in a lower volume of distribution for ethanol, and thus higher blood alcohol levels from a given level of consumption. Preliminary results indicate that only younger women (<50 years of age) seem to have significantly lower gastric ADH than men, in biopsy specimens from the antrum and corpus of the stomach; after age 50 this difference was no longer detectable (Table 1). Older women probably have even higher gastric ADH activities than men of similar age, because gastric ADH activity decreased with age only in men. Like Frezza et al. (1990), Seitz and colleagues (1990) found significantly elevated blood ethanol concentrations in younger (21 to 37 years of age) nonalcoholic women as compared to younger (27 to 37 years) nonalcoholic men, but these results were reversed in subjects over 50 years of age, and the highest blood ethanol levels were observed in men over 60. However, changes in the relative metabolic rates of older male and female drinkers do not protect women against the cumulative effects of drinking across the lifespan.

Gender Differences in Alcohol-Induced Liver Disease

The male to female ratio of mortality has been more than 2:1 for all cases of cirrhosis, and it is even greater when restricted to alcoholic cirrhosis (Hällen & Krook, 1963; Jolliffe & Jellinek, 1941). However, there is evidence that the progression to more severe liver injury is accelerated in women

(Rankin, 1977), a pattern that will become of greater concern if there is any convergence of men's and women's lifetime drinking patterns. Wilkinson and associates (1969) found women to be more susceptible than men to the development of alcoholic cirrhosis. Other studies also found the incidence of chronic advanced liver disease to be higher among women than among men for a similar history of alcohol abuse (Maier et al., 1979; Morgan & Sherlock, 1977; Nakamura et al., 1979). Pequignot et al. (1974, 1978) also have shown that a daily intake of alcohol as low as 40 g in men and only 20 g in women resulted in a statistically significant increase in the incidence of cirrhosis in a well-nourished population.

How being female potentiates alcohol-induced liver damage is not known. Some of women's vulnerability could be hormonal, since both endogenous and exogenous (i.e., contraceptive) female hormones have been shown to result in some impairment of liver function in a significant number of women (Allan & Tyler, 1967; Kappas, 1967; Larsson-Cohn, 1967; Pihl et al., 1968; Saleh & Abd-el-Hay, 1977). It is conceivable that an interaction between some of these hormone-related changes in the liver and those induced by ethanol may result in more severe liver damage. Alternatively, or in addition, some gender dependent biochemical differences may increase vulnerability to the hepatotoxicity of ethanol. For instance, sex-specific cytochrome P450 has been identified as a cause of sex- and species-related differences in drug toxicity in rats (Kato & Yamazoe, 1992). Differences in the expression levels of sex-specific cytochrome P450 possibly may contribute to greater drug and alcohol toxicity in women.

We have found that male and female rats differ in how the hepatic acid binding protein responds to alcohol. We previously reported that feeding alcohol-containing diets to rats (Baraona et al., 1975, 1977) and baboons (Savolainen et al., 1984) increases the amount of protein in the liver. More recently, we found that fatty acid-binding protein is a major contributor to the ethanol-induced increase in liver cytosolic proteins in male rats (Pignon et al., 1987). This increase in liver fatty acid binding protein (L-FABP) may play a role in protecting the livers of male rats against the excess accumulation of free fatty acids, by binding these acids and thereby making them less reactive. We then found a much smaller increase of cytosolic fatty acid-binding capacity in female rats (58%) than in males (161%) (Shevchuk et al., 1991). The increase in female rats was barely sufficient for binding the large increase of fatty acids produced by ethanol in the females. A possible implication for women who consume large amounts of alcohol is that their small (and probably inadequate) increases in liver fatty acid binding and esterification during alcohol consumption may increase their risks of a harmful accumulation of fatty acids in the liver. This accumulation could potentially increase the vulnerability of women drinkers to alcohol-induced hepatotoxicity.

Another possible risk to women from alcohol's effect on the liver is that alcohol may reduce the activity of NA^+, K^+ ATPase, a hepatic plasma membrane enzyme. This enzyme is important for maintaining the correct balance of sodium and potassium inside and outside of cells. When ethanol was administered to rats in concentrations ranging from 8 to 90 Mm, it did not significantly inhibit the enzyme's activity in male rats (Yamada et al., 1985), but in female rats the ethanol produced an eightfold decrease of NA^+, K^+ ATPase activity (Pascale et al., 1989).

Women may be more vulnerable than men to pathological effects of alcohol on the liver as well as on other tissues. Such vulnerability may include higher risks of breast cancer (Longnecker et al., 1988; Lowenfels & Zevola, 1989) and gastric ulcer (Rabinovitz et al., 1989). Although chronic alcoholism is related to brain damage in both sexes, Mann and colleagues (1992) found that alcohol-related brain shrinkage was similar in alcoholic men and women even though the women had significantly shorter periods of exposure to ethanol. Gender differences in benzodiazepine binding sites in alcoholic cirrhosis have also been reported (Dodd, 1995). These findings indicate the importance of determining whether women are more vulnerable to acute and chronic effects of alcoholism on many tissues and organs.

In conclusion, gender differences in response to alcohol, suspected for centuries, are now beginning to be objectively documented. One of the most striking differences is the increased bioavailability of alcohol in women. This basic gender difference is important not merely among women who develop alcoholism, but also among the much larger number of women who engage in social drinking. It is now clear that an alcohol intake that may be considered moderate and innocuous in men is not necessarily so in women. Gender also affects some of the pathologic actions of ethanol. The greater susceptibility of women to alcohol-related liver injury was discussed in detail, but there are likely to be important gender differences in the responses of other tissues to alcohol consumption. Further studies are needed to investigate such gender differences in tissue sensitivity to alcohol intake, and to unravel the mechanisms involved. In the meanwhile, it is important to make women aware that alcohol may affect them differently and more powerfully than it affects men.

Acknowledgments

This chapter has been supported by the Department of Veterans Affairs and by Department of Health and Human Services grant AA05934.

References

Allan, J.S., & Tyler, E.T. (1967). Biochemical findings in long-term oral contraceptive usage. I. Liver function studies. *Fertility and Sterility, 18,* 112-123.

Arthur, M.J.P., Lee, A., & Wright, R. (1984). Sex differences in the metabolism of ethanol and acetaldehyde in normal subjects. *Clinical Science, 67,* 397-401.

Baraona, E., Leo, M.A., Borowsky, S.A., & Lieber, C.S. (1975). Alcoholic hepatomegaly: Accumulation of protein in the liver. *Science, 190,* 794-795.

Baraona, E., Leo, M.A., Borowsky, S.A., & Lieber, C.S. (1977). Pathogenesis of alcohol-induced accumulation of protein in the liver. *Journal of Clinical Investigation, 60,* 546-554.

Caballeria, J., Baraona, E., & Lieber, C.S. (1987). The contribution of the stomach to ethanol oxidation in the rat. *Life Sciences, 41,* 1021-1027.

Caballeria, J., Frezza, M., Hernandez-Munoz, R., DiPadova, C., Korsten, M.A., Baraona, E., & Lieber, C.S. (1989). Gastric origin of the first-pass metabolism of ethanol in humans: Effect of gastrectomy. *Gastroenterology, 97,* 1205-1209.

Carter, E.A., & Isselbacher, K.J. (1971). The role of microsomes in the hepatic metabolism of ethanol. *Annals of the New York Academy of Sciences, 179,* 282-294.

Cederbaum, A.I., Pietruszko, R., Hempel, J., Becker, F.F., & Rubin, E. (1975). Characterization of a nonhepatic alcoholic dehydrogenase from rat hepatocellular carcinoma and stomach. *Archives of Biochemistry and Biophysics, 171,* 348-360.

Cole-Harding, S., & Wilson, J.R. (1987). Ethanol metabolism in men and women. *Journal of Studies on Alcohol, 48,* 380-387.

Corti, B., & Ibrahim, J. (1990). Women and alcohol: Trends in Australia. *Medical Journal of Australia, 152,* 625-632.

Cripps, A.W. & Williams, V.J. (1975). The effect of pregnancy and lactation on food intake, gastrointestinal anatomy and the absorptive capacity of the small intestine in the albino rat. *British Journal of Nutrition, 33,* 17-32.

Datta, S., Hay, V.M., & Pleuvry, B.J. (1974). Effects of pregnancy and associated hormones in mouse intestine *in vivo* and *in vitro. Pleugers Archives, 346,* 87-93.

Dietary Guidelines. (1995). *Nutrition and your health: Dietary guidelines for Americans* (4th ed.). Washington, D.C.: U.S. Department of Agriculture & U.S. Department of Health and Human Services.

DiPadova, C., Worner, T.M., Julkunen, R.J.K., & Lieber, C.S. (1987). Effects of fasting and chronic alcohol consumption on the first-pass metabolism of ethanol. *Gastroenterology, 92,* 1169-1173.

DiPadova, C., Roine, R., Frezza, M., Gentry, R.T., Baraona, E., & Lieber, C.S. (1992). Effects of ranitidine on blood alcohol levels after ethanol ingestion: Comparison with other H_2-receptor antagonists. *Journal of the American Medical Association, 267,* 83-86.

Dodd, P.R. (1995). Benzodiazepine binding sites in alcoholic cirrhotics: Evidence for gender differences. *Metabolic Brain Disease, 10,* 93-104.

Engel, J.A. (1985). Influence of age and hormones on the stimulatory and sedative effects of ethanol. In U. Rydberg, C. Alling, J. Engel, B. Pernow, L.A. Pellborn, & S. Rossner (Eds.), *Alcohol and the Developing Brain* (pp. 57-67). New York: Raven.

Frezza, M., DiPadova, C., Pozzato, G., Terpin, M., Baraona, E., & Lieber, C.S. (1990). High blood alcohol levels in women: The role of decreased gastric alcohol dehydrogenase activity and first-pass metabolism. *New England Journal of Medicine, 322,* 95-99.

Fukunaga, T., Sillanaukee, P., & Eriksson, C.J.P. (1993). Occurrence of blood acetaldehyde in women during ethanol intoxication. Preliminary findings. *Alcoholism: Clinical and Experimental Research, 17,* 1198-1200.

Gomberg, E.S.L. (1993). Women and alcohol: Use and abuse. *Journal of Nervous and Mental Disease, 181,* 211-219.

Halsted, C.H., Robles, E.A., & Mezey, E. (1973). Distribution of ethanol in the human gastrointestinal tract. *American Journal of Clinical Nutrition, 26,* 831-834.

Hahn, H.K.J., & Burch, R.E. (1983). Impaired ethanol metabolism with advancing age. *Alcoholism: Clinical and Experimental Research, 7,* 299-301.

Hällen, J., & Krook, H. (1963). Follow-up studies on an unselected ten-year material of 360 patients with liver cirrhosis in one community. *Acta Medica Scandinavica, 173,* 479–493.

Hempel, J.D., & Pietruszko, R. (1979). Human stomach alcohol dehydrogenase: Isoenzyme composition and catalytic properties. *Alcoholism: Clinical and Experimental Research, 3,* 95–98.

Hernández-Muñoz, R., Caballeria, J., Baraona, E., Uppal, R., Greenstein, R., & Lieber, C.S. (1990). Human gastric alcohol dehydrogenase: Its inhibition by H_2-receptor antagonists, and its effect on the bioavailability of ethanol. *Alcoholism: Clinical and Experimental Research, 14,* 946–950.

Hill, S.Y. (1995). Mental and physical health consequences of alcohol use in women. In M. Galanter (Ed.), *Recent developments in alcoholism, vol. 12: Alcoholism and women. The effect of gender* (pp. 181–197). New York: Plenum.

Holmes, R.S., Courtney, Y.R., & VandeBerg, J.L. (1986). Alcohol dehydrogenase isozymes in baboons: Tissue distribution, catalytic properties and variant phenotypes in liver, kidney, stomach, and testis. *Alcoholism: Clinical and Experimental Research, 10,* 623–630.

Jolliffe, N., & Jellinek, E.M. (1941). Vitamin deficiencies and liver cirrhosis in alcoholism: Part VII. Cirrhosis of the liver. *Quarterly Journal of Studies on Alcohol, 2,* 544–583.

Jones, B.M., & Jones, M.K. (1976). Male and female intoxication levels for three alcohol doses or do women really get higher than men? *Alcohol Technical Report, 5,* 11–14.

Julia, P., Farres, J., & Pares, X. (1987). Characterization of three isoenzymes of rat alcohol dehydrogenase: Tissue distribution and physical and enzymatic properties. *European Journal of Biochemistry, 162,* 179–189.

Julkunen, R.J.K., DiPadova, C., & Lieber, C.S. (1985a). First pass metabolism of ethanol—A gastrointestinal barrier against the systemic toxicity of ethanol. *Life Sciences, 37,* 567–573.

Julkunen, R.J.K., Tannenbaum, L., Baraona, E., & Lieber, C.S. (1985b). First pass metabolism of ethanol: An important determinant of blood levels after alcohol consumption. *Alcohol, 2,* 437–441.

Kappas, A. (1967). Estrogens and the liver. *Gastroenterology, 52,* 113–116.

Kato, R., & Yamazoe, Y. (1992). Sex-specific cytochrome P450 as a cause of sex- and species-related differences in drug toxicity. *Toxicology Letters, 64/65,* 661–667.

Lamboeuf, Y., De-Saint-Blanquat, G., & Derache, R. (1981). Mucosal alcohol dehydrogenase- and aldehyde dehydrogenase-mediated ethanol oxidation in the digestive tract of the rat. *Biochemical Pharmacology, 30,* 542–545.

Lamboeuf, Y., La Droitte, P., & De-Saint-Blanquat, G. (1983). The gastrointestinal metabolism of ethanol in the rat. Effect of chronic alcohol intoxication. *Archives Internationales de Pharmacodynamie et de Therapie, 261,* 157–169.

Larsson-Cohn, U. (1967). The 2 hour sulfobromophtalein retention test and the transaminase activity during oral contraceptive therapy. *American Journal of Obstetrics and Gynecology, 98,* 188–193.

Lee, L., Schmidt, K.L., Tornwall, M.S., Henagan, J.M., & Miller, T.A. (1992). Gender differences in ethanol oxidation and injury in the rat stomach. *Alcohol, 9,* 421–425.

Lieber, C.S. (Ed.). (1992). Medical and nutritional complications of alcoholism: Mechanisms and management. New York: Plenum.

Lim, R.T., Jr., Gentry, R.T., Ito, D., Yokoyama, H., Baraona, E., & Lieber, C.S. (1993). First pass metabolism of ethanol in rats is predominantly gastric. *Alcoholism: Clinical and Experimental Research, 17,* 1337–1344.

Lin, G.W.J., & Lester, D. (1980). Significance of the gastrointestinal tract in the *in vivo* metabolism of ethanol in the rat. In R.G. Thurman (Ed.), *Alcohol and aldehyde metabolizing systems-IV. Advances in Experimental Medicine and Biology: vol. 132* (pp. 281-286). New York: Plenum.

Longnecker, M.P., Berlin, J.A., Orza, M.J., & Chalmers, T.C. (1988). A meta-analysis of alcohol consumption in relation to risk of breast cancer. *Journal of the American Medical Association, 260,* 652-656.

Lowenfels, A.B., & Zevola, S.A. (1989). Alcohol and breast cancer: An overview. *Alcoholism: Clinical and Experimental Research, 13,* 109-111.

Maier, K.P., Haag, S.G., Peskar, B.M. & Gerok, W. (1979). Verlaufsformen alkoholischer Lebererkrankungen. *Klinische Wochenschrift, 57,* 311-317.

Maly, I.P., & Sasse, D. (1991). Intraacinar profiles of alcohol dehydrogenase and aldehyde dehydrogenase activities in human liver. *Gastroenterology, 101,* 1716-1723.

Mann, K., Batra, A., Günthner, A., & Schroth, G. (1992). Do women develop alcoholic brain damage more readily than men? *Alcoholism: Clinical and Experimental Research, 16,* 1052-1056.

Marshall, A.W., Kingstone, D., Boss, M., & Morgan, M.Y. (1983). Ethanol elimination in males and females: Relationship to menstrual cycle and body composition. *Hepatology, 3,* 701-706.

Mercer, P.W., & Khavari, K.A. (1990). Are women drinking more like men? An empirical examination of the convergence hypothesis. *Alcoholism: Clinical and Experimental Research, 14,* 461-466.

Mezey, E., Potter, J.J., & Diehl, A.M. (1986). Depression of alcohol dehydrogenase activity in rat hepatocyte culture by dihydrotestosterone. *Biochemical Pharmacology, 35,* 335-339.

Mishra, L., Sharma, S., Potter, J.J., & Mezey, E. (1989). More rapid elimination of alcohol in women as compared to their male siblings. *Alcoholism: Clinical and Experimental Research, 13,* 752-754.

Morgan, M.Y., & Sherlock, S. (1977). Sex-related differences among 100 patients with alcoholic liver disease. *British Medical Journal, 1,* 939-941.

Nakamura, S., Takezawa, Y., Sato, T., Kera, K., & Maeda, T. (1979). Alcoholic liver disease in women. *Tohoku Journal of Experimental Medicine, 129,* 351-355.

Parrish, K.M., Higuchi, S., & Dufour, M.C. (1991). Alcohol consumption and the risk of developing liver cirrhosis: Implications for future research. *Journal of Substance Abuse, 3,* 325-335.

Pascale, R., Daino, L., Garcea, R., Frassetto., S., Ruggiu, M.E., Vannini, M.G., Cozzolino, P., & Feo, F. (1989). Inhibition by ethanol of rat liver plasma membrane (Na^+, K^+) ATPase: Protective effect of S-adenosyl-L-methionine, L-methionine, and *N*-acetylcysteine. *Toxicology and Applied Pharmacology, 97,* 216-229.

Pequignot, G., Chabert, C., Eydoux, H., & Corcoul, M.A. (1974). Increase in the risk of cirrhosis as a function of alcohol intake. *Revue de l'Alcoolisme, 20,* 191-202.

Pequignot, G., Tuyns, A.J., & Berta, J.L. (1978). Ascitic cirrhosis in relation to alcohol consumption. *International Journal of Epidemiology, 7,* 113-120.

Pestalozzi, D.M., Bühler, R., von Wartburg, J.P., & Hess, M. (1983). Immunohistochemical localization of alcohol dehydrogenase in the human gastrointestinal tract. *Gastroenterology, 85,* 1011-1016.

Pignon, J.P., Bailey, N.C., Baraona, E., & Lieber, C.S. (1987). Fatty acid-binding protein: A major contributor to the ethanol-induced increase in liver cytosolic proteins in the rat. *Hepatology, 7,* 865-871.

Pihl, E., Rais, O., & Zeuchner, E. (1968). Functional and morphological liver changes in women taking oral contraceptives: A clinical and ultrastructural study with special reference to the occurrence of cholestasis. *Acta Chirurgica Scandinavica, 134,* 639-650.

Rabinovitz, M., Van Thiel, D.H., Dindzans, V., & Gavaler, J.S. (1989). Endoscopic findings in alcoholic liver disease. Does gender make a difference? *Alcohol, 6,* 465-468.

Rankin, J.G. (1977). The natural history and management of the patient with alcoholic liver disease. In M.M. Fisher & J.G. Rankin (Eds.), *Alcohol and the Liver* (pp. 365-381). New York: Plenum.

Roine, R.P., Gentry, R.T., Lim, Jr., R.T., Baraona, E., and Lieber, C.S. (1991). Effect of concentration of ingested ethanol on blood alcohol levels. *Alcoholism: Clinical and Experimental Research, 15,* 734-738.

Saleh, F.M., & Abd-El-Hay, M.M. (1977). Liver function tests after the use of long-acting progestational contraceptives. *Contraception, 16,* 409-416.

Savolainen, M.J., Baraona, E., Pikkarainen, P., & Lieber, C.S. (1984). Hepatic triacyglycerol synthesizing activity during progression of alcoholic liver injury in the baboon. *Journal of Lipid Research, 25,* 813-820.

Scott, L.D., Lester, R., Van Thiel, D.H., & Wald, A. (1983). Pregnancy related changes in small intestinal myoelectric activity in the rat. *Gastroenterology, 84,* 301-305.

Seitz, H.K., Egerer, G., & Simanowski, U.A. (1990). High blood alcohol levels in women. *New England Journal of Medicine, 323,* 58. (Letter to the Editor)

Shevchuk, O., Baraona, E., Ma, X.L., Pignon, J.P., & Lieber, C.S. (1991). Gender differences in the response of hepatic fatty acids and cytosolic fatty acid-binding capacity to alcohol consumption in rats. *Proceedings of the Society for Experimental Biology and Medicine, 198,* 584-590.

Sutker, P.B., Goist Jr., K.C., & King, A.R. (1987). Acute alcohol intoxication in women: Relationship to dose and menstrual cycle phase. *Alcoholism: Clinical and Experimental Research, 11,* 74-79.

Teschke, R., & Wiese, B. (1982). Sex-dependency of hepatic alcohol metabolizing enzymes. *Journal of Endocrinological Investigation, 5,* 243-250.

Van Thiel, D.H. (1991). Gender differences in susceptibility and severity of alcohol-induced liver disease. (RSA presidential address) (pp. 9-18). In H. Kalant, J.M. Khanna, & Y. Israel (Eds.), Advances in biomedical alcohol research. Oxford: Pergamon Press.

Van Thiel, D.H., Gavaler, J.S., Joshi, S.H., Sara, R.K., & Stremple, J. (1977). Heartburn of pregnancy. *Gastroenterology, 72,* 666-668.

Van Thiel, D.H., Gavaler, J.S., & Stremple, J. (1976). Lower esophageal sphincter pressure in women using sequential oral contraceptives. *Gastroenterology, 71,* 232-235.

Van Thiel, D.H., Gavaler, J.S., & Stremple, J.F. (1979). Lower esophageal sphincter pressure during the normal menstrual cycle. *American Journal of Obstetrics and Gynecology, 134,* 64-69.

Vestal, R.E., McGuire, E.A., Tobin, J.D., Andres, R., Norris, A.H., & Mezey, E. (1977). Aging and ethanol metabolism. *Clinical Pharmacology and Therapeutics, 21,* 343-354.

Wagner, J.G. (1986). Lack of first-pass metabolism of ethanol at blood concentrations in the social drinking range. *Life Sciences, 39,* 407-414.

Wald, A., Van Thiel, D.H., Hoechstetter, L., Gavaler, J.S., Egler, K.M., Verm, R., Scott, L., & Lester, R. (1982). Effect of pregnancy on gastrointestinal transit. *Digestive Diseases and Sciences, 27,* 1015-1018.

Wilkinson, P., Santamaria, J.N., & Rankin, J.G. (1969). Epidemiology of alcoholic cirrhosis. *Australian Annals of Medicine, 18,* 222-226.

Yamada, S., Mak, K.M., & Lieber, C.S. (1985). Chronic ethanol consumption alters rat liver plasma membranes and potentiates release of alkaline phosphatase. *Gastroenterology, 88,* 1799-1806.

CHAPTER 4

Childbearing and Alcohol Use

KRISTI-ANNE TOLO PASSARO AND RUTH E. LITTLE

Although the adverse effects of drinking during pregnancy were recorded in the Old Testament book of Judges and in the writings of Aristotle, fetal alcohol syndrome was first described in the medical literature only 25 years ago. Throughout the first half of the twentieth century, the problems noted among the children of alcoholics were ascribed to genetic damage or to poor home environment. Even as recently as the mid-1960s, it was commonly believed that *no* amount of alcohol consumed during pregnancy would adversely affect fetal development. Since that time, however, professional and public opinions on the topic have shifted dramatically, as reflected in the surgeon general's 1981 recommendation that women abstain from drinking alcohol during pregnancy (U.S. Surgeon General, 1981).

This chapter will evaluate the short- and long-term effects of heavy and moderate maternal drinking during pregnancy. It will also include an evaluation of the effects of maternal drinking during lactation and will review what is known about the effects of paternal drinking on pregnancy outcomes. The chapter will conclude with analyses of the J-shaped risk curve for drinking before and during pregnancy using data collected as part of an ongoing, large-scale British longitudinal study of pregnancy and childhood.

Alcohol Consumption and Pregnancy Outcome

Fetal Alcohol Syndrome

The adverse effects of very heavy maternal alcohol consumption during pregnancy on offspring were first reported by Lemoine et al. in 1968 and, independently, by Jones et al. in 1973. The name *fetal alcohol syndrome* (FAS) was first assigned to these effects in 1973 (Jones & Smith, 1973). Critics of these initial reports argued that the physical and developmental abnormalities attributed to alcohol were more likely produced by the intake of other drugs (such as nicotine or diazepam) or by the poor diets characteristic of heavy drinking and alcoholic women (Clarren & Smith, 1978). In time, however, the results of hundreds of studies conducted in humans and animals have provided incontrovertible evidence that ethanol itself can be harmful to developing embryos and fetuses.

In 1980 the Research Society on Alcoholism's Fetal Alcohol Study Group recommended that the following three clinical manifestations should be present for a diagnosis of fetal alcohol syndrome: (1) growth deficiency; (2) altered morphogenesis (that is, structural development); and (3) central nervous system dysfunction (Rosett, 1980). The growth retardation associated with FAS can begin pre- or postnatally, although the former is more common. Infants and children with FAS are usually at least two standard deviations below the mean for weight, length, and/or head circumference. Children with FAS generally have very characteristic facial abnormalities, particularly in the upper lip and eye regions, although variation in facial appearance does exist among these children. The third criterion required for a diagnosis of FAS is often manifested as mental retardation, the syndrome's most debilitating feature. The average intelligence quotient of children with FAS is well below the normal mean IQ of 100. However, a broad spectrum of IQs can be found among them, ranging from very severely retarded to approximately normal. In general, the IQs of children with FAS are inversely related to the extent of their physical abnormalities (Clarren & Smith, 1978).

Fetal alcohol syndrome is usually thought to occur only among the offspring of women who are alcoholics or who are regular, heavy drinkers or bingers (Streissguth, 1978). The level of heavy drinking required to produce FAS is difficult to define, particularly since individual maternal and fetal characteristics can influence the effects of a given amount of alcohol on a developing fetus (Clarren and Smith, 1978). In 1977 the National Institute on Alcohol Abuse and Alcoholism (NIAAA) reported that habitual consumption of the equivalent of six hard drinks per day during pregnancy poses a serious threat to a fetus (see Warren, 1977). The dividing line between the amount of alcohol required to produce FAS and the amount associated with less severe fetal effects remains controversial, however, and may never be precisely determined. The effects of moderate levels of alcohol consumption during pregnancy are discussed in the following section.

In the United States and Canada, fetal alcohol syndrome occurs at an overall rate of approximately two to three cases per 1,000 live births (A.P. Streissguth, personal communication). This rate is comparable to that of Down syndrome or spina bifida (Little & Wendt, 1991). The birth prevalence of FAS is considerably higher in certain population subgroups, however. Native American populations are particularly affected: in one isolated population, one of every eight liveborn children was diagnosed with FAS (Robinson et al., 1987).

In the past two decades, the clinical manifestations of FAS in infancy and early childhood have been well described. Little is known about the long-term effects of heavy maternal drinking during pregnancy, but two recent reports of the results of long-term follow-up studies of children with FAS provide important information about what happens to these children as they grow up. In 1991, Streissguth et al. reported on the growth, facial morphology, and level of central nervous system functioning of FAS patients followed into adolescence and adulthood. The heights and head circumferences of teenagers and adults with FAS tended to remain well below normal, but the FAS patients studied did experience some catch-up growth in terms of weight. The characteristic facial features of children with FAS became less distinctive in adolescence and adulthood. However, the average IQ of the teens and adults with FAS followed by Streissguth and colleagues was still in the mentally retarded range, and average academic functioning remained poor. Measures of adaptive behavior corresponded to age levels considerably below chronologic ages, even among nonretarded subjects. The investigators concluded that the "developmental and cognitive handicaps [associated with FAS] persist as long in life as these patients have been studied" (Streissguth et al., 1991, p. 1966).

The French physician who first described FAS in 1968 has also recently published the results of a long-term follow-up study of children with FAS (Lemoine & Lemoine, 1992). Lemoine and Lemoine noted changes in the faces of maturing FAS patients—continued development of the nose and chin, and sometimes even overgrowth—similar to what Streissguth et al. (1991) reported. The French researchers also found that the height and weight of adults with FAS were not as exceptionally low as in childhood, but the relatively small head size associated with FAS in childhood persisted among adults. Lemoine and Lemoine also found that intellectual retardation and serious psychological and behavioral problems persisted among adults with FAS, corroborating Streissguth's findings.

Moderate Maternal Drinking and Reproductive Outcome

While the relationship between heavy maternal alcohol use during pregnancy and fetal alcohol syndrome is well established, the effects of more moderate levels of maternal drinking on birth size, gestational age, pregnancy loss, and other reproductive outcomes are less clear. As in the case of heavy drinking, levels of drinking characterized as "moderate" vary among studies, ranging from a few drinks per week to four or more drinks per day, with drinking levels in most studies falling somewhere in the middle. We will review the current state of knowledge on the effects of moderate drinking and will discuss possible explanations for the discrepancies in the existing literature.

Numerous investigators have found moderate maternal alcohol consumption during pregnancy to be related to reductions (generally of 100 to 200 grams) in infant birth weight (e.g., Brooke et al., 1989; Little et al., 1986; Martin et al., 1980; Mills et al., 1984; Ogston and Parry, 1992; Rosett et al., 1983;

Virji, 1991), but many other investigators have not found any such effects of moderate drinking (e.g., Day et al., 1989; Ernhart et al., 1985; Kline et al., 1987; Marbury et al., 1983; McDonald et al., 1992b; Sulaiman et al., 1988; Walpole et al., 1990). Some researchers have found effects on birth weight at average maternal drinking levels of approximately one drink per day (Little et al., 1986), whereas others have not seen such reductions even among women drinking up to four drinks a day (Kaminski et al., 1976). Two recent reports have found moderate maternal drinking to be related to lowered birth weight only among women who smoke (Brooke et al., 1989; Haste et al., 1991); however, an earlier study including only nonsmoking women also found an association between moderate drinking and reduced birth weight (Little et al., 1986). A 1992 report of the results of a multicenter project conducted in seven European countries indicated that decreases in infant birth weight were found among women drinking at least the equivalent of approximately 10 to 12 drinks per week, but investigators did not find differences in this relationship by maternal smoking status (Ogston & Parry, 1992).

Data relating moderate maternal drinking during pregnancy to gestational age at delivery are also contradictory. Some researchers report that moderate drinkers deliver earlier in pregnancy (e.g., Berkowitz, 1981; Halmesmaki et al., 1987b; Little et al., 1986; Rosett et al., 1983; Sulaiman et al., 1988) and others report no association between moderate drinking and gestational age (e.g., Coles et al., 1985; Marbury et al., 1983; Mills et al., 1984; Shiono et al., 1986; Virji & Cottington, 1991). Among studies that have found an association with gestational age, effect sizes are typically rather small (e.g., a difference of 0.5 to 1.5 days).

Findings about moderate maternal drinking and miscarriage or stillbirth are also inconsistent. While numerous investigators have found drinking to be associated with higher risk of pregnancy loss (e.g., Anokute, 1986; Armstrong et al., 1992; Kline et al., 1980; Russell & Skinner, 1988; Sokol et al., 1980), many others have not found the same association (e.g., Grisso et al., 1984; Halmesmaki et al., 1989; Kaminski et al., 1981; Marbury et al., 1983; Parazzini et al., 1990; Walpole et al., 1990). A recent study of more than 35,000 pregnancies found a nonlinear dose-response relationship between maternal drinking and miscarriage, with the rate of loss beginning to increase among women drinking only one to two drinks a week in early pregnancy (Armstrong et al., 1992). Other studies have found increased rates of miscarriage only among women drinking an average of at least one drink per day (Anokute, 1986; Harlap & Shiono, 1980).

In studies of drinking during pregnancy and congenital anomalies, some have found a connection (e.g., Day et al., 1989; Ernhart et al., 1985, 1987; Graham et al., 1988; Rosett et al., 1983; Rostand et al., 1990) and others have not (e.g., Coles et al., 1985; Grisso et al., 1984; Halmesmaki et al., 1987b; Kaminski et al., 1981; Marbury et al., 1983; Mills & Graubard, 1987), with considerable variation among studies in the range of drinking levels included and in the types and categorization of anomalies examined. A recent study of nearly 90,000 pregnancies found moderate maternal drinking during pregnancy to be unrelated to any of several categories of birth defects, with the possible exception of musculoskeletal defects for women consuming seven or more drinks a week (McDonald et al., 1992a).

Several groups of researchers have found maternal drinking during pregnancy, even at nonabusive levels, to be associated with poorer infant performance on the Bayley Scales of Infant Development, particularly on the Mental Development Index (e.g., Fried & Watkinson, 1988; Graham et al., 1988; Jacobson et al., 1993; O'Connor et al., 1986; Parry & Ogston, 1992; Streissguth et al., 1980). Jacobson et al. (1993) recently reported that the effects of moderate drinking during pregnancy on Bayley Scale scores previously reported in white, middle-class infants (Streissguth et al., 1980) are also seen in the infants of black, inner-city women who drink at least once daily. However, other recent studies of moderate maternal drinking during pregnancy and Bayley scores found no associations between the two (Forrest et al., 1991; Greene et al., 1991; Richardson et al., 1989).

Other neurobehavioral problems such as tremulousness, decreased sucking, neonatal hyperactivity, and electroencephalogram abnormalities have also been identified in the offspring of moderate drinkers (e.g., Coles et al., 1985; Ioffe et al., 1984; Martin et al., 1979; Scher et al., 1988; Smith et al., 1986). A variety of other reproductive outcomes, including Apgar scores and newborn sleep state regulation, appeared to be adversely affected by moderate maternal drinking during pregnancy in some, but not all, investigations (e.g., Kaminski et al., 1981; Marbury et al., 1983; Ogston & Parry, 1992; Streissguth et al., 1981; Sulaiman et al., 1988; Walpole et al., 1990).

To make useful interpretations of the inconsistent findings summarized above, the best strategy is not simply to choose sides and ignore the contrary evidence, but rather to consider possible explanations why research on moderate drinking during pregnancy might produce conflicting results.

Most studies of moderate alcohol consumption and reproductive outcome to date have focused on average levels of drinking within specified periods of time (e.g., per week or per day). However, the importance of peak blood alcohol concentrations has been demonstrated both in rodents (Bonthius & West, 1990; Brown et al., 1979; Kelly et al., 1989; West et al., 1989) and in nonhuman primates (Clarren et al., 1988). In the few studies of binge drinking among nonalcoholic women, binges did not adversely affect birth size (Jones et al., 1984; Tolo and Little, 1993) but were associated with neonatal electroencephalogram abnormalities (Ioffe & Chernick, 1988) and neurobehavioral deficits (Streissguth et al., 1989). The use of average measures of ethanol exposure may mask variations between women in terms of their *pattern* of alcohol use. Assume, for example, that sporadic peak exposures to ethanol are associated with neurobehavioral problems in offspring but chronic lower doses are not. In that situation, two studies whose cohorts both consume an *average* of one drink a day (and which use only a measure of average daily alcohol intake in their analyses) may produce very different results if one cohort is made up predominantly of women with a single binge episode once a week and the other consists primarily of women who regularly consume one drink each day. This scenario might occur when study cohorts are drawn from populations that differ in their drinking patterns (and thus in their proportions of binge drinkers) for cultural or other reasons.

Research on effects of moderate drinking during pregnancy must consider not only patterns of peak consumption but also the timing of alcohol use relative to the stages of pregnancy. *In utero* ethanol exposures in early pregnancy would be expected to affect embryonic survival and organogenesis, while impairments of somatic growth and neurologic development are more plausible results of late pregnancy alcohol exposure. In addition, women drinking during late pregnancy are likely to have consumed alcohol in early and mid-pregnancy as well; for the offspring of these women, therefore, both timing and duration of alcohol exposure need to be considered. It is also important to recognize that drinking patterns typically change over the course of pregnancy (Hook, 1978; Little et al., 1990), so that reports of pre-pregnancy (or post-pregnancy) drinking patterns may not accurately reflect levels of drinking throughout pregnancy.

Women's drinking prior to pregnancy may also have implications for reproductive outcomes. Infants born to alcoholic women who abstain during pregnancy have lower mean birth weight than those born to nonalcoholic women with only low levels of drinking in pregnancy, suggesting a persistent effect of pre-pregnancy heavy drinking (Little et al., 1980). It has also been shown repeatedly, however, that pre-pregnancy abstainers tend to be at slightly higher risk of adverse pregnancy outcomes compared to light drinkers (e.g., Brooke et al., 1989; Forrest et al., 1991; Little & Weinberg, 1993; McDonald et al., 1992b; Mills et al., 1984; Shiono et al., 1986). This pattern is manifested as a J-shaped curve for pre-pregnancy drinking and adverse reproductive outcomes, with infants of light drinkers faring slightly better than those of total abstainers and much better than those of heavy drinkers. The pattern is also seen for drinking during pregnancy, although less consistently. A similar curve has been observed for a variety of nonreproductive outcomes, particularly coronary heart disease mortality (e.g., Boffetta & Garfinkel, 1990; Lazarus et al., 1991; Rimm et al., 1991; Shaper et al., 1988). The J-curve for maternal drinking and pregnancy outcome will be discussed in greater detail in the second section of this chapter.

Some inconsistencies in research on moderate drinking during pregnancy may result from limitations in how data on drinking are obtained and analyzed. Studies that ask about maternal drinking retrospectively are susceptible to recall biases, since study participants are aware of their pregnancy outcomes at the time of exposure reporting. Drinking may also be measured imprecisely or inaccurately if the terms used to ask about drinking patterns are not well defined. For example, the specification of a "binge" as consumption of "at least five drinks on any single occasion" (Streissguth et al., 1989, p. 477) will produce more precise and more accurate responses than the description of binging as drinking "to the point of feeling 'drunk'" (Jones et al., 1984, p. 114A). Since there are no standardized cutpoints used in defining light and moderate drinkers, studies may also generate conflicting results simply through the use of different categorizations of alcohol variables. Finally, failure to control for confounding variables that may affect pregnancy outcomes (e.g., smoking), and low statistical power from small clinical samples, may also contribute to inconsistencies in research findings (see Little & Wendt, 1991, for further discussion).

Race and socioeconomic status (SES) may modify how moderate alcohol consumption relates to pregnancy outcomes. The risk of fetal alcohol effects appears to differ between the infants of lower and middle-class women (Streissguth & LaDue, 1985), and the risk of fetal alcohol syndrome clearly varies according to racial or ethnic background (Chavez et al., 1989). Whether the risk of adverse pregnancy outcomes associated with moderate maternal drinking differs by race is less clear. We are aware of only two studies on this topic that have been conducted in predominantly black, lower SES populations (Coles et al., 1985; Jacobson et al., 1993); both found moderate maternal drinking during pregnancy to be associated with neurobehavioral deficits in offspring. If race and SES do modify relationships between moderate drinking and pregnancy outcome, failure to take these characteristics into account may lead to apparently conflicting findings.

Before we consider the possible effects of moderate maternal drinking in any greater detail, we should review two other possible influences of drinking on childbearing, influences that have received much less attention than drinking during pregnancy.

Effects of Maternal Drinking during Lactation

Breast-feeding women have traditionally been counseled that moderate consumption of alcohol will enhance their ability to produce and to let down milk (Davidson et al., 1981; Fildes, 1986; Walter, 1975). However, only minimal attention has been paid to the adverse effects that maternal drinking during lactation may have on infant health and development, despite the fact that infants have only a limited ability to metabolize alcohol (Pikkarainen & Raiha, 1967). Since the infant brain continues to develop during the postpartum period, exposure to ethanol at this critical period is of concern.

Alcohol consumed by lactating women is transferred to their infants via breast milk in concentrations that are comparable to the levels of ethanol present in the peripheral blood of drinking women. However, the actual amount of ethanol transmitted represents only a small fraction of the amount consumed by the mother (Kesaniemi, 1974; Lawton, 1985). In a recent study, Mennella and Beauchamp (1991) estimated that approximately 0.5–3.3% of an experimentally administered maternal dose of ethanol (one drink) was actually transmitted to the breast-feeding infant.

In several studies conducted in laboratory animals, ethanol exposure through breast milk has been associated with a variety of adverse outcomes in newborn offspring, including decreased body weight (Abel, 1974; Borges & Lewis, 1982; DaSilva et al., 1980; Detering et al., 1979; Swanberg & Wilson, 1979), reduced viability (Baer & Crumpacker, 1977), hypoactivity (Buckalew, 1978), developmental aberrations (Kelly et al., 1987), and altered brain growth and development (Borges & Lewis, 1982; Diaz & Samson, 1980; Rawat, 1977). In addition, maternal consumption of ethanol has been shown to alter milk composition in rodents (Vilaro et al., 1987).

The existing data on the effects of maternal drinking during lactation in humans are sparse. In addition to two case reports of adverse infant outcomes associated with ethanol transmission via breast milk (Anderson, 1977; Binkiewicz et al., 1978), only one population-based study has been published on this topic. In 1989, Little et al. reported that maternal alcohol consumption during the first three months after delivery was associated with delayed motor development in infants at one year of age, with a dose-response curve beginning at levels of consumption as low as one drink per day during lactation. This relationship remained even after the potentially confounding effects of more than 100 covariates were taken into account. Among infants who were exclusively breast-fed, the relationship was particularly strong, whereas no such association was found among bottle-fed infants. Infant mental development was not adversely affected by maternal drinking during lactation. Because binge drinking during lactation was not associated with developmental delays, the authors concluded that the effects of maternal drinking during lactation on infant motor development were most likely produced by the accumulation of multiple small doses of ethanol in the breast-fed infant; such accumulation has also been noted for other drugs consumed by lactating women, including diazepam and caffeine (Le Guennec & Billon, 1987; Peterson & Bowes, 1983; Wilson et al., 1986).

In 1991, Mennella and Beauchamp reported the results of an experimental study demonstrating that the infants of women who consumed a single alcoholic drink prior to nursing consumed less breast milk that their unexposed counterparts, even though both groups' feedings were similar in length and frequency, and though the exposed infants actually sucked more frequently at the beginning of feeding periods. They also found that maternal alcohol intake altered the odor of breast milk, particularly within the first hour following consumption. Mennella and Beauchamp's results suggest that, although the volume of ethanol transmitted to the infant may be small, it is sufficient to alter milk composition, as indicated by the change in smell and (presumably) taste.

Paternal Drinking and Pregnancy Outcome

Alcohol's adverse effects on reproductive functioning among male alcohol abusers have been well documented (e.g., Brzek, 1987; Valimaki & Ylikahri, 1983). Alcohol has been shown to interfere with testicular function (Anderson et al., 1989), even at blood alcohol concentrations considerably below the usual legal limit for driving under the influence of alcohol (Salonen, 1986). However, little is known about whether paternal alcohol consumption has any biologically mediated effect on pregnancy *outcome*.

Several rodent studies have demonstrated increased rates of embryonic and fetal death (Badr & Badr, 1975; Klassen & Persaud, 1976; Mankes et al., 1982), decreased litter sizes (Abel, 1989; Anderson et al., 1978; Mankes et al., 1982; Tanaka et al., 1982), and reduced pup weights (Mankes et al., 1982) in untreated females mated to ethanol-consuming males when compared to those mated with untreated males. Other studies have found no such differences (Abel & Moore, 1987; Abel & Tan, 1988; Anderson et al., 1981; Randall et al., 1982). Additional animal studies have found paternal preconceptional alcohol administration to be related to reduced offspring activity level (Abel & Tan, 1988) and to increased susceptibility of offspring to infection (Berk et al., 1989; Hazlett et al., 1989).

While the existing animal literature related to paternal alcohol consumption and reproductive outcome is suggestive (though conflicting), the available epidemiologic data on the topic are sparse. Three studies of paternal alcohol consumption have found no effects on pregnancy loss. However, all three studies had methodological limitations: reliance on the mother's recall of how the father drank before pregnancy, potential selection biases from using only hospitalized miscarriage cases, and (except for Windham et al., 1992) failure to control for other variables that might have affected pregnancy outcomes.

Two studies of how paternal drinking affected birth size produced conflicting results. Little and Sing (1987) found paternal drinking in the month of conception (as reported by the mother after delivery) to be associated with reduced infant birth weight (and to be an even better predictor of birth weight than maternal alcohol use), even after controlling for the effects of a variety of variables. In contrast, Savitz et al. (1992) did not find men's drinking during their partners' pregnancy to be related to birth weight or to gestational age in a population demographically similar to that studied by Little and Sing. Savitz et al. (1992) noted, however, that fewer than 2% of their study participants drank the mean amount of alcohol consumed by Little and Sing's subjects.

The biologic mechanisms by which father's drinking habits may affect reproductive outcomes are not well understood. Paternal exposures could contribute directly to adverse reproductive outcomes by means of *de novo* mutations in germ cells or sperm (Cohen, 1986; Soyka & Joffe, 1980). In animals, ethanol consumption by males has been shown to produce alterations in sperm chromosomes and DNA (Abel et al., 1988; Hunt, 1987; Pylkkanen & Salonen, 1987). Paternal contributions to adverse reproductive outcomes may also occur through the secretion of toxicants into the seminal fluid (Cohen, 1986; Soyka & Joffe, 1980), with adverse effects on spermatozoal characteristics, fertilization, implantation, or fetal development.

Maternal Drinking and Pregnancy Outcome: The J-Shaped Curve

Epidemiologic studies of maternal alcohol use and pregnancy outcome over the last 20 years have repeatedly shown a J-curve of risk for the spectrum of drinking before and after conception. Slightly lower birth weight and slightly higher rates of preterm delivery, congenital malformations, Apgar scores, and stillbirth have been reported for infants of abstainers relative to those of light drinkers (e.g., Brooke et al., 1989; Forrest et al., 1991; Little & Weinberg, 1993; McDonald et al., 1992b; Mills et al., 1984; Shiono et al., 1986). Because the difference in risk between abstaining and light drinking is small, many authors ignore it or attribute it to chance. Others cite the increased risk among abstainers as evidence that no dose-response relationship between maternal drinking and birth outcome exists (e.g., Shiono et al., 1986).

We have previously analyzed the J-curve phenomenon using data from the United States (Little & Wendt, 1991). The sharp decrease in drinking after conception in U.S. women has restricted variability in these samples. Some degree of decrease is expected because of the endogenous aversion to alcoholic beverages that occurs after conception, as shown by early studies conducted before general knowledge of fetal alcohol effects (Hook, 1978). However, in the United States, the natural decline in drinking during pregnancy has been supported and intensified by recent legislative and educational policy decisions that have brought strong and widespread warnings to pregnant women about alcohol consumption.

To investigate the J-curve more thoroughly, we analyzed data on nearly 9,000 women in England who had a broader spectrum of drinking habits both before and after conception than found in previous U.S. samples. The group is relatively homogeneous culturally and ethnically, and generally at low risk of adverse pregnancy outcome. These factors permitted us to explore the J-curve phenomenon more carefully than has been possible in earlier studies.

The data for these analyses are from the Avon Longitudinal Study of Pregnancy and Childhood (ALSPAC) conducted by the University of Bristol (England). ALSPAC is one of a multinational set of investigations initiated by the World Health Organization, known collectively as the European Longitudinal Study of Pregnancy and Childhood (ELSPAC). ALSPAC was designed to study all pregnant residents of Avon County, England (excluding the Bath Health District), whose pregnancies ended between April 1, 1991 and December 31, 1992. Avon County has both urban and rural sections and is demographically similar to England as a whole, except for having a larger proportion of higher SES residents. Over 90% of all pregnancies occurring in the study area during the specified time period were enrolled. The sample used in these analyses was restricted to women who had delivered live singletons, who were not users of any illegal drug (excluding marijuana), and who had no missing alcohol use data. There were 8,895 women and infants in the final sample.

For the ALSPAC study, efforts were made to recruit participants as early as possible during pregnancy, preferably at their first prenatal visit. Enrolled pregnant women were asked to complete several mailed, self-administered questionnaires during the pregnancy. The information on drinking habits used in this study was obtained in a questionnaire sent at approximately 18 weeks of gestation. Participants reported frequency of alcohol consumption (and, for daily drinkers, quantity of alcohol consumed per day) before conception and during the first three months of pregnancy. They also reported the number of binge days (where a binge was defined as consumption of approximately four or more drinks) occurring during a one-month period prior to the receipt of the questionnaire (or approximately during the fourth month of gestation). The questionnaires also provided data on smoking habits before and during pregnancy, marijuana use, caffeine intake (from coffee, tea, and cola), gravidity, parity, and maternal age and weight. Information on birth outcomes was obtained from hospital delivery records, and gestational age was calculated from last menstrual period.

Analyses used continuous measures of birth weight and gestational age, and also dichotomies indicating low birth weight (<2,500 grams) or preterm birth (<37 completed weeks of gestation). We do not report probability values for any statistical tests used because the focus of the analysis is on replicating previously observed patterns in a large sample, rather than on evaluating the probability that observed differences are due to chance.

Table 1 presents drinking patterns before conception and in the earlier part of pregnancy. The decline in drinking after conception is clear: the proportion of abstainers rises from 8% to 46%. Table 2 shows birth weight and gestational age of the infants by these drinking patterns. In general, mean birth

TABLE 1
Drinking Patterns Before Conception and in Early Pregnancy

	n	Percent[1]
Before conception		
Abstained from drinking	684	8
Drank less than once a week	3,444	39
Drank 1 to 6 days a week	3,812	43
Drank daily, 1 to 2 drinks	812	9
Drank daily, 3 or more drinks	143	2
First three months of pregnancy		
Abstained from drinking	4,058	46
Drank less than once a week	3,496	39
Drank 1 to 6 days a week	1,187	13
Drank daily, 1 to 2 drinks	130	2
Drank daily, 3 or more drinks	24	*
Fourth month of pregnancy[2]		
No binges in previous month	7,416	83
1 to 2 binges in previous month	793	9
3 to 4 binges in previous month	321	4
More than 4 binges in previous month	365	4

[1]Numbers may not add to 100% due to rounding.
[2]A "binge" was defined as consumption of four or more drinks on a single day. This question was asked in reference to the month preceding receipt of the questionnaire, which was sent at 18 weeks of gestation.
*Less than 0.5%.

weight decreases as frequency and amount of drinking increase, both before and in early pregnancy. The J-curve is apparent for drinking before conception, with total abstainers having infants of lower birth weight than infants of light and moderate drinkers; in fact, the mean weight of abstainers' infants is only two grams greater than that of infants whose mothers were in the highest drinking group (three or more drinks daily). Infants of preconception abstainers were more likely to be of low birth weight or to be born preterm than infants of women who drank before pregnancy.

The J-curve is also suggested for drinking *during* pregnancy (Table 2). To clarify the contribution of pre-pregnancy abstainers to the curve seen for pregnancy drinking, we considered change in drinking between the two periods (Table 3). Pregnancy drinking was categorized by the approximate degree of risk incurred by various drinking patterns, with "low risk" defined as drinking less than daily (with no binges) and "high risk" defined as daily drinking and/or binging. Virtually all preconception abstainers remained abstinent after conception (667 of 684). Preconception drinkers who were in the

TABLE 2

Birth Weight and Gestational Age by Drinking Patterns Before Conception and in Early Pregnancy

	BIRTH WEIGHT (g)		GESTATIONAL AGE (days)	
	Mean (SD)	% LBW[1]	Mean (SD)	% Preterm[1]
Before conception (n_1/n_2)[2]				
Abstained from drinking (670/649)	3,325 (541)	6.7	279 (14.2)	7.7
Drank less than once a week (3,343/3,354)	3,414 (496)	3.9	280 (13.3)	6.2
Drank 1 to 6 days a week (3,726/3,722)	3,412 (484)	3.3	280 (12.7)	5.2
Drank daily; 1 to 2 drinks (795/784)	3,374 (535)	4.9	280 (13.0)	6.6
Drank daily; 3 or more drinks (141/132)	3,323 (511)	6.4	280 (12.5)	6.1
First three months of pregnancy(n_1/n_2)[2]				
Abstained from drinking (3,956/3,937)	3,396 (510)	4.3	280 (13.4)	6.1
Drank less than once a week (3,400/3,414)	3,411 (479)	3.6	280 (12.7)	5.6
Drank 1 to 6 days a week (1,167/1,146)	3,411 (506)	3.7	280 (13.2)	6.3
Drank daily; 1 to 2 drinks (128/124)	3,254 (577)	6.2	279 (13.1)	6.4
Drank daily; 3 or more drinks (24/20)	3,172 (492)	8.3	279 (17.7)	10.0
Fourth month of pregnancy[3] (n_1/n_2)[2]				
No binges in previous month (7,233/7,216)	3,405 (495)	3.9	280 (13.0)	5.9
1 to 2 binges in previous month (772/761)	3,390 (507)	3.6	279 (13.4)	6.0
3 to 4 binges in previous month (314/312)	3,416 (525)	3.5	280 (13.5)	6.4
More than 4 binges in previous month (356/352)	3,330 (533)	6.5	280 (13.5)	5.4

[1]Low birth weight (LBW) was defined as birth weight less than 2,500 grams; preterm birth was defined as birth before 37 completed weeks of gestation.
[2]Numbers in parentheses represent valid sample sizes for birth weight (n_1) and gestational age (n_2) calculations for each row.
[3]A "binge" was defined as consumption of four or more drinks on a single day.

TABLE 3
Risk Level of Early Pregnancy Drinking by Drinking Status Prior to
Conception, in percent

	PRECONCEPTION DRINKING STATUS		
	Abstained (N = 684)	Drank < Daily (N = 7,256)	Drank Daily (N = 955)
Risk level of early pregnancy drinking[1]			
No drinking	98	41	23
Low risk	2	43	37
High risk	*	16	40

[1]Low risk = drinking less than daily, no binges. High risk = drinking daily, or binge.
*Less than 0.5%.

higher drinking categories before pregnancy were more likely to be high risk drinkers during pregnancy.

The birth weight and gestational age values associated with various drinking patterns are given in Table 4. Among women who did not drink in early pregnancy, preconception abstainers had smaller babies than women who drank before pregnancy. In fact, women who abstained before conception (even the small proportion that drank during pregnancy) had infants with lower mean birth weights than any other group; their babies were also more likely to be of low birth weight or to be born preterm. The slight J-curve suggested for drinking during pregnancy in the unstratified sample (Table 2) is again suggested when restricted to preconception drinkers (Table 4), but it is not clearly defined; there seems to be no clear penalty attached to abstinence during pregnancy. However, effects of shifting to abstinence early in pregnancy may be obscured by variation in when abstinence began (and was recalled) relative to the date of conception.

The results described here are not due to confounding by covariates mentioned earlier (smoking, marijuana use, caffeine intake, gravidity, parity, or maternal age and weight). When each of these variables was used to stratify the sample, the patterns reported here were apparent in almost every stratum. We did not see strong differences in the patterns for smokers and nonsmokers that have been described elsewhere (e.g., in Little & Wendt, 1991).

Possible explanations for the J-curve relationships between drinking and pregnancy outcomes have been that (1) abstinent women include recovering alcoholics, past problem drinkers, or women with medical problems; (2) abstinent women may have lower SES than drinkers; and (3) self-reports of

TABLE 4
Birth Weight and Gestational Age for Preconception Abstainers and Drinkers by Risk Level of Drinking in Early Pregnancy[1]

	BIRTH WEIGHT (g)		GESTATIONAL AGE (days)	
	Mean (SD)	% LBW	Mean (SD)	% Preterm
Abstainer before conception (n_1/n_2)[2]				
No drinking in early pregnancy (653/633)	3,325 (542)	6.6	278 (14.3)	7.9
Low- or high-risk drinking in early pregnancy[3] (17/16)	3,325 (527)	11.8	284 (9.3)	0.0
Drinker before conception (n_1/n_2)[2]				
No drinking in early pregnancy (3,117/3,114)	3,406 (504)	4.0	280 (13.3)	5.9
Low-risk drinking in early pregnancy (3,397/3,405)	3,421 (477)	3.4	280 (12.5)	5.6
High-risk drinking in early pregnancy (1,491/1,473)	3,381 (515)	4.2	280 (13.4)	6.0

[1]Low-risk drinking = less than daily drinking in first trimester and no binges reported in preceding month. High-risk drinking = daily drinking in first trimester or binge(s) reported in preceding month.
[2]Numbers in parentheses represent valid sample sizes for birth weight (n_1) and gestational age (n_2) calculations for each row.
[3]Low- and high-risk pregnancy drinking categories are combined due to small numbers.

abstinence may be systematically biased (e.g., by denial) (Little & Wendt, 1991). We now suggest that a biological mechanism involving placental functioning could contribute to the presence of the J-curve. The placenta is the source of fetal nutrition. Small doses of alcohol consumed prior to conception may improve placental functioning, perhaps by influencing the development of placental vasculature. Infants of women who are light drinkers before conception might thus be expected to have a slight developmental advantage compared to infants of preconception abstainers.

This hypothesis could be evaluated with careful prospective studies, perhaps using biological markers of placental functioning such as estriol. Fetal and placental weights have been shown to correlate directly with estriol excretion (Chang et al., 1977). If our hypothesis is correct, light preconception drinkers should have higher estriol levels (indicating better placental functioning) than preconception abstainers. It is interesting to note that lower estriol levels have already been reported in pregnant chronic alcohol abusers (Halmesmaki et al., 1987a), as would be expected given the decrements in fetal development seen in their infants.

We propose this hypothesis with some trepidation. It is not intended to serve as a rationale for using alcohol, particularly during pregnancy. The clinical implications of the J-curve are minimal, for the differences in risk from abstaining versus light drinking prior to conception are small. Rather, the hypothesis is proposed because it may provide insight into the mechanism by which alcohol influences human growth *in utero.*

In this chapter, we have summarized current knowledge about several possible effects of alcohol use on childbearing. The short-term manifestations of the fetal alcohol syndrome have been thoroughly described in the literature, but further studies of the long-term sequelae of this syndrome are needed. In addition, studies of moderate maternal drinking and pregnancy outcome that pay careful attention to the timing and pattern of women's drinking, as well as those that evaluate the long-term neurobehavioral functioning of children born to moderate drinkers, will contribute to an improved understanding of the effects of nonabusive maternal drinking on child health and development. It is also clear that effects of maternal drinking during lactation and paternal drinking before a partner's pregnancy are not yet adequately understood. Finally, studies that investigate our hypothesized biological mechanism for the J-curve will serve to clarify the reasons for its existence in numerous studies.

Acknowledgments

We gratefully acknowledge the statistical assistance of Dr. John Noss. We are extremely grateful to all the mothers who took part, to the midwives for their cooperation and help in recruitment, and to the whole ALSPAC team of interviewers, computer technicians, laboratory technicians, clerical workers, research scientists, volunteers, and managers who continue to make the study possible. This study could not have been undertaken without the financial support of the Wellcome Trust, the Department of Health, the Department of the Environment, British Gas, and other companies. The ALSPAC study is part of the WHO-initiated European Longitudinal Study of Pregnancy and Childhood.

References

Abel, E.L. (1974). Alcohol ingestion in lactating rats: Effects on mothers and offspring. *Archives Internationales de Pharmacodynamie et de Therapie, 210,* 121-127.

Abel, E.L. (1989). Paternal and maternal alcohol consumption: Effects on offspring in two strains of rats. *Alcoholism: Clinical and Experimental Research, 13,* 533-541.

Abel, E.L., & Moore, C. (1987). Effects of paternal alcohol consumption in mice. *Alcoholism: Clinical and Experimental Research, 11,* 533-535.

Abel, E.L., & Tan, S.E. (1988). Effects of paternal alcohol consumption on pregnancy outcome in rats. *Neurotoxicology and Teratology, 10,* 187-192.

Abel, E.L., Zajac, C.S., Waselewsky, D.R. & Smith, D.I. (1988). Effects of male alcohol consumption on sperm DNA and on offspring behavior and hematology. *Teratology, 37,* 519.

Anderson, P.O. (1977). Drugs and breast feeding. *Drug Intelligence & Clinical Pharmacy, 11,* 208-223.

Anderson, R.A., Jr., Berryman, S.H., Phillips, J.F., Feathergill, K.A., Zaneveld, L.J.D., & Russell, L.D. (1989). Biochemical and structural evidence for ethanol-induced impairment of testicular development: Apparent lack of Leydig cell involvement. *Toxicology and Applied Pharmacology, 100,* 62-85.

Anderson, R.A., Jr., Beyler, S.A., & Zaneveld, L.J.D. (1978). Alterations of male reproduction induced by chronic ingestion of ethanol: Development of an animal model. *Fertility and Sterility, 30,* 103-105.

Anderson, R.A., Jr., Furby, J.E., Oswald, C., & Zaneveld, L.J.D. (1981). Teratological evaluation of mouse fetuses after paternal alcohol ingestion. *Neurobehavioral Toxicology and Teratology, 3,* 117-120.

Anokute, C.C. (1986). Epidemiology of spontaneous abortions: The effects of alcohol consumption and cigarette smoking. *Journal of the National Medical Association, 78,* 771-775.

Armstrong, B.G., McDonald, A.D., & Sloan, M. (1992). Cigarette, alcohol, and coffee consumption and spontaneous abortion. *American Journal of Public Health, 82,* 85-87.

Badr, F.M., & Badr, R.S. (1975). Induction of dominant lethal mutation in male mice by ethyl alcohol. *Nature, 253,* 134-136.

Baer, D.S., & Crumpacker, D.W. (1977). Fertility and offspring survival in mice selected for different sensitivities to alcohol. *Behavior Genetics, 7,* 95-103.

Berk, R.S., Montgomery, I.N., Hazlett, L.D., & Abel, E.L. (1989). Paternal alcohol consumption: Effects on ocular response and serum antibody response to pseudomonas aeruginosa infection in offspring. *Alcoholism: Clinical and Experimental Research, 13,* 795-798.

Berkowitz, G.S. (1981). An epidemiologic study of pre-term delivery. *American Journal of Epidemiology, 113,* 81-92.

Binkiewicz, A., Robinson, M.J., & Senior, B. (1978). Pseudo-Cushing syndrome caused by alcohol in breast milk. *Journal of Pediatrics, 93,* 965-967.

Boffetta, P., & Garfinkel, L. (1990). Alcohol drinking and mortality among men enrolled in an American Cancer Society prospective study. *Epidemiology, 1,* 342-348.

Bonthius, D.J., & West, J.R. (1990). Alcohol-induced neuronal loss in developing rats: Increased brain damage with binge exposure. *Alcoholism: Clinical and Experimental Research, 14,* 107-118.

Borges, S., & Lewis, P.D. (1982). A study of alcohol effects on the brain during gestation and lactation. *Teratology, 25,* 283-289.

Brooke, O.G., Anderson, H.R., Bland, J.M., Peacock, J.L., & Stewart, C.M. (1989). Effects on birth weight of smoking, alcohol, caffeine, socioeconomic factors, and psychosocial stress. *British Medical Journal, 298,* 795-801.

Brown, N.A., Goulding, E.H., & Fabro, S. (1979). Ethanol embryotoxicity: Direct effects on mammalian embryos in vitro. *Science, 206,* 573-575.

Brzek, A. (1987). Alcohol and male fertility (preliminary report). *Andrologia, 19,* 32-36.

Buckalew, L.W. (1978). Effect of maternal alcohol consumption during nursing on offspring activity. *Research Communications in Psychology, Psychiatry and Behavior, 3,* 353-358.

Chang, A., Abell, D., Beischer, N., & Wood, C. (1977). Trial of intravenous therapy in women with low urinary estriol excretion. *American Journal of Obstetrics and Gynecology, 127,* 793-799.

Chavez, G.F., Cordero, J.F., & Becerra, J.E. (1989). Leading major congenital malformations among minority groups in the United States, 1981-1986. *Journal of the American Medical Association, 261,* 205-209.

Clarren, S.K., Astley, S.J., & Bowden, D.M. (1988). Physical anomalies and developmental delays in nonhuman primate infants exposed to weekly doses of ethanol during gestation. *Teratology, 37,* 561-569.

Clarren, S.K., & Smith, D.W. (1978). The fetal alcohol syndrome. *New England Journal of Medicine, 298,* 1063-1067.

Cohen, F.L. (1986). Paternal contributions to birth defects. *Nursing Clinics of North America, 21,* 49-64.

Coles, C.D., Smith, I., Fernhoff, P.M., & Falek, A. (1985). Neonatal neurobehavioral characteristics as correlates of maternal alcohol use during gestation. *Alcoholism: Clinical and Experimental Research, 9,* 454-460.

DaSilva, V.A., Ribiero, M.J., & Masur, J. (1980). Developmental, behavioral and pharmacological characteristics of rat offspring from mothers receiving ethanol during gestation or lactation. *Developmental Psychobiology, 13,* 653-660.

Davidson, S., Alden, L., & Davidson, P. (1981). Changes in alcohol consumption after childbirth. *Journal of Advances in Nursing, 6,* 195-198.

Day, N.L., Jasperse, D., Richardson, G., Robles, N., Sambamoorthi, U., Taylor, P., Scher, M., Stoffer, D., & Cornelius, M. (1989). Prenatal exposure to alcohol: Effect on infant growth and morphologic characteristics. *Pediatrics, 84,* 536-541.

Detering, N., Reed, W.D., Ozand, P.T., & Karahasan, A. (1979). The effects of maternal ethanol consumption in the rat on the development of their offspring. *Journal of Nutrition, 109,* 999-1009.

Diaz, J., & Samson, H.H. (1980). Impaired brain growth in neonatal rats exposed to ethanol. *Science, 208,* 751-753.

Ernhart, C.B., Abraham, W.W., Linn, P.L., Sokol, R.J., Kennard, M.J., & Filipovich, H.F. (1985). Alcohol-related birth defects: Syndromal anomalies, intrauterine growth retardation, and neonatal behavioral assessment. *Alcoholism: Clinical and Experimental Research, 9,* 447-453.

Ernhart, C.B., Sokol, R.J., Martier, S., Moron, P., Nadler, D., Ager, J.W., & Wolf, A. (1987). Alcohol teratogenicity in the human: A detailed assessment of specificity, critical period, and threshold. *American Journal of Obstetrics and Gynecology, 156,* 33-39.

Fildes, V.A. (1986). *Breasts, bottles and babies: A history of infant feeding.* Edinburgh: Edinburgh University Press.

Forrest, F., Florey, C. du V., Taylor, D., McPherson, F., & Young, J.A. (1991). Reported social alcohol consumption during pregnancy and infants' development at 18 months. *British Medical Journal, 303,* 22-26.

Fried, P.A., & Watkinson, B. (1988). 12- and 24-month neurobehavioural follow-up of children prenatally exposed to marijuana, cigarettes and alcohol. *Neurotoxicology and Teratology, 10,* 305-313.

Graham, J.M., Hanson, J.W., Darby, B.L., Barr, H.M., & Streissguth, A.P. (1988). Independent dysmorphology evaluations at birth and 4 years of age for children exposed to varying amounts of alcohol in utero. *Pediatrics, 81,* 772-778.

Greene, T., Ernhart, C.B., Ager, J., Sokol, R., Martier, S., & Boyd, T. (1991). Prenatal alcohol exposure and cognitive development in the preschool years. *Neurotoxicology and Teratology, 13,* 57-68.

Grisso, J.A., Roman, E., Inskip, H., Beral, V., & Donovan, J. (1984). Alcohol consumption and outcome of pregnancy. *Journal of Epidemiology and Community Health, 38,* 232-235.

Halmesmaki, E., Autti, I., Granstrom, M.L., Stenman, U.H., & Ylikorkala, O. (1987a). Estradiol, estriol, progesterone, prolactin, and human chorionic gonadotropin in pregnant women with alcohol abuse. *Journal of Clinical Endocrinology and Metabolism, 64,* 153-156.

Halmesmaki, E., Raivio, K.O., & Ylikorkala, O. (1987b). Patterns of alcohol consumption during pregnancy. *Obstetrics and Gynecology, 69,* 594-597.

Halmesmaki, E., Valimaki, M., Roine, R., Ylikahri, R., & Ylikorkala, O. (1989). Maternal and paternal alcohol consumption and miscarriage. *British Journal of Obstetrics and Gynaecology, 96,* 188-191.

Harlap, S., & Shiono, P.H. (1980). Alcohol, smoking, and incidence of spontaneous abortions in the first and second trimester. *Lancet (2),* 173-176.

Haste, F.M., Anderson, H.R., Brooke, O.G., Bland, J.M., & Peacock, J.L. (1991). The effects of smoking and drinking on the anthropometric measurements of neonates. *Paediatric and Perinatal Epidemiology, 5,* 83-92.

Hazlett, L.D., Barrett, R.P., Berk, R.S., & Abel, E.L. (1989) Maternal and paternal alcohol consumption increase offspring susceptibility to pseudomonas aeruginosa ocular infection. *Ophthalmic Research, 21,* 381-7.

Hook, E.B. (1978). Dietary cravings and aversions during pregnancy. *American Journal of Clinical Nutrition, 31,* 1355-1362.

Hunt, P.A. (1987). Ethanol-induced aneuploidy in male germ cells of the mouse. *Cytogenetics and Cell Genetics, 44,* 7-10.

Ioffe, S., & Chernick, V. (1988). Development of the EEG between 30 and 40 weeks gestation in normal and alcohol-exposed infants. *Developmental Medicine and Child Neurology, 30,* 797-807.

Ioffe, S., Childiaeva, R., & Chernick V. (1984). Prolonged effects of maternal alcohol ingestion on the neonatal electroencephalogram. *Pediatrics, 74,* 330-335.

Jacobson, J.L., Jacobson, S.W., Sokol, R.J., Martier, S.S., Ager, J.W., & Kaplan-Estrin, M.G. (1993). Teratogenic effects of alcohol on infant development. *Alcoholism: Clinical and Experimental Research, 17,* 174-183.

Jones, K.L., Chernoff, G.F., & Kelley, C.D. (1984). Outcome of pregnancy in women who "binge" drink during the first trimester of pregnancy. *Clinical Research, 32,* 114A (Abstract).

Jones, K.L., & Smith, D.W. (1973). Recognition of the fetal alcohol syndrome in early infancy. *Lancet, 2,* 999-1001.

Jones, K.L., Smith, D.W., Ulleland, C.N., & Streissguth, P. (1973). Pattern of malformation in offspring of chronic alcoholic mothers. *Lancet, 1,* 1267-1271.

Kaminski, M., Franc, M., Lebouvier, M., du Mazaubrun, C., & Rumeau-Rouquette, C. (1981). Moderate alcohol use and pregnancy outcome. *Neurobehavioral Toxicology and Teratology, 3,* 173-181.

Kaminski, M., Rumeau-Rouquette, C., & Schwartz, D. (1976). Consommation d'alcool chez les femmes enceintes et issue de la grossesse [Alcohol consumption among pregnant women and outcome of pregnancy]. *Revue d'Epidemiologie, Médecine Sociale et Sante Publique, 24,* 27-40. English translation by Little, R.E., & Schinzel, A. (1978). Alcohol consumption in pregnant women and the outcome of pregnancy. *Alcoholism: Clinical and Experimental Research, 2,* 155-163.

Kelly, S.J., Black, A.C., Jr., & West, J.R. (1989). Changes in the muscarinic cholinergic receptors in the hippocampus of rats exposed to ethyl alcohol during the brain growth spurt. *Journal of Pharmacology & Experimental Therapeutics, 249,* 798-804.

Kelly, S.J., Hulsether, S.A., & West, J.R. (1987). Alterations in sensorimotor development: Relationship to postnatal alcohol exposure. *Neurotoxicology and Teratology, 9,* 243-251.

Kesaniemi, Y.A. (1974). Ethanol and acetaldehyde in the milk and peripheral blood of lactating women after ethanol administration. *Journal of Obstetrics and Gynaecology of the British Commonwealth, 81,* 84-86.

Klassen, R.W., & Persaud, T.V.N. (1976). Experimental studies on the influence of male alcoholism on pregnancy and progeny. *Experimentelle Pathologie, 12,* 38-45.

Kline, J., Shrout, P., Stein, Z., Susser, M., & Warburton, D. (1980). Drinking during pregnancy and spontaneous abortion. *Lancet, 2,* 176-180.

Kline, J., Stein, Z., & Hutzler, M. (1987). Cigarettes, alcohol and marijuana: Varying associations with birthweight. *International Journal of Epidemiology, 16,* 44-51.

Lawton, M.E. (1985). Alcohol in breast milk. *Australian and New Zealand Journal of Obstetrics and Gynaecology, 25,* 71-73.

Lazarus, N.B., Kaplan, G.A., Cohen, R.D., & Leu, D.J. (1991). Change in alcohol consumption and risk of death from all causes and from ischaemic heart disease. *British Medical Journal, 303,* 553-556.

Le Guennec, J.C., & Billon, G. (1987). Delay in caffeine elimination in breast-fed infants. *Pediatrics, 79,* 264-268.

Lemoine, P., Haronsseau, H., Borteyru, J.P., & Menuet, J.C. (1968). Les enfants de parents alcooliques. Anomalies observees. A propos de 127 cas. *Ouest-Medical, 21,* 476-482.

Lemoine, P., & Lemoine, P. (1992). Avenir des enfants de mères alcooliques (étude de 105 cas retrouvés à l'age adulte) et quelques constatations d'interet prophylactique. *Annales de Pédiatrie (Paris), 39,* 226-235.

Little, R.E., Anderson, K.W., Ervin, C.H., Worthington-Roberts, B., & Clarren, S.K. (1989). Maternal alcohol use during breast-feeding and infant mental and motor development at one year. *New England Journal of Medicine, 321,* 425-430.

Little, R.E., Asker, R.L., Sampson, P.D., & Renwick, J.H. (1986). Fetal growth and moderate drinking in early pregnancy. *American Journal of Epidemiology, 123,* 270-278.

Little, R.E., Lambert, M.D., & Worthington-Roberts, B. (1990). Drinking and smoking at three months postpartum by lactation history. *Paediatric and Perinatal Epidemiology, 4,* 290-302.

Little, R.E., & Sing, C.F. (1987). Father's drinking and infant birth weight: Report of an association. *Teratology, 36,* 59-65.

Little, R.E., Streissguth, A.P., Barr, H.M., & Herman, C.S. (1980). Decreased birth weight in infants of alcoholic women who abstained during pregnancy. *Journal of Pediatrics, 96,* 974-977.

Little, R.E., & Weinberg, C.R. (1993). Risk factors for antepartum and intrapartum stillbirth. *American Journal of Epidemiology, 137,* 1177-1189.

Little, R.E., & Wendt, J.K. (1991). The effects of maternal drinking in the reproductive period: An epidemiologic review. *Journal of Substance Abuse, 3,* 187-204.

Mankes, R.F., LeFevre, R., Benitz, K.F., Rosenblum, I., Bates, H., Walker, A.I., Abraham, R., & Rockwood, W. (1982). Paternal effects of ethanol in the Long-Evans rat. *Journal of Toxicology and Environmental Health, 10,* 871-878.

Marbury, M.C., Linn, S., Monson, R., Schoenbaum, S., Stubblefield, P.G., & Ryan, K.J. (1983). The association of alcohol consumption with outcome of pregnancy. *American Journal of Public Health, 73,* 1165-1168.

Martin, D.C., Martin, J.C., Streissguth, A.P., & Lund, C.A. (1979). Sucking frequency and amplitude in newborns as a function of maternal drinking and smoking. In M. Galanter (Ed.), *Currents in alcoholism, Vol. 5* (pp. 359-366). New York: Grune and Stratton.

Martin, D.C., Barr, H.M., & Streissguth, A.P. (1980). Birth weight, birth length, and head circumference related to maternal alcohol, nicotine and caffeine use during pregnancy. *Teratology, 21,* 54A.

McDonald, A.D., Armstrong, B.G., & Sloan, M. (1992a). Cigarette, alcohol, and coffee consumption and congenital defects. *American Journal of Public Health, 82,* 91-93.

McDonald, A.D., Armstrong, B.G., & Sloan, M. (1992b). Cigarette, alcohol, and coffee consumption and prematurity. *American Journal of Public Health, 82,* 87-90.

Mennella, J.A., & Beauchamp, G.K. (1991). The transfer of alcohol to human milk: Effects on flavor and the infant's behavior. *New England Journal of Medicine, 325,* 981-985.

Mills, J.L., & Graubard, B.I. (1987). Is moderate drinking during pregnancy associated with an increased risk for malformations? *Pediatrics, 80,* 309-314.

Mills, J.L., Graubard, B.I., Harley, E.E., Rhoads, G.G., & Berendes, H.W. (1984). Maternal alcohol consumption and birth weight: How much drinking during pregnancy is safe? *Journal of the American Medical Association, 252,* 1875-1879.

O'Connor, M.J., Brill, N.J., & Sigman, M. (1986). Alcohol use in primiparous women older than 30 years of age: relation to infant development. *Pediatrics, 78,* 444-450.

Ogston, S.A., & Parry, G.J. (1992). EUROMAC. A European concerted action: maternal alcohol consumption and its relation to the outcome of pregnancy and child development at 18 months. Results—strategy of analysis and analysis of pregnancy outcome. *International Journal of Epidemiology, 21,* S45-71.

Parazzini, F., Bocciolone, L., La Vecchia, C., Negri, E., & Fedele, L. (1990). Maternal and paternal moderate daily alcohol consumption and unexplained miscarriages. *British Journal of Obstetrics and Gynaecology, 97,* 618-22.

Parry, G.J., & Ogston, S.A. (1992). EUROMAC. A European concerted action: maternal alcohol consumption and its relation to the outcome of pregnancy and child development at 18 months. Results—child development at age 18 months. *International Journal of Epidemiology, 21,* S72-78.

Peterson, R.G., & Bowes, W.A., Jr. (1983). Drugs, toxins, and environmental agents in breast milk. In M.C. Neville and M.R. Neifert (Eds.), *Lactation: Physiology, nutrition, and breast-feeding.* New York: Plenum Press.

Pikkarainen, P.H., & Raiha, N.C. (1967). Development of alcohol dehydrogenase activity in the human liver. *Pediatric Research, 1,* 165-168.

Pylkkanen, L., & Salonen, I. (1987). Concomitant mutagenicity of ethanol and x-ray irradiation in the mouse male germ cells. *Alcohol, 4,* 401-404.

Randall, C.L., Burling, T.A., Lochry, E.A., & Sutker, P.B. (1982). The effect of paternal alcohol consumption on fetal development in mice. *Drug and Alcohol Dependence, 9,* 89-95.

Rawat, A.K. (1977). Developmental changes in the brain levels of neurotransmitters as influenced by maternal ethanol consumption in the rat. *Journal of Neurochemistry, 28,* 1175-1182.

Richardson, G.A., Day, N.L., & Taylor, P.M. (1989). The effect of prenatal alcohol, marijuana, and tobacco exposure on neonatal behavior. *Infant Behavior and Development, 12,* 199-209.

Rimm, E.B., Giovannucci, E.L., Willett, W.C., Colditz, G.A., Ascherio, A., Rosner, B., & Stampfer, M.J. (1991). Prospective study of alcohol consumption and risk of coronary disease in men. *Lancet, 338,* 464-468.

Robinson, G.C., Conry, J.L., & Conry, R.R. (1987). Clinical profile and prevalence of fetal alcohol syndrome in an isolated community in British Columbia. *Canadian Medical Association Journal, 137,* 203-207.

Rosett, H.L. (1980). A clinical perspective of the fetal alcohol syndrome. *Alcoholism: Clinical and Experimental Research, 4,* 119-122.

Rosett, H.L., Weiner, L., Lee, A., Zuckerman, B., Dooling, E., & Oppenheimer, E. (1983). Patterns of alcohol consumption and fetal development. *Obstetrics and Gynecology, 61,* 539-546.

Rostand, A., Kaminski, M., Lelong, N., Dehaene, P., Delestret, I., Klein-Bertrand, C., Querleu, D., & Crepin, G. (1990). Alcohol use in pregnancy, craniofacial features, and fetal growth. *Journal of Epidemiology and Community Health, 44,* 302-306.

Russell, M., & Skinner, J.B. (1988). Early measures of maternal alcohol misuse as predictors of adverse pregnancy outcomes. *Alcoholism: Clinical and Experimental Research, 12,* 824-830.

Salonen, I. (1986). Exposure to ethanol during capacitation impairs the fertilizing ability of human spermatozoa in vitro. *International Journal of Andrology, 9,* 259-70.

Savitz, D.A., Zhang, J., Schwingl, P., & John, E.M. (1992). Association of paternal alcohol use with gestational age and birth weight. *Teratology, 46,* 465-471.

Scher, M.S., Richardson, G.A., Coble, P.A., Day, N.L., & Stoffer, D.S. (1988). The effects of prenatal alcohol and marijuana exposure: Disturbances in neonatal sleep cycling and arousal. *Pediatric Research, 24,* 101-105.

Shaper, A.G., Wannamethee, G., & Walker, M. (1988). Alcohol and mortality in British men: Explaining the U-shaped curve. *Lancet, 2,* 1267-1273.

Shiono, P.H., Klebanoff, M.A., & Rhoads, G.G. (1986). Smoking and drinking during pregnancy: Their effects on preterm birth. *Journal of the American Medical Association, 255,* 82-4.

Smith, I.E., Coles, C.D., Lancaster, J., Fernhoff, P.M., & Falek, A. (1986). The effect of volume and duration of prenatal ethanol exposure on neonatal physical and behavioral development. *Neurotoxicology and Teratology, 8,* 375-381.

Sokol, R.J., Miller, S.I., & Reed, G. (1980). Alcohol abuse during pregnancy: An epidemiological model. *Alcoholism: Clinical and Experimental Research, 4,* 135-145.

Soyka, L.F., and Joffe, J.M. (1980). Male mediated drug effects on offspring. In R. Schwarz & S.J. Yaffe (Eds.), *Drug and chemical risks to the fetus and newborn.* New York: Alan R. Liss.

Streissguth, A.P. (1978). Fetal alcohol syndrome: An epidemiologic perspective. *American Journal of Epidemiology, 107,* 467-478.

Streissguth, A.P. (1986). The behavioral teratology of alcohol: Performance, behavioral, and intellectual deficits in prenatally exposed children. In J.R. West (Ed.), *Alcohol and Brain Development* (pp. 3-44). New York: Oxford University Press.

Streissguth, A.P., Aase, J.M., Clarren, S.K., Randels, S.P., LaDue, R.A., & Smith, D.F. (1991). Fetal alcohol syndrome in adolescents and adults. *Journal of the American Medical Association, 265,* 1961-1967.

Streissguth, A.P., Barr, H.M., Martin, D.C., & Herman, C.S. (1980). Effects of maternal alcohol, nicotine, and caffeine use during pregnancy on infant mental and motor development at 8 months. *Alcoholism: Clinical and Experimental Research, 4,* 152-164.

Streissguth, A.P., Bookstein, F.L., Sampson, P.D., & Barr, H.M. (1989). Neurobehavioral effects of prenatal alcohol: Part III. PLS analysis of neuropsychologic tests. *Neurotoxicology and Teratology, 11,* 493-507.

Streissguth, A.P., & LaDue, R.A. (1985). Psychological and behavioral effects in children prenatally exposed to alcohol. *Alcohol Health & Research World, 10,* 6-12.

Streissguth, A.P., Martin, D.C., Martin, J.C., & Barr, H.M. (1981). The Seattle longitudinal prospective study on alcohol and pregnancy. *Neurobehavioral Toxicology and Teratology, 3,* 223-233.

Streissguth, A.P., Martin, D.C., Barr, H.M., Sandman, B.M., Kirchner, G.L., & Darby, B.L. (1984). Intrauterine alcohol and nicotine exposure: Attention and reaction time in 4-year-old children. *Developmental Psychology, 20,* 533-541.

Sulaiman, N.D., Florey, C.D., Taylor, D.J., & Ogston, S.A. (1988). Alcohol consumption in Dundee primigravidas and its effects on outcome of pregnancy. *British Medical Journal, 296,* 1500-1503.

Swanberg, K.M., & Wilson, J.R. (1979). Genetic and ethanol-related differences in maternal behavior and offspring viability in mice. *Developmental Psychobiology, 12,* 61-66.

Tanaka, H., Suzuki, N., & Arima, M. (1982). Experimental studies on the influence of male alcoholism on fetal development. *Brain Development, 4,* 1-6.

Tolo, K.A., & Little, R.E. (1993). Occasional binges by moderate drinkers: Implications for birth outcomes. *Epidemiology, 4,* 415-420.

United States Surgeon General. (1981). Surgeon general's advisory on alcohol and pregnancy. *FDA Drug Bulletin, 11,* 9-10.

Valimaki, M., & Ylikahri, R. (1983). The effect of alcohol on male and female sexual function. *Alcohol and Alcoholism, 18,* 313-320.

Vilaro, S., Vinas, O., Remesar, X., & Herrera, E. (1987). Effects of chronic ethanol consumption on lactational performance in rats: Mammary gland and milk composition and pups' growth and metabolism. *Pharmacology, Biochemistry and Behavior, 27,* 333-339.

Virji, S.K. (1991). The relationship between alcohol consumption during pregnancy and infant birthweight: An epidemiologic study. *Acta Obstetricia et Gynecologica Scandinavica, 70,* 303-8.

Virji, S.K., & Cottington, E. (1991). Risk factors associated with preterm deliveries among racial groups in a national sample of married mothers. *American Journal of Perinatology, 8,* 347-353.

Walpole, I., Zubrick, S., & Pontre, J. (1990). Is there a fetal effect with low to moderate alcohol use before or during pregnancy? *Journal of Epidemiology and Community Health, 44,* 297-301.

Walter, M. (1975). The folklore of breastfeeding. *Bulletin of the New York Academy of Medicine, 51,* 870-876.

Warren, K.R. (Ed.). (1977). *Critical review of the fetal alcohol syndrome.* Rockville, MD: National Institute on Alcohol Abuse and Alcoholism (distributed by the National Clearinghouse for Alcohol and Drug Information, Rockville, MD).

West, J.R., Goodlett, C.R., Bonthius, D.J., & Pierce, D.R. (1989). Manipulating peak blood alcohol concentrations in neonatal rats: Review of an animal model for alcohol-related developmental effects. *Neurotoxicology, 10,* 347-365.

Wilson, J.T., Hinson, J.L., Brown, R.D., & Smith, I.J. (1986). A comprehensive assessment of drugs and chemical toxins excreted in breast milk. In M. Hamosh and A.S. Goldman (Eds.), *Human lactation 2: Maternal and environmental factors* (pp. 395-423). New York: Plenum Press.

Windham, G.C., Fenster, L., Swan, S.H. (1992). Moderate maternal and paternal alcohol consumption and the risk of spontaneous abortion. *Epidemiology, 3,* 364-70.

CHAPTER 5

Gender Differences in the Genetic Contribution to Alcoholism Risk and to Alcohol Consumption Patterns

ANDREW C. HEATH, WENDY S. SLUTSKE, AND
PAMELA A.F. MADDEN

One of the most contentious issues in research on gender and alcohol use concerns the evaluation of genetic influences, and whether these influences are stronger in men than in women, as some have suggested (e.g., Cloninger et al., 1988; McGue, 1994). Evidence for a genetic influence derives from several sources, including studies of monozygotic and dizygotic twin pairs, studies of alcoholic and control biologic parents and their adopted-away offspring, and genetic association studies comparing alcoholic cases and controls. We shall have little to say about association studies, beyond a brief discussion of the methodologic problems which these involve, since the number of such studies continues to grow rapidly, while their methodologic uncertainties persist. We shall review in greater detail the empirical findings from twin and adoption studies, and then review the assumptions used in estimating the "heritability" of alcoholism (that is, the magnitude of the genetic contribution to alcoholism risk) before summarizing estimates of the heritability of alcoholism in men and women from the different studies. Finally, we shall consider the pathways by which a genetic influence on alcoholism risk may arise, and the extent to which genetic factors also influence normal variation in alcohol consumption patterns in men and women.

Genetic Association Studies

The strongest case for a genetic involvement in the etiology of a disorder is established when a specific genetic risk factor or protective factor is identified. In studies of Japanese populations, associations between an inherited deficiency of alcohol metabolism (ALDH2 deficiency) and (1) increased facial flushing, (2) decreased frequency of alcohol consumption, and (3) decreased frequency of alcoholism and alcoholic liver disease have been reported (reviewed in Agarwal & Goedde, 1990). Compared to individuals of European ancestry, a much higher proportion of Asians experience reactions such as facial flushing and increased heart rate after ingestion of only moderate amounts of alcohol, a difference that has been attributed to the high prevalence among Asians of a deficiency in an enzyme involved in the metabolism of alcohol. In a case-control study of alcoholic liver disease patients, only 3 out of 23 cases, but 28 out of 49 controls exhibited ALDH2 deficient genotypes. In a series of Japanese alcoholics, only 5% had the ALDH2 deficiency, compared to 42% of healthy controls. Similar results have been obtained in Chinese alcoholics and controls (Thomasson et al., 1993). While this provides a convincing demonstration of how a simple genetic defect may have an important effect on alcohol-related behaviors (a protective effect in this example), no such genetic deficiency has been demonstrated in non-Asian populations.

Typically, researchers have sought evidence for an association between genetic markers and alcoholism in two ways: First, case-control studies compare allele frequencies at a candidate genetic locus in a series of alcoholics and matched controls ("genetic association" studies). Second, linkage studies examine whether alcoholism and a genetic marker segregate together within families (i.e., whether, within any given family, alcoholics all have one particular allele at a genetic locus). (An allele is one of a group of two or more genes that have been found to occur at a given genetic locus; each individual has two alleles at every locus, one inherited from the mother, the second inherited from the father.) There have been no replicated linkage findings in the alcoholism field. However, in case-control research, considerable excitement was generated by the report of a significant genetic association between alcoholism and the D_2 dopamine receptor (DRD2) gene by Blum et al. (1990), who reported that some 69% of a series of alcoholics, but only 20% of controls, carried the A1 allele at the DRD2 locus. Attempts to replicate this finding have produced both positive (Amadeo et al., 1993; Blum et al., 1991; Comings et al., 1991; Parsian et al., 1991) and negative findings (Arinami et al., 1993; Bolos et al., 1990; Cook et al., 1992; Gerlernter et al., 1991; Goldman et al., 1993; Schwab et al., 1991; Turner et al., 1992).

In any case-control study, failure to appropriately match cases and controls can lead to artifactual findings. This is especially the case in genetic association studies, because differences in allele frequency for individuals from different ethnic backgrounds will generate spurious associations if cases and controls are imperfectly matched; and the A1 allele in particular shows pronounced differences in frequency across different populations (Barr & Kidd, 1993). A research strategy for circumventing this problem (the "haplotype relative risk" approach; Falk & Rubinstein, 1987) requires obtaining DNA samples from alcoholic cases and both parents in order to compare the frequencies of those alleles which the parents transmitted and those which the parents did not transmit to the alcoholics. Unfortunately, there are practical problems in using this strategy for genetic studies of alcoholism because of the association between alcoholism and increasing mortality risk. To date, no studies using this strategy have been published. Even in those case-control studies that have reported a significant association of the A1 allele with alcoholism, the A1 allele has often (Arinami, 1993; Blum et al., 1991; Parsian et al., 1991), but not always (Cook et al., 1992), been associated with alcoholism severity (typically defined as the presence of alcohol-related medical complications), raising the possibility that the DRD2 locus may be involved in the progression of alcoholism rather than its onset. At the present time, we are forced to conclude that significant genetic associations with alcoholism have not yet been conclusively established for non-Asian populations. We may also note that female alcoholics have constituted a small percentage of those used in genetic association studies, with results typically not reported separately by gender (McGue & Slutske, 1993).

Empirical Findings from Twin and Adoption Studies

Findings from studies of alcoholism in twin pairs (Allgulander et al., 1990, 1991, 1992; Caldwell & Gottesman, 1991; Heath & Martin, 1994; Hrubec & Omenn, 1981; Kaij, 1960; Kaprio et al., 1987; Kendler et al., 1992; Koskenvuo et al., 1984; McGue et al., 1992; Pickens et al., 1991; Prescott et al., 1994; Romanov et al., 1991), adoptees (Cadoret, 1994; Cadoret et al., 1985, 1987; Cloninger et al., 1981, 1988; Goodwin et al., 1973, 1974, 1977a,b), and half-siblings (Schuckit et al., 1972) are consistent with a genetic contribution to the risk of developing alcohol-related problems. With the exception of a single small sample twin study conducted in the United Kingdom (Gurling et al., 1984), studies have consistently found a higher probandwise concordance (the probability that an alcoholic twin will also have an alcoholic co-twin) in monozygotic twin pairs (identical twin pairs, who are genetically identical) than in dizygotic twin pairs (fraternal twin pairs, who are genetically no more alike than ordinary full siblings), which is what would be predicted if there were a genetic influence on alcoholism risk. With the exception of a small-sample adoption study conducted in the United States (see Roe & Burks, 1945), a study of female Danish adoptees by Goodwin et al. (1977a,b), and a recently reported study in Iowa (Cadoret, 1994), alcoholism risk in adoptees has been found to be positively associated with alcoholism risk in the biological parents, an association which would also be predicted if there is a genetic contribution to alcoholism risk. Findings have more often been significant for men than for women, and reported estimates of heritability (the percentage of the total variation in alcoholism risk attributable to genetic effects; see below) have sometimes been higher for men than for women, leading to a widespread view that genes play a more important role in alcoholism in men than in women (e.g., Cloninger et al., 1981; McGue, 1994). Before accepting this view, however, it may be helpful to review the methods that are typically used to estimate the magnitude of the genetic contribution to alcoholism risk, and to reexamine in detail the findings reported in individual studies.

Evidence for a genetic contribution to alcoholism risk has in the past derived from three basic types of research design: (1) record linkage studies that have matched official records of alcoholism treatment or alcohol-related problems with registers of twins or adoptees; (2) epidemiologic surveys that have interviewed or surveyed by mailed questionnaire a community sample of twin pairs (no such surveys of adoptee samples have been published); and (3) hybrid studies in which a "proband" is identified from treatment or other records, and the history of alcoholism in the proband and in the proband's co-twin (in the case of studies of twins) or adopted-away offspring are directly assessed by interview or questionnaire. (The term "proband" is used by geneticists for individuals identified for a genetic study from hospital or clinic or official records.) This hybrid strategy is the one most commonly used in genetic studies, since it avoids the high costs associated with identifying cases from large community samples.

Record Linkage Studies

Results from six major record linkage studies have been reported, five conducted in Scandinavian countries and one in the United States. Kaij (1960) matched records of male twin births from two counties in Sweden to temperance board records, and identified male like-sex monozygotic (MZ) and dizygotic (DZ) twin pairs in which at least one twin had been registered with the local temperance board. In Sweden at that time, community temperance boards were notified of cases of "intemperance," and were responsible for imposing fines or supervising treatment or involuntary hospitalization, this latter sanction being applied only in the most chronic cases. Using the broadest criterion of at least one registration, or more restrictive definitions, significantly higher probandwise concordances were observed in MZ than in DZ twin pairs (e.g., 61% versus 39% for the broadest criterion), both risks being substantially higher than the risk to an unselected male from the population (reported as 7.7% by Kaij, based on an earlier Swedish census study). Because twins were identified because of social problems with alcohol—Kaij (1960) notes that doctors would be unlikely to report their patients unless they were unable to help them—we must be cautious about overgeneralizing from this study (cf., Kaij and Dock, 1975): some individuals with severe alcohol-related problems may never have been registered, and others may have been registered after a transient episode. Furthermore, it is likely that cases of alcoholism associated with a history of antisocial behavior were overrepresented in the temperance board records: Amark (1951) reported a very high percentage of criminals (44%) in male alcoholics identified through Stockholm Temperance Board materials. However, twins with at least one registration were over five times more likely to be diagnosed as alcoholic at follow-up interview (Kaij, 1960), and hospitalized alcoholics were more than four times more likely to be registered than the general male population of Sweden (56% versus 12.4%; Amark, 1951).

The Stockholm adoption study of Bohman, Cloninger, and colleagues (Bohman, 1978; Bohman et al., 1981; Cloninger et al., 1981, 1985, 1988) also made use of the Swedish temperance board system for case-finding. In contrast to the Kaij study, this study provides information about the genetic contribution to alcoholism risk in women as well as in men. All births to unwed mothers in Stockholm over the period 1930–49 were identified, and selected for further study if the biological father had been identified, and the adoption had occurred by age 3, with placement to a nonrelative. Alcoholism in the biological and adoptive parents was assessed using temperance board registrations as mild (single registration), moderate (2-3 registrations), or severe (more than 3 registrations, compulsory treatment, or psychiatric hospitalization with a diagnosis of alcoholism), with additional information available from child welfare registers and the State Criminal Board (Cloninger et al., 1985). We shall focus on the same broad criterion of 1 + temperance board registrations used with the Kaij (1960) study. From the data presented by Cloninger et al. (1985) we can compute that approximately 32% of the biological fathers, but only 4.7% of the biological mothers, were alcoholic by this criterion. There was random mating for alcoholism in this population of unwed parents, i.e., that biological father's risk of alcoholism was not associated with biological mother's risk (tetrachoric correlation, $r = 0.06$, standard error $= 0.07$) (see Jöreskog & Sorbom, 1988, for a more detailed discussion of interpretation of the tetrachoric correlation). In contrast, in less than 4% of the adoptive families was either parent alcoholic. If we contrast these risks to the frequency of registration in men reported for Swedish males based on a census conducted in 1964 (approximately a 14% prevalence, cited in Kaij & Dock, 1975), then we see that the biological fathers had unusually high rates, and the adoptive fathers unusually low rates, of alcoholism, implying that the adoptees would be at increased genetic risk, but exposed to low-risk family environments.

For the adoptees in the Stockholm study, additional information was used from the National Health Insurance Board, with medical records sought for any adoptees for whom required sick leave reports indicated at least two weeks sick leave with a psychiatric diagnosis (Cloninger, 1990; Cloninger et al., 1985, 1988). When all the adoptees were evaluated using this expanded database in 1972 (aged 23–43), 17.5% of the sons and 3.4% of the daughters were identified as alcoholic. Of those adoptees with a psychiatric diagnosis of alcoholism identified from National Health insurance records, 58% of men, but only 29% of women, had at least one temperance board registration (Cloninger et al., 1985), consistent with the hypothesis that temperance board records may have omitted many alcoholics who did not display antisocial behavior. Risk of alcoholism in the adoptees, in either men or women, was not significantly associated with alcoholism risk in the adoptive parents. Among adoptive sons, alcoholism was significantly more common in the sons of alcoholic biologic fathers (23% lifetime prevalence) and in the sons of alcoholic biologic mothers (28%) than in the sons of nonalcoholic parents (15%). Among adoptive daughters, alcoholism was significantly more common in the daughters of alcoholic mothers (9.8% lifetime prevalence) but not in the daughters of alcoholic fathers (3.9%), compared to the daughters of nonalcoholic parents (2.8%). Thus, these adoption data agree with the twin data from Kaij in supporting a genetic contribution to problems with alcohol in men, but also demonstrate an association between daughter's alcoholism risk and biological mother's alcoholism risk (Bohman et al., 1981).

Additional record linkage studies have been conducted in Finland and Sweden, which have involved matching national birth certificate-derived twin registers (Kaprio et al., 1978; Medlund et al., 1977) to hospitalization records. Since this procedure excludes outpatient contacts, it presumably identifies only the most severe alcoholics. The Swedish study, reported by Allgulander et al. (1990, 1991, 1992), involved matching 12,844 twin pairs born 1926-58 (Medlund et al., 1977) to ICD-8 psychiatric inpatient discharge codes for the period 1969-83. Based on diagnoses for all inpatient admissions (Allgulander et al., 1992), probandwise concordances were 21.4% for MZ female pairs, 8.9% for DZ female pairs, 13.2% for MZ male pairs, and 7.9% for DZ male pairs, and were substantially higher than the overall prevalence of alcoholism-related hospitalization (0.5% for women, 1.7% for men). Although the authors reported significant evidence for a genetic contribution to alcoholism risk both in men and in women, with an even stronger genetic influence in women than in men, based on the multiple admission data (Allgulander et al., 1992), reanalysis of their data reveals that it is not possible to reject the hypothesis of no genetic effects at the conventional 5% significance level (see below).

Two articles have reported twin pair concordances for ICD-8 hospital discharge codes using twins from the Finnish twin register (Kaprio et al., 1978), a register of twin pairs born in Finland between 1880 and 1957, and alive in 1967. The first study, which used a sample of 16,649 twin pairs where both twins were alive at the beginning of 1972, reported results of matching to hospital discharge records and death certificates for the period 1972-79, and reported results for alcoholism (ICD-8 code 303), but not for alcohol-abuse associated diseases (Koskenvuo et al., 1984). Reported age-adjusted hospitalization rates for alcoholism for the period 1972-79 were 1.9% in men and 0.2% in women. Probandwise concordances were 23.1% in MZ male twin pairs, and 10.8% in DZ like-sex male twin pairs; but no concordant female like-sex pairs were observed. Because the power to resolve genetic and environmental effects in twin data is weakened by low prevalence rates (Neale & Cardon, 1992), even with the very large initial sample size the hypothesis of no genetic effects could not be rejected at the 5% significance level in these data. Male alcoholism in this sample was highly familial (the MZ tetrachoric correlation was 0.6), but the possibility that the correlation was purely the result of shared environmental influences cannot be excluded. A second article (Romanov et al., 1991) examined alcohol-related discharges for the period 1972–85, and included alcoholic liver disease, alcoholic psychosis, and alcohol intoxication as well as alcoholism, but was restricted to male twins from pairs where the residence of both twins was known ($N = 5,526$ pairs). Probandwise concordance rates for alcoholism as defined in this chapter (i.e., including alcohol-related discharges) were 19.7% for MZ male pairs and 12.1% for DZ male pairs, which may be contrasted with the overall population prevalence of 2.5%. The authors reported finding significant evidence for genetic effects on alcoholism risk. However, if their data are reanalyzed correctly (see below), we find that the hypothesis that twin pair resemblance is entirely explained by shared environmental influences, with no genetic influence, cannot be rejected.

Finally, a recent study by Kendler et al. (in press) has confirmed the earlier work of Kaij (1960), by demonstrating higher MZ than DZ concordances for temperance board registrations in a national sample of Swedish male twins born 1902–49. A total of 13.2% of MZ twins and 14.6% of DZ twins had one or more temperance board registrations. However, if one twin had a temperance board registration, the probability that the co-twin was also registered was 47.9% for MZ, but only 32.8% for DZ co-twins, consistent with an important genetic influence on this measure of alcohol problems.

Only a single comparable record-linkage study has been conducted in the United States, and that too was restricted to male like-sex twin pairs. Hrubec and Omenn (1981) reviewed Veterans Administration medical records of 13,486 male twin pairs from the NAS/NRC Veterans Twin panel, a panel of twin pairs who were identified through their service in the Second World War and who were followed up at least through age 50. The lifetime prevalence for alcoholism and alcoholic psychosis in this sample was reported as 2.63% in MZ twins and 3.12% in DZ twins, a difference in prevalence that was marginally significant. A higher prevalence in dizygotic than in monozygotic twins would be expected if there were genetic influence on alcoholism risk and also a systematic loss of alcoholic twins from the sample, perhaps because of alcohol-related illness or mortality or because twins with very early onset alcoholism were excluded from military service even in time of war. (Greater loss of monozygotic twins is expected because a twin pair was more likely to be lost to the sample if both twins were alcoholic than if only one twin was alcoholic; and the genetic hypothesis predicts that there would be more concordant alcoholism in monozygotic than in dizygotic twin pairs.) The observed difference is unlikely to cause any serious statistical bias in estimates of the genetic contribution to alcoholism risk in these data. Probandwise concordances were 26.3% for MZ male pairs and 11.9% for DZ male pairs. The evidence for genetic effects in these data is highly significant ($p < .001$). As with the Swedish and Finnish studies using hospital discharge records, it is likely that only severe cases of alcoholism were detected. For example, 22.7% of those diagnosed as alcoholic also had a diagnosis of liver cirrhosis.

Reliance on data from hospital discharges or other medical records has both advantages and disadvantages. Alcoholism cases identified in community surveys (cf., Robins & Regier, 1991; Kessler et al., 1994) include many individuals with a history of only mild problems (see Heath, Bucholz et al., 1994). Hospital discharge or medical records identify severe alcoholics, the group likely to have the greatest utilization of health services. Some have argued that identifying probands through inpatient treatment, by identifying severe cases, ensures that more "genetic" cases are selected (e.g., Goodwin et al., 1994). At least in the case of the Hrubec and Omenn study, however, selection of cases identified through the VA system is apparently oversampling cases with medical complications, so that we cannot exclude the possibility that we are observing genetic influences on the development of medical complications of alcoholism, rather than of alcoholism per se.

The Finnish data do not give any indication of a genetic contribution to severe alcoholism in women. However, given the very low prevalence of alcohol-related hospital discharges in Finnish women (0.2%), even if severe alcoholism in women had a heritability of 60%, we would require a sample of 54,000 female like-sex twin pairs (larger than the entire population of female twins in Finland) to have an 80% chance of rejecting the hypothesis of no genetic effects at the 5% significance level (cf., Neale & Cardon, 1992)! The Swedish hospitalization data do show the predicted higher MZ than DZ concordance in female like-sex pairs, but this difference is not significant either in women or in men. The Swedish data using temperance board registrations were also consistent with a genetic contribution to risk of alcohol problems in both men and women. These data, which used an outcome measure that was more likely to include cases with social rather than medical complications from alcohol use, imply that genetic vulnerability contributes to more than just medical complications of alcoholism. This is an issue to which we shall return later.

In sum, the data from record linkage studies, using either temperance board registrations or hospital discharge or medical record diagnoses, are consistent with a genetic contribution to alcoholism risk in men, though in some studies the hypothesis of no genetic influence could not be rejected. The Swedish adoption data also suggest a genetic effect in women as well.

General Population Surveys

To date, results have been published from only one large-sample genetic-epidemiologic survey that has assessed alcoholism by structured psychiatric interview: a survey of female like-sex MZ and DZ twin pairs ($N=1,030$ pairs) from the Virginia Twin Register (Kendler et al., 1992). Analyses are in progress for two other surveys: (1) a survey by telephone interview of 6,000 twins from the Australian National Health and Medical Research Council twin panel (a volunteer panel) that obtained data from 1,429 female like-sex and 607 male like-sex pairs (Heath et al., 1993); and (2) a survey by telephone interview of some 3,300 male like-sex twin pairs from the Vietnam-era twin panel (Tsuang et al., 1994; cf., Eisen et al., 1989). Twins in the Virginia study were identified from birth records, and were eligible for interview if they had participated in at least one prior mailed questionnaire study. Interviews were conducted by social workers and other clinically trained interviewers using the Structured Clinical Interview for DSM-III-R (Spitzer et al., 1987). Results from the Virginia survey have been reported for three diagnostic classifications: (1) narrow (DSM-III-R alcohol dependence, but with the additional requirement of symptoms of tolerance or withdrawal); (2) intermediate (DSM-III-R alcohol dependence); and (3) broad (at least one problem with alcohol that was not limited to an isolated incident). For each of these classifications, higher MZ than like-sex DZ probandwise concordances were observed (26.2% versus 11.9%; 31.6% versus 24.4%; 46.9% versus 31.5%), consistent with a genetic influence. For each classification significant familial aggregation was observed; but only for the broadest classification could the hypothesis of no genetic effects be rejected at the 5% significance level by the most stringent likelihood-ratio chi-square criterion (Kendler et al., 1992). Once again, lifetime prevalence of alcoholism was lower in MZ than in DZ twins for all alcoholism classifications (e.g., 8.1% versus 10.2% for "intermediate" alcoholism), which again may be explained by undersampling of alcoholics.

One other interview-based survey for which data have been published assessed problems with alcohol in a community sample of 902 male like-sex twin pairs in Finland in 1958-59 (Partanen et al., 1966). Nondiagnostic assessments of problems with alcohol were used. As reviewed elsewhere (Heath, 1995), this survey found evidence for a substantial genetic contribution to individual differences in alcohol consumption patterns, but little genetic influence on measures of adverse social consequences of alcohol use or arrests for drunkenness.

Several twin surveys have assessed problems with alcohol by mailed questionnaire. Many of these surveys have used nondiagnostic assessments of alcohol-related problems (e.g., Heath & Martin, 1994; Kaprio et al., 1987), though Feighner criteria for alcoholism (Feighner et al., 1972) have sometimes been applied (Heath et al., 1993; Prescott et al., 1994). Prescott et al.

(1994) surveyed a volunteer panel of older American twins, recruited through the American Association of Retired Persons. For Feighner definite/ probable alcoholism, they found no significant evidence for genetic effects on lifetime alcoholism, either in 217 male like-sex twin pairs (MZ probandwise concordance rate = 44.4%, DZ = 15.4%, with these rates not differing significantly because of small sample size) or in 966 female like-sex pairs (20% versus 15%). In a mailed questionnaire survey of Australian twins (Heath et al., 1993), conducted in 1989-92, self-report data on problems with alcohol were obtained from two twin cohorts: a cohort of pairs born 1895-1964 who had been surveyed previously in 1981 ("1981 cohort"), and a new cohort of pairs born 1964-71 ("1989 cohort"). Problems with alcohol were coded according to Feighner criteria. Using the broad category of definite/probable alcoholism, the 1981 cohort showed no significant difference in probandwise concordance rates, either for male like-sex pairs (49.5% versus 44.4% for MZ versus DZ pairs) or for female like-sex pairs (23.9% versus 19.7%), although there was a trend in the predicted direction. In the 1989 cohort, data for male like-sex pairs (albeit based on small sample sizes) also failed to show evidence for genetic influence; indeed, the probandwise concordance was higher in DZ than in MZ pairs (67.7% versus 54.6%). However, there was highly significant evidence for a genetic influence in young women (probandwise concordances of 52.9% for MZ female pairs versus 34.2% for DZ female pairs).

General population surveys to evaluate the genetic contribution to alcoholism risk have many of the same advantages and disadvantages as general community surveys in conventional epidemiology. They avoid confounding risk-factors for the disorder with risk-factors for treatment-seeking, or risk-factors for a poor outcome. They also avoid problems with the overrepresentation of individuals with multiple disorders in treatment samples (Berkson's bias; see Berkson, 1946). The cases identified in a community survey will include a higher proportion of individuals with mild or transient problems. This may be an advantage, if we wish to predict which individuals who develop problems with alcohol recover successfully, and which individuals progress to the point where extensive treatment is required. It may be a disadvantage, if we are primarily interested in severe cases of alcoholism. General population surveys suffer from the important disadvantage of requiring very large sample sizes for adequate power to detect significant genetic influences on alcoholism risk. Of the published studies, significant evidence for genetic influence on problems with alcohol has been obtained only in the 1989 cohort of the Australian twin panel (using self-report questionnaire data), and for a broadly defined problem-drinking measure (assessed by interview) in the Virginia study. However, in the majority of studies, probandwise concordances were higher for MZ twin pairs than for DZ twin pairs, consistent with the hypothesis of a genetic contribution to alcoholism risk.

Hybrid Studies

A number of studies have examined the risk of alcoholism in adopted-away offspring or co-twins of probands, as ascertained through treatment facilities or official records. Kaij (1960) conducted follow-up interviews wherever possible with the twins he had evaluated using Swedish temperance board records. However, since Kaij interviewed both members of a twin pair himself, the possibility of unintentional biases, particularly when interviewing the second member of a monozygotic twin pair, cannot be ruled out. In contemporary research it is now required that interviews be conducted by interviewers who are "blind," i.e., have no knowledge of the alcoholism or other psychiatric history of other family members.

Goodwin and colleagues (1973, 1974, 1977a,b) examined the risk of alcoholism in adopted-away children whose biological parents who had been hospitalized with an alcoholism diagnosis in Copenhagen, Denmark. In addition to the adopted-away sons ($n = 55$) and daughters ($n = 49$) of alcoholic parents, they also interviewed control adoptees ($n = 78$ adopted sons, $n = 47$ adopted daughters), and nonadopted offspring of the alcoholic biological parents ($n = 20$ sons, $n = 81$ daughters). The adoptees were identified from records of all adoptions to nonfamily adoptive parents during the period 1924–47, and were included only if adoption had occurred within the first six months of life. Although sample sizes were small, the methodology was sound: interviews were conducted by psychiatrists blind to the psychiatric family history of the interviewees, and standardized diagnostic criteria were used for assessment. For the adopted sons of alcoholics (Goodwin et al., 1973, 1974), the lifetime risk of alcoholism was significantly greater in probands than in male control adoptees (18% versus 5%), but did not differ from the risk to the nonadopted biological offspring of the alcoholic parents (i.e., the biological siblings of a subsample of the high-risk adoptees—17% lifetime prevalence). Adopted-away sons of alcoholics were less likely to report a history of alcoholism in their adoptive fathers (12% for possible or definite alcoholism) than were control adoptees (22%). These findings are consistent with the hypothesis that parent-offspring resemblance for alcoholism risk is determined by shared genetic factors rather than by shared environmental risk-factors. In contrast, only 2% of adopted-away daughters of alcoholics received a lifetime diagnosis of alcoholism, compared to 4% of control adoptees, and 3% of nonadopted daughters of alcoholics (Goodwin et al., 1977a,b), so there was no evidence for a genetic contribution to alcoholism risk in women.

Interview follow-up data have been reported for alcoholic twin probands and their co-twins identified from a single hospital in the United Kingdom (Gurling et al., 1984), as well as for twin series ascertained through hospitals in St. Louis, Missouri (Caldwell & Gottesman, 1991), and through treatment facilities in Minnesota (McGue et al., 1992; Pickens et al., 1991). The British study found no significant evidence for genetic influence in either men or women. Based on interview assessments of the alcohol dependence syndrome (Edwards et al., 1977), the proportion of affected co-twins of affected male probands was 33% in MZ and 30% in DZ pairs, while corresponding proportions in female pairs were 8% in MZ and 13% in DZ pairs (Gurling et al., 1984). Both the St. Louis study and the Minnesota study of Pickens et al. obtained assessments of DSM-III alcohol abuse or dependence using the DIS (Robins et al., 1985). We present results here for the broad category "abuse or dependence," which more closely approximates DSM-III-R dependence. In the St. Louis study, probandwise concordance rates for DSM-III abuse or dependence were 68% for MZ male pairs and 46% for DZ like-sex male pairs, a significant difference consistent with a genetic influence on male alcoholism; but the concordance rates of 47% for MZ female and 42% for DZ female like-sex pairs were not significantly different. The St. Louis study also obtained data from DZ unlike-sex pairs (which are useful for testing for sex-specific genetic or environmental risk-factors): 33% of the female co-twins of male probands with alcohol abuse or dependence, and 58% of the male co-twins of female probands, also met criteria for DSM-III abuse or dependence. In the Minnesota study, concordance rates for DSM-III abuse or dependence were 76% in MZ male and 61% in DZ male like-sex pairs, and 36% and 25% for MZ and DZ female like-sex pairs. Once again, in the Minnesota study, the hypothesis of no genetic effects on alcoholism risk in women could not be rejected at the 5% significance level. In men, although the concordance rate in MZ male pairs was significantly higher than the concordance rate in DZ pairs, interpretation of this difference is problematic because of differences in the age distribution of the two zygosity groups. Small differences in age distribution are not a problem in epidemiologic and record-linkage studies, where age effects will be confounded with shared environmental rather than genetic effects (since both MZ and DZ pairs are perfectly correlated for age). However, they do become important in proband studies, in which appropriate estimates of the prevalence of alcoholism in the general population must be derived from external sources. Although the MZ male pairs were younger than the DZ male pairs, because of the trend for more problems in younger age groups (see Robins & Regier, 1991), the predicted lifetime prevalence for males of the same age distribution as the MZ twins was higher than the predicted lifetime prevalence for males of the same age as the DZ twins (Pickens et al., 1991). Once this effect is taken into account, the evidence for a genetic influence on male alcoholism risk (at least as assessed by DSM-III abuse or dependence) is also nonsignificant (see below).

McGue et al. (1992) reported results of a mailed questionnaire survey of Minnesota twins ascertained through treatment facilities, including a subset of those twins reported by Pickens et al. The McGue study had the largest sample size of all the twin studies using a hybrid strategy. A self-report questionnaire was used to assess DSM-III abuse or dependence. This study found no evidence for a genetic contribution to alcoholism risk in women, and somewhat inconsistent evidence for a genetic influence in men (as we review in more detail below). Probandwise concordances were 39% for MZ female like-sex pairs, 42% for DZ female pairs, 76% for MZ male pairs, and 53% for DZ male pairs; the latter difference was significant, but was also confounded with an age difference as in the Pickens et al. study. Data from unlike-sex pairs showed that 78% of the male co-twins of female probands, and 31% of the female co-twins of male probands, also met criteria for DSM-III alcohol abuse or dependence.

The first adoption study of alcoholism was conducted in the United States by Roe and Burks (1945). However, sample size in that study (32 adopted-away offspring of alcoholic biological parents and 25 control adoptees) were too small to be useful: no cases of alcoholism were identified in either experimental or control groups, so no definitive conclusions could be drawn. More recently, Cadoret has conducted a series of adoption studies in Iowa (Cadoret, 1994; Cadoret et al., 1985, 1987). Findings from the first two of these studies appear to support a genetic contribution to alcoholism risk, though preliminary reports of two more recent studies indicate negative findings (Cadoret, 1994).

In a Lutheran Social Services sample, Cadoret et al. (1985) identified from adoption agency records (1) adoptees with evidence of alcohol-related problems in first-degree biologic family members (e.g., a relative who was described as a heavy drinker with a social, legal, occupational, or medical problem due to drinking); (2) adoptees with evidence of antisocial behaviors in biologic relatives, as indicated by at least two behaviors from a list that ranged from "associating with children of bad reputation" to being a convicted felon; and (3) control adoptees with no evidence of psychiatric, substance abuse, or behavior problems in biologic relatives. First-degree biologic relatives included older siblings as well as parents. Adoptees were assessed by interview. In the total sample of adoptees, 29.1% of men and 9.2% of women met definite or possible criteria for DSM-III alcohol abuse or dependence; but rates of alcoholism were significantly elevated in adoptees whose biologic relatives had alcohol problems (61.1% of men, 33.3% of women), consistent with the hypothesis of a genetic influence in both genders. In adopted men, alcoholism was also significantly more common in adoptees with a history of alcoholism in the adoptive family (48.0%), with a similar though nonsignificant trend in the adoptive women (17.4%), suggesting an environmental influence also of parental alcoholism.

The second study (Cadoret et al., 1987) was an interview follow-up of a sample of male adoptees recruited through Iowa's Children's and Family Services either as control adoptees, or because at least one biologic parent showed evidence of any psychiatric or behavior disturbance. Once again alcoholism in the adoptees was significantly associated with both alcohol-related problems in biologic parents and alcohol-related problems in the adoptive parents. In both samples, there was also a significant association between antisocial personality disorder (ASPD) in male adoptees and their biologic relatives, and between ASPD and alcoholism in the adoptees themselves, but no significant cross-association between antisocial behaviors in the biologic first-degree relatives and alcoholism in the male adoptees, nor between alcoholism in the biologic relatives and ASPD in the adoptees.

Genetic studies using samples ascertained through alcoholic probands have an important advantage: they are substantially cheaper than studies using community-based samples. However, as we shall see below, if we are interested in quantifying the magnitude of the genetic influence on alcoholism risk, data from proband-based samples are much more difficult to interpret. The published adoption data from the Danish and Iowa studies are in agreement in suggesting a genetic influence on alcoholism risk in men, but inconsistent in their conclusions concerning women. The twin studies have consistently failed to find evidence for a genetic influence on female alcoholism, but two of the three interview-based studies appear to confirm a genetic influence on male alcoholism.

Gender Differences in the Magnitude of the Genetic Influence on Alcoholism Risk

Record Linkage or Epidemiologic Data

Although studies more often fail to find significant evidence for a genetic contribution to alcoholism in women than in men, this does not constitute evidence for a weaker genetic influence in women. Failure to reject the null hypothesis of no genetic influence may result merely from low statistical power, given the lower prevalence of alcohol problems in women than in men. The lower the population prevalence, the larger the sample size that is needed to reject the hypothesis of no genetic influence (Neale & Cardon, 1992). What we should ask is whether, in a given study, the heritability estimates obtained for women are significantly lower than those for men. And as a first step toward quantifying the genetic influence on alcoholism risk in a given dataset, we should make explicit the assumptions of our genetic model.

If we assume that alcoholism is a disorder of complex etiology, influenced by multiple environmental risk factors and perhaps also multiple genetic risk factors, then it is plausible to postulate a continuum of risk or "liability" to alcoholism in the general population, with an individual's alcoholism risk (liability score) being the sum or product of his or her genetic and environmental risk factors. If we could measure all those risk factors directly, from the central limit theorem in statistics, we would anticipate that the distribution of liability scores would be approximately normal. Thus, even though we

FIGURE 1
Assumptions Used in the Genetic Analysis of Alcoholism data: (a)
Threshold and (b) Multiple-Threshold Models; (c) Severity and (d) Two-
Process Models for Analysis of Data from Clinically Ascertained Samples

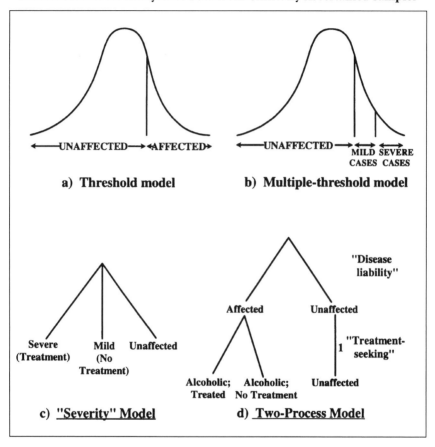

measure only a binary trait—presence or absence of alcoholism—it is reasonable to hypothesize a continuous underlying liability distribution, with individuals who exceed some "threshold" becoming alcoholic (Falconer, 1965; see Figure 1a). Likewise for a polychotomous measure of alcoholism severity, we may imagine an underlying continuum with multiple thresholds (Reich et al., 1975; Figure 1b)—those individuals with the most extreme liability scores would become the severe cases, those with intermediate scores the mild cases, and those below the lowest threshold would be unaffected. In fact, we do not need to be able to observe "liability" scores directly, provided that our assumption that they are normally distributed is correct. Predicted proportions of pairs concordant and discordant for alcoholism will vary as a function of both population prevalence and twin-pair liability correlation. For a given population prevalence, higher correlations will lead to higher proportions of concordant alcoholic pairs; and likewise for a given correlation, a higher population prevalence will lead to a higher proportion of concordant alcoholics. Thus, we can obtain estimates of twin-pair correlations from the two-way contingency tables cross-classifying the affection status (presence or absence of a history of alcoholism) of twin and co-twin. (These are the same assumptions used by psychometricians [e.g., Olsson, 1979; Jöreskog and Sorbom, 1988] to estimate "tetrachoric" or "polychoric" correlations from ordinal data. This approach was adopted much earlier by geneticists—e.g., Pearson, 1900.)

Data from a record-linkage study or general population survey may be summarized in two-way contingency tables, cross-classifying the affection status of one relative (e.g., biological parent or first-born twin) by the affection status of another (e.g., adopted-away offspring or second-born twin). The adoption data in Table 1, for example, are temperance board registration data on biological parents and their adopted-away offspring reported for the Swedish adoption study by Cloninger (1990; see also Cloninger et al., 1981, 1988). Binary classifications have been used for all relationships except father-son, for which we use the trichotomous classification of no registrations/1 registration/2 or more registrations reported in Cloninger et al. (1988). (Trichotomous classifications have not been reported for the other relationships, presumably because fewer mothers and daughters had two or more registrations, so that some of the cells of the 3×3 tables would have been extremely sparse.)

We can use standard statistical software packages such as PRELIS2 (Jöreskog and Sorbom, 1993) to estimate tetrachoric or polychoric correlations from these two-way tables. Without going into technical details, the expected proportions of relatives who are concordant unaffected, concordant affected, or discordant for alcoholism, are a function of the population prevalence for each class of relative, and the tetrachoric correlation between the relatives, i.e., their correlation for liability to alcoholism. Thus, from the observed two-way tables it is possible to obtain maximum likelihood estimates of the tetrachoric or polychoric correlations and population frequencies. When we estimate polychoric correlations from the contingency tables of Table 1, the estimates that we obtain (and the standard errors of these estimates) are 0.19 ($SE = 0.06$) for biological father–adopted-away son; 0.17 ($SE = 0.11$) for biological mother–adopted-away son; 0.29 ($SE = 0.13$) for biological mother–adopted-away daughter; and 0.06 ($SE = 0.10$) for biological father–adopted-away daughter. The two unlike-sex correlations are nonsignificant, whereas the mother-daughter and father-son correlations are both significant. With three or more ordinal categories, as we have for the father-son data, we also obtain a goodness-of-fit chi-square, which tests whether the

TABLE 1

Adoption and twin data on the familial aggregation of alcoholism risk. Adoption data are two-way contingency tables for Swedish temperance board registration in the Swedish adoption study of alcoholism (adapted from Cloninger et al., 1988, and Cloninger, 1990). Twin data are numbers of affected and unaffected co-twins of alcoholic twin probands reported in the studies of Pickens et al. (1991), Caldwell and Gottesman (1991), and McGue et al. (1992).

ADOPTION DATA

ADOPTED-AWAY SONS

	None	One	Recurrent
Biological father			
None	504	39	51
One	82	5	9
Recurrent	125	20	27

	None	One or more
Biological mother		
None	688	142
One or more	23	9

ADOPTED-AWAY DAUGHTERS

	None	One or more
Biological father		
None	587	19
One or more	295	12
Biological mother		
None	836	26
One or more	46	5

TWIN DATA

Co-twin:	PICKENS ET AL. (1991)		CALDWELL & GOTTESMAN (1991)		MCGUE ET AL. (1992)	
	Unaffected	Affected	Unaffected	Affected	Unaffected	Affected
MZ males	12	38	9	19	20	65
DZ like-sex males	25	39	14	12	44	52
MZ females	20	11	9	8	27	17
DZ like-sex females	18	6	14	10	25	18
DZ unlike-sex male probands	–	–	8	11	5	18
DZ unlike-sex female probands	–	–	27	13	45	20

Note: Sample of McGue et al. overlaps with that of Pickens et al.

assumptions of the multiple threshold model are justified: we obtain a chi-square value of 3.33, on 3 degrees of freedom, which is nonsignificant. Since this is a goodness-of-fit chi-square, it tests whether the observed data are consistent with what we would predict under the model, and a significant chi-square would indicate *failure* of the model. In the present example, the nonsignificant chi-square indicates that the data are consistent with the hypothesis that males with 0, 1, or 2+ temperance board registrations are ordered along a continuum of severity.

If there is no selective placement, i.e., no tendency for offspring of alcoholics to be adopted into more high-risk environments than offspring of nonalcoholics, the correlation between biological parent and adopted-away offspring will be entirely determined by their genetic relationship. From quantitative genetic theory (e.g., Bulmer, 1980), since a parent and his or her biological child share half their genes in common, and since there is no evidence for an association between alcoholism in biological mothers and in biological fathers in these data, we may write $r_{PO} = 1/2$ VAG, where r_{PO} denotes the parent-offspring correlation, and VAG is the proportion of the variance in liability to alcoholism that is explained by genetic effects (strictly, by additive genetic effects, i.e., excluding nonadditive effects such as genetic dominance, which do not contribute to parent-offspring resemblance); this is the so-called narrow-sense heritability of alcoholism. If the heritability of alcoholism varies as a function of gender, we would have to estimate separate heritabilities from the father-son and mother-daughter correlations, with the unlike-sex father-daughter and mother-son correlations predicted to be $1/2$ $VAG_m^{1/2}$ $VAG_f^{1/2}$, where $VAG_m^{1/2}$ $VAG_f^{1/2}$ is the geometric mean of the male like-sex and female like-sex heritabilities. Thus, at face value, the father-son and mother-daughter correlations from the Swedish adoption project are suggesting a higher heritability of alcoholism in women (58%) than in men (38%).

One further step is necessary before we can have confidence in this conclusion of a stronger genetic influence on alcoholism in women than in men: we must test whether the four correlations that we have estimated are significantly heterogeneous, or whether they are in fact consistent with a single heritability estimate that is the same for men and women. This can be done most conveniently using software packages that allow us to estimate a single correlation (or equivalently, heritability) for the four two-way contingency tables (e.g., Neale, 1992). When we do this, our goodness-of-fit chi-square is 4.84 on 3 degrees of freedom. The difference between this chi-square value, and the value obtained when we estimated four separate correlations, is a likelihood-ratio chi-square which tests whether the model estimating a single correlation gives a significantly worse fit than the four-correlation model, i.e., which tests whether the four correlations are significantly heterogeneous. In fact, we find that the likelihood-ratio chi-square is nonsignificant ($\chi^2 = 1.51$, $df = 3$, $p > .05$), and obtain an overall heritability estimate of 37%. (If a newspaper article said that alcoholism has a heritability of 37%, many ordinary readers might wrongly conclude that 37% of children of alcoholics develop alcoholism themselves. The heritability describes what proportion of the variation in alcoholism risk that we observe in a particular population is explained by genetic differences between individuals.) As one final step, we may compute 95% confidence limits on this point estimate of heritability, which gives us important additional information about the precision (or imprecision) of our estimate of the genetic contribution to alcoholism risk. To do this, we find those values for the heritability, above and below our point estimate, which lead to a just significant likelihood-ratio chi-square, i.e., which give a poorer fit to the data by approximately 3.84 chi-square units. For the Swedish adoption data, we find a 95% confidence interval of 19–56%. In other words, if we drew repeated samples from this same population, we would expect our heritability estimate from these new samples to fall within the range of 19–56% nineteen times out of twenty.

In analyzing twin data from record linkage or general community surveys, our approach will be essentially the same as for adoption data, except that we must allow for the fact that members of a twin pair may have similar alcoholism risks because of shared environmental as well as shared genetic risk factors. We may express the polychoric correlation between monozygotic twin pairs (r_{MZ}) and between dizygotic twin pairs (r_{DZ}) as a function both of the heritability of alcoholism (VAG) and of the contribution of environmental risk-factors shared by twin pairs growing up in the same family (which we shall denote by VSE, an abbreviation for variance due to shared environmental influences): r_{MZ} = VAG + VSE (since identical twin pairs share identical genotypes as well as the same family environments); r_{DZ} = 1/2 VAG + VSE (since fraternal twin pairs on average share only half their genes in common, but share the same family environment). These parameters may be estimated from monozygotic and dizygotic twin-pair contingency tables in the same manner as with adoption data, and the goodness-of-fit chi-square obtained under the full model allowing for both genetic and environmental causes of twin pair resemblance may be compared to chi-squares for models that assume either no genetic influence on alcoholism risk (fixing VAG = 0) or no shared environmental influence (fixing VSE = 0), by likelihood-ratio chi-square test, in order to test the significance of each parameter. Some published analyses of twin-pair data on alcoholism have tested the significance of genetic or shared environmental effects on alcoholism risk not by likelihood-ratio chi-square, but by comparing the estimates of VAG and VSE (from a model that includes both) to their standard errors (e.g., Allgulander et al., 1992; Romanov et al., 1991). For technical reasons reviewed elsewhere (see Neale et al., 1989; Neale & Cardon, 1992), such a procedure can give misleading results, and it appears to have led a number of researchers to report evidence for a significant genetic influence erroneously.

Analyzing Data from Samples Ascertained Through Probands

In analyzing data from samples ascertained through probands, we are still able to estimate tetrachoric or polychoric correlations, and to obtain estimates of genetic and environmental parameters. In order to do so, however, we must perform an "ascertainment correction," a procedure that entails making strong, and in some studies untestable, assumptions. Two alternative assumptions that have been used by different investigators, at least implicitly, are summarized by the two probability trees in Figures 1c and 1d. The first model is a "severity" model which assumes that alcoholics identified through hospitals or other treatment facilities are more extreme in their genetic liability than alcoholics identified in the general community (Goodwin et al., 1994). The second model is a two-process model which assumes that one set of genetic or environmental risk factors determines which individuals become alcoholic, and a second set of risk factors determines the conditional probability that an individual who becomes alcoholic will also receive treatment.

Also presented in Table 1 are the results of the three U.S. twin studies that used clinically ascertained samples, one conducted in St. Louis (Caldwell & Gottesman, 1991) and two in Minnesota (McGue et al., 1992; Pickens et al., 1991). In data from a community sample we would observe proportions of pairs who are concordant unaffected, discordant for alcoholism, or concordant affected. In data from samples ascertained through a proband, we, of course, observe only the proportions of co-twins who are unaffected versus affected. Let us consider first the model of Figure 1d, which assumes that alcoholics who receive treatment are a random sample of all alcoholics; we will further assume that the probability that an alcoholic who is a twin will receive treatment is unrelated to his co-twin's alcoholism status. If we know the prevalence of alcoholism in the general population (for example, from epidemiologic surveys such as the ECA or NCS study; see Kessler et al., 1994; Robins & Regier, 1991), then for a given twin-pair tetrachoric correlation we can estimate the proportions of twin pairs in the general population who would be predicted to be concordant affected (A), discordant (B), and concordant unaffected (C). Because the alcoholic twin probands are assumed to be a random sample of all alcoholics, where one twin is a proband we can derive the expected proportion of those pairs in which the co-twin is also affected: $2A/(2A+B)$. Thus, provided that we have information about the population prevalence of alcoholism from external sources, the proportions of unaffected and affected co-twins of alcoholic twin probands are all that we need to estimate the MZ and DZ twin-pair tetrachoric correlation, and in turn to estimate the importance of genetic factors.

The critical importance of the assumptions that are made when analyzing data from a proband-based study can be illustrated by comparing the correlations that are obtained using different sets of assumptions. When inspecting twin-pair correlations, it is helpful to remember four simple points: (1) the MZ correlation provides a direct estimate of the total variance in risk that can be explained by both genetic and shared environmental factors, so that $1\text{-}r_{MZ}$ estimates the contribution of environmental influences not shared by members of a twin pair (as well as diagnostic error, if twin pairs are assessed and diagnosed independently) to variance in risk of alcoholism; (2) twice the difference in the monozygotic and dizygotic correlations (i.e., $2\,[r_{MZ}-r_{DZ}]$) estimates the contribution of additive genetic effects to variance in risk; (3) $(2r_{DZ}-r_{MZ})$ estimates the contribution of shared environment to variance in risk of alcoholism; (4) a negative estimate obtained under (3) indicates that nonadditive genetic effects are important. Although these estimates lack desirable properties of estimates obtained by appropriate statistical techniques (e.g., they do not tell us whether particular effects are significant), they provide a useful "first impression" of what a dataset may show.

Using ECA data weighted for the age distribution observed for each zygosity group, Pickens et al. (1991) estimated population prevalences for DSM-III alcohol abuse and/or dependence: 30.7% for male MZ twins (i.e., for males in the general population with an age distribution similar to that which they observed for their MZ male pairs), 27.4% for male DZ twins, 9.7% for female MZ twins, and 7.9% for female DZ twins. Using these data together with the proportions of affected and unaffected twins from Table 1, under the model of Figure 1d the estimated tetrachoric correlations are 0.86, 0.69, 0.55, and 0.42. Caldwell and Gottesman calculated prevalences of 24.0%, 25.6%, and 25.7% for male twins from MZ, DZ like-sex, and DZ opposite-sex pairs, and corresponding female prevalences of 6.1%, 5.7%, and 5.4%, respectively (Caldwell, 1992). Tetrachoric correlations estimated from their data for MZ male, DZ like-sex male, MZ female, DZ like-sex female, and opposite-sex pairs ascertained either through female or through male probands are: 0.81, 0.45, 0.76, 0.71, 0.41, and 0.99, respectively. The two latter correlations are significantly heterogeneous ($\chi^2=9.12$, $df=1$, $p < .001$), even though we would expect them to be the same if the ascertainment correction used was appropriate. McGue et al. report prevalences for male and female like-sex MZ and DZ pairs (29.8% and 28.1% for the males, 9.0% and 9.2% for the females), and for co-twins from unlike-sex pairs, but not for probands from opposite-sex pairs (opposite-sex pairs with male probands are on average older than pairs with female probands). We have therefore interpolated approximate values for the latter twins. Estimated tetrachoric correlations from this dataset are 0.87, 0.56, 0.61, 0.65, 0.69, and 0.99, respectively, with two latter correlations not being significantly heterogeneous (pooled correlation $r=0.75$, $\chi^2=2.20$, $df=1$, $p > .05$). The estimated correlations from these studies lead toward conclusions that genetic influences and nonshared environmental influences may be more important in men than in women, and shared environmental influences more important in women than in men.

The analyses of the preceding paragraph were all predicated on the implicit assumption that treated alcoholics are a random sample of all alcoholics. Let us consider the alternative "severity" model in Figures 1b and 1c, whereby individuals who receive treatment have more extreme liability values (i.e., are further along the liability continuum), and milder cases of alcoholism remain untreated and have intermediate values between the unaffecteds and treated alcoholics. Only a comparatively small proportion of individuals who met criteria for alcohol abuse or dependence in the ECA study had alcohol-related treatment contacts (McEvoy et al., 1983, report lifetime figures of 21.7% for male alcoholics and 27.1% for female alcoholics). In data from an epidemiologic twin study of alcoholism, if we were to take into account treatment-seeking, our data-summary would consist of a set of 3×3 contingency tables, with categories unaffected, mild and untreated, and severe and treated. Assuming an overall prevalence of alcoholism of approximately 30% in men but 9% in women, for the two Minnesota datasets, prevalences of treated and untreated alcoholism would be 6.5% and 23.5% in men, and 2.44% and 6.56% in women, respectively. Let us suppose that our twin probands are a random sample of the treated alcoholics. In effect, we are only observing a single row of the 3×3 contingency table, corresponding to the "severe" alcoholic twins. The appropriate prevalence to assume for the probands will thus be 6.5% for men rather than 30%, and 2.44% for women rather than 9%. For the co-twins, unless we distinguish explicitly between those with and those without a treatment-history, we are in effect collapsing the two alcoholic categories together into a single "affected" category, so the appropriate prevalences for the co-twins will still be 30% for women and 9% for men.

How much do estimates of twin-pair tetrachoric (or polychoric) correlations change when we use the assumptions of the severity model (Figure 1c) rather than the two-process model (Figure 1d)? To examine this question, we have reanalyzed the twin-pair data in Table 1, assuming prevalences of 6.5% or 2.44% for treated male and female twins from the two Minnesota samples, and recomputing prevalences for probands from the data in Caldwell (1992), assuming the same proportions of treated and untreated twins as reported by McEvoy et al. (1983). Thus, we have ignored age differences in treatment-seeking, about which we have no information. We have retained the same prevalence estimates for the co-twins used in the previous analyses. Twin-pair tetrachoric correlations were estimated according to the severity model, for MZ male, DZ male, MZ female, DZ female, and also for DZ unlike-sex pairs ascertained through female versus male probands (only for Caldwell & Gottesman, 1991, and McGue et al., 1992). The respective correlations for Caldwell and Gottesman were .54, .28, .60, .58, .33, .61; for Pickens et al., .57, .44, .41,

.33; and for McGue et al., .58, .35, .46, .49, .55, .57. Clearly, changing to the assumptions of the severity model markedly reduces the estimates of twin tetrachoric correlations. Of course, without data from an epidemiologic twin study of treated and untreated alcoholism, we cannot say which of models 1c and 1d, or some intermediate model, best represents the truth. We may note, however, that the abnormally high estimates for the DZ unlike-sex correlation obtained under the two-process model for data from male probands and their female co-twins (0.99 for both St. Louis and Minnesota datasets) do not occur under the severity model.

The different assumptions of the two models also lead to substantially different conclusions about the importance of the genetic contribution to alcoholism risk in men and women. Consider what happens when we apply the two models to the data of McGue et al. (1992). The two-process model does not adequately fit the data, if we include unlike-sex as well as like-sex pairs in the analyses ($p<.01$ in all cases). If we analyze only data from the four like-sex twin groups, we obtain heritability estimates that are significantly higher in men than in women ($\chi^2=6.43$, $df=1$, $p=.01$); the heritability estimates obtained (with 95% confidence intervals) are 0% (0–47%) for women and 62% (22-94%) for men. In contrast, using the severity model, we obtain a good fit for a model allowing for both genetic and shared environmental influences on alcoholism risk, even when we analyze data from all six zygosity groups ($\chi^2=7.92$, $df=4$, $p=.10$). In this analysis we do not find significant sex differences in the heritability of alcoholism ($\chi^2=3.62$, $df=2$, $p>.05$); and the overall heritability estimate for men and women is only 18% (0–40%). For data from Caldwell and Gottesman (1991), a two-process model gives an overall heritability estimate of 22% for men and women (0-57%), while a severity model gives a heritability estimate of 13% (0–44%). In a reanalysis of the Pickens et al. (1991) data, our heritability estimate for men and women also decreases, from 33% (0–70%) in a two-process model to 23% (0–52%) in a severity model.

A Summary of Estimates of the Genetic Contribution to Alcoholism Risk

Now that we have reviewed the individual studies cited to support a genetic contribution to alcoholism risk, and the methods used to quantify the heritability of alcoholism, we can reexamine the evidence for a gender difference in the importance of genetic factors. In Figure 2 we summarize point estimates for the heritability of alcoholism, for each of the major twin or adoption studies from which we could derive such estimates, as well as 95% confidence intervals for each estimate. In some cases estimates will differ from those reported by the original authors because we used slightly different analytic methods here. In some cases we have been able to compute only approximate estimates, for example because no estimates of population

FIGURE 2
Estimates (and 95% Confidence Intervals) of the Genetic Contribution to Alcoholism Risk from Twin and Adoption Studies

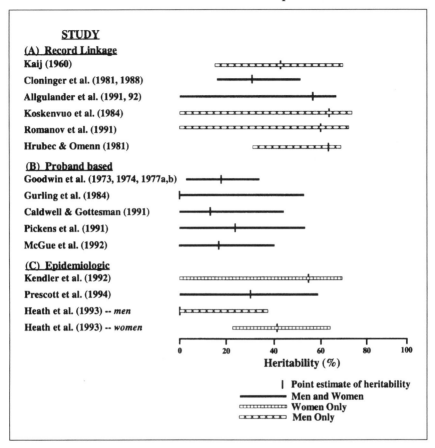

prevalence were available (e.g., Gurling et al., 1984). Separate estimates are reported for men and women only for those cases where we found a significant sex difference in the genetic contribution to alcoholism in that study. In the case of studies using samples ascertained through alcoholic probands, we have used a severity model even where a two-process model was used by the original authors.

Several datapoints in Figure 2 require clarification. For data from Kaij (1960) we have used the broadest criterion of one or more temperance board registrations. From Kendler et al. (1992) we have taken the DSM-III-R alcohol dependence data, rather than the narrower or broader diagnoses. Data from Heath et al. (1993) are for estimates pooled across 1981 and 1989 birth cohorts, since there was no significant heterogeneity as a function of cohort, once we allowed for gender differences in the heritability of alcoholism. We have not presented analyses of the Iowa adoption studies, since we could not separate risk to adopted-away offspring of control biologic parents from risk to adopted-away offspring of nonalcoholic biologic parents oversampled because of the presence of other psychopathology.

From Figure 2 we may draw several important conclusions. With the exception of a mailed questionnaire survey of alcohol-related problems that failed to find a significant genetic influence on alcoholism in men (Heath et al., 1993), there is no evidence from within-study comparisons for a significantly higher heritability of alcoholism in women than in men. (Of course, it is still possible that a meta-analysis of these data would yield modest but significant gender differences.) For individual studies, confidence intervals on estimates of the genetic contribution to alcoholism risk are extremely broad, both for studies that have failed to find significant heritability, and for studies that have reported that genetic factors are important. Despite this, point estimates of alcoholism heritability derived from the record-linkage studies and the single interview-based epidemiologic study (Kendler et al., 1992) are all substantial (range=43–63%), and the confidence intervals from these studies all overlap in the range of 30–55%, consistent with a moderately large genetic contribution to alcoholism risk. Estimates derived from the samples ascertained through an alcoholic proband, under a severity model, are substantially lower, falling in the range of 0–31%, with confidence intervals overlapping in the range of 3–40%. As noted above, using a two-process model would lead to higher heritability estimates, but would require that data from unlike-sex twin pairs be discarded in the case of the McGue study. Still different assumptions, perhaps taking into account the role of psychiatric comorbidity in determining treatment access, would also lead to different estimates, a fact that emphasizes the uncertainty of estimates derived from proband-based samples. Finally, the questionnaire surveys of community samples have yielded quite variable results, although interpretation of these data must be cautious in view of the limited validity data for such questionnaire assessments of alcohol problems in genetic research. Overall, it appears that there is indeed a genetic contribution to alcoholism risk, though the magnitude of this contribution is estimated very imprecisely in any single study. However, the case for a higher heritability of alcoholism in men than in women is far from compelling. Our reanalysis does raise the important issue that, while from the epidemiologic data it appears that genetic influences on alcoholism risk are important, from the clinically ascertained samples it appears possible that there are important environmental barriers determining who receives care for an alcohol-related problem.

What are the Pathways from Genotype to Alcoholism Risk in Men versus Women?

The statement that there may be a genetic contribution to alcoholism risk has been interpreted by some as implying a narrow medical-genetic model for the inheritance of alcoholism (e.g., Billings, 1990). However, it seems unlikely that a model based on the inheritance of rare monogenic Mendelian disorders is of any relevance to the familial transmission of a complex disorder of multifactorial etiology such as alcoholism. A behavioral genetic perspective (e.g., Heath, 1993; McGue, 1994) that recognizes that there may be multiple pathways to alcoholism, with some pathways perhaps more important in men, and others in women, is likely to be more appropriate. In this section, therefore, we review some of the possible explanations for how a genetic influence arises.

Genetics, Personality, and Psychopathology

Various theorists have hypothesized that differences in temperament or personality are important mediators of genetic influence on alcoholism risk (e.g., Cloninger, 1987; Tarter, 1988). Cloninger (1987), for example, has postulated the existence of at least two types of alcoholism, with differing personality profiles. Behavioral genetic studies comparing (1) twin pairs reared apart and together (Langinvainio et al., 1984; Pedersen, 1993; Pedersen et al., 1988; Shields, 1962; Tellegen et al., 1988); (2) biological parent-offspring and adoptive parent-offspring resemblance (Eaves et al., 1989; Loehlin, 1992; Scarr et al., 1981); (3) MZ and DZ twin pairs reared together (Eaves & Eysenck, 1975; Floderus-Myrhed et al., 1980; Heath et al., 1994; Loehlin & Nichols, 1976; Martin & Jardine, 1986; Rose et al., 1988); and (4) MZ and DZ twin pairs and their offspring (Eaves et al., 1994; Leohlin, 1992; Price et al., 1982) have yielded consistent support for an important genetic contribution to personality differences. Family resemblance for personality, in both men and women, appears to be largely determined by shared genes rather than by shared environment (Eaves et al., 1989; Loehlin, 1992). However, the extent to which personality differences per se, rather than merely antisocial personality disorder, predict future differences in alcoholism risk remains controversial (Barnes, 1983; Nathan, 1988). Nonetheless, as reviewed recently by Sher (1991), measures of behavioral undercontrol (e.g., impulsivity, rebelliousness, aggressiveness) appear to be precursors of alcoholism risk in men, and are elevated in adult male and female offspring of alcoholics. Although the evidence is weaker, measures of emotionality (e.g., neuroticism) may also be associated with elevated alcoholism risk (Sher, 1991), particularly in women. To date, there have been few attempts to integrate research on the inheritance of personality differences with genetic research on alcoholism, although this is likely to change as publications emerge from the Minnesota, Virginia, and Australian twin studies. The substantial comorbidity observed between alcoholism and other psychiatric disorders (e.g., Robins and Regier, 1991) raises the likelihood that at least some genetic influences will be mediated through risk of other disorders. The Virginia twin study, for example, has reported a moderate genetic correlation between risk of major depression and alcoholism in women (Kendler et al., 1992) and a strong genetic correlation between the personality trait neuroticism and risk of major depression (Kendler et al., 1993b), raising the possibility that a genetic association between alcoholism risk and neuroticism may be found.

Genetic Influences on Alcohol Consumption Patterns

A growing literature indicates that there are important genetic influences on drinking patterns of alcohol users from general community (i.e., not exclusively alcoholic) samples, and that these genetic influences are at least as important in women as in men (reviewed in Heath, 1995). These data derive primarily from large-sample epidemiologic twin studies conducted in Finland (Kaprio et al., 1992; Partanen et al., 1966), Sweden (Medlund et al., 1977), Australia (Heath & Martin, 1994; Jardine & Martin, 1984), the United Kingdom (Clifford et al., 1984), and the United States (Carmelli et al., 1993; Heath, 1995). Almost without exception, these studies have found significant evidence for a genetic contribution to differences in alcohol consumption patterns, both in men and (where included in the sample) in women. (The single exception is the analysis of the 1981 survey of the Australian twin panel reported by Jardine and Martin, 1984, which found no significant evidence for a genetic influence on weekly consumption or 7-day diary measures for men aged 31 and older.) Substantial genetic influences have been found for measures of frequency (how often an individual uses alcohol), quantity (how much he/she drinks on occasions when alcohol is taken), typical weekly consumption, and frequency of excessive drinking. With the exception of the early Finnish study of male twins by Partanen et al. (1966), and the study of World War II veteran male twins by Carmelli et al. (1993), all of these studies have included twins of both genders, and have found the importance of genetic factors to be at least as great in women as in men.

These findings raise the possibility that because of inherited, perhaps physiological, differences (see also below), some individuals will experience the effects of even small amounts of alcohol as aversive, and so will be less likely to develop problems with alcohol, whereas others will find the effects of alcohol to be very rewarding, and so will be more likely to progress to become heavy drinkers. Thus, the genetics of alcohol exposure (Heath, 1993) may constitute an important component of the developmental pathway leading to alcoholism. Understanding the genetic contribution to differences in consumption level, however, may also help us better understand the phenomenon of long-term excessive alcohol consumption by nonalcoholics. It is important that we not forget that excessive consumption per se is an important risk factor for a variety of serious medical conditions (e.g., USDHHS, 1994), including alcoholic liver disease, pancreatitis, hypertension, cardiomyopathy, cardiac arrhythmias, stroke, oral cancers, menstrual cycle dysfunction, and, in the case of women drinking during pregnancy, fetal injury.

Genetic Effects on Alcohol Sensitivity

In U.S. populations, researchers have examined differences between adult offspring of alcoholics and controls in response to a challenge dose of alcohol, in an attempt to identify physiological responses that may mediate a genetic influence on alcoholism risk (Schuckit, 1980a). With rare exceptions (e.g., Lex et al., 1988), this research has focused almost exclusively on possible mediators of alcoholism in men. Decreased body sway after alcohol challenge has been reported in those with a positive family history of alcoholism (Schuckit, 1985), although others have reported increased body sway (Lipscomb et al., 1979; McCaul et al., 1991). A meta-analysis of self-report measures of intoxication (Pollock, 1992) confirms the hypothesis that sons of alcoholics experience less intense intoxication in response to an acute dose of alcohol than do controls. Follow-up data reported by Schuckit (1993) also confirm that reduced intoxication in response to alcohol challenge is a predictor of future development of problems with alcohol. This finding is consistent with the hypothesis that there are genetically determined protective reactions to alcohol (i.e., feelings of intoxication) which are diminished in alcoholics compared to nonalcoholics. However, since alcohol-challenge experiments are never conducted with alcohol-naive subjects, the possibility that these results are the consequence of differing degrees of tolerance developed by offspring of alcoholics versus controls cannot be excluded. Data from an alcohol challenge twin study conducted in Australia confirm an important genetic contribution, in women as well as men, to differences in subjective intoxication (Neale & Martin, 1989) and body sway (Martin, 1990; Martin et al., 1985) after alcohol challenge, but also demonstrate significant genetic correlations between these measures and prior experience with alcohol (Heath & Martin, 1992), raising questions about the direction of causation of this association (Heath & Martin, 1991; Neale & Cardon, 1992).

Conclusions

From our review of the literature concerning a possible genetic contribution to alcoholism, we may conclude that the evidence is fairly consistent that genes do play some role in the inheritance of alcoholism. However, estimates of the strength of that genetic influence are highly variable from study to study, and differ markedly between those studies using clinically ascertained samples and those studies using epidemiologic or record-linkage strategies. Evidence for a gender difference in the genetic contribution to alcoholism risk from within-study comparisons, the most sensitive test for a gender difference, is almost entirely lacking. However, it is possible that a meta-analysis of these data would detect such a difference. Data on normal variation in alcohol consumption patterns suggest that the genetic influence on level of alcohol use is at least as important in women as in men. We have identified several possible behavioral pathways by which genetic influences on alcoholism may arise. Unfortunately, since few studies have been interested in the mediators or moderators of a genetic influence on alcoholism risk, we can say very little at this time about the relative importance of such pathways in men versus women. Methods for tackling questions about the size and pathways of genetic influences are now well established, however, and a new generation of studies is now providing data that should help to answer these questions.

Acknowledgments

Supported in part by NIH grants AA07535 and AA07728, and by postdoctoral training grant MH17104.

References

Agarwal, D.P., & Goedde, H.W. (1990). Human aldehyde dehydrogenases: Genetic implications in alcohol sensitivity, alcohol-drinking habits, and alcoholism. In C.R. Cloninger & H. Begleiter (Eds.), *Genetics and biology of alcoholism* (pp. 253–263). Plainview, NY: Cold Spring Harbor Laboratory Press.

Allgulander, C., Nowak, J., & Rice, J.P. (1990). Psychopathology and treatment of 30,344 twins in Sweden: I. The appropriateness of psychoactive drug treatment. *Acta Psychiatrica Scandinavica, 82*, 420–426.

Allgulander, C., Nowak, J., & Rice, J.P. (1991). Psychopathology and treatment of 30,344 twins in Sweden: II. Heritability estimates of psychiatric diagnosis and treatment in 12,884 twin pairs. *Acta Psychiatrica Scandinavica, 83*, 12–15.

Allgulander, C., Nowak, J., & Rice, J.P. (1992). Psychopathology and treatment of 30,344 twins in Sweden. *Acta Psychiatrica Scandinavica, 86*, 421–422.

Amadeo, S., Abbar, M., Fourcade, M.L., Waksman, G., Leroux, M.G., Madec, A., Selin, M., Champiat, J.-C., Brethome, A., Leclaire, Y., Castelnau, D., Venisse, J.-L., & Mallet, J. (1993). D2 dopamine receptor gene and alcoholism. *Journal of Psychiatric Research, 27*, 173–179.

Amark, C. (1951). A study in alcoholism: Clinical, social-psychiatric and genetic investigations. *Acta Psychiatrica et Neurologica Scandinavica, Supplementum 70*, 1-283.

Arinami, T., Itokawa, M., Komiyama, T., Mitsushio, H., Mori, H., Mifune, H., Hamaguchi, H., & Toru, M. (1993). Association between severity of alcoholism and the A1 allele of the dopamine D2 receptor gene TaqI A RFLP in Japanese. *Biological Psychiatry, 33*, 108-114.

Barnes, G.E. (1983). Clinical and personality characteristics. In B. Kissin & H. Begleiter (Eds.), *The pathogenesis of alcoholism: Psychosocial factors* (vol. 6, pp. 113-196). New York: Plenum.

Barr, C.L., & Kidd, K.K. (1993). Population frequencies of the A1 allele at the dopamine D2 receptor locus. *Biological Psychiatry, 34*, 204-209.

Berkson, J. (1946). Limitations of the application of fourfold table analysis to hospital data. *Biometrics Bulletin, 2*, 47-53.

Billings, P.R. (1990). Brewing genes and behavior: The potential consequences of genetic screening for alcoholism. In C.R. Cloninger & H. Begleiter (Eds.), *Genetics and biology of alcoholism* (pp. 333-350). Plainview, NY: Cold Spring Harbor Laboratory Press.

Blum, K., Noble, E.P,,. Sheridan, P.J., Finley, O., Montgomery, A., Ritchie, T., Ozkaragoz, T., Fitch, R.J., Sadlack, F., Sheffield, D., Dahlmann, T., Halbardier, S., & Nogami, H. (1991). Association of the A1 allele of the D2 dopamine receptor gene with severe alcoholism. *Alcohol, 8*, 409-416.

Blum, K., Noble, E.P., Sheridan, P.J., Montgomery, A., Ritchie, T., Jagadeeswaran, P., Nogami, H., Briggs, A.H., & Cohn, J.B. (1990). Allelic association of human dopamine D2 receptor gene in alcoholism. *Journal of the American Medical Association, 263*, 2055-2060.

Bohman, M. (1978). Some genetic aspects of alcoholism and criminality: A population of adoptees. *Archives of General Psychiatry, 35*, 269-276.

Bohman, M., Sigvardsson, S., & Cloninger, C.R. (1981). Maternal inheritance of alcohol abuse: Cross-fostering analysis of adopted women. *Archives of General Psychiatry, 38*, 965-969.

Bolos, A.M., Dean, M., Lucas-Derse, S., Ramsburg, M., Brown, G.L., & Goldman, D. (1990). Population and pedigree studies reveal a lack of association between the dopamine D2 receptor gene and alcoholism. *Journal of the American Medical Association, 264*, 3156-3160.

Bulmer, M.G. (1980). *Mathematical theory of quantitative genetics*. New York: Oxford University press.

Cadoret, R., Troughton, E., & Woodworth, G. (1994). Evidence of heterogeneity of genetic effect in Iowa adoption studies. *Annals of the New York Academy of Sciences, 708*, 59-71.

Cadoret, R.J., O'Gorman, T.W., Troughton, E., & Heywood, E. (1985). Alcoholism and antisocial personality: Interrelationships, genetic and environmental factors. *Archives of General Psychiatry, 42*, 161-167.

Cadoret, R.J., Troughton, E., & O'Gorman, T.W. (1987). Genetic and environmental factors in alcohol abuse and antisocial personality. *Journal of Studies on Alcohol, 48*, 1-8.

Caldwell, C.B. (1992). Unpublished Ph.D. thesis, University of Virginia.

Caldwell, C.B., & Gottesman, I.I. (1991). Sex differences in the risk for alcoholism: A twin study. *Behavior Genetics, 21*, 563.

Carmelli, D., Heath, A.C., & Robinette, D. (1993). Genetic analysis of drinking behavior in World War II veteran twins. *Genetic Epidemiology, 10*, 201-213.

Clifford, C.A., Fulker, D.W., Gurling, H.M.D., & Murray, R.M. (1984). A genetic and environmental analysis of a twin family study of alcohol use, anxiety, and depression. *Genetic Epidemiology, 1,* 47-52.

Cloninger, C.R. (1987). Neurogenetic adaptive mechanisms in alcoholism. *Science, 236,* 410-416.

Cloninger, C.R. (1990). Genetic epidemiology of alcoholism: Observations critical in the design and analysis of linkage studies. In C.R. Cloninger & H. Begleiter (Eds.), *Genetics and biology of alcoholism* (pp. 105-133). Plainview, NY: Cold Spring Harbor Laboratory Press.

Cloninger, C.R., Bohman, M., & Sigvardsson, S. (1981). Inheritance of alcohol abuse: Cross-fostering analysis of adopted men. *Archives of General Psychiatry, 38,* 861-868.

Cloninger, C.R., Bohman, M., Sigvardsson, S., & Von Knorring, A.L. (1985). Psychopathology in adopted-out children of alcoholics: The Stockholm Adoption Study. In M. Galanter (Ed.), *Recent developments in alcoholism, Vol. 3* (pp. 37-51). New York: Plenum.

Cloninger, C.R., Reich, T., Sigvardsson, S., Von Knorring, A.L., & Bohman, M. (1988). Effects of changes in alcohol use between generations on inheritance of alcohol abuse. In R.M. Rose & J.E. Barrett (Eds.), *Alcoholism: Origins and outcome* (pp. 49-74). New York: Raven.

Comings, D.E., Comings, B.G., Muhleman, D., Dietz, G., Shahbahrami, B., Tast, D., Knell, E., Kocsis, P., Baumgarten, R., Kovacs, B.W., Levy, D.L., Smith, M., Borison, R.L., Evans, D., Klein, D.N., MacMurray, J., Tosk, J.M., Sverd, J., Gysin, R., & Flanagan, S.D. (1991). The dopamine D_2 receptor locus as a modifying gene in neuropsychiatric disorders. *Journal of the American Medical Association, 266,* 1793-1800.

Cook, B.L., Wang, Z.W., Crowe, R.R., Hauser, R., & Freimer, M. (1992). Alcoholism and the D_2 receptor gene. *Alcoholism: Clinical and Experimental Research, 16,* 806-809.

Eaves, L., & Eysenck, H. (1975). The nature of extraversion: A genetical analysis. *Journal of Personality and Social Psychology, 32,* 102-112.

Eaves, L.J., Eysenck, H.J., & Martin, N.G. (1989). *Genes, culture and personality: An empirical approach.* London: Academic Press.

Eaves, L.J., Heath, A.C., Neale, M.C., Hewitt, J.K., & Martin, N.G. (1994). Sex differences and non-additivity in the effects of genes on personality. Unpublished manuscript.

Edwards, G., Gross, M.M., Keller, M., Moser, J., & Room, R. (1977). *Alcohol related disabilities,* WHO Offset Publication No. 32. Geneva: World Health Organization.

Eisen, S., Neuman, R., Goldberg, J., Rice, J., & True, W. (1989). Determining zygosity in the Vietnam era twin registry: An approach using questionnaires. *Clinical Genetics, 35,* 423-432.

Falconer, D.S. (1965). The inheritance of liability to certain diseases, estimated from the incidence among relatives. *Annals of Human Genetics, 29,* 51-76.

Falk, C.T., & Rubinstein, P. (1987). Haplotype relative risks: An easy reliable way to construct a proper control sample for risk calculations. *Annals of Human Genetics, 51,* 227-233.

Feighner, J.P., Robins, E., Guze, S.B., Woodruff, R.A., Jr., Winokur, G., & Munoz, R. (1972). Diagnostic criteria for use in psychiatric research. *Archives of General Psychiatry, 26,* 57-63.

Floderus-Myrhed, B., Pedersen, N., & Rasmuson, I. (1980). Assessment of heritability for personality, based on a short-form of the Eysenck personality inventory: A study of 12,898 twin pairs. *Behavior Genetics, 10,* 153-162.

Gelernter, J., O'Malley, S., Risch, N., Kranzler, H.R., Krystal, J., Merikangas, K., Kennedy, J.L., & Kidd, K.K. (1991). No association between an allele at the D_2 dopamine receptor gene (DRD2) and alcoholism. *Journal of the American Medical Association, 266,* 1801-1807.

Goldman, D., Brown, G.L., Albaugh, B., Robin, R., Goodson, S., Trunzo, M., Akhtar, L., Lucas-Derse, S., Long, J., Linnoila, M., & Dean, M. (1993). DRD2 dopamine receptor genotype, linkage disequilibrium, and alcoholism in American Indians and other populations. *Alcoholism: Clinical and Experimental Research, 17,* 199-204.

Goodwin, D.W., Knop, J., Jensen, P., Gabrielli, Jr., W.F., Schulsinger, F., & Penick, E.C. (1994). Thirty-year follow-up of men at high risk for alcoholism. *Annals of the New York Academy of Sciences, 708,* 97-101.

Goodwin, D.W., Schulsinger, F., Hermansen, L., Guze, S.B., & Winokur, G. (1973). Alcohol problems in adoptees raised apart from alcoholic biological parents. *Archives of General Psychiatry, 28,* 238-243.

Goodwin, D.W., Schulsinger, F., Knop, J., Mednick, S., & Guze, S.B. (1977a). Alcoholism and depression in adopted-out daughters of alcoholics. *Archives of General Psychiatry, 34,* 751-755.

Goodwin, D.W., Schulsinger, F., Knop, J., Mednick, S., & Guze, S.B. (1977b). Psychopathology in adopted and nonadopted daughters of alcoholics. *Archives of General Psychiatry, 34,* 1005-1009.

Goodwin, D.W., Schulsinger, F., Møller, N., Hermansen, L., Winokur, G., & Guze, S.B. (1974). Drinking problems in adopted and nonadopted sons of alcoholics. *Archives of General Psychiatry, 31,* 164-169.

Gurling, H.M.D., Oppenheim, B.E., & Murray, R.M. (1984). Depression, criminality and psychopathology associated with alcoholism: Evidence from a twin study. *Acta Geneticae Medicae et Gemellologiae, 33,* 333-339.

Heath, A.C. (1993). What can we learn about the determinants of psychopathology and substance abuse from studies of normal twins? In T.J. Bouchard, Jr. & P. Propping (Eds.), *Twins as a tool of behavioral genetics* (pp. 273-285). Chichester: John Wiley & Sons Ltd.

Heath, A.C. (1995). Genetic influences on drinking behavior in humans. In H. Begleiter & B. Kissin (Eds.), *Alcohol and alcoholism: Vol. 1. The Genetic factors and alcoholism.* Oxford: Oxford University Press.

Heath, A.C., Bucholz, K.K., Dinwiddie, S.H., Madden, P.A.F., Dunne, M.P., Statham, D., & Martin, N.G. (1993). *Contribution of genetic factors to risk of alcohol problems in women.* Presented at the annual meeting of the Behavior Genetics Association, July 13-16, Sydney, Australia.

Heath, A.C., Bucholz, K.K., Slutske, W.S., Madden, P.A.F., Dinwiddie, S.H., Dunne, M.P., Statham, D.B., Whitfield, J.B., Martin, N.G., & Eaves, L.J. (1994). The assessment of alcoholism in surveys of the general community: What are we measuring? Some insights from the Australian twin panel interview survey. *International Review of Psychiatry, 6,* 295-307.

Heath, A.C., Cloninger, C.R., & Martin, N.G. (1994). Testing a model for the genetic structure of personality: A comparison of the personality systems of Cloninger and Eysenck. *Journal of Personality and Social Psychology, 66,* 762-775.

Heath, A.C., & Martin, N.G. (1991). Intoxication after an acute dose of alcohol: An assessment of its association with alcohol consumption patterns by using twin data. *Alcoholism: Clinical and Experimental Research, 15,* 122-128.

Heath, A.C., & Martin, N.G. (1992). Genetic differences in psychomotor performance decrement after alcohol: A multivariate analysis. *Journal of Studies on Alcohol, 53,* 262-271.

Heath, A.C., & Martin, N.G. (1994). Genetic influences on alcohol consumption patterns and problem drinking: Results from the Australian NH&MRC twin panel follow-up survey. *Annals of the New York Academy of Sciences, 708*, 72-85.

Heath, A.C., Neale, M.C., Kessler, R.C., Eaves, L.J., & Kendler, K.S. (1992). Evidence for genetic influences on personality from self-reports and informant ratings. *Journal of Personality and Social Psychology, 63*, 85-96.

Hrubec, Z., & Omenn, G.S. (1981). Evidence of genetic predisposition to alcoholic cirrhosis and psychosis: Twin concordances for alcoholism and its biological end points by zygosity among male veterans. *Alcoholism: Clinical and Experimental Research, 5*, 207-215.

Jardine, R., & Martin, N.G. (1984). Causes of variation in drinking habits in a large twin sample. *Acta Geneticae Medicae et Gemellologiae, 33*, 435-450.

Jöreskog, K., & Sorbom, D. (1988). *PRELIS: A program for multivariate data screening and data summarization. A preprocessor for LISREL* (2nd ed.). Mooresville, IN: Scientific Software.

Jöreskog, K.G., & Sorbom, D. (1993). *PRELIS 2 user's reference guide.* Chicago, IL: Scientific Software International.

Kaij, L. (1960). *Alcoholism in twins: Studies on etiology and sequels of abuse of alcohol.* Stockholm: Almqvist and Wiksell.

Kaij, L., & Dock, J. (1975). Grandsons of alcoholics: A test of sex-linked transmission of alcohol abuse. *Archives of General Psychiatry, 32*, 1379-1381.

Kaprio, J., Koskenvuo, M., Langinvainio, H., Romanov, K., Sarna, S., & Rose, R.J. (1987). Genetic influences on use and abuse of alcohol: A study of 5,638 adult Finnish twin brothers. *Alcoholism: Clinical and Experimental Research, 11*, 349-356.

Kaprio, J., Sarna, S., Koskenvuo, M., & Rantasalo, I. (1978). The Finnish Twin Registry: Formation and compilation, questionnaire study, zygosity determination procedures, and research program. *Progress in Clinical and Biological Research, 24*, 179-184.

Kaprio, J., Viken, R., Koskenvuo, M., Romanov, K., & Rose, R.J. (1992). Consistency and change in patterns of social drinking: A 6-year follow-up of the Finnish twin cohort. *Alcoholism: Clinical and Experimental Research, 16*, 234-246.

Kendler, K.S., Heath, A.C., Neale, M.C., Kessler, R.C., & Eaves, L.J. (1992). A population-based twin study of alcoholism in women. *Journal of the American Medical Association, 268*, 1877-1882.

Kendler, K.S., Heath, A.C., Neale, M.C., Kessler, R.C., & Eaves, L.J. (1993a). Alcoholism and major depression in women: A twin study of the causes of comorbidity. *Archives of General Psychiatry, 50*, 690-698.

Kendler, K.S., Neale, M.C., Kessler, R.C., Heath, A.C., & Eaves, L.J. (1993b). A longitudinal twin study of personality and major depression in women. *Archives of General Psychiatry, 50*, 853-862.

Kendler, K.S., Prescott, C.A., Neale, M.C., & Pedersen, N.L. (in press). Temperance Board Registration for alcohol abuse in a national sample of Swedish male twins born 1902-1949.

Kessler, R.C., McGonagle, K.A., Zhao, S., Nelson, C.B., Hughes, M., Eshleman, S., Witchen, H.U., & Kendler, K.S. (1994). Lifetime and 12-month prevalence of DSM-III-R psychiatric disorders in the United States: Results from the National Comorbidity Study. *Archives of General Psychiatry, 51*, 8-19.

Koskenvuo, M., Langinvainio, J., Kaprio, J., Lonnqvist, J., & Tienari, P. (1984). Psychiatric hospitalization in twins. *Acta Geneticae Medicae et Gemellologiae, 33*, 321-332.

Langinvainio, H., Kaprio, J., Koskenvuo, M., & Lonnqvist, J. (1984). Finnish twins reared apart. III. Personality factors. *Acta Geneticae Medicae et Gemellologiae, 33*, 259-264.

Lex, B.W., Lukas, S.E., Greenwald, N.E., & Mendelson, J.H. (1988). Alcohol-induced changes in body sway in women at risk for alcoholism: A pilot study. *Journal of Studies on Alcohol, 49*, 346-356.

Lipscomb, T.R., Carpenter, J.A., & Nathan, P.E. (1979). Static ataxia: A predictor of alcoholism? *British Journal of Addiction, 74*, 289-294.

Loehlin, J.C. (1992). *Genes and environment in personality development:Individual differences and development series, Vol. 2.* Newbury Park, CA: Sage Publications.

Loehlin, J.C., & Nichols, R.C. (1976). *Heredity, environment, and personality:A study of 850 sets of twins.* Austin: University of Texas Press.

Martin, N.G. (1990). Twin studies of alcohol consumption, metabolism, and sensitivity. In C.R. Cloninger & H. Begleiter (Eds.), *Genetics and biology of alcoholism* (pp. 15-29). Plainview, NY: Cold Spring Harbor Laboratory Press.

Martin, N.G., & Jardine, R. (1986). Eysenck's contributions to behavior genetics. In S. Modgil and C. Modgil (Eds.), *Hans Eysenck: Consensus and controversy* (pp. 13-62). Lewes, Sussex: Falmer Press.

Martin, N.G., Oakeshott, J.G., Gibson, J.B., Starmer, G.A., Perl, J., & Wilks A.V. (1985). A twin study of psychomotor and physiological responses to an acute dose of alcohol. *Behavior Genetics, 15*, 305-347.

McCaul, M.E., Turkkan, J.S., Svikis, D.S., & Bigelow, G.E. (1991). Familial density of alcoholism: Effects on psychophysiological responses to ethanol. *Alcohol, 8*, 219-222.

McEvoy, L., Robins, L.N., & Helzer, J.E. (1983). *Alcoholism and mental health services: Who comes to treatment?* Paper presented at the annual meeting of the American Public Health Association, Dallas, Texas, November 15.

McGue, M. (1994). Genes, environment, and the etiology of alcoholism. In *The development of alcohol problems:Exploring the biopsychosocial matrix of risk* (NIAAA Research Monograph No. 26; NIH Publication No. 94-3495). Rockville, MD: National Institutes of Health.

McGue, M., Pickens, R.W., & Svikis, D.S. (1992). Sex and age effects on the inheritance of alcohol problems: A twin study. *Journal of Abnormal Psychology, 101*, 3-17.

McGue, M., & Slutske, W. (1993). *The inheritance of alcoholism in women.* Paper presented at the National Institute of Alcohol Abuse and Alcoholism Working Group for Prevention Research on Women and Alcohol, Rockville, MD, September 13-14.

Medlund, P., Cederlof, R., Floderus-Myrhed, B., Friberg, L., & Sorensen, S. (1977). A new Swedish twin registry. *Acta Medica Scandinavica Supplement 600.*

Nathan, P.E. (1988). The addictive personality is the behavior of the addict. *Journal of Consulting and Clinical Psychology, 56*, 183-188.

Neale, M.C. (1992). *Mx statistical modeling.* Department of Psychiatry, Medical College of Virginia.

Neale, M.C., & Cardon, L.R. (1992). *Methodology for genetic studies of twins and families, NATO ASI Series.* Dordrecht, The Netherlands: Kluwer Academic Publishers.

Neale, M.C., Heath, A.C., Hewitt, J.K., Eaves, L.J., & Fulker, D.W. (1989). Fitting genetic models with LISREL: Hypothesis testing. *Behavioral Genetics, 19*, 63-78.

Neale, M.C., & Martin, N.G. (1989). The effects of age, sex, and genotype on self-report drunkenness following a challenge dose of alcohol. *Behavior Genetics, 19*, 63-78.

Olsson, U. (1979). Maximum-likelihood estimation of the polychoric correlation coefficient. *Psychometrika, 44*, 443-460.

Parsian, A., Todd, R.D., Devor, E.J., O'Malley, K.L., Suarez, B.K., Reich, T., & Cloninger, C.R. (1991). Alcoholism and alleles of the human D_2 dopamine receptor locus: Studies of association and linkage. *Archives of General Psychiatry, 48*, 655-663.

Partanen, J., Bruun, K., & Markkanen, T. (1966). Inheritance of drinking behavior: A study on intelligence, personality, and use of alcohol of adult twins. Helsinki, Finland: Finnish Foundation for Alcohol Studies.

Pearson, K. (1900). Mathematical contribution to the theory of evolution: VII. On the correlation of characters not quantitatively measurable. *Philosophical Transactions of the Royal Society of London, Series A 195*, 1-47.

Pedersen, N.L. (1993). Genetic and environmental continuity and change in personality. In T.J. Bouchard & P. Propping, (Eds.), *Twins as a tool of behavioral genetics* (pp. 147-164). Chichester: John Wiley & Sons.

Pedersen, N.L., Plomin, R., McClearn, G.E., & Friberg, L. (1988). Neuroticism, extraversion, and related traits in adult twins reared apart and reared together. *Journal of Personality and Social Psychology, 55*, 950-957.

Pickens, R.W., Svikis, D.S., McGue, M., Lykken, D.T., Heston, L.L., & Clayton, P.J. (1991). Heterogeneity in the inheritance of alcoholism: A study of male and female twins. *Archives of General Psychiatry, 48*, 19-28.

Pollock, V.E. (1992). Meta-analysis of subjective sensitivity to alcohol in sons of alcoholics. *American Journal of Psychiatry, 149*, 1534-1538.

Prescott, C.A., Hewitt, J.K., Truett, K.R., Heath, A.C., Neale, M.C., & Eaves, L.J. (1994). Genetic and environmental influences on lifetime alcohol-related problems in a volunteer sample of older twins. *Journal of Studies on Alcohol, 55*, 184-202.

Price, R.A., Vandenberg, S.G., Iyer, H., & Williams, J.-S. (1982). Components of variation in normal personality. *Journal of Personality and Social Psychology, 43*, 328-340.

Reich, T., Cloninger, C.R., & Guze, S.B. (1975). The multifactorial model of disease transmission: I. Description of the model and its use in psychiatry. *British Journal of Psychiatry, 127*, 1-10.

Robins, L.N., Orvaschel, H., Anthony, J., Blazer, D., Burnam, A., & Burke, J. (1985). The diagnostic interview schedule. In W.W. Eaton & L.G. Kessler (Eds.), *Epidemiologic methods in psychiatry: The NIMH epidemiologic catchment area program.* Orlando, FL: Academic Press.

Robins, L.N., & Regier, D.A. (1991). *Psychiatric disorders in America: The epidemiologic catchment area study.* New York: Free Press.

Roe, A., & Burks, B.S. (1945). *Adult adjustment of foster children of alcoholic and psychotic parentage and the influence of the foster home: No. 3. Memoirs of the section on alcohol studies.* New Haven, CT: Yale University/Quarterly Journal of Studies on Alcohol.

Romanov, K., Kaprio, J., Rose, R.J., & Koskenvuo, M. (1991). Genetics of alcoholism: Effects of migration on concordance rates among male twins. *Alcohol and Alcoholism, Suppl. 1*, 137-140.

Rose, R.J., Koskenvuo, M., Kaprio, J., Sarna, S., & Langinvainio, H. (1988). Shared genes, shared experiences, and similarity of personality: Data from 14,288 adult Finnish co-twins. *Journal of Personality and Social Psychology, 54*, 161-171.

Scarr, S., Webber, P.L., Weinberg, R.A., & Wittig, M.A. (1981). Personality resemblance among adolescents and their parents in biologically related and adoptive families. *Journal of Personality and Social Psychology, 40*, 885-898.

Schuckit, M.A. (1980). Alcoholism and genetics: Possible biological mediators. *Biological Psychiatry, 15*, 437-447.

Schuckit, M.A. (1985). Ethanol-induced changes in body sway in men at high alcoholism risk. *Archives of General Psychiatry, 42*, 375-379.

Schuckit, M.A. (1993). *A prospective study of the role of alcohol sensitivity in the vulnerability to alcoholism.* Paper presented at the annual meeting of the Research Society on Alcoholism, San Antonio, Texas, June 19-24.

Schuckit, M.A., Goodwin, D.W., & Winokur, G. (1972). A study of alcoholism in half siblings. *American Journal of Psychiatry, 128*, 1132-1136.

Schwab, S., Soyka, M., Niederecker, M., Ackenheil, M., Scherer, J., & Wildenauer, D.B. (1991). Allelic association of human D2-receptor DNA polymorphism ruled out in 45 alcoholics. *American Journal of Human Genetics, Supplement 49*, 203.

Sher, K.J. (1991). *Children of alcoholics: A critical appraisal of theory and research.* Chicago: University of Chicago Press.

Shields, J. (1962). *Monozygotic twins: Brought up apart and brought up together.* Oxford: Oxford University Press.

Spitzer, R.L., Williams, J.B., & Gibbon, M. (1987). *Structured clinical interview for DSM-III-R.* New York: Biometrics Research Dept., New York State Psychiatric Interview.

Tarter, R.E. (1988). Are there inherited behavioral traits that predispose to substance abuse? *Journal of Consulting and Clinical Psychology, 56*, 189-196.

Tellegen, A., Lykken, D.T., Bouchard, T.J., Jr., Wilcox, K.J., Segal, N.L., & Rich, S. (1988). Personality similarity in twins reared apart and together. *Journal of Personality and Social Psychology, 54*, 1031-1039.

Thomasson, H.R., Crabb, D.W., Edenberg, H.J., & Li, T.-K. (1993). Alcohol and aldehyde dehydrogenase polymorphisms and alcoholism. *Behavior Genetics, 23*, 131-136.

Tsuang, M.T., Lyons, M.J., Eisen, S.A., Goldberg, J., True, W.R., Meyer, J.M., & Eaves, L.J. (1994). Genetic influence on abuse of illicit drugs: A study of 3,297 twin pairs. Unpublished manuscript.

Turner, E., Ewing, J., Shilling, P., Smith, T.L., Irwin, M., Schuckit, M., & Kelsoe, J.R. (1992). Lack of association between an RFLP near the D2 dopamine receptor gene and severe alcoholism. *Biological Psychiatry, 31*, 285-290.

U.S. Department of Health and Human Services (1994). *Eighth special report to the U.S. Congress on alcohol and health* (NIH Pub. No. 94-3699). Washington, DC: U.S. Government Printing Office.

SECTION III

Life Experiences and Women's and Men's Drinking

Introductory Note

The four chapters in this section share a common expectation: that women's drinking differs from men's not simply because of biology but also because of individual experience. Gender is expected to modify not only the experiences people have but also how those experiences influence alcohol use and its effects. However, the findings in these chapters suggest that effects of learning and life events on drinking are often not gender-specific. Learning and life experiences often influence men's and women's drinking more similarly than differently, and do not readily explain much of the gender differences in drinking. Furthermore, to predict and explain women's and men's drinking behavior, variations in women's experiences (and in men's) may be more important than contrasts between women's and men's lives.

Barnes and associates investigate whether differences in family and peer socialization of male and female adolescents explain why boys drink more heavily and more frequently than girls. Analyses of their Buffalo, N.Y., sample reveal differences in the upbringing of sons and daughters. Parents monitor daughters more closely than sons, and sons have more deviant friends than daughters do, patterns that would tend to magnify gender differences in heavy drinking. However, parental support and monitoring, and drinking and deviance by peers, have similar effects on female and male adolescent drinking. Also, after controlling for parental and peer socialization, there is still a significant gender difference in frequency of heavy drinking, a difference that increases with age. Something more than the influence of parents and peers causes female and male adolescent drinking patterns to diverge.

White and Huselid focus their attention not on how adolescents are taught, but on the lessons adolescents learn about gender. They theorize that adolescent drinking is influenced by what adolescents learn about how women and men should behave. Learning an ideology favoring traditional separations of men's and women's roles may magnify differences in how male and female adolescents drink, by encouraging them to conform to traditional gender-differentiated drinking norms. Furthermore, learning to behave according to traditional gender roles may influence how adolescents cope with problems and emotional distress, and gender-related coping patterns might influence adolescent use of alcohol. In past research, and in White and Huselid's analysis here of a large longitudinal survey of New Jersey adolescents, adolescent drinking behavior shows the predicted relationships with gender-role ideology more consistently than with gender-role behavior. However, gender-role ideology and behavior explain only a fraction of male-female differences in adolescent alcohol use and its consequences.

Cooper's research team also wants to know how coping with distress may influence women's and men's drinking behavior. They raise the possibility that men may drink more than women because men experience more stress than women, and/or because men cope with stress in ways that encourage the use of alcohol. Past research suggests that stressful life experiences, and a habit of coping with problems by trying to ignore or escape them (avoidance coping), may lead to greater use and abuse of alcohol. However, past research also suggests that women experience more stress than men related to stressful experiences of people in their social networks, and that women are more likely than men to use avoidance coping. Using data from large regional samples of both adolescents and adults, Cooper et al. confirm what previous research led them to expect. Women experience as much personal stress as do men, and greater stress associated with events in their social networks. Women also report higher levels of avoidance coping than do men. And both avoidance coping and stress related to social networks are associated with greater use and abuse of alcohol. These findings suggest not only that gender differences in drinking are not explained by stress and coping, but that stress and coping, as research has measured them, may actually conceal or obscure differences in how women and men use alcohol. Reasons for gender differences in alcohol apparently lie elsewhere.

In all these chapters, life experiences and learning that are thought to cause women to drink differently from men also influence some women to drink differently from others. Differences among women that affect their risks of alcohol-related problems and alcoholism are the focus of Gomberg's chapter. Gomberg argues that we need to know more about how women's alcohol problems and alcoholism are affected by *when* their drinking problems arise (at what age and what stage of the life cycle). A large Michigan sample of women being treated for alcoholism allows Gomberg to compare younger (under 40) and older (40+) alcoholic women with each other and with age-matched women who did not have alcohol-related problems. The women whose drinking problems began early in life also began to drink at younger ages and entered treatment at younger ages than other patients. In comparisons of older and younger alcoholic women, the older women are less likely to work outside the home, to drink in public places, and to get in trouble with authorities, family, and friends. These age differences may make it harder to recognize alcohol problems in older women than among women under 40. The younger alcoholic women also report higher rates of assaults, drinking-related arrests, and attempted suicide than the older women. In comparisons with age-matched women who have no alcohol-related problems, the older alcoholic women are more likely to be divorced, separated, or widowed, and the younger alcoholic women are more likely to report childhood problems of impulse control (such as trouble with school authorities and running away from home). In general, the alcoholic women left school and home earlier than did the nonalcoholic women, and are more likely to be in lower status jobs or unemployed. It appears that an accumulation of troubles and disadvantages make some women more vulnerable to alcoholism than others. However, it is not yet clear to what extent the negative experiences that contribute to or accompany women's alcoholism differ from the experiences of male alcoholics.

CHAPTER 6

Family Socialization Effects on Alcohol Abuse and Related Problem Behaviors among Female and Male Adolescents

GRACE M. BARNES, MICHAEL P. FARRELL, AND
BARBARA A. DINTCHEFF

While male and female adolescents do not differ greatly in their rates of abstention from alcohol, it has been well documented that males are far more likely than females to be heavier drinkers and to have alcohol-related problems (Barnes & Welte, 1986a,b; Johnston et al., 1991; Windle, 1991). This gap between male and female heavier drinking becomes larger as adolescents progress from early to late adolescence. Even though there has been a substantial decline in alcohol consumption over the past decade, the pattern of differences between the genders has remained (Barnes et al., 1993).

Furthermore, it has been shown that adolescent alcohol abuse is part of a larger syndrome of other problem behaviors including illicit drug use and delinquency (Barnes & Welte, 1986a; Donovan & Jessor, 1985). Consistent with their heavy drinking, adolescent males have higher mean levels than females do of "externalizing" problem behaviors, such as delinquency (e.g., Elliott et al., 1985) and illicit drug use (e.g., Johnston et al., 1991). On the other hand, empirical studies show that females have higher levels than males do of certain "internalizing" problem outcomes, such as depressive symptoms (e.g., Windle, 1992a,b).

A major challenge for research is to account for the gender differences in heavy drinking, delinquency, and depression. Although there is no lack of sound empirical research showing gender differences in adolescent alcohol abuse and related problem outcomes, there is a dearth of research directed toward an understanding of the similarities and differences in the antecedent pathways to alcohol abuse for male and female adolescents. Thompson and Wilsnack (1984), in their review of patterns and influences on drinking and drinking problems among female adolescents, note that few studies examining general influences on adolescent drinking differentiate how boys and girls are influenced, and even fewer studies attempt to interpret observed gender differences.

There is strong theoretical and empirical evidence showing the importance of parent-child relationships and socialization in the family on the development of a wide range of adolescent behaviors, including alcohol abuse, illicit drug abuse, and delinquency (see Barnes, 1990; Barnes & Farrell, 1992; Farrell & Barnes, 1993). Even given genetic predispositions to the development of some types of alcoholism (Goodwin, 1984; Schuckit, 1987), most young people are raised in families where members hold certain attitudes and expectations about alcohol and where adults serve as role models for various types of drinking behaviors. In addition to serving as role models for alcohol-related behaviors, parents are powerful agents of socialization more generally conceived. Thus, various aspects of parenting, for example, the levels and quality of support, monitoring, and communication, can be expected to exert important influences on the development of adolescent alcohol abuse and related problem behaviors.

In a conceptual model elaborated elsewhere (Barnes, 1990), family socialization is seen as the link between individual factors (psychological and biological) and the larger culture (including sociodemographic and family structural factors). In this model, the young person learns social behaviors, including drinking behaviors, during the socialization process by ongoing interactions with significant others, especially parents and adolescent peers, who play an increasingly important role during adolescence. However, parent-child relationships are seen as particularly potent and primary, occurring early in development. Furthermore, parent-child interactions may serve as a basis for the adolescent's choice of friendships with peers. In their extensive review of the parent-child interaction literature, Maccoby and Martin (1983) note that the parent-child bond is unique among human relationships. Unlike other relationships, the tie is enduring throughout the child's development, and even in adulthood the tie is seldom severed. Maccoby and Martin (1983) further note that the parent-child bond is unique in its initial asymmetry with the inherent differential power between parents and children. While there are undoubtedly bidirectional effects whereby adolescents' behaviors affect parental behaviors, most of the existing theory and empirical research supports a "social mold" perspective, with parents exerting powerful influences on the development of their children (Peterson & Rollins, 1987). Therefore, if adolescent outcomes are shaped by socialization, do differences in the socialization experiences of girls and boys account for gender differences in their drinking behavior, delinquency, and psychological distress?

This process of interaction and socialization in the family occurs within a larger context—involving a particular family structure, a racial/ethnic identity, specific socioeconomic circumstances, and indeed gender role expectations. Many researchers have argued for comprehensive models to explain adolescent alcohol abuse, linking individual/genetic attributes and sociodemographic/structural factions with interaction processes among significant others (Barnes, 1990; Jessor, 1987, 1992; Zucker, 1979; Zucker & Gomberg, 1986). However, most empirical studies have examined a limited set of personality/individual variables or a limited set of parenting variables for their effects on adolescent outcomes. Thus, the literature abounds with studies that have not taken into account critical context/sociodemographic factors such as race, socioeconomic status, family structure, and gender. The many conflicting findings in the field of family socialization on adolescent development are due, in part, to lack of attention to both "person and context" variables in explaining complex adolescent risk behaviors (cf., Jessor, 1992).

In this chapter, family socialization effects on male and female alcohol abuse will be examined using data from an ongoing longitudinal study of adolescents and their families. The sampling was designed to be representative of general population adolescents and their parents in western New York State; thus, the sample reflects the diversity of demographic and family factors in the area. Respondents were first interviewed in 1989–90 and then reinterviewed one year later in 1990–91. This chapter addresses the following central question: Are sociodemographic, family socialization, and peer influences on adolescent alcohol abuse, delinquency, and psychological distress the same or different for female and male adolescents? The analyses here assess adolescent problem behaviors at Time 2, using a series of Time 1 sociodemographic, family, and peer predictor variables.

Method

Sampling

A representative household sample of 699 adolescents and their families in Buffalo, N.Y., and its surrounding suburbs and towns was obtained by means of random-digit-dial (RDD) telephone procedures on a computer-assisted telephone interviewing (CATI) network.[1] The criteria for inclusion into the sample were that the household have at least one adolescent between 13 and 16 years old at Time 1 and at least one parent (biological or surrogate). African-American families were oversampled ($n = 210$) to allow sufficient subsample for meaningful analysis.

After eligibility was determined, interviews were carried out by trained, two-person interviewing teams in the respondents' homes. Both mothers and fathers (biological and surrogate) of the target adolescents were included in the study, depending upon the family composition. Families were paid $50 at Time 1 and $75 at Time 2. Using stringent follow-up procedures, the Time 1 completion rate was 71% of eligible families and 77% for African-American families. Furthermore, a comparison of the demographic characteristics of the sample with available census data revealed that the sample closely resembled the characteristics of the population in the metropolitan Buffalo,

N.Y., area. Of the original 699 adolescents and their families, 658 (94%) were retained in the sample one year later at Time 2. Analysis of those who dropped out of the study versus those who remained in the sample showed no evidence of bias in the wave 2 sample. Additional information on the methodology and detailed sociodemographic characteristics of the African-American and white samples have been presented elsewhere (see Barnes & Farrell, 1992; Barnes et al., 1991a).

Dependent Measures

For the present multivariate analysis, three Time 2 dependent measures were derived for adolescents.

Frequent heavy drinking (past year). Frequent heavy drinking was measured from questions about the frequency of having five or more drinks of beer, wine, or distilled spirits. Frequent heavy drinking represents the number of days in the past year that the adolescent drank five or more drinks of an alcoholic beverage (based on the beverage consumed most often).

Adolescent deviant behavior (number of deviant acts in past year). Seventeen questions covered a variety of relatively minor deviant acts, such as staying out later than parents said and skipping a day of school without a real excuse, as well as more serious deviance, such as having sexual relations with someone; beating up someone on purpose; breaking into a house, business, or car; and taking something of value that did not belong to him/her. Two items regarding the use of marijuana and other illicit drugs also were included in this deviance scale, but not items about extreme drinking, to avoid overlap with the "heavy drinking" dependent variable. Questions about conflict in the family were deleted from the deviance scale to avoid overlap with independent variables such as the measure of parental support. For the 17-item deviance scale, interitem consistency (alpha) was .74.

Adolescent psychological distress. Adolescents' psychological distress was measured with responses to nine items indicating how often in the past year adolescents were bothered or troubled by the following: feeling too tired to do things; having trouble going to sleep or staying asleep; feeling unhappy, sad, or depressed; feeling hopeless about the future; feeling nervous or tense; daydreaming; worrying too much about things; having headaches; and having nightmares. Response categories were frequently, sometimes, hardly ever, and never (alpha = .77).

Independent Measures

A series of self-explanatory sociodemographic variables were measured including adolescent race (white and other versus African-American), age, family structure (living with two biological parents versus single parent and other arrangements), and the mother's years of education. (Father's education was also measured but is not analyzed here, because inclusion of single-parent, female-headed households meant that data for fathers was more often missing.)

Two measures of parental problem drinking were used in analyses here:

Mother's heavy drinking. This variable was derived from a mother's report of the number of days in the past year she consumed five or more drinks at a sitting, based on the beverage she consumed most frequently.

Father's problem drinking. Due to the large number of households with no father present, it was not possible to use the same self-report measure of heavy drinking as was used for mothers. Therefore, a dichotomous variable (0,1) was constructed to indicate whether or not a father was a problem drinker. Where an adolescent's father was interviewed, he was classified as a problem drinker if he reported three or more alcohol-related social problems or signs of alcohol dependence in the past year (e.g., trouble with police, boss, or friends because of drinking; driving while impaired; having blackouts; drinking in the morning), or if he reported an average daily consumption over three drinks per day based on quantity-frequency measures of beer, wine, and spirits. In situations where the father was not interviewed, he was classified as a problem drinker if the mother classified him as a problem drinker or an alcoholic drinker. (It should be noted that this variable is used not as a clinical diagnosis of alcohol abuse or dependence, but to indicate the upper end of the ranges of drinking and alcohol-related problems, as in other general population surveys of adults [cf., Barnes et al., 1991b; Hilton, 1988].)

Key parental socialization variables include the following independent variables measured at Time 1. These variables have been operationalized based on previous theory and empirical research (e.g., Barnes, 1990; Barnes & Farrell, 1992; Rollins & Thomas, 1979).

Support. Support is defined as behaviors toward adolescents indicating to them that they are valued and loved. An eight-item scale was used (alpha = .80) with items such as: "When you do something well, how often does your mother give you praise or encouragement for what you do?" "How much do you rely on your mother for advice and guidance?" "How often does your mother give you a hug, a kiss, or a pat on the back?" (The father's support scale was based on a separate set of items asked in the same manner as for mother.)

Monitoring. This two-item scale comprises an aspect of parental control. The items were: "How often do you tell your parents where you're going to be after school?" "How often do you tell your parents where you're really going when you go out evenings and weekends?" There were five response choices ranging from "always" to "never." The alpha for the two-item scale was .64.

Positive communication with mother. Barnes and Olson's (1982) 20-item communication scale was used to measure parent-adolescent interaction. Examples of items are (1) "I am very satisfied with how my mother and I talk together," and (2) "If I were in trouble, I could tell my mother." Response choices on a five-point Likert scale ranged from "strongly disagree" to "strongly agree." Reversed coding of negatively worded items produced a scale of positive adolescent-mother communication (alpha = .87). (Parallel items were used to construct a scale of adolescent-father communication.)

Emotional autonomy. Adolescents' emotional autonomy is the process whereby adolescents increase independence from parents while remaining tied to them. A low level of emotional autonomy indicates a substantial amount of emotional conflict as an adolescent strives for independence. Emotional autonomy was measured by an eight-item scale, with response choices on a five-point Likert scale ranging from "strongly agree" to "strongly disagree" (alpha =.76) (Bray et al., 1984). Examples of items are (1) "I often get so emotional with my parents that I cannot think straight," and (2) "My parents frequently try to change some aspect of my personality."

Peer variables as reported by the adolescent include the following independent variables:

Peer (vs. parent) orientation. This is a two-item scale: (1) "If you had a serious decision to make, like whether or not to continue in school or whether or not to get married, whose opinion would you value most . . . ?" (2) "With regard to your present outlook on life . . . whose views have had a greater impact on you . . . ?" Response choices were: "parents most," "parents and friends equally," and "friends most" (alpha = .68).

Closest friend's drinking. Closest friend's drinking is measured as the estimated average ounces of absolute alcohol consumed per day, based on adolescent responses to two questions: the closest friend's frequency of drinking any kind of alcohol beverage, and the average number of drinks the friend consumed per sitting. A dichotomous friend's drinking variable is also used to examine interaction effects. One category includes abstainers and infrequent drinkers, i.e., those who drink no more than once a month and drink no more than one drink on an occasion. The other category includes all other drinkers.

Closest friend's deviance (past 12 months). The closest friend's deviance scale is a condensed version (12 items) of the adolescent deviance scale described above. The major difference is that more general response categories were used ("never," "seldom," "sometimes," and "frequently"), since adolescents would not necessarily know the exact number of times that their friends had engaged in various behaviors (alpha = .79).

Results

Descriptive Analyses

Table 1 gives Time 1 and Time 2 means for male and female adolescents on sociodemographic, parental, and peer socialization factors, and behavior out-

TABLE 1
Mean Comparisons of Sociodemographic Measures, Socialization Measures,
and Alcohol Abuse and Related Problem Behaviors for Male and Female
Adolescents at Times 1 and 2
(Weighted Data)

	TIME 1			TIME 2		
	Male ($n = 324$)	Female ($n = 375$)		Male ($n = 301$)	Female ($n = 357$)	
Sociodemographic measures						
Adolescent age (years)	14.5	14.5	NS	15.5	15.5	NS
Proportion with two biological parents in household	0.56	0.57	NS	0.52	0.55	NS
Mother's education (years)	13.2	13.4	NS	13.4	13.4	NS
Family income ($ thousands)	35.9	34.4	NS	38.7	38.5	NS
Parental socialization measures						
Adolescent reports of:						
Mother support (8-40)	27.2	27.4	NS	26.4	27.8	**
Father support (8-40)	25.3	23.5	***	24.5	23.1	**
Parental monitoring (0-8)	5.8	6.5	***	5.3	6.1	***
Communication with mother (20-100)	66.1	64.3	NS	63.5	63.3	NS
Communication with father (20-100)	64.2	61.1	**	60.9	60.2	NS
Emotional autonomy (8-40)	26.5	25.9	NS	26.7	26.5	NS
Mother reports of:						
Mother support (8-40)	30.7	31.2	NS	30.2	31.4	***
Parental monitoring (0-8)	7.1	7.4	***	6.8	7.2	***
Communication: Adolescent & mother (20-100)	76.9	77.9	NS	79.3	79.5	NS
Father reports of ($n = \sim396$):						
Father support (8-40)	29.1	27.9	**	29.1	28.3	NS
Parental monitoring (0-8)	7.0	7.2	NS	6.7	6.9	NS
Communication: Adolescent & father (20-100)	75.9	74.6	NS	77.2	76.4	NS
Peer socialization measures						
Peer orientation (2-6)	3.4	3.8	***	3.5	3.8	***
Closest friend's support (6-30)	22.2	25.2	***	22.7	25.6	***
Proportion whose closest friend is a drinker	0.37	0.42	NS	0.59	0.55	NS
Closest friend's absolute alcohol (oz./day)	0.12	0.08	NS	0.19	0.16	NS
Closest friend's deviance (0-36)	7.6	6.7	*	8.9	7.5	***
Adolescent behavioral measures						
Proportion drinkers	0.53	0.47	NS	0.65	0.64	NS
Average absolute alcohol (oz./day)	0.16	0.11	NS	0.32	0.14	***

TABLE 1
(continued)

	TIME 1			TIME 2		
	Male (n = 324)	Female (n = 375)		Male (n = 301)	Female (n = 357)	
No. days drank 5+ drinks						
alcohol (past year)	9.1	4.9	*	13.7	5.4	***
Times drunk (past year)	3.0	2.9	NS	6.7	4.0	**
Deviant acts (no. in past year)						
(0-180)	27.3	25.8	NS	32.1	28.5	*
Expanded Deviance Scale						
(T2 only) (0-255)				41.5	30.8	***
Psychological distress (9-36)	21.7	23.7	***	22.2	23.5	***

*$p \leq .05$.   **$p \leq .01$.   ***$p \leq .001$.

come measures. These comparisons are important because there are few representative longitudinal, general population studies that assess how parenting is perceived both by adolescent children and their parents.

Sociodemographic factors. None of the sociodemographic characteristics in Table 1 differ significantly for male and female adolescents. The average age for both sexes was 14.5 years at Time 1 and 15.5 at Time 2. Slightly more than half of both males and females were living with both biological parents at both times of the survey.

Parental socialization factors. At Time 1, both adolescents and mothers perceived that mothers gave the same level of support to male and female children. One year later, daughters reported slightly more maternal support than sons, a pattern also reported by mothers themselves. At both Time 1 and Time 2, sons reported more support from fathers than daughters did, consistent with what fathers also reported. (However, one must be cautious about interpreting fathers' reports, because only a subsample of fathers were interviewed, primarily due to family structure.) It is noteworthy that both mothers and fathers consistently said they gave more support to their adolescents than adolescents reported receiving.

At both Time 1 and Time 2, male and female adolescents and their mothers all reported greater parental *monitoring* of whereabouts and activities of daughters than of sons. As in reports of parental support, parents reported more monitoring than adolescents reported receiving. The only clear gender differences in relations with parents were the differences in support and monitoring. Sons' and daughters' communications with either parent and emotional autonomy were not significantly different.

Peer socialization factors. Females and males did differ significantly in peer orientation and support from closest friends. Female adolescents relied more on friends' opinions (peer orientation) and reported more support from their closest friends than males did. Gender differences in closest friends' drinking were not significant, but males reported higher levels of deviance among closest friends than females did.

Adolescent outcomes. Consistent with earlier research, male and female adolescents did not differ greatly in the prevalence of drinking, but males reported consuming larger amounts of alcohol and more frequently drinking heavily and getting drunk than females did. This pattern was clearer at Time 2, when the adolescents were 14 to 17 years old. As in previous studies, the males also reported higher levels of deviance, whereas females reported higher levels of psychological distress.

Multivariate Analyses

A multivariate analysis of variance (MANOVA)[2] was carried out to examine the effect of Time 1 sociodemographic, parent, and peer socialization variables on adolescent alcohol abuse and other related problem outcomes at Time 2. The MANOVA results in Table 2 allow for examination of the dependent variables taken together as a syndrome in addition to consideration of individual outcomes. The analysis has the added advantage of having Time 2 dependent variables measured one year later than predictor (independent) variables. Predictor variables were entered into the analysis sequentially, based on the study's theoretical model, first taking into account race and other sociodemographic factors, then entering family and peer socialization factors. Each independent variable listed was tested for significance while controlling for the variables listed previously.

As reported from this sample and other studies, African-American adolescents have less heavy drinking and deviance than white adolescents (Barnes et al., 1994; Welte & Barnes, 1987). Psychological distress is also less prevalent among African-American than white adolescents. Increasing age is a highly significant predictor of increasing heavy drinking and deviance among adolescents, although age does not predict greater levels of psychological distress. Family structure and mother's education have no significant effects on any of the three adolescent dependent variables.

Measures of mothers' heavy drinking and fathers' problem drinking do not show a significant main effect on adolescent heavy drinking or deviance in this general population sample. However, there is an indication that fathers characterized as problem drinkers have adolescents with greater levels of psychological distress than do fathers who are not problem drinkers.

After controlling for demographic characteristics and parental drinking patterns, higher levels of maternal support and parental monitoring predicted lower levels of heavy drinking and deviance among adolescents a year later. Maternal support also predicted lower levels of adolescent distress. Distress and deviance were also higher among adolescents who had previously reported less emotional autonomy from their parents.

TABLE 2
Multivariate Analysis (MANOVA) with Time 1 Sociodemographic and Socialization Predictors of Time 2 Adolescent Frequent Heavy Drinking, Deviance and Psychological Distress (Sequential Method)

Time 1 Independent Variables	MULTIVARIATE F: 3 Dependent Variables Taken Together	UNIVARIATE F: Frequent Heavy Drinking (Time 2)	Deviance (Time 2)	Psychological Distress (Time 2)	Interpretation & Direction of Effect
Race White and other African-American	7.9***	7.3**	10.8***	14.8***	African-Americans have less heavy drinking, deviance, and psychological distress than whites
Adolescent age (13–16 years)	11.3***	10.2***	32.8***	NS	As adolescents get older, heavy drinking and deviance increase; age does not predict distress
Family structure Two biological parents Single parent and other	NS	NS	NS	NS	Family structure has no significant effect on adolescent problem behaviors and distress
Mother's education (years)	NS	NS	NS	NS	Mother's education has no observed effect on adolescent problem behaviors and distress
Mother's heavy drinking (no. days 5+ drinks/past year)	NS	NS	NS	NS	There is no observable effect of mother's heavy drinking on adolescent problem outcomes
Father problem drinker (0, 1)	NS	NS	NS	5.6*	Father's problem drinking is associated with greater adolescent distress

TABLE 2 (continued)

Time 1 Independent Variables	MULTIVARIATE F 3 Dependent Variables Taken Together	UNIVARIATE F Frequent Heavy Drinking (Time 2)	Deviance (Time 2)	Psychological Distress (Time 2)	Interpretation & Direction of Effect
Mother support (8–40)	15.6***	4.6*	45.4***	6.2**	Higher levels of mother support are associated with lower levels of all problem outcomes
Parental monitoring (0–8)	32.0***	39.2***	88.0***	NS	Higher parental monitoring is associated with less problem behavior, but is not related to distress
Emotional autonomy (8–40)	18.2***	NS	10.1**	52.9***	Low levels of autonomy are highly associated with distress and deviance
Closest friend's support (6–30)	2.9*	5.0*	NS	4.3*	The more support from the closest friend, the more heavy drinking and distress
Peer orientation (2–6)	2.7*	NS	8.1**	NS	Greater levels of peer orientation are related to higher levels of deviance
Closest friend's drinking (oz. per day)	32.1***	95.8***	20.2***	NS	Closest friend's drinking predicts adolescent drinking and deviance
Closest friend's deviance (no. in past year)	20.4***	6.8**	58.6***	NS	Friend's deviance predicts adolescent heavy drinking and deviance

TABLE 2 (continued)

Time 1 Independent Variables	MULTIVARIATE F	UNIVARIATE F			Interpretation & Direction of Effect
	3 Dependent Variables Taken Together	Frequent Heavy Drinking (Time 2)	Deviance (Time 2)	Psychological Distress (Time 2)	
Gender	15.9***	20.4***	22.6***	9.1**	After taking into account all of the above factors, gender remains a significant predictor of outcomes. Being female is predictive of higher distress while being male is predictive of higher levels of heavy drinking and deviance
(All the above main effects were entered as interactions with gender with the resulting significant interactions)					
Significant interactions with gender					
Age × Gender	NS	3.5 (p = .06)	NS	NS	Age has a stronger effect on heavy drinking among males than females
Father Problem Drinker × Gender	NS	NS	NS	6.2**	Father's problem drinking has a stronger effect on distress for females than for males
Friend's Alcohol Use × Gender	NS	NS	NS	5.2*	Friend's alcohol use and friend's deviance both show a stronger effect on distress among males than among females
Friend's Deviance × Gender	NS	NS	NS	7.0**	

* $p \leq .05$.　** $p \leq .01$.　*** $p \leq .001$.

In addition to these critical influences of parental socialization on adolescent outcomes, peer influences are also important factors in adolescent outcomes. Friend's drinking (as reported by the adolescent) is a particularly powerful predictor of adolescent drinking, and friend's deviance is a highly significant predictor of adolescent deviance.

When the variable gender was entered first into this same analysis, it had a strong effect on outcomes as noted in the descriptive analysis in Table 1. For the present analysis, gender was entered as the last main effect to examine whether or not it still accounted for variance in outcomes after taking into account all of the other sociodemographic, parent, and peer socialization variables. Gender per se remains a significant predictor of outcomes. In a separate analysis (not shown), adolescent's weight (in pounds) was entered just before gender to take into account some of the biological differences in body composition of adolescent males and females, which might, in turn, explain why males drink more heavily than females. After controlling for weight and the other variables, gender remained highly significant as an independent variable. In short, male and female adolescents do drink differently, and it is not just because of differences in weight and demographics, and not just because of differences in how they are raised and how they make friends.

A primary purpose of this analysis was to determine whether adolescent males and females differ in how sociodemographic and socialization variables predict adolescent drinking, deviance, and distress. To evaluate whether main effects of the independent variables were similar for males and females, interaction terms for all independent variables and gender were entered into the analysis after the main effects.[3] Most interaction effects were not statistically significant. This indicates that parental support and monitoring, for example, and peer role models for drinking and deviance have a similar impact on both male and female outcomes.

There were a few noteworthy interactions with gender. Age has a stronger relationship to heavy drinking for males than for females. This is evidenced in the bivariate relationship depicted in Figure 1, where there is no difference in heavy drinking among males and females at 14 years old, but after that male rates of heavy drinking increase rapidly whereas female rates change little.

Two other interactions between alcohol variables and gender have significant effects on psychological distress at Time 2. As depicted in Figure 2, daughters but not sons are likely to be more distressed if their fathers are problem drinkers. In contrast, Figure 3 shows that male adolescents but not females are likely to be more distressed if their best friends are moderate or heavy drinkers.

Discussion

This research and that of numerous other investigators have clearly established that there are gender differences in heavy drinking, deviant behavior, and psychological distress in adolescence. We have attempted to learn

FIGURE 1
Interaction of Age and Gender on Frequency of Heavy Drinking (Time 2)

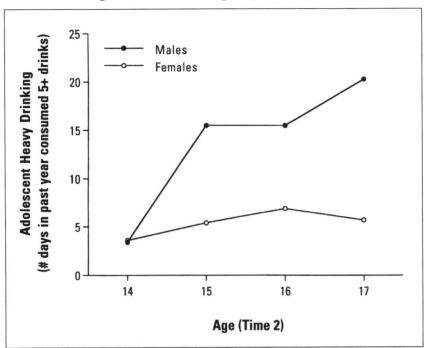

whether there are differences in parental and peer socialization of male and female adolescents, and whether such differences in socialization explain gender differences in adolescent outcomes. The socialization differences may be manifested in at least two ways. First, socialization patterns (e.g., support, monitoring, and peer modeling) may be different for males and females, but may have the same relationships to outcomes for both genders. Second, parents and peers may have stronger influences on outcomes for one gender that is more responsive to their socialization.

In general, we have not found as many differences in socialization for males and females as might be expected from the theoretical literature or popular notions. For example, communication with mother and father shows no differences at either point in time, according to independent reports from adolescents, mothers, and fathers. Likewise, emotional autonomy, an aspect of the process of becoming independent from parents, shows no significant gender differences. This lack of difference is consistent with some recent reports (cf., Steinberg, 1987). These gender similarities may represent some historical changes toward more equality in socialization of girls and boys. More than likely, previous conflicting findings are due to methodological limitations of research, including convenience samples and small sample sizes. The present

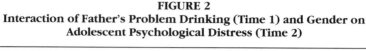

FIGURE 2
Interaction of Father's Problem Drinking (Time 1) and Gender on
Adolescent Psychological Distress (Time 2)

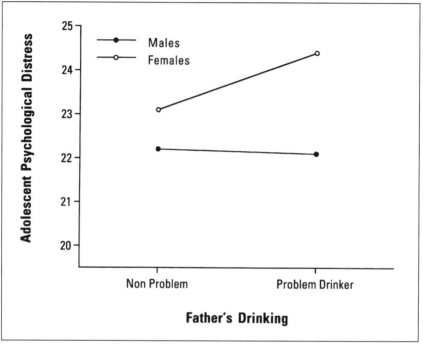

study relies on a randomly selected, general population sample of adolescents representing a full spectrum of demographic diversity in a metropolitan area.

Nonetheless, we do observe some gender differences in socialization. There is evidence that daughters receive more maternal support than do sons, while fathers show more support for sons than daughters. The importance of fathers in the socialization of children is an understudied area that has recently been brought to the forefront (e.g., see Cath et al., 1989). Although we did not find a main effect of family structure on adolescent outcomes, future research should examine how family structure influences paternal socialization and whether this relationship is different for male and female adolescents.

The second major component of parental socialization, namely, monitoring, shows a clear and consistent gender difference. Given that males are monitored less than females and that lower levels of monitoring are strongly predictive of problem behaviors, it is reasonable to conclude that increases in monitoring for boys would produce decreases in alcohol abuse and deviant behavior. This finding has strong implications for family prevention efforts.

FIGURE 3
Interaction of Closest Friend's Drinking (Time 1) and Gender on Adolescent Psychological Distress (Time 2)

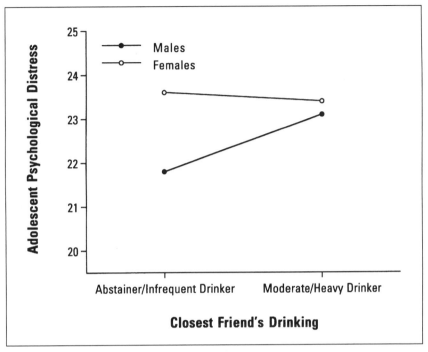

Another clear gender difference is in peer socialization. Females rely more on their closest friends for advice on important decisions and receive more generalized support in their friendships than do males. This is consistent with other research showing that girls are more concerned about relationships and intimacy (Papini et al., 1990; Richards & Larson, 1989; Smith & Pasternoster, 1987). On the other hand, males have closest friends with higher levels of deviance than do females, and this variable, along with friend's drinking, is strongly related to heavy drinking and deviance even after the parental variables have been taken into account. Consistent with control theory (e.g., Hirschi, 1969), family factors may influence the choice of peers. Where parent-child interaction is problematic, adolescents are likely to withdraw from the family and rely more heavily on the influence of peer subcultures (e.g., Barnes et al., 1987; Barnes & Windle, 1987). Similarly, other scientists have shown that parental closeness discouraged drug use both directly and through its impact on peer-related variables, especially the choice of nondrug-using friends (e.g., Brook et al., 1990; Jacob & Leonard, 1994; Kandel & Andrews, 1987).

In addition to gender differences in the levels of various socialization factors, we examined interaction effects to assess whether or not demographic and socialization factors predicted outcomes in a different pattern for males and females. Basically, we find that the main effects of parenting and peer socialization are equally important in predicting heavy drinking and deviance among both males and females. However, there is an indication that age has a stronger effect on heavy drinking among males than females. For many adolescent males, movement into adult roles seems to include adoption of a culture of heavy drinking.

The other gender interactions we observe occur with parental drinking and peer variables showing a differential effect on psychological distress, but not heavy drinking and deviance. Having a problem-drinking father has a significant impact on the psychological distress of girls. This finding may again relate to the concept that females are more sensitive to relationships within the family. While parents have been shown to be models for development of various drinking patterns (see Barnes, 1990, for a review), the measures of alcohol *abuse* by mothers and fathers do not show main effects on adolescent heavy drinking and deviance. It may be that the effects of a problem-drinking parent are manifested in problematic drinking later in young or middle adulthood (Barnes & Welte, 1990). We also have preliminary evidence from our longitudinal analysis of subsequent waves of data that parenting mediates the relationship between parents' problem drinking and adolescent problem outcomes. In other words, parents who are problem drinkers provide less support and monitoring for their adolescents, and lower levels of support and monitoring in turn influence adolescent alcohol misuse.

In spite of the significant effects of parent and peer socialization, there remain gender differences in alcohol abuse, deviance, and distress. After taking into account this vast array of variables, as well as body weight, gender per se still has significant effects on outcomes. This is consistent with the recent findings of Huselid and Cooper (1992), who examined gender roles as mediators of sex differences in adolescent alcohol abuse. Using a large, random sample of adolescents, they found that sex differences in alcohol measures remained significant even though the gender roles mediated some of the gender effect on alcohol consumption.

While we have measured socialization by way of a variety of social interactions among adolescents, parents, and closest friends, there may be a more symbolic, generalized socialization that we have not adequately assessed. This type of socialization occurs from media and cultural scripts linking drinking behavior among young males to the development of masculinity. Losh-Hesselbart (1987), in her review of the development of gender roles, notes that modeling (social learning) does not only occur through concrete figures such as parents, siblings, and peers, but there are also symbolic presentations, including media models, that are important in developing behaviors. For example, she notes that heavy television viewers are more gender-stereotyped than light viewers and that boys more often than girls imitate same-sex models in the media.

While media representations of drinking may influence drinking and beverage preferences among young people, the media messages are likely to be reflective of the larger cultural notions regarding the functions and meanings of drinking. We need clearer definitions and ways of measuring these broader cultural norms associated with heavy drinking and adolescent male development.

Acknowledgments

This research was supported by National Institute on Alcohol Abuse and Alcoholism grant R01-AA06925. The authors gratefully acknowledge the contributions of Lois Uhteg and the interviewing staff for careful and complete data collection, and thank Audrey Topinko for her excellent work in preparing the manuscript for publication.

Notes

1. Given that over 96% of family households in this area have telephones, random-digit-dial (RDD) is a cost-effective means of obtaining a random sample of households. Furthermore, it is an efficient method of screening for eligibility of respondents for inclusion in a sample where a specific population group, such as adolescents, is required.
2. Multiple dependent variables were used because the behaviors of interest are significantly correlated; i.e., correlations between deviance and frequent heavy drinking and deviance and psychological distress are .50 and .26, respectively; and the correlation between the alcohol abuse variable and psychological distress is lower than the others (.14), although it is statistically significant. MANOVA allows the investigator to consider the effects of independent variables separately for each dependent variable as well as the joint effects on the dependent variables taken together. Unlike path modeling techniques, MANOVA also allows the investigator to easily examine interaction effects among independent variables, particularly among each independent variable and gender.
3. To facilitate probing interactions with gender by minimizing the multicollinearity between independent variables and interaction terms, we made use of Aiken and West's (1991) procedures for centering the independent variables by setting the mean of each continuous independent variable to zero.

References

Aiken, L.S., & West, S.G. (1991). *Multiple regression: Testing and interpreting interactions.* Newbury Park, CA: Sage.

Barnes, G.M. (1990). Impact of the family on adolescent drinking patterns. In R.L. Collins, K.E. Leonard, & J.S. Searles (Eds.), *Alcohol and the family: Research and clinical perspectives* (pp. 137-161). New York: Guilford.

Barnes, G.M., & Farrell, M.P. (1992). Parental support and control as predictors of adolescent drinking, delinquency, and related problem behaviors. *Journal of Marriage and the Family, 54,* 763-776.

Barnes, G.M., Farrell, M.P., & Banerjee, S. (1994). Family influences on alcohol abuse and other problem behaviors among black and white adolescents in a general population sample. *Journal of Research on Adolescence, 4*(2), 183-201.

Barnes, G.M., Farrell, M.P., Welch, K.W., Uhteg, L., & Dintcheff, B. (1991a). *Description and analysis of methods used in the Family and Adolescent Study.* Buffalo, NY: Research Institute on Alcoholism.

Barnes, G.M., Farrell, M.P., & Windle, M. (1987). Parent-adolescent interactions in the development of alcohol abuse and other deviant behaviors. *Family Perspectives, 21*(4), 321-335.

Barnes, G.M., & Welte, J.W. (1986a). Adolescent alcohol abuse: Subgroup differences and relationships to other problem behaviors. *Journal of Adolescent Research, 1,* 79-94.

Barnes, G.M., & Welte, J.W. (1986b). Patterns and predictors of alcohol use among 7-12th grade students in New York State. *Journal of Studies on Alcohol, 47,* 53-62.

Barnes, G.M., & Welte, J.W. (1990). Prediction of adults' drinking patterns from the drinking of their parents. *Journal of Studies on Alcohol, 51,* 523-527.

Barnes, G.M., Welte, J.W., & Dintcheff, B. (1991b). Drinking among subgroups in the adult population of New York State: A classification analysis using CART. *Journal of Studies on Alcohol, 52,* 338-344.

Barnes, G.M., Welte, J.W., & Dintcheff, B. (1993). Decline in alcohol use among 7-12th grade students in New York State, 1983-1990. *Alcoholism: Clinical and Experimental Research, 17,* 797-801.

Barnes, G.M., & Windle, M. (1987). Family factors in adolescent alcohol and drug abuse. *Pediatrician—International Journal of Child and Adolescent Health, 14,* 13-18.

Barnes, H., & Olson, D.H. (1982). Parent-adolescent communication. In D.H. Olson, H.I. McCubbin, H. Barnes, A. Larsen, M. Muxen, & M. Wilson (Eds.), *Family inventories* (pp. 33-48). St. Paul, MN: University of Minnesota, Family Social Science.

Bray, J.H., Williamson, D.S., & Malone, P.E. (1984). *Personal authority in the family manual.* Houston, TX: Texas Women's University, Houston Center.

Brook, J.S., Brook, D.W., Gordon, A.S., Whiteman, M., & Cohen, P. (1990). The psychosocial etiology of adolescent drug use: A family interactional approach. *Genetic, Social, and General Psychology Monographs, 116*(2), 111-267.

Cath, S.H., Gurwitt, A., & Gunsberg, L. (1989). *Fathers and their families.* Hillsdale, NJ: Analytic Press.

Donovan, J.E., & Jessor, R. (1985). Structure of problem behavior in adolescence and young adulthood. *Journal of Consulting and Clinical Psychology, 53*(6), 890-904.

Elliott, D.S., Huizinga, D., & Ageton, S.S. (1985). *Explaining delinquency and drug use.* Newbury Park, CA: Sage.

Farrell, M.P., & Barnes, G.M. (1993). Family systems and social support: A test of the effects of cohesion and adaptability on the functioning of parents and adolescents. *Journal of Marriage and the Family, 55,* 119-132.

Goodwin, D.W. (1984). Studies of familial alcoholism: A growth industry. In D.W. Goodwin, K.T. Van Dusen, & S.A. Mednick (Eds.), *Longitudinal research in alcoholism.* Boston: Kluwer-Nijhoff.

Hilton, M.E. (1988). Trends in U.S. drinking patterns: Further evidence from the past 20 years. *British Journal of Addiction, 83,* 269-278.

Hirschi, T. (1969). *Causes of delinquency.* Berkeley, CA: University of California Press.

Huselid, R.F., & Cooper, M.L. (1992). Gender roles as mediators of sex differences in adolescent alcohol use and abuse. *Journal of Health and Social Behavior, 33,* 348-362.

Jacob, T., & Leonard, K. (1994). Family and peer influences in the development of adolescent alcohol abuse. In *The development of alcohol problems: Exploring the biopsychosocial matrix of risk* (NIAAA Research Monograph No. 26; NIH Publication No. 94-3495). Rockville, MD: National Institutes of Health.

Jessor, R. (1987). Problem-behavior theory, psychosocial development, and adolescent problem drinking. *British Journal of Addiction, 82,* 331-342.

Jessor, R. (1992). Risk behavior in adolescence: A psychosocial framework for understanding and action. *Developmental Review, 12,* 374-390.

Johnston, L.D., O'Malley, P.M., & Bachman, J.G. (1991). *Drug use among American high school seniors, college students and young adults, 1975-1990: Vol. 1. High school seniors* (DHHS Publ. No. ADM 91-1813). Washington, DC: U.S. Government Printing Office.

Kandel, D.B., & Andrews, K. (1987). Processes of adolescent socialization by parents and peers. *International Journal of the Addictions, 22,* 319-342.

Losh-Hesselbart, S. (1987). Development of gender roles. In M.B. Sussman & S.K. Steinmetz (Eds.), *Handbook of marriage and the family* (pp. 535-563). New York: Plenum Press.

Maccoby, E.E., & Martin, J.A. (1983). Socialization in the context of the family: Parent-child interaction. In E.M. Hetherington (Ed.), *Handbook of child psychology: Vol. IV. Socialization, personality, and social development* (pp. 1-101). New York: John Wiley & Sons.

Papini, D.R., Farmer, F.F., Clark, S.M., Micka, J.C., & Barnett, J.K. (1990). Early adolescent age and gender differences in patterns of emotional self-disclosure to parents and friends. *Adolescence, 25,* 959-976.

Peterson, G.W., & Rollins, B.C. (1987). Parent-child socialization. In M.B. Sussman & S.K. Steinmetz (Eds.), *Handbook of marriage and the family* (pp. 471-507). New York: Plenum Press.

Richards, M.H., & Larson, R. (1989). The life space and socialization of the self: Sex differences in the young adolescent. *Journal of Youth and Adolescence, 18,* 617-626.

Rollins, B.C., & Thomas, D.L. (1979). Parental support, power, and control techniques in the socialization of children. In W.R. Burr, R. Hill, F.I. Nye, & I.L. Reiss (Eds.), *Contemporary theories about the family* (Vol. 1, pp. 317-364). New York: Free Press.

Schuckit, M.A. (1987). Biological vulnerability to alcoholism. *Journal of Consulting and Clinical Psychology, 55,* 301-309.

Smith, D.A., & Paternoster, R. (1987). The gender gap in theories of deviance: Issues and evidence. *Journal of Research in Crime and Delinquency, 24,* 140-172.

Steinberg, L. (1987). Recent research on the family at adolescence: The extent and nature of sex differences. *Journal of Youth and Adolescence, 16,* 191-197.

Thompson, K.M., & Wilsnack, R.W. (1984). Drinking and drinking problems among female adolescents: Patterns and influences. In S.C. Wilsnack & L.J. Beckman (Eds.), *Alcohol problems in women: Antecedents, consequences, and intervention* (pp. 37-65). New York: Guilford.

Welte, J.W., & Barnes, G.M. (1987). Alcohol use among adolescent minority groups. *Journal of Studies on Alcohol, 48,* 329-336.

Windle, M. (1991). Alcohol use and abuse: Some findings from the National Adolescent Student Health Survey. *Alcohol Health & Research World, 15,* 5-10.

Windle, M. (1992a). A longitudinal study of stress buffering for adolescent problem behaviors. *Developmental Psychology, 28,* 522-530.

Windle, M. (1992b). Temperament and social support in adolescence: Interrelations with depressive symptoms and delinquent behaviors. *Journal of Youth and Adolescence, 21,* 1-21.

Zucker, R.A. (1979). Developmental aspects of drinking through the young adult years. In H.T. Blane and M.E. Chafetz (Eds.), *Youth, alcohol, and social policy* (pp. 91-146). New York: Plenum.

Zucker, R.A., & Gomberg, E.S.L. (1986). Etiology of alcoholism reconsidered: The case for a biopsychosocial process. *American Psychologist, 41,* 783-793.

CHAPTER 7

Gender Differences in Alcohol Use during Adolescence

HELENE RASKIN WHITE AND REBECCA FARMER HUSELID

The purpose of this chapter is to explore the relationship between gender and alcohol use during adolescence. The chapter is divided into two major sections. In the first section we review recent data from studies of U.S. adolescents attending junior high, high school, and college to determine the extent of gender differences in drinking patterns, problems, and motivations. In the second section we examine gender-role explanations for these differences both theoretically and empirically. In concluding, we summarize methodological problems with existing studies and present an agenda for future research.

Differences Associated with Biological Sex

Although early studies of adolescents reported that males drank more than females, data collected during the 1970s began to indicate that the gender differential was disappearing (Wechsler & McFadden, 1976). These findings suggested a convergence in drinking patterns for young males and females based upon a hypothesis that young females were increasing their use at a faster rate than males and, thus, catching up to males (Temple, 1987). It was assumed that these changes resulted from the women's liberation movement, which led to relaxed gender-role stereotypes in regard to many behaviors including drinking. Thus, it was postulated that as normative pressures against female drinking were relaxed, gender differences in opportunities to drink, motives for drinking, and alcohol consumption would also decline. Specifically, this convergence was expected to result from increased drinking by women, in part because higher aspirations and liberated roles were expected to create greater stress among women and an increased need to drink to relieve this stress (Berkowitz & Perkins, 1987; Engs & Hanson, 1990; Temple, 1987; Wilsnack & Wilsnack, 1978). The supporters of the "convergence hypothesis" predicted that gender differences in patterns of use and related problems would become smaller or nonexistent in younger cohorts and in groups least committed to traditional gender roles (Robbins, 1989, p.117).

Recent data clearly support a convergence hypothesis in terms of lifetime and annual prevalence rates (i.e., the percentage of youths drinking at least once during their lifetime or during the last year, respectively) for both college students (Johnston et al., 1992b; O'Hare, 1990) and younger adolescents (Johnston et al., 1992a; White et al., 1993). An illustration of this finding is shown in Table 1, which presents data from the "Monitoring the Future" study (Johnston et al., 1992a,b) and the NIDA "National Household Survey" (National Institute on Drug Abuse, 1991). As can be seen in Table 1, the extent of alcohol use among adolescents is widespread. By the 8th grade more than half of all adolescents have used alcohol in the last year and by their senior year this rate increases to more than three-fourths. Frequent drinking is relatively rare. Except among male high school seniors, 2% or less of all adolescents drink daily and about 5% to 6% drink weekly. On the other hand, high quantity drinking is common. More than one-fifth of high school seniors and one-third of college students report drinking five or more drinks per occasion in the last two weeks.

Using these national data, we computed chi-square statistics for differences in prevalence rates for males and females. (These statistics are only approximations given that they are based on estimated numbers of respondents.) The data show that prevalence rates are almost identical for males and females. Only one statistically significant gender difference was found (among 12th-grade students) and that difference was less than 3%. While it is generally agreed that prevalence rates (i.e., the numbers using alcohol) are similar for males and females, the data on consumption (i.e., quantity and frequency), drinking problems, and alcohol-related expectancies clearly indicate that there are still gender differences. These differences are discussed below.

Alcohol Use Patterns

Most studies indicate that young males tend to drink more frequently than young females (Beck & Summons, 1987; Engs & Hanson, 1990; Perkins, 1992; Tortu et al., 1988), although some studies suggest that these rates may also be converging (Berkowitz & Perkins, 1987; Wechsler & McFadden, 1976; Windle & Barnes, 1988). The inconsistency in findings across studies may result from differences in measurement. For example, Wechsler and McFadden (1976) measured frequency as a dichotomy of drinking more than or less than 10 times in the last year, while others measure it as a continuous variable. The Johnston et al. (1992a,b) data indicate that significantly more male than female high school and college students drank alcohol daily, while the NIDA study (National Institute on Drug Abuse, 1991) found no significant differences in weekly drinking among youth (see Table 1).

It has consistently been reported that males drink in greater quantities than females (Barnes & Welte, 1986; Beck & Summons, 1987; Engs & Hanson, 1990; Perkins, 1992; Schall et al., 1992). However, when one controls for body weight, the findings are less consistent (Ratliff & Burkhart, 1984; Schall et al., 1992). Berkowitz and Perkins (1987) suggest that most males and females drink similar amounts, but there is a small subset of males who drink in extreme quantities and frequencies. Thus, when one compares means for males and females, males appear to be heavier drinkers, but it may be only a small subset of male drinkers who bring up the mean considerably.

Most studies of heavy drinking, which usually combine frequency and quantity, find that males drink more heavily than do females (Brennan et al., 1986; Ferrence, 1980; O'Hare 1990). A study of New York State adolescents, however, found no difference between boys and girls in terms of a quantity-frequency measure of consumption (Windle & Barnes, 1988). The data in Table 1 from the Johnston et al. (1992a,b) study show that significantly more males than females drank five or more drinks on at least one occasion in the last two weeks in both the high school and college samples. According to Johnston et al. (1992a,b), the gap in heavy drinking has narrowed over the last several years. The narrowing is due to decreases in heavy drinking by males, rather than to the increases in drinking by women that were expected by proponents of the convergence hypothesis.

Differences in beverage preference (i.e., favorite beverage) have also been noted across studies (Engs & Hanson, 1990). Beer is generally preferred by young males, while young females prefer wine (Engs & Hanson, 1990) or distilled spirits (Schall et al., 1992). Beck and Summons (1987) found that male adolescents drank significantly greater quantities of beer, wine, and distilled spirits than did females, and that males drank beer and wine more often than did females, but found no significant differences in the frequency of use of distilled spirits. Our own analyses of the Rutgers Health and Human Development Project (HHDP)[1] data indicated that, at each age level and each test occasion, males reported drinking significantly more beer than did females, and in later adolescence (18-24 years old) males also drank significantly more distilled spirits than did females. In contrast, there were no statistically significant gender differences in terms of wine quantity. In terms of frequency, males drank beer more frequently than did females, older females drank wine more frequently than did older males, and there was no gender difference in frequency of drinking distilled spirits (data not presented, but available from the authors upon request).

Gender differences interact with other demographic variables such as age and ethnicity. Existing studies indicate that differences in prevalence rates (use vs. no use) between adolescent males and females are most pronounced around 12 or 13 years old (Barnes & Welte, 1986; Ferrence 1980), but differences in heavy drinking become more pronounced with advancing age (Barnes & Welte, 1986). Schall et al. (1992) found significant gender differ-

TABLE 1
Gender Differences In Prevalence, Frequency, and Quantity
of Alcohol Use in National Survey Data (in percent)

| Measures | 1991 NATIONAL SAMPLE OF HIGH SCHOOL STUDENTS[1] | | | 1991 NATIONAL SAMPLE OF COLLEGE STUDENTS[2] | 1990 NATIONAL HOUSEHOLD SAMPLE OF ADOLESCENTS[3] |
	Grade 8	Grade 10	Grade 12	College	12–17 Years Old
Annual prevalence					
Males	54.4	71.8	79.0	89.2	40.8
Females	53.6	72.9	76.2	87.6	41.1
χ^2	1.08	2.21	16.53*	0.82	0.02
Daily use					Weekly use
Males	0.7	2.3	5.3	6.0	5.6
Females	0.3	0.4	1.6	2.5	4.5
χ^2	13.5*	99.84*	149.05*	10.85*	1.33
5+ Drinks per occasion within the last 2 weeks					
Males	14.3	26.4	37.8	52.3	
Females	11.4	19.5	21.2	34.9	
χ^2	32.45*	98.47*	482.65*	43.26*	

[1] Johnston et al., 1992a, Vol I. Adapted from Tables 52 and 54, pp. 142 and 144.
[2] Johnston et al., 1992b, Vol II. Adapted from Tables 8 and 9, pp. 59 and 61.
[3] National Institute on Drug Abuse, 1991. Adapted from Tables 13-A and 21-A, pp. 83 and 117.

*$p < .001$.

ences in heavy drinking among Anglo and Hispanic college students, but not among Asian, African, or Native American students.

Problem Drinking

Problem drinking in adolescence is generally defined in terms of heavy drinking, as a function of quantity and frequency (discussed above), or, alternatively, by the number of times intoxicated or number of alcohol-related negative consequences experienced (White, 1987). For these latter two indicators of problem drinking, most studies indicate that males score higher than females.

In the majority of studies of college students, males report getting intoxicated more often than females (Brennan et al., 1986; Engs & Hanson, 1990). In contrast, Windle and Barnes (1988) found no significant difference between male and female high school students in the number of times intoxicated in the last year. The lack of a significant gender difference in this latter study may reflect the fact that the sample is younger than most of the others studied, which could forecast a historical change for this new cohort of youth, or that the sample is from the Northeast where more liberal gender role attitudes might exist. Carr and collegues (1990) found that while male and female high school athletes drank at the same frequency, males got intoxicated significantly more often than females.

In general, the literature also suggests that male adolescents (White & Labouvie, 1989) and college students (Brennan et al., 1986; Engs & Hanson, 1990; Perkins, 1992; Ratliff & Burkhart, 1984) experience more alcohol-related problems than females, although some studies report no differences (e.g., O'Hare, 1990). The gender differential in reporting alcohol-related problems appears to be larger for white students and smaller for African-Americans (Curtis et al., 1990), probably reflecting gender-by-ethnicity interactions in drinking patterns.

When researchers examine specific types of consequences they find that males are significantly more likely to experience consequences such as fighting, nervousness due to drinking, physical injuries, family problems related to use, sexual problems, problems with school work and the law, and automobile accidents (O'Hare 1990; Perkins, 1992; Wechsler & Isaac, 1991), while the genders do not differ in terms of consequences such as blackouts, damaged friendships, self-injury, and engaging in behavior they would not have if they had not been drinking (Hughes & Dodder, 1983; Perkins, 1992; Wechsler & Isaac, 1991). Robbins (1989) suggests that a "styles of deviance perspective" is most applicable to explaining gender differences in substance abuse problems. Among youth 12 to 17 years old, she found that substance use, including alcohol use, was related more strongly to intrapsychic problems in females and to problems in psychosocial functioning among males.

Alcohol Use Expectancies and Motivations

The data indicate that, in general, adolescent males and females use alcohol for the same reasons. Both genders report drinking for sociability reasons and to meet arousal, experiential, and disinhibition needs (Berkowitz & Perkins, 1987; Ratliff & Burkhart, 1984). However, there are some drinking motivations and expectancies that differ between males and females. For example, college women expect more cognitive-physical impairments than men. Women may experience these effects more readily because they reach higher blood alcohol concentrations per dose than men do (Leigh, 1987; Rohsenow, 1983), or they may be more sensitive to greater social disapproval of women than men for showing effects of alcohol consumption (Landrine et al., 1988). Other gender differences in reasons for drinking are that male adolescents are more likely to report social cohesion reasons for alcohol use (Newcomb et al., 1988) and male adolescents are more likely to report greater social pressures to drink (Windle & Barnes, 1988). The findings are inconsistent with regard to whether or not gender differences exist in escape reasons for drinking (Berkowitz & Perkins, 1987; Newcomb et al., 1988; Ratliff & Burkhart, 1984; Rohsenow, 1983) and expectancies for more nastiness or aggressive behavior from drinking (Leigh, 1987; Ratliff & Burkhart, 1984; Rohsenow, 1983).

In addition, there appear to be gender differences in the relationship between expectancies/motivations and alcohol use patterns. For example, levels of use, intoxication, and use-related problems are more strongly related to personal psychological motivations (e.g., relief of stress, alter negative self-image, cope with personal problems) for female high school students than for males (Carman & Holmgren, 1986; Newcomb et al., 1988; Windle & Barnes, 1988). Thus, these findings support the assumption that because of the stigma against female heavy drinking, young women who drink heavily are more likely to do so to relieve stress or in response to a specific precipitating event (Ratliff & Burkhart, 1984).

Correlates and Contexts of Alcohol Use

Although the gender differential exists in terms of patterns of alcohol use and problems, some studies indicate that there are no gender differences in the theoretical predictors of drinking for male and female adolescents (Jessor & Jessor, 1977; White et al., 1986). In contrast, other studies indicate that certain variables better predict male alcohol-use involvement (such as impulsivity, rebelliousness, undercontrol, anxiety, decision-making ability) (Robins & Smith, 1980; Tortu et al., 1988), whereas other variables better predict female use (such as neurotic and depressive symptoms, parental and peer influences, somatic problems) (Berkowitz & Perkins, 1987; Johnson & Marcos, 1988; Robins & Smith, 1980; Tortu et al., 1988). Studies have also found gender differences in drinking locations and contexts (see Berkowitz & Perkins, 1987; Engs & Hanson, 1990; O'Hare, 1990). (The literature on correlates and predictors of adolescent drinking behaviors is large enough to fill a whole chapter and cannot be reviewed here. The interested reader is referred to Bucholz, 1990, and Kandel, 1980, for reviews.)

Summary

Overall, the data reviewed above indicate that males and females differ in their drinking patterns, problems, and expectancies. The fact that findings are not consistent across studies probably reflects differences in the measurement of alcohol-related variables, as well as differences in samples (e.g., age, ethnicity, region of country, etc.). Recent data suggest that there may be a narrowing of the gender differential in terms of frequency and heavy drinking, especially among younger cohorts. This narrowing appears to result from less frequent and less heavy drinking by males rather than from increases in use by females. Thus, if the current trends continue, we may see even a further convergence in the next decade. Nevertheless, the gender gap is currently significant and in the following section we examine gender-role explanations for this gap.

Gender Roles and Alcohol Use

Physiological sex differences in body weight, body water content, and metabolism that produce lower dose-related blood alcohol concentrations in males may partially account for the heavier drinking of males (Corrigan, 1985; Ferrence, 1980; Frezza et al., 1990; McCrady, 1988). However, culturally-defined gender-role norms are believed to be at least as important as biology in explaining gender differences in drinking patterns and outcomes (Heath, 1991). This may be particularly true during adolescence when drinking habits are initiated and gender-role expectations may be particularly salient (Hill & Lynch, 1983).

Sociocultural norms regarding alcohol use clearly differ between males and females. For instance, heavy drinking and intoxication are viewed as more socially acceptable for males than females and are more consistent with traditional male gender roles (e.g., Gomberg, 1982; Landrine et al., 1988; Lemle & Mishkind, 1989). Adolescents apparently share these double-standards, as boys believe that drinking enhances their social image among peers, whereas girls view their drinking as socially undesirable (Chassin et al., 1985).

These cultural gender norms may influence drinking through various mechanisms. Gender differences in parental supervision and control (Barnes, 1990) and in peer support for drinking (Harford & Grant, 1987) may influence the availability of opportunities to drink as well as the social consequences of drinking. However, one's personal gender-role identity may have a more stable and direct influence on one's drinking pattern than situational constraints imposed by parents or peers. Individuals vary in the extent to which their own gender-role identity and belief system resembles cultural gender stereotypes (Bem, 1981). Therefore, particularly during adolescence, internalized gender roles may predict drinking better than biological sex (Chomak & Collins, 1987), and may in fact account for gender differences in adolescent alcohol use (Horwitz & White, 1987).

In this section we focus on gender-role (GR) explanations of gender differences in adolescent drinking. A major complication in reviewing the literature on gender roles and alcohol use is that a multitude of diverse GR measures have been used. This review will focus on two dimensions of internalized gender roles: *gender-role attributes,* or personality traits associated with masculinity and femininity[2] and *gender-role ideology*, or attitudes toward the rights and social roles of men and women.[3]

It is important to distinguish among the diverse gender-role measures because research indicates that GR personality attributes, GR ideology, and preference for gender-linked behaviors are not highly intercorrelated (Orlofsky, 1981), and may be differentially related to alcohol use and abuse. In fact, studies that have included multiple GR measures have not always found them similarly related to drinking patterns (e.g., Snell et al., 1987; Zucker et al., 1981). Thus, one test of the adequacy of theoretical models in this area is the extent to which the model provides a comprehensive and parsimonious account of relationships between drinking and various aspects of GR identity.

In the following subsections we present two theoretical models of gender role–alcohol relationships and review empirical support for these models. Then we examine evidence that gender roles mediate (or account for) gender differences in drinking outcomes, including new analyses of the HHDP dataset.

Theoretical Models of Gender Roles and Alcohol Use

Conventionality model. Two predominant conventionality explanations have been offered to explain why internalized gender roles would be expected to influence alcohol use. Congruence models propose that individuals with conventional or "sex-typed" gender roles will conform to cultural gender norms for behavior more often than less conventional persons (Bem, 1974). Cultural standards tolerate or even encourage heavy drinking among males, but discourage and stigmatize heavy alcohol use among females (Landrine et al., 1988). Therefore, males who identify with traditionally masculine attributes would be expected to drink more heavily, and females who identify with traditionally feminine attributes would be expected to drink less heavily, compared with their less conventional counterparts.

Conversely, deviance models propose that rejection of traditional gender-role characteristics leads to adoption of behavior patterns typical of the opposite sex as a form of rebellion against conventional norms (Wilsnack & Wilsnack, 1978). Thus, females who have adopted masculine attributes would be expected to drink more, and males who have adopted feminine attributes to drink less, than their conventionally sex-typed counterparts.

Although they focus on opposite ends of the continuum, both congruence and deviance models share the assumption that it is the conventionality of gender-role identity that explains the relationship between gender roles and alcohol use. Furthermore, both models predict the same empirical pattern when gender roles are used as continuous measures: masculine attributes should be positively or directly related to drinking and feminine attributes should be negatively or inversely related to drinking. In other words, highly masculine males and females would be expected to drink more than those low on masculinity. Conversely, highly feminine males and females should drink less than low femininity individuals. Therefore, we consider both congruence and deviance models "conventionality" explanations of gender role–alcohol use relations.

The conventionality model predicts that the effects of GR ideology will differ by gender, because more traditional attitudes should predict conformity to cultural drinking norms that are more supportive of drinking by males than by females. Thus, traditional males would be expected to drink much more heavily than traditional females, whereas less traditional males and females should exhibit relatively similar drinking patterns. In other words, traditional GR attitudes should predict greater alcohol use among males, but less drinking among females.

Functional-value model. An alternative explanation for relationships between gender-role attributes and drinking patterns (Huselid & Cooper, 1992) is based on Spence's (1984) premise that gender-role attribute scales assess personality traits, not larger concepts of gender-role identity. That is, the masculinity dimension measures instrumental traits and femininity measures expressive traits. The functional-value model proposes that GR attributes may be related to drinking patterns because of their functional, adaptive value as personality traits.

Consistent with this interpretation, instrumentality has been found to serve as an active, adaptive style of coping with problematic situations (Hamilton & Fagot, 1988; Towbes et al., 1989). Similarly, expressive attributes may buffer the effects of life stress on alcohol use (Snell et al., 1987). Thus, instrumentality and expressivity may be inversely correlated with alcohol use and drinking problems because highly instrumental or expressive individuals may be less likely to drink to cope with stressful life situations than individuals low in these attributes.

In contrast, less socially desirable aspects of traditional masculinity (e.g., arrogance, overcontrol of emotion) and femininity (e.g., overly dependent, nagging) may not be adaptive. These traits can make it harder to get along with other people and can provoke negative reactions that make a person feel unpopular, devalued, or incompetent. These adverse social effects of undesirable gender attributes may lead adolescents to seek solace or escape in *greater* substance use. Thus, unlike the conventionality model, the functional-value model predicts differential relationships between desirable and undesirable GR attributes and drinking outcomes. However, the functional explanation does not account for the effects of traditional GR ideology on drinking.

In summary, the two major gender-role theories suggest that gender roles predict drinking because individuals with conventional GR identities conform to cultural double-standards regarding alcohol use (Bem, 1981) or, in contrast, because desirable GR personality traits prevent excessive or problematic drinking, whereas undesirable GR attributes make one more vulnerable to problem drinking (Spence, 1984). These theories not only predict different empirical patterns as summarized in the next paragraph, but also have distinct implications regarding how gender roles may influence the development of drinking problems. The conventionality model suggests that gender roles determine how comfortable we are deviating from cultural gender norms, and thus influence our behavior directly, particularly in a social context. However, the functional model suggests that GR socialization influences our personality traits, which in turn influence how easily we feel stressed and how likely we are to use alcohol or other drugs to cope with stress. In other words, the functional explanation suggests that gender roles influence drinking patterns indirectly, through their influence on stress and coping processes.

Both the conventionality and functional models predict an inverse relationship between positively valued feminine traits and alcohol use, but make contrasting predictions for the effects of socially undesirable feminine attributes on drinking. Similarly, both models predict a direct association between undesirable masculine traits and alcohol outcomes, but make opposite predictions for valued masculine attributes. In the following section, we examine the empirical evidence consistent with these two theoretical models.

Empirical Evidence

Feminine attributes. As stated above, both models predict inverse relationships between alcohol use and desirable feminine attributes such as emotional warmth and concern for others. Although femininity has not reliably predicted whether adolescents drink or abstain (Huselid & Cooper, 1992; Wilsnack & Wilsnack, 1978), these attributes have consistently predicted less alcohol consumption (quantity and frequency of use), particularly among females (Huselid & Cooper, 1992; Snell et al., 1987; Wilsnack & Wilsnack, 1978). Similar findings have been obtained with other GR measures. Among college students, preference for feminine gender-role behaviors has been inversely related to alcohol consumption (Chomak & Collins, 1987), as has a bipolar femininity measure (Parker, 1975).

A similar inverse relationship has also been obtained between femininity and drinking problems in adolescence (Horwitz & White, 1987; Huselid & Cooper, 1992; Koch-Hattem & Denman, 1987; Wilsnack & Wilsnack, 1978). Finally, expressive attributes have also been inversely related to a composite measure of alcohol/drug use and delinquency among males (Spence et al., 1979). In sum, consistent with both theoretical models, feminine expressive attributes have predicted less alcohol use and drinking problems across a number of adolescent samples using several different femininity measures.

Fewer studies have examined the effects of undesirable feminine attributes on drinking, although given the contrasting theoretical predictions this is a promising area for future research. Socially undesirable feminine traits should be inversely related to drinking based on the conventionality model, but directly related to drinking from the functional-value perspective. The Extended Personal Attribute Questionnaire (Spence et al., 1979) measures two negative feminine attributes—one dimension characterized by being "spineless" and overly dependent on others, the other tapping chronic complaining or whining. Surprisingly, both dimensions have predicted greater alcohol use among males, but not among females (Snell et al., 1987; Spence et al., 1979).

Masculine attributes. Several personality attributes have been associated with traditional masculinity, including both socially desirable (e.g., instrumentality) and undesirable traits (e.g., aggressiveness, overcontrol of emotion). According to the conventionality model, both types of masculine traits should predict greater alcohol use. However, the functional-value model predicts that only dysfunctional attributes will increase drinking, whereas adaptive attributes will be associated with less drinking. Consistent with both models, undesirable masculine traits have been associated with heavy and problematic alcohol use among adolescent males (Mosher & Sirkin, 1984; Wilsnack & Wilsnack, 1980) and across both genders (Snell et al., 1987; Spence et al., 1979).

In contrast, the effects of socially desirable masculine attributes appear to vary between alcohol outcomes. Consistent with the conventionality model, instrumentality has been associated with being a drinker rather than a nondrinker, but only among males (Huselid & Cooper, 1992; Lapp, 1984; Wilsnack & Wilsnack, 1980). However, consistent with the functional-value model, instrumental attributes have been inversely related to alcohol-related problems (Horwitz & White, 1987; Huselid & Cooper, 1992; Koch-Hattem & Denman, 1987). Finally, instrumentality has been unrelated to the quantity and frequency of alcohol use among adolescents (Huselid & Cooper, 1992; Snell et al., 1987; Wilsnack & Wilsnack, 1980).

In sum, masculine instrumental attributes have been found to increase the likelihood that a male adolescent will be a drinker, do not predict the amount of alcohol adolescents drink, and yet decrease the likelihood that adolescents experience drinking problems. These mixed findings may reflect qualitative differences between these outcomes, with the most serious negative outcomes inversely related to adaptive traits (i.e., instrumentality) as the functional-value model predicts, but with normative experiences such as trying alcohol directly related to adaptive traits. The failure to find a consistent relationship between adaptive traits and quantity-frequency measures may reflect the fact that these measures encompass the full range of use, from an occasional drink to heavy drinking. These findings, indicating that gender roles are differentially related to various alcohol outcomes, underscore the need for researchers to examine a wide range of drinking behaviors recognizing that not all drinking is excessive or problematic.

In addition, the association of instrumentality and alcohol use may be clarified by using less global, more context-specific measures of instrumentality. Wills and associates (1989) found various dimensions of assertiveness differentially related to substance use. General assertiveness, which is similar to the masculinity measures, was unrelated to use. However, the ability to assertively resist pressure to drink was inversely related to use, and assertiveness in social or dating situations was directly related to substance use. Moreover, this study indicates that male and female adolescents differ not only in overall levels of general assertiveness, but also in the contexts in which they feel comfortable asserting themselves. Girls may be more comfortable refusing alcohol than boys, which may explain why alcohol-specific assertiveness predicted actual alcohol use more accurately among girls than among boys.

Gender-role ideology. The relationship between GR ideology and alcohol use provides a clear test of the conventionality model, because these scales directly tap the conventionality of GR beliefs. Moreover, GR ideology is not generally considered a functional personality attribute, and therefore these effects are not subject to a functional-value interpretation.

The conventionality model predicts that traditional GR beliefs should be directly related to alcohol use among males, and inversely related to alcohol use among females. Data on females are consistent with this prediction. Across adolescent and young adult age groups, nondrinkers or light drinkers hold more traditional GR attitudes than heavier drinkers (Parker, 1975; Zucker et al., 1981). Similarly, young women who hold nontraditional or egalitarian attitudes about domestic roles consume more alcohol than more traditional women, even after controlling for employment status, education, and other demographic variables (Parker & Harford, 1992). Not surprisingly, female adolescents who specifically believe that drinking is less appropriate for women are less likely to drink, and this attitude is also inversely related to alcohol consumption and problem drinking among drinkers (Wilsnack & Wilsnack, 1978).

Fewer studies have considered the effects of GR attitudes on male adolescents' alcohol use or abuse. A national sample of young adult males found no association between attitudes toward domestic roles and either alcohol consumption or alcohol-related problems (Parker & Harford, 1992). However, other studies have found the predicted relationship between traditional beliefs and heavier drinking. Among males, endorsement of "macho" attitudes toward women and toward male roles has been directly associated with alcohol use (Mosher & Sirkin, 1984; Pleck et al., 1994), as has the traditional view that men should not help with household chores (Wilsnack & Wilsnack, 1980). Finally, a recent study including both genders found the expected gender-by-GR ideology interaction (Huselid & Cooper, 1992). Traditional GR ideology was directly related to alcohol use, heavy drinking, and drinking problems among male adolescents, whereas among females these relation-ships were inverse in direction, but nonsignificant. Thus, overall, the findings support the conventionality model prediction that females with traditional gender-role attitudes drink less, whereas males with conventional gender-role attitudes drink more than their nonconventional counterparts.

Summary. This review of the literature reveals partial support for both functional-value and conventionality explanations of gender-role effects on drinking. Consistent with the functional-value model and in contrast to con-ventionality hypotheses, masculine instrumental attributes have been con-sistently inversely related to drinking problems, and undesirable aspects of femininity have been directly related to drinking, at least among males. On the other hand, the GR ideology findings provide unambiguous support for the conventionality model. Traditional GR attitudes have been directly related to drinking among males and inversely related among females, indi-cating that the conventionality of GR beliefs predicts how closely personal drinking habits conform to cultural norms. However, both explanations can account for the robust findings obtained—that alcohol outcomes are in-versely related to positive valued feminine traits and directly related to nega-tive aspects of masculinity. In sum, it remains unclear whether gender-role attributes are related to alcohol use because they represent adoption of a con-ventional or nonconventional gender-role identity, or because they have func-tional value as coping strategies. Resolution of the theoretical debate will require additional research.

Gender Roles as Mediators of Gender Differences

Implicit in the literature on gender roles and alcohol use is the assumption that internalized gender roles account for gender differences in drinking. De-spite the face validity of this idea, there is little empirical evidence directly testing the extent to which gender differences are "mediated" or reduced by controlling for gender roles. Such analyses would remove the "variance" or variability in drinking behavior that is explained by gender-role characteris-tics and observe whether biological sex differences are smaller in magnitude than they were initially. Complete mediation exists if gender roles account for a large proportion of the gender differences and male/female differences in alcohol use are no longer significant after removing gender-role effects (Baron & Kenny, 1986). In this subsection, we review existing data and present new analyses testing the hypothesis that gender roles mediate gender differences in adolescent drinking.

Chomak and Collins (1987) found that a GR behavior measure (preference for gender-linked hobbies, occupations) accounted for more variance in total alcohol use and in beer drinking (11–12%) than did biological sex. Unfortu-nately, few other studies have compared the variance accounted for by gender and gender roles. However, in a formal test of the GR mediation hypothesis, Huselid and Cooper (1992) found that gender-role attributes and ideology substantially mediated the gender-alcohol relationship. Gender differences in the frequency of alcohol use and in drinking to intoxication were eliminated by controlling for gender roles. Gender differences in quantity consumed, frequency of heavy drinking (five or more drinks per occasion), and drinking problems were also reduced, but remained statistically significant after removing gender-role effects. The standardized regression coefficients for alcohol use were reduced by amounts ranging from 26% to 71%, whereas for drinking problems the coefficients were reduced by a more modest 16%. Thus, these findings suggest that gender roles account for a substantial portion of gender differences in alcohol use, although the magnitude of the effect may vary between alcohol measures. Interestingly, the extent to which gender roles mediated gender differences did not vary across age groups (13 to 19) or by ethnicity (i.e., African-American vs. white). Of course, these findings must be replicated before they can be generalized.

To this end, we briefly summarize new analyses on this issue using longitudinal data from the HHDP described previously (see footnote 1). Given that both gender roles and drinking patterns change during the course of adolescence, the mediation hypothesis is examined cross-sectionally and results compared across time. Analyses were conducted on 1,270 primarily white, middle- and working-class respondents at three points in time, separated by three years. Respondents ranged from 12 to 18 years of age at Time 1, 15 to 21 at Time 2, and 18 to 24 at Time 3, thereby providing data on the transition from adolescence into early adulthood.

Multiple regression analyses[4] were conducted following procedures described previously (Huselid & Cooper, 1992) and using similar measures of both gender roles and alcohol use. As shown in Table 2, results indicated only weak mediation effects, with reductions ranging from 0% to 28% in the coefficients for gender when GR effects were removed. After controlling for age and race, the variance accounted for by both gender and gender roles was modest (1% to 7%), but the effects of gender per se increased longitudinally with age. Gender roles mediated gender effects on frequency of drinking from late adolescence on, and mediated problems at all ages. That is, gender-related rules of behavior were most likely to influence how often a young person would drink and the likelihood that that person would experience negative consequences due to drinking.

Tests of the mediation hypothesis using beverage-specific measures revealed more consistent GR mediation effects for beer drinking than for wine or distilled spirits. The findings suggested that beer is not only the most strongly gender-linked alcoholic beverage, but is also most reliably related to internalized gender roles. As with overall alcohol use, gender and gender roles accounted for more variance in beer drinking as respondents grew older. (These data are not presented here but are available from the authors upon request.)

The pattern of GR effects on alcohol outcomes indicates few significant effects of masculine and feminine attributes on alcohol use. In three instances, traditional gender ideology is positively related to heavy drinking and drinking problems. This results because more heavy drinking and related problems occur among young men, and men have more traditional gender role attitudes. This observation is made clear by the significant gender by GR ideology interactions obtained across all measures, consistent with the conventionality model. Probes of these interactions revealed the predicted pattern: traditional attitudes were directly related to drinking among males and inversely related to drinking among females. Therefore, these findings support the conventionality model.

Conclusions and Suggestions for Future Research

Although studies have demonstrated a gender differential in alcohol use, caution must be used when interpreting these differences for several reasons. For example, some research suggests that males underreport drinking more often than females and that males as compared to females more often indicate that their reports are unreliable (Ferrence, 1980). Thus, the gender differential may be even larger than the data suggest. Similarly, women may either be more perceptive in their attribution of problems and, thus, report proportionally higher rates of problems than men, or because of the stigma associated with female drinking they may be less likely to report negative consequences related to alcohol use (Robbins, 1989; Wilsnack & Wilsnack, 1978). In addition, lists of alcohol-related expectancies and problems are often biased in favor of higher reports by males. In many studies, the consequence lists are slanted toward socially disruptive (externalized) negative consequences and exclude less visible negative consequences such as depression and unwanted sex, which are more often experienced by young women (Berkowitz & Perkins, 1987; Ferrence, 1980). Further, female adolescents often drink with male companions who may protect them from some adverse consequences of their use, such as driving under the influence. Therefore, future research needs to explore a broader range of motivations and consequences.

The data presented above also indicate that gender differences vary by beverage type, with beer drinking more strongly related to gender and gender roles than wine or spirits. Thus, studies that rely on overall alcohol consumption may overlook interesting gender differences in drinking preferences that would be clarified by future research examining beverage types separately. In addition, given that women reach higher dose-related blood alcohol concentrations (BACs) than men due to differences in body weight and metabolism (Frezza et al., 1990), quantity measures should take these factors

TABLE 2
Significant Standardized Regression Coefficients (Betas) for Gender Controlling for Gender Roles

Alcohol Measures	TIME 1				TIME 2				TIME 3			
	Freq.	Quan.	Intox.	Prob.	Freq.	Quan.	Intox.	Prob.	Freq.	Quan.	Intox.	Prob.
Step 1: Age and Race												
R^2	.45***	.37***	.44***	.39***	.27***	.10***	.19***	.17***	.05***	.04***	.05***	.04***
Step 2: Gender												
R^2 change	.01***	.02***	.01***	.01***	.02***	.05***	.01***	.02***	.04***	.07***	.03***	.04***
β	.09***	.14***	.08***	.10***	.13***	.22***	.10***	.12***	.19***	.26***	.17***	.20***
Step 3: Gender Roles												
R^2 change	—[1]	.01*	—[1]	.01**	—[1]	.01*	—[1]	.01*	.01**	—[1]	—[1]	.01*
β gender controlling for gender roles	.09***	.11***	.09***	.07**	.11***	.19***	.10***	.10**	.14***	.23***	.15***	.15***
Percent reduction in beta for gender	0%	19%	0%	28%	21%	15%	2%	19%	27%	12%	11%	27%
β Femininity (Fem.)									-.07*		-.07*	-.10**
β Masculinity (Masc.)		.07**				.08**			.08**			
β GR ideology				.08**				.07*				
Step 4: Interactions												
R^2 change	—[1]	.01**	—[1]	—[1]	.01**	.01***	—[1]	.01*	.01*	.01**	—[1]	.01*
β Fem. × Gender												
β Masc. × Gender												
β Ideology × Gender	.09**	.12***	.09**	.09*	.15***	.14***	.09**	.13***	.13***	.15***	.11*	.10*

Notes: Gender was coded: 0 = female, 1 = male. Masculine and feminine attributes were assessed by the PAQ (Spence et al., 1974). The GR ideology measure (adapted from Kirkpatrick, 1936) was coded so that higher scores indicate more traditional attitudes. Alcohol measures were log transformed prior to analysis to reduce skewness and kurtosis.
* $p < .05$. ** $p < .01$. *** $p < .001$.
[1]R^2 change less than .01.

into account. For example, typical BACs could be computed rather than relying on number of drinks consumed. Additional research in this area may provide support for the idea that gender-linked beverage preferences are related to physiological gender differences. For instance, researchers have suggested that women prefer wine because it has lower alcohol content than distilled spirits and fewer calories than beer, thus by drinking wine they can avoid becoming intoxicated or full as quickly as with other alcoholic beverages (Chomak & Collins, 1987).

Our review of the literature indicates that gender continues to be a reliable predictor of adolescent drinking patterns and this fact may be due in part to internalized gender roles. However, the extent of these mediating effects may differ depending on the alcohol use and GR measures used, thus these findings must be replicated before the magnitude of the effects can be evaluated. Future research could also extend current findings by using GR measures that include negative aspects of masculine and feminine roles, particularly since "macho" aggressive attributes and attitudes appear to be robust predictors of problematic alcohol use among male adolescents. In addition, a full understanding of the etiology of gender differences in drinking may require studies of possible mediators such as physiological factors and gender differences both in drinking opportunities and in social reactions to drinking behavior.

Additional tests of the mediation hypothesis would also provide a better indication of whether GR effects are robust enough to have clinically meaningful effects on alcohol use and abuse, or on other expressions of deviance (e.g., drug abuse, delinquency) in adolescence and into adulthood. Our analyses suggest that young women with nontraditional or egalitarian attitudes toward women's roles drink more heavily than young women with traditional beliefs, and young men with traditional attitudes drink more heavily than those with less traditional views. However, it is not clear whether these differences in alcohol use during adolescence are related to the development of alcohol-related problems later on. Thus, at present we must be cautious in drawing conclusions about the effects of gender roles in adolescence on later alcohol abuse.

The theoretical issues raised by this review also require further study. Robust findings have been obtained where conventionality and functional value predictions are identical, and contradictory results have been observed where predictions differ. This pattern suggests that individual differences may moderate whether gender roles predict drinking because of their functional value, or because they reflect conformity to gender norms. For example, recent evidence suggests that conventionality predictions apply more accurately to sex-typed individuals (high masculine-low feminine males; high feminine-low masculine females), whereas functional-value predictions are supported among those with a balance of masculine and feminine traits (Huselid & Cooper, 1993). Based upon these findings, we might expect that masculine men who lack socially desirable feminine characteristics would be at higher risk for developing alcohol-related problems than androgynous men who have both socially valued masculine and feminine attributes. It would be interesting to determine if these same findings would apply to masculine (cross-sex typed) females.

Additional research testing potential moderators of these two theoretical mechanisms may improve our understanding of why gender roles are related to alcohol use. Such research might help identify GR attributes that put individuals at high or low risk for alcohol-related problems regardless of biological sex, which, in turn, could inform prevention and intervention efforts. In addition, new research could be designed to more directly test assumptions underlying both models. For instance, more research is needed to test the functional-value premise that instrumental and expressive attributes are closely related to coping styles and that they buffer the effects of stress on alcohol use. Of course, alcohol use is only one of many possible responses to stress. Therefore, the functional value of gender roles in buffering stress should be examined across a wider range of outcomes including depression and delinquency (Horwitz & White, 1987).

Finally, the extant literature on gender roles and alcohol use is cross-sectional, therefore causal relationships between these variables are unclear. Prospective research designs, such as the HHDP, are needed to determine whether GR characteristics predict subsequent drinking patterns, or vice-versa. These temporal relationships could best be tested using structural equation modeling techniques that control for a major problem inherent in longitudinal research, that is, that measurement error is correlated across time. Our next step is to do this type of analysis with the HHDP data.

In sum, our reading of the literature leads us to conclude that both biological sex and gender roles have substantial effects on adolescent drinking patterns. However, much remains to be learned about *how* and *why* alcohol use is linked to gender and gender roles. Thus, future research that specifically examines the theoretical underpinnings of these relationships using longitudinal research designs, more comprehensive gender-role measures, and powerful data analytic techniques would provide valuable information on the development of gender-role identity and on gender differences in drinking patterns during adolescence. Most importantly, this research may reveal causal mechanisms linking gender and gender norms with substance use and abuse.

Acknowledgments

Preparation of this chapter was supported in part by grants from the National Institute on Drug Abuse (DA/AA-03095), the Alcoholic Beverage Medical Research Foundation, and the National Institute of Mental Health (MH16242). The authors thank Drs. Firoozeh Vali and Allan Horwitz for their comments and suggestions.

Notes

1. The Rutgers Health and Human Development Project (HHDP) is a longitudinal study of the development of alcohol and drug using behaviors from adolescence into adulthood. Subjects were originally identified by a random telephone survey in New Jersey. Interested participants and their parents were interviewed in their homes and subsequently came to the test site for a full day of testing. The subjects were tested initially between 1979 and 1981 (Time 1) at the ages of 12, 15, and 18 ($N=1,380$). Subjects were retested in 1982-84 (Time 2) and again in 1985-87 (Time 3) for a 92% completion rate across all three measurement occasions. Overall, the data suggest that the sample of participants is most representative of nonminority adolescents living in a metropolitan, working- and middle-class environment. (For more information about the study, see Pandina et al., 1984.)
2. For two decades, the predominant GR measures have assessed personality attributes associated with concepts of masculinity and femininity. Although masculinity and femininity were originally assessed as opposite poles on a single continuum, this view has been criticized (e.g., Constantinople, 1973) and such measures have been largely replaced with scales that assess these as two separate dimensions. The most widely used measures are the Bem Sex Role Inventory (BSRI; Bem, 1974) and Personal Attributes Questionnaire (PAQ; Spence et al., 1974). On both measures, masculinity is characterized by instrumental traits (e.g., active, confident), whereas femininity taps socioemotional or expressive qualities (e.g., warm, kind). Both measures have been criticized for focusing exclusively on socially desirable attributes, which led to the development of measures that also tap negative aspects of traditional gender roles (e.g., Spence et al., 1979).
3. Measures of gender-role ideology include attitudes toward feminism or female roles (e.g., Smith et al., 1975) and toward male roles (Snell, 1986), as well as items assessing traditional occupational choices or the importance of fulfilling traditional family roles (Wilsnack et al., 1986).
4. Multiple regression is a method by which we attempt to predict the occurrence or magnitude of a single dependent variable (e.g., times intoxicated) from a number of independent variables (e.g., age, race, gender, masculinity, femininity, and gender role ideology). We look at how much variation (the amount of variance, R^2) in each dependent variable is explained by different sets of predictors. In addition, in these hierarchical regression analyses, we look at the change in variance that occurs as we add new independent variables to the model. We also examine the standardized regression coefficients (beta weights), which tell us how much change in the dependent variable is predicted by each independent variable after controlling for all the other independent variables in the model. A coefficient of 1.0 implies that one standard deviation of change in the predictor would produce one standard deviation of change in the dependent variable. Interaction effects imply that two variables occurring together have an effect that differs from the sum of their separate effects.

References

Barnes, G.M. (1990). Impact of the family on adolescent drinking patterns. In R.L. Collins, K.E. Leonard, & J.S. Searles (Eds.), *Alcohol and the family: Research and clinical perspectives* (pp. 137-161). New York: Guilford.
Barnes, G.M., & Welte, J.W. (1986). Patterns and predictors of alcohol use among 7-12th grade students in New York state. *Journal of Studies on Alcohol, 47*, 53-62.

Baron, R. M., & Kenny, D.A. (1986). The moderator-mediator variable distinction in social psychological research: Conceptual, strategic, and statistical considerations.
Journal of Personality and Social Psychology, 51, 1173-1182.

Beck, K.H., & Summons, T.G. (1987). Adolescent gender differences in alcohol beliefs
and behaviors. *Journal of Alcohol and Drug Education, 33*(1), 31-44.

Bem, S.L. (1974). The measurement of psychological androgyny. *Journal of Consulting and Clinical Psychology, 42*, 155-162.

Bem, S.L. (1981). Gender Schema Theory: A cognitive account of sex typing. *Psychological Review, 88*, 354-364.

Berkowitz, A.D., & Perkins, H.W. (1987). Recent research on gender differences in collegiate alcohol use. *Journal of American College Health, 36*, 123-129.

Brennan, A.F., Walfish, S., & AuBuchon, P. (1986). Alcohol use and abuse in college students: I. A review of individual and personality correlates. *International Journal
of the Addictions, 21*, 449-474.

Bucholz, K.K. (1990). A review of correlates of alcohol use and alcohol problems in
adolescence. In M. Galanter (Ed.), *Recent developments in alcoholism: Vol. 8.
Combined alcohol and other drug dependence* (pp. 111-123). New York: Plenum.

Carman, R.S., & Holmgren, C. (1986). Gender differences in the relationship of drinking motivations and outcomes. *Journal of Psychology, 120*, 375-378.

Carr, C.N., Kennedy, S.R., & Dimick, K.M. (1990). Alcohol use among high school athletes: A comparison of alcohol use and intoxication in male and female high school
athletes and non athletes. *Journal of Alcohol and Drug Education, 36*(1), 39-43.

Chassin, L., Tetzloff, C., & Hershey, M. (1985). Self-image and social-image factors in
adolescent alcohol use. *Journal of Studies on Alcohol, 46*, 39-47.

Chomak, S., & Collins, R.L. (1987). Relationship between sex-role behaviors and alcohol consumption in undergraduate men and women. *Journal of Studies on Alcohol, 48*, 194-201.

Constantinople, A. (1973). Masculinity-femininity: An exception to the famous dic-
tum? *Psychological Bulletin, 80*, 389-407.

Corrigan, E.M. (1985). Gender differnces in alcohol and other drug use. *Addictive Behaviors, 10*, 313-317.

Curtis, K., Genaro, S., Roberts, A., & Kayson, W.A. (1990). Effects of sex, race and year
in college on self-reported drinking-related problem behaviors. *Psychological Reports, 66*, 871-874.

Engs, R.C., & Hanson, D.J. (1990). Gender differences in drinking patterns and problems among college students: A review of the literature. *Journal of Alcohol and
Drug Education, 35* (2), 36-47.

Ferrence, R.G. (1980). Sex differences in the prevalence of problem drinking. In O.J.
Kalant (Ed.), *Research advances in alcohol and drug problems: Vol. 5. Alcohol
and drug problems in women* (pp. 69-124). New York: Plenum.

Frezza, M., DiPadova, C., Pozzato, G., Terpin, M., Baraona, E., & Lieber, C.S. (1990).
High blood alcohol levels in women: The role of decreased gastric alcohol dehydrogenase activity and first-pass metabolism. *New England Journal of Medicine,
322*, 95-99.

Gomberg, E.S.L. (1982). Historical and political perspective: Women and drug use.
Journal of Social Issues, 38, 9-23.

Hamilton, S., & Fagot, B.I. (1988). Chronic stress and coping styles: A comparison of
male and female undergraduates. *Journal of Personality and Social Psychology,
55*, 819-823.

Harford, T.C., & Grant, B.F. (1987). Psychosocial factors in adolescent drinking contexts. *Journal of Studies on Alcohol, 48*, 551-557.

Heath, D.B. (1991). Women and alcohol: Cross-cultural perspectives. *Journal of Substance Abuse, 3*, 175-185.

Hill, J.P., & Lynch, M.E. (1983). The intensification of gender-related role expectations during early adolescence. In J. Brooks-Gunn & A.C. Petersen, *Girls at puberty: Biological and psychosocial perspectives* (pp. 201-28). New York: Plenum Press.

Horwitz, A.V., & White, H.R. (1987). Gender role orientations and styles of pathology among adolescents. *Journal of Health and Social Behavior, 28*, 158-170.

Hughes, S.P., & Dodder, R.A. (1983). Alcohol consumption patterns among college populations. *Journal of College Student Personnel, 24*, 257-264.

Huselid, R.F., & Cooper, M.L. (1992). Gender roles as mediators of sex differences in adolescent alcohol use and abuse. *Journal of Health and Social Behavior, 33*, 348-362.

Huselid, R.F., & Cooper, M.L. (1993, August). *Sex-type as moderator of internalized and externalized distress.* Paper presented at American Psychological Association meetings in Toronto, Canada.

Jessor, R., & Jessor, S.L. (1977). *Problem behavior and psychosocial development: A longitudinal study of youth.* New York: Academic Press.

Johnson, R.E., & Marcos, A.C. (1988). Correlates of adolescent drug use by gender and geographic location. *American Journal of Drug and Alcohol Abuse, 14*, 51-63.

Johnston, L.D., O'Malley, P.M., & Bachman, J.G. (1992a). *Smoking, drinking, and illicit drug use among American secondary school students, college students, and young adults, 1975-1991: Vol. I. Secondary school students* (NIH Publication No. 93-3480). Rockville, MD: National Institute on Drug Abuse.

Johnston, L.D., O'Malley, P.M., & Bachman, J.G. (1992b). *Smoking, drinking, and illicit drug use among American secondary school students, college students, and young adults, 1975-1991: Vol.II. College students and young adults* (NIH Publication No. 93-3481). Rockville, MD: National Institute on Drug Abuse.

Kandel, D.B. (1980). Drug and drinking behavior among youth. *Annual Review of Sociology, 6*, 235-285.

Kirkpatrick, C. (1936). The construction of a belief-pattern scale for measuring attitudes towards feminism. *Journal of Social Psychology, 7*, 421-437.

Koch-Hattem, A., & Denman, D. (1987). Factors associated with young adult alcohol abuse. *Alcohol and Alcoholism, 22*, 181-192.

Landrine, H., Bardwell, S., & Dean, T. (1988). Gender expectations for alcohol use: A study of the significance of the masculine role. *Sex Roles, 19*, 703-712.

Lapp, J.E. (1984). Psychotropic drug and alcohol use by Montreal college students: Sex, ethnic and personality correlates. *Journal of Alcohol and Drug Education, 30* (1), 18-26.

Leigh, B.C. (1987). Beliefs about the effects of alcohol on self and others. *Journal of Studies on Alcohol, 48*, 467-475.

Lemle, R., & Mishkind, M.E. (1989). Alcohol and masculinity. *Journal of Substance Abuse Treatment, 6*, 213-222.

McCrady, B.S. (1988). Alcoholism. In E.A. Blechman & K.O. Brownell (Eds.), *Handbook of behavioral medicine for women* (pp. 356-368). New York: Pergamon.

Mosher, D.L., & Sirkin, M. (1984). Measuring a macho personality constellation. *Journal of Research in Personality, 18*, 150-163.

National Institute on Drug Abuse. (1991). *National household survey on drug abuse: Population estimates 1990* (DHHS Publication No. ADM 91-1732). Washington, DC: U.S. Government Printing Office.

Newcomb, M.D., Chou, C-P., Bentler, P.M., & Huba, G.J. (1988). Cognitive motivations for drug use among adolescents: Longitudinal tests of gender differences and predictors of change in drug use. *Journal of Counseling Psychology, 35*, 426-438.

O'Hare, T.M. (1990). Drinking in college: Consumption patterns, problems, sex differences and legal drinking age. *Journal of Studies on Alcohol, 51*, 536-541.

Orlofsky, J.L. (1981). Relationship between sex role attitudes and personality traits and the sex role behavior scale-1: A new measure of masculine and feminine role behaviors and interests. *Journal of Personality and Social Psychology, 40*, 927-940.

Pandina, R.J., Labouvie, E.W., & White, H.R. (1984). Potential contributions of the life span developmental approach to the study of adolescent alcohol and drug use: The Rutgers Health and Human Development Project, a working model. *Journal of Drug Issues,14*, 253-268.

Parker, D.A., & Harford, T.C. (1992). Gender-role attitudes, job competition and alcohol consumption among women and men. *Alcoholism: Clinical and Experimental Research, 16*, 159-165.

Parker, F.B. (1975). Sex-role adjustment and drinking disposition of women college students. *Journal of Studies on Alcohol, 36*, 1570-1573.

Perkins, H.W. (1992). Gender patterns in consequences of collegiate alcohol abuse: A 10-year study of trends in an undergraduate population. *Journal of Studies on Alcohol, 53*, 458-462.

Pleck, J.H., Sonenstein, F.L., & Ku, L.C. (1994). Problem behaviors and masculinity ideology in adolescent males. In R. Ketterlinus & M.E. Lamb (Eds.), *Adolescent problem behaviors* (pp. 165-186). Hillsdale, NJ: Erlbaum.

Ratliff, K.G., & Burkhart, B.R. (1984). Sex differences in motivations for and effects of drinking among college students. *Journal of Studies on Alcohol, 45*, 26-32.

Robbins, C. (1989). Sex differences in psychosocial consequences of alcohol and drug abuse. *Journal of Health and Social Behavior, 30*, 117-130.

Robins, L.N., & Smith, E.M. (1980). Longitudinal studies of alcohol and drug problems: Sex differences. In O.J. Kalant (Ed.), *Research advances in alcohol and drug problems: Vol 5. Alcohol and drug problems in women* (pp. 203-232). New York: Plenum.

Rohsenow, D.J. (1983). Drinking habits and expectancies about alcohol's effects for self versus others. *Journal of Consulting and Clinical Psychology, 51*, 752-756.

Schall, M., Kemeny, A., & Maltzman, I. (1992). Factors associated with alcohol use in university students. *Journal of Studies on Alcohol, 53*, 122-136.

Smith, E.R., Ferree, M.M., & Miller, F.D. (1975). A short scale of attitudes toward feminism. *Representative Research in Social Psychology, 6*, 51-56.

Snell, W.E. (1986). The masculine role inventory: Components and correlates. *Sex Roles, 15*, 443-455.

Snell, W.E. Jr., Belk, S.S., & Hawkins, R.C. (1987). Alcohol and drug use in stressful times: The influence of the masculine role and sex-related personality attributes. *Sex Roles, 16*, 359-373.

Spence, J.T. (1984). Masculinity, femininity, and gender-related traits: A conceptual analysis and critique of current research. *Progress in Experimental Personality Research, 13*, 1-97.

Spence, J.T., Helmreich, R.L., & Holahan, C.K. (1979). Negative and positive components of psychological masculinity and femininity and their relationships to self-reports of neurotic and acting out behaviors. *Journal of Personality and Social Psychology, 37*, 1673-1682.

Spence, J.T., Helmreich, R.L., & Stapp, J. (1974). The Personal Attributes Questionaire: A measure of sex-role stereotypes and masculinity-femininity. *Journal Supplement Abstract Service Catalog of Selected Documents in Psychology, 4*, 43.

Temple, M. (1987). Alcohol use among male and female college students: Has there been a convergence? *Youth and Society, 19*, 44-72.

Tortu, S., Bettes, B.A., Baker, E., & Botvin, G.J. (1988, November). Gender differences in correlates of substance use: Implications for prevention. Paper presented at the 116th annual meeting of the American Public Health Association, Boston, MA.

Towbes, L.C., Cohen, L.H., & Glyshaw, K. (1989). Instrumentality as a life-stress moderator for early versus middle adolescents. *Journal of Personality and Social Psychology, 57*, 109-119.

Wechsler, H., & Isaac, N. (1991). *Alcohol and the college freshman:"Binge" drinking and associated problems*. Washington, DC: AAA Foundation for Traffic Safety.

Wechsler, H., & McFadden, M. (1976). Sex differences in adolescent alcohol and drug use: A disappearing phenomenon. *Journal of Studies on Alcohol, 37*, 1291-1301.

White, H.R. (1987). Longitudinal stability and dimensional structure of problem drinking in adolescence. *Journal of Studies on Alcohol, 48*, 541-550.

White, H.R., Hansell, S., & Brick, J. (1993). Alcohol use and violent behavior among youth. *Alcohol Health & Research World, 17*, 144-150.

White, H.R., Johnson, V., & Horwitz, A. (1986). An application of three deviance theories to adolescent substance use. *International Journal of the Addictions, 21*, 347-366.

White, H.R., & Labouvie, E.W. (1989). Towards the assessment of adolescent problem drinking. *Journal of Studies on Alcohol, 50*, 30-37.

Willis, T.A., Baker, E., & Botvin, G.J. (1989). Dimensions of assertiveness: Differential relationships to substance use in early adolescence. *Journal of Consulting and Clinical Psychology, 57*, 473-478.

Wilsnack, R.W., & Wilsnack, S.C. (1980). Drinking and denial of social obligations among adolescent boys. *Journal of Studies on Alcohol, 41*, 1118-1133.

Wilsnack, R.W., & Wilsnack, S.C. (1978). Sex roles and drinking among adolescent girls. *Journal of Studies on Alcohol, 39*, 1855-1874.

Wilsnack, S.C., Klassen, A.D., & Wright, S.I. (1986). Gender-role orientations and drinking among women in a national survey. *Proceedings of the 34th International Congress on Alcoholism and Drug Dependence* (pp. 242-255). Edmonton, Alberta, Canada: Alberta Alcohol and Drug Abuse Commission.

Windle, M., & Barnes, G.M. (1988). Similarities and differences in correlates of alcohol consumption and problem behaviors among male and female adolescents. *International Journal of the Addictions, 23*, 707-728.

Zucker, R.A., Battistich, V.A., & Langer, G.B. (1981). Sexual behavior, sex-role adaptation and drinking in young women. *Journal of Studies on Alcohol, 42*, 457-465.

CHAPTER 8

Gender, Stress, Coping, and Alcohol Use

M. Lynne Cooper, Michael R. Frone, Marcia Russell, and Robert S. Peirce

M en drink more and experience more drinking-related problems than do women, both in adolescence (Barnes & Welte, 1986; Lex, 1991) and as adults (Hilton, 1987; Lex, 1991). To date, efforts to explain these differences have focused on gender role socialization factors, which have proven only partially successful in accounting for male-female differences in alcohol use and abuse (e.g., Huselid & Cooper, 1992). Thus, other factors need to be considered if we are to understand more adequately the underlying source of gender differences in alcohol involvement. Both stress and coping factors have been cited as potentially useful explanatory mechanisms (e.g., Cooper et al., 1992a; Huselid & Cooper, 1992). That is, if men lead more stressful lives or use more maladaptive forms of coping than women, these differences may account for their relatively greater alcohol use. The present study therefore examines in a systematic manner the extent to which stress and coping factors can account for—or mediate—gender differences in alcohol involvement among both adolescents and adults.

Mediation is defined as the mechanism through which one variable (a presumed cause) affects another (the presumed effect); thus mediation addresses the question of how or why specific effects occur (Baron & Kenny, 1986). For example, men may experience more work-related or financial stress, which, in turn, may cause them to drink more heavily than women. Or, alternatively, men may be more likely than women to cope with the stresses they experience in negative or maladaptive ways, and this in turn may lead to a greater reliance on alcohol as a coping mechanism. Thus, taking account of gender differences in stress and coping may help to explain why men drink more and experience more alcohol-related problems than do women.

According to Baron and Kenny (1986), we should expect stress and coping factors to mediate gender differences in alcohol involvement to the extent that: (1) males report higher levels of stress and more maladaptive coping, and (2) stressors and maladaptive coping are both positively related to alcohol involvement. However, reviews of relevant research suggest that the second condition may be valid, but the first condition is unlikely to occur.

Gender Differences in Stress and Coping

Examination of the stress and coping literatures suggests that where gender differences are found, they tend to favor males. For example, although most studies find no gender differences in the number of negative life events occurring to oneself (referred to as *self-events*), both adolescent and adult females have reported significantly more negative events occurring to others in their social networks (referred to as *network events*; for reviews, see Compas & Phares, 1991; Wethington et al., 1987).

Coping, defined as cognitive and behavioral efforts to master, reduce, or tolerate the internal and/or external demands created by a stressful event or situation (Folkman & Lazarus, 1980), can be categorized into at least two broad types: (1) active or approach coping and (2) avoidance coping. Although alternative categorizations exist (e.g., problem vs. emotion-focused coping; Folkman & Lazarus, 1980), active vs. avoidant coping is a widely recognized coping dimension (e.g., Carver et al., 1989; Suls & Fletcher, 1985; Weidner & Collins, 1993) that we believe is particularly relevant for understanding alcohol use. Active coping includes strategies aimed at dealing directly with a problem through either cognitive or behavioral means. Regardless of the specific strategy chosen, individuals attempting to cope actively recognize that a problem exists and that coping effort is required. In contrast, avoidance coping represents a failure to confront a problem by denying its existence, minimizing its severity, diverting attention away from it, and/or venting one's negative feelings.[1]

Research on gender differences in coping behavior suggests that males report higher levels of active coping, whereas females report greater use of avoidance coping (for a review, see Weidner & Collins, 1993). In the only consistent exception to this pattern, females appear more likely than males to use active forms of coping that involve seeking help from others (Belle, 1987; Miller & Kirsch, 1987). Given that active, problem-focused coping has been associated with positive emotional outcomes and avoidance coping with more negative ones (e.g., Aldwin & Revenson, 1987; Carver et al., 1989), these data suggest that females relative to males tend to use more maladaptive forms of coping, with the exception of support seeking, which is more commonly used by females and may be more adaptive.

Stress and Alcohol Involvement

According to tension reduction theory (TRT; Conger, 1956), people drink alcohol for its tension-reducing properties. Tension refers here to various negative emotional states that could plausibly serve as aversive sources of motivation, such as fear, anxiety, distress, or depression. Hypothetically, stress should lead to increased or problematic drinking because people use alcohol to cope with the negative emotions generated by stressful experiences.

As previously indicated, empirical evidence generally supports a link between stressors and heavy or abusive drinking (for reviews, see Cappell & Greeley, 1987; Pohorecky, 1991; Sher, 1987; Young et al., 1990). For example, Wills (1986) found that negative events were significantly positively related to several indices of alcohol use across two different adolescent samples in both concurrent and prospective analyses. In addition, follow-up studies conducted among recovering alcoholics also support a link between the experience of intervening stressful events and relapse (for reviews, see Billings & Moos, 1983; Marlatt & Gordon, 1985). Thus, although negative findings have been reported (e.g., Cooke & Allan, 1984; Stone et al., 1985), substantial empirical evidence suggests that negative events may lead to increased or problematic alcohol use.

These studies, however, either did not examine network events or failed to analyze their data separately for events that happened to oneself vs. events that happened to others. Thus, the above conclusions regarding stressor effects on alcohol use most likely pertain to negative self-relevant events only. In fact, we know of only one study that specifically examined network events (O'Doherty & Davies, 1988). Surprisingly, this study found that heavy drinkers reported significantly fewer network events than non-heavy drinkers. This unexpected finding may indicate that problem alcohol users have fewer meaningful ties or more strained ties with friends and family, and thus are less likely to be aware of and/or to experience negative emotional consequences as a result of problems occurring to these significant others. However, insufficient detail was provided about the sample, measures, and analyses used in this study to evaluate fully their finding. Thus, it remains unclear whether and, if so, how negative events occurring to socially significant others will be associated with alcohol involvement in a heterogeneous community sample of drinkers.

Coping and Alcohol Involvement

At least two distinct theoretical perspectives provide a basis for postulating that alcohol involvement should be negatively related to active coping and positively related to avoidance coping. First, tension reduction models posit that individuals drink alcohol to relieve tension or negative emotions. Thus, to the extent that negative emotions are reduced by active coping and exacerbated by avoidance coping (as discussed above), alcohol involvement should be reduced by active coping and increased by avoidance coping, indirectly via the experience of negative emotions. The study of cognitive expectancies about alcohol's effects provides a second perspective that leads to similar predictions. Because alcohol is widely believed to possess a range of properties that facilitate problem avoidance (e.g., helping to forget one's problems, decreasing negative mood; Brown et al., 1980), drinking seems especially likely to be used as a problem avoidance strategy and thus should be positively correlated with other avoidant strategies. Alcohol is also widely expected to impair cognitive processing and behavior (e.g., Brown et al., 1980). Thus, alcohol use seems likely to be viewed as antagonistic to the successful execution of active coping strategies, and so is likely to be negatively associated with active coping.

Examination of the empirical literature provides general support for the prediction that coping strategies are related to alcohol use, although the data more strongly support the deleterious effects of avoidance coping than the beneficial effects of active coping. For example, in a two-year follow-up study, recovering alcoholics who relapsed were more likely to use avoidance coping than either their abstinent counterparts or a matched community control group (Moos et al., 1981); these groups did not differ, however, in their use of active coping strategies (Moos et al., 1981). Similarly, Moos et al. (1990) found that older (aged 55–65) problem drinkers were distinguished from older non-problem drinkers by their greater reliance on several forms of avoidance coping, whereas the problem drinkers differed from non-problem drinkers (in the expected direction) on only one of four active coping strategies. Wills (1985) also observed inconsistent relationships between indices of active coping (e.g., problem solving, cognitive coping, physical exercise) and alcohol use among adolescents.

Unlike the relatively straightforward predictions for avoidance coping, the theoretical and empirical bases for predicting a relationship between support seeking and alcohol involvement are equivocal. On the one hand, measures of perceived social support and social integration have been consistently positively related to adaptive outcomes (Cohen & Wills, 1985), and support seeking has been conceptually and empirically related to other adaptive forms of coping including active coping (Moos et al., 1986). Furthermore, the only studies we know of that examined the link between support seeking and alcohol involvement found significant inverse relationships in both adults (Stone et al., 1985) and adolescents (Wills, 1985). Among adolescents, however, there was less alcohol use only among those who sought support from their parents. On the other hand, supportive others may be sought as a diversion or in order to vent one's negative feelings, which may be maladaptive (Carver et al., 1989). Moreover, both support seeking and receipt have been positively related to stress and distress (Cohen & Hoberman, 1983; Williams & Williams, 1983).

Thus, both theory and research indicate that avoidance coping should be positively related to heavy or abusive drinking. In contrast, predictions for active coping and support seeking are more tenuous. However, to the extent that both are conceived as generally adaptive strategies, we would expect them to be negatively related.

Summary and Integration of Predicted Relationships

The pattern of expected relationships is summarized in Figure 1. As shown in the upper portion of Figure 1, we expect females to report more network events than males, but to report similar levels of self-events. In turn, we expect both self- and network events to be positively related to alcohol involvement. Although the prediction for network events lacks empirical support, network events theoretically should be related to heavier drinking to the extent that these events precipitate the experience of negative emotions.

If stressful events (both self- and network) are related to gender and drinking in the ways predicted in Figure 1, they will not mediate (reduce or

FIGURE 1
Hypothetical Relationships among Gender, Stress,
Coping, and Alcohol Outcomes

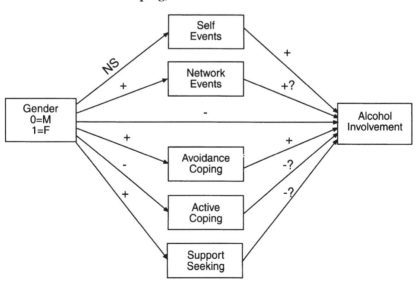

Note: NS indicates that no significant difference is hypothesized; + and − indicate that significant positive and negative effects, respectively, are hypothesized.

eliminate) gender differences in alcohol-related outcomes, for two reasons. First, self-events cannot account for gender differences in alcohol-related outcomes if men and women do not experience different levels of these events. Second, if network events are positively related both to being a woman and to alcohol involvement, these events may *suppress* (or hide) rather than mediate the effects of gender on alcohol involvement.[2] Hypothetically, women's greater experience of network events should lead them to drink more, which in turn would counteract and obscure other ways that being a woman tends to reduce alcohol use. Another way to think about this is that if women experienced as few network events as men do, they would drink less than they actually do, whereas if men experienced as many network events as women do, they would drink even more than they actually do. To the extent that stressful events and their effects occur as hypothesized in Figure 1, the *total* effect of gender on alcohol involvement will be composed of a *negative direct effect* plus a *positive indirect effect* via network events. This will make the total effect of gender (observed in bivariate analyses of gender and alcohol involvement) smaller than its direct effect, because direct and indirect effects with opposite signs tend to cancel each other.

As shown in the lower portion of Figure 1, we expect women to report higher levels of avoidance coping and support seeking, but lower levels of active coping. In turn, avoidance coping should be positively related to alcohol involvement, whereas active coping and support seeking should be negatively related. To the extent that these patterns occur, support seeking should mediate the gender-alcohol link. Hypothetically, women engage in more support-seeking behavior which, in turn, leads to lower alcohol involvement; thus greater support seeking on the part of women should at least partly explain why they are less involved with alcohol than men are. In contrast, both avoidance coping and active coping should function as suppressor variables. Women relative to men are expected to use more avoidant and less active coping which, in turn, should be related to *more, not less* alcohol involvement. Thus, if women relied on active coping as much as men do, and on avoidant coping as little as men do, we would expect women to drink less than they actually do. Likewise, if men relied on avoidant coping as much as women do, and on active coping as little as women do, we would expect men to drink even more than they do.

To the extent that data support these predictions, gender differences in stress and coping are unlikely to explain gender differences in alcohol involvement. Except for effects of support seeking, which are hypothesized to mediate gender differences in alcohol involvement, we expect that controlling for stress and coping factors will *increase* unexplained gender differences in alcohol use and abuse due to gender. To test these predictions, we will use survey data from separate samples of adolescent and adult drinkers.

Method

Adolescent Sample

Sample and procedure. In 1989–90, the first author conducted a survey of community-residing adolescents to study interrelationships among risky behaviors (including alcohol use and high risk sex) and psychosocial factors predisposing adolescents to engage in risky behaviors. Random-digit-dial techniques were used to identify a representative sample of adolescents, aged 13 to 19, residing within the city limits of Buffalo, New York. Telephone exchanges concentrated in primarily African-American areas of the city were oversampled. Face-to-face interviews were completed with 2,052 adolescents, for an 81% completion rate. Interviews were conducted by 30 professionally trained interviewers using a structured interview schedule. Ninety-five percent of the interviews were conducted in private interview rooms on the campus of the State University of New York at Buffalo; the remaining respondents ($n=110$) were interviewed in private in their homes. The average interview length was two hours, and respondents were paid $25 for their participation.

The data analyzed here were obtained from a subset of 1,114 respondents who reported drinking within the past six months and who provided complete data on all measures. Respondents ranged in age from 13 to 19 (mean [$\pm$SD] = 17.3 ± 1.9). About half of the respondents were male (46.3%); one-third were African-American (32.3%). A majority of the parents or caregivers of these adolescents had completed high school (34.1%) or some college (33.8%); 11.9% had not completed high school, and 20.2% had obtained at least a bachelor's degree.

Measures. All measures included in the present analyses were administered by the interviewer in a fixed order. Table 1 (above the diagonal) presents descriptive information, estimates of internal consistency reliability (Cronbach's alpha), and partial correlations among all measures.

1. *Demographic variables.* Age (measured in years and months), race (coded 0 = non-white, 1 = white), and parental socioeconomic status were assessed and included in all analyses as control variables. Parental SES was measured by a standardized composite of two variables: parent education (highest grade of school or year of college completed by a custodial caregiver) and parent employment status (coded 0 = sole or both caregivers were unemployed, 1 = either or both were employed).

2. *Stressful life events.* Respondents were presented a list of 30 events gleaned from the Adolescent Perceived Events Scale (Compas et al., 1987), and were asked to indicate whether any of the events had occurred to them personally, to members of their family, or to their friends. Representative self-events included "had a serious illness" and "ended an important love relationship." Representative network events included "serious illness or injury of a friend/family member" and "friend/family member became pregnant or

TABLE 1
Partial Correlations, Controlling for Age, Race, SES/Education, and Descriptive Information for Study Variables
(Adolescent Sample [N = 1,114] is Above Diagonal; Adult Sample [N = 1,336] is Below Diagonal)

	1	2	3	4	5	6	7	8	9	10	Mean	SD	Reliability (α)
1. Gender	-	.02	-.12***	-.17***	-.18***	.01	.11***	.17***	.12***	.22***	0.54	0.50	-
Alcohol outcomes													
2. Drink to cope	-.11***	-	.31***	.37***	.41***	.15***	.19***	.30***	.11***	.06	1.57	0.75	.83
3. Usual consumption	-.29***	.37***	-	.68***	.41***	.14***	.08**	.15***	-.02	-.03	0.70	1.43	-
4. Freq. drink 5+	-.33***	.36***	.61***	-	.53***	.19***	.15***	.14***	-.03	-.01	1.88	2.37	-
5. Alcohol problems	-.19***	.37***	.45***	.43***	-	.24***	.21***	.20***	-.00	.00	0.79	1.10	-
Stressors													
6. Self-events	.03	.12***	.16***	.07*	.18***	-	.38***	.20***	.11**	.08*	1.85	1.56	-
7. Network events	.07*	.05	.03	.01	.09**	.12***	-	.24***	.12***	.09**	2.27	1.99	-
Coping													
8. Avoidance	.05	.28***	.13***	.11***	.21***	.20***	.07**	-	.15***	.00	0.03	2.11	.51
9. Active	.05*	.07*	-.01	-.02	.02	.09**	.06*	.12**	-	.42***	-0.01	1.76	.71
10. Support seeking	.12***	.01	-.03	-.04	.03	.07*	.14***	.04	.30***	-	2.48	0.75	.60
Mean	0.62	1.38	0.77	1.66	0.33	1.04	0.39	0.23	-0.01	1.90			
SD	0.49	0.48	1.49	2.40	1.06	1.36	0.79	2.31	1.79	0.49			
Reliability (α)	-	.81	-	-	-	-	-	.66	.78	.53			

Note: Gender is coded 0 = male, 1 = female.
*p < .05. **p < .01. ***p < .001.

had a child." For each event that had occurred, respondents were then asked to rate its overall impact on their life using a scale of -3 (extremely undesirable) to $+3$ (extremely desirable). From these ratings, separate indices counting the number of negative (ratings of -3, -2, -1) self- and network events were derived.

3. *Coping.* Six coping scales were administered: Anger-In and Anger-Out subscales of Spielberger's Anger Expression scale (Spielberger et al., 1985), and Avoidance Coping, Active Cognitive Coping, Active Behavioral Coping, and Support Seeking subscales of the Health and Daily Living Form Coping Response Index (Moos et al., 1986). The anger coping scales assess how individuals typically react or behave when they feel angry or upset. Anger-In assesses the extent to which respondents suppress or avoid dealing with angry feelings (e.g., "Boil inside, but don't show it"), while Anger-Out measures the degree to which individuals engage in aggressive behaviors when motivated by angry feelings (e.g., "slam doors," "say nasty things"; 6 items each). The remaining four other coping scales assess specific coping strategies used to deal with a recently experienced stressful event. Respondents were asked to recall and briefly describe such an event or situation, and then rated the extent to which they used each of 32 coping strategies (not at all, somewhat, a great deal) to deal with this event/situation. From these items, four indexes were derived. Active Behavioral Coping (9 items) assesses the extent to which subjects engaged in direct action and problem-solving (e.g., "Tried to find out more about the situation"). Active Cognitive Coping (11 items) assesses the use of cognitive strategies to reframe or reinterpret the situation (e.g., "Tried to see the positive side of the situation"). Avoidance Coping (7 items) assesses reliance on avoidance, denial, or tension reduction (e.g., "Kept my feelings to myself" and "Avoided being with people in general").[3] Support Seeking assesses the extent to which subjects sought help and support from others (e.g., "Talked with a friend about the problem").

To determine if these measures reflected the two hypothesized coping domains, the six measures were subjected to a principal components factor analysis with oblique rotation.[4] As expected, the analysis extracted two factors with eigenvalues greater than 1.0. Active coping measures and support seeking loaded on the first factor, with factor regression coefficients $\geq .69$. The other three measures loaded on an avoidant, emotion-focused coping factor with loadings $\geq .51$. Based on these results, composite measures of Active Coping (comprising the Active Cognitive and Active Behavioral scales) and Avoidance Coping (comprising the Anger-In, Anger-Out, and Avoidance Coping scales) were created by computing the mean of the means for relevant scales.[5] Because of anticipated gender differences in support seeking vs. active coping, support seeking was scored separately from the Active Coping composite. Scale scores were standardized before constructing the composite measures, because response formats and/or variances differed across scales.

4. *Alcohol outcomes.* Four alcohol-related outcomes were examined: (a) drinking to cope, (b) average alcohol consumption, (c) frequency of heavy drinking, and (d) drinking problems.

Drinking to cope (Cooper, 1994) was assessed by a five-item scale in which respondents reported the frequency of drinking to manage or cope with negative emotions (e.g., to forget your worries, to cheer up when you're in a bad mood). Items were answered on a four-point scale ranging from "almost never/never" to "almost always/always."

Average alcohol consumption during the past six months was computed from two standard items, assessing frequency of drinking (on a nine-point scale ranging from "less than once a month during the past six months" to "every day") and average number of drinks consumed per drinking occasion. Responses were converted into average number of drinks per day, where one drink was defined as 12 ounces of beer, 4 ounces of wine, or 1 ounce of distilled spirits (all approximately 0.5 ounces of absolute alcohol). Frequency of heavy drinking (defined as five or more drinks on a single occasion) was assessed by a single item using the same nine-point ordinal scale described above.

Drinking problems were assessed by four items in which respondents rated the frequency (0 = "never" to 4 = "5 or more times") of problems resulting from their alcohol use, in the following life domains: with parents, friends, dating partners, or at school or work. An index was derived by counting how many types of problems occurred one or more times in the past six months. Six-month abuse items were developed by Jessor and colleagues (1989).

Adult Sample

Sample and procedure. In 1986, we conducted a survey of community-residing adults to study the interrelationships among stress, alcohol use, and hypertension. Respondents were drawn from a random sample of adult (≥ 19 years old) household residents in Erie County, New York, stratified on race (African-American, non-African-American) and education (less than high school, high school, some college). Face-to-face interviews were completed with 1,933 adults for a 78% completion rate. Interviews were conducted by 27 professionally trained interviewers using a structured interview schedule. All interviews were conducted in respondents' homes. Average interview length was 90 minutes, and respondents were paid $25 for participation.

The data analyzed here were obtained from a subset of 1,336 respondents who reported drinking within the past 12 months and who provided complete data on all measures. Respondents ranged in age from 19 to 87 (mean

[±SD] age = 40.3 ± 15.3). Less than half of the respondents were male (38.5%), half were African-American (50.2%), a little more than half were employed (55.5%), and just under half were married or living as married (45.7%). About 16.1% of the sample had not completed high school, whereas 33.3% had completed high school, 34.4% had completed some college, and 16.2% had obtained at least a bachelor's degree.

Measures. All measures were administered in a fixed order by the interviewer, and are conceptually and/or operationally parallel to those used in the adolescent sample. Table 1 (below the diagonal) presents descriptive information and partial correlations for the major study variables.

1. *Demographic variables.* Age (in years), race (coded 0 = non-white, 1 = white), and education (coded as the highest year of school or college completed by the respondent) were assessed and used as control variables in all analyses, as previously described for the adolescent sample.

2. *Stressors.* Fifty-two events were selected from the PERI Life Events Scale (Dohrenwend et al., 1978) and organized into eight life domains (work, love and marriage, children, finances, health and illness, criminal and legal matters, household, school). Respondents indicated whether they had experienced each event during the past year, and also indicated whether a subset of 21 events had occurred to significant others during this time period. For each event that had occurred, respondents rated its impact on their life on a scale from 1 (extremely negative) to 6 (extremely positive). The responses were used to compute the number of self-rated negative life events (rated 1 to 3) that had occurred to oneself and to significant others.

3. *Coping.* Coping measures for the adult sample were identical to those in the adolescent study. Factor analysis of these measures (by the procedures described earlier) yielded results essentially identical to those obtained from the adolescent sample. Two factors were extracted with eigenvalues greater than 1.0. Both active coping measures and support seeking loaded on the first factor with factor regression coefficients ≥.54; the remaining measures loaded on an avoidant, emotion-focused coping factor with loadings ≥.55. The procedures used in the adolescent sample were used to create composite measures of Active Coping and Avoidance Coping, and Support Seeking was retained as a separate scale.

4. *Alcohol outcome measures.* As in the adolescent sample, we examined four drinking outcomes among the adults. Drink to cope was assessed by a five-item measure similar to that used for the adolescents (for details, see Cooper et al., 1992b). Average alcohol consumption during the past 12 months was estimated from standard quantity-frequency questions employed in the National Health and Leisure Time Survey (Wilsnack et al., 1984). Responses were converted into average number of drinks per day, using the same definitions of drinks as in the adolescent study. Frequency of heavy drinking during the past 12 months (operationally defined as drinking five or

more drinks on a single occasion) was assessed on a nine-point scale ranging from "never" to "5 or more times a week."

Drinking problems were assessed by 17 items from the National Institute of Mental Health Diagnostic Interview Schedule (Robins et al., 1981), designed to yield data for DSM-III diagnoses of alcohol abuse and dependence. Representative problems included going on "binges or benders," losing a job because of drinking, and having "blackouts" or the "shakes." In the present study, an index of drinking problems was computed by counting the total number of problems that occurred one or more times in the past 12 months (see Robins et al., 1981, for validity data).

Data Analyses

The expected pattern of bivariate relationships (Figure 1) led us to predict both suppression effects (via network events, avoidance coping, active coping) and mediation effects (via support seeking). Because suppression and mediation are alternative types of intervening variable processes (Bollen, 1989), similar procedures can be used to examine both processes. To demonstrate either suppression or mediation, we must show that the independent variable (gender) is significantly related to the intervening variables (stress and coping), and that the intervening variables are significantly related to the outcomes (alcohol use and abuse; Baron & Kenny, 1986; Cohen & Cohen, 1983). To show mediation (Baron & Kenny, 1986), additional conditions are necessary: (1) the independent variable must be significantly related to the outcome, and (2) the magnitude of the relationship between the independent variable and the outcome must be reduced or eliminated by controlling for the hypothesized mediators. These conditions do *not* apply to suppressor relationships. With regard to the first criterion, suppression may mask a simple relationship between the independent and outcome variables *if* the direct and indirect effects are of opposing signs *and* of nearly equal magnitude (Bollen, 1989). Hence suppression—but not mediation—may occur in the absence of a significant link between gender and alcohol outcome. With regard to the second condition, the magnitude of the gender-alcohol outcome relationship should be increased by controlling for a suppressor variable, but decreased by controlling for a mediating variable. These conditions will be tested using a combination of analysis of covariance, partial correlations, and hierarchical multiple regression.

Results

Table 2 summarizes mean gender differences in stress, coping, and alcohol outcomes for the adolescent and adult samples. As expected, male adolescents reported significantly higher levels of alcohol involvement than female

TABLE 2
Gender Differences in Stress, Coping, and Alcohol Variables

| | ADOLESCENT SAMPLE | | ADULT SAMPLE | |
	Males ($n = 516$)	Females ($n = 598$)	Males ($n = 514$)	Females ($n = 822$)
Alcohol outcomes				
Drink to cope	1.55	1.58	1.45	1.34***
Usual consumption	0.88	0.55***	1.32	0.44***
Freq. drink 5+	2.29	1.54***	2.65	1.04***
Alcohol problems	1.00	0.61***	0.58	0.17***
Stressors				
Self-events	1.83	1.87	0.99	1.08
Network events	2.03	2.47***	0.33	0.43*
Coping				
Avoidance	−0.35	0.36***	0.10	0.31
Active	−0.23	0.18***	−0.14	0.06*
Support seeking	2.30	2.64***	1.82	1.94***

Note: Means are adjusted for age, race, and SES/education.
*$p < .05$. **$p < .01$. ***$p < .001$.

adolescents on all alcohol measures except for drinking to cope (where no gender difference was found). Similarly, among the adults, men reported significantly higher levels on all alcohol outcomes than did women. Thus, gender was related to alcohol outcomes in the expected manner, with the exception of adolescent drinking to cope.

Also, as hypothesized, both adolescent and adult females reported significantly more negative events in their social networks than their male counterparts did. Moreover, as expected, no gender difference was observed in the number of self-events. There were significant gender differences in all coping measures, except for avoidance coping by adults. As hypothesized, female adolescents and adults reported higher levels of avoidance coping and support seeking than their male counterparts did. However, contrary to prediction, females in both samples reported significantly higher levels of active coping. Thus, with the exceptions of active coping in both samples and avoidance coping in the adult sample, gender was related to the intervening stress and coping factors in the expected manner.

However, examination of the partial correlations in Table 1 indicates that stressful events and coping strategies were not uniformly related to alcohol outcomes in the expected manner. Self-events were significantly positively related to all alcohol measures in both the adolescent (above the diagonal) and adult (below the diagonal) samples, as expected. In the adolescent sample, network events were also significantly positively correlated with all alcohol

FIGURE 2a
Summary of Empirical Tests Assessing Viability of Mediational Hypotheses among Adolescents

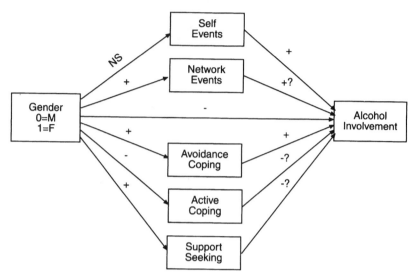

Note: NS indicates no significant relationship; + and – indicate significant positive and negative relationships, respectively.

outcomes. In the adult sample, however, network events were significantly positively related to drinking problems, but were unrelated to other alcohol outcomes. The partial correlations between the coping and alcohol variables reveal that Avoidance Coping was significantly positively correlated with all alcohol outcomes in both samples, as predicted. However, active coping and support seeking were generally not significantly related to the alcohol measures in either the adult or the adolescent sample. The sole exception to this pattern was a small but significant *positive* correlation between active coping and drinking to cope in both samples.

Figures 2a and 3a summarize the results of these preliminary tests for the adolescent and adult samples, respectively. Considered collectively, these analyses support only a subset of the hypothesized indirect effects. As shown in Figure 2a, gender had reliable indirect effects[6] on all alcohol outcomes via network events and avoidance coping in the adolescent sample, and an indirect effect on drinking to cope via active coping. As shown in Figure 3a, gender had a reliable indirect effect on alcohol-related problems via network events in the adult sample, and an indirect effect on drinking to cope via active coping. The direction of the obtained indirect effects suggests that, in both samples, controlling for these intervening variables should *increase* the magnitude of the direct effect of gender on alcohol outcomes. Thus, these factors seem likely to act as suppressors of gender-

FIGURE 2b
Estimated Model Predicting Alcohol Use and Problems among Adolescents

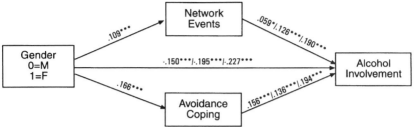

Note: Coefficients for the dependent measures are provided in the following order: usual consumption, frequency of drinking 5+, and drinking problems.

*$p < .05$.   ***$p < .001$.

alcohol relationships.[7] No support was found for the only hypothesized mediated relationship (via support seeking), because the presumed mediator was not significantly related to any of the alcohol outcomes in either sample.

The final test necessary to determine whether the stress and coping variables suppress relationships between gender and alcohol outcomes is to estimate the *direct* effect of gender on each alcohol outcome after controlling for the relevant intervening variables (as summarized above). Figures 2b, 2c, and 3b show results of these analyses. These figures indicate that the direct effects of gender on alcohol outcomes remain significant and negative (except for drinking to cope in the adolescent sample), whereas all indirect effects are positive. These effects are summarized in Table 3 together with the total effect of gender on each alcohol outcome. Comparison of the total effects of gender with the corresponding direct effects of gender (presented in

FIGURE 2c
Estimated Model Predicting Drink to Cope among Adolescents

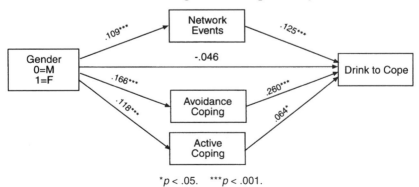

*$p < .05$.   ***$p < .001$.

FIGURE 3a
**Summary of Empirical Tests Assessing Viability of Mediational Hypotheses
among Adults**

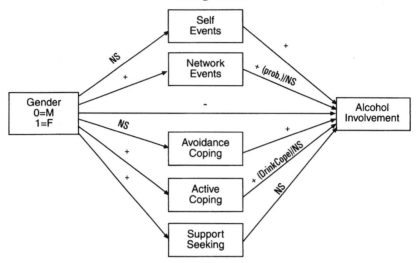

Note: NS indicates no significant relationships; + and − indicate significant positive and negative relationships, respectively.

the first and last lines, respectively, of the top and bottom portions of Table 3) supports the hypothesized suppressor effects. In each case, the direct effect is *larger* than the total effect of gender (particularly among adolescents), due to the countervailing influence of the indirect effects. Thus, taking these

FIGURE 3b
Estimated Models among Adults

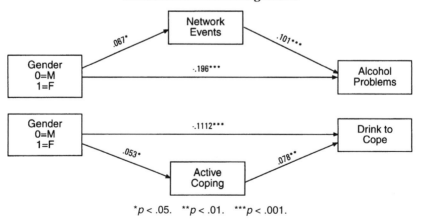

*p < .05.   **p < .01.   ***p < .001.

TABLE 3
Decomposition of the Gender Effect on Alcohol Outcomes

	Drink to Cope	Usual Consumption	Freq. Drink 5+	Alcohol Problems
Adolescent sample				
Total gender effect[1]	.019	−.118***	−.158***	−.174***
Indirect via:				
Network events	.014	.006	.014	.021
Avoidance coping	.043	.026	.023	.032
Active coping	.008	–	–	–
Total indirect	.065	.032	.037	.053
Direct	−.046	−.150***	−.195***	−.227***
Adult sample				
Total gender effect[1]	−.108***	−.289***	−.326***	−.189***
Indirect via:				
Network events	–	–	–	.007
Active coping	.004	–	–	–
Total indirect	.004	–	–	.007
Direct	−.112***	–	–	−.196***

[1]Total effect is indexed by the regression coefficient (beta) for gender controlling for age, race, and the composite parent SES measure in the adolescent sample, and for age, race, and respondent education in the adult sample.
***$p < .001$.

differences into account serves to increase rather than decrease gender differences in alcohol involvement, as expected.

Discussion

The present study examined the notion that stress and coping could at least partially account for gender differences in alcohol involvement among both adolescents and adults. Contrary to initial expectation, however, consideration of relevant theory and empirical literature led us to propose that stress and coping factors obscure rather than explain gender differences in alcohol involvement. Results of our analyses supported this hypothesis, indicating that significant effects of stress and coping increased the magnitude of unexplained gender differences in alcohol outcomes, particularly among adolescents. Accordingly, gender differences in stress and coping—at least as measured in the present study—cannot be used to explain gender differences in alcohol involvement. Thus, the question of how or why men drink more and experience more drinking-related problems than woman remains unanswered by the present study.

Although stress and coping factors examined in the present study failed to explain gender differences in alcohol outcomes, other types or dimensions of coping may prove useful in explaining these differences. For example, in an earlier study conducted with our adolescent sample, we found that the gender-linked attributes of expressivity (more common among females) and emotional control (more common among males) produced substantial but not complete reductions in the magnitude of the relationships between gender and several alcohol-related outcomes (Huselid & Cooper, 1992). Although expressivity and emotional control are not coping strategies per se, they have clear implications for styles or characteristic ways of coping. Expressive individuals are thought to be more empathic and emotionally open, and thus may be better able to utilize social support and to cope constructively with distressing emotions. In contrast, individuals high in emotional control are hypothesized to be less comfortable expressing their emotions, and thus may be more likely to repress or deny troubling emotions and less likely to ask for or accept support in times of need. Alcohol, because of its well-known capacity to anesthetize negative emotions, may be particularly attractive to individuals low in expressiveness and high in emotional control, who are prone to suppress rather than express negative emotions. Thus, the findings on expressivity and emotional control (Huselid & Cooper, 1992) suggest that considering a broader range of coping styles and behaviors could reveal coping responses that do mediate gender differences in alcohol-related outcomes.

Likewise the present study examined only one type of stressor, acute stressful life events. Thus, it seems plausible that exposure to other types of stressors, such as chronic stressors or more minor hassles and everyday problems, might instead mediate gender differences in alcohol involvement. However, available evidence also fails to support this possibility, indicating that females report higher levels of everyday problems (Cooper et al., 1992a), work-family conflict (e.g., Frone et al., 1992; Simon, 1992), family stressors (e.g., Simon, 1992), and financial strain (Albino & Tedesco, 1984). Thus, chronic stressors also seem likely to obscure rather than explain gender differences in alcohol outcomes. However, findings on gender differences in job stressors are mixed, and appear to vary as a function of the specific occupations sampled and stressor dimensions examined (cf., Albright et al., 1992; Barnett et al., 1993; Lambert, 1991; Loscocco & Spitze, 1990; Nelson & Hitt, 1992), so it is possible that certain types of chronic job-related stress may help to explain the male excess in drinking among employed individuals.

An alternative possibility not considered in the present study is that men and women differ *not* in their exposure to stressors, but in how the emotional impact of stressors alters their drinking behavior. According to this possibility, men are more likely than women to experience adverse alcohol-related outcomes as a result of exposure to life stressors. This possibility is consistent with differences in gender socialization processes, by which women are socialized to internalize distress (i.e., to turn it inward), whereas men are socialized to externalize (or act out) their distress (for reviews, see Cooper et al., 1992a; Huselid & Cooper, 1992). Hypothetically, therefore, differences in socialization make it more likely that women will internalize stress-related effects (e.g., by becoming depressed), whereas men under stress will use alcohol and exhibit alcohol-related problems.

Earlier research on our adult sample supports the idea that the relationship between stress and alcohol-related outcomes differs across men and women (Cooper et al., 1992a). We found that alcohol use and drinking problems were predicted by interactions of gender with life events and gender with everyday problems, such that both stressor measures were more strongly related to alcohol outcomes among males than among females. We also found a consistent pattern of three-way gender-by-stressor-by-avoidance coping interactions in which life events were strongly related to alcohol pathology among the subset of men who were high in avoidance coping, but were essentially unrelated to alcohol pathology among low-avoidance-coping men and among women, regardless of their coping style. These findings suggest that differences in how stressors are related to alcohol use may do more to explain gender differences in alcohol involvement than differences in exposure to stress or in coping per se.

Unlike research on acute stressful life events, however, research on chronic stressors provides little support for the notion that males are more likely than females to drink to cope with stress. For example, in an earlier study conducted with our adult sample (Frone et al., 1993), we found no indication that the magnitude of the relationship between work-family conflict and alcohol use differed across males and females. Similarly, data reported by Parker and Farmer (1988) and House et al. (1986) suggest little difference in the magnitude of work stressor effects on alcohol-related outcomes across gender groups. Indeed, data reported by Wilsnack (1992) suggest that drinking among women may be even more strongly related to some forms of chronic stress than is drinking among their male counterparts. Specifically, he reports that unwanted role statuses (defined as having an unwanted role or not having a desired role) are more consistently related to alcohol outcomes among women than among men. In contrast, in the only study to provide evidence of greater male vulnerability to the effects of chronic stressors, this author and colleagues found that financial strains were significantly positively related to the use of alcohol to cope among males, but not among females (Peirce et al., 1994).

It is worth noting that the bivariate relationships observed in our data generally conformed to predictions and were largely consistent across both samples. Both samples showed the expected pattern of gender differences in network events, avoidance coping, support seeking, and all alcohol outcomes (except for drinking to cope in the adolescent sample). Also, as anticipated, males and females failed to differ on self-events in either sample. However, contrary to expectation, females in both samples reported higher levels of active coping than males. This finding, though discrepant with most empirical evidence, has been previously reported for the particular measure used in the present study (Moos, 1992), and may therefore reflect some peculiarity specific to this operationalization of the active coping construct.

Both theory and research also indicated that negative self-events and avoidance coping should be positively related to alcohol outcomes, and these predictions were supported across both samples. In contrast, the weak predictions advanced for network events, active coping, and support seeking received mixed support. Although network events were consistently positively related to all alcohol outcomes among adolescents, as hypothesized, they were related to only one of four outcomes among adults. One reason why network events were more strongly related to adverse alcohol outcomes among adolescents may be that adolescents' lives are more enmeshed with those of their peers and their well-being is more dependent on their family. Accordingly, disruptions in the adolescent's social network may be more stressful and therefore more likely to be associated with increased alcohol use. This interpretation is consistent with the fact that adolescents reported more than seven times as many negative network events than adults (means = 2.93 vs. 0.39, respectively).[8]

Finally, neither active coping nor support seeking was related to alcohol outcomes in either sample, except for the unexpected positive link between active coping and drinking to cope. As suggested earlier, the lack of relationship between support seeking and alcohol outcomes is consistent with the notion that support can be sought for various reasons, only some of which are adaptive. Effects of support may also depend on the characteristics of the individuals from whom the support is sought. For example, seeking support from heavy-drinking friends may encourage companionate drinking, whereas seeking support from a nondrinking friend might reduce alcohol use. These considerations suggest that more detailed information on the nature of support seeking might reveal systematic but opposing relationships between support seeking and alcohol outcomes.

The conflicting findings for active coping may also reflect a need for more refined measurement and analyses. For example, research indicates that although active coping strategies are usually adaptive, they may be maladaptive if employed in situations that cannot be changed (Forsythe & Compas, 1987). This suggests the possibility that additional information on relevant dimensions of the stressor, such as its controllability or tractableness, might clarify the relationship between active coping and alcohol involvement. Moreover, the notion that the beneficial effects of active coping vary with stressor type raises the additional possibility that the range of available coping alternatives—or one's coping flexibility—may be a more critical determinant of alcohol-related outcomes than use of any one strategy or type of strategy per se.

Furthermore, to the extent that use of active coping strategies is responsive to variability in the nature of the stressor, use of a situation-specific coping measure, such as the one used in the present study, may have limited ability to predict behaviors (e.g., global measures of alcohol use) that are not specifically tied to that situation. However, we obtained similarly weak results in an earlier study using a trait-type measure of active coping style (John Henryism) (Cooper et al., 1988), thus tending to undermine this interpretation. Finally, we also cannot dismiss the possibility that active, problem-focused coping (including support seeking) failed to predict alcohol outcomes because, as we have argued elsewhere (Cooper et al., 1988), this particular coping dimension is not a potent determinant of drinking behavior.

In sum, the present study found that neither stressful events nor coping strategies could explain gender differences in alcohol involvement. In fact, some negative events (those occurring to others in one's social network) and reliance on some forms of coping actually obscured rather than explained gender differences in alcohol involvement. Thus, future research will need to consider either a broader range of stress and coping factors or other explanatory mechanisms to gain insight into the reasons why males typically drink more and experience more alcohol-related problems than do females.

Acknowledgments

This research was supported by National Institute on Alcohol Abuse and Alcoholism grant AA08047 awarded to M. Lynne Cooper and grant AA05702 awarded to Marcia Russell. Thanks to Pamela Mudar and Cheryl A. Burkett, respectively, for their invaluable assistance in data analysis and manuscript preparation.

Notes

1. Although avoidant coping strategies may be adaptive in certain types of situations (e.g., in those that cannot be changed; see Lazarus & Folkman, 1991, for a thoughtful discussion of this issue) and in the short run (Suls & Fletcher, 1985), chronic reliance on avoidant forms of coping has been associated prospectively with long-term negative outcomes (Aldwin & Revenson, 1987; Aspinwall & Taylor, 1992). Thus, in the present study, our use of the term refers to a tendency to rely on avoidant coping strategies across a range of situations regardless of their appropriateness, rather than to the occasional situationally appropriate use of an avoidance coping strategy.
2. Suppression is said to occur when the relationship between two independent or causal variables (gender and network events) is hiding or suppressing their real relationship with a third variable (alcohol outcomes; Cohen & Cohen, 1983).

3. One item, "Tried to reduce tension by drinking more," was omitted from this scale to avoid explicit confounding with our alcohol criterion measures.
4. Factor analysis is a generic term for a number of different but related mathematical and statistical techniques designed to investigate the nature of the relationships between variables in a specified set. The major purposes of factor analysis are to determine whether a set of variables can be described in terms of a number of "dimensions" or "factors" smaller than the number of variables, and to determine what these dimensions (factors) are; that is, to indicate what trait or characteristic each of them represents. For a more in-depth discussion of this procedure, see Lindeman et al. (1980; chapter 8) or Gorsuch (1983).
5. As we have argued elsewhere (Cooper et al., 1992a), both Anger-In and Anger-Out may be regarded as avoidant strategies to the extent that they represent attempts to avoid rather than confront or deal with the problematic situation. Moreover, consistent with findings reported in several other studies (e.g., Collins & Hailey, 1989), Anger-In and Anger-Out were positively correlated ($r = .62, p < .001$). Although somewhat counterintuitive, their positive relationship may reflect a style of coping that is characterized by avoidance or denial of problems alternating with occasional outbursts of anger that may or may not be directed at the real source of the problem.
6. Indirect effects are obtained by multiplying coefficients on paths leading from gender to the intervening variables by coefficients on paths leading from the intervening variables to their respective alcohol outcomes. According to Cohen and Cohen (1983), an indirect effect may be considered reliable when the direct effects comprising it (in this case, the direct effect of gender on the intervening variable, and of the intervening variable on the alcohol outcome) are both statistically significant.
7. Interestingly, although we anticipated that active coping would act as a suppressor variable, this hypothesis was based on the assumption that males would report higher levels of active coping and active coping would be negatively related to alcohol outcomes. However, we found just the opposite pattern: females reported higher levels of active coping, and active coping was positively related to drink to cope in both samples. Thus, although the data support the predicted suppression effect, they do so for reasons opposite to those we anticipated.
8. This difference is unlikely to reflect a simple reporting bias in that adults reported slightly more self-events than adolescents (means = 1.04 vs. 0.89, respectively).

References

Albino, J.E., & Tedesco, L.A. (1984). Women's health issues. In A.U. Rickel, M. Gerrard, & I. Iscoe (Eds.), *Social psychological problems of women*. New York: Hemisphere.

Albright, C.L., Winkelby, M.A., Ragland, D.R., Fisher, J., & Syme, S.L. (1992). Job strain and prevalence of hypertension in a biracial population of urban bus drivers. *American Journal of Public Health, 82*, 984-989.

Aldwin, C.M., & Revenson, T.A. (1987). Does coping help? A reexamination of the relation between coping and mental health. *Journal of Personality and Social Psychology, 53*, 337-348.

Aspinwall, L.G., & Taylor, S.E. (1992). Modeling cognitive adaptation: A longitudinal investigation of the impact of individual differences and coping on college adjustment and performance. *Journal of Personality and Social Psychology, 63*, 989-1003.

Barnes, G.M., & Welte, J.W. (1986). Patterns and predictors of alcohol use among 7-12th grade students in New York State. *Journal of Studies on Alcohol, 47*, 53-62.

Barnett, R.C., Marshall, N.L., Raudenbush, S.W., & Brennan, R.T. (1993). Gender and the relationship between job experiences and psychological distress: A study of dual-earner couples. *Journal of Personality and Social Psychology, 64,* 794-806.

Baron, R.M., & Kenny, D.A. (1986). The moderator-mediator variable distinction in social psychological research: Conceptual, strategic, and statistical considerations. *Journal of Personality and Social Psychology, 51,* 1173-1182.

Belle, D. (1987). Gender differences in the social moderators of stress. In R.C. Barnett, L. Biener, & G.K. Baruch (Eds.), *Gender and stress* (pp. 257-277). New York: Free Press.

Billings, A.G., & Moos, R.H. (1983). Psychosocial processes of recovery among alcoholics and their families: Implications for clinicians and program evaluators. *Addictive Behaviors, 8,* 205-218.

Bollen, K.A. (1989). *Structural equations with latent variables.* New York: John Wiley & Sons.

Brown, S.A., Goldman, M.S., Inn, A., & Anderson, L.R. (1980). Expectations of reinforcement from alcohol: Their domain and relation to drinking patterns. *Journal of Consulting and Clinical Psychology, 48,* 419-426.

Cappell, H., & Greeley, J. (1987). Alcohol and tension reduction: An update on research and theory. In H.T. Blane and K.E. Leonard (Eds.), *Psychological theories of drinking and alcoholism* (pp. 15-54). New York: Guilford.

Carver, C.S., Scheier, M.F., & Weintraub, J.K. (1989). Assessing coping strategies: A theoretically based approach. *Journal of Personality and Social Psychology, 56,* 267-283.

Cleary, P.D. (1987). Gender differences and stress related disorders. In R.C. Barnett, L. Biener, & G.K. Baruch (Eds.), *Gender and stress* (pp. 39-72). New York: Free Press.

Cohen, J., & Cohen, P. (1983). *Applied multiple regression/correlation analysis for the behavioral sciences* (2nd ed.). Hillsdale, NJ: Lawrence Erlbaum Associates.

Cohen, S., & Hoberman, H.M. (1983). Positive events and social support as buffers of life change stress. *Journal of Applied Social Psychology, 13,* 99-125.

Cohen, S., & Wills, T.A. (1985). Stress, social support, and the buffering hypothesis. *Psychological Bulletin, 98,* 310-357.

Collins, S.W., & Hailey, B.J. (1989). The anger-expression scale: Correlations and the State Trait Personality Inventory and Subscale correlations. *Educational and Psychological Measurement, 49,* 447-455.

Compas, B.E., Davis, G.E., Forsythe, C.J., & Wagner, B.M. (1987). Assessment of major and daily stressful events during adolescence: The Adolescent Perceived Events Scale. *Journal of Consulting and Clinical Psychology, 55,* 534-541.

Compas, B.E., & Phares, V. (1991). Stress during childhood and adolescence: Sources of risk and vulnerability. In E.M. Cummings, A.L Greene, & K.H. Karraker (Eds.), *Life-span developmental psychology: Perspectives on stress and coping* (pp. 111-129). Hillsdale, NJ: Lawrence Erlbaum Associates.

Conger, J.J. (1956). Alcoholism: Theory, problem and challenge. II. Reinforcement theory and the dynamics of alcoholism. *Quarterly Journal of Studies on Alcohol, 17,* 296-305.

Cooke, D.J., & Allan, C.A. (1984). Stressful life events and alcohol abuse in women: A general population study. *British Journal of Addiction, 79,* 425-430.

Cooper, M.L. (1994). Motivations for alcohol use among adolescents: Development and validation of a four-factor model. *Psychological Assessment, 6,* 117-128.

Cooper, M.L., Russell, M., & George, W.H. (1988). Coping, expectancies, and alcohol abuse: A test of social learning formulations. *Journal of Abnormal Psychology, 97,* 218-230.

Cooper, M.L., Russell, M., Skinner, J.B., Frone, M.R., & Mudar, P. (1992a). Stress and alcohol use: Moderating effects of gender, coping and alcohol expectancies. *Journal of Abnormal Psychology, 101,* 139-152.

Cooper, M.L., Russell, M., Skinner, J.B., & Windle, M. (1992b). Development and validation of a three-dimensional measure of drinking motives. *Psychological Assessment, 4,* 123-132.

Dohrenwend, B.S., Krasnoff, L., Askenasy, A.R., & Dohrenwend, B.P. (1978). Exemplification of a method for scaling life events: The PERI Life Events Scale. *Journal of Health and Social Behavior, 19,* 205-229.

Folkman, S., & Lazarus, R.S. (1980). An analysis of coping in a middle-aged community sample. *Journal of Health and Social Behavior, 21,* 219-239.

Forsythe, C.J., & Compas, B.E. (1987). Interaction of cognitive appraisals of stressful events and coping: Testing the goodness of fit hypothesis. *Cognitive Therapy & Research, 11,* 473-485.

Frone, M.R., Russell, M., & Cooper, M.L. (1992). Prevalence of work-family conflict: Are work and family boundaries asymmetrically permeable? *Journal of Organizational Behavior, 13,* 723-729

Frone, M.R., Russell, M., & Cooper, M.L. (1993). Relationship of work-family conflict, gender and alcohol expectancies to alcohol use/abuse. *Journal of Organizational Behavior, 14,* 545-558.

Gorsuch, R.L. (1983). *Factor analysis,* (2nd ed.). Hillsdale, NJ: Lawrence Erlbaum.

Hilton, M.E. (1987). Drinking patterns and drinking problems in 1984: Results from a general population survey. *Alcoholism: Clinical and Experimental Research, 11,* 167-175.

House, J.S., Strecher, V., Metzner, H.L., & Robbins, C.A. (1986). Occupational stress and health among men and women in the Tecumseh Community Health Study. *Journal of Health and Social Behavior, 27,* 62-77.

Huselid, R. F., & Cooper, M.L. (1992). Gender roles as mediators of sex differences in adolescent alcohol use and abuse. *Journal of Health and Social Behavior, 33,* 348-362.

Jessor, R., Donovan, J.E., & Costa, F.M. (1989). *Health Behavior Questionnaire.* Boulder, CO: Institute of Behavioral Science, University of Colorado.

Lambert, S.J. (1991). The combined effects of job and family characteristics on the job satisfaction, job involvement, and intrinsic motivation of men and women workers. *Journal of Organizational Behavior, 12,* 341-363.

Lazarus, R.S., & Folkman, S. (1991). The concept of coping. In A. Monat & R.S. Lazarus (Eds.), *Stress and coping: An anthology* (pp. 189-206). New York: Columbia University Press.

Lex, B.W. (1991). Gender differences and substance abuse. In N.K. Mello (Ed.), *Advances in substance abuse: Vol. 4. Behavioral and biological research* (pp. 225-296). London: Jessica Kingsley.

Lindeman, R.H., Merenda, P.F., & Gold, R.Z. (1980). *Introduction to bivariate and multivariate analysis.* Glenview, IL: Scott Foresman and Co.

Loscocco, K.A., & Spitze, G. (1990). Working conditions, social support, and well-being of female and male factory workers. *Journal of Health and Social Behavior, 31,* 313-327.

Marlatt, G.A., & Gordon, J.R. (Eds.). (1985). *Relapse prevention: Maintenance strategies in the treatment of addictive behaviors.* New York: Guilford.

Miller, S.M., & Kirsch, N. (1987). Sex differences in cognitive coping with stress. In R.C. Barnett, L. Biener, & G.K. Baruch (Eds.), *Gender and stress* (pp. 278-307). New York: Free Press.

Moos, R.H., (1992). Stress and coping theory and evaluation research: An integrated perspective. *Evaluation Review, 16* (5), 534-553.

Moos, R.H., Brennan, P.L., Fondacaro, M.R., & Moos, B.S. (1990). Approach and avoidance coping responses among older problem and nonproblem drinkers. *Psychology and Aging, 5*, 31-40.

Moos, R.H., Cronkite, R.C., Billings, A.G., & Finney, J.W. (1986). *Health and Daily Living Form Manual (rev. ed.).* Palo Alto, CA: Social Ecology Laboratory, Veterans Administration and Stanford University Medical Centers.

Moos, R.H., Finney, J.W., & Chan, D.A. (1981). The process of recovery from alcoholism. I. Comparing alcoholic patients and matched community controls. *Journal of Studies on Alcohol, 42*, 383-402.

Nelson, D.L., & Hitt, M.A. (1992). Employed women and stress: Implications for enhancing women's mental health in the workplace. In J.C. Quick, L.R. Murphy, & J.J. Hurrell, Jr. (Eds.), *Stress & well-being at work: Assessments and interventions for occupational mental health* (pp. 164-177). Washington, DC: American Psychological Association.

O'Doherty, F., & Davies, J.B. (1988). Life events, stress, and addiction. In S. Fisher & J. Reason (Eds.), *Handbook of life stress, cognition and health* (pp. 287-300). New York: John Wiley & Sons.

Parker, D.A., & Farmer, G.C. (1988). The epidemiology of alcohol abuse among employed men and women. In M. Galanter (Ed.), *Recent developments in alcoholism, Vol. 6* (pp. 113-130). New York: Plenum.

Peirce, R.S., Frone, M.R., Russell, M., & Cooper, M.L. (1994). Relationship of financial strain and psychosocial resources to alcohol use and abuse: The mediating role of negative affect and drinking motives. *Journal of Health and Social Behavior, 35,* 291-308.

Pohorecky, L.A. (1991). Stress and alcohol interaction: An update of human research. *Alcoholism: Clinical and Experimental Research, 15*, 438-459.

Robins, L.N., Helzer, J.E., Croughan, J., & Ratcliff, K.S. (1981). National Institute of Mental Health Diagnostic Interview Schedule: Its history, characteristics, and validity. *Archives of General Psychiatry, 38*, 381-389.

Robins, L.N., Helzer, J.E., Croughan, J., Williams, J.B.W., & Spitzer, R.L. (1985). *NIMH Diagnostic Interview Schedule: Version IIIA* (Public Health Service No. ADM-T-42-3[4-85]). Rockville, MD: National Institute of Mental Health.

Sher, K.J. (1987). Stress response dampening. In H.T. Blane & K.E. Leonard (Eds.), *Psychological theories of drinking and alcoholism* (pp. 227-271). New York: Guilford.

Simon, R.W. (1992). Parental role strains, salience of parental identity and gender differences in psychological distress. *Journal of Health and Social Behavior, 33,* 25-35.

Spielberger, C.D., Johnson, E.H., Russell, S.F., Crane, R.J., Jacobs, G.A., & Worden, T.J. (1985). The experience and expression of anger: Construction and validation of an anger expression scale. In M.A. Chesney & R.H. Rosenman (Eds.), *Anger and hostility in cardiovascular and behavioral disorders* (pp. 5-30). Washington, DC: Hemisphere.

Stone, A.A., Lennox, S., & Neale, J.M. (1985). Daily coping and alcohol use in a sample of community adults. In S. Shiffman & T.A. Wills (Eds.), *Coping and substance use* (pp. 199-222). New York: Academic Press.

Suls, J., & Fletcher, B. (1985). The relative efficacy of avoidant and nonavoidant coping strategies: A meta-analysis. *Health Psychology, 4*, 249-288.

Weidner, G., & Collins, R.L. (1993). Gender, coping and health. In H.W. Krohne (Ed.), *Attention and avoidance: Strategies in coping with aversiveness* (pp. 241-265). Seattle, WA: Hogrefe & Huber.

Wethington, E., McLeod, J.D., & Kessler, R.C. (1987). The importance of life events for explaining sex differences in psychological distress. In R.C. Barnett, L. Biener, & G.K. Baruch (Eds.), *Gender and stress* (pp. 144-154). New York: Free Press.

Williams, K.B., & Williams, K.D. (1983). Social inhibition and asking for help: The effects of number, strength, and immediacy of potential help givers. *Journal of Personality and Social Psychology*, *44*, 67-77.

Wills, T.A. (1985). Stress, coping, and tobacco and alcohol use in early adolescence. In S. Shiffman & T.A. Wills (Eds.), *Coping and substance use* (pp. 67-94). New York: Academic Press.

Wills, T.A. (1986). Stress and coping in early adolescence: Relationships to substance use in urban school samples. *Health Psychology*, *5*, 503-529.

Wilsnack, R.W. (1992). Unwanted statuses in women's drinking. *Journal of Employee Assistance Research*, *1*, 239-270.

Wilsnack, S.C., Klassen, A.D., & Wilsnack, R.W. (1984). Drinking and reproductive dysfunction among women in a 1981 national survey. *Alcoholism: Clinical and Experimental Research*, *8*, 451-458.

Young, R.M., Oei, T.P.S., & Knight, R.G. (1990). The tension reduction hypothesis revisited: An alcohol expectancy perspective. *British Journal of Addiction*, *85*, 31-40.

CHAPTER 9

Alcohol Abuse:
Age and Gender Differences

EDITH S. LISANSKY GOMBERG

Measurements of drinking behaviors in the United States have found consistent contrasts between male and female drinking, from the pioneering work of Cahalan, Cisin, and Crossley (1969) to more recent analysis of national survey results (Clark & Hilton, 1991). Males are more likely to drink than females, and they are more likely to drink heavily and more likely to become problem drinkers. Findings about age differences have also been fairly consistent. Among both men and women, younger drinkers are more likely to be heavy drinkers than middle-aged or elderly drinkers (Clark & Hilton, 1991), although there are exceptions to this trajectory among African-Americans and Hispanic-Americans (Spiegler et al., 1989). Among women in the general population, those under 40 tend to drink more than older women and, by age 50, the percentage of heavy drinkers among women drops precipitously (Gomberg, 1982a).

Women are not a homogeneous population (Scarf, 1980), and there are variations in the patterns and problems of women's drinking that relate to ethnicity, education, marital status, and employment:

Ethnicity. More women abstain from alcohol among three minority groups (African-American, Hispanic-American and Asian-American) than among whites (Spiegler et al., 1989). Effects of aging on drinking vary from group to group. For example, the proportion of African-American women who are abstainers increases as women enter their 40s; among white women, abstinence shows a similar rise at age 60 and older. At the other end of the drinking spectrum, frequent or heavy drinkers are significantly more common among white women than among African-American women up to age 40, but after that the differences are smaller (Herd, 1988, 1993).

Education. An early national survey found that abstinence was much more likely among women least educated (grammar school), and that women with some college experience were more likely to use alcohol (Cahalan et al., 1969). The proportion of women who were heavy drinkers, however, was approximately the same for all educational groups, although fewer college graduates were heavy drinkers. More recent research has confirmed that the less educated are more likely to be abstainers (Clark & Hilton, 1991), while high school graduates are the educational subgroup most likely to be frequent/heavy drinkers.

Marital status. The proportion of women who drink is highest among the never-married; the proportion of frequent/heavy drinkers is highest in this group as well (Clark & Hilton, 1991). This pattern is undoubtedly linked with age, because single women are often young, and it is younger women involved in dating/mating behavior who are particularly likely to drink frequently or heavily. At the other end of the age spectrum, it is not surprising that high percentages of widowed women abstain from alcohol, and relatively few drink heavily.

Employment. Women are more likely to use alcohol if they are employed, but employment status has little effect on the proportion of women drinkers who drink heavily (Williams & DeBakey, 1992). Effects of employment on women's drinking are unclear (Wilsnack & Wilsnack, 1992), perhaps in part because of historical changes in women's work roles.

The Life Cycle

Life-historical studies of drinking careers have been more prominent and informative for men's lives (Levinson et al., 1978; Vaillant, 1977) than for women's. However, there have been several longitudinal studies which have included both male and female participants (Block, 1971; Eichorn et al., 1981; Pandina et al., 1984), and the Oakland Growth Studies (Eichorn et al., 1981) have produced a number of reports about alcohol and drug use by both males and females (Block et al., 1988; Jones, 1968, 1971, 1981). Historical and epidemiological data indicate that risks of alcohol-related problems are higher for men than for women at all ages, and some studies have found that women develop alcohol problems at later ages than men do (Gomberg, 1976; Parrella & Filstead, 1988).[1]

Drawing conclusions, however, about gender differences in the life course of alcohol-related problems is difficult because of *historical* change. Women have experienced dramatic changes not only in gender norms for drinking behavior, but also in many other roles that affect their opportunities to drink. The growth of women's employment outside the home, and in the diversity of women's occupations, is one example of the historical changes in women's roles that have affected how they use and abuse alcohol. Such changes mean that drinking patterns across the lifespan of one cohort of women may not be very useful for predicting how drinking patterns change during the lives of later cohorts.

The difficulties of evaluating how drinking changes across the lifespan are increased because the scarcity of long-term longitudinal studies makes it necessary to rely heavily on data from cross-sectional studies, where drinking patterns of people of all different ages are measured at one point in time. Using data from such studies to compare men or women in their 30s, 40s, 50s, and 60s confounds effects of aging with effects from having different historical experiences. Nevertheless, three types of cross-sectional studies have become essential sources of information about how age and drinking are related.

First, epidemiological studies have gathered data on the drinking patterns in the general population from adolescence to old age, including measures of drinking frequencies and quantities and of alcohol-related problems (e.g., Hilton, 1988, 1991; Johnston et al., 1993). Second, studies in clinical populations have gathered data on ages of onset for drinking problems or for alcoholism, and the relationships of ages of onset with positive family history (Cloninger et al., 1981) and with comorbidity (Hesselbrock et al., 1984; Schuckit & Monteiro, 1988; Schuckit et al., 1969). Third, other clinical studies of patients dependent on drugs or alcohol have compared age subgroups on demographic characteristics, drinking behaviors, and drinking consequences (Gomberg, 1982b, 1986; Harrison, 1989; Harrison & Belille, 1987). The third type is really a variant of age-at-onset studies, because younger alcohol or drug dependent people will, for the most part, have younger ages of onset for alcohol problems.

Age-at-Onset Studies

The idea that *age at onset* of problem drinking is critical for distinguishing different groups of alcoholic patients is not new. Knight (1937) distinguished essential and reactive alcoholism: essential or primary alcoholism is characterized by early onset, a family history of alcoholism, and "psychopathic personality disorder," whereas reactive alcoholism is associated with later onset, lower rates of family alcoholism, and "neurotic disorder." Cloninger's more recent typology using age at onset (Cloninger, 1987; Cloninger et al., 1981) has generated a good deal of research. Cloninger's Type 1 alcoholism is characterized by later onset, psychological dependence, and stronger contributions of environmental influences; Type 2 alcoholism is characterized by earlier onset, stronger family history, and more antisocial behavior.

Other research has confirmed that early onset of alcoholism is associated with more severe problems. Lee and DiClimente (1985) reported that early onset alcoholics exhibited more social role maladaptation and more severe alcoholism symptoms. A study by von Knorring et al. (1985) found that early onset alcoholics demonstrated more psychosocial impairment, criminality, and drug problems than late onset alcoholics. More recently, Irwin and associates (1990) found that earlier age at onset was correlated with histories of problems with alcohol, drugs, and childhood criminality. It should be noted, however, that some negative results have been reported. Worobec et al. (1990) did not find an association between earlier onset and a more severe course of alcoholism among research subjects who were children of alcoholics. Nevertheless, Schuckit (1991, p. 512) concludes that "most data going back to the 1950s demonstrate a much more severe course of alcohol and other substance-related difficulties in alcoholics who developed their alcohol-related life impairments in their early twenties." Although Schuckit describes age at onset as "the best documented of the demographic divisions" among alcoholics, he concludes that it is questionable whether age at onset identifies "unique and distinct subtypes."

Parrella and Filstead (1988) raise the question of how to *define* age at onset. They selected five life events as possible criteria: getting drunk regularly, realizing that alcohol gave relief, family and friends noting the problem, the first attempt to stop drinking, and the point at which the individual first thought he/she had a drinking problem. These events are reported sequentially by problem drinkers, with getting drunk regularly a pattern that typically develops earliest, and self-realization of the drinking problem typically developing last. The five indicators are reported in the same sequence by both female and male patients, although the events occur later for women. Obviously, measurement of age at onset will vary depending on the criteria used.

During the 1960s, several investigators reported data suggesting that age at onset would be a good basis for subtyping women alcoholics (Cramer & Blacker, 1963; Curlee, 1969; Kinsey, 1966). Kinsey (1966) differentiated three subgroups: women with early onset and rapid development, women with early onset and slower development, and women with later onset and rapid development. Commenting on these, Gomberg (1976, p. 134) thought it necessary to see how the proposed subgroups "relate to therapy and prognosis . . . and to sex roles, constraints, social class, and changes over time."

In studies of alcohol abuse among older people (60 and over), differences between early onset and late or recent onset are a major issue (Gomberg, 1982a, 1990a). Subgroups of early onset and late onset alcohol abusers among the elderly have been observed in clinical studies (Gaitz & Baer, 1971; Glatt & Rosin, 1964; Merry, 1980; Wilkinson, 1971), epidemiological research (Abraham & Patterson, 1978–79; Holzer et al., 1984), and even among Skid Row male alcohol abusers (Cohen & Sokolovsky, 1989). Early onset alcoholics among the elderly are those for whom problem drinking began in adolescence or in their 20s or 30s. A recent report (Gomberg, 1995a) finds that in a group of elderly male alcoholics in treatment, the mean age at onset was 27.0. For a comparable group of elderly women alcohol abusers in treatment, the mean age at onset was 46.2. Epidemiological research on the general population supports this gender difference: among elderly respondents who reported alcohol-related problems within the last six months, less than one-third of the men reported onset after age 40, but more than half of the women reported such "late onset" (Holzer et al., 1984).

There are at least two major questions about what distinguishes early and late onset alcohol abuse among the elderly. First, there is the problem of defining when onset is "late." Late onset may be defined as "an onset of alcohol problems after the age of 40" (Schuckit, 1977), after age 50 (Schonfeld & Dupree, 1991), after age 55 (Fitzgerald & Mulford, 1992), or "over age 60" (Moos & Finney, 1984). Sometimes, investigators write about those "who begin to drink excessively in their later years" (Moos & Finney, 1984), or "late in life" (Cohen, 1975). In our current data collection at an alcohol research center mandated for research on alcohol and aging, the term "recent onset" has been substituted and defined as onset that occurred within the last 10 years.

Second, there is the possibility that early and late onset differ not only in age but also in precipitating causes. Are those who manifest late or recent onset responding to stress, e.g., bereavement, retirement, illness? Late onset alcohol abusers have, in fact, been defined as "reactive alcoholics" (Gomberg, 1982a). An early epidemiological study of an urban residential area (Bailey et al., 1965) found that a large number of widowers could be labeled as "probable alcoholics." A study of a clinical sample of middle to upper class male alcoholics (Finlayson et al., 1988) noted, in addition to effects of bereavement, the critical role of retirement in late onset. On the other hand, a recent general population survey of the elderly found late life stress unrelated to heavy drinking (Welte & Mirand, 1992).

Late onset may be more important among elderly alcoholics seeking treatment because of its prevalence in this population and its implications for treatment outcomes. Clinical studies have estimated that about one-third of elderly alcohol abusers had late onsets (Wilkinson, 1971; Zimberg, 1974). Moos and Finney (1984) found that 33.6% of the 440 elderly alcohol abusers whom they studied reported that their problem drinking had begun within the past two years. Late onset may also be related to better prognosis, treatment attendance, and treatment completion (Atkinson, 1995; Atkinson et al., 1990; Schonfeld & Dupree, 1991).

Chronological Age Studies

Studies of alcohol or drug abusers by age group go back to early reports of "generational differences" among drug abusers, which agreed in describing younger addicts as manifesting more "socially disapproved modes of behavior" (Brotman et al., 1972). A comparison of younger and older male alcoholic patients in a veterans hospital (mean ages 23.8 and 48.4, respectively) found that the younger men reported more family history of alcoholism, more drug use, lower Minnesota Multiphasic Personality Inventory (MMPI) (Swenson et al., 1973) scores for depression, and higher scores on the MMPI Psychopathic

Deviate Scale (Gomberg, 1982b). Comparisons of age groups of alcoholic women in treatment (Harrison, 1989; Harrison & Belille, 1987) show similarly that drug abuse, eating disorders, childhood antisocial behaviors, suicide attempts, and abusive relationships were more prevalent among the younger women.

In a national general population survey, Wilsnack and Cheloha (1987) examined specific configurations of social roles associated with problem drinking among women in the age groups 21 to 34, 35 to 49, 50 to 64, and 65 and older. The authors concluded that women's problem drinking throughout the lifespan is related to age-specific patterns of "role deprivation": a lack of marital and work roles when young, and losses or limitations of work, parenting, and/or marital roles in middle and old age that leave them more dependent on the companionship of drinkers. Gomberg and Turnbull (1990) examined role deprivation patterns for different age groups of women alcoholics in treatment. Women in their 20s did not fit the pattern described by Wilsnack and Cheloha (i.e., being unmarried and lacking a full-time employment role), but women in their 40s did show "irreversible" losses of marital and childrearing roles.

The Michigan Study of Alcoholic Women in Treatment[2]

Because most previous studies of alcoholic women had compared them only with alcoholic men, a study was undertaken to compare alcoholic women of different age groups with age-matched groups of nonalcoholic women (Gomberg, 1986). The reasoning was that men and women were members, in a sense, of different subcultures, and were socialized quite differently. The search for what distinguishes alcoholic women from women who do not develop alcohol-related problems had to be conducted by comparing subgroups of women.

Subjects. The study interviewed women from treatment facilities in six counties in southeastern Michigan.[3] The 21 inpatient and outpatient treatment centers that recruited patients for the study drew from urban, suburban, and rural areas. A total of 301 women patients agreed to be interviewed; the refusal rate was 7%. Patients were seen after detoxification (1–2 weeks). There were 99 women in the 20–29 age group, 108 women in the 30–39 age group and 94 women in the 40–49 age group. The 301 patients are described below as *alcoholic* or *clinic* women.

Age at onset. Among the women in their 20s, the mean age at onset was 19.6, and 43% of these young patients dated onset during their adolescent years. Mean age at onset was 28.3 for the women in their 30s, and 36.5 for the women in their 40s. The estimated duration of problem drinking was five years for the women in their 20s, seven years for those in their 30s, and nine years for those in their 40s.

Control group. In order to match more effectively, selection of the control women was delayed until half the alcoholic women had been interviewed. After several selection methods were considered and rejected, the control women were selected *by nomination:* the alcoholic women were asked to suggest a friend, acquaintance, or neighbor who might agree to be interviewed and who did not have problems related to alcohol. The control women interviewed included 34 women in their 20s, 53 in their 30s, 50 in their 40s. The mean ages of the three patient age groups were, respectively, 24.9, 35.1, and 45.1; the three matched control age groups had very similar mean ages of 24.0, 34.6, and 45.0. Although the oldest group of respondents (alcoholics and controls) reported somewhat less parental education than the younger two groups, there were no significant differences between the oldest group and the younger groups in the economic status of the families during the respondents' childhoods.

The interview schedule. A list of variables was assembled from the literature on female alcoholism. The final interview schedule also included items from three other sources: the Connors Collection of alcohol study questionnaires, housed at the Rutgers Center of Alcohol Studies Library; instruments used by the Institute for Social Research in mental health research (Veroff et al., 1981); and the National Institute of Mental Health's Diagnostic Interview Schedule (DIS) (Robins et al., 1985). After the interview schedule had been pretested with clinic clients and reviewed both by clinical social workers and recovering women alcoholics, the final version included items about childhood and adolescent experience; drinking history; social supports; marital, parenting, and work roles; health; drug use; and psychiatric symptoms.

Hypotheses. Two major hypotheses for the research were based on earlier work with younger and older male alcoholics (Gomberg, 1982b). The hypotheses were that (1) younger problem drinkers with earlier onset would show greater impulsivity and more indicators of antisocial personality, and (2) older problem drinkers with later onset would manifest more depressive features. However, in light of what has been learned about gender socialization and the later onset of women's problem drinking, the research team was prepared to find that female alcoholics might not show the same age differences as male alcoholics.

Results

Early histories. Clinic and control women did not differ in the negative life events of their early years but they did show strong differences in reports of early life affective responses (Gomberg, 1989a): in conflict with parents, childhood depression, and feelings of deprivation, the clinic women—not surprisingly—reported significantly more. The clinic women reported significantly more early life problems linked to difficulties in impulse control:

strong differences in early temper tantrums, enuresis, running away from home, "cutting" school, expulsion/suspension from school, dropping out before the completion of 12th grade, and early suicide attempts (Gomberg, 1989a). Of the clinic women, 62% left their family of origin before the age of 20, compared with 42% of control women.

Difficulties in impulse control, however, were significantly more common among the younger patients. When the clinic women were compared with their nonalcoholic age peers, the women in their 40s showed little difference in early life problems, but the alcoholic/clinic women below the age of 40 did report significantly more history of early life temper tantrums, runaways, and difficulties with school authorities than did the age-matched control women.

Family histories, positive and negative. Are the children of alcoholics more likely to manifest early onset of alcohol-related problems? Generally, the literature has reported such a relationship among male alcoholics. For example, in a study of younger and older male alcoholics (Gomberg, 1982b), there was a clear association between the frequency of reported alcoholism in the parent(s) and early onset. In the Michigan study, respondents were asked about the drinking patterns of fathers, mothers, siblings, and other relatives during the respondents' growing-up years. The differences between the alcoholic women in their 20s, 30s, and 40s were small and nonsignificant. The alcoholic women with no family history of problem drinking reported a mean age at onset of 29.6; those with a family history of problem drinking a mean age at onset of 26.4—a nonsignificant difference. The relationship between a family history of problem drinking and early onset *does not* hold up for women, at least not in this sample (Gomberg, 1991a).

Predicting early onset for women. What, then, may be the predictors of early onset of alcohol-related problems among women? A number of possible variables were evaluated by regression analysis (Gomberg, 1988a). As Table 1 shows, the best predictors were earlier age of first intoxication and the use of marijuana and/or other drugs during early adolescence. Lesser predictors were temper tantrums during childhood and reported unhappiness while growing up. As is often the case in predicting aberrant behavior, the best predictors are early samples of the behavior itself.

Predicting later onset for women. While the mean age at onset of the youngest group of alcoholic women was 19.6, the mean age at onset of the 40s group was 36.5. Most of the alcoholic women in their 40s were born in the 1930s, suggesting that, as a cohort, they were raised with more traditional views of female roles than were the younger alcoholics. They were significantly more condemning of women's drinking than were the younger alcoholics. They were less likely to be in the workplace than their age-matched controls (39% versus 69%). They did not differ from the control women of the same age in reports of childhood problems linked to difficulties in impulse

TABLE 1
Predicting Early Age at Onset among Alcoholic Women in Treatment

Variable	Beta	SE	p
Model 1			
Age at first intoxication	−.41956	.056	.001
Marijuana/drug use, 13–15	.31464	.048	.001
Temper tantrums	.12940	.051	.01
Age began smoking	.00053	.054	
Positive family history	.01746	.049	
$R^2 = .435$			
Model 2			
Age at first intoxication	−.41488	.048	.001
Marijuana/drug use, 13–15	.30560	.048	.001
Temper tantrums	.15336	.046	.001
$R^2 = .436$			
Model 3			
Age at first intoxication	−.40309	.048	.001
Marijuana/drug use, 13–15	.34427	.048	.001
Temper tantrums	.14411	.046	.01
Happy/unhappy while growing up	−.10049	.044	.05
$R^2 = .446$			

control, but they reported significantly more "nervous problems," fears, and phobias during their earlier years. One hypothesis is that coping mechanisms, particularly for dealing with frustration, are less adequate among those women who will belatedly become alcoholic.

The alcoholic women in their 40s differed from age-matched control women in marital, sexual, and reproductive histories. Thirty-seven percent of the alcoholic women were divorced, separated, or widowed, compared with 18% of the age-matched controls. The alcoholic women were less likely than controls to report that their husbands were good sex partners, and more likely to report a history of miscarriage or hysterectomy (Gomberg, 1986). Such unhappy or frustrating experiences might interact with poor coping resources to increase risks of "reactive" alcoholism, but it is unclear how much the undesirable experiences may have resulted from alcoholism rather than causing it.

Role behaviors. Although the alcoholic and control women came from similar backgrounds and socioeconomic levels of family origin, the alcoholic women left school at an earlier age, left home at an earlier age, and married at an earlier age than did the control women. The long-term consequence of such decisions was, inevitably, lower occupational status. Furthermore, as shown in Table 2, the alcoholic women were more likely than other women to be unemployed (looking for work) or staying at home, as a concomitant or

TABLE 2
Employment Status and Occupations of Clinic
and Control Women (in percent)

	Working	Unemployed	Homemaker
Clinic women			
19–29 years	68.9	22.2	8.9
30–39 years	56.5	15.7	27.8
40–49 years	39.6	17.6	42.9
Control women			
21–29 years	78.1	9.4	12.5
30–39 years	81.1	5.7	13.2
40–49 years	71.4	4.1	24.5

For % homemakers, clinic women vs. controls: $\chi^2 = 10.9$, df $= 2$, $p < .01$

OCCUPATIONS OF EMPLOYED CLINIC AND CONTROL WOMEN

	Prof.	Mgrs.	Clerical	Sales	Craft/ operative	Service/ labor
Clinic women	24.5	8.8	22.0	5.7	19.5	19.5
Control women	33.0	16.5	27.2	5.8	2.9	14.6

($\chi^2 = 19.6$, df $= 5$, $p < .001$)

consequence of their drinking. Alcoholic and control women differed significantly in both employment status and occupational levels.

The alcoholics reported more marital disruption than the control women, and were more likely to be married to a heavy or problem drinker. Both of these patterns have been found consistently in studies of alcoholic women (Busch & Feuerlein, 1975; Gomberg, 1979, 1991b; Johnson, 1982; Lisansky, 1957; Mulford, 1977; Schuckit, 1972; Wanberg & Knapp, 1970; Wilsnack et al., 1984). Alcoholic and control women did not differ in numbers of children, but the alcoholic women were more likely to have had a miscarriage or hysterectomy, and the alcoholic women in their 30s reported three times as many children "born with problems" as the nonalcoholic women in the same age group.

Use of other drugs. The alcoholic women began smoking at an earlier age, were more likely to be current smokers (82%, compared with 34% of control women), and were more likely to be heavy smokers (40%, compared with 4%). The younger an alcoholic woman was, the more likely she was to be a smoker. Alcoholic women reported significantly more use than control women of medication including minor tranquilizers, stimulants, sedatives, and analgesics. Alcoholic women also reported use of several illicit drugs (cocaine, hallucinogens, and heroin) significantly more often than control women, although there were no differences in reported use of marijuana

(Gomberg, 1989b). Age comparisons within the sample of alcoholic women indicate that the older women were more likely than the younger women to use a drug prescribed by a physician (Gomberg, 1995b). The younger women alcoholics were more likely to use stimulants, sedatives, hallucinogens, cocaine, and heroin than were the older alcoholics. The younger women were also more likely to use drugs and alcohol together than were the older women.

Implications of drinking in public vs. drinking at home. All the alcoholic women reported that much of their drinking was done at home. However, those in their 20s did more drinking in public places than did the older women alcoholics. Furthermore, a larger proportion of the younger women were employed outside the home (69% versus 40% of older women), so their drinking or its effects might be more visible. When the alcoholic women were asked about drinking in the workplace, 14% of those in high-level occupations, 21% of those in middle-level occupations, and 36% of those in low-level occupations reported drinking at work. If drinking by younger women alcoholics is more visible, it is perhaps not surprising that they arouse "more social concern and hostility" (Gomberg, 1988b). The younger women alcoholics also reported more trouble with legal authorities and more rejection by family and friends than did the older women alcoholics.

Violent events. The respondents were also queried about violent events occurring in the last two years. The alcoholic women reported more assaults, more arrests, more robberies, more suicide attempts, and more automobile accidents than the control women. Violence directed toward one's husband (hitting or throwing things) was reported by 50% of the alcoholic women and by 30% of the controls. When age groups of alcoholic women were compared, the youngest group always reported more violence. For example, 22% of the youngest women reported assaults within the last two years as compared with 5% of middle-aged alcoholic women. Twice as many of the younger alcoholic women (42%) reported arrests associated with their drinking compared to alcoholic women in their 40s (21%). There seems to be an association between drinking in more visible, public places and violent experiences (Gomberg, 1990b).

Depression. Factor analysis of the 48 interview items dealing with depression yielded four factors: depressed mood, low self-esteem, negative perceptions of childhood, and somatic symptoms (Turnbull & Gomberg, 1988). While the factor structure did not differ between alcoholic and control women (Turnbull & Gomberg, 1990), alcoholic women had significantly higher scores on depression (Gomberg, 1986). When age groups of alcoholic women were compared, the youngest subgroup had slightly *higher* scores on all four factors of depression. Thus, one of the starting hypotheses, that older problem drinkers would show more depressive features than younger ones, was clearly *not* supported among the alcoholic women studied.

TABLE 3
Precentages of Women Reporting Suicide Attempts

	All Cases	20–29	30–39	40–49
Alcoholic	40.0	50.5	43.0	25.5
Control	8.8	8.8	9.4	8.0
χ^2	43.5	18.3	18.4	6.4
Significance	.0000	.0000	.0000	.0000

Age differences (20s vs. 30s vs. 40s)
  Alcoholic women: χ^2 = 13.15, significance = .0014
  Control women: χ^2 = .66, significance = .9673

Suicide attempts. As shown in Table 3, a significantly higher percentage of alcoholic women (40.0%) than control women (8.8%) reported having made suicide attempts (Gomberg, 1989c). Age differences in rates of attempted suicide were minimal in the control group, but were striking among the alcoholics. Suicide attempts were reported by 25.5% of the middle-aged alcoholic women, 43.0% of those in their 30s, and 50.5% of the youngest sub-

TABLE 4
Events Occurring Before Entering Treatment: All Clinic Women and Clinic
Women by Age Group (in percent)

	All Clinic	Age 20–29	Age 30–39	Age 40–49	p
Recent pretreatment events					
Increasing depression	87.8	90.9	89.8	82.8	
Blackouts, DTs, etc.	67.4	55.6	59.3	42.4	<.05
Marital/love problems	65.4	61.6	72.2	62.4	
Relatives fed up	52.4	55.6	59.3	42.4	<.05
Trouble with police	21.3	33.3	13.9	17.1	<.01
Suicide attempt	21.0	22.2	26.9	14.0	
R was very sick	23.7	25.3	26.9	18.3	
Death of a loved one	24.0	18.2	22.2	32.3	
Child-related events*					
Problems with a child	47.0	45.4	50.0	46.1	
Child moved away					
from home	34.1	22.7	21.1	58.4	<.001
Job-related events					
Recent warning at work	16.6	22.4	15.0	12.2	
Lost job within last two years	21.6	34.3	17.6	12.8	<.001
Changed job, worse job,					
within last two years	10.0	18.2	6.5	5.3	<.01

*Percentages calculated as % of women in each age group who have had children.

group. Thus, not only were alcoholic women more likely than controls to attempt suicide, but the youngest alcoholics were at greatest risk.

Entry into treatment. The alcoholic women were given a list of events and asked, "During the months before you stopped drinking and got into treatment this time, were any of the following things going on?" The most frequently cited events were increasing depression, symptoms such as blackouts, and problems in close interpersonal relationships. Work-connected problems and difficulties with the police preceded entry into treatment significantly more often among the youngest alcoholics than among the older subgroups. The younger alcoholics were also more likely to report blackouts and rejection by family members just prior to entering treatment. Among the alcoholic women in their 40s who had children, more than half cited "child moved away from home" as a stressful event preceding entry into treatment.

Some Implications for Treatment

The findings reported here, as well as other research and clinical reports on alcoholic women, have some broad implications for treatment strategies. Clearly, treatment plans must be differentiated for women at different stages of life. For *middle-aged women* (who used to be the great majority of those seen in treatment), important components of treatment may include reconstructing social networks, evaluating the positive and negative features of family structure, and offering support and encouragement for the development of marketable skills. "Lost roles" (Wilsnack & Cheloha, 1987) do seem to be of primary importance: in the research reported here, when alcoholic women in their 40s were compared with nonalcoholic women of the same age, the alcoholic women were significantly more likely to be divorced or separated (34% vs. 12%, respectively), unemployed (18% vs. 4%), and distressed by a child's recent move away from home (55% vs. 34%). The loss of marital and childbearing roles may be irreversible, but these women's lives need to be restructured in terms of job, volunteer work, and other meaningful activities.

Among the *youngest alcoholics,* the mending of social networks (and particularly ties with family and friends) needs to be a primary issue in treatment. The youngest alcoholics are the most likely to report broken communication with parents and friends (Gomberg, 1988b), and they may narrow their social contacts to the people with whom they drink. The loss of social ties needs to be reversed, particularly because it may contribute to the relatively high rates of depression and suicide attempts among young alcoholic women. These young women tend to engage in less denial than older alcoholics (Gomberg, 1986), so reality-oriented therapies dealing with their use of other drugs and their limited control over impulses may be beneficial.

Gender and Elderly Alcohol Abuse

Recent research on male and female alcohol abusers in treatment who are age 55 or older (Gomberg, 1995a; Gomberg & Nelson, 1992) has confirmed some relationships of age, gender, and alcohol abuse suggested by earlier research on drinking and roles across the lifespan. Three patterns from the research deserve emphasis here. First, the often reported finding of more marital disruption among female alcoholics than among male alcoholics had a unique pattern among elderly patients. More older men were divorced or separated than older women, but far more of the older women were widowed (51% of the women, 18% of the men). Thus, elderly alcoholics may reflect the finding in the general population that among older people who live alone, women are more likely to be living alone because of widowhood.

Second, the research upheld the generalization that women enter treatment after fewer years of problem drinking than men have experienced. Among the older female alcoholics studied, 38% reported that the onset of problem drinking occurred within the past 10 years, whereas only 4% of the male alcoholics reported the onset that recently. A similar gender difference in age of onset of problem drinking has been reported by elderly respondents in epidemiological studies of the general population (e.g., Holzer et al., 1984).

Third, gender differences in elderly alcoholics' use of prescribed psychoactive drugs were consistent with gender comparisons throughout the lifespan (Gomberg, 1995a; Mellinger et al., 1984; Robbins & Clayton, 1989). The older alcoholic women studied were likely to be more frequent or heavier users of prescribed psychoactive drugs than the older men, and the women reported more tolerance and more dependence on prescription drugs than did the men (Gomberg, 1995a).

Research Recommendations

The age and gender patterns described here raise many important questions about the development of alcohol-related problems and alcoholism. Three questions in particular deserve high priority in alcohol research:

First, a pattern of early family and school problems, drinking-related arrests, and other drug use is most characteristic of the youngest alcoholic women. This suggests that to some extent antisocial personality disorder affects alcohol problems in young women as it does in young men. The relationship between antisocial personality disorder, early onset of alcohol problems, and youthful alcoholism among young women needs closer study (Zucker & Gomberg, 1996).

Second, alcohol-related problems peak for many women and men in late adolescence/early adulthood (Clark & Hilton, 1991; Fillmore, 1987; Fillmore et al., 1991). Nevertheless, as the Michigan study and research on older alcoholics show, women's and men's alcoholism often persists into middle or old age, or begins then. In research on how maturation processes affect alcohol use (e.g., Miller-Tutzauer et al., 1991; Schulenberg et al., 1993), it is important to determine why these processes fail to protect some women and men against a continuation or later onset of problem drinking.

Finally, the research literature emphasizes the poorer prognosis of male and female early onset alcoholics. This may reflect clinical research in which later onset (and older) alcoholics respond better to treatment (e.g., Atkinson, 1995). Among problem drinkers in the general population, young women may modify their own drinking more readily than older women (e.g., Fillmore et al., 1991; Wilsnack & Wilsnack, 1991). The question raised by these contrasting patterns is, why might treatment interventions be both more necessary and more beneficial for older (and later onset) female problem drinkers? Research to answer this question could have important implications for efforts to orient treatment to age and gender differences in alcohol abuse.

Notes

1. Studies that do not find later onset of alcohol-related problems in women than in men (Griffin et al., 1989; Piazza et al., 1989; Prescott et al., 1994) suggest that gender differences in age of onset may vary with the age and clinical or nonclinical settings of problem drinker samples.
2. Funded by National Institute on Alcohol Abuse and Alcoholism grant AA04143; a grant from the Rackham School of Graduate Studies, University of Michigan; and from a National Institutes of Health Biomedical Research Grant to the vice president for research, University of Michigan. Participants included Elizabeth M. Douvan, Mary Ellen Colten, Susan Timmer, Joanne E. Turnbull, Rebecca Schilit, and David M. Klingel.
3. Patients were middle and upper income women, all white. They were diagnosed by clinic staff as alcohol abusers or alcohol-dependent, based on DSM-III (American Psychiatric Association, 1980) criteria.

References

Abraham, R.B., & Patterson, R.D. (1978-79). Psychological distress among the community elderly: Prevalence, characteristics and implications for service. *Internal Journal of Aging and Human Development, 9,* 1-18.

American Psychiatric Association Task Force on Nomenclature and Statistics. (1980). Diagnostic and statistical manual of mental disorders (DSM-III). Washington, DC: Author.

Atkinson, R.M. (1995). Treatment programs for aging alcoholics. In T.P. Beresford & E.S.L. Gomberg (Eds.), *Alcohol and aging* (pp. 186-210). New York: Oxford University Press.

Atkinson, R.M., Tolson, R.L., & Turner, J.A. (1990). Late versus early onset problem drinking in older men. *Alcoholism: Clinical and Experimental Research, 14,* 574-579.

Bailey, M.B., Haberman, P.W., & Alksne, H. (1965). The epidemiology of alcoholism in an urban residential area. *Quarterly Journal of Studies on Alcohol, 26,* 19-40.

Block, J. (1971). *Lives through time.* Berkeley: Brancroft Books.

Block, J., Block, J.H., & Keyes, S. (1988). Longitudinally foretelling drug usage in adolescence: Early childhood personality and environmental precursors. *Child Development, 59,* 336-355.

Brotman, R.E., Suffet, S.L., & Shah, R. (1972). Generational differences among drug abuse patients. *International Journal of the Addictions, 7,* 219-235.

Busch, H., & Feuerlein, W. (1975). Sozialpsychologische Aspeke in Ehen von Alkoholikerinnen [Sociopsychological aspects in marriages of alcoholic women]. *Schweizer Archiv fur Neurologie, 116,* 329-341.

Cahalan, D., Cisin, I.H., & Crossley, H.M. (1969). *American drinking practices: A national study of drinking behavior and attitudes* (Monograph No. 6). New Brunswick, NJ: Rutgers Center of Alcohol Studies.

Clark, W.B., & Hilton, M.E. (Eds.). (1991). *Alcohol in America: Drinking practices and problems.* Albany, NY: State University of New York Press.

Cloninger, C.R.(1987). Neurogenetic adaptive mechanisms in alcoholism. *Science, 236,* 410-416.

Cloninger, C.R., Bohman, M., & Sigvardsson, S. (1981). Inheritance of alcohol abuse: Cross-fostering analysis of adopted men. *Archives of General Psychiatry, 38,* 861-868.

Cohen, C.I., & Sokolovsky, J. (1989). *Old men of the bowery: Strategies for survival among the homeless.* New York: Guilford Press.

Cohen, S. (1975). Drug use in the aging patient. *Lex et Sci, 11,* 217-221.

Cramer, M.J., & Blacker, E. (1963). "Early" and "late" problem drinkers among female prisoners. *Journal of Health and Human Behavior, 4,* 282-290.

Curlee, J. (1969). Alcoholism and the "empty nest." *Bulletin of Menninger Clinic, 33,* 165-171.

Eichorn, D.H., Clausen, J.A., Haan, N., Honzik, M.P., & Mussen, P.H. (Eds.). (1981). *Present and past in middle life.* New York: Academic Press.

Fillmore, K.M. (1987). Women's drinking across the adult life course as compared to men's. *British Journal of Addiction, 82,* 801-811.

Fillmore, K.M., Hartka, E., Johnstone, B.M., Leino, E.V., Motoyoshi, M., & Temple, M.T. (1991). A meta-analysis of life course variation in drinking. *British Journal of Addiction, 86,* 1221-1268.

Finlayson, R.E., Hurt, R.D., Davis, Jr., L.J., & Morse, R.M. (1988). Alcoholism in elderly persons: A study of the psychiatric and psychosocial features of 216 inpatients. *Mayo Clinic Proceedings, 63,* 761-768.

Fitzgerald, J.L., & Mulford, H.A. (1992). Elderly vs. younger problem drinker "treatment" and recovery experiences. *British Journal of Addiction, 87,* 1281-1291.

Gaitz, C.M., & Baer, P.E. (1971). Characteristics of elderly patients with alcoholism. *Archives of General Psychiatry, 24,* 372-378.

Glatt, M.M., & Rosin, A.J. (1964). Aspects of alcoholism in the elderly. *Lancet, 2,* 472-473.

Gomberg, E.S. (1976). Alcoholism in women. In B. Kissin & H. Begleiter (Eds.), *The biology of alcoholism: Volume 4. Social aspects of alcoholism* (pp. 117-166). New York: Plenum.

Gomberg, E.S. (1979). Problems with alcohol and other drugs. In E.S. Gomberg & V. Franks (Eds.), *Gender and disordered behavior: Sex differences in psychopathology* (pp. 204-240). New York: Brunner/Mazel.

Gomberg, E.S.L. (1982a). Alcohol use and alcohol problems among the elderly. In NIAAA, *Special population issues* (pp. 263-290) (NIAAA Alcohol and Health

Monograph No. 4; DHHS Publication No. ADM 82-1193). Washington, DC: U.S. Government Printing Office.

Gomberg, E.S.L. (1982b). The young male alcoholic: A pilot study. *Journal of Studies on Alcohol, 43,* 683-701.

Gomberg, E.S.L. (1986). Women and alcoholism: Psychosocial issues. In *Women and alcohol: Health-related issues* (pp. 78-120) (NIAAA Research Monograph No.16; DHHS Publication No. ADM 86-1139). Washington, DC: U.S. Government Printing Office.

Gomberg, E.S.L. (1988a). Predicting age at onset for alcoholic women. *Alcoholism: Clinical and Experimental Research, 12,* 337 (abstract).

Gomberg, E.S.L. (1988b). Alcoholic women in treatment: The question of stigma and age. *Alcohol and Alcoholism, 23,* 507-514.

Gomberg, E.S.L. (1989a). Alcoholic women in treatment: Early histories and early problem behaviors. *Advances in Alcohol & Substance Abuse, 8,* 133-147.

Gomberg, E.S.L. (1989b). Alcoholism in women: Use of other drugs. *Alcoholism: Clinical and Experimental Research, 13,* 338 (abstract).

Gomberg, E.S.L. (1989c). Suicide risk among women with alcohol problems. *American Journal of Public Health, 79,* 1363-1365.

Gomberg, E.S.L. (1990a). Drugs, alcohol, and aging. In L.T. Kozlowski et al. (Eds.), *Research advances in alcohol and drug problems, Volume 10* (pp. 171-213). New York: Plenum.

Gomberg, E.S.L. (1990b). Alcoholic women in treatment: Report of violent events. *Alcoholism: Clinical and Experimental Research, 14,* 312 (abstract).

Gomberg, E.S.L. (1991a). Comparing alcoholic women with positive vs negative family history. *Alcoholism: Clinical and Experimental Research, 15,* 363 (abstract).

Gomberg, E.S.L. (1991b). Women and alcohol: Psychosocial aspects. In D.J. Pittman and H.R. White (Eds.), *Society, culture, and drinking patterns reexamined* (pp. 263-284). New Brunswick, NJ: Rutgers Center of Alcohol Studies.

Gomberg, E.S.L. (1995a). Older women and alcohol: Use and abuse. In M. Galanter (Ed.), *Recent developments in alcoholism: Vol. 12. Alcoholism and women: The effect of gender* (pp. 61-79). New York: Plenum.

Gomberg, E.S.L., (1995b). Health care provision for men and women. In M.V. Seeman (Ed.), *Gender and psychopathology.* Washington, DC: American Psychiatric Association.

Gomberg, E.S.L., & Nelson, B.W. (1992, June). *Gender differences among older alcoholics in treatment.* Presentation at the Research Society on Alcoholism meeting, San Diego, CA.

Gomberg, E.S.L. & Turnbull, J.E. (1990). Alcoholism in women: Pathways to treatment. *Alcoholism: Clinical and Experimental Research, 14,* 312 (abstract).

Griffin, M.L., Weiss, R.D., Mirin, S.M., & Lange, U. (1989). A comparison of male and female cocaine abusers. *Archives of General Psychiatry, 46,* 122-126.

Harrison, P.A. (1989). Women in treatment: Changing over time. *International Journal of the Addictions, 24,* 655-671.

Harrison, P.A., & Belille, C.A. (1987). Women in treatment: Beyond the stereotype. *Journal of Studies on Alcohol, 48,* 574-578.

Herd, D. (1988). Drinking by black and white women: Results from a national survey. *Social Problems, 35,* 493-505.

Herd, D. (1993). An analysis of alcohol-related problems in black and white women drinkers. *Addictions Research, 1,* 181-198.

Hesselbrock, M.N., Hesselbrock, V.M., Babor, T.F., Stabenau, J.R., Meyer, R.E., & Weidenman, M. (1984). Antisocial behavior, psychopathology and problem drinking in the natural history of alcoholism. In D.W. Goodwin, K.T. Van Dusen, & S.A.

Mednick (Eds.), *Longitudinal research in alcoholism* (pp. 197–214). Boston: Kluwer-Nijhoff.

Hilton, M.E. (1988). Trends in U.S. drinking patterns: Further evidence from the past 20 years. *British Journal of Addiction, 83,* 269–278.

Hilton, M.E. (1991). The demographic distribution of drinking patterns in 1984. In W.B. Clark and M.E. Hilton (Eds.), *Alcohol in America: Drinking practices and problems* (pp. 73–86). Albany, NY: State University of New York Press.

Holzer, C.E., Robins, L.N., Myers, J.K., Weissman, M.M., Tischler, G.L., Leaf, P.J., Antohony, J., & Bednarski, P.B. (1984). Antecedent and correlates of alcohol abuse and dependence in the elderly. In NIAAA, *Nature and extent of alcohol problems among the elderly* (pp. 217–244) (NIAAA Research Monograph No. 14; DHHS Publication No. ADM 84-1321). Washington, DC: U.S. Government Printing Office.

Irwin, M., Schuckit, M., & Smith, T.L. (1990). Clinical importance of age at onset in type 1 and type 2 primary alcoholics. *Archives of General Psychiatry, 47,* 320–324.

Johnson, P.B. (1982). Sex differences, women's roles and alcohol use: Preliminary national data. *Journal of Social Issues, 38,* 93–116.

Johnston, L.D., O'Malley, P.M., & Bachman, J.G. (1993). National survey results on drug use from the "Monitoring the Future Study, 1975–1992" (2 volumes, National Institute on Drug Abuse, NIH Publication Nos. 93-3597 & 93-3598). Washington, DC: U.S. Government Printing Office.

Jones, M.C. (1968). Personality correlates and antecedents of drinking patterns in adult males. *Journal of Consulting and Clinical Psychology, 32,* 2–12.

Jones, M.C. (1971). Personality antecedents and correlates of drinking patterns in women. *Journal of Consulting and Clinical Psychology, 36,* 61–69.

Jones, M.C. (1981). Midlife drinking patterns: Correlates and antecedents. In D.H. Eichorn et al. (Eds.), *Present and past in middle life* (pp. 223–242). New York: Academic Press.

Kinsey, B.A. (1966). *The female alcoholic: A social psychological study.* Springfield, IL: Charles C Thomas.

Knight, R.P. (1937). Psychodynamics of chronic alcoholism. *Journal of Nervous and Mental Disease, 86,* 538–548.

Lee, G.P., & DiClimente, C.C. (1985). Age of onset versus duration of problem drinking on the Alcohol Use Inventory. *Journal of Studies on Alcohol, 46,* 398–402.

Levinson, D.J., Darrow, C.N., Klein, E.B., Levinson, M.H., & McKee, B. (1978). *The seasons of a man's life.* New York: Knopf.

Lisansky, E.S. (1957). Alcoholism in women: Social and psychological concomitants: I. Social history data. *Quarterly Journal of Studies on Alcohol, 18,* 588–623.

Mayfield, D.G. (1974). Alcohol problems in the aging patient. In W.E. Fann and G.L. Maddox (Eds.), *Drug Issues in Geropsychiatry,* Baltimore: Williams and Wilkins.

Mellinger, G.D., Balter, M.B., & Uhlenhuth, E.H. (1984). Prevalence and correlates of the long-term regular use of anxiolytics. *Journal of the American Medical Association, 251,* 375–379.

Merry, J. (1980). Alcoholism in the aged. *British Journal of Alcohol and Alcoholism, 15,* 56–57.

Miller-Tutzauer, C., Leonard, K.E., & Windle, M. (1991). Marriage and alcohol use: A longitudinal study of "maturing out." *Journal of Studies on Alcohol, 52,* 434–440.

Moos, R.H. & Finney, J.W. (1984). A systems perspective on problem drinking among older adults. In: G. Maddox, L.N. Robins, & N. Rosenberg (Eds.), *Nature and extent of alcohol problems among the elderly* (pp. 151–172) (NIAAA Research Monograph No. 14; DHHS Publ. No. ADM 84-1321). Washington, DC: U.S. Government Printing Office.

Mulford, H.A. (1977). Women and men problem drinkers: Sex differences in patients served by Iowa's community alcoholism centers. *Journal of Studies on Alcohol, 38,* 1624-1639.

Pandina, R.J., Labouvie, E.W., & White, H.R. (1984). Potential contributions of the life span developmental approach to the study of adolescent alcohol and drug use: The Rutgers Health and Human Development Project—A working model. *Journal of Drug Issues, 14,* 253-268.

Parrella, D.P., & Filstead, W.J. (1988). Definition of onset in the development of onset-based alcoholism typologies. *Journal of Studies on Alcohol, 49,* 85-92.

Piazza, N.J., Vrbka, J.L., & Yeager, R.D. (1989). Telescoping of alcoholism in women alcoholics. *International Journal of the Addictions, 24,* 19-28.

Prescott, C.A., Hewitt, J.K., Truett, K.R., Heath, A.C., Neale, M.C., & Eaves, L.J. (1994). Genetic and environmental influences on lifetime alcohol-related problems in a volunteer sample of older twins. *Journal of Studies on Alcohol, 55,* 184-202.

Robbins, C., & Clayton, R.R. (1989). Gender-related differences in psychoactive drug use among older adults. *Journal of Drug Issues, 19,* 207-219.

Robins, L.N., Helzer, J.E., Croughan, J., Williams, J.B.W., & Spitzer, R.L. (1985). *National Institute of Mental Health Diagnostic Interview Schedule: Version IIIA* (Public Health Service No. ADDM-T-42-3 [4-85]). Washington, DC.

Scarf, M. (1980). *Unfinished business: Pressure points in the lives of women.* New York: Doubleday.

Schonfeld, L., & Dupree, L.W. (1991). Antecedents of drinking for early- and late-onset elderly alcohol abusers. *Journal of Studies on Alcohol, 52,* 587-592.

Schuckit, M.A. (1972). The alcoholic woman: A literature review. *Psychiatry in Medicine, 3,* 37-43.

Schuckit, M.A. (1977). Geriatric alcoholism and drug abuse. *Gerontologist, 17,* 168-174.

Schuckit, M.A. (1991). Importance of subtypes in alcoholism. *Alcohol and Alcoholism, 26, Suppl.1,* 511-514.

Schuckit, M.A., & Monteiro, M.G. (1988). Alcoholism, anxiety and depression. *British Journal of Addiction, 83,* 1373-1380.

Schuckit, M., Pitts, Jr., F.N., Reich, T., King, L.J., & Winokur, G. (1969). Alcoholism: I. Two types of alcoholism in women. *Archives of General Psychiatry, 20,* 301-306.

Schulenberg, J., Wadsworth, K.N., O'Malley, P.M., Bachman, J.G., Abata, A.T., & Johnston, L.D. (1993). The impact of personality and social context on trajectories of binge drinking during the transition to young adulthood. Presentation at the 1993 conference of the Society for Research on Child Development, New Orleans, LA.

Spiegler, D., Tate, D., Aitken, S. & Christian C. (Eds.). (1989). Alcohol use among U.S. ethnic minorities (NIAAA Research Monograph No. 18; DHHS Publication No. ADM 89-1435). Washington, DC: U.S. Government Printing Office.

Swenson, W.M., Pearson, J.S., & Osborne, D. (1973) *An MMPI source book: Basic item, scale, and pattern data on 50,000 medical patients.* Minneapolis, MN: University of Minnesota Press.

Turnbull, J.E., & Gomberg, E.S.L. (1988). Impact of depressive symptomatology on alcohol problems in women. *Alcoholism: Clinical and Experimental Research, 12,* 374-381.

Turnbull, J.E., & Gomberg, E.S.L. (1990). The structure of depression in alcoholic women. *Journal of Studies on Alcohol, 51,* 148-155.

Vaillant, G.E. (1977). *Adaptation to life.* Boston: Little Brown and Co.

Vaillant, G.E. (1983). *The natural history of alcoholism.* Cambridge, MA: Harvard University Press.

Veroff, J., Kulka, R.A., & Douvan, E. (1981). *Mental health in America: Patterns of help-seeking from 1957 to 1976.* New York: Basic Books.

Von Knorring, L., Palm, U., & Andersson, H.-E. (1985). Relationship between treatment outcome and subtype of alcoholism in men. *Journal of Studies on Alcohol, 46,* 388-391.

Wanberg, K.W., & Knapp, J. (1970). Differences in drinking symptoms and behavior of men and women alcoholics. *British Journal of Addiction, 64,* 347-355.

Welte, J.W., & Mirand, A.L. (1992). *Alcohol use by the elderly: Patterns and correlates.* A report on the Erie County Elder Drinking Survey. Buffalo, NY: Research Institute on Addictions.

Wilkinson, P. (1971). Alcoholism in the aged. *Journal of Geriatrics, 59*-64.

Williams, G.D., & DeBakey, S.F. (1992). Changes in levels of alcohol consumption: United States, 1983-1988. *British Journal of Addiction, 87,* 643-648.

Wilsnack, R.W., & Cheloha, R. (1987). Women's roles and problem drinking across the lifespan. *Social Problems, 34,* 231-248.

Wilsnack, R.W., & Wilsnack, S.C. (1992). Women, work, and alcohol: Failures of simple theories. *Alcoholism: Clinical and Experimental Research, 16,* 172-179.

Wilsnack, R.W., Wilsnack, S.C., & Klassen, A.D. (1984). Women's drinking and drinking problems: Patterns from a 1981 national survey. *American Journal of Public Health, 74,* 1231-1238.

Wilsnack, S.C., & Wilsnack, R.W. (1991). Epidemiology of women's drinking. *Journal of Substance Abuse, 3,* 133-157.

Worobec, T.G., Turner, W.M., O'Farrell, T.J., Cutter, H.S., Bayog, R.D., & Tsuang, M.T. (1990). Alcohol use by alcoholics with and without a history of parental alcoholism. *Alcoholism: Clinical and Experimental Research, 14,* 887-892.

Zimberg, S. (1974). The elderly alcoholic. *Gerontologist, 14,* 221-224.

Zucker, R.A, & Gomberg, E.S.L. (1996). *Alcoholism and anti-social personality in women.* Manuscript submitted for publication.

SECTION IV

Interpersonal Relationships and Women's and Men's Drinking

Introductory Note

The preceding chapters looked within individuals for explanations of women's and men's alcohol consumption and its effects. In this section the authors argue that the causes and consequences of men's and women's drinking arise not just from individual characteristics but also from social interaction and relationships. Women and men may share many beliefs about alcohol and its effects, but their drinking behavior diverges because of differences in what men and women believe about other people, and in how they behave toward other people. These chapters suggest that men's and women's drinking behavior and social relationships are likely to affect each other reciprocally, in two important ways. First, social relationships may influence alcohol consumption in ways that then change those social relationships. For example, painful marital problems may lead some partners to use alcohol as an emotional bandage, a coping strategy that may make the marital problems worse. Second, in relationships each person's drinking behavior and its effects may elicit responses from others that encourage or discourage such alcohol use. For example, choice of romantic or marital partners may depend partly on compatible drinking patterns (assortative mating). The reciprocity of drinking and social interaction means that the drinking behavior of two people in any close and long-lasting relationship cannot be understood adequately as behavior of separate individuals, but should be viewed as a product of their partnership.

The chapter on sexuality and alcohol use by Wilsnack et al. provides evidence for many of the above ideas, from the research literature and from a 1981 national survey. Women and men share some views of drinking and sexuality: a majority expect drinking to facilitate their sexual behavior or pleasure, and report positive effects of alcohol on their sexuality and emotional intimacy. Among both women and men, heavier drinkers have more positive views of alcohol's effects on sexuality and more liberal attitudes toward sexual activity. However, connections between sex and alcohol may contribute to some undesirable reciprocal relationships, particularly for women. Heavy drinking may lead to higher risks of sexual dysfunction, and higher risks of sexual assault. The evidence suggests that women trying to overcome sexual dysfunction or to cope with traumatic assault experiences may then rely more heavily on alcohol. What the chapter cannot describe as clearly is how drinking affects sexual interaction in *couples*. For example, there have been relatively few studies about how men interpret women's drinking as a signal to make sexual advances, or about the quality and risks of sexual relations when couples drink together.

Couples are the major focus of Roberts and Leonard's chapter on marriage and alcohol. Their chapter begins with two consistent findings in the research literature: among both men and women, getting married is associated with reduced drinking (for reasons still uncertain), but marital conflict and dissolution are associated with heavier drinking (although gender effects and the direction of causality are still uncertain). Using a longitudinal study of newlyweds, Roberts and Leonard investigate how the interlocking drinking patterns of husband and wife are related to the quality of marital life. In the five types of drinking partnerships discovered, marriages in which husbands and wives drink together in similar ways (quantity and frequency) are relatively harmonious, whereas husbands and wives who have discrepant drinking patterns report greater marital discord and more binge drinking (relatively heavy consumption per drinking occasion). Many couples with well-matched drinking patterns may have started out that way because of assortative mating. However, Roberts and Leonard find little support for the idea that men influence women's drinking more than women influence men's. Instead, they argue that the development of drinking partnerships in marriage is a reciprocal process in which each spouse influences the other.

Kantor and Asdigian's chapter on the linkage between drinking and domestic violence further demonstrates the need to understand relationships and not just individuals in order to explain causes and consequences of alcohol use. The women and men in their national survey of marital partners have quite similar expectations about how drinking can lead to more assertive and aggressive behavior. Heavier drinkers, both female and male, have a greater tendency to believe that drinking makes aggressive or violent behavior more likely and more forgivable. However, domestic assaults did not result simply from individual beliefs about alcohol or even individual drinking behavior. Most domestic assaults were not preceded by drinking, but did involve mutual aggression, from the viewpoint of the men and women who reported becoming violent. What drinking by either partner may do is to make it easier for the more aggressive or less inhibited spouse(s) to get into a reciprocal escalation of conflict that results in violence. Alcohol use and its expected effects become part of the harmful social interaction. And the fact that women who abuse alcohol are more likely to be victims of marital violence suggests that a vicious circle can develop, whereby women in violent relationships may seek solace from alcohol, which may increase or perpetuate the risks of becoming involved in further marital violence.

A vicious circle of relational problems and substance abuse is how the Stone Center relational model would explain women's alcohol and drug problems, as applied by Covington and Surrey. Their chapter argues that women may use alcohol and other substances to help them make or maintain social connections, or to cope with the pain from relational losses or problems. Such use may include drinking to keep company with a heavy-drinking partner, or to help change one's behavior or feelings to meet a partner's needs or desires. If valued relationships disintegrate or become distressful, women may drink to reduce the pain of feeling isolated or trapped, to numb feelings of self-blame for relationship failures, or to help make it possible to behave in expected ways when they could not do so otherwise (as in sexual situations). Coping by drinking or using other drugs may then further damage relationships, or may lead women to abandon social contacts as they become more dependent on intoxication, increasing the social isolation that motivates or facilitates further self-medicative substance use. An implication for treatment is that substance-abusing women may benefit greatly from joining mutual-help groups of women with similar problems, where they can become socially reconnected in an environment where they can share their pain. Such a treatment approach requires more attention to the relational context of substance abuse than many traditional treatment approaches (such as 12-step programs) have been able to offer. This is one way in which analysis of gender-related antecedents of alcohol problems may indicate more promising ways to prevent or treat those problems.

CHAPTER 10

Sexuality, Gender, and Alcohol Use

SHARON C. WILSNACK, JOSEPH J. PLAUD, RICHARD W. WILSNACK,
AND ALBERT D. KLASSEN

R esearch on relationships between sexual experience and alcohol use and abuse has typically looked in only one direction and at only one gender at a time. The research literature on how alcohol affects sexual function reports either on men or on women, without direct gender comparisons. Most of the laboratory investigations of how alcohol affects sexual function have used male subjects (for reviews, see Crowe & George, 1989; Hull & Bond, 1986; Lang, 1985), perhaps because of the earlier availability of devices for measuring physiological sexual arousal in males. In contrast, recent clinical and epidemiological research on how sexual experience and sexual problems affect alcohol use has been based on samples consisting only or predominantly of women (e.g., Beckman & Ackerman, 1995; Klassen & Wilsnack, 1986; Norris, 1994, in press). Multivariate analyses have yielded relatively robust cross-sectional and longitudinal relationships between aspects of sexual experience and women's drinking (e.g., S. Wilsnack, 1991; S. Wilsnack et al., 1991). However, the scarcity of comparable data on men leaves open the question of whether these "new" predictors of women's drinking are unique to women, more important for women than for men, or perhaps also strongly associated with drinking and problem drinking among men.

This chapter addresses questions about sexuality, gender, and alcohol use in two sections. The first section presents an overview of past research on alcohol use and adult female and male sexuality. The rapidly growing literature on adolescent drinking and sexuality needs and deserves a separate review elsewhere. The second section of this chapter reports new analyses of data from a U.S. national study of women's drinking. The inclusion of a male comparison sample in one phase of this study permits an examination of gender similarities and differences in relationships between drinking behavior and sexual experience.

PAST RESEARCH ON ALCOHOL AND SEXUALITY

Sexuality-Related Alcohol Expectancies

Across cultures and historical periods, people have consistently expected intoxicants such as alcohol to improve or facilitate sexual activity (see, e.g., Crowe & George, 1989; Klassen & Wilsnack, 1986; Roehrich & Kinder, 1991; Sandmaier, 1980). Contemporary surveys suggest that these associations persist. In 1970, for example, 68% of women and 45% of men in a popular magazine survey reported that alcohol increased their sexual enjoyment (Athanasiou et al., 1970). A pioneering study of alcohol expectancies (Brown et al., 1980) found that positive associations between drinking and sex and romance formed one of six major expectancy factors in a large sample of young adults. In our own 1981 U.S. national survey, 60% of female drinkers and 61% of male drinkers reported that they felt less inhibited about sex when they drank alcohol (see detailed discussion below). In a follow-up survey 10 years later, the same proportion of female drinkers—60%—reported alcohol-related sexual disinhibition (S. Wilsnack, 1995). Changes in gender roles and in sexual attitudes and behavior apparently have not altered the conviction of many U.S. women and men that drinking alcohol can have beneficial effects on sexual behavior and sexual pleasure.

Physiological and Cognitive Effects of Alcohol on Sexual Arousal

Effects of Alcohol Consumption

Laboratory studies of how alcohol consumption affects physiological indices of sexual function have generally found that alcohol intake reduces physiological sexual arousal for both genders, especially at higher levels of consumption. Increasing amounts of alcohol have been associated in male social drinkers with decreased penile tumescence (Briddell & Wilson, 1976; Farkas & Rosen, 1976) and increased latency to ejaculation (Malatesta et al., 1979); male alcoholics also responded to increasing blood alcohol levels with decreased penile tumescence (Wilson et al., 1978). The fewer studies of female social drinkers have found parallel effects of alcohol on arousal, with progressive amounts of alcohol producing reductions in vaginal blood flow (Wilson & Lawson, 1976a, 1978) and increased latency and decreased intensity of orgasmic response (Malatesta et al., 1982).

Although larger doses of alcohol typically depress physiological sexual arousal in both women and men, effects of alcohol on *cognitive* or *subjective* sexual arousal are not as clear or uniform. Among men, low to moderate alcohol intake may increase self-reported sexual arousal, in contrast to physiological effects, while higher doses of alcohol produce a suppression of self-reported sexual arousal, consistent with physiological effects (Malatesta et al., 1979; Wilson & Lawson, 1976b). Some studies of males have found that alcohol consumption leads to more indiscriminate arousal by a variety of erotic stimuli (Langevin et al., 1985) and decreases the ability to cognitively suppress arousal (Wilson & Niaura, 1984).

Although men have lower self-reported sexual arousal at high levels of consumption, studies of women have generally found that increasing consumption leads them to report *greater* sexual arousal (Malatesta et al., 1982; Wilson & Lawson, 1976a, 1978). Self-reports of greater sexual arousal at higher levels of alcohol intake may result because drinkers interpret the nonspecific excitatory physiological effects of alcohol as *sexual* arousal (McCarty et al., 1982); women may be more likely to make such an interpretation if they are less aware than men of physiological cues that drinking has reduced sexual arousal (Wilson & Lawson, 1978). An alternative explanation is suggested by a recent finding that alcohol increases testosterone levels in female but not male drinkers (Eriksson et al., 1994). To the extent that increased testosterone levels can produce heightened feelings of sexual arousal, this could provide a physiological explanation for the gender difference in subjective effects of alcohol.

Effects of Alcohol Expectancy Set

Studies using a balanced-placebo design (in which subjects do not know whether they are actually drinking alcohol or merely an alcohol-flavored placebo) have generally found that *alcohol expectancy set* (the belief that they have consumed alcohol) increases both physiological and subjective sexual arousal in men, regardless of the actual alcohol content of their drinks (Briddell & Wilson, 1976; Farkas & Rosen, 1976; Wilson & Lawson, 1976b). These effects of expectancy set appear to be heightened when men report higher levels of guilt about sexual expression, and when sexual stimuli are less socially acceptable (Lang et al., 1980; Lansky & Wilson, 1981).

In two studies of female social drinkers (Wilson & Lawson, 1976a, 1978), women's *belief* that they had consumed alcohol did not affect either their physiological or their self-reported sexual arousal. Given that women and men share generally positive expectancies that alcohol will enhance sexual functioning, the fact that these expectancies are less likely to increase actual physiological or subjective sexual arousal in women than in men may reflect the greater personal inhibitions and social risks of open sexual expression in women (Crowe & George, 1989).

Alcohol Consumption and Sexual Behavior

General Population Studies

The positive expectancies about drinking and sexuality discussed above suggest that alcohol consumption might increase a drinker's likelihood of engaging in sexual activity. This prediction would be consistent with findings of positive correlations between alcohol consumption and the reported frequency of sexual activity in both women and men (e.g., Anderson & Dahlberg, 1992; Cooper, 1992; Leigh, 1990) and between heavier drinking and more liberal sexual behavior in women (Klassen & Wilsnack, 1986).

Despite these positive correlational findings, general population studies of men and women have not resolved *how* alcohol use affects sexual activity. Much recent research on this issue has tried to determine whether alcohol use increases the likelihood of sexual activity that risks transmission of HIV, i.e., sexual intercourse without condoms, particularly with multiple partners (see reviews by Cooper, 1992, and by Donovan & McEwan, 1995). There are at least three ways that alcohol use might be associated with high-risk sexual activity: First, the intoxicating or disinhibiting effects of alcohol at the time of sexual activity could make sexual partners neglect condom use. Most studies of specific sexual events among drinking/nondrinking adults find no connection from drinking to unprotected sexual intercourse (Harvey & Beckman, 1986; Gold & Skinner, 1992; Perry et al., 1994; Temple et al., 1993; Weatherburn et al., 1993). In one British study (Gold et al., 1992) greater intoxication preceded unsafe sexual encounters, and in one U.S. study (Trocki & Leigh, 1991) intoxication predicted subsequent unsafe sexual activity among heterosexual women and homosexual men, but not among heterosexual men, but both of these studies had very low response rates (24%). However, research on adolescent samples has found stronger associations between drinking and subsequent unprotected intercourse (Cooper et al., 1994; Robertson & Plant, 1988).

Second, regular or heavy drinking, and drinking in connection with sexual activity, may be part of a risk-taking lifestyle that includes engaging in unprotected sexual activity with multiple partners. This could help explain the repeated findings in general population surveys of correlations between measures of alcohol use and participation in risky sexual activity (e.g., Anderson & Dahlberg, 1992; Hingson et al., 1990; Leigh et al., 1994; McEwan et al., 1992; Parker et al., 1994). Marin and Flores (1994) reported from a survey of sexually active Latinas that use of alcohol prior to sex was associated with having more sexual partners, but did not adversely affect condom use.

Third, the effects of alcohol consumption, particularly among potential sexual partners, may make individuals more likely to engage in subsequent sexual intercourse. To the extent that such sexual activity is likely to be unprotected regardless of alcohol consumption, drinking that increases sexual activity would thereby increase unsafe sex (Strunin & Hingson, 1992). This effect of drinking would be consistent with research showing widespread beliefs that alcohol facilitates sexual functioning, and may also help explain findings that alcohol use is more strongly associated with sexual activity involving new partners (Temple & Leigh, 1992; Temple et al., 1993).

As a whole, the research on alcohol use and sexual behavior strongly suggests that any positive associations between drinking and sexual activity (including high-risk sex) are more complex than would be predicted by simple disinhibiting effects of alcohol. The associations may depend on characteristics of the drinker (including gender and sexual orientation), the drinker's partner (who may or may not also be drinking), and the quality of the relationship that would be influenced by alcohol use (e.g., duration, intimacy, power balance). For example, alcohol hypothetically may have a more powerful influence on risky sexual activity among younger drinkers in less stable dating relationships than among older drinkers in long-established romantic partnerships (Cooper, 1992).

One complexity of the association between drinking and sexual activity is that an individual's use of alcohol may indicate his or her sexual availability or assertive sexuality to a potential sexual partner, who may then act on that perception. Evidence that alcohol serves as a sexual signal comes mainly from research in which young adults evaluate verbal descriptions of dating situations or first encounters. In several studies, reported drinking by a woman led evaluators of both genders to view her as more sexually active or receptive (Garcia & Kushner, 1987; George et al., 1988; George et al., 1995), although men's perception of sexual cues in women's drinking may be contingent on men's own expectations that alcohol has disinhibiting effects (George et al., 1995). Men's reported drinking on a first date increased women's predictions that sexual intercourse would occur (Corcoran & Bell, 1990), and reported drinking by either men or women on a first date made it more likely to both male and female evaluators that the drinking individual would initiate sexual intercourse (Corcoran & Thomas, 1991). However, in studies based on brief descriptions of hypothetical situations, alcohol may be a more powerful sexual signal than in the social situations where potential partners actually meet.

Clinical Studies

In contrast to the complex and sometimes inconsistent findings from studies of women and men in the general population, studies of alcoholic women in treatment samples have more consistently found significant associations between self-reported drinking and sexual activity. For example, Beckman (1979) found that alcoholic women in treatment were more likely than both nonalcoholic women and women receiving treatment for other psychiatric disorders to report that drinking increased sexual desire, sexual activity, and sexual enjoyment. Covington and Kohen (1984) also found that alcoholic women were more likely than nonalcoholic women to report that drinking facilitated sexual activity. The majority of a sample of 61 middle-class recovering alcoholic women reported that they always or sometimes used alcohol to facilitate sexual activity, and 80% reported that when drinking they perceived that alcohol improved their sexual functioning; these women engaged in much more sexual activity with partners (but with less frequent orgasms) during active alcoholism than either before or after the period of alcohol dependence (Apter-Marsh, 1984). In a large clinical study of alcoholic women (Turnbull & Gomberg, 1991), one of several factors of drinking-related consequences included self-reports of feeling more sexy, more willing or eager to have sex, and of greater enjoyment of sex.

Clinical research on alcoholic *men* has evaluated effects of drinking on male sexual dysfunction (see below), but has rarely studied how alcohol's sexual effects are experienced by male alcoholics. Although some clinical reports have described alcoholic men who believe that they must be drunk in order to be potent or sexually functional (McCarthy, 1984; O'Farrell, 1990), there have been few efforts to measure such beliefs empirically. What evidence there is provides little support for assuming that male alcoholics perceive the sexual benefits of drinking that may motivate female alcoholics to drink. A small U.S. sample of male alcoholics in treatment reported somewhat more frequent and more satisfying sexual activity during abstinence than when drinking (Nirenberg et al., 1990). In a study of patients with sexual dysfunction or disorder (Fagan et al., 1988), among those classified as probable alcoholics by high scores on the Michigan Alcoholism Screening Test (MAST), the men reported less "joy and vigor" in their sex lives than the women; among the patients without probable alcoholism, the men reported more "joy and vigor" than the women. In a Danish sample of alcoholic men being treated with disulfiram (Jensen, 1984), half of the patients said that acute alcohol intake diminished their sexual problems, but the men reported no significant difference in coital activity or masturbation before and after treatment.

Clearly, more research is needed to clarify whether perceptions of alcohol-enhanced sexuality play a greater role in the development of alcohol abuse in women than in men. If such a gender difference exists, contributing factors might include (1) greater alienation of male alcoholics' wives or partners than among female alcoholics' partners, many of whom may be alcohol abusers themselves; and (2) more directly deleterious effects of heavy alcohol consumption on male than on female sexual function. (As discussed below, women can generally perform sexually even when sexual interest or orgasmic responsiveness is absent, whereas alcohol-induced erectile impairment makes sexual intercourse more difficult for males.)

Methodological Limitations of Sexuality and Alcohol Research

Potential sensitivity about reporting sexual experiences creates some unique methodological difficulties for research on sexuality that need to be taken into consideration in interpreting findings. Low participation rates in many studies of sexual behavior—as low as 13% in some laboratory studies of alcohol effects on women's sexual response (Crowe & George, 1989), and in the 20%s in some general population surveys (Trocki & Leigh, 1991)—may limit generalization of their results. Furthermore, there is considerable evidence that individuals who volunteer for sex research studies (e.g., Wolchik et al., 1985), including alcoholic patients (e.g., Nirenberg et al., 1991), differ in important ways from the larger group of nonvolunteers. An additional concern is whether patterns of bias in volunteers are similar or different for women and for men. These methodological considerations necessitate caution in interpreting gender similarities and differences in existing studies, and underscore the importance of developing better techniques for enhancing participation rates and sample representativeness in future studies in this area (see, e.g., Laumann et al., 1994).

Sexual Dysfunction and Alcohol Abuse

Female Problem Drinkers and Alcoholics

Alcoholic women in treatment typically report elevated rates of sexual dysfunction and sexual dissatisfaction, compared with nonalcoholic women in the general population (e.g., Beckman, 1979; Covington & Kohen, 1984; Schaefer & Evans, 1987), and compared with women receiving treatment for non-alcohol-related problems (Beckman, 1979; Peterson et al., 1984). Although the clinical retrospective method of these studies makes temporal sequences of heavy drinking and sexual problems difficult to determine, it seems likely that excessive drinking may be both an attempt to self-medicate sexual problems and the cause of worsened sexual difficulties (S. Wilsnack, 1984, 1991).

The available *longitudinal* data suggest that sexual dysfunction may contribute to the chronicity of problem drinking among women in the general population. In longitudinal multivariate analyses of five-year follow-up data from women showing signs of problem drinking in 1981, a higher level of sexual dysfunction in 1981 was the single strongest predictor of continued problem drinking in 1986 (S. Wilsnack et al., 1991). Furthermore, women problem drinkers who divorced or separated between 1981 and 1986 were more likely to experience remission of problem drinking if the marriages they had left had been sexually dysfunctional (Klassen et al., 1991).

Male Alcoholics

Although information about alcohol consumption and sexual functioning among men in the general population is limited, clinical studies of alcoholic men typically report elevated rates of sexual dysfunction. A review of nine studies of male alcoholics in treatment (Schiavi, 1990) found that rates of erectile dysfunction ranged from 8% to 54% and lack of sexual desire from 31% to 58%. In the small number of studies that included nonalcoholic control groups, alcoholic men were significantly more likely than controls to report sexual dysfunctions, particularly disorders of sexual desire and arousal (Jensen, 1979, 1984; Tan et al., 1984; Whalley, 1978). From the perspective of clinicians treating sexual problems, Fagan et al. (1988) found that among 145 consecutive patients (predominantly male) presenting with sexual dysfunction or disorders, 29% had MAST scores in the probable alcoholic range.

Findings in such studies may be affected by uncontrolled factors such as other medical conditions and medications (e.g., disulfiram [Antabuse]) that are common in alcoholic populations and are known to impair sexual functioning. Indeed, in one study where sexual dysfunction was clearly more prevalent in alcoholic men (63%) than in nonalcoholic controls (10%), half of the alcoholic men claimed that their sexual problems started the same day they began treatment, and believed that Antabuse was the cause (Jensen, 1984). Cirrhosis and other liver damage related to alcohol abuse have been identified as contributing to sexual dysfunction through disturbance of sex hormone metabolism, although there is some debate about whether this is the most important way that alcohol affects sex hormone levels (Bannister et al., 1987; Gavaler et al., 1983; Valimaki et al., 1990). In studies of both male and female alcoholics, probable reciprocal associations among sexual dysfunction, other relationship problems, and alcohol abuse are virtually impossible to disentangle (Schiavi, 1990; S. Wilsnack, 1984). For example, some research suggests that men's alcohol abuse may increase their sexual problems by alienating their sexual partners or exacerbating conflicts with their partners (Nirenberg et al., 1990; O'Farrell, 1990; O'Farrell et al., 1991). Despite these complexities, the high rates of sexual difficulties in clinical samples of alcoholic women and alcoholic men suggest that both substance abuse treatment professionals and marital and sex therapists should be educated about the potentially destructive reciprocal interactions between sexual and relationship dysfunction and abuse of alcohol and other drugs.

Alcohol Use and Sexual Orientation

Drinking Patterns among Gay Men and Lesbians

Early studies of alcohol use among sexual minorities reported high rates of alcohol-related problems—averaging around 30% in most studies—among both lesbians and gay men (e.g., Fifield et al., 1977; Lohrenz et al., 1978; Saghir & Robins, 1973). However, many of these studies obtained their samples at least in part through gay bars, thus overrepresenting bar patrons and presumably overrepresenting heavier drinking persons.

As one byproduct of the AIDS epidemic, samples more representative of communities of gay men have been surveyed about a range of sexual and health behaviors, including alcohol use. These studies indicate that homosexual men use alcohol somewhat more than do heterosexual men (on some measures), but have overall rates of alcohol abuse substantially lower than those in earlier studies that used bar-based convenience samples. For example, Stall and Wiley (1988) classified 19% of self-identified gay men and 11% of heterosexual men in a San Francisco sample as heavy drinkers, but most other drinking measures did not differ between the two groups. In a New York City sample of gay men surveyed in 1986 and 1987 (Martin et al., 1989), alcohol consumption was relatively modest and stable (an average of 5 drinks per week among nonabstainers), and rates of DSM-III alcohol abuse/dependence declined from 12% in 1986 to 9% in 1987. Declining rates of alcohol and drug use have been reported in other studies of gay men as well (e.g., Remien et al., 1990); the declines appear to reflect normative changes regarding substance use and other risk behaviors within the gay community, motivated by both general and HIV-specific health concerns (Paul et al., 1991).

Although AIDS has motivated representative sampling mainly of gay men rather than lesbians, four studies have systematically surveyed lesbians about their drinking behavior. McKirnan and Peterson (1989a) in 1985–86 attempted to obtain a more representative sample of both gay men and lesbians by recruiting 3,400 respondents (748 women) from several sources in Chicago, including readers of a gay newspaper, community and health organizations, and gay cultural events. Judging from comparisons with respondents in a 1979 U.S. national survey (Clark & Midanik, 1982), abstaining from alcohol was less common among lesbians than among all women in the general population (15% vs. 34%), and less common among gay men than among all men in the general population (13% vs. 23%). Although rates of heavy drinking (more than 60 drinks per month) were similar for lesbians and all general population women (9% and 7%) and for gay and all general population men (17% and 21%), both lesbians and gay men were more likely to report alcohol dependence symptoms (both 23%) than women (8%) or men (16%) in the 1979 U.S. national survey. Lesbians and older homosexuals had more elevated rates of dependence symptoms, relative to the general population, than gay men and younger homosexuals did. These age and gender differences may reflect a greater physiological and/or cultural vulnerability of female and older homosexuals to risks of alcohol problems as a consequence of consistent, even if not "heavy," drinking (McKirnan & Peterson, 1989a).

In a national study of lesbian health concerns conducted in 1984–85 (Bradford & Ryan, 1987), 83% of the 1,917 lesbian respondents reported drinking at least occasionally, 6% reported drinking daily, and 14% indicated that they were worried about their alcohol use. These rates are only slightly higher than those for all women in our 1981 national survey, a small difference that may be accounted for by the higher educational and occupational level of the lesbian sample. Interestingly, in both the Chicago and the national lesbian samples, drinking did not decline with age as it does in the general population of women. Instead, daily drinking in the national lesbian sample increased steadily with age, from 3% of respondents aged 17–24 to 21% of respondents aged 55 and older. In the Chicago survey, both lesbians and gay men showed significantly less reduction in alcohol dependence symptoms with advancing age than did women and men in the 1979 national general population sample used for comparisons.

A more recent comparison of 55 lesbian and bisexual women with 373 heterosexual women in a random household sample of San Francisco residents aged 18–50 (Bloomfield, 1993) found no significant differences between the two groups in drinking levels or drinking patterns. However, a higher proportion of lesbian and bisexual women (13%) than of heterosexual women (3%) described themselves as recovered or recovering alcoholics. Although *longitudinal* or repeated cross-sectional data on lesbian drinking patterns are not available, the relatively low rates of daily drinking among younger respondents in the national lesbian health survey, and the relatively high proportion of lesbians in the San Francisco sample reporting recovery from alcoholism, may reflect a recent cohort shift among lesbians toward less problematic use of alcohol. The feminist and gay rights movements of the 1970s may have contributed to such a shift by increasing awareness of substance abuse problems among lesbians, by promoting positive self-identities and normative support for abstinence, and by creating social alternatives to the gay bar (Hastings, 1982; Paul et al., 1991).

Risk Factors for Substance Abuse in Lesbians and Gay Men

Personal and social-environmental risk factors believed to contribute to alcohol and drug abuse in lesbians and gay men include internalized homophobia and conflict about sexual orientation, isolation and alienation resulting from societal discrimination and oppression, underemployment and other role constraints, and the prominent role of the gay bar in homosexual communities (Deevey & Wall, 1992; Fifield et al., 1977; Paul et al., 1991; Ziebold & Mongeon, 1982). Additional risk factors that may be particularly relevant to lesbians include heavy-drinking partners, a history of physical or sexual abuse, and relationship violence (Hughes & Wilsnack, 1994; Schilit et al., 1990; Underhill & Wolverton, 1993).

In one of the few studies to evaluate empirically these hypothesized risk factors for gay and lesbian drinking, McKirnan and Peterson (1989b) tested the general hypothesis that stress due to (1) intra- or interpersonal conflict about sexual orientation and (2) societal discrimination based on sexual orientation would be related to alcohol abuse among gay men and lesbians, particularly among those who were vulnerable to substance abuse because of (1) tension-reduction alcohol expectancies and (2) use of bars as a primary social setting. Conflict due to sexual orientation had no relationship to alcohol or drug use. Measures of sexual orientation-based discrimination, negative affectivity (low self-esteem, alienation, and depression), and overall stress *were* significantly related to alcohol and drug abuse, but only among high-vulnerability gay men, not among low-vulnerability gay men or among lesbians.

McKirnan and Peterson interpret their findings as reflecting in part a greater stigmatization of male than of female homosexuality. However, since lesbians may be faced with discrimination related both to gender *and* to sexual orientation (e.g., Hall, 1990), it is not immediately clear why measures of societal discrimination would not show significant associations with their drinking as well as that of gay men. The lack of significant findings among women may result more from the smaller number of lesbians sampled, and the smaller number who would socialize regularly at bars. The McKirnan and Peterson study illustrates how the development of alcohol abuse may depend not only on the stress confronting the drinker but also on the availability of alcohol as a means of coping with stress.

Alcohol Use and Sexual Victimization

Sexual Victimization in Childhood

Studies of females. Numerous clinical studies have found elevated rates of childhood sexual abuse in the histories of alcoholic women in treatment (e.g., Covington & Kohen, 1984; Rohsenow et al., 1988; Russell & Wilsnack, 1991), and elevated rates of alcohol abuse and dependence in female psychiatric patients with histories of childhood sexual abuse (e.g., Pribor & Dinwiddie, 1992; Roesler & Dafler, 1993; Swett & Halpert, 1994; Yellowlees & Kaushik, 1994). In a recent series of studies, women in treatment for alcohol-related problems had significantly higher rates of both physical and sexual abuse in childhood than did (1) women in a general household sample, or (2) women without alcohol problems but receiving other mental health services (Miller et al., 1993). Relationships between childhood victimization and adult alcohol abuse persisted after controlling for demographic characteristics and parental alcohol problems. These patterns suggest a specific link between sexual victimization in childhood and women's risks of subsequent alcohol abuse, a risk not explained by family history of alcohol problems or other background characteristics.

Childhood sexual abuse also predicts alcohol use or abuse among individuals not in treatment, but most studies reporting this association have sampled adolescents (e.g., Berenson et al., 1992; Hernandez, 1992). However, data from our 1991 national survey suggest that associations between childhood sexual abuse and problem drinking are also strong among adult women in the general population. We defined childhood sexual abuse (CSA) as sexual activity occurring before age 18 that (1) was unwanted and/or (2) involved a partner five or more years older (after Wyatt, 1985; Wyatt et al., 1993). After controlling for age, ethnicity, and parental education, we found significant relationships between a history of CSA and 1991 measures of problem drinking, lifetime use of illicit drugs and psychoactive prescription drugs, anxiety, depression, binge eating, vaginismus, and early onset of sexual experience (S. Wilsnack et al., in press; Wonderlich et al., 1996). These nationally representative data support findings from clinical and adolescent studies, and suggest that experiences of childhood sexual abuse may be an important risk factor for problem drinking and other long-term adverse consequences in women.

Studies including males. According to most estimates, female victims of CSA outnumber male victims by a ratio between 1.5:1 and 3:1 (Finkelhor, 1994; Finkelhor & Dziuba-Leatherman, 1994). Nevertheless, many male children are sexually abused, and clinical observation suggests that such abuse may be a risk factor for later alcohol and drug abuse by men as well as women (Lew, 1990). Perhaps because CSA is less prevalent among males than females, empirical studies of CSA and its consequences have often omitted men. However, in one study of Maine substance abuse inpatients, histories of physical sexual abuse before age 17 appeared to be significantly more common among both men (18%) and women (74%) than estimated CSA rates in the general New England population (Rohsenow et al., 1988).

A second study that included men is a 20-year follow-up of 611 young adult women and men who experienced court-substantiated child abuse (physical or sexual) or neglect between 1967 and 1971, and 457 nonabused/nonneglected controls matched on gender, age, race, and social class background (Widom et al., 1995). After controlling for parental substance abuse, childhood poverty, age, and race, a history of childhood victimization (abuse or neglect) was significantly associated with women's but not men's symptoms of alcohol abuse and dependence. When women's types of victimization were analyzed separately, neglect was the only significant predictor of alcohol abuse/dependence symptoms. Although the prospective design of this study is a major strength, generalization of the findings is limited by the sample characteristics (including low SES, high alcohol involvement, and extensive criminal activity of both abused and control subjects) and by the reliance on incomplete and potentially biased records of childhood abuse and neglect.

Sexual Victimization in Adulthood

Alcohol use as a risk factor for sexual assault. Adult men are so rarely victims of reported sexual aggression (Dunn & Gilchrist, 1993; Lipscomb et al., 1992) that most of the recent research on the epidemiology and antecedents of sexual assault focuses exclusively on women (e.g., Abbey et al., 1996; Alexander et al., 1994; American College of Obstetrics and Gynecology, 1993; George et al., 1992). One clear pattern in such research is that a woman's risk of being sexually assaulted is increased when either the perpetrator of the assault or the woman victim has been drinking (e.g., Martin, 1992; Muehlenhard & Linton, 1987; Norris, 1994). Drinking by the *perpetrator* may reduce inhibitions against socially unacceptable behavior and allow the perpetrator to attribute responsibility for his behavior to alcohol rather than to himself (Pernanen, 1991; Richardson & Campbell, 1982). Drinking by the *victim* may increase her risk of sexual assault directly by impairing her alertness and judgment about high-risk companions or situations and her physical ability to resist attack, and indirectly via social perceptions that women drinking are more sexually accessible (Abbey et al., 1994; Corcoran & Thomas, 1991; George et al., 1995). Women as well as men may be less likely to perceive sexual aggression if assault or rape occurs when the assailant and victim had been drinking together (Norris & Cubbins, 1992). Alcohol use, so often a part of social interaction between women and men, is even more frequently involved in sexual assaults: current estimates are that between one-third and three-quarters of sexual assaults involve alcohol consumption by the perpetrator, the victim, or both (Collins & Messerschmidt, 1993; Koss et al., 1988). Better knowledge about how actual and perceived drinking by women and their companions affects sexually aggressive behavior would be valuable in efforts to reduce alcohol-related sexual victimization.

Sexual assault as a risk factor for alcohol abuse. Sexual victimization in adulthood (as in childhood) may increase women's risks of *subsequent* alcohol or other drug abuse. A 1990 national telephone survey asked 4,008 adult women about their experiences of violent victimization, including sexual assault and rape (Kilpatrick et al., 1992). Rape victims who had experienced rape-related post-traumatic stress disorder (PTSD) were much more likely (20.1%) than nonvictims (1.5%) to report two or more major alcohol-related problems. A majority (79%) of rape victims in this cross-sectional survey retrospectively reported a later age for their first alcohol intoxication than for their first rape. In analyses of two subsequent reinterviews of the 1990 sample, although findings for rape were not reported separately from other forms of violent assault, the data suggest that experiences of violent victimization are more likely to precede and predict alcohol dependence than to result from it (Kilpatrick et al., 1994).

ALCOHOL USE AND SEXUAL EXPERIENCE: GENDER COMPARISONS FROM A U.S. NATIONAL SURVEY

A number of the sexual behaviors discussed in this chapter were measured and analyzed in our own 1981-91 national longitudinal study of women's drinking. Associations between sexual experience and drinking behavior among *women* in that study have been reported elsewhere (Klassen & Wilsnack, 1986; S. Wilsnack, 1991; and throughout this chapter). The availability of a male comparison sample in the 1981 survey allows parallel analyses of alcohol-sexuality connections among men, and permits some preliminary conclusions about gender similarities and differences in these associations.

Method

Sample

The 1981 sample of 911 women, and a comparison sample of 396 men, were designed to be representative of U.S. adults (21 and older) in non-institutional residences in the 48 contiguous states. To ensure sufficient numbers of heavier drinking women, the female sample was stratified to oversample women drinking four or more drinks per week. Completion rates were 89% for moderate and heavier drinking women (4+ drinks/week), 83% for lighter drinking and abstaining women, and 66% for men. Additional information about the 1981 sample design can be found in R. Wilsnack et al. (1984). The subsequent five- and 10-year follow-up surveys are described in S. Wilsnack et al. (1991 and 1994, respectively).

Measures

Drinking measures. The primary drinking measure used in the present analyses is based on respondents' self-reported use of beer, wine, and distilled spirits during the 30 days prior to the interview. This *30-day quantity-frequency index* combines information about drinking frequency, drinking quantity, typical size of drinks, and ethanol (absolute alcohol) content for each of the three beverage types, producing an estimate of respondents' average consumption of ounces of ethanol per day. Respondents reporting 1 oz. or more of daily ethanol consumption (roughly two or more standard drinks of beer, wine or spirits) were classified as heavier drinkers; respondents reporting 0.22 to 0.99 oz. per day were classified as moderate drinkers; and respondents who had consumed alcoholic beverages at least once in the past 30 days but whose reported ethanol consumption was less than 0.22 oz. per day were classified as lighter drinkers. The abstainer category included respondents who had never consumed alcoholic beverages and those who had not done so for at least one year. A final category consisted of respondents who had consumed alcoholic beverages in the past 12 months but not in the past 30 days. Because these "temporary abstainers" were more likely than lighter drinkers to report a variety of drinking-related problems and symptoms (R. Wilsnack et al., 1984; S. Wilsnack et al., 1984), they are analyzed here as a separate category.

Drinkers may on occasion engage in episodes of especially heavy drinking, which may have unusually serious consequences. Therefore, a second measure, of *heavy episodic drinking,* is based on respondent reports of how often in the past 12 months they had consumed six or more drinks in a single day.

A third drinking measure, *total daily consumption,* takes into account both the quantity and frequency of drinking in the past 30 days and the frequency of heavy drinking episodes (6+ drinks/day), to estimate average daily ethanol consumption over the past 12 months. More detailed descriptions of the drinking measures are provided in R. Wilsnack et al. (1984).

Sexual behavior. Questions about sexual attitudes, sexual experience, and perceived effects of drinking on sexuality were developed for the 1981 survey, drawing upon a 1970 national sexuality survey (Klassen et al., 1989). Questions about sexual dysfunction were based on Kaplan's (1974, 1979) classifications of female and male sexual dysfunctions. For women these included lifetime lack of sexual interest, lifetime lack of orgasm, low frequency of orgasm, and vaginismus[1]; for men these included inability to achieve or maintain an erection, premature ejaculation, and delayed ejaculation. All sexuality questions were asked in a self-administered handout completed near the end of the 90-minute face-to-face interviews; interviewers (female for all female respondents and most male respondents) were available to answer questions or assist respondents if asked. After completing the sexuality handout, the respondent placed it in a sealed "privacy envelope" identified only by a code number to assure full confidentiality.

Hypotheses

We expected women and men to show similar patterns of association between drinking levels and perceived sexuality-related effects of drinking, sexual attitudes, and sexual behaviors. We also expected that heavier drinkers (1) would perceive more positive effects of drinking on sexuality, and (2) would have more liberal sexual attitudes and behaviors. Any gender differences were expected to show stronger alcohol-sexuality associations in women. If both alcohol use and sexual expression are subject to greater personal inhibition and social suppression in women than in men (Klassen & Wilsnack, 1986), the "disinhibiting" effects of alcohol may have a greater functional utility and strength for women.

Predicting gender differences in associations between drinking levels and sexual *dysfunction* is complicated by women's and men's physiological differences in the ability to engage in sexual intercourse despite the presence of sexual dysfunctions. Women whose sexual interest is low or absent, or who experience infrequent orgasm or none at all, can still engage in sexual intercourse. In contrast, male sexual problems such as inability to attain or maintain an erection typically prevent men from initiating or completing sexual intercourse. These physiological differences may in turn influence how alcohol is used in relation to sexual performance. A woman with lack of sexual interest or anorgasmia may drink heavily in an attempt to make an uncomfortable or distressing sexual interaction easier or more tolerable. A sexually distressed man who drinks heavily is likely to further impair his ability to function sexually. These gender differences would lead one to expect a stronger association between sexual dysfunction and drinking levels among women, because women can use alcohol instrumentally for at least *two* sexuality-linked reasons—to make sexual activity more enjoyable or more tolerable, and to medicate general feelings of distress about sexuality—whereas men will primarily use alcohol only for the latter reason.

Data Analysis

Calculations of the percentages, cross-tabulations, and measures of association reported here involved statistical weighting that took into account variations in response rates and the stratified oversampling of moderate-to-heavy drinking women (see R. Wilsnack et al., 1984, for details). However, tests of statistical significance were based on actual numbers of respondents in each sample or subsample. Some percentages and Ns presented here differ in minor ways from previously published data for women in the 1981 sample (e.g., Klassen & Wilsnack, 1986, Tables I-IV). The discrepancies are due to the removal of six of the original 917 female cases. During longitudinal follow-up, these cases were found to contain errors in data coding or respondent classification that could not be corrected.

Simple comparisons between the female and male samples used the standard significance test for differences between proportions, based on the

approximate normal distribution of such differences (e.g., Loether & Mc-
Tavish, 1980). Logistic regression was used to examine possible gender differences in patterns of association between drinking levels and sexuality
variables. The logit of each outcome was modeled as a function of gender,
linear trend in drinking level, and their interaction; significance of the interaction was assessed via the Pearson chi-square statistic for the difference between models with and without the interaction. Because of the large number
of tests, the reader is cautioned that there may be some Type I error among
the significant results; because of the complexity of the analyses and the preliminary nature of the investigation, no attempt was made to control the overall error rate. Our interpretations of findings, however, emphasize patterns of
findings that are consistent across multiple variables rather than individual or
isolated findings more likely to result from Type I error.

Results

Drinking Behavior of Female and Male Samples

Table 1 shows the distributions of the 1981 female and male samples on
two measures of drinking behavior. On the 30-day quantity-frequency index
(Table 1a), women were significantly more likely than men to be long-term
abstainers or lighter drinkers, and significantly less likely than men to drink
moderately or heavily. Women were also considerably less likely than men to
engage in heavy episodic drinking (Table 1b)—drinking six or more drinks in
a single drinking day ($p < .0001$ for proportions of women vs. men reporting one or more heavy drinking episodes). Women's and men's age distributions did not differ, so gender differences in drinking levels were unlikely to
be confounded by age differences in drinking behavior.

In general, the distributions of drinking levels and patterns for women and
men in the 1981 national survey are similar to those in other surveys conducted in the 1970s and 1980s (Ferrence, 1980; Hilton, 1988; S. Wilsnack
et al., 1994). And men's higher levels of drinking and heavier drinking than
women's are consistent with virtually every recent gender comparison of
adult drinkers (Ferrence, 1980; Fillmore et al., 1991; R. Wilsnack et al., 1995).

Perceived Effects of Drinking on Sexual Feelings and Emotional Intimacy

Table 2a shows how women and men in each of three 30-day drinking levels (light, moderate, heavy) responded to four questions about the perceived
effects of drinking on sexual inhibition, sexual pleasure, and emotional closeness. Perhaps the strongest impression of these responses is the *similarity*
of women's and men's reports. A majority of women drinkers indicated that

TABLE 1
Sample Distributions on Drinking Indexes

(a) 30-Day Quantity-Frequency Index

	Women (N = 911)	Men (N = 396)
Abstained at least past 12 months	39.1 (214)	24.9* (97)
Abstained the past 30 days	9.6 (73)	11.7 (48)
Lighter Drinker: < 0.22 oz. ethanol/day	31.0 (245)	17.9* (68)
Moderate Drinker: 0.22-0.99 oz. ethanol/day	14.5 (261)	28.1** (113)
Heavier Drinker: 1+ oz. ethanol/day	5.7 (108)	17.3* (66)

(b) Heavy Episodic Drinking: "Thinking about your use of alcoholic beverages in the last 12 months, how often did you have six or more drinks of wine, beer, or liquor in a single day?"

	Women (N = 911)	Men (N = 396)
Abstained at least past 12 months	39.1 (214)	24.9* (97)
Never in past 12 months	40.8 (366)	26.4** (105)
1-3 times in past 12 months	7.9 (106)	10.5 (40)
4-11 times in past 12 months	5.8 (100)	11.7 (48)
1-3 times/month	1.7 (36)	9.5 (39)
1-2 times/week	2.7 (43)	9.1 (33)
3+ times/week	2.1 (40)	8.0 (31)

Note: Percentages are based on weighting; *n*'s (in parentheses) are actual numbers of cases in each subgroup. Subgroup *n*'s may not total sample *N* because of missing data. *p < .05; **p < .01 for female-male comparisons (2-tailed tests for differences between proportions).

TABLE 2

Perceived Effects of Drinking on Sexuality and Interpersonal Closeness among Current Drinkers, by 30-Day Quantity-Frequency Level

Questions	Gender	Overall	Lighter Drinkers	Moderate Drinkers	Heavier Drinkers
(a) How true is it that when you drink . . . . (% sometimes or usually true)					
1. You feel less inhibited about sex?	Women	60 (529)	56 (166)	63 (256)	68 (107)
	Men	61 (242)	51 (64)	61 (113)	70[a] (65)
2. Sexual activity is more pleasurable for you?	Women	44 (523)	39 (164)	47 (254)	56[a,e] (105)
	Men	44 (243)	29 (65)	39 (112)	68[d,e] (66)
3. You feel closer to a person you share drinks with?	Women	61 (531)	60 (167)	61 (257)	67[e] (107)
	Men	67 (243)	50 (64)	70 (113)	79[c,e] (66)
4. You find it easier to be open with other people?	Women	70 (536)	65 (172)	73 (257)	81[a] (107)
	Men	74 (244)	61 (65)	74 (113)	85[b] (66)

(b) Have any of the following ever happened to you? (% yes)

1.	You became sexually forward when you had been drinking?	Women	22**** (542)	20 (176)	21**** (259)	28** (107)
		Men	39 (233)	22 (54)	42 (113)	49^b (66)
2.	You became less particular in your choice of sexual partners when you had been drinking?	Women	8**** (543)	4**** (176)	11**** (259)	12^a,** (108)
		Men	31 (232)	24 (53)	33 (113)	31 (66)
3.	Someone who was drinking became sexually aggressive toward you?	Women	60* (542)	62** (176)	58 (258)	58 (108)
		Men	52 (233)	38 (54)	57 (113)	56 (66)
	Total unweighted *n*	Women	544	176	260	108
		Men	247	68	113	66

Note: Percentages are based on weighting; *n*'s (in parentheses) are actual numbers of cases in each subgroup. Respondents who reported no alcohol consumption in the past 12 months are excluded.

$^a p < .05$; $^b p < .01$; $^c p < .001$; $^d p < .0001$ for association between drinking levels and perceived effects (Tau$_b$, 2-tailed).

$^e p < .05$ for Gender × Drinking Level interaction in logistic regression analyses.

$^* p < .05$; $^{**} p < .01$; $^{***} p < .001$; $^{****} p < .0001$ for female-male comparisons (2-tailed tests for differences between proportions).

drinking had positive effects on their sexual inhibitions and on their feelings of being close to and open with other people; a large minority felt that drinking made sexual activity more pleasurable. The proportion of women drinkers reporting these positive effects increased as drinking levels increased, with these associations statistically significant for feelings of sexual pleasure and emotional openness.

Men were just as likely as women to report positive effects of drinking on sexuality and intimacy. Like women, men who drank more heavily were more likely to report positive effects of drinking on sexuality and intimacy; these associations were statistically significant for all four perceived effects. In fact, contrary to expectations, logistic regression analyses showed that as drinking levels increased, men showed a significantly greater increase than women in the prevalence of perceived positive effects of alcohol on sexual pleasure and feelings of closeness.

The questions about sexuality and intimacy asked respondents how regularly they experienced various effects "*when you drink.*" Therefore, positive relationships between drinking levels and reported effects are unlikely to result merely because heavier drinkers drink more frequently and thus experience drinking effects of all kinds more often. Instead, the positive relationships suggest that expecting drinking to reduce sexual inhibitions, to enhance sexual pleasure, and to increase interpersonal closeness may motivate both women and men to drink more heavily.

Reported Effects of Drinking on Sexual Assertiveness and Choice of Sexual Partners

Table 2b shows that men were more likely than women to report becoming sexually forward and less particular about the choice of sexual partners when they had been drinking. The gender differences are large and statistically significant for all comparisons except lighter drinkers' self-reports of sexual assertiveness. Clearly, these data do not support a stereotype of alcohol-induced sexual assertiveness or "promiscuity" in women (e.g., Blume, 1991). If anything, they suggest that such behavior may occur more frequently in men.

What may seem surprising is that among moderate and heavier drinkers, men were as likely as women to report experiencing sexually aggressive behavior from someone else who had been drinking. There are several possible reasons for this unexpected finding: First, the term "sexually aggressive" was not defined for respondents. Hypothetically it could range from spontaneous flirtation to unwanted and even violent sexual imposition, and men and women may have different ideas of what sexually aggressive behavior toward themselves would include. Second, the frequency of sexually aggressive encounters was not measured; women may experience many more such encounters than men do. Third, men may be inclined to interpret women's drinking and women's behavior while drinking as sexual overtures that justify men's own sexual assertiveness "in response." This would be consistent with studies of how drinking may be interpreted as a signal of sexual availability (Corcoran & Thomas, 1991; George et al., 1988).

Drinking, Sexual Attitudes, and Sexual Behavior

Table 3 summarizes relationships between 30-day drinking levels and four sexual behaviors and attitudes. Consistent with previous research (e.g., Klassen et al., 1989; Laumann et al., 1994; Oliver & Hyde, 1993), men reported substantially higher rates of premarital sexual experience and masturbation than did women, and more liberal attitudes toward sexual relations between an unmarried man and woman. Women and men had similar views about the possibility of enjoying sexual activity with a same-sex partner.

Among both men and women, moderate and heavier drinkers reported higher rates of premarital sex and more liberal attitudes toward sexual relations between unmarried persons, when compared with long-term abstainers and lighter drinkers (χ^2s = 16.66-53.52, $df = 1$, all p's < .001, for moderate and heavier drinkers vs. abstainers and lighter drinkers). Female moderate and heavier drinkers also reported higher rates of masturbation ($\chi^2 = 15.46$, $df = 1$, $p < .001$) and more positive attitudes toward same-gender sexual activity ($\chi^2 = 5.40$, $df = 1$, $p < .05$), compared with female long-term abstainers and lighter drinkers. Excluding temporary abstainers, both women and men showed a strong monotonic relationship between drinking levels and tolerance of sexual relations between an unmarried woman and man who love each other (Tau$_b$ = .323 for women, .238 for men, p's < .0001). These positive associations between heavier drinking and more liberal sexual attitudes and behavior may reflect (1) disinhibiting effects of heavier alcohol consumption on sexual behavior, and/or (2) effects of a generalized moral value system that influences both drinking behavior and sexual expression (Klassen & Wilsnack, 1986).

Both male and female *temporary abstainers* (who drank in the past year but not the past 30 days) differed from longer term abstainers, showing less traditional or conservative responses to most of the sexual behavior and attitude questions. In earlier analyses of female respondents, we have found that the temporary abstainers include many respondents who previously drank at heavier levels, and whose recent abstention may be a reaction to earlier alcohol-related problems (S. Wilsnack et al., 1984). Temporary abstainers with relatively recent histories of heavy drinking might be expected to resemble moderate and heavier drinkers more than they resemble long-term or lifetime abstainers in sexuality and other characteristics.

TABLE 3
Sexual Behavior and Sexual Morality, by 30-Day Q-F Level

Questions	Gender	Overall	Abstainers	Temporary Abstainers	Lighter Drinkers	Moderate Drinkers	Heavier Drinkers
1. Sexual relations before marriage? (% yes)	Women	42**** (841)	27**** (189)	45**** (67)	49* (233)	60**** (249)	53**** (103)
	Men	82 (347)	73 (77)	84 (42)	67 (66)	90 (98)	93 (64)
2. Ever came to a sexual climax by yourself (masturbation)? (% yes)	Women	39**** (768)	31**** (164)	52 (63)	37**** (218)	49**** (229)	57**** (94)
	Men	79 (305)	77 (64)	68 (38)	77 (57)	79 (87)	88 (59)
3. If no question of right or wrong, might sex with another woman/man be enjoyable for you? (% yes)	Women	9 (772)	6 (161)	17 (64)	8 (223)	13 (231)	10 (93)
	Men	8 (300)	5 (61)	10 (36)	9 (56)	8 (87)	9 (60)

4.	How do you feel about an unmarried man and unmarried woman who love each other having sexual relations? (% not wrong at all)	Women	35**** (884)	18* (210)	35** (73)	42 (242)	52 (254)	74 (105)
		Men	54 (385)	31 (94)	62 (46)	55 (67)	61 (112)	67 (66)
Total unweighted n		Women	911	214	73	245	261	108
		Men	396	97	48	68	113	66

Notes: Percentages are based on weighting; *n*'s (in parentheses) are actual numbers of cases in each subgroup. Quantity-frequency data were missing for 10 women and 4 men (unweighted cases). Further variation in *n*'s is due to missing data for individual sexuality questions.

*$p < .05$; **$p < .01$; ***$p < .001$; ****$p < .0001$ for female-male comparisons (2-tailed tests for differences between proportions).

TABLE 4a
Female Sexual Dysfunction by Total Consumption Level

Questions	Overall	Abstainers	Temporary Abstainers	Lighter Drinkers	Moderate Drinkers	Heavier Drinkers	TEMPORARY ABSTAINERS Infreq. Drinking	TEMPORARY ABSTAINERS > Infreq. Drinking
Sexual Dysfunction Index:								
Never any sexual interest or enjoyment, lack or low frequency of orgasm, or vaginismus (% 1 or more)	35 (806)	35 (173)	40 (67)	37 (200)	28 (238)	38 (128)	30 (29)	57* (38)
1. I have never had any interest or enjoyment in sexual relations (% true)	5 (798)	9 (169)	6 (66)	3 (199)	1 (237)	5 (127)	1 (29)	15* (37)
2. I have never come to a sexual climax (had orgasm) with a partner (% true)	6 (789)	5 (166)	5 (65)	6 (200)	5 (231)	7 (127)	0 (28)	15* (37)
3. When having sex with a partner, about how regularly have you come to a sexual climax? (% saying 25% of the time or less)	25 (768)	26 (158)	27 (64)	25 (197)	20 (229)	28 (120)	18 (29)	43* (35)
4. Sexual relations have sometimes been so physically painful I could not have intercourse (% true)	17 (805)	16 (174)	22 (66)	19 (201)	13 (237)	14 (127)	18 (29)	28 (37)
Total unweighted *n*	891	206	72	211	253	135	32	40

Notes: Percentages are based on weighting; *n*'s (in parentheses) are actual numbers of cases in each subgroup. Women who reported they had never had a sexual partner are excluded. Consumption category *n*'s do not sum to 891 due to 14 cases (unweighted) for which total consumption data were missing or inadequate. Further variations in subgroup *n*'s are due to missing data for individual sexuality questions.

*$p < .05$ for temporary abstainers with histories of more than infrequent drinking vs. infrequent-drinking temporary abstainers (2-tailed tests for differences between proportions).

Drinking and Sexual Dysfunction

Drinking levels and female sexual dysfunctions. Tables 4a and 4b compare rates of several types of sexual dysfunction for women and men across levels of total daily consumption, a measure of average consumption over the past 12 months that takes into account the quantity and frequency of drinking in the past 30 days, as well as the frequency of heavy drinking episodes (6+ drinks in a drinking day). This 12-month consumption measure showed somewhat more consistent relationships to the sexual dysfunction measures than did the 30-day quantity-frequency measure, possibly because of the longer term or lifetime framework of most of the sexual dysfunction questions.

Table 4a shows that women's levels of sexual dysfunction do not increase monotonically as their levels of alcohol consumption increase. Although percentage differences are small for some of the four dysfunctions, there is a consistent curvilinear pattern. In almost all cases, women who were moderate drinkers reported lower rates of sexual dysfunction than heavier drinkers, and lower rates than lighter drinkers or temporary or long-term abstainers. Moderate drinkers were significantly lower than all other women combined on reported lack of sexual interest ($\chi^2 = 4.74$, $df = 1$, $p < .05$). On an index combining lack of sexual interest, lack or low frequency of orgasm with a partner, and vaginismus, moderate drinkers' lower scores approached but did not reach statistical significance ($\chi^2 = 3.41$, $df = 1$, $p = .065$, for moderate drinkers vs. all other women).

There are several possible reasons why women who drink moderately might report fewer sexual problems: First, women who abstain or drink little may be more likely to experience personal and social inhibition of sexuality as well as alcohol use, while women who drink very heavily may be at risk of being caught in a vicious circle of alcohol abuse and sexual problems. Second, moderate levels of alcohol consumption may have mildly facilitative effects on women's sexual functioning. Third, women's moderation in drinking may reflect a more general moderation in personality and lifestyle that reduces risks of problems associated with either drinking or sexual activity. If replicated with other samples, a curvilinear relationship between alcohol consumption and women's sexual problems would parallel Lipton's (1994) data, showing lower levels of depressive symptoms among moderate drinkers than among heavier drinkers or abstainers.

Most alcoholic women in clinical studies consume considerably more alcohol than the two standard drinks per day that defined heavier drinking in this general population study. For this reason, we examined rates of sexual dysfunction among women in the most extreme categories of the drinking measures. On the measure of heavy episodic drinking, the small number of women who reported consuming six or more drinks in a day three or more

TABLE 4b
Male Sexual Dysfunction by Total Consumption Level

Questions	Overall	Abstainers	Temp. Abstain.	Lighter Drinkers	Moderate Drinkers	Heavier Drinkers	TEMPORARY ABSTAINERS	
							Infreq. Drinking	> Infreq. Drinking
Erectile Problems Index (% 1 or more erectile problems)	12 (340)	11 (74)	22[a] (41)	13 (52)	10 (92)	8 (81)	18 (8)	23 (33)
There have been at least *two months or more*, when my partner and I had a problem with my . . . (% true)								
1. Not getting an erection	8 (340)	6 (74)	15 (41)	9 (52)	9 (92)	4 (81)	0 (8)	20 (33)
2. Losing an erection *before* intercourse	7 (339)	8 (74)	14[a] (41)	6 (51)	6 (92)	4 (81)	9 (8)	16 (33)
3. Losing an erection *during* intercourse	8 (338)	9 (72)	13 (41)	9 (52)	6 (92)	6 (81)	18 (8)	12 (33)
Orgasm Problems Index (% 1 or more orgasm problems)	38 (340)	35 (74)	43 (41)	33 (52)	34 (92)	48* (81)	18 (8)	49 (33)
There have been at least *two months or more* when during sex with a partner, . . . (% true)								
4. I frequently came to a climax too soon	34 (339)	31 (73)	33 (41)	31 (52)	32 (92)	43* (81)	9 (8)	40 (33)
5. I frequently had trouble coming to a climax	10 (339)	9 (73)	12 (41)	9 (52)	9 (92)	14 (81)	9 (8)	12 (33)
Total unweighted *n*	394	96	48	55	106	85	10	38

Notes: Percentages are based on weighting; *n*'s (in parentheses) are actual numbers of cases in each subgroup. Two men who reported they had never had a sexual partner are excluded. Consumption category *n*'s do not sum to 394 due to 4 cases (unweighted) for which total consumption data were missing or inadequate. Further variations in subgroup *n*'s are due to missing data for individual sexuality questions.

[a]$p < .05$ for temporary abstainers vs. all others (chi-square and Fisher's exact tests, 2-tailed).

*$p < .05$ for heavier drinkers vs. all others (chi-square test, 1-tailed).

days per week (unweighted $n = 40$) were higher than all other women combined on all four of the sexual dysfunctions, but the only comparison that approached statistical significance was lack of sexual interest (reported by 15.2% of women consuming 6+ drinks 3+ days/week vs. 4.9% of all other women, Fisher's exact test $p = .063$). The lack of strong relationships between sexual dysfunctions and drinking levels in this general population sample of women suggests that the threshold above which alcohol consumption is strongly linked to an increase in sexual problems may be quite high, reached by many alcoholic women but only a small proportion of women drinkers in the general population.

Female temporary abstainers. Women who were temporarily abstaining from alcohol were the most likely to report one or more sexual dysfunctions. In an effort to understand why, we subdivided the temporary abstainers into two groups: (1) those who had done only "infrequent drinking" in the past 12 months (never more than one drink a month), and who said they had never felt a need to cut down on their drinking; and (2) the other temporary abstainers, who had consumed more than one drink a month during the past year, and/or who said they had at some time felt they should reduce their alcohol consumption. The right-hand column of Table 4a shows that those temporary abstainers with histories of more than minimal drinking were exceptionally likely to report lack of sexual interest or pleasure and lack or infrequency of orgasm from sex with a partner (all p's $< .05$ for these temporary abstainers vs. temporary abstainers reporting histories of only infrequent drinking). If many of these women had previously perceived an association between problems with sexuality and problems with their own alcohol use (as a cause and/or consequence), their recent cessation of drinking could reflect an attempt to reduce one or both types of problems.

Drinking levels and male sexual dysfunctions. Contrary to predictions based on alcoholic samples, reported erectile problems were slightly (although nonsignificantly) *less* common among heavier drinkers than among other men (Table 4b). Even at more extreme levels of consumption, men who consumed six or more drinks three or more days a week were slightly (but not significantly) less likely than men drinking less to report difficulty attaining an erection or loss of erection prior to intercourse. The relatively low rates of erectile dysfunctions among heavier drinking men suggest that it may be incorrect to generalize observed erectile problems in alcoholic men (with frequent liver involvement) to the larger population of men who drink heavily. It is possible that the psychologically disinhibiting effects of moderate to heavy alcohol consumption may reduce risks of psychogenic erectile problems in some men, whereas more extreme levels of consumption produce physiologically deleterious effects on erectile function.

Dysfunctions of orgasm and ejaculation, on the other hand, were significantly associated with heavier drinking. Compared with all other men, heavier drinkers were more likely to report reaching orgasm too soon and more likely to report at least one of the two orgasm/ejaculation problems. At more extreme levels of consumption, men who consumed six or more drinks three or more days per week (unweighted $n = 31$) were significantly more likely than other men to report reaching a climax too soon (48.3% vs. 33.1%, $\chi^2 = 2.74$, $df = 1$, $p < .05$) and having trouble coming to a climax (23.1% vs. 9.1%, Fisher's exact test $p = .021$). Men in this extreme group were substantially more likely (64.3%) than all other men (37.7%) to report at least one of the two ejaculation problems ($\chi^2 = 7.58$, $df = 1$, $p < .01$). The fact that problems of ejaculation timing increased with drinking levels whereas erectile problems did not suggests that it may be more constructive to *differentiate* the sexual problems that men experience as a result of drinking, rather than raising oversimplified questions of whether or not drinking impairs men's sexuality.

Male temporary abstainers. One notable feature of male sexual dysfunction patterns is the elevated rates of nearly all dysfunctions among temporary abstainers.[2] This group exceeded all other abstention and drinking categories on all three of the individual erectile problems and on the erectile problems summary score; differences were statistically significant for erectile failure before intercourse and for the erectile problems index. Temporary abstainers were also slightly higher than all other groups except heavier drinkers on the two orgasm problems and their summary index, although differences were not statistically significant. The elevated sexual dysfunction rates among temporary abstainers, present for both women and men, support the interpretation that this group contains individuals whose current abstention is motivated by a history of alcohol-related sexual and other problems.

Discussion

Associations between women's and men's drinking and sexuality are more similar than different in the comparisons here. A majority of both women and men reported positive effects of alcohol on sexuality and emotional intimacy, and for both genders these positive effects were more prevalent at higher drinking levels. Although men were more likely than women to acknowledge becoming more sexually forward or less particular about sexual partners when drinking, men were nearly as likely as women to report experiencing sexually aggressive behavior from another person who had been drinking. And both men and women showed strong associations between higher drinking levels and more liberal sexual attitudes and behaviors.

Women's and men's connections between drinking and sexual dysfunction differed somewhat. Heavier drinking had only nonsignificant positive relationships to female sexual dysfunction, suggesting that links between drinking and sexual dysfunction reported in clinical studies of alcoholic women may occur only at relatively extreme levels of alcohol consumption. Men, in contrast, were significantly more likely to have ejaculation/orgasm problems, but not erectile problems, at the higher drinking levels measured in the present survey. Both women and men who had consumed alcohol in the past year but not in the past month reported more sexual problems than other drinkers and long-term abstainers; conceivably their current abstention was in part an attempt to reduce earlier sexual and other problems that they perceived as alcohol-related.

Where gender differences were found, men typically showed stronger connections between drinking and sexual behavior than did women. Specifically, men had significantly stronger positive associations than women between drinking levels and perceived positive effects of drinking on feelings of emotional closeness and sexual pleasure (Table 2a), and men were significantly more likely than women to report becoming more sexually assertive and less particular in choice of sexual partners when drinking (Table 2b). Because women's sexuality has historically been subject to greater social constraints than men's, and because open expression of female sexuality carries greater social risks, it is possible that alcohol's effects on sexual feelings—even if experienced equally by women and men—may not be as freely expressed in women drinkers as in men (see also Crowe & George, 1989).

In earlier analyses of the 1981 survey data, several drinking-related problems thought to be more characteristic of women than men (e.g., impairment of household work by drinking, drinking-related problems with children, and drinking-related accidents in the home) were reported by relatively large numbers of *men* (S. Wilsnack et al., 1986). In similar fashion, the analyses of sexual experience and drinking reported here show how correlates or predictors of alcohol use may not be as gender-specific as earlier expected, but rather may contribute to a more comprehensive understanding of antecedents and consequences of alcohol use in both women and men.

CONCLUSIONS: SOME IMPLICATIONS FOR RESEARCH AND PRACTICE

The studies summarized here, including our own, show how complex the relationships are between drinking and sexual behavior. These relationships do not fit neatly into a few patterns or theories. However, the findings here do suggest some basic perspectives that could benefit future research and interventions dealing with problems arising from the combination of alcohol and sexuality: First, associations of drinking with sexual activity or expected sexual benefits do not occur in only one gender, or in opposite directions for women and men. Instead, research indicates that when gender differences occur at all, men and women usually differ only in the degrees to which they connect drinking patterns with sexual behaviors or benefits. Efforts to study or intervene in problems involving both alcohol and sexuality should avoid assuming that women's and men's problems are at opposite poles.

Second, it is important to show how beliefs about alcohol and sex may increase risks of sexual aggression and victimization. For example, widespread beliefs (among both men and women) that drinking increases sexual assertiveness or responsiveness, or that drinking signals sexual interest, may create a cultural milieu in which social drinking facilitates sexual imposition or makes such imposition seem more forgivable.

Third, problems of sexual aggression or sexual dysfunction are often entangled with problems of alcohol abuse, with each type of problem potentially aggravating the other. Therefore, professionals who hope to help people with alcohol problems or problems of sexual victimization or sexual dysfunction should try not to isolate these, but to discover and understand how these several kinds of problems may interlock.

Fourth, individual-level analyses of how drinking influences sexual behavior (and vice versa) are fundamentally incomplete. Links between alcohol and sex typically arise in social relationships, in which each person's alcohol use or its effects on sexuality influences what the other person does or experiences. Better understanding of the interactions of alcohol and sexuality requires more than an individualistic perspective.

These perspectives may seem unlikely to provoke any arguments. However, the study of alcohol and sexuality is at such an early stage that adoption of even such mild suggestions could help advance both research and clinical practice beyond myths and ideological habits. We hope for such benefits.

Acknowledgments

The 1981–1991 national longitudinal survey of women's drinking reported in this chapter was supported by research grant R37-AA04610 from the National Institute on Alcohol Abuse and Alcoholism, National Institutes of Health. We are grateful to T. Robert Harris and Perry W. Benson for assistance with statistical data analysis.

Notes

1. The question intended to assess vaginismus did not ask explicitly about vaginal muscle spasms preventing intercourse, since many women (especially those never treated for sexual dysfunction) might not know whether "vaginal spasms" were the cause of their difficulties. Instead, the question stated, "Sexual relations have sometimes been so physically painful for me that I *could not* have intercourse." Positive responses to this question (which was endorsed by 16.7% of 1981 female respondents who had ever had sex with a partner) presumably include some conditions in addition to vaginal spasms that can create pain and prevent intercourse.
2. The smaller number of male than female temporary abstainers, particularly the small number of males who had always been infrequent drinkers (unweighted $N = 8$), made it preferable to analyze the male temporary abstainers as one group rather than subdividing them into previously-heavier and always-minimal current abstainers.

References

Abbey, A., Ross, L.T., & McDuffie, D. (1994). Alcohol's role in sexual assault. In R.R. Watson (Ed.), *Drug and alcohol abuse reviews: Vol. 5. Addictive behaviors in women* (pp. 97-123). Totowa, NJ: Humana.

Abbey, A., Ross, L.T., McDuffie, D., & McAuslan, P. (1996). Alcohol and dating risk factors for sexual assault among college women. *Psychology of Women Quarterly, 20,* 147-169.

Alexander, B.H., Franklin, G.M., & Wolf, M.E. (1994). The sexual assault of women at work in Washington State, 1980 to 1989. *American Journal of Public Health, 84,* 640-642.

American College of Obstetrics and Gynecology (1993). Sexual assault: ACOG Technical Bulletin Number 172—September 1992. *International Journal of Gynecology and Obstetrics, 42,* 67-72.

Anderson, J.E., & Dahlberg, L.L. (1992). High-risk sexual behavior in the general population: Results from a national survey, 1988-1990. *Sexually Transmitted Diseases, 19,* 320-325.

Apter-Marsh, M. (1984). The sexual behavior of alcoholic women while drinking and during sobriety. *Alcoholism Treatment Quarterly 1* (No. 3), 35-48.

Athanasiou, R., Shaver, P., & Tavris, C. (1970, July). Sex: Once again a functional religion—Report on more than 20,000 responses to 101 questions on sexual attitudes and practices. *Psychology Today,* 37-52.

Bannister, P., Oakes, J., Sheridan, P., & Losowsky, M.S. (1987). Sex hormone changes in chronic liver disease: A matched study of alcoholic versus non-alcoholic liver disease. *Quarterly Journal of Medicine, 63,* 305-313.

Beckman, L.J. (1979). Reported effects of alcohol on the sexual feelings and behavior of women alcoholics and nonalcoholics. *Journal of Studies on Alcohol, 40,* 272-282.

Beckman, L.J., & Ackerman, K.T. (1995). Women, alcohol, and sexuality. In M. Galanter et al. (Eds.), *Recent developments in alcoholism:Vol. 12. Alcoholism and women* (pp. 267-285). New York: Plenum.

Berenson, A.B., San Miguel, V.V., & Wilkinson, G.S. (1992). Violence and its relationship to substance use in adolescent pregnancy. *Journal of Adolescent Health, 13,* 470-474.

Bloomfield, K. (1993). A comparison of alcohol consumption between lesbians and heterosexual women in an urban population. *Drug and Alcohol Dependence, 33,* 257-269.

Blume, S.B. (1991). Sexuality and stigma. The alcoholic woman. *Alcohol Health & Research World, 15,* 139-146.

Bradford, J., & Ryan, C. (1987). *The National Health Care Survey: Final report.* Washington, DC: National Lesbian and Gay Health Foundation.

Briddell, D.W., & Wilson, G.T. (1976). Effects of alcohol and expectancy set on male sexual arousal. *Journal of Abnormal Psychology, 85,* 225-234.

Brown, S.A., Goldman, M.S., Inn, A., & Anderson, L.R. (1980). Expectations of reinforcement from alcohol: Their domain and relation to drinking patterns. *Journal of Consulting and Clinical Psychology, 48,* 419-426.

Clark, W.B., & Midanik, L. (1982). Alcohol use and alcohol problems among U.S. adults: Results of the 1979 national survey. In National Institute on Alcohol Abuse and Alcoholism, *Alcohol consumption and related problems* (pp. 3-52) (Alcohol and Health, Monograph No. 1; DHHS Publication No. ADM 82-1190). Washington, DC: U.S. Government Printing Office.

Collins, J.J., & Messerschmidt, P.M. (1993). Epidemiology of alcohol-related violence. *Alcohol Health & Research World, 17*, 93-100.

Cooper, M.L. (1992). Alcohol and increased behavioral risk for AIDS. *Alcohol Health & Research World, 16* (No. 1), 64-72.

Cooper, M.L., Peirce, R.S., & Huselid, R.F. (1994). Substance use and sexual risk taking among black adolescents and white adolescents. *Health Psychology, 13*, 251-262.

Corcoran, K.J., & Bell, B.G. (1990). Opposite sex perceptions of the effects of alcohol consumption on subsequent sexual activity in a dating situation. *Psychology, 27* (2), 7-11.

Corcoran, K.J., & Thomas, L.R. (1991). The influence of observed alcohol consumption on perceptions of initiation of sexual activity in a college dating situation. *Journal of Applied Social Psychology, 21*, 500-507.

Covington, S.S., & Kohen, J. (1984). Women, alcohol, and sexuality. *Advances in Alcohol and Substance Abuse, 4* (1), 41-56.

Crowe, L.C., & George, W.H. (1989). Alcohol and human sexuality: Review and integration. *Psychological Bulletin, 105* (3), 374-386.

Deevey, S., & Wall, L.J. (1992). How do lesbian women develop serenity? *Health Care for Women International, 13*, 199-208.

Donovan, C., & McEwan, R. (1995). A review of the literature examining the relationship between alcohol use and HIV-related sexual risk-taking in young people. *Addiction, 90*, 319-328.

Dunn, S.F.M., & Gilchrist, V.J. (1993). Sexual assault. *Primary Care: Clinics in Office Practice, 20*, 359-373.

Eriksson, C.J., Fukunaga, T., & Lindman, R. (1994). Sex hormone response to alcohol. *Nature, 369*, 711.

Fagan, P.J., Schmidt, C.W., Jr., Wise, T.N., & Derogatis, L.R. (1988). Alcoholism in patients with sexual disorders. *Journal of Sex and Marital Therapy, 14*, 245-252.

Farkas, G.M., & Rosen, R.C. (1976). Effect of alcohol on elicited male sexual response. *Journal of Studies on Alcohol, 37*, 265-272.

Ferrence, R.G. (1980). Sex differences in the prevalence of problem drinking. In: O.J. Kalant (Ed.), *Research advances in alcohol and drug problems: Vol. 5. Alcohol and drug problems in women* (pp. 69-124). New York: Plenum.

Fifield, L.H., Latham, J.D., & Phillips, C. (1977). *Alcoholism in the gay community: The price of alienation, isolation, and oppression.* Los Angeles: Gay Community Services Center.

Fillmore, K.M., Hartka, E., Johnson, B.M., Leino, E.V., Motoyoshi, M., & Temple, M.T. (1991). A meta-analysis of life course variation in drinking. *British Journal of Addiction, 86*, 1221-1268.

Finkelhor, D. (1994). The international epidemiology of child sexual abuse. *Child Abuse and Neglect, 18*, 409-417.

Finkelhor, D., & Dziuba-Leatherman, J. (1994). Victimization of children. *American Psychologist, 49*, 173-183.

Garcia, L.T., & Kushner, K. (1987). Sexual inferences about female targets: The use of sexual experience correlates. *Journal of Sex Research, 23*, 252-256.

Gavaler, J.S., Urso, T., & Van Thiel, D.H. (1983). Ethanol: Its adverse effects upon the hypothalamic-pituitary-gonadal axis. *Substance and Alcohol Actions/Misuse, 4*, 97-110.

George, L.K., Winfield, I., & Blazer, D.G. (1992). Sociocultural factors in sexual assault: Comparison of two representative samples of women. *Journal of Social Issues, 48*, 105-125.

George, W.H., Cue, K.L., Lopez, P.A., Crowe, L.C., & Norris, J. (1995). Self-reported alcohol expectancies and postdrinking sexual inferences about women. *Journal of Applied Social Psychology, 25,* 164-186.

George, W.H., Gournic, S.J., & McAfee, M.P. (1988). Perceptions of postdrinking female sexuality: Effects of gender, beverage choice, and drink payment. *Journal of Applied Social Psychology, 18,* 1295-1317.

Gold, R.S., Karmiloff-Smith, A., Skinner, M.J., & Morton, J. (1992). Situational factors and thought processes associated with unprotected intercourse in heterosexual students. *AIDS Care, 4,* 305-323.

Gold, R.S., & Skinner, M.J. (1992). Situational factors and thought processes associated with unprotected intercourse in young gay men. *AIDS, 6,* 1021-1030.

Hall, J.M. (1990). Alcoholism in lesbians: Developmental, symbolic interactionist, and critical perspectives. *Health Care for Women International, 11,* 89-107.

Harvey, S.M., & Beckman, L.J. (1986). Alcohol consumption, female sexual behavior, and contraceptive use. *Journal of Studies on Alcohol, 47,* 327-332.

Hastings, P. (1982, August). Alcohol and the lesbian community: Changing patterns of awareness. *Drinking and Drug Practices Surveyor, 18,* 3-7.

Hernandez, J.T. (1992). Substance abuse among sexually abused adolescents and their families. *Journal of Adolescent Health, 13,* 658-662.

Hilton, M.E. (1988). Trends in U.S. drinking patterns: Further evidence from the past 20 years. *British Journal of Addiction, 83,* 269-278.

Hingson, R.W., Strunin, L., Berlin, B.M., & Heeren, T. (1990). Beliefs about AIDS, use of alcohol and drugs, and unprotected sex among Massachusetts adolescents. *American Journal of Public Health, 80,* 295-299.

Hughes, T.L., & Wilsnack, S.C. (1994). Research on lesbians and alcohol: Gaps and implications. *Alcohol Health & Research World, 18,* 202-205.

Hull, J.G., & Bond, C.F., Jr. (1986). Social and behavioral consequences of alcohol consumption and expectancy: A meta-analysis. *Psychological Bulletin, 99,* 347-360.

Jensen, S.B. (1979). Sexual function and dysfunction in alcoholics. *British Journal of Sexual Medicine, 10,* 29-31.

Jensen, S.B. (1984). Sexual function and dysfunction in younger married alcoholics: A comparative study. *Acta Psychiatrica Scandinavica, 69,* 543-549.

Kaplan, H.S. (1974). *The new sex therapy: Active treatment of sexual dysfunctions* (Vol. 1). New York: Brunner/Mazel.

Kaplan, H.S. (1979). *Disorders of sexual desire and other new concepts and techniques in sex therapy.* New York: Brunner/Mazel.

Kilpatrick, D.G., Edmonds, C.N., & Seymour, A.K. (1992). *Rape in America: A report to the nation.* Arlington, VA: National Victim Center.

Kilpatrick, D.G., Resnick, H.S., Saunders, B.E., Best, C.L., & Epstein, J. (1994, June). *Violent assault and alcohol dependence among women: Results of a longitudinal study.* Paper presented at the annual meeting of the Research Society on Alcoholism, Maui, Hawaii.

Klassen, A.D., Williams, C.J., & Levitt, E.E. (1989). *Sex and morality in the U.S.: An empirical enquiry under the auspices of the Kinsey Institute* (H.J. O'Gorman, Ed.). Middletown, CT: Wesleyan University Press.

Klassen, A.D., & Wilsnack, S.C. (1986). Sexual experience and drinking among women in a U.S. national survey. *Archives of Sexual Behavior, 15,* 363-392.

Klassen, A.D., Wilsnack, S.C., Harris, T.R., & Wilsnack, R.W. (1991, March). *Partnership dissolution and remission of problem drinking in women: Findings from a U.S. longitudinal survey.* Paper presented at the Symposium on Alcohol, Family and Significant Others, Social Research Institute of Alcohol Studies and Nordic Council for Alcohol and Drug Research, Helsinki, Finland.

Koss, M.P., Dinero, T.E., Seibel, C.A., & Cox, S.L. (1988). Stranger and acquaintance rape: Are there differences in the victim's experience? *Psychology of Women Quarterly, 12,* 1-24.

Lang, A.R. (1985). The social psychology of drinking and human sexuality. *Journal of Drug Issues, 15,* 273-289.

Lang, A.R., Searles, J., Lauerman, R., & Adesso, V. (1980). Expectancy, alcohol, and sex guilt as determinants of interest in and reaction to sexual stimuli. *Journal of Abnormal Psychology, 89,* 644-653.

Langevin, R., Ben-Aron, M.H., Coulthard, R., Day, D., Hucker, S.J., Purins, J.E., Roper, V., Russon, A.E., & Webster, C.D. (1985). The effect of alcohol on penile erection. In R. Langevin (Ed.), *Erotic preference, gender identity, and aggression in men: New research studies* (pp. 101-111). Hillsdale, NJ: Erlbaum.

Lansky, D., & Wilson, G.T. (1981). Alcohol, expectations, and sexual arousal in males: An information processing analysis. *Journal of Abnormal Psychology, 90,* 35-45.

Laumann, E.O., Gagnon, J.H., Michael, R.T., & Michaels, S. (1994). *The social organization of sexuality: Sexual practices in the United States.* Chicago: University of Chicago Press.

Leigh, B.C. (1990). "Venus gets in my thinking": Drinking and female sexuality in the age of AIDS. *Journal of Substance Abuse, 2,* 129-145.

Leigh, B.C., Temple, M.T., & Trocki, K.F. (1994). The relationship of alcohol use to sexual activity in a U.S. national sample. *Social Science and Medicine, 39,* 1527-1535.

Lew, M. (1990). *Victims no longer: Men recovering from incest and other sexual child abuse.* New York: Harper & Row (Perennial Library).

Lipscomb, G.H., Muram, D., Speck, P.M., & Mercer, B.M. (1992). Male victims of sexual assault. *Journal of the American Medical Association, 267,* 3064-3066.

Lipton, R.I. (1994). The effect of moderate alcohol use on the relationship between stress and depression. *American Journal of Public Health, 84,* 1913-1917.

Loether, H.J., & McTavish, D.G. (1980). *Descriptive and inferential statistics: An introduction* (2nd ed.). Boston: Allyn & Bacon.

Lohrenz, L.J., Connelly, J.C., Coyne, L., & Spare, K.E. (1978). Alcohol problems in several Midwestern homosexual communities. *Journal of Studies on Alcohol, 39,* 1959-1963.

Malatesta, V.J., Pollack, R.H., Crotty, T.D., & Peacock, L.J. (1982). Acute alcohol intoxication and female orgasmic response. *Journal of Sex Research, 18,* 1-17.

Malatesta, V.J., Pollack, R.H., Wilbanks, W.A., & Adams, H.E. (1979). Alcohol effects on the orgasmic-ejaculatory response in human males. *Journal of Sex Research, 15,* 101-107.

Marin, B.V., & Flores, E. (1994). Acculturation, sexual behavior, and alcohol use among Latinas. *International Journal of the Addictions, 29,* 1101-1114.

Martin, J.L., Dean, L., Garcia, M., & Hall, W. (1989). The impact of AIDS on a gay community: Changes in sexual behavior, substance use and mental health. *American Journal of Community Psychology, 17,* 269-293.

Martin, S.E. (1992). The epidemiology of alcohol-related interpersonal violence. *Alcohol Health & Research World, 16,* 230-237.

McCarthy, B.W. (1984). Returning to drinking as a result of erectile dysfunction. In D.J. Powell (Ed.), *Alcoholism and sexual dysfunction: Issues in clinical management* (pp. 33-34). New York: Haworth.

McCarty, D., Diamond, W., & Kaye, M. (1982). Alcohol, sexual arousal, and the transfer of excitation. *Journal of Personality and Social Psychology, 42,* 977-988.

McEwan, R.T., McCallum, A., Bhopal, R.S., & Madhok, R. (1992). Sex and the risk of HIV infection: The role of alcohol. *British Journal of Addiction, 87,* 577-584.

McKirnan, D.J., & Peterson, P.L. (1989a). Alcohol and drug use among homosexual men and women: Epidemiology and population characteristics. *Addictive Behaviors, 14,* 545-553.

McKirnan, D.J., & Peterson, P.L. (1989b). Psychosocial and cultural factors in alcohol and drug abuse: An analysis of a homosexual community. *Addictive Behaviors, 14,* 555-563.

Miller, B.A., Downs, W.R., & Testa, M. (1993). Interrelationships between victimization experiences and women's alcohol use. *Journal of Studies on Alcohol* (Suppl. No. 11), 109-117.

Muehlenhard, C.L., & Linton, M.A. (1987). Date rape and sexual aggression in dating situations: Incidence and risk factors. *Journal of Counseling Psychology, 34,* 186-196.

Nirenberg, T.D., Liepman, M.R., Begin, A.M., Doolittle, R.H., & Broffman, T.E. (1990). The sexual relationship of male alcoholics and their female partners during periods of drinking and abstinence. *Journal of Studies on Alcohol, 51,* 565-568.

Nirenberg, T.D., Wincze, J.P., Bansal, S., Liepman, M.R., Engle-Friedman, M., & Begin, A. (1991). Volunteer bias in a study of male alcoholics' sexual behavior. *Archives of Sexual Behavior, 20,* 371-379.

Norris, J. (1994). Alcohol and female sexuality: A look at expectancies and risks. *Alcohol Health & Research World, 18,* 197-201.

Norris, J. (in press). Alcohol consumption and female sexuality: A review. In E. Taylor, J. Howard, P. Mail, & M. Hilton (Eds.), *Prevention research on women and alcohol.* Washington, DC: U.S. Government Printing Office.

Norris, J., & Cubbins, L.A. (1992). Dating, drinking, and rape: Effects of victim's and assailant's alcohol consumption on judgments of their behavior and traits. *Psychology of Women Quarterly, 16,* 179-191.

O'Farrell, T.J. (1990). Sexual functioning of male alcoholics. In R.L. Collins, K.E. Leonard, & J.S. Searles (Eds.), *Alcohol and the family: Research and clinical perspectives* (pp. 244-271). New York: Guilford.

O'Farrell, T.J., Choquette, K.A., & Birchler, G.R. (1991). Sexual satisfaction and dissatisfaction in the marital relationships of male alcoholics seeking marital therapy. *Journal of Studies on Alcohol, 52,* 441-447.

Oliver, M.B., & Hyde, J.S. (1993). Gender differences in sexuality: A meta-analysis. *Psychological Bulletin, 114,* 29-51.

Parker, D.A., Harford, T.C., & Rosenstock, I.M. (1994). Alcohol, other drugs, and sexual risk-taking among young adults. *Journal of Substance Abuse, 6,* 87-93.

Paul, J.P., Stall, R., & Bloomfield, K.A. (1991). Gay and alcoholic: Epidemiologic and clinical issues. *Alcohol Health & Research World, 15,* 151-160.

Pernanen, K. (1991). *Alcohol in human violence.* New York: Guilford.

Perry, M.J., Solomon, L.J., Winett, R.A., Kelly, J.A., Roffman, R.A., Desiderato, L.L., Kalichman, S.C., Sikkema, K.J., Norman, A.D., Short, B., et al. (1994). High risk sexual behavior and alcohol consumption among bar-going gay men. *AIDS, 8,* 1321-1324.

Peterson, J.S., Hartsock, N., & Lawson, G. (1984). Sexual dissatisfaction of female alcoholics. *Psychological Reports, 55,* 744-746.

Pribor, E.F., & Dinwiddie, S.H. (1992). Psychiatric correlates of incest in childhood. *American Journal of Psychiatry, 149,* 52-56.

Remien, R, Rabkin, J., Williams, J., Bradbury, M., Ehrhardt, A., & Gorman, J. (1990, May). *Cessation of substance use disorders in gay men.* Paper presented at the 143rd annual meeting of the American Psychiatric Association, New York, NY (Cited in Paul et al., 1991).

Richardson, D., & Campbell, J.L. (1982). Alcohol and rape: The effect of alcohol on attributions of blame for rape. *Personality and Social Psychology Bulletin,* *8,* 468-476.

Robertson, J.A., & Plant, M.A. (1988). Alcohol, sex and risks of HIV infection. *Drug and Alcohol Dependence, 22,* 75-78.

Roehrich, L., & Kinder, B.N. (1991). Alcohol expectancies and male sexuality: Review and implications for sex therapy. *Journal of Sex and Marital Therapy, 17,* 45-54.

Roesler, T.A., & Dafler, C.E. (1993). Chemical dissociation in adults sexually victimized as children: Alcohol and drug use in adult survivors. *Journal of Substance Abuse Treatment, 10,* 537-543.

Rohsenow, D.J., Corbett, R., & Devine, D. (1988). Molested as children: A hidden contribution to substance abuse? *Journal of Substance Abuse Treatment, 5,* 13-18.

Russell, S.A., & Wilsnack, S.C. (1991). Adult survivors of childhood sexual abuse: Substance abuse and other consequences. In P. Roth (Ed.), *Alcohol and drugs are women's issues: Vol. 1. A review of the issues* (pp. 61-70). Metuchen, NJ: Women's Action Alliance & Scarecrow Press.

Saghir, M.T., & Robins, E. (1973). *Male and female homosexuality: A comprehensive investigation.* Baltimore: Williams & Wilkins.

Sandmaier, M. (1980). *The invisible alcoholics: Women and alcohol abuse in America.* New York: McGraw-Hill.

Schaefer, S., & Evans, S. (1987). Women, sexuality and the process of recovery. In E. Coleman (Ed.), *Chemical dependency and intimacy dysfunction* (pp. 91-120). New York: Haworth.

Schiavi, R.C. (1990). Chronic alcoholism and male sexual dysfunction. *Journal of Sex and Marital Therapy, 16,* 23-33.

Schilit, R., Lie, G.Y., & Montagne, M. (1990). Substance use as a correlate of violence in intimate lesbian relationships. *Journal of Homosexuality, 19*(3), 51-65.

Stall, R., & Wiley, J. (1988). A comparison of alcohol and drug use patterns of homosexual and heterosexual men: The San Francisco men's health study. *Drug and Alcohol Dependence, 22,* 63-73.

Strunin, L., & Hingson, R. (1992). Alcohol, drugs, and adolescent sexual behavior. *International Journal of the Addictions, 27,* 129-146.

Swett, C., & Halpert, M. (1994). High rates of alcohol problems and history of physical and sexual abuse among women inpatients. *American Journal of Drug and Alcohol Abuse, 20,* 263-272.

Tan, E.T.H., Johnson, R.H., Lambie, D.G., Vijayasenan, M.E., & Whiteside, E.A. (1984). Erectile impotence in chronic alcoholics. *Alcoholism: Clinical and Experimental Research, 8,* 297-301.

Temple, M.T., & Leigh, B.C. (1992). Alcohol consumption and unsafe sexual behavior in discrete events. *Journal of Sex Research, 29,* 207-219.

Temple, M.T., Leigh, B.C., & Schafer, J. (1993). Unsafe sexual behavior and alcohol use at the event level: Results of a national survey. *Journal of Acquired Immune Deficiency Syndromes, 6,* 393-401.

Trocki, K.F., & Leigh, B.C. (1991). Alcohol consumption and unsafe sex: A comparison of heterosexuals and homosexual men. *Journal of Acquired Immune Deficiency Syndromes, 4,* 981-986.

Turnbull, J.E., & Gomberg, E.S.L. (1991). The structure of drinking-related consequences in alcoholic women. *Alcoholism: Clinical and Experimental Research, 15,* 29-38.

Underhill, B.L., & Wolverton, T. (1993). *Creating visibility: Providing lesbian-sensitive and lesbian-specific alcoholism recovery services.* Los Angeles: Alcoholism Center for Women.

Valimaki, M., Pelkonen, R., Harkonen, M., Tuomala, P., Koistinen, P., Roine, R., & Ylikahri, R. (1990). Pituitary-gonadal hormones and adrenal androgens in non-cirrhotic female alcoholics after cessation of alcohol intake. *European Journal of Clinical Investigation, 20,* 177-181.

Weatherburn, P., Davies, P.M., Hickson, F.C., Hunt, A.J., McManus, T.J., & Coxon, A.P. (1993). No connection between alcohol use and unsafe sex among gay and bisexual men. *AIDS, 7,* 115-119.

Whalley, L.J. (1978). Sexual adjustment of male alcoholics. *Acta Psychiatrica Scandinavica, 58,* 281-298.

Widom, C.S., Ireland, T., & Glynn, P.J. (1995). Alcohol abuse in abused and neglected children followed-up: Are they at increased risk? *Journal of Studies on Alcohol, 56,* 207-217.

Wilsnack, R.W., Vogeltanz, N.D., Wilsnack, S.C., et al. (1995, June). *Alcohol consumption and adverse drinking consequences: Descriptive findings from the International Research Group on Gender and Alcohol.* Paper presented at the 21st Annual Epidemiology Symposium of the Kettil Bruun Society for Social and Epidemiological Research on Alcohol, Porto, Portugal.

Wilsnack, R.W., Wilsnack, S.C., & Klassen, A.D. (1984). Women's drinking and drinking problems: Patterns from a 1981 national survey. *American Journal of Public Health, 74,* 1231-1238.

Wilsnack, S.C. (1984). Drinking, sexuality, and sexual dysfunction in women. In S.C. Wilsnack & L.J. Beckman (Eds.), *Alcohol problems in women: Antecedents, consequences, and intervention* (pp. 189-227). New York: Guilford.

Wilsnack, S.C. (1991). Sexuality and women's drinking: Findings from a U.S. national study. *Alcohol Health & Research World, 15,* 147-150.

Wilsnack, S.C. (1995). Alcohol use and alcohol problems in women. In A.L. Stanton & S.J. Gallant (Eds.), *Psychology of women's health: Progress and challenges in research and application* (pp. 381-443). Washington, DC: American Psychological Association.

Wilsnack, S.C., Klassen, A.D., Schur, B.E., & Wilsnack, R.W. (1991). Predicting onset and chronicity of women's problem drinking: A five-year longitudinal analysis. *American Journal of Public Health, 81,* 305-318.

Wilsnack, S.C., Klassen, A.D., & Wilsnack, R.W. (1984). Drinking and reproductive dysfunction among women in a 1981 national survey. *Alcoholism: Clinical and Experimental Research, 8,* 451-458.

Wilsnack, S.C., Vogeltanz, N.D., Klassen, A.D., & Harris, T.R. (in press). Childhood sexual abuse and women's substance abuse: National survey findings. *Journal of Studies on Alcohol.*

Wilsnack, S.C., Wilsnack, R.W., & Hiller-Sturmhofel, S. (1994). How women drink: Epidemiology of women's drinking and problem drinking. *Alcohol Health & Research World, 18,* 173-181.

Wilsnack, S.C., Wilsnack, R.W., & Klassen, A.D. (1986). Epidemiological research on women's drinking, 1978-1984. In National Institute on Alcohol Abuse and Alcoholism, *Women and alcohol: Health-related issues* (pp. 1-68). (NIAAA Research Monograph No. 16; DHHS Publication No. ADM 86-1139). Washington, DC: U.S. Government Printing Office.

Wilson, G.T., & Lawson, D.M. (1976a). Effects of alcohol on sexual arousal in women. *Journal of Abnormal Psychology, 85,* 489-497.

Wilson, G.T., & Lawson, D.M. (1976b). Expectancies, alcohol, and sexual arousal in male social drinkers. *Journal of Abnormal Psychology, 85,* 587-594.

Wilson, G.T., & Lawson, D.M. (1978). Expectancies, alcohol, and sexual arousal in women. *Journal of Abnormal Psychology, 87,* 358-367.

Wilson, G.T., Lawson, D.M., & Abrams, D.B. (1978). Effects of alcohol on sexual arousal in male alcoholics. *Journal of Abnormal Psychology, 87,* 609-616.

Wilson, G.T., & Niaura, R.S. (1984). Alcohol and the disinhibition of sexual responsiveness. *Journal of Studies on Alcohol, 45,* 219-224.

Wolchik, S.A., Braver, S.L., & Jensen, K. (1985). Volunteer bias in erotica research: Effects of intrusiveness of measure and sexual background. *Archives of Sexual Behavior, 14,* 93-107.

Wonderlich, S.A., Wilsnack, R.W., Wilsnack, S.C., & Harris, T.R. (1996). Childhood sexual abuse and bulimic behavior in a nationally representative sample. *American Journal of Public Health, 86,* 1082-1086.

Wyatt, G.E. (1985). The sexual abuse of Afro-American and white-American women in childhood. *Child Abuse and Neglect, 9,* 507-519.

Wyatt, G.E., Newcomb, M.D., & Riederle, M. (1993). *Sexual abuse and consensual sex: Women's developmental patterns and outcomes.* Newbury Park, CA: Sage.

Yellowlees, P.M., & Kaushik, A.V. (1994). A case-control study of the sequelae of childhood sexual assault in adult psychiatric patients. *Medical Journal of Australia, 160,* 408-411.

Ziebold, T.O., & Mongeon, J.E. (1982). Introduction: Alcoholism and the homosexual community. *Journal of Homosexuality, 7* (4), 3-7.

CHAPTER 11

Gender Differences and Similarities in the Alcohol and Marriage Relationship

LINDA J. ROBERTS AND KENNETH E. LEONARD

According to a recent national survey, 73% of married men and 63% of married women drink alcohol (Hilton, 1991). Thus, for a substantial majority of couples, drinking is woven into the fabric of married life. Although researchers have recently turned their attention to the links between alcohol use and the family, this burgeoning literature has concentrated on the effects of parental alcoholism on child outcomes, and surprisingly little research has been directed specifically at the marital bond. How does alcohol use affect marital functioning and the quality of the marital relationship? Conversely, how do marital events and the quality of the marital relationship affect drinking? What impact does becoming married have on drinking levels and patterns?

As has been emphasized throughout this volume, these important questions cannot be adequately answered with research that relies exclusively on *male* subjects. Nor is it enough to simply incorporate female subjects; the possibility of a differential relationship between alcohol and marriage as a function of gender needs to be addressed. The purpose of this chapter is to evaluate the existing literature on marriage and alcohol with respect to the issue of gender differences. Is drinking woven into the fabric of marriage differently for husbands and wives?

Reviewing the literature on any scientific issue is like trying to solve a jigsaw puzzle. The reviewer tries to piece studies together into a coherent picture, culling out studies that are weak or do not belong. For the issue of "gender, marriage, and alcohol," the puzzle-solving task is difficult. To begin with, there is no clear picture of what the results of studies should be—no strong conceptual or theoretical foundation to guide and integrate research on this issue. Furthermore, there are a lot of missing pieces. Studies of alcohol and marriage are relatively scarce, and very few examine both male and female partners. Most of the existing studies are only small pieces of the puzzle, brief research on small and nonrepresentative samples. Longitudinal or experimental research with large representative samples of both men and women is very rare.

To improve our ability to accurately describe the "picture" emerging from the integration of the existing puzzle pieces, we will add to the box some preliminary data analyses and unpublished papers from our current work with a large sample of couples in the early years of marriage. This research project, referred to as the Buffalo Newlywed Study (BNS), was designed to estimate the prevalence of alcohol-related marital violence in the first three years of marriage and to examine a social learning model of the relationship between alcohol use and marital violence. However, since the study included extensive assessments of both alcohol variables and indices of marital functioning collected over time and from both spouses, it provides an ideal dataset for addressing a variety of questions concerning the interrelationships of drinking and marriage.

Couples were recruited for the study as they applied for a marriage license at City Hall in Buffalo, New York. This recruitment strategy provided a heterogeneous sample that is generally representative of the urban area in which the couples reside. For example, 70% of the subjects are Caucasian, 25% African-American, and 5% are Hispanic. The sample is predominantly Catholic (50%), 12% did not complete high school, and 25% were college graduates (for further details, see Leonard & Senchak, 1992). Data were collected from subjects at three time points: an initial assessment at the time of marriage (Time 1), a one-year follow-up (Time 2), and a three-year follow-up (Time 3). The preliminary reports from this dataset presented here involve 475 couples who had completed both Time 1 and Time 2 assessments.[1]

Although the Newlywed Study is limited to young, newly married couples, this period is critical for the marriage-alcohol relationship. During the early years of marriage, a couple must lay the groundwork for a stable marital bond, and it is during this period that the bond is the most fragile. Newly married couples must negotiate a satisfactory division of roles and responsibilities, develop their ability to resolve the inevitable conflicts they will face, and learn ways to maintain closeness and rapport. Since drinking is heaviest in young adulthood, it is precisely these important developmental tasks that have the strongest potential to affect and be affected by alcohol use. The transition to marriage is also an important event with respect to drinking behavior. As couples marry, a "drinking partnership" is forged from the premarital drinking habits of two separate individuals. A couple establishes norms and rules for drinking behavior in their shared household (e.g., is alcohol served with meals, kept in the house, offered to guests, etc.). Moreover, the shared domicile increases each partner's sphere of influence over the other; each partner becomes a salient feature of the other's drinking context, thereby establishing pathways for direct influence through modeling and social reinforcement.

Incorporating data from the Newlywed Study where appropriate, we will focus on three broad areas of the gender, marriage, and alcohol puzzle: the reciprocal relationships between alcohol and marriage per se (marital status and the transition to marriage); the reciprocal relationships between alcohol and marital functioning; and the establishment of the marital "drinking partnership."

Marital Status and the Transition to Marriage

Beginning with Durkheim's analysis of suicide, researchers have suggested that marriage offers protection from a variety of mental health problems, including alcohol-related problems. As early as 1944, Bacon reported that men arrested for inebriety were less likely to be married than age-adjusted general population rates. Early descriptions of problem-drinking women also noted that many of the women were unmarried, usually divorced or separated (e.g., Gomberg, 1986; Lisansky, 1957).

Several epidemiological studies have examined the relationship between alcohol problems and marital status (Cahalan et al., 1969; Clark & Midanik, 1982; Hilton, 1991; Johnson, 1982; Wechsler et al., 1978; Whitehead & Layne, 1987; Wilsnack et al., 1986). For males, the results in Table 1 are consistent across studies—married men are less likely to be heavy drinkers than single or divorced/separated men. Most studies have found heavy drinking most common among divorced/separated men, but two studies found heavy drinking slightly more common among single men. The percentages of heavy drinking males differed from study to study, partly because of variations in how heavy drinking is defined, and also because of methodological and geographical differences. Nevertheless, it is clear that married men are less likely to engage in heavy drinking.

In general, the relationship of marital status to drinking patterns is similar among women—married women exhibit the lowest prevalence of heavier drinking. However, being married often has a weaker effect on heavy drinking among women than it does among men. Furthermore, in three studies single women had the highest prevalence of heavy drinking, while in four studies divorced or separated women had the highest prevalence. Thus, though married women are less likely to drink heavily, relationships between drinking and marital status among women may be more complex than any simple protective effect of getting married.

Several problems of measurement and analysis make it unwise to draw simple conclusions about marriage and alcohol use from these epidemiological studies. First single, married, and divorced individuals differ from one another in ways other than marital status. For example, single individuals, whether men or women, are considerably younger on average than married or divorced individuals. Thus, some of the apparent effects of marriage may be effects of age. Being married will also often entail more role responsibilities than many unmarried individuals have. For example, many of those married

TABLE 1
Rates of Heavy Drinking by Gender and Marital Status

	MEN (%)			WOMEN (%)		
	Married	Single	Div./ sep.	Married	Single	Div./ sep.
Cahalan et al. (1969)[1]	21	28	25	4	7	11
Clark & Midanik (1982)[2]	17	31	29	5	8	6
Hilton (1991)[2]	20	24	27	5	9	4
Wilsnack et al. (1986)[2]	14	18	29	5	9	7
Johnson (1982)[3]	17	39	44	9	11	15
Wechsler et al. (1978)[1]	33	50	58	10	12	24
Whitehead & Layne (1987)[4]	12	16	27	11	16	28

[1]Heavy drinkers defined according to complex classification system including frequency, modal quantity, and maximum quantity.
[2]Sixty drinks per month or more, or average daily consumption of 2 drinks or more.
[3]Approximate blood alcohol concentration per day calculated as daily consumption/ $(.14 \times \text{lbs.})$ for men and daily consumption/ $(.12 \times \text{lbs.})$ for women. These figures were calculated from tables presented in Johnson's article.
[4]Typical quantity of 6 or more drinks for men, 4–5 drinks or more for women.

will have childrearing responsibilities. This is far less likely among those single and is gender-imbalanced among the divorced or separated.

Another problem is the definition of marital status. Some studies include cohabiting in the same category as married, though there is evidence to suggest that the drinking patterns of these two groups may be quite different (Helzer et al., 1991; Wilsnack et al., 1984). Also, among people classified as married, individuals in their first marriage may drink differently from individuals who have remarried, but differences in alcohol use between the first-married and remarried have not been adequately studied. Finally, the most problematic aspect of these studies is their cross-sectional nature; the processes underlying the associations between marital status and drinking have not been addressed. For example, it is not clear from these studies whether marriage reduces the risk of heavy drinking for men and women or whether high-risk individuals are less likely to marry and more likely to divorce than low-risk individuals.

Several longitudinal studies (Bachman et al., 1984; Horwitz & White, 1991; Miller-Tutzauer et al., 1991; Power & Estaugh, 1990; Roberts et al., 1992b) have provided data more appropriate for describing causal relationships between drinking and the transition to marriage. One general conclusion from these studies is that early adolescent alcohol consumption does not lead to delays in marriage for males or females. For example, Bachman et al. (1984) found no differences in high school drinking or drug use between students who were living with a spouse one to three years after high school and those living in other arrangements. Power and Estaugh (1990) analyzed the results of a survey of young people born in Great Britain in 1958 and reassessed at ages 7, 11, 16, and 23. Their findings indicated that marital status at age 23 was not related to drinking at age 16 for males or females, except that the heaviest male drinkers at age 16 were actually more likely to have married by age 23.

While adolescent drinking does not appear to be related to subsequent marriage, whether *early adult* drinking is related to the likelihood of marriage is unclear. Horwitz and White (1991) examined drinking and marriage among a cohort identified in adolescence and assessed at ages 21 and 24. Their results suggested that both men and women who were married by age 24 had fewer alcohol-related problems at age 21 than subjects who were single at age 24. In contrast, in an analysis of data from the Youth Cohort of the National Longitudinal Survey of Labor Market Experience, Miller-Tutzauer et al. (1991) found that men and women who would marry in two years manifested similar levels of alcohol consumption as men and women who would still be single in two years. This study also reported that there appeared to be a decline in drinking in the year immediately preceding marriage. In contrast to drinking levels, the analyses of drinking problems did not reveal significant shifts either before or at the time of marriage. Taken together, these studies suggest that drinking levels do not seem to impede the transition to marriage. While drinking problems during adolescence are not strongly related to marriage, the occurrence of such problems in early adulthood seems to delay marriage. Among those who do marry, there may be a period of time preceding marriage that is characterized by lighter drinking; however, whether this reduced drinking is the result of an intimate, premarital relationship and/or whether this reduced drinking enables a transition to marriage is unclear. Perhaps both processes occur.

The longitudinal studies found that becoming married by the time of follow-up predicted lower alcohol consumption than would be expected from an individual's previous drinking level (Bachman et al., 1984; Power & Estaugh, 1990). Horwitz and White (1991) found that marital status at the time of the follow-up was predictive of drinking at the follow-up independent of drinking at the initial assessment, although this effect of marriage was significant only for women. The long follow-up periods and the uncertainty concerning the exact time of marriage within the interval between assessments leave the issue of whether couples reduce their drinking in response to marriage per se unresolved. However, Miller-Tutzauer et al. (1991) examined subjects on a year-by-year basis and found that in the year prior to marriage, men and women drank more than those who had already married. From the year prior to the year of marriage, men and women reduced their drinking and did not differ from those who had been married longer. This study thus provides the strongest support for the hypothesis that the transition to marriage results in a reduction in drinking and that this is equally true for males and females.

Although men and women appear to respond to marriage similarly in terms of gross estimates of drinking, heavy drinking, or drinking problems, there may be differences if specific drinking patterns or contexts of drinking are considered. Preliminary analyses examining drinking from the year prior to marriage to the first year of marriage have been conducted with BNS data (Roberts et al., 1992b,c). Although it is not possible to unambiguously attribute these changes to marriage because there was no comparison sample of couples who did not marry, the results are nonetheless suggestive.

Consistent with the hypothesis that marriage can serve a protective function with respect to alcohol consumption and problems, both husbands and wives reported lower daily consumption and fewer alcohol-related problems during the first year of marriage in contrast to the year before marriage (see Table 2). While the direction of change in alcohol use was the same for both sexes, marriage produced more significant changes for women. No significant changes were evident for husband's typical quantity per occasion, frequency of drinking beer or wine, nor usual frequency of drunkenness. In contrast, the wives showed significant reductions on every consumption measure. Both men and women increased their drinking at home and decreased the quantity consumed in the presence of their partner. While women significantly decreased the amount they typically drank when their husband was not present, this reduction was not statistically significant for men.

In summary, there is evidence to suggest that temporally remote drinking patterns do not influence the onset of marriage. However, reduced levels of drinking appear to characterize the time period just before marriage. Whether this reduction results from or enables the development of a relationship with marital potential is unclear. The reduction appears to continue at least until after the couple is wed, but may not continue beyond the first year. Evidence for gender differences is inconclusive. Some studies have comparable effects of marriage on men's and women's drinking, but at least one study suggests that marriage may reduce women's but not men's alcohol problems. The Newlywed Study suggests that a decline in drinking over the first year of marriage is more evident among women, but that both men and women evidence similar reductions in alcohol problems and scores on the Alcohol Dependence Scale over this time.

TABLE 2
Husbands' and Wives' Drinking Behaviors at the Time of Marriage (Time 1)
and One-Year Anniversary (Time 2)

	MEN			WOMEN		
	Time 1	Time 2		Time 1	Time 2	
Alcohol consumption						
Average daily oz. of ethanol	0.73	0.67	*	0.30	0.20	***
Typical quantity	4.38	4.33		3.32	2.83	***
Days per month consumed beer	6.27	5.94		2.19	1.89	†
Days per month consumed wine	0.93	0.78		1.26	1.02	*
Days per month consumed spirits	1.68	1.38	**	1.08	0.75	**
Risky and problem drinking						
Days per month 6 or more	1.83	1.56	†	0.66	0.36	**
Days per month intoxicated	1.29	1.17		0.66	0.33	***
Alcohol problems	1.69	1.36	***	0.79	0.43	***
Alcohol Dependence Scale	3.69	2.85	***	2.47	1.76	***
Drinking context						
% QFI with partner present	0.61	0.62		0.70	0.67	*
% QFI at home	0.48	0.64	**	0.59	0.81	**
Typical quantity partner present	3.83	3.64	*	2.64	2.25	***
Typical quantity partner not present	3.53	3.34		1.92	1.58	**

†$p < .10.$ *$p < .05.$ **$p < .01.$ ***$p < .001.$

Marital Functioning and the Quality of the Marital Relationship

Although the evidence suggests that getting married may reduce risks of alcohol-related problems, the relationships between *being married* and drinking are much more complex and poorly understood. Marriage can be either a stress or a support, increasing risks or offering protection from negative physical and mental health outcomes (Bromet & Moos, 1977; Gove et al., 1983; Pearlin et al., 1981).

For both husbands and wives, heavy drinking has been implicated as a cause of marital dissolution (Burns, 1984; Glatt, 1961; Kinsey, 1966; Power & Estaugh, 1990; Straus & Bacon, 1951) and of marital problems including conflict, infidelity, and violence (see Orford, 1990). However, there is also evidence for effects in the reverse direction, that is, drinking may increase as a *consequence* of marital difficulties or dissolution (Dahlgren, 1979; Magura & Shapiro, 1988; Mulford, 1977; Wilsnack & Cheloha, 1987). To complicate matters further, some researchers have reported that alcohol use may actually be adaptive for some couples, even when one of the partners is an identified problem drinker (Dunn et al., 1987; Holmila, 1988; Jacob et al., 1983; Steinglass et al., 1977).

The research literature does not help much to untangle these complex relationships, and says even less about gender differences in how marriage and drinking interrelate. Most of the research on marital functioning and drinking has been carried out with male problem drinkers. Nonetheless, many investigators suggest that women's drinking is more closely linked to marital/family functioning than is men's (e.g., Curlee, 1967; Gomberg, 1976; Jacob & Seilhamer, 1991; Perodeau, 1984).

The evidence for gender differences in relationships between drinking and marital functioning is circumstantial and weak. For example, it has been reported that wives are more likely to cite marital and family difficulties as the cause of their drinking (Beckman, 1975; Lisansky, 1957), to develop drinking problems after marriage (Noel et al., 1991), to drink at home (Wanberg & Horn, 1970), and to have less tolerant partners who are more likely to end the marriage (Corrigan, 1980; Dahlgren, 1979; Williams & Klerman, 1984). As Gomberg (1976) intimates, this presumed gender difference may be grounded as much in assumptions about gender roles as in sound research evidence: "From the research literature (and from common sense knowledge of social roles) the generalization can be made that men seem to feel the consequences of their alcoholism in the work situation; women within the family" (p. 620). Women are seen as more likely to experience marital and family problems due to drinking and as more likely to drink in response to marital and family difficulties. Before examining evidence for gender differences in the causal relationships suggested here, we will examine the evidence for the simpler assertion that the link between drinking and family dysfunction is stronger for females than for males.

The Cross-Sectional Association of Marital Dysfunction and Drinking for Husbands and Wives

Ten studies were found that reported cross-sectional relationships between alcohol use and marital functioning for both husbands and wives, in clinical samples (Bromet & Moos, 1977; Dahlgren, 1979; Mulford, 1977; Noel et al., 1991; Steinglass et al., 1987), clinical samples with a matched control group (Brennan & Moos, 1990; Perodeau & Kohn, 1989), and community samples (Holmila, 1988; Horowitz & White, 1991; Schwarz & Wheeler, 1992). In the clinical samples, female problem drinkers consistently reported more stress, conflict, and disharmony in their marriages than did male problem drinkers (Brennan & Moos, 1990; Dahlgren, 1979; Mulford, 1977; Perodeau & Kohn, 1989).[2] They were also less likely to view their spouse as a confidant (Mulford, 1977) or a source of support (Brennan & Moos, 1990), and more likely to attribute their drinking to the behavior of their partner (Dahlgren, 1975).

However, there are problems with interpreting these findings as gender differences. First, it is well known that the drinking behavior of *partners* tends to be different for male and female problem drinkers: female problem drinkers are much more likely to be married to male problem drinkers than vice versa (Bromet & Moos, 1976; Hall et al., 1983; Lisansky, 1957; Mulford, 1977). In Dahlgren's (1979) study, 50% of her female alcoholic subjects had husbands who were alcoholic; in Mulford's (1977) study, 49% of the wives as compared to 6% of the husbands had heavy drinking partners. More reported marital problems for female than for male problem drinkers may have as much to do with their partner's drinking as their own.

The apparently stronger association between female problem drinking and self-reported marital disharmony might also result from gender-specific reporting biases. Consistent with this interpretation, Dahlgren (1975) has argued that because heavy drinking is more stigmatized for women, women are more likely to attribute their heavy drinking to causes—such as marital conflict—that are likely to elicit sympathy rather than condemnation. Perodeau and Kohn (1989), however, found evidence to suggest that it may be male self-reports that are biased—male problem drinkers may underreport their marital difficulties. In their study, female but not male alcoholics' self-reports were found to be congruent with therapists' rating of the marriage. There is further evidence to suggest that the stronger association between marital functioning and drinking for females than for males is based on a gender difference in *perceptions* or self-reports of the marriage rather than on objective behavioral differences. In studies in which *observer* reports (by partner, children, or behavioral coding) of marital functioning were examined, no differences were found in the marital functioning of male and female problem drinkers (Bromet & Moos, 1977; Perodeau & Kohn, 1989; Steinglass et al., 1987).[3] Both groups were found, however, to have poorer marital and family functioning than their non-problem-drinking counterparts (Brennan & Moos, 1990; Perodeau & Kohn, 1989).

When studies using general population or community samples are examined, the assertion by previous reviewers that the "gender, alcohol, and marriage puzzle" depicts a stronger marital functioning/alcohol link for females than males is directly challenged. Despite considerable variability in methodology, subject characteristics, and assessment measures, in the three studies we found addressing this issue with nonclinical samples, husband drinking was uniformly associated with marital dysfunction, whereas wife drinking was either not associated (Holmila, 1988; Horowitz & White, 1991) or negatively associated (Schwarz & Wheeler, 1992). This observed association, however, may not signify anything more than the well-known fact that males drink substantially more than females and have more alcohol-related problems. These studies of community samples are not able to address the issue of whether male and female *problem drinking* may have differential effects on the marriage.

In summary, despite a prevailing belief that female problem drinking has a stronger association with marital/family dysfunction than does male problem drinking, there does not appear to be solid evidence supporting this belief. Although female problem drinkers do report more marital dysfunction than males, spouses report marital dysfunction in both cases, and it is simply not clear what accounts for the differences found in male and female alcoholics' self-reports of their marital functioning.

The Direction of Influence between Marital Functioning and Drinking in Husbands and Wives

Olenick and Chalmers (1991) attempted to learn whether drinking led to or resulted from marital problems, by examining *perceptions* of the sequence of drinking and marital problems reported by female and male problem and non-problem drinkers. With problem and non-problem drinkers combined, females were more likely to report that drinking followed marital problems, while males were more likely to report that their drinking provoked marital problems. However, there was also a significant group-by-gender interaction. Among problem drinkers, women were more likely than men to report drinking as a result of marital conflict, while among non-problem drinkers, men were more likely than women to report that they drank subsequent to marital problems.

Although these results are suggestive, the self-report methodology leaves open the possibility that the results reflect gender-specific reporting biases rather than different processes. Unfortunately, very few studies have used longitudinal, observational, or experimental designs to study the processes linking marital functioning with alcohol use. We were unable to find *any* such studies comparing male and female *problem* drinkers. We did, however, find two longitudinal studies that examined marital functioning and drinking among *non-problem-drinking* husbands and wives (Cronkite & Moos, 1984; Romelsjo et al., 1991).

Both of these studies were designed to examine stressful life situations, including marital strain, as longitudinal predictors of alcohol outcomes. Romelsjo et al. (1991) obtained self-reports of marital strain and problems in their Human Population Laboratory (HPL) study, and Cronkite and Moos (1984) used each partner's report of the spouse's depressed mood, physical symptoms, and drinking. Cronkite and Moos conducted a one-year follow-up and used typical quantity as the drinking outcome, while the HPL cohort was followed for nine years, with a quantity-frequency index as the outcome measure. Although Cronkite and Moos found some support for the generalization that female drinking is more affected by marital strain (here partner's depressed mood) than is male drinking, Romelsjo et al. found the opposite: male but not female reports of alcohol use increased if marital strain was reported nine years earlier. With the results of the only studies in this area inconsistent, little can be concluded about the effects of marital functioning on drinking except that the assertion of a greater effect for females is premature.

TABLE 3
Significant Longitudinal Predictors of Husband and Wife Perceptions of
Marital Intimacy

	HUSBAND MARITAL INTIMACY		WIFE MARITAL INTIMACY	
	R^2 Change	Beta	R^2 Change	Beta
T1 Intimacy	.16***	.40***	.22***	.47***
Sociodemographics				
entered as block	.03*		.03**	
Partner problem drinking	.01*		.00	
Alcohol problems		− .04		
Dependence symptoms		− .14†		
Own problem drinking	.02*		.00	
Alcohol problems		− .22		
Dependence symptoms		− .25†		
Partner consumption	.01*		.00	
Typical amount		.02		
Frequency		.14**		
Own consumption	.00		.02***	
Typical amount				.04
Frequency				.17***

†$p < .10$.   *$p < .05$.   **$p < .01$.   ***$p < .001$.

We were unable to locate *any* studies that examined the impact of drinking on the marital functioning of males and females. Therefore, to address
this important issue, we undertook some preliminary analyses of data from
the Newlywed Study. We used drinking behavior to predict reported intimacy one year after marriage in hierarchical regression analyses that first
controlled for reported intimacy at the time of marriage. The criterion variable was the residual change in marital intimacy[4] over the course of the first
year of marriage. Separate regressions were completed for husbands and
wives, and variables were entered in blocks. After a set of sociodemographic variables, partner's problem drinking (dependence symptoms and
alcohol problems) was entered, followed by own problem drinking, partner's consumption (frequency and typical quantity), and own consumption. The results are presented in Table 3. A husband's marital intimacy was
likely to be lower if he perceived either himself or his wife as a problem
drinker the year before. In contrast, a wife's marital intimacy was unrelated
to her perceptions of problem drinking (her own or her partner's) a year
earlier. However, more frequent drinking by wives appeared to have a positive impact on marital functioning, because it predicted greater intimacy
by both partners' reports.

The Drinking Partnership and Marital Outcomes

Given that husbands generally drink more frequently than their wives, one interpretation of the positive effects of wives' frequent drinking on marital harmony is that frequent-drinking wives try to drink *with* their husbands so that drinking is done together rather than alone. The positive effect may depend on what kind of *drinking partnership* develops in the marriage. The studies reviewed so far have examined the relationship between marital functioning and the husband's and wife's drinking patterns *considered separately*. However, drinking is incorporated into the fabric of a marriage in diverse ways, and it may be the drinking partnership rather than the independent effects of one partner's drinking that is critical to marital functioning. Recent research (Holmila, 1988; Perodeau & Kohn, 1989; S. Wilsnack & R. Wilsnack, 1990) provides some support for this complex approach to the interrelationship of alcohol and marital functioning. For example, among women who drink, the highest level of marital satisfaction is reported by wives whose husbands also drink occasionally rather than frequently or not at all (S. Wilsnack & R. Wilsnack, 1990). More positive marital functioning has also been found among couples who drink together rather than apart, or who have nondiscrepant drinking frequencies (Gleiberman et al., 1992; Holmila, 1988; R. Wilsnack & S. Wilsnack, 1990).

As we use the term here, the "drinking partnership" refers not only to the match, or lack thereof, between husband and wife drinking levels, but also to the patterning and contexts of their mutual drinking. Drinking partnerships may vary from a pattern in which the partners have one or two drinks each night, together, in the privacy of their home, to a pattern in which each partner drinks one night each week, separately, at a bar with his/her own friends. Although the overall consumption levels in the two partnerships may be similar, the drinking may have divergent effects on the marriage. As a first step in exploring drinking partnerships and marital outcomes in the Newlywed Study, we used cluster analysis to identify a typology of drinking partnerships and related these cluster profiles to various indices of marital functioning (Roberts et al., 1992a).

Six drinking level and drinking context variables were used to identify the drinking partnership profiles: husband's and wife's drinking frequency, husband's and wife's typical quantity per occasion, percentage of couple's total drinking done in each other's presence, and the percentage of couple's drinking done in the home. Figure 1 presents the five-cluster solution derived from a *k*-means iterative partitioning of the data (see Roberts et al., 1992c, for further details). Clusters 1 and 3 are comprised of couples with compatible, light, and infrequent drinking styles. The two clusters differ, however, in drinking context. Couples in Cluster 1 are "social drinkers," drinking primarily out of the home and not with one another, while couples in Cluster 3 are

FIGURE 1
Five Couple Drinking Profiles

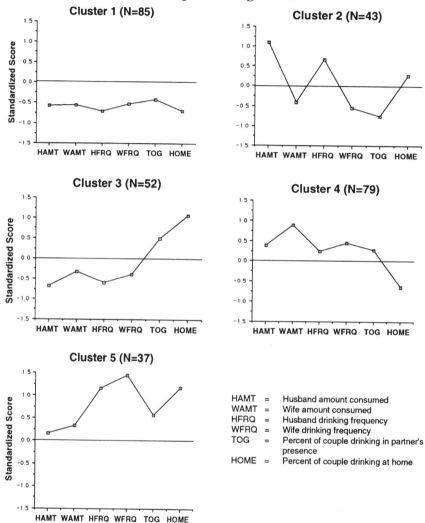

"intimate drinkers," drinking primarily with one another and in their own home. Cluster 5 is similar to Cluster 3 in the "intimate" context of drinking and the compatability of husband and wife consumption patterns, but couples in this group consume more alcohol. Cluster 5 has marked elevations in frequency but not quantity of drinking for both husband and wife. Although partners in Cluster 4 also drink at levels above the mean, the opposite pattern is characteristic of their profile: quantity is somewhat greater than frequency.

Cluster 4 also differs from 5 in that the couples tend to drink out of the home. Cluster 2 has the most discrepant husband and wife drinking levels, with husband's drinking level elevated and drinking occurring separately.

The five clusters differed significantly on indices of marital functioning. Consistent with the importance of the partnership as compared to overall consumption levels, clusters characterized by high levels of consumption were not uniformly associated with marital dysfunction. For example, couples in Cluster 5 were characterized by high marital adjustment, high marital intimacy, and positive problem-solving behavior, although both partners consumed alcohol in quantities above the mean and more frequently than partners in any other cluster. However, their drinking was done in an "intimate" context. Clusters 2 and 4 were the groups most consistently associated with less optimal marital functioning and with more problematic drinking behavior. Cluster 2 and, to a lesser extent, Cluster 4, were characterized by *discrepant* partner consumption patterns, and in both cases the elevated spouse showed a pattern of "binge" drinking, i.e., a pattern of higher quantity than frequency of consumption. It is important to note that these relationships between the drinking partnerships and marital functioning held after statistically controlling for husband and wife quantity-frequency measures. This strongly suggests that there is something about a couple's drinking partnership independent of overall estimates of alcohol consumption that makes a difference in both husbands' and wives' perceptions of their marital quality.

Establishing the Drinking Partnership: Assortative Mating and Partner Influence

A substantial body of evidence supports the notion that spouses' drinking behaviors are positively associated (e.g., Cahalan et al., 1969; Corbett et al., 1991; Hall et al., 1983). However, *how and why* partners' drinking habits are associated, and further, whether there are gender differences in the paths to their association, is less clear. As discussed earlier, a number of studies have documented that female problem drinkers are more likely than male problem drinkers to be married to problem-drinking partners (Bromet & Moos, 1976; Hall et al., 1983; Lisansky, 1957; Mulford, 1977). This observed difference is at least in part attributable to the higher proportion of heavy drinking males in the general population. Nonetheless, this gender discrepancy has been interpreted to suggest that there is a greater likelihood of assortative mating for alcoholism among females than among males, or, alternatively, that husband's drinking exerts a greater influence on wife's drinking than vice versa.

Jacob and Bremer (1986) have previously reviewed the evidence for a gender difference in assortative mating among alcoholics. They found 10 studies that reported assortative mating rates for both male and female alcoholics, allowing for direct gender comparisons. Across the studies, the average assortative mating rate for women was 34% (range = 16-55%), whereas the average rate for men was 12% (range = 0-33%). That is, the rate of alcoholism among the male spouses of alcoholics was nearly three times the rate of alcoholism among the female spouses of alcoholics. However, as Jacob and Bremer argue, this mirrors the difference in base rates of alcoholism. If this is true, and if the base rates for marriage are comparable for male and female alcoholics (and at present there is no evidence that this is not the case), *there can be no gender differences in assortative mating rates.* It is the different *base rates* for alcoholism for men and women and not the number of observed matings that determine the final assortative mating rate. Thus, the popular contention that there are differential assortative mating rates for alcoholism based on gender is unwarranted.

Another popular explanation for the differential rates of heavy drinking among partners of male and female problem drinkers is based on the notion that husbands' drinking habits exert greater influence on their wives' drinking than wives' habits exert on their husbands' drinking. Gomberg (1976) has concluded that "we know that the social contagion of alcoholism goes from husband to wife significantly more frequently than it goes in the other direction" (p. 617). Again, however, at issue is whether there is a gender difference here other than the well-established difference in base rates of heavy drinking for males and females. Is it more likely that husbands' heavy drinking will operate as a risk factor for wives than that wives' more moderate drinking will operate as a protective factor for their husbands?

Despite a paucity of empirical data that would address this question, there has been a tendency to conclude that even among non-problem-drinking spouses, the direction of influence in drinking habits is from husband to wife (e.g., Cahalan, 1970; Jacob & Seilhamer, 1991; White et al., 1991). The evidence for such a conclusion is suggestive at best. A number of studies have shown that wives' drinking is strongly associated with their perceptions of their husbands' drinking (Haer, 1955; Hammer & Vaglum, 1989; Wilsnack et al., 1984). In an early study, for example, Haer (1955) found a stronger association between female reports of their own drinking and their perceptions of their partner's drinking than between males and their perceptions of their partner's drinking, leading him to suggest that the husband may "play the role of leader in establishing drinker norms." More recently, in a study of almost 4,000 Norwegian women, Hammer and Vaglum (1989) report that husbands' consumption (as reported by the wives) explained 48% of the variance in wives' drinking levels. Wilsnack et al. (1984) reported a similarly strong association in their U.S. national study. In neither of these large studies, however, were the comparable associations reported for husbands so that any implications could be drawn about a gender difference. Interestingly, in a subsequent paper, Wilsnack et al. (1987) compared husband and wife reports and noted:

"We expected to find that women were more influenced by a spouse's drinking than men were; however, the association between current drinking and spouse's perceived drinking level was stronger for men than women" (p. 103).

Even with appropriate gender comparisons, these correlational self-report studies contribute little to an understanding of spousal influence on drinking; longitudinal studies are needed. We were able to find only two longitudinal studies that examined influences of spousal drinking for both male and female subjects. In a study assessing factors influencing the stress-illness relationship among 267 married couples, Cronkite and Moos (1984) examined the effects of spouse behaviors, such as typical quantity of alcohol consumed, depressed mood, and physical symptoms, on alcohol consumption one year later, controlling for baseline consumption levels. Contrary to popular conceptions, these researchers found that wife's alcohol consumption (typical quantity consumed) was a predictor of her husband's subsequent alcohol consumption, but that husband's consumption did not predict wife's subsequent consumption.

Using a similar longitudinal design, but multiple drinking indices, Roberts et al. (1992b) examined cross-partner effects between husbands and wives in the Newlywed Study. Husband's drinking predicted wife's frequency, frequent heavy, and typical quantity, while wife's drinking predicted husband's frequency and dependence symptoms. Interestingly, the wife's Time 1 drinking frequency was negatively related to her husband's Time 2 dependence symptoms, suggesting that a frequent-drinking wife may moderate a husband's problem drinking over time. Thus, neither longitudinal study supported the prevailing assumption that husband's influence would be stronger than wife's in the establishment of the drinking partnership. At least during the first year of marriage, there is, instead, evidence for reciprocal influence processes.

Summary

A review such as this usually concludes by describing the "picture" emerging from the assembled puzzle-pieces of information and by identifying where information is missing or details of the picture need closer attention. However, the literature on alcohol, marriage, and gender lacks information on many major questions. Whole sections of the puzzle are missing, and the picture is hard to define. Part of the reason for the dearth of research findings is the complexity of the questions that need to be answered. As Jacob and Seilhamer (1982) have noted, "The impact of alcoholism on marital functioning and the influence of marital relationships on the development and maintenance of alcoholism represent enormously challenging problems for theorists, researchers, and clinicians alike" (p. 114). It is even more complicated to try to find patterns in both male *and* female problem *and* non-problem drinking. Nonetheless, we will briefly describe what can be pieced together about gender differences in relationships between marriage and alcohol use, with the caveat that conclusions based on the limited available research must be provisional.

The Evidence for Gender Differences

Despite common conceptions to the contrary, there is little empirical evidence for strong gender differences in how marriage is related to alcohol use. Adolescent alcohol use does not appear to delay the entry into marriage for either men or women. However, there is some evidence suggesting that male heavy drinkers will marry earlier (Power & Estaugh, 1990) and other evidence suggesting that female heavy drinkers are more likely to enter cohabiting relationships (Bachman et al., 1984). Drinking apparently declines prior to marriage among both men and women; it is unclear whether this decline results from an intimate relationship or facilitates marriage, or both. The transition to marriage appears to have a protective effect on drinking and drinking problems for both men and women, although there is some preliminary evidence to suggest that the effect is more pervasive for women. In the context of an ongoing marital relationship, wives do not seem to be more likely to use alcohol in response to marital strain, nor do they appear to suffer more negative marital consequences due to their drinking. Further, the evidence does not suggest that wives are more influenced by their husbands' drinking than husbands are influenced by their wives' drinking. In short, drinking patterns and problems of both men and women are associated with marriage, marital functioning, and the behavior of marital partners, and the similarities of these associations for men and women far outweigh the differences.

However, the fundamental gender difference in drinking behavior—the fact that men are more likely than women to drink, to drink heavily, and to become alcoholic—leads to different marital experiences for wives than for husbands. Because of this gender difference, wives are more likely to have problem-drinking partners than are husbands. Women are rarely married to men who drink less than they do. Consequently, husbands are likely to influence wives to drink more, while wives are likely to influence their husbands to drink less. The heavier drinking by husbands is more likely to harm marital functioning than the lighter drinking by wives, and frequent-drinking wives are more likely to have drinking styles that match or are congruent with the drinking styles of their husbands. In methodological terms, there is a confound between gender and the drinking behavior of the spouse such that in examining gender, alcohol, and marriage, one must always consider the drinking behavior of the spouse. Beyond the fundamental gender difference in drinking, however, patterns of drinking in relation to marriage cannot be explained by the sex, gender role, or marital role of any one partner.

Future Directions

How can we account for the discrepancy between the general expectations for a gender effect and the absence of strong empirical support for such an effect? As we have alluded to in previous sections, few studies have been specifically designed to examine gender differences in the alcohol and marriage area. Moreover, overly simplistic views of alcohol, gender roles, and marriage have guided many investigators in this area. For example, much of the speculation concerning the differential impact of women's drinking versus men's drinking on marital and family functioning is rooted in the assumption that women's responsibilities are centered around the home and family, while men's responsibilities are more occupation-oriented. While this characterization of role differentiation may be generally accurate, it also neglects the considerable overlap between husband and wife roles. Many women today have occupational responsibilities, even if their husband's occupation plays a more central role in the life of the family. Similarly, most men have home and family responsibilities, even though the extent and precise nature of these responsibilities may differ from their wives' responsibilities.

Furthermore, it is important to recognize that home/family and occupational domains are interrelated and interdependent. Problems at work related to drinking will have direct and indirect effects on marital functioning for both partners. Drinking-related problems at home can have adverse consequences at work that rebound to further strain the marital relationship. If alcohol impairs role performances, the adverse effects on marital functioning may not make gender distinctions. In short, the absence of major gender effects in the alcohol and marriage area may stem from weaknesses in the conceptual and theoretical bases for hypothesizing gender differences in this area.

From our perspective, another major reason that gender differences in the alcohol/marriage relationships have not been found is that the search for gender differences has looked at behavior of husbands and wives separately instead of the interactions of their behavior. In examining the impact of one spouse's drinking on the partner's satisfaction, it is necessary to consider the partner's drinking; the interaction of the two drinking patterns may be of more importance than the main effects of the individual drinking patterns. Further, we have speculated that the combination of husband and wife drinking can take on several different configurations. It is the configuration of the couple's alcohol consumption and the context in which their joint drinking pattern develops that are critical elements for understanding the interrelationships between marriage and alcohol use.

The failure to adequately conceptualize the relationship of gender to alcohol and marriage and the nonlinear effects of husband and wife drinking lead us to suggest that the most promising research avenues will not involve simple gender comparisons. Instead, our understanding of the gender, marriage, and alcohol puzzle may be improved most by focusing on the functional requirements of marriages and how these requirements influence and are influenced by individual drinking patterns and the drinking partnership.

Acknowledgments

This research was supported by National Institute on Alcohol Abuse and Alcoholism grants R01-AA07183 to Kenneth E. Leonard and K21-AA00149 to Linda J. Roberts. At the time this research was conducted, Linda J. Roberts was with the Research Institute on Addictions, New York State Office of Alcoholism and Substance Abuse Services, Buffalo, N.Y.

Notes

1. The BNS staff approached 1,400 eligible couples and successfully screened 76%. Of these, only 10% refused to participate in the longitudinal study. Complete data were obtained from approximately 77% of the couples who agreed to participate. Analyses were undertaken to determine the extent to which the participating sample deviates from the overall population of newlywed couples applying for marriage licenses. To the extent that couples who refuse the initial screening interview at the courthouse are similar to couples who refuse but then agree to provide minimal sociodemographic information, our sample may very slightly overrepresent the young, lower-to-middle-class couples. However, the overall impact of these differences was quite minimal, with the significant correlations ranging from $r = .06$ to $r = .11$. Couples who agreed to participate but failed to provide complete data were more likely to be African-American; younger couples, couples living together prior to marriage, couples with higher husband income, and couples in which the wife was unemployed were more likely to provide complete data. Once again, however, the impact of these biases is likely to be relatively small, given that effect sizes, as measured by Pearson's R, were quite small ($r = .07$ to .11).

   One-year follow-up data were collected from at least one spouse in 84% of couples, and complete data from both spouses were collected from 76% of the couples. Follow-up of older, white, and highly educated couples was significantly higher than follow-up for younger, black, and less educated couples. However, an examination of the demographic breakdown of the completed sample nonetheless suggests a reasonably good representation of younger, African-American, and less educated couples. For further details on sample characteristics and study procedures, see Leonard and Roberts (in press).

2. The results of a recent study by Noel et al. (1991) found instead that female alcoholics reported better marital satisfaction and role functioning than male alcoholics. However, subjects in this study were sampled from couples who presented for alcohol/*marital* therapy, and this may have resulted in a sample that is significantly different than that of the other studies.

3. The results of the Noel et al. study were again somewhat different. Rather than finding no differences, these researchers found that the partners of female alcoholics were more satisfied than the partners of males and that in videotaped interactions with their partners, females functioned more positively.

4. Marital intimacy was assessed with a modified version of the Miller Social Intimacy Scale (Miller & Lefcourt, 1982). The scale assesses the overall degree of closeness, affection, and personal disclosure in the marriage.

References

Bachman, J.G., O'Malley, P.M., & Johnston, L.D. (1984). Drug use among young adults: The impacts of role status and social environment. *Journal of Personality and Social Psychology, 47*, 629-645.

Bacon, S.D. (1944). Inebriety, social integration, and marriage. *Quarterly Journal of Studies on Alcohol, 5*, 86-125.

Beckman, L.J. (1975). Women alcoholics: A review of social and psychological studies. *Journal of Studies on Alcohol, 36*, 797-824.

Brennan, P.L., & Moos, R.H. (1990). Life stressors, social resources, and late-life problem drinking. *Psychology and Aging, 5*, 491-501.

Bromet, E., & Moos, R.H. (1976). Sex and marital status in relation to the characteristics of alcoholics. *Journal of Studies on Alcohol, 37*, 1302-1312.

Bromet, E., & Moos, R.H. (1977). Environmental resources and the posttreatment functioning of alcoholic patients. *Journal of Health and Social Behavior, 18*, 326-338.

Burns, A. (1984). Perceived causes of marriage breakdown and conditions of life. *Journal of Marriage and the Family, 46*, 551-562.

Cahalan, D. (1970). *Problem drinkers: A national survey.* San Francisco, CA: Jossey-Bass.

Cahalan, D., Cisin, I.H., & Crossley, H.M. (1969). *American drinking practices: A national study of drinking behavior and attitudes* (Monograph No. 6). New Brunswick, NJ: Rutgers Center of Alcohol Studies.

Clark, W.B., & Midanik, L. (1982). Alcohol use and alcohol problems among U.S. adults: Results of the 1979 national survey. In NIAAA, *Alcohol consumption and related problems* (Alcohol and Health Monograph No. 1, pp. 3-52; DHHS Publication No. ADM 82-1190). Washington, DC: U.S. Government Printing Office.

Corbett, K., Mora J., & Ames, G. (1991). Drinking patterns and drinking-related problems of Mexican-American husbands and wives. *Journal of Studies on Alcohol, 52*, 215-223.

Corrigan, E.M. (1980). *Alcoholic women in treatment.* New York: Oxford University Press.

Cronkite, R.C., & Moos, R.H. (1984). The role of predisposing and moderating factors in the stress-illness relationship. *Journal of Health and Social Behavior, 25*, 372-393.

Curlee, J. (1967). Alcoholic women: Some considerations for further research. *Bulletin of the Menninger Clinic, 31*, 154-163.

Dahlgren, L. (1975). Special problems in female alcoholism. *British Journal of Addictions, 70* (Suppl. 1), 18-24.

Dahlgren, L. (1979). Female alcoholics: IV. Marital situation and husbands. *Acta Psychiatrica Scandinavia, 59*, 59-69.

Dunn, N.J., Jacob, T., Hummon, N., & Seilhamer, R.A. (1987). Marital stability in alcoholic-spouse relationships as a function of drinking pattern and location. *Journal of Abnormal Psychology, 96*, 99-107.

Glatt, M.M. (1961). Drinking habits of English (middle class) alcoholics. *Acta Psychiatrica Scandinavia, 37*, 88-113.

Gleiberman, L., Harburg, E., DiFranceisco, W., & Schork, A. (1992). Familial transmission of alcohol use: V. Drinking patterns among spouses, Tecumseh, Michigan. *Behavior Genetics, 22,* 63-79.

Gomberg, E.S. (1976). The female alcoholic. In R.E. Tarter & A.A. Sugerman (Eds.), *Alcoholism: Interdisciplinary approaches to an enduring problem* (pp. 603-636). Reading, MA: Addison-Wesley.

Gomberg, E.S.L. (1986). Women and alcoholism: Psychosocial issues. In NIAAA, *Women and alcohol: Health-related issues* (Research Monograph No. 16, pp. 78-120; DHHS Publication No. ADM 86-1139). Washington, DC: U.S. Government Printing Offices.

Gove, W.R., Hughes, M., & Style, C.B. (1983). Does marriage have positive effects on the psychological well-being of the individual? *Journal of Health and Social Behavior, 24,* 122-131.

Haer, J.L. (1955). Drinking patterns and the influence of friends and family. *Quarterly Journal of Studies on Alcohol, 16,* 178-185.

Hall, R.L., Hesselbrock, V.M., & Stabenau, J.R. (1983). Familial distribution of alcohol use: II. Assortative mating of alcoholic probands. *Behavior Genetics, 13,* 373-382.

Hammer, T., & Vaglum, P. (1989). The increase in alcohol consumption among women: A phenomenon related to accessibility or stress? A general population study. *British Journal of Addiction, 84,* 767-775.

Helzer, J.E., Burnam, A., & McEvoy, L.T. (1991). Alcohol abuse and dependence. In L.N. Robins & D.A. Reiger (Eds.), *Psychiatric disorders in America: The epidemiologic catchment area study* (pp. 81-115). New York: Free Press.

Hilton, M.E. (1991). The demographic distribution of drinking patterns in 1984. In W.B. Clark & M.E. Hilton (Eds.), *Alcohol in America: Drinking practices and problems* (pp. 73-86). Albany, NY: State University of New York Press.

Holmila, M. (1988). *Wives, husbands and alcohol: A study of informal drinking control within the family.* Helsinki, Finland: Finnish Foundation for Alcohol Studies.

Horwitz, A.V., & White, H.R. (1991). Becoming married, depression, and alcohol problems among young adults. *Journal of Health and Social Behavior, 32,* 221-237.

Jacob, T., & Bremer, D.A. (1986). Assortative mating among men and women alcoholics. *Journal of Studies on Alcohol, 47,* 219-222.

Jacob, T., Dunn, N.J., & Leonard, K. (1983). Patterns of alcohol abuse and family stability. *Alcoholism: Clinical and Experimental Research, 7,* 382-385.

Jacob, T., & Seilhamer, R.A. (1982). The impact on spouses and how they cope. In J. Orford and J. Harwin (Eds.), *Alcohol and the family* (pp. 114-126). London, Canberra: Croom Helm.

Jacob, T., & Seilhamer, R.A. (1991). Alcoholism and the family. In D.J. Pittman & H.R. White (Eds.), *Society, culture, and drinking patterns reexamined* (pp. 613-649). New Brunswick, NJ: Rutgers Center of Alcohol Studies.

Johnson, P.M. (1982). Sex differences, women's roles and alcohol use: Preliminary national data. *Journal of Social Issues, 38*(2), 93-116.

Kinsey, B.A. (1966). *The female alcoholic: A social psychological study.* Springfield, IL: Charles C Thomas.

Leonard, K.E., & Roberts, L.J. (in press). Marital aggression, quality, and stability in the first year of marriage: Findings from the Buffalo Newlywed Study. In T.N. Bradbury (Ed.), *The developmental course of marital dysfunction.* New York: Cambridge University Press.

Leonard, K.E., & Senchak, M. (1992). Alcohol and premarital aggression among newlywed couples. *Journal of Studies on Alcohol,* Suppl. No. 11, 96-108.

Lisansky E. (1957). Alcoholism in women: Social and psychological concomitants. I. Social history data. *Quarterly Journal of Studies on Alcohol, 18,* 588-623.

Magura, M., & Shapiro, E. (1988). Alcohol consumption and divorce: Which causes which? *Journal of Divorce, 12,* 127-136.

Miller, R.S., & Lefcourt, H.M. (1982). The assessment of social intimacy. *Journal of Personality Assessment, 46,* 514-518.

Miller-Tutzauer, C., Leonard, K.E., & Windle, M. (1991). Marriage and alcohol use: A longitudinal study of "maturing out." *Journal of Studies on Alcohol, 52,* 434-440.

Mulford, H.A. (1977). Women and men problem drinkers: Sex differences in patients served by Iowa's community alcoholism centers. *Journal of Studies on Alcohol, 38,* 1624-1639.

Noel, N.E., McCrady, B.S., Stout, R.L., & Fisher-Nelson, H. (1991). Gender differences in marital functioning of male and female alcoholics. *Family Dynamics of Addictions Quarterly, 1,* 31-38.

Olenick, N.L., & Chalmers, D.K. (1991). Gender-specific drinking styles in alcoholics and nonalcoholics. *Journal of Studies on Alcohol, 52,* 325-330.

Orford, J. (1990). Alcohol and the family. In L.T. Kozlowski, H.M. Annis, H.D. Cappell, F.B. Glaser, M.S. Goodstadt, Y. Isreal, H. Kalant, E.M. Sellers, & E.R. Vingilis (Eds.), *Research advances in alcohol and drug problems* (Vol. 10, pp. 81-155). New York: Plenum Press.

Pearlin, L.I., Menaghan, E.G., Lieberman, M.A., & Mullan, J.T. (1981). The stress process. *Journal of Health and Social Behavior, 22,* 337-356.

Perodeau, G.M. (1984). Married alcoholic women: A review. *Journal of Drug Issues, 14,* 703-719.

Perodeau, G.M., & Kohn, P.M. (1989). Sex differences in the marital functioning of treated alcoholics. *Drug and Alcohol Dependence, 23,* 1-11.

Power, C., & Estaugh, V. (1990). The role of family formation and dissolution in shaping drinking behaviour in early adulthood. *British Journal of Addiction, 85,* 521-530.

Roberts, L.J., Leonard, K.E., & Senchak, M. (1992a, June). *Couple drinking style and marital functioning: A cluster analytic approach.* Paper presented at the annual meeting of the Research Society on Alcoholism, La Jolla, CA.

Roberts, L.J., Leonard, K.E., & Senchak, M. (1992b, October). *Alcohol use and the transition to marriage.* Paper presented at the symposium on "Transitions in Alcohol Consumption: The Third Decade of Life," 21st Annual International Medical Advisory Conference, La Jolla, CA.

Roberts, L.J., Leonard, K.E., & Senchak, M. (1992c, November). *Changes in drinking patterns during a life transition: Husbands and wives in their first year of marriage.* Paper presented at the annual convention of the Association for the Advancement of Behavior Therapy, Boston, MA.

Romelsjo, A., Lazarus, N.B., Kaplan, G.A., & Cohen, R.D. (1991). The relationship between stressful life situations and changes in alcohol consumption in a general population sample. *British Journal of Addiction, 86,* 157-169.

Schwarz, J.C., & Wheeler, D.S. (1992). Dependency conflict, marital threat, and alcohol consumption in a middle-aged sample. *The Journal of Genetic Psychology, 153,* 249-267.

Steinglass, P., Bennett, L.A., Wolin, S.J., & Reiss, D. (1987). *The alcoholic family.* New York: Basic Books.

Steinglass, P., Davis, D.I., & Berenson, D. (1977). Observations of conjointly hospitalized "alcoholic couples" during sobriety and intoxication: Implications for theory and therapy. *Family Process, 16,* 1-16.

Straus, R., & Bacon, S.D. (1951). Alcoholism and social stability. *Quarterly Journal of Studies on Alcohol, 12,* 231-260.

Wanberg, K.W., & Horn, J.L. (1970). Alcoholism symptom patterns of men and women: A comparative study. *Quarterly Journal of Studies on Alcohol, 31,* 40-61.

Wechsler, H., Demone, H.W., Jr., & Gottlieb, N. (1978). Drinking patterns of Greater Boston adults: Subgroup differences on the QFV index. *Journal of Studies on Alcohol, 39,* 1158-1165.

White, H.R., Bates, M.E., & Johnson, V. (1991). Social reinforcement and alcohol consumption. In W.M. Cox (Ed.), *Why people drink: Parameters of alcohol as a social reinforcer* (pp. 233-261). New York: Gardner.

Whitehead, P.C., & Layne, N. (1987). Young female Canadian drinkers: Employment, marital status and heavy drinking. *British Journal of Addiction, 82,* 169-174.

Williams, C.N., & Klerman, L.V. (1984). Female alcohol abuse: Its effects on the family. In S.C. Wilsnack & L.J. Beckman (Eds.), *Alcohol problems in women* (pp. 280-312). New York: Guilford.

Wilsnack, R.W., & Cheloha, R. (1987). Women's role and problem drinking across the life span. *Social Problems, 34,* 231-248.

Wilsnack, R.W., & Wilsnack, S.C. (1990, June). *Husbands and wives as drinking partners.* Paper presented at the 16th Annual Alcohol Epidemiology Symposium of the Kettil Bruun Society for Social and Epidemiological Research on Alcohol, Budapest, Hungary.

Wilsnack, R.W., Wilsnack, S.C., & Klassen, A.D. (1984). Women's drinking and drinking problems: Patterns from a 1981 national survey. *American Journal of Public Health, 74,* 1231-1238.

Wilsnack, R.W., Wilsnack, S.C., & Klassen, A.D. (1987). Antecedents and consequences of drinking and drinking problems in women: Patterns from a U.S. national survey. In P.C. Rivers (Ed.), *Nebraska symposium on motivation, 1986: Alcohol and addictive behavior* (pp. 85-158). Lincoln, NE: University of Nebraska Press.

Wilsnack, S.C., & Wilsnack, R.W. (1990, June). *Marital drinking and the quality of marital relationships: Patterns from a U.S. longitudinal survey.* Paper presented at the 35th International Institute on the Prevention and Treatment of Alcoholism, International Council on Alcohol and Addictions, Berlin, Federal Republic of Germany.

Wilsnack, S.C., Wilsnack, R.W., & Klassen, A.D. (1986). Epidemiological research on women's drinking, 1978-1984. In NIAAA, *Women and alcohol: Health-related issues.* (Research Monograph, No. 16, pp. 1-68; DHHS Publication No. ADM 86-1139). Washington, DC: U.S. Government Printing Office.

CHAPTER 12

Gender Differences in Alcohol-Related Spousal Aggression

GLENDA KAUFMAN KANTOR AND NANCY L. ASDIGIAN

Statements by battered women such as, "He only beat me when he was drunk," illustrate typical expectations about alcohol's aggression-invoking potential as well as alcohol's salience in explanations of wife beating. A substantial literature has established alcohol use by husbands as a major risk marker in assaults on wives (e.g., Hotaling & Sugarman, 1986; Kaufman Kantor & Straus, 1987, 1989; Leonard, 1984; Leonard & Blane, 1992; Leonard & Jacob, 1988; Leonard et al., 1985). However, both the initial statement and the majority of research reflect a primary emphasis on intoxicated aggression by the husband. The possibility of similar behaviors by female partners is generally disregarded. This suggests a need for further study of the context of spousal aggression for both husbands and wives. For example, it is important to determine whether the meaning of alcohol-related violence differs by gender, and if women's drinking or aggression contributes to their victimization. This chapter will consider gender differences in both alcohol-related beliefs about aggression and alcohol-related aggressive behaviors toward spouses.

Gender, Drunkenness, and Aggression

Traditional definitions of femininity endow women with higher moral sensibilities than men (Frieze et al., 1978), and are inconsistent with portrayals of drunken aggression committed by women. First, conventional stereotypes typically cast males in the role of aggressive perpetrators and females as passive victims. Second, drunkenness by women is a strong violation of gender role norms (Sandmaier, 1980), largely influenced by societal expectations about women's maternicity. The hand that rocks the cradle is supposed to be a steady one. However, drunkenness by men, even in its more negative public manifestation such as bar fights, while not always condoned, is more consistent with approved "macho" behavior.

Given widely held beliefs that aggression is primarily a masculine behavior, it is not surprising that research on aggression by women is relatively recent. Maccoby and Jacklin's (1974) comprehensive review of gender differences among children found few sex differences except for aggressive behaviors. More recent reviews investigating gender differences in adult aggressive behavior suggest either inconsistencies or fewer sex differences in aggression, or identify factors that mediate gender-aggression relationships (Eagly & Steffen, 1986; Frodi et al., 1977). Eagly and Steffen (1986) concluded in their meta-analysis that women's and men's beliefs about the consequences of their aggression is the major factor accounting for variability in sex differentiated aggressive behavior. Greenblat (1983) has found greater normative approval for wives slapping husbands than the reverse because it is believed that women are less likely to do physical harm than men.

Aggression by wives has been studied less than that of husbands, and findings of equal rates of violence by wives (Stets & Straus, 1990; Straus, 1993; Straus et al., 1980) have been regarded as controversial and have been challenged by some feminist scholars (Dobash et al., 1992; Pleck et al., 1977–78). Underlying the concerns of the feminist protest is the belief that such a focus detracts from the more serious problems of battered women. Kaufman Kantor and Straus (1987) have argued that aggression by husbands and wives cannot be equated because of the greater potential for physical injury by husbands given their greater size and strength; women are six times more likely to require medical care for injuries sustained in family violence (Stets & Straus, 1990). Furthermore, women are less able than men to leave violent relationships because of numerous social constraints including greater economic dependency and responsibility for children.

Alcohol-Aggressor Effects vs. Alcohol-Victimization Effects

Research that considers the possibility of alcohol-related aggression by females or by both partners is rare and lacks consistent results. In an early paper on drinking patterns and spousal violence, Kaufman Kantor and Straus (1986) reported that husband's drinking was strongly associated with violence by both husbands and wives. A more recent study designed specifically to examine women's assaultiveness towards partners reported a modest but significant association between women's alcoholism and their assaults on partners (Sommer et al., 1992). However, neither of these studies controlled for the drinking and violence of the partner. Miller and associates (1991) found that wife victimizations were more severe when both partners were drinking, and that alcoholic women engaged in less severe and less chronic violence than their alcoholic spouses. In contrast to the studies suggesting that women may also be assaultive when drinking, Frieze and Schafer (1984) found aggression by women under the influence to be uncommon and attributed women's aggression to the husband's drinking and violence.

The few studies that have considered drinking by the wife as a contributing factor to her victimization (e.g., Frieze & Schafer, 1984; Miller et al., 1989) have largely found an increase in wife assaults when women are under the influence. Our examination of the aggression-intoxication association has focused on both "alcohol-aggressor" effects (i.e., the link between drinking and perpetration of intra-family violence) (Kaufman Kantor & Straus, 1987) and on "drug-alcohol victimization" effects (i.e., the link between substance abuse and being a victim of wife-beating) (Kaufman Kantor & Straus, 1989). In the alcohol-aggressor study (Kaufman Kantor & Straus, 1987), we tested a theoretical model of wife abuse, including occupational class, drinking patterns, and approval of violence, and found a strong association between alcohol abuse by the husband and assaults on the wife.

The alcohol-victimization study (Kaufman Kantor & Straus, 1989), which controlled for several additional etiological variables, confirmed our earlier alcohol-aggressor findings and found that women who abused alcohol or other drugs were much more likely than nonabusers to be victims of marital violence. However, both the alcohol-aggressor study and the alcohol-victimization study concluded that other factors, such as cultural traditions legitimizing violence against women, are important determinants of wife assaults. Research suggesting that males increase their aggression towards women who violate gender role expectations (Frodi et al., 1977) provides at least a partial explanation of why intoxicated women are at risk for victimization.

Explanatory Model of Alcohol and Aggression

Our analysis of gender differences in alcohol-related aggression is informed by a social learning perspective (e.g., Bandura, 1986) that views the family as a training ground for the acquisition of normative attitudes regarding gender-typed behavior, appropriate alcohol use, and the legitimacy of violence. From this perspective, individuals learn a script for alcohol-related violence by observing the behaviors of others, e.g., that aggression is both a "natural" and forgivable consequence of drinking. A common belief, referred to as "time-out" behavior, is that men learn to become intoxicated in order to justify aggression or otherwise unacceptable behaviors (e.g., Gelles, 1974).

The exact mechanism producing the alcohol-violence linkage, including the existence of a psycho-pharmacological basis for disinhibition, is not well understood. Disinhibition is a complex process resulting from the perceptual and cognitive effects of alcohol. For example, the ability to interpret the behaviors of others is one of several cognitive processes that may be impaired. But mediating variables such as contextual factors present in the interaction of individuals and expectancies about alcohol's effects must also be considered (Blum, 1981; Boyatzis, 1983; Pernanen, 1981, 1991; Powers & Kutash, 1982).

Gender and Aggressive Alcohol Cognitions

A large body of evidence indicates that the pharmacological action of alcohol cannot completely account for the behavioral effects of drinking (see Marlatt & Rohsenow, 1980, for a review). This recognition has prompted researchers to explore the impact of alcohol expectancies on drinking-related behavior. Alcohol expectancies refer to the beliefs that individuals hold about the behavioral, emotional, cognitive, and physical effects of drinking. The strength of these expectancies has been demonstrated in experimental studies that show subjects ingesting a placebo disguised as alcohol will manifest some of the same alcohol-related behaviors as those ingesting genuine alcohol beverages (Marlatt & Rohsenow, 1980). Alcohol consumption is believed to be motivated, in part, by attempts to achieve the desirable consequences that drinking is expected to bring about (Goldman et al., 1987).

Although gender differences in alcohol expectancies have been examined in a number of studies, researchers have not systematically explored the specific alcohol-related beliefs held by males and females (cf., Critchlow, 1986; Leigh, 1987). Studies that have considered gender differences in alcohol expectancies have been inconsistent in their findings regarding aggressive alcohol expectancies (e.g., Brown et al., 1980; Leigh, 1987; Rohsenow, 1983; Rohsenow & Bachorowski, 1984). Moreover, analyses of gender differences in expectancies about alcohol's effects on aggression have only examined overall scores on expectancy indexes (e.g., Brown et al., 1980; Leigh, 1987). If important differences exist between males and females in the form or content of beliefs about alcohol-related violence, such analyses would obscure those differences. For example, it is possible that women associate drinking with increased levels of verbal aggression, whereas men associate drinking with elevated levels of physical aggression. In this study we attempt to extend previous alcohol expectancy research by conducting a more fine-grained analysis of gender differences in beliefs about the violent consequences of drinking.

Research Objectives

Investigators have often hypothesized that intimate partners who engage in alcohol-related violence expect alcohol to increase aggression, or that violent partners expect to be excused for their behavior while drunk. However, few studies have subjected these hypotheses to empirical verification or provided a gender analysis of alcohol-aggressor or alcohol-victimization relationships. Therefore, this study will consider the following questions:

- Are there gender-based cognitive differences in expectancies of alcohol-related aggression and norms of alcohol-related behavior (i.e., legitimation of alcohol related aggression)?
- Are the relations among drinking, violence, aggressive alcohol expectancies, and violence norms similar for men and women?
- Are there gender-based behavior differences in alcohol-related marital assaults (drinking at the time of violence)?

We consider these questions by first examining overall gender differences in the beliefs and characteristics that are central to this study. Next, we explore the factor structure of aggressive alcohol expectancies and norms legitimizing alcohol-related violence among females and males. We then turn to an examination of the similarities of relations among drinking, violence, aggressive alcohol expectancies, and alcohol-violence norms for women and men. Our final analyses examine gender differences in episodes where drinking occurred at the time of spousal aggression.

Method

Sample

The data used to examine the research questions were obtained in 1992 as part of a national study on alcohol–family violence relationships. Interviews were conducted with a national probability sample of 1,970 persons, including an oversample of 800 Hispanic persons, who were living with a member of the opposite sex as a couple. One member of each household, either the husband or the wife, was randomly selected.[1] Interviews lasted approximately 45 minutes and were completely confidential. Interviewers were of the same language group that was predominant in the sampling area for which they were responsible. The overall response rate for all eligible individuals was 75.4%. All analyses contained in this chapter were weighted to compensate for any unequal probabilities of selection resulting from the sampling process and any biases resulting from nonresponse, screening, or eligibility processes.

The analyses used in this chapter are based on the subsample of respondents who are nonabstainers ($N = 1,446$).[2] Such individuals are defined in this study as those who drank any amount in the past year, or those who if abstinent this year had a history of at least one episode of heavy drinking in prior years. Nonabstainers represent 73.4% of the total research sample.

Violence Measures

Physical aggression was measured with the Conflict Tactics Scale (CTS) (Straus, 1979, 1990). The CTS asks respondent to think of situations in the past year when they had a disagreement or were angry with their spouse and to indicate how often they engaged in each of the acts included in the CTS. The list starts with items for the "reasoning" subscale of the CTS (such as "discussed the issue"), followed by items in the "verbal aggression" subscale (such as "insulted or swore at him/her"), and then violent acts (threw something at the other; pushed, grabbed or shoved; slapped or spanked; kicked, bit or hit with fist; hit or tried to hit with something; beat up the other; threatened with a knife or gun; used a knife or gun). The same questions are repeated asking respondents to report on their partner's behavior. We categorized respondents into violent and nonviolent groups based on whether they engaged in one or more acts of physical violence against their spouse during the previous year.

The Conflict Tactics Scale (Straus, 1979, 1990) is the most widely used instrument for measuring intra-family aggression, and it is described by experts as "the current yardstick in the field" (Jaffe et al., 1990). Factor analyses by investigators using diverse populations have consistently revealed a factor structure consisting of a reasoning factor, a verbal/symbolic aggression factor, and either a single violence factor or two violence factors, the second measuring life-threatening attacks with a knife or gun (e.g., Barling et al, 1987; Hornung et al., 1981; Jorgensen, 1977). Overall, there is an accumulation of evidence that the CTS has a stable factor structure, moderate reliability and concurrent validity, and strong evidence of construct validity (summarized in Straus, 1990).

Alcohol Measures

Quantity and frequency. Respondents provided data for several measures of drinking behavior, such as the average quantity and frequency of alcohol consumption, as well as reports on their partner's drinking. Despite concerns about the validity of self-reports and spousal reports of drinking, centering on inaccuracies or biases of recall (Babor et al., 1987), there is a substantial literature validating use of these measures (Maisto et al., 1979; Polich, 1982; Van Hasselt et al., 1985).

Heavy drinking. The criterion used to designate "heavy drinking" was four drinks per sitting for women and five drinks per sitting for men, where these amounts represent the typical quantity per drinking occasion. Although these cutting points are somewhat arbitrary and may be lower than consumption levels of some clinical alcoholics, they are consistent with gender differences in alcohol consumption levels that might lead to intoxication or alcohol-related problems. For example, women develop higher blood alcohol concentrations than men after drinking equivalent amounts of alcohol (Frezza et al., 1990), thus making them more susceptible to intoxication. The cutting points are also similar to those used in survey research (e.g., Leonard & Blane, 1992; Wilsnack et al., 1987).

Alcohol expectancy concepts. Eight items from the arousal and power sub-scale of the Alcohol Expectancy Questionnaire (AEQ) (Brown et al., 1980) were used to measure beliefs about alcohol's effects (e.g., "After a few drinks it is easier to pick a fight"). The AEQ is a widely used instrument with high internal consistency and test-retest reliability (Cronbach's alpha = .72 to .92) (Brown et al., 1980). We also developed additional violence legitimation items to measure the processes used to excuse alcohol-related misconduct (see Table 1 for a list of all items). Respondents used a 4-point scale ("strongly agree" to "strongly disagree") to rate all items on the basis of their own thoughts, feelings, and beliefs about drinking, and their own experiences when drinking.

Drinking at Time of Violence Measure

The measure of drinking at the time of violence (DTV) replicates the measure used in the 1985 National Family Violence Survey (Kaufman Kantor & Straus, 1987). It is based on the survey question, "Were either you or your partner drinking or intoxicated at the time of (the most severe act of conflict behavior by the respondent or partner)?"

Control Variables

We included other variables in the analyses because of their potential relevance to either drinking or violence. In certain analyses these variables included alcohol consumption and aggression by the partner. Age and family income were also controlled in multivariate analyses. Family income was defined as total family income from all sources before taxes.

Results

Gender Differences in Respondent Characteristics and Alcohol Cognitions

Descriptive information for violent and nonviolent male and female respondents on demographic, cognitive, and behavioral characteristics used in this study appear in Table 1.[3] The data in Table 1, Part A, replicate previous research findings regarding gender differences in alcohol consumption levels. Among both violent and nonviolent respondents, men were significantly more likely than women to drink heavily. However, there was less of a discrepancy in heavy

TABLE 1
Characteristics of Violent and Nonviolent Men and Women

	VIOLENT		NONVIOLENT	
	Men ($n = 82$)	Women ($n = 105$)	Men ($n = 704$)	Women ($n = 555$)
Part A				
Respondent drinking				
% Heavy drinking	30.7	18.3*	13.9	7.0**
Family income				
% Less than $24,999	32.2	23.7	25.8	23.7
Respondent age				
(mean years)	37.0	36.0	48.0	46.0**
Spousal violence				
% Partner violent	85.8	66.3**	4.6	3.2
Part B				
Expected effects of alcohol (% agree)				
1. Easier to pick fight	40.8	43.5	23.0	24.0
2. Lose temper easily	37.6	24.0*	17.3	14.6
3. More outspoken/opinionated	45.9	47.4	38.4	35.0
4. Argue point more forcefully	27.5	28.9	20.3	20.1
5. Aroused/physically excited	27.5	33.4	20.7	27.8**
6. Increases female aggression	43.6	45.2	31.5	30.2
7. Easier to act impulsively	42.9	34.8	31.9	31.0
8. Feel powerful to influence	12.0	5.3	6.6	3.2**
Alcohol effects legitimate (% agree)				
1. Making allowances for drunken acts	32.8	36.0	36.0	26.5***
2. Forgiving crazy behavior	12.8	18.5	11.7	12.4
3. Equal punishment for violent drunks	89.2	81.8	88.6	84.9*

Note: In this table, all variables, with the exception of respondent age, are dichotomized.
*$p < .05$.   **$p < .01$.   ***$p < .001$.

drinking levels between violent men and women, and violent individuals had higher rates of heavy drinking regardless of their gender.

Men's and women's family incomes did not differ reliably, although violent men were most likely to have below-median family incomes. Consistent with the age disparities typical of American couples, the men in our sample were slightly older than the women, although the difference was significant only among nonviolent respondents. Violent respondents were younger than nonviolent respondents, consistent with results of other studies (e.g., Kaufman Kantor and Straus, 1989; Straus et al., 1980; Suitor et al., 1990).

The most striking pattern in Part A of Table 1 is the apparent mutuality of partner assaults. The overwhelming majority of respondents who used violence against their partners reported that their partners also used violence against them. Although this was true for both sexes, mutual violence was more frequently reported by men than by women. Assaultive women were significantly less likely than assaultive men to report violence by their partners, suggesting that men are less likely than women to retaliate in response to a partner's assault. Very few nonviolent respondents, regardless of gender, reported being assaulted by their partners.

Aggressive Alcohol Expectancies

Part B of Table 1 examines gender differences on the alcohol cognition measures (dichotomized into "agree" and "disagree" categories) separately for violent and nonviolent respondents. Looking first at the respondents who engaged in spousal violence during the previous year, it can be seen that men and women did not differ on most aggressive alcohol expectancy items. Violent men were, however, significantly more likely than violent women to believe that alcohol leads to loss of temper ($p < .05$). These men were also somewhat more likely to believe that alcohol gives an increased sense of power and influence over others ($p < .10$) and facilitates impulsive behavior ($p < .13$).

Few nonviolent respondents expected alcohol to enhance feelings of power and influence, but the men were twice as likely as the women to expect this ($p < .01$). Nonviolent women, however, were significantly more likely than men to believe that alcohol increases physical arousal and excitability ($p < .01$). This finding may reflect the fact that women associate alcohol intoxication with a reduction in sexual inhibitions.

Violence Legitimation

Inspection of the lower portion of Table 1, Part B, shows that violent men and women did not differ in the degree to which they viewed alcohol as a legitimate excuse for engaging in misconduct. Since both men and women in this group drank more heavily than their nonviolent counterparts (see Table 1, Part A), the expectancy findings suggest that personal alcohol use may help to rationalize the violent behavior of both genders. In contrast, nonviolent men and women differed in their views of what drinking legitimates, but the differences were inconsistent. Compared with nonviolent women, nonviolent men were more likely to believe that allowances should be made for drinking-related misconduct, but less likely to favor greater leniency towards alcohol-related aggression (i.e., more likely to believe that drunken violence should be punished as harshly as other violence).

Overall, the bivariate analyses showed that expectancies about alcohol's effects on aggression were influenced less by gender than by whether a respondent had engaged in violence against a spouse during the previous year. This is perhaps not surprising, considering that violent men and women were more than twice as likely to be heavy drinkers as nonviolent men and women were. Because spousal violence is much less normative for women than it is for men, women may find it as necessary as men to attribute their violent behavior to the effects of alcohol.

As a supplement to these bivariate analyses, we also compared men's and women's responses to each expectancy and legitimation item in multivariate analyses of covariance (MANCOVAs) that statistically controlled for effects of family income, age, drinking, and violence by husbands and wives. The results showed that men were more likely than women to associate drinking with heightened feelings of power and influence over others (means [± SD] = 1.75 ± 0.65 and 1.54 ± 0.57, respectively) and irritability/shortness of temper (means = 1.97 ± 0.74 and 1.84 ± 0.72, respectively). These findings suggest that alcohol consumption, by enhancing feelings of male dominance and making men more easily provoked, creates a set of conditions conducive to male-perpetrated aggression. However, scores on the three violence legitimation items did not differ between male and female respondents when gender differences in demographic characteristics, drinking, and violence levels were held constant.

Factor Structure of Alcohol Cognitions

We factor analyzed the aggressive expectancy and violence legitimization items separately for male and female respondents, so that we could examine gender differences in the underlying dimensions of alcohol cognitions. In both analyses, responses to the eight expectancy items and the three violence legitimation items were subjected to a principal components factor analysis using varimax rotation. The purpose of the rotation is to achieve simplified, interpretable factors. Rotated item loadings (>.40) from the factor solutions obtained for males and females are presented in Table 2.

Factor structure for males. Looking first at the results for males, it can be seen that two factors emerged. For men, Factor 1 was comprised of all of the aggressive expectancy items and thus represents beliefs about the disinhibiting effects of alcohol on arousal, and on assertive and antagonistic behavior. All of the violence legitimation items loaded onto Factor 2. The dimension being tapped by this factor is one of perceived responsibility for drunken behavior.

TABLE 2
Aggressive Alcohol Expectancy and Violence Legitimation Factors for Men and Women

Item	MEN (wtd *n* = 748)		WOMEN (wtd *n* = 640)		
	Factor 1	Factor 2	Factor 1	Factor 2	Factor 3
Easier to pick fight	.74	–	–	.73	–
Lose temper easily	.73	–	–	.85	–
More outspoken or opinionated	.72	–	.63	–	–
Argue point more forcefully	.66	–	.55	.49	–
Aroused/physically excited	.64	–	.67	–	–
Increases female aggressiveness	.59	–	.65	–	–
Easier to act impulsively	.58	–	.68	–	–
Feel powerful to influence others	.55	–	–	.47	–
Make allowances for behavior of drunks	–	.74	–	–	.77
Forgive crazy behavior of drunks	–	.73	–	–	.56
Equal punishment for those who punch others while drunk	–	.36	–	–	.47
Eigenvalue	3.82	1.05	3.97	1.03	0.62
% of variance	34.80	9.60	36.10	9.40	5.60

Factor structure for females. An examination of the factor structure obtained for females reveals a different pattern. The expectancy items loaded onto two factors rather than one. The first expectancy factor included items that primarily reflect beliefs about the disinhibiting effects of drinking on arousal (e.g., physical arousal/excitement) and assertive behavior (e.g., impulsiveness, outspokenness). The second expectancy factor represents beliefs about alcohol-induced hostility or antagonistic behaviors (picking fights, short temper, argumentativeness, ready to exert power over others). A third factor, although relatively weak in strength, was comprised of the violence legitimation items.

Why did men link alcohol's effects on arousal and self-assertion with its effects on hostile and antagonistic behavior, whereas women did not? One possibility is that men assume that drinking-related self-assertion leads to, or is synonymous with, adversarial relations with other people, because men try to dominate and control others, whereas women do not assume that alcohol-related self-assertion has to lead to power struggles and hostility. Another possibility is that women distinguish the kind of self-assertion that does not violate their ideas of what a woman is, from hostile behavior that seems more of a trait of men than of women. These ideas might help explain why the women here associated "female aggressiveness" when drinking with assertiveness, but associated being argumentative also with alcohol's effects on hostility.

Relations among Alcohol Use, Spousal Violence, Aggressive Alcohol Expectancies, and Violence Legitimation

The preceding analyses provided important information about the content and structure of alcohol cognitions among men and women, but not about the interrelationships among drinking, alcohol cognitions, and spousal violence. We carried out additional analyses to determine whether men and women with higher levels of alcohol consumption who had also used violence against their partners had higher scores on measures of aggressive alcohol expectancies and violence legitimation. If beliefs about alcohol-related aggression and/or adherence to norms legitimizing drunken violence play a role in spousal abuse, we would expect scores on these measures to be highest among individuals who both drink heavily and have been violent to their partners.

Analysis of male expectancies. The first two analyses were performed separately on the expectancy and violence legitimation data for male respondents. Husband-to-wife violence during the previous year (none vs. any) and drinking level (less than five vs. five or more drinks per drinking occasion) served as the between-subjects factors in both analyses. Family income and respondent age were used as covariates.[4] Men who drank more heavily, and those who used violence against their wives, were more likely to agree that alcohol increases aggressive behavior overall ($F = 4.65$, $df = 8/706$, $p < .0001$, and $F = 2.78$, $df = 8/706$, $p < .01$, respectively). In addition, Table 3 shows that men who reported both drinking heavily and recently assaulting their wives most strongly expected alcohol to increase verbal aggression (i.e., "arguing a point more forcefully") ($F = 12.92$, $df = 1/713$, $p < .001$).

Analysis of male violence legitimation. Overall, men's perception that drinking makes violence forgivable was greater among the heavier drinkers ($F = 2.80$, $df = 3/672$, $p < .05$) but was not significantly related to men's reported use of violence against their wives. Analyses of individual items (see Table 3) revealed inconsistent interaction effects. If heavy drinking men had assaulted their wives they were more likely to want less punishment for drunken violence ($F = 8.40$, $df = 1/674$, $p < .01$), but they did not want special tolerance for the behavior of drunks ($F = 4.13$, $df = 1/674$, $p < .05$).

Analysis of female expectancies. We next evaluated whether differences in women's alcohol expectancies and violence legitimation were related to

TABLE 3
Adjusted Means for Significant Interactions of Drinking and Violence from
Male and Female Analyses

Item	Drinks per Day	Violence to Partner	
		None	Any
Men			
Argue point more	<5	2.05	2.18
forcefully	5+	1.85	2.69
Equal punishment for			
those who punch	<5	1.87	1.97
others while drunk	5+	2.01	1.63
Make allowances for	<5	2.15	2.47
behavior of drunks	5+	2.24	2.14
Women			
More outspoken or	<4	2.26	2.28
opinionated	4+	2.25	2.97

wife-to-husband violence during the previous year (none vs any) and drinking level (less than four vs. or more drinks per drinking occasion). Family income and respondent age again served as covariates in both analyses. Overall, women agreed more strongly that alcohol increases aggression if they were heavier drinkers ($F = 3.54$, $df = 8/584$, $p < .001$) and if they had used violence against their husbands ($F = 2.96$, $df = 8/584$, $p < .01$). As shown in Table 3, one expectancy showed a significant interaction effect. Heavy drinking women who had also been violent towards their husbands were very strongly convinced that drinking made them more outspoken and opinionated ($F = 7.61$, $df = 1/591$, $p < .01$).

Analysis of female violence legitimation. Among women, as among men, overall perceptions that drinking may make violence forgivable were significantly associated with heavier drinking ($F = 4.03$, $df = 3/582$, $p < .01$) but not with violence towards one's spouse. Women who were heavy drinkers were more likely than their moderate drinking counterparts to agree that drunken individuals should be forgiven for deviant behavior ($F = 9.95$, $df = 1/584$, $p < .01$) and that allowances should be made for drunken behavior ($F = 7.06$, $df = 1/584$, $p < .01$). No other differences on the violence legitimation items were observed among female respondents.

Drinking at the Time of Violence

A more direct way to analyze links between alcohol and spousal aggression is to examine situations where drinking immediately preceded violence between spouses. Table 4 shows reports of who was drinking at the time of the most severe incident of violence between spouses in the year prior to the survey. Alcohol consumption was *not* an antecedent to the violence reported by almost three-quarters of the couples in the total sample, and in over two-thirds of the couples where the respondent was a drinker. However, in reports of drinking at the time of violence, husbands were more than twice as likely to be drinking as wives. It was rare for wives to be the only persons drinking during episodes of assaults. A violent episode in which the woman was drinking was typically a situation where both partners had been drinking at the time. These findings hold true regardless of the respondent's own drinking pattern.

We also conducted subsequent multivariate analyses to determine whether drinking patterns or perceptions of violence increased the odds that the husband or wife would engage in alcohol-related violence. Separate logistic regression equations were estimated for husbands and wives. The dichotomous dependent measure was drinking at the time of violence toward one's partner (yes/no). Thus, we examined separately the profiles of men assaulting wives, and wives assaulting husbands. The independent variables were the summed Alcohol Expectancy Scale, the summed Legitimation Scale, usual number of drinks consumed by husband, usual number of drinks consumed by wife, age, family income, and the partner's violence rate.

Predicting male alcohol-related aggression. The results of the equation for men, shown in Table 5, show that a wife's drinking significantly increased the likelihood that her husband would engage in alcohol-related aggression. No other predictors had significant effects. However, the overall model provided a good fit to the data and correctly identified just over half (52.2%) of those men likely to be assaultive under the influence.

TABLE 4
Drinking at the Time of Spousal Violence (in percent)

	Full Sample ($n = 292$)[1]	Nonabstainers Only ($n = 242$)[2]
No, neither were drinking	73.5	68.8
Yes, husband only was drinking	14.7	17.6
Yes, wife only was drinking	2.4	2.2
Yes, both were drinking	9.4	11.4

[1]Excludes 1,664 cases of no physical conflict and 11 cases with missing data on the physical violence or drinking at the time of violence variables.
[2]Excludes 1,664 cases of no physical conflict, 48 cases of physical conflict in which both partners were abstainers, and 16 cases with missing data on the physical violence, drinking at the time of violence, or alcohol consumption variables.

TABLE 5
Logistic Regression Analyses of Drinking at the Time of Violence (DTV)

Variable	MEN (wtd n = 71)						WOMEN (wtd n = 95)					
	B	SE	Wald	df	p	Exp(B)[1]	B	SE	Wald	df	p	Exp(B)
AEQ Scale	.13	.08	2.19	1	.14	1.13	.59	.20	8.78	1	.003	1.80
Violence legitimation	−.28	.23	1.39	1	.24	0.76	−.75	.38	3.99	1	.05	0.47
Resp. drinking	.07	.13	0.31	1	.58	1.07	.47	.23	4.16	1	.04	1.60
Part. drinking	.52	.20	7.02	1	.01	1.68	.26	.19	1.81	1	.18	1.29
Family income	−.00	.00	1.75	1	.19	1.00	−.00	.00	0.24	1	.62	1.00
Resp. age	.005	.03	0.02	1	.90	1.00	.11	.04	5.90	1	.02	1.11
Part. viol. rate	−.16	.97	0.03	1	.87	1.00	−.68	.94	0.53	1	.47	0.51
	χ^2			df		p	χ^2			df		p
Model chi-square[2]	23.62			7		.001	36.91			7		0.00
Goodness of fit[3]	63.57			64		.49	52.74			87		1.00
%DTV correctly identified	52.17						40.00					
%Not DTV correctly identified	85.71						96.30					

[1] Exp(B) shows how much the odds of DTV change as each predictor variable increases by one unit. Values greater than 1 indicate that the odds of DTV increase with increases in each predictor variable. Values less than 1 indicate that the odds of DTV decrease with increases in each of the predictor variables. Values of 1 indicate that the odds of DTV remain the same when each of the predictor variables increases in value.

[2] The model chi-square is an omnibus test of the null hypothesis that the coefficients for all of the variables in the logistic regression model are zero. A significant chi-square value indicates that the null hypothesis can be rejected.

[3] The goodness-of-fit statistic tests the difference between the observed and model-predicted probabilities of drinking at the time of violence. A nonsignificant value for the goodness-of-fit statistic indicates that the difference between observed and predicted probabilities are no larger than what would be expected by chance.

Predicting female alcohol-related aggression. Table 5 shows that several factors predicted which women were likely to be involved in alcohol-related aggression against their partners. The significant predictors of women's alcohol-related violence were their alcohol expectancies (AEQ scores), heavy drinking, age, and norms legitimating alcohol-related violence.

The findings indicate that women drinking when they assaulted their husbands believed that alcohol increases aggression, but did not believe that intoxication excuses bad behavior. Even though there were more predictors of alcohol-related assaults by wives, the predictors explained less of the risk of alcohol-related violence than for husbands. The main reason for this explanatory weakness is that only a very small number of women engaged in alcohol-related aggression (weighted $n = 15$). The women's analysis correctly identified less than half (40.0%) of the women who assaulted their husbands while drinking. The women's statistical model provides an excellent fit to the data as indicated by the nonsignificant goodness-of-fit measure. However, as with men, the fit is good because the model is better at predicting which women were *not* likely to be involved in alcohol-related violence.

Discussion

Gender and Alcohol Cognitions

Our factor analyses demonstrated important gender differences in beliefs and expectations about the consequences of alcohol consumption. Those findings suggested that men do not distinguish the effects of alcohol on arousal and disinhibition from the effects of alcohol on verbal and physical aggression. Women, on the other hand, appear to psychologically segregate the arousing and disinhibiting effects of drinking from effects specifically on aggression. One possible explanation of this finding is that women perceive certain effects of alcohol as less consistent with their self-images (or ideas of feminity) than other effects. Specifically, women seem to distinguish between alcohol as a disinhibitor and alcohol as a cause of antagonistic and aggressive behavior in a way that men do not. These differences contrast somewhat with the findings of previous research (Leigh, 1987) showing that similar alcohol expectancy factors emerge for men and women.

Our factor analysis results are, however, consistent with Frieze and Schafer's (1984) suggestion that men interpret or label the increases in physiological arousal that arise from alcohol consumption as aggressive impulses. The cognitive model of reactions to alcohol put forth by Frieze and Schafer proposes that the source of initial alcohol-induced elevations of physiological arousal (e.g., vasodilation, increased heart rate) can be ambiguous, and the physical sensations that arise from alcohol consumption are therefore susceptible to cognitive labeling. Men, because they are socialized into strong, powerful roles, are more apt to misattribute those sensations as feelings of aggression or dominance. Through repeated experiences with these feelings, males may come to expect a heightened sense of power and aggression when they drink and, in turn, may act on those feelings by striking out against others.

Our analysis of gender differences in specific alcohol cognitions provided additional evidence consistent with this argument. The only alcohol expectancies that differed between men and women pertained to drinking-related increases in irritability and feelings of domination/power. Males were more likely than females to associate alcohol consumption with being short-tempered as well as with feeling powerful over others. The findings suggest that alcohol consumption enhances feelings of male dominance and increases the ease with which men are provoked to hostility. For men, this would seem to support Room's (1980, p. 8) contention that alcohol is "an instrument of intimate domination."

Gender Influences on Drinking at the Time of Violence

In light of the gender differences in drinking behavior and aggressive alcohol cognitions described above, our finding that husbands engage in more drinking-related spousal violence than wives do is perhaps not surprising (see Table 4). The assaults that women do perpetrate against their husbands tend to be more highly tied to mutual drinking than to instances in which wives are drinking alone. An important caveat in interpreting these results is that much of the spousal aggression in our study is mutual.

Logistic regression analyses indicate that alcohol-related assaults on wives were more likely when both partners were heavy drinkers. Typical consumption levels of wives were the only significant predictors of husbands' alcohol-related assaults on wives. One possible explanation of these findings is that marriages between heavy drinking partners may be more discordant, conflict-ridden relationships, thus increasing the probability of physical assaults. Drinking-related assaults by wives against husbands were also predictable from women's own consumption patterns and from their aggressive alcohol expectancies. However, the results concerning the characteristics of women drinking at the time of assaults against husbands must be interpreted with caution because the findings are based on a very small number of women.

Gender and "Time-Out" Behavior

Individuals who hold aggressive expectancies about alcohol do not necessarily drink solely or mainly in order to manifest aggressive behavior. There is some evidence to support Gelles's (1974) contention that men drink in order to be violent (i.e., their expectancies that alcohol will make them more aggressive and hostile). However, that argument oversimplifies the complexity of alcohol-violence relationships, and represents only one possible scenario. First, it assumes malevolent intention, and ignores the myriad of factors potentially present in a drinking situation, such as the drinking or aggression by a partner. Second, it is also possible to simultaneously hold competing expectancies (Rohsenow & Bachorowski, 1984). For example, individuals may choose to drink or get drunk in order to forget their troubles. But because each drinking situation is comprised of multiple situational variables such as the amount drunk, partner's drunkenness, and issues that are raised by either partner when drinking, aggression is not an inevitable consequence of drunkenness.

The fact that heavy drinking women are likely to believe in alcohol's disinhibiting properties suggests that they are not all that dissimilar from heavy drinking men. Because drinking and violence are less normative for females, women who engage in such behaviors may have even more need than men for beliefs in the disinhibiting effects of alcohol. Research on the disinhibiting effects of alcohol on women has mainly considered the link between alcohol and sexuality, and has shown, among women associating sexual pleasure with drinking, greater effects of expectancies than for men (Lindman, 1992). That is, the greater the inhibition conflict, or more forbidden the behavior, the stronger the expectancy effect.

The Intoxicated Dyad

One limitation of this study is that the data on couples are based on the reports of only one member of the couple. Although this is typical of the majority of studies done on spousal violence, it also suggests a need for research based on dyads. Another limitation is that men typically disclose less of their violent behavior, particularly less of their severe violence, than do women (Stets & Straus, 1990). Nevertheless, the results here provide important data on areas neglected by previous research.

Our analyses suggest that there is a high degree of mutuality of aggression. This does not preclude the possibility that the husband is the only drunken aggressor, but that is only one potential scenario. For example, drinking by either partner may lead to conflicts in which the husband resorts eventually to violence, which then provokes defensive violence by the wife. The frequent verbal abuse inflicted by a drunken spouse may also incite a woman to acts of retaliatory aggression. Although women are less likely than men to consume large amounts of alcohol, there is also a strong correlation between partners' drinking patterns (Kaufman Kantor & Straus, 1989). For female heavy drinkers, this means they are more likely to have a heavy drinking male partner. Such women are at increased risks for victimization for a number of reasons, including their violation of traditional gender role norms by becoming intoxicated and by their increased use of aggression. Women drinking to intoxication are also at risk because they may feel they deserved to be beaten due to their drunkenness or aggression. Women believing they provoked the violence or were responsible for the violence may perpetuate these patterns by avoidance of help-seeking because of guilt and shame.

When couples in the general population get into conflicts, a process of reciprocal escalation may be intensified or catalyzed by the use of alcohol. What helps escalate conflict is the physiological effect of alcohol on cognitive perception, leading to misperceived communications and a heightened perception of threat (e.g., Boyatzis, 1977; Lang et al., 1975). Individuals under the influence may feel "disinhibited" to air previously unarticulated grievances, and thus may engage in greater verbal aggression which, in turn, may cue verbal and physical aggression by their partners. Moreover, when women are physically aggressive towards their spouses, in spite of the greater normative approval for wives slapping husbands, they risk their husbands' retributive and potentially more injurious aggression. This can be magnified when intoxication lessens restraints and distorts interpretations of behavior.

The results of this study also do not rule out the possibility that the etiology of the drinking violence relationships for men and women is attributable to their histories of victimization. Higher rates of physical and sexual abuse have been found for men and women with substance abuse problems (Dembo et al., 1989; Kaufman Kantor, 1990; Wilsnack, 1991). Such studies supporting a social learning framework suggest that aggressive behaviors may be independent of alcohol's effects, or that violent victimizations may lead to substance abuse which, in turn, increases aggression. A history of alcohol-linked violent socialization is an important etiological consideration that should be accounted for in all future studies of alcohol-related violence.

Whether or not individuals of either gender engage in drunken aggression towards their spouses may be mediated by their incorporation of cultural expectancies about these behaviors (e.g., that any violence or drunken violence towards a loved one is acceptable, that power differentials in relationships may be maintained through coercive means, or that alcohol and violence are irrevocably linked). Thus, when future research investigates how men and women learn to engage in alcohol-related violence against their spouses, such research must include the larger cultural context that weds alcohol to aggression.

Acknowledgments

The research reported here was supported by National Institute on Alcohol Abuse and Alcoholism grant R01-AA09070. We are grateful to the members of the Family Research Laboratory Violence Seminar for their comments on the manuscript, to Jana Jasinski for her assistance with data management, and to Kyle Ruonala and Tara Leary for their assistance in manuscript preparation.

Notes

1. The practice of interviewing only one member of each household is consistent with those in previous national surveys on family violence (Straus and Gelles, 1990; Straus et al., 1980). It is done to minimize the possibility of retaliatory violence to a woman that might result if her partner discovered that she reported his assaults. It has been assumed that the possibility of wife assaults as a consequence of the family violence research process could be more likely if the husband had knowledge of the questions being asked of his wife.
2. We selected nonabstaining respondents (both current and former drinkers) for this chapter because individual perceptions and experiences with alcohol are central to the major questions which we examine.
3. The sample sizes reported in this table and in all other tables are based on weighted *n*'s. The net effect of the weighting process is that the effective sample size is reduced. Two-tailed tests of significance are used for all analyses.
4. Lower scores on the family income covariate were associated with higher levels of agreement on the expectancy and legitimation items in both the male and female analyses. However, the age covariate showed a different pattern for males and females. Among men, being younger was related to higher levels of aggressive alcohol expectancies and violence legitimation. Among women, being older tended to be associated with more aggressive alcohol expectancies and greater violence legitimation.

References

Babor, T.F., Stephens, R.S., & Marlatt, G.A. (1987). Verbal report methods in clinical research on alcoholism: Response bias and its minimization. *Journal of Studies on Alcohol, 48,* 410-424.

Bandura, A. (1986). *Social foundations of thought and action: A social cognitive theory.* Englewood Cliffs, NJ: Prentice Hall.

Barling, J., O'Leary, K.D., Jouriles, E.N., Vivian, D., MacEwen, K.E. (1987). Factor similarity of the Conflict Tactics Scales across samples, spouses, and sites: Issues and implications. *Journal of Family Violence, 2* (1), 37-55.

Blum, R.H. (1981). Violence, alcohol, and setting: An unexplored nexus. In J.J. Collins, Jr. (Ed.), *Drinking and crime: Perspectives on the relationships between alcohol consumption and criminal behavior* (pp. 110-42). New York: Guilford.

Boyatzis, R.E. (1977). Alcohol and interpersonal aggression. In M.M. Gross (Ed.), *Alcohol intoxication and withdrawal: IIIb. Studies in alcohol dependence (Advances in experimental medicine and biology series, Vol. 85B)* (pp. 345-374). New York: Plenum.

Boyatzis, R.E. (1983). Who should drink what, when and where if looking for a fight. In E. Gottheil, K.A. Druley, T.E. Skoloda, & H.M. Waxman (Eds.), *Alcohol, drug abuse and aggression* (pp. 314-29). Springfield, IL: Charles C Thomas.

Brown, S.A., Goldman, M.S., Inn, A., & Anderson, L.R. (1980). Expectations of reinforcement from alcohol: Their domain and relation to drinking patterns. *Journal of Consulting and Clinical Psychology, 48,* 419-426.

Brown, S.A., Christiansen, B.A., & Goldman, M.S. (1987). The Alcohol Expectancy Questionnaire: An instrument for the assessment of adolescent and adult alcohol expectancies. *Journal of Studies on Alcohol, 48,* 483-491.

Critchlow, B. (1986). The powers of John Barleycorn: Beliefs about the effects of alcohol on social behavior. *American Psychologist, 41,* 751-764.

Dembo, R., Williams, L., La Voie, L., Berry, E., Getreu, A., Wish, E.D., Schmeidler, J., & Washburn, M. (1989). Physical abuse, sexual victimization, and illicit drug use: Replication of a structural analysis among a new sample of high-risk youths. *Violence and Victims, 4,* 121-138.

Dobash, R.P., Dobash, R.E., Wilson, M., & Daly, M. (1992). The myth of sexual symmetry in marital violence. *Social Problems, 39* (1), 71-91.

Eagly, A.H., & Steffen, V.J. (1986). Gender and aggressive behavior: A meta-analytic review of the social psychological literature. *Psychological Bulletin, 100,* 309-330.

Frezza, M., DiPadova, C., Pozzato, G., Terpin, M., Baraona, E., & Lieber, C.S. (1990). High blood alcohol levels in women: The role of decreased gastric alcohol dehydrogenase activity and first-pass metabolism. *New England Journal of Medicine, 322,* 95-99.

Frieze, I.H., & Schafer, P.C. (1984). Alcohol use and marital violence: Female and male differences in reactions to alcohol. In S.C. Wilsnack & L.J. Beckman (Eds.), *Alcohol problems in women:Antecedents, consequences, and interventions* (pp. 260-279). New York: Guilford.

Frieze, I.H., Parsons, J.E., Johnson, P.B., Ruble, D.N., & Zellman, G.L. (1978). *Women and sex roles:A social psychological perspective.* New York & London: W.W. Norton.

Frodi, A., Macaulay, J., & Thome, P.R. (1977). Are women always less aggressive than men? A review of the experimental literature. *Psychological Bulletin, 84,* 634-660.

George, W.H., & Norris, J. (1991). Alcohol, disinhibition, sexual arousal, and deviant sexual behavior. *Alcohol Health & Research World, 15,* 133-138.

Gelles, R.J. (1974). *The violent home:A study of physical aggression between husbands and wives.* Beverly Hills, CA: Sage.

Goldman, M.S., Brown, S.A., & Christiansen, B.A. (1987). Expectancy theory: Thinking about drinking. In H.T. Blane & K.E. Leonard (Eds.), *Psychological theories of drinking and alcoholism* (pp. 181-226). New York: Guilford.

Greenblat, C. (1983). A hit is a hit . . . or is it? Approval and tolerance of the use of physical force by spouses. In D. Finkelhor, R.J. Gelles, G.T. Hotaling, & M.A. Straus (Eds.), *The dark side of families: Current family violence research* (pp. 235-60). Beverly Hills, CA: Sage.

Hornung, C.A., McCullough, B.C., Sugimoto, T. (1981). Status relationships in marriage: Risk factors in spouse abuse. *Journal of Marriage and the Family, 43,* 675-692.

Hotaling, G.T., & Sugarman, D.B. (1986). An analysis of risk markers in husband to wife violence: The current state of knowledge. *Violence and Victims, 1* (2), 101-124.

Jaffe, P.G., Wolfe, D.A., Wilson, S.K. (1990). *Children of battered women.* Newbury Park, CA: Sage.

Jorgensen, S.R. (1977). Societal class heterogamy, status striving, and perceptions of marital conflict: A partial replication and revision of Pearlin's Contingency Hypothesis. *Journal of Marriage and the Family, 39,* 653-689.

Kaufman Kantor, G. (1990). *Parental drinking, violence and child aggression.* Paper presented at the annual meeting of the American Psychological Association, Boston, MA.

Kaufman Kantor, G., & Straus, M.A. (1989). Substance abuse as a precipitant of wife abuse victimizations. *American Journal of Drug and Alcohol Abuse, 15* (2), 173-189.

Kaufman Kantor, G., & Straus, M.A. (1987). The "drunken bum" theory of wife beating. *Social Problems, 34* (3), 213-230.

Kaufman Kantor, G., & Straus, M.A. (1986). *Drinking patterns and spousal violence.* Paper presented at the National Alcoholism Forum conference on "Alcohol and the Family," San Francisco, CA.

Lang, A.R., Goeckner, D.J., Adesso, V.J., & Marlatt, G.A. (1975). Effects of alcohol on aggression in male social drinkers. *Journal on Abnormal Psychology, 84,* 508-518.

Leigh, B.C. (1987). Beliefs about the effects of alcohol on self and others. *Journal of Studies on Alcohol, 48,* 467-475.

Leonard, K.E. (1984). Alcohol consumption and escalatory aggression in intoxicated and sober dyads. *Journal of Studies on Alcohol, 45,* 75-80.

Leonard, K.E., & Blane, H.T. (1992). Alcohol and marital aggression in a national sample of young men. *Journal of Interpersonal Violence, 7,* 19-30.

Leonard, K.E., Bromet, E.J., Parkinson, D.K, Day, N.L., & Ryan, C.M. (1985). Patterns of alcohol use and physically aggressive behavior in men. *Journal of Studies on Alcohol, 46,* 279-282.

Leonard, K.E., & Jacob, T. (1988). Alcohol, alcoholism, and family violence. In V.B. Van Hasselt, R.L. Morrison, A.S. Bellack, & M. Hersen (Eds.), *Handbook of family violence* (pp. 383-406). New York: Plenum.

Lindman, R. (1992). Alcohol and female disinhibition. In K. Björkqvist & P. Niemelä (Eds.), *Of mice and women* (pp. 241-249). New York: Academic Press, Inc. (Harcourt Brace Jovanovich).

Maccoby, E.E., & Jacklin, C.N. (1974). *The psychology of sex differences.* Stanford: Stanford University Press.

Maisto, S.A., Sobell, L.C., & Sobell, M.B. (1979). Comparison of alcoholics' self-reports of drinking behavior with reports of collateral informants. *Journal of Consulting and Clinical Psychology, 47,* 106-112.

Marlatt, G.A., & Rohsenow, D.J. (1980). Cognitive processes in alcohol use: Expectancy and the balanced-placebo design. In N.K. Mello (Ed.), *Advances in substance abuse: Behavioral and biological research* (Vol. 1, pp. 159-199). Greenwich, CT: JAI Press.

Miller, B.A., Downs, W.R., & Gondoli, D.M. (1989). Spousal violence among alcoholic women as compared to a random household sample of women. *Journal of Studies on Alcohol, 50,* 533-540.

Miller, B.A., Downs, W.R., Testa, M., & Keil, A. (1991, November). *Thematic analyses of severe spousal violence incidents: Women's perceptions of their victimization.* Paper presented at the annual meeting of the American Society of Criminology, San Francisco, CA.

Pernanen, K. (1991). *Alcohol in human violence.* New York: Guilford.

Pernanen, K. (1981). Theoretical aspects of the relationship between alcohol use and crime. In J.J. Collins, Jr. (Ed.), *Drinking and crime: Perspectives on the relationships between alcohol consumption and criminal behavior* (pp. 1-69). New York: Guilford.

Pleck, E., Pleck, J.H., Grossman, M., & Bart, P.B. (1977-78). The battered data syndrome: A comment on Steinmetz's article. *Victimology: An International Journal, 2,* 680-684.

Polich, J.M. (1982). The validity of self-reports in alcoholism research. *Addictive Behaviors, 7,* 123-132.

Powers, R.J., & Kutash, I.L. (1982). Alcohol, drugs, and partner abuse. In M. Roy (Ed.), *The abusive partner: An analysis of domestic battering* (pp. 39-75). New York: Van Nostrand Reinhold.

Rohsenow, D.J. (1983). Drinking habits and expectancies about alcohol's effects for self versus others. *Journal of Consulting and Clinical Psychology, 51,* 752-756.

Rohsenow, D.J., & Bachorowski, J.A. (1984). Effects of alcohol and expectancies on verbal aggression in men and women. *Journal of Abnormal Psychology, 93,* 418-432.

Room, R. (1980). *Alcohol as an instrument of intimate domination.* Paper presented at the annual meeting of the Society for the Study of Social Problems, New York.

Sandmaier, M. (1980). *The invisible alcoholics: Women and alcohol abuse in America.* New York: McGraw-Hill.

Sommer, R., Barnes, G.E., & Murray, R.P. (1992). Alcohol consumption, alcohol abuse, personality and female perpetrated spouse abuse. *Personality and Individual Differences, 13* (12), 1315-1323.

Stets, J.E., & Straus, M.A. (1990). Gender differences in reporting marital violence and its medical and psychological consequences. In M.A. Straus & R.J. Gelles (Eds.), *Physical violence in American families: Risk factors and adaptations to violence in 8,145 families* (pp. 151-166). New Brunswick, NJ: Transaction.

Straus, M.A. (1979). Measuring intrafamily conflict and violence: The Conflict Tactics (CT) Scales. *Journal of Marriage and the Family, 41,* 75-88.

Straus, M.A. (1990). The Conflict Tactics Scales and its critics: An evaluation and new data on validity and reliability. In M.A. Straus & R.J. Gelles (Eds.), *Physical violence in American families: Risk factors and adaptations to violence in 8,145 families* (pp. 133-148). New Brunswick, NJ: Transaction.

Straus, M.A. (1993). Physical assaults by wives: A major social problem. In R.J. Gelles & D. Loseke (Eds.), *Current controversies on family violence* (pp. 67-87). Newbury Park, CA: Sage.

Straus, M.A., & Gelles, R.J. (1990). *Physical violence in American families: Risk factors and adaptations to violence in 8,145 families.* New Brunswick, NJ: Transaction.

Straus, M.A., Gelles, R.J., & Steinmetz, S.K. (1980). *Behind closed doors: Violence in the American family.* Newbury Park, CA: Sage.

Suitor, J.J., Pillemer, K., & Straus, M.A. (1990). Marital violence in a life course perspective. In M.A. Straus and R.J. Gelles (Eds.), *Physical violence in American families: Risk factors and adaptations to violence in 8,145 families* (pp. 305-317). New Brunswick, NJ: Transaction.

Van Hasselt, V.B., Morrison, R.L., & Bellack, A.S. (1985). Alcohol use in wife abusers and their spouses. *Addictive Behaviors, 10,* 127-135.

Wilsnack, S.C. (1991). Sexuality and women's drinking: Findings from a U.S. national study. *Alcohol Health & Research World, 15,* 147-150.

Wilsnack, R.W., Wilsnack, S.C., & Klassen, A.D. (1987). Antecedents and consequences of drinking and drinking problems in women: Patterns from a U.S. national survey. In P.C. Rivers (Ed.), *Alcohol & addictive behavior: Nebraska Symposium on Motivation, Vol. 34, 1986* (pp. 85-158). Lincoln, NE: University of Nebraska Press.

CHAPTER 13

The Relational Model of Women's Psychological Development: Implications for Substance Abuse

STEPHANIE S. COVINGTON AND JANET L. SURREY

Over the past two decades, new conceptualizations of women's psychological development have been evolving which emphasize the centrality of relationships in women's lives (Belenky et al., 1986; Gilligan, 1982; Jordan et al., 1991; Miller, 1976). This relational perspective has sought to describe development from women's perspective, using language and concepts derived from women's experience. Since women in this culture have been the "carriers" of certain aspects of the total human experience, specifically carrying responsibility for the care and maintenance of relationships, this model attempts to articulate the strengths as well as the problems arising for women from this relational orientation. Theorists and clinicians at the Stone Center at Wellesley College have been developing this theoretical perspective as a base for creating relational models of healing and empowerment for women.

Traditional theories of psychology have described development as the pathway from childlike dependence to mature independence, emphasizing the importance of a self-sufficient, clearly differentiated, autonomous self. These models have more likely been representative of men's experience. The concepts of separation, individuation, and self-development characterize the models as a basis for clinical practice and treatment. In contrast, the relational model views development as growth with and toward connection, positing healthy connection with other persons as the means and goal of psychological development.

In this chapter, we present an overview of the relational model and explore its application to the understanding, treatment, and prevention of substance abuse in women. We have found this model to be extremely useful in conceptualizing the contexts and meanings of substance abuse in women's lives and particularly helpful in suggesting new treatment models. It is also a useful frame for evaluating what is beneficial and what may be harmful to women in traditional treatment programs and models of recovery.

The Stone Center Relational Model

The Stone Center model was built on the early work of Jean Baker Miller who published *Toward a New Psychology of Women* in 1976. Miller proposed that women's psychological development differed in fundamental ways from the traditional model of development derived from men's experience. She suggested that for women the primary motivation throughout life is toward establishing a basic sense of connection to others. She wrote that women feel a sense of self and self-worth when their actions arise out of connection with others and lead back into, not away from, connections. The experience of psychological connection is based on empathy and mutuality in relationships. Connection is experienced as a feeling of mutual presence and joining in a relational process. The "relationship" develops a new, unique, and always changing existence that can be described, experienced, and nurtured.

Women's relational yearnings and the centrality of relationship for women's psychological health has often been pathologized when viewed through the lens of traditional, "self-" centered models. Descriptions of women's dependency, passivity, caretaking fixations, and (most recently) codependency reflect this misunderstanding and distortion of women's relational orientation.

The Stone Center relational model describes the attributes and qualities of relationships that foster growth and healthy development. From the perspective of this model, healthy connections with other human beings are mutual, creative, energy-releasing, and empowering for all participants, and are fundamental to women's psychological well-being. Psychological problems or so-called pathologies can be traced to disconnections or violations within relationships, arising at personal/familial levels as well as at the sociocultural level.

Mutuality is a fundamental aspect of healthy, growth-promoting relationships, and is more than equality, reciprocity, and intimacy. It suggests a way of being-in-relation which includes the whole person. This has been called a relational attitude, orientation, or stance. Each person can represent her feelings, thoughts, and perceptions in the relationship and can *move with* and *be moved by* the feelings, thoughts, and perceptions of the other. Mutual influence, mutual impact, and mutual responsiveness characterize such relationships, which can be described as forward *moving* and dynamic processes. The possibility of change and movement is always present.

When a relationship moves from disconnection to mutual connection, each person feels a greater sense of personal authenticity as well as a sense of "knowing" or "seeing" the other. This experience of mutual empathy requires that each person have the capacity for empathic connecting. Empathy is a complex, highly developed ability to join with another at a cognitive and affective level without losing connection with one's own experience. Openness to growth through empathic joining within the relational process is fundamental to mutual relationships.

Mutual empowerment describes a process of relational interaction where each person grows in psychological strength or power. This has been described as "power-with-others," as distinguished from "power-over" others, which has been the traditional structure of relationships, where one person (or group of persons) has been dominant and the other subordinate, or one person (or group of persons) has been assigned the task of fostering the psychological development of others. Historically, women have been assigned the task of fostering the psychological development of others, including men and children.

Miller (1986) has described five psychological outcomes of healthy growth-fostering relationships for all participants. These are: (1) increased zest and vitality, (2) empowerment to act, (3) knowledge of self and other, (4) self-worth, and (5) a desire for more connection.

The relational perspective does not idealize women or relationships. The remainder of this chapter discusses ways in which women's motives for connection can lead them toward substances and substance abuse in a culture where they have been given the primary responsibility for relationship, yet where important relationships, institutions, and political systems are frequently far from mutually empathic and mutually empowering.

Substance Use in and as Relationship

From the perspective of the Stone Center model, women frequently begin to use substances in ways that initially seem to be in the service of making or maintaining connections, and to try to feel connected, energized, loved, or loving when that is not the whole truth of their experience (Surrey, 1991). Women often use substances to deal with hurt and pain in their relationships and also to try to provide for others (especially children) a safe and loving relational context. Women also turn to drugs in the context of relationships with drug-abusing partners—to feel joined or connected through the use of drugs. Women may actually use mind-altering substances to try to stay psychologically connected with someone who is using drugs.

Further, women may begin to use substances to maintain relationships, often to try to alter themselves to fit the relationships available. Miller (1990) has described this basic relational paradox—when a woman cannot move a relationship towards mutuality, she begins to change herself to maintain the relationship. Stiver (1990) has written about children of "dysfunctional" families who frequently turn to substances to alter themselves to adapt to the disconnections within the family, thus giving the illusion of being in relationship when one is not or is only partially in relationship.

Miller (1990) has described the outcomes of disconnections, that is, non-mutual or abusive relationships, which she terms a "depressive spiral." These are: diminished zest or vitality, disempowerment, unclarity or confusion, diminished self-worth, and a turning away from relationships. This depressive spiral lays a foundation for the use of substances to provide what relationships are not providing, for example, energy, a sense of agency and control, relief from confusion and negative feelings, a sense of self-worth, and the energy to work on relationships.

This turning toward the abuse of substances in the service of maintaining relationships, dealing with pain in relationships, or providing for others has tragic consequences, as the abuse of substances leads to diminished opportunities for practice and growth in real connection. When such relational development is constricted, there develops a vicious circle of increased isolation which in turn leads to further use of substances. In Alcoholics Anonymous this is described as a progressive disease of isolation. Theologian Dorothy Soelle (1978) described this alienation or disconnection from relationships as spiritual death or "death by bread alone," biological life without that which is most truly human—real connectedness to others.

One way of viewing addiction is as a kind of relationship. The addicted woman is in a relationship with alcohol, other drugs, food, sex, money, or another person, that is characterized by obsession, compulsion, nonmutuality, and an imbalance of power. It is a kind of love relationship in which the object of addiction becomes the focus of a woman's life. Addicted women frequently use relational imagery to describe their drug use, for example: "Alcohol was my true love, I never went to bed without Jack Daniels"; "My most passionate affair was with cocaine"; or "Food was my mother, my friend, whom I turned to for solace and comfort, who was always there for me when I needed it."

The drug of choice seems at first a good friend, bringing with it a positive, soothing experience and feelings of comfort or euphoria. Over time, however, the drug becomes "necessary for the addict's peace of mind or continued existence" (Byington, 1993, p. 4). It becomes the organizing principle of the addict's life, causing her life to become more constricted and externally focused. The friend then becomes lethal and toxic. "I turned to Valium, but then Valium turned on me." Such imagery is frequently heard in women describing the progression of their addiction. We could speak of addiction as a contraction of connection and recovery as an expansion of connection (Covington & Beckett, 1988).

If we contrast this with what we know about healthy relationships, we see that addictive relationships lack growth-producing characteristics. In the Stone Center model, healthy relationships are characterized by a mutuality of involvement: both parties move with and are moved by the thoughts, feelings, and perceptions of the other.

In addiction, however, there is no mutuality of involvement; a woman gives nothing of her true self to the object of her addiction. Paradoxically, she ends up giving up herself, but not in any mutually beneficial way. According to Diane Byington (1993):

Addiction is considered to have occurred when a relationship with a drug is pursued and believed by the individual to be essential in spite of continuing negative consequences to her. In addiction, the relationship with the drug is at least as important to the individual as relationships with people. (p. 5)

Another aspect of addiction as relationship is the experience the addict has when recovery begins—when the relationship is over. When the addict gives up the object of her addiction, she experiences grief and loss. As with the ending of any relationship, there is a myriad of intense feelings. The grieving experience is generally characterized by anger, loss, and a drive to fill the void.

Relational Underpinnings of Substance Abuse

The Stone Center model draws attention to aspects of the familial and cultural relational context that lay the groundwork for the development of substance abuse in women. The particular drug (legal or illegal) or coping behavior a woman chooses is multiply determined by genetics; physiological makeup; familial history; ethnic, race, or class factors; availability; chance; and many other factors. We appreciate that once a person is addicted, all attention needs to be paid to the withdrawal and recovery from that particular substance. However, it is also crucial to address the relational and cultural context in which the substance abuse develops, and the implications for psychotherapy, prevention, and treatment programs.

At least five patterns of relational disconnection may foster substance abuse and increase risks of relapse in women: (1) nonmutual relationships; (2) effects of isolation and shaming; (3) limiting relational images; (4) abuse, violation, and systemic violence; and (5) distortion of sexuality.

Nonmutual Relationships

Rather than focusing on women's "pathological" or problematic orientation toward caretaking or maintenance of relationships, we believe the focus should be on the failures of mutuality in relationships as the source of problems. Women's desire to make and then to maintain connection becomes problematic when it is one-sided or distorted and not mutual. Over time, the impact of nonmutuality leads to confusion, distorted relational patterns such as compulsive caretaking, or retreat from real relationships. The primary relationships in our culture have not been rooted in the search for mutuality. In particular, the male-female relationship has been historically rooted in a power-over, nonmutual model. Further, the idealized images of "good mothers" have left mothers struggling to try to fit themselves to such unrealistic images without a relational context of mutuality for themselves. The media and culture promote the use of drugs or substances to solve all problems, including relationship problems such as these.

Effects of Isolation and "Shaming"

Many writers have described American culture as very alienated. Community, familial, and religious structures are breaking down, and lifestyle demands and lack of support for child care lead to increasing isolation of individuals and families, with little time or opportunity for community building. In fact, women who are at high risk for drug abuse are frequently socially isolated—single parents, unemployed, or recently separated, divorced, or widowed (Finkelstein, 1993; Finkelstein & Derman, 1991; Wilsnack et al., 1986).

From a clinical perspective, psychological isolation occurs when there is some failure of the relational context to validate and respond to a woman's experience or her attempts at connection. Miller (1990) has described the state of "condemned isolation" where a woman feels isolated in her important relationships, and feels that she is the problem; that she is condemned to be isolated, with no possibility of changing this situation. In our clinical experience, this terrible state of shame and condemned isolation is highly correlated with drug use, as drugs become a way of coping with feelings that are seemingly beyond the scope of what is human and what could possibly be brought into connection with any good outcome. Such feelings may come to feel increasingly monstrous, crazy, evil, or dangerous.

Women are highly prone to isolation when "shaming" occurs. Jordan and colleagues (1991) have described the tremendous degree of cultural shaming around women's yearnings for connection, sexuality, and emotionality. Women are prone to develop a sense of personal deficiency—"something is wrong with me"—thus taking responsibility for problematic relationships and seeking all kinds of ways to change or alter themselves. In nonmutual relationships, women often become the "carriers" of the disavowed feelings of others, thus carrying the pain, anger, or fear of those with whom they are connected.

Limiting Relational Images

The culture, as well as individual families, often promotes distorted or limiting images of what it is to be healthy, worthwhile, physically attractive, or successful. Psychological theories both reflect and shape cultural images of what is healthy. Women internalize images of what one must look like, act like, or even feel like to be worthy of connection.

Women often use drugs to manipulate their bodies and selves into these problematic images of self in relationship. An old Jefferson Airplane song, "One pill makes you larger and one pill makes you small," describes such changes. Women often use substances to alter mood, intensity, body size, or emotional tone to fit such cultural images. We regulate ourselves when we feel too big (too angry, sexual, passionate, powerful, needy) or too small (too fearful, childlike, dependent, or vulnerable). Polydrug use is often related to such relational images—different drugs may be used to achieve different changes—and is a frequent characteristic of addicted women. Self-help book authors and medical professionals are frequently complicit in this enterprise of encouraging women to change themselves to fit cultural images. According to recent studies, medical doctors prescribe approximately 60% of psychoactive drugs, 70% of antidepressants, and 80% of amphetamines to women (Galbraith, 1991). In order to alter the self in this way, a woman's sensitivity to body, feelings, and deep levels of knowing must be cut off. This alienation from self is supported by a pervasive cultural disrespect for the body, especially real adult women's bodies (e.g., Kilbourne, 1991).

Abuse, Violation, and Systemic Violence

Another source of relational disconnection that contributes to the development of substance abuse, addiction, and relapse in women is the experience of abuse and violence.

It is estimated that four million American women are victims of domestic violence each year (see *Nation's Health,* 1994). According to one estimate (Kilpatrick et al., 1992), approximately 639,500 rapes occurred among American women aged 18 and older in 1992. By age 18, as many as 38% of all female children in this country have been sexually abused, in comparison to 7% of male children (Russell, 1984). With the increased acknowledgment of childhood sexual abuse of boys and girls, the gender differences are often minimized or overlooked. While both male and female children are at risk for abuse, females are at much higher risk than males for interpersonal violence throughout their adolescence and adult lives.

While all women are at risk of being abused, the risk of childhood abuse is higher for women raised in an alcoholic family, and the risk of being abused as an adult is higher for women who have an alcoholic male partner. In one study (Faller, 1988), 67% of sexually aggressive acts against children and 39% of such acts against women had involved alcohol use. Other studies estimate that between 70% and 80% of husbands who batter their wives use alcohol (Coleman & Strauss, 1983; Roberts, 1988), and that 35% of incest perpetrators are heavy drinkers (Crewsden, 1988).

Women who have been abused are in turn at greater risk to abuse alcohol and other drugs. One national study found that 70% of battered women were frequent drinkers (Roberts, 1988). A study of alcoholic women and matched nonalcoholic women (Covington & Kohen, 1984) revealed that 74% of the alcoholic women had experienced sexual abuse, 52% had experienced physical abuse and 72% had experienced emotional abuse. By comparison, 50% of the nonalcoholic subjects reported sexual abuse, 34% reported physical abuse, and 44% reported emotional abuse. Moreover, the alcoholic women were found to have been abused sexually, physically, and emotionally by more perpetrators, more frequently, and for longer periods of time than their non-alcoholic counterparts. The alcoholic women also reported more incidents of incest and rape.

Women recovering from childhood molestation, rape, or battering are teaching us about the impact of such trauma on relational development. When early parental relationships are abusive, violating, and dangerous, all future relationships are impacted. The very high rate of substance abuse and addiction among survivors of abuse and violence suggests the likelihood of turning to substance abuse when healthy relationships are unavailable and when faith or trust in the possibility of growth in human connection is impaired. The use of alcohol and other drugs has become a way for women to deal with the emotional pain resulting from earlier abuse by someone close to them, someone they trusted.

Personal violence toward women must be understood in the larger societal context of systemic violence and oppression. We would include in the factors contributing to substance abuse the impact of racism, classism, heterosexism, and ageism, as these intersect with sexism for women.

Distortion of Sexuality

Sexuality is at the core of the relational self (Covington, 1991; Jordan, 1987; Schnarch, 1991). Since female sexuality has historically been defined by men, and women have been silenced about their own experience, few women feel totally comfortable with this aspect of themselves.

Linking sexuality to substance abuse, Wilsnack and associates (1991) found sexual dysfunction to be the best single predictor of women's chronic problems with alcohol over a five-year study period. Given the association between substance abuse and sexual abuse, a woman's sexual dysfunction may be connected to early childhood abuse and/or to current domestic abuse. Women who have been abused often use alcohol or drugs in a self-medicating way in order to numb the emotional pain of the abuse experience. This can create a spiraling relationship where many women, believing that alcohol and drugs reduce sexual inhibition and facilitate sexual pleasure, drink or use substances to alleviate the sexual difficulties they are experiencing. But alcohol and drugs, which decrease physiological sexual arousal and interfere with orgasm in women, only exacerbate the problem. Thus, substance abuse can become both a cause and a consequence of sexual dysfunction (Covington, 1986, 1993).

Addiction is often defined as a physical, emotional, social, and spiritual disease. Our definition of sexual health is the integration of all these aspects of self; therefore, addiction can have an impact on every aspect of sexuality. Physically, alcohol and drugs can affect hormonal cycles and deaden the senses, thus diminishing the pleasure of the physical sexual experience. They can also increase the likelihood of sexual dysfunction.

Emotionally, several areas can be impacted. As discussed earlier, many women use alcohol and drugs in order to establish and maintain relationships. Sexuality, relationship, and mood-altering drugs become interconnected at an early age. For example, girls are often given their first alcohol and drugs by someone with whom they are emotionally involved, whereas boys are more likely to have their first alcohol/drug experience with their peers and to buy the alcohol themselves. Girls, therefore, often are in relationships with their "supplier." Adolescent and adult women who are in relationships with chemically dependent men often begin to drink and use drugs in order to join their male partner in his drug experiences.

Emotional connection can also be impaired by dissociation, a common defense mechanism used by people who have been abused. The dissociative process often begins as a result of the abuse experience, then later becomes part of the ongoing defense structure. Alcohol and drugs play a role in that they can recreate the dissociative experience. Dissociation has a very serious impact on relationships and on one's capacity for intimacy, because, when a person is dissociated, she is essentially "not there"—not present in the relationship nor capable of deep connection. Women who have been sexually abused often dissociate during sexual encounters.

Socially, one need only look to liquor commercials to see the strong association between sex and alcohol. Through its advertising, the liquor and beer industry essentially promises more romance, more fun and more sex in your life if you drink a particular brand. Studies of high school students have shown that girls very often have their first sexual experience and their first drinking experience at the same time. Not surprisingly, alcohol is the drug of choice for seduction purposes, and many people in our society still see alcohol as an aphrodisiac, despite physiological evidence to the contrary (Kilbourne, 1991).

Implications for Treatment

Alcoholics Anonymous as a Recovery Model for Women

As discussed above, relational disconnections may propel women into substance abuse. Conversely, the creation of positive, mutually enhancing connections may be exceptionally useful as an approach for helping women to break out of patterns of substance abuse. This principle is illustrated by the widespread use of mutual-help groups to recover from drug and alcohol abuse. Women are joining Alcoholics Anonymous and other 12-step programs in increasing numbers (Alcoholics Anonymous World Services, 1990). Many 12-step groups today have a majority of women members (for example, Overeaters Anonymous, Al-Anon, Codependents Anonymous).

Strengths. Self-help or, more accurately, mutual-help groups have made many important contributions to the recovery field for women, as they provide a growth-fostering relational context. They offer their members social support through the creation of a caring community. People come together voluntarily to discuss a common problem and to share their experiences, feelings, and coping techniques. Face-to-face interactions are stressed and members are taught to transform negative self-images into positive ones.

Mutual-help groups reflect the relational model in their design. Their structure is nonauthoritarian and nonlinear. Mutuality is emphasized. There are no supervisors, no professionally trained staff, who wield either authority or knowledge. Nor do such programs rely on outsiders for financial support or legitimacy. The sharing that occurs in mutual-help groups is not dependent on hierarchy or status. In this way, it is very different from the dominant culture. It is also in contrast to the power differential that is usually inherent in the therapist-client relationship. The value of participation in a program like Alcoholics Anonymous (AA) is twofold: one benefits by giving as well as by receiving. A woman is valued both for what she shares for herself and for what she offers to others.

A major advantage of mutual-help groups for women is that they are free and, in most urban communities, readily available throughout most parts of the day. It is in this respect that they are most unlike conventional problem-solving techniques, where help is provided only on occasion, almost exclusively as a response to a specific request from a particular individual.

Twelve-step programs of recovery are based on a relational psychology and spirituality that are very congruent with the Stone Center relational model. The core relational movement from isolation to connection is basic to recovery. Asking for help, sharing one's experience, strength, and hope, speaking authentically, accepting vulnerability, and being there for others—the typical ingredients of a 12-step meeting—are basic steps in building connection.

Reaching out for connection at the moment when the momentum of the past is drawing one into isolation and into the addictive process is the core relational movement of healing. The AA slogan, "You're as sick as you are secret," makes this point. The program teaches that sharing and bearing pain together is the only possible alternative to drug or alcohol use. This emphasis on the necessity of relationship and mutuality to work constructively with emotions is also congruent with Stone Center theory and, thus, in the authors' experience, highly beneficial for women.

Another relational benefit of mutual-help programs is the alcohol- and drug-free social activities they offer, and the opportunities to make new friends who are similarly committed to living free of addiction.

Of great value within the 12-step program are special groups for women only. Women attending same-sex groups are freed from the pressure to remain attractive to males while revealing feelings of shame or remorse about some previous or current behavior or thought. They are more easily able to talk about childhood experiences of oppression or abuse by males. And they are able to discuss their current lives more openly, talking about their lovers, husbands, and families to other women who will not find fault with their interpretations of reality. In these settings women's shared relational strengths greatly foster mutual empowerment.

Another important contribution made by 12-step programs is their holistic vision of health. The physical, emotional, and spiritual aspects of addiction are all seen as important. This challenges clinicians to pay attention to all aspects of a woman's recovery and to become comfortable integrating spirituality into the therapeutic setting, as well as working with the physical and sociopolitical levels.

Limitations. For all its contributions, the 12-step model also has some limitations. Part of the current wave of criticism of Alcoholics Anonymous and similar programs (e.g., Rieff, 1991) stems from their insistence on the locus of pathology within the individual and individual change as the solution to life's problems.

In AA, alcoholism and other problems that may be related to one's drinking are not viewed in a social context. AA ideology does not encourage attention to the relational, cultural, or sociopolitical factors that foster substance abuse. Little attention is paid to the fact that, especially for women, the larger context contributes to the abuse of substances, and an awareness of these factors is essential to women in recovery.

AA is not designed to address specific life issues that contribute to a woman's substance abuse. For example, issues of rape, battering, or incest often prevent a woman from achieving comfortable or long-lasting sobriety. As much as they may threaten her attempts at sobriety, these problems are unlikely to find resolution at AA meetings. Repeated relapse can be the signal that a woman requires more than a self-help or mutual-help program can offer; she needs the help and care of a trained professional who will work with her—with concurrent use of the recovery group—to prevent repeated returns to drinking.

Another limitation of Alcoholics Anonymous and other recovery programs is their use of outdated language. Much of the AA literature was written 20 to 50 years ago and is overtly sexist in its content and connotations. Despite use of the gender-neutral phrase "Higher Power," the 12 steps of AA repeatedly mention God as a masculine entity. Although people are encouraged to define God in their own terms, some argue that the very concept of God or Higher Power is patriarchal and therefore sexist. Many women have difficulty accepting the patriarchal theology and language of the programs, and professionals need some background in feminist theology (e.g., Plaskow & Christ, 1989) to help clients deal with these contradictions.

One might argue that AA meetings are only places to find out about alcoholism and recovery from it, and that they need not be "politically correct." But it is also true that, for people to "hear" things fully, they must be said in appropriate ways using nonoffensive language.

Newer groups, such as Women for Sobriety and Save Our Selves, have gone out of their way to correct this language bias. And, to their credit, some traditional 12-step groups have taken it upon themselves to review their literature, substituting gender-neutral pronouns. There is also a movement seeking to have AA's "Big Book" rewritten in its entirety to become nonsexist. Although the possibility of this occurring any time soon is rather remote, there is certainly evidence of a recognition that some of the program's materials are limited in their appeal.

Another aspect of 12-step language that has proved troublesome for many people is the word "powerless," which appears in the very first step: AA members are called upon to admit that they are powerless over alcohol. Critics of AA say that to urge women to admit their powerlessness over alcohol—and, by elaboration, their powerlessness in the program, over people, places, and things—is to set them up as victims who are discouraged from taking control over their own lives (see Berenson, 1991). These critics are missing one of the enduring paradoxes of AA that perhaps contributes to its success in many people's lives: that admitting where you are powerless in life actually empowers you. It allows you to identify areas of your life in which you do have power and control. For example, an alcoholic woman in an abusive relationship may admit to her powerlessness over drinking and, once sober, realize that she does wield important power in other areas of her life. She does not have the power to change the behavior of her abuser, but she may find she has the power to leave him.

When people get to AA, it is because they are in fact powerless to bring about desired feelings or to accomplish their goals without using alcohol. Removing alcohol from their lives with an admission of powerlessness over it is not the passivity and immobilization that typically characterizes a victim. Rather, it is taking a positive action to realistically assess one's own capacity for change and potential for growth.

Codependence

Another useful illustration of the limitations of the 12-step model is the concept of codependence. Women are defining themselves as "codependent" in increasing numbers and seeking treatment in 12-step programs or specialized treatment centers.

Originally, the term referred to people whose lives were significantly affected by living with chemically dependent people, especially "over-functioning" for the addicted family member or being obsessed with trying to control him or her. To help people focus on their own lives and issues, therapists coined the term "codependency" to define a disease or syndrome inherent in the person him- or herself which significantly affects all of that person's relationships. The disease is believed to be related to growing up in a "dysfunctional" family, or experiencing abuse or less-than-nurturing parenting as a child (Mellody et al., 1989). Characteristics of codependence vary across writers. Symptoms include "caretaking, low self-worth, obsession, controlling behavior, denial, external referencing, weak boundaries, lack of trust, anger, and sexual problems" (Beattie, 1987).

One concern about the codependency movement is that the syndrome's definition is so inclusive, yet so vague, that nearly everyone in the culture fits the criteria. Another is that, since women in the culture are *expected* to be the primary caretakers of others and of relationships, codependency appears to be highly gender-linked. Rather than affirming and revisioning women's potential strength in relationships, and validating their motive for connection, the codependency concept tends to pathologize their relational orientation, thus putting women in a cultural double bind.

The codependent label reflects an intrapsychic paradigm, that the disease is in the individual, not in the relationship. For women, taking sole responsibility for problems in a relationship does not enhance psychological development. As we have discussed, the Stone Center paradigm seeks to locate problems in the movement of the relationship and to study the impact of non-mutual, abusive, or disconnected relationships.

Current applications of the concept of codependency are for the most part highly individualistic and separate from any sociocultural or political framework. This leaves no room for studying how women are socialized in patriarchal culture or for any power-analysis of relationships. The effects of trauma, abuse, and power-over relationships could produce many of the symptoms of codependency, which could in extreme forms represent aspects of posttraumatic stress disorder. Further, this model incorrectly suggests that full recovery is possible in an interpersonal and societal system that promotes and continuously creates such symptomatic responses.

Recovery from codependency is often seen as requiring a strengthening of self, for example, solidifying boundaries, focusing on one's own needs, putting oneself first, and esteeming oneself from within. All of these have value as long as the importance of the relational context is also acknowledged, with healthy mutual connection regarded as both the healing energy and the goal of recovery—as both the means and the end.

Specialized Treatment Programs for Women

In general, existing substance abuse treatment programs are not gender sensitive. Some of the limitations of Alcoholics Anonymous become magnified in traditional psychiatric settings where the structures are hierarchical and nonmutual. Such a medical model is antithetical to the relational model. Women's unique patterns of substance abuse and psychological recovery have not been the basis for the design of these programs.

Beth Glover Reed (1987, p. 152) explains that the reasons addiction recovery programs have been designed primarily for men are complex:

> Many of the reasons are related to the social acceptability of various drugs at different times in history, and the types of social and personal costs that society wants to reduce or control. Others are related to stereotypic views of women and men, as well as general knowledge about women within the social sciences and human services. The researchers, theorists and policymakers are predominantly men, as were the majority of those within drug dependence programs (e.g., Henderson & Anderson, 1982). In research studies, women were either ignored, combined with men for data analysis, assumed to be the opposite of the men, or their results were so puzzling that they were called unpredictable and, thus, not interpreted.

Reed (1987, p. 151) also states that developing effective treatment services for women requires more than merely adding new components or staff training to existing programs:

> The primary barriers to the provision of more women-oriented services are theoretical, administrative and structural, and also involve policy and funding decisions. Assumptions about drug dependence, some key policy areas and funding patterns, as well as the structures, practices and culture of existing treatment organizations must be examined.

Not only do we lack treatment programs designed especially for women, but we have treatment programs designed especially for men, and women are expected to fit into them. Moreover, within the traditional programs, we have a lack of gender-specific groups. This is an important point because studies have found markedly different patterns of small-group interaction between men and women in same-gender and mixed-gender groups.

One study, for example, looked at men in group together, women in group together, and men and women in group together (Aries, 1976). Findings indicate that, when men and women group together, the women help facilitate the men's talking about their own experiences more, and women share their experiences and feelings less than when they are in an all-female group.

Studies of mixed-gender alcoholic groups have produced similar results. Priyadarsini (1986) found that compared to alcoholic women, alcoholic men more frequently took the initiative in introducing topics for discussion, choosing the topics and issues discussed, and regulating the level of affectivity exhibited.

Nicolina Fedele and Elizabeth Harrington (1990) concluded that the connection forged by women's group interactions have an essential role in women's treatment: "For where women gather together, there exists a potentially rich relational context to foster growth" (p. 10). In mixed-gender settings, it is also essential to provide specialized groups for women on such topics as trauma, body image, sexuality, and empowerment strategies.

Whenever possible, specialized treatment programs for women are the preferred treatment setting. Programs built on an appreciation and application of the relational model are extremely effective and powerful, based on the authors' clinical experience and observation. Programs are most successful when the relational model provides the underlying treatment philosophy, shapes the dynamics of staff and patient relationships, and is reflected in the patterns of staff interactions and decision making.

References

Alcoholics Anonymous World Services. (1990, Fall). Triennial surveys profile AA membership over the years. *About AA*, pp. 1-2.

Aries, E. (1976). Interaction patterns and themes of male, female, and mixed groups. *Small Group Behavior*, 7, 7-18.

Beattie, M. (1987). *Codependent no more*. Center City, MN: Hazelden Foundation.

Belenky, M.F., Clinchy, B.M., Goldberger, N.R., & Tarule, J.M. (1986). *Women's ways of knowing: The development of self, voice and mind*. New York: Basic Books.

Berenson, D. (1991). Powerlessness: Liberating or enslaving? Responding to the feminist critique of the twelve steps. In C. Bepko (Ed.), *Feminism and addiction* (pp. 67-84). Binghamton, NY: Haworth.

Byington, D. (1993). *Love and drugs*. Unpublished manuscript, Graduate School of Social Work, University of Denver.

Coleman, D.H., & Strauss, M.A. (1983). Alcohol abuse and family violence. In E. Gottheil, K.A. Druley, T.E. Skolada, & H.M. Waxman (Eds.), *Alcohol, drug abuse and aggression* (pp. 104-124). Springfield, IL: Charles C Thomas.

Covington, S.S. (1986). Facing the clinical challenges of women alcoholics: Physical, emotional & sexual abuse. *Focus on Family and Chemical Dependence, 9*, 10-11, 37, 42-44.

Covington, S.S. (1991). *Awakening your sexuality: A guide for recovering women*. San Francisco: Perennial Library.

Covington, S.S. (1993). Alcohol addiction and sexual dysfunction. In E.M. Freeman (Ed.), *Substance abuse treatment: A family systems perspective* (pp. 189-216). Newbury Park, CA: Sage.

Covington, S., & Beckett, L. (1988). *Leaving the enchanted forest: The path from relationship addiction to intimacy*. San Francisco: Harper & Row.

Covington, S.S., & Kohen J. (1984). Women, alcohol, and sexuality. *Advances in Alcohol and Substance Abuse, 4*, 41-56.

Crewsden, J. (1988). *By silence betrayed: Sexual abuse of children in America*. Boston: Little, Brown.

Faller, K.C. (1988). *Child sexual abuse: An interdisciplinary manual for diagnosis, case management and treatment*. New York: Columbia University Press.

Fedele, N.M., & Harrington, E.A. (1990). *Women's groups: How connections heal* (Work in Progress No. 47). Wellesley, MA: Stone Center, Working Paper Series.

Finkelstein, N. (1993, July). The relational model. In D. Kronstadt, P.F. Green, & C. Marcus (Eds.), *Pregnancy and exposure to alcohol and other drug use* (pp. 126-163). Washington, DC: U.S. Department of Health and Human Services, Substance Abuse and Mental Health Services Administration, Center for Substance Abuse Prevention.

Finkelstein, N., & Derman, L. (1991). Single-parent women: What a mother can do. In P. Roth (Ed.), *Alcohol and drugs are women's issues* (pp. 78-84). Metuchen, NJ: Scarecrow.

Galbraith, S. (1991). Women and legal drugs. In P. Roth (Ed.), *Alcohol and drugs are women's issues* (pp. 150-154). Metuchen, NJ: Scarecrow.

Gilligan, C. (1982). *In a different voice: Psychological theory and women's development.* Cambridge, MA: Harvard University Press.

Henderson, D.C., & Anderson, S.C. (1982). Treatment of alcoholic women. *Focus Women, 3,* 34-48.

Jordan, J. (1987). *Clarity in connection: Empathic knowing, desire, and sexuality* (Work in Progress No. 29). Wellesley, MA: Stone Center, Working Paper Series.

Jordan, J.V., Kaplan, A., Miller, J.B., Stiver, I., & Surrey, J. (1991). *Women's growth in connection: Writings from the Stone Center.* New York: Guilford Press.

Kilbourne, J. (1991). The spirit of the Czar: Selling addictions to women. In P. Roth (Ed.), *Alcohol and drugs are women's issues* (pp. 10-22). Metuchen, NJ: Scarecrow.

Kilpatrick, D.G., Edmonds, C.N., & Seymour, A.K. (1992). *Rape in America: A report to the nation.* Arlington, VA: National Victim Center.

Mellody, P., Miller, A.W., & Miller, J.K. (1989). *Facing codependence: What it is, where it comes from, how it sabotages our lives.* New York: Harper & Row.

Miller, J.B. (1976). *Toward a new psychology of women.* Boston: Beacon Press.

Miller, J.B. (1986). *What do we mean by relationships?* (Work in Progress No. 22). Wellesley, MA: Stone Center, Working Paper Series.

Miller, J.B. (1990). *Connections, disconnections, and violations* (Work in Progress No. 33). Wellesley, MA: Stone Center, Working Paper Series.

Nation's Health (1994, May/June). Shalala: Domestic abuse epidemic in U.S. *Nation's Health.*

Plaskow, J., & Christ, C. (Eds.). (1989). *Weaving the visions: New patterns in feminist spirituality.* San Francisco: Perennial Library.

Priyadarsini, S. (1986). Gender-role dynamics in an alcohol therapy group. In D.L. Strug, S. Priyadarsini, & M.M. Hyman (Eds.) *Alcohol interventions: Historical and sociocultural approaches* (pp. 179-196). Binghamton, NY: Haworth.

Reed, B.G. (1987). Developing women-sensitive drug dependence treatment services: Why so difficult? *Journal of Psychoactive Drugs, 19,* 151-164.

Rieff, D. (1991, October). Victims, all? *Harper's Magazine,* 49-56.

Roberts, A.R. (1988). Substance abuse among men who batter their mates: The dangerous mix. *Journal of Substance Abuse Treatment, 5,* 83-87.

Russell, D.E.H. (1984). *Sexual exploitation: Rape, child sexual abuse, and workplace harassment.* Beverly Hills, CA: Sage.

Schnarch, D.M. (1991). *Constructing the sexual crucible: An integration of sexual and marital therapy.* New York: Norton.

Soelle, D. (1978). *Death by bread alone.* Philadelphia, PA: Fortress Press.

Stiver, I. (1990). *Dysfunctional families and wounded relationships* (Work in Progress No. 38). Wellesley, MA: Stone Center, Working Paper Series.

Surrey, J. (1991). *Women and addiction: A relational perspective* (colloquium presented). Wellesley, MA: Stone Center.

Wilsnack, S.C., Klassen, A.D., Schur, B.E., & Wilsnack, R.W. (1991). Predicting onset and chronicity of women's problem drinking: A five-year longitudinal analysis. *American Journal of Public Health, 81,* 305–317.

Wilsnack, S.C., Wilsnack, R.W., & Klassen, A.D. (1986). Epidemiological research on women's drinking, 1978-1984. In National Institute on Alcohol Abuse and Alcoholism, *Women and alcohol: Health-realted issues* (pp. 1-68) (NIAAA Research Monograph No. 16; DHHS Publication No. ADM 86-1139). Washington, DC: U.S. Government Printing Office.

Social Contexts and Women's and Men's Drinking

Introductory Note

The causes and consequences of women's and men's drinking may depend not only on interpersonal relationships of the drinkers, as argued in the preceding chapters, but also on the larger social contexts in which drinking occurs. The chapters in this section examine how social settings and social groups may modify men's and women's alcohol use and its effects. A recurrent theme is that whenever men and women are expected to differ in their social behavior, these expectations will modify how they use alcohol and how they behave when drinking. As a result, connections between drinking behavior and ethnic identity, employment, and crime are often not the same for women as for men. The combined effects of gender and social contexts can be described but are often difficult to explain, because current theories of alcohol use are too simple for the complex patterns observed, and too little has been learned yet about how women's drinking varies in different social settings.

Oversimplified ideas about social influences on drinking are a major problem addressed by the chapter on ethnic variation by Gilbert and Collins. Although women more often abstain and less often drink heavily than men in U.S. ethnic minorities, the gender gaps vary among the subgroups within broad ethnic categories. In the United States, contrasts between men's and women's drinking appear greater among Koreans and Filipinos than among Japanese, and greater among the Navajo than among the Sioux. Heavy drinking by middle-aged men is more prevalent among Mexican-Americans and African-Americans than other ethnic categories. Reasons for such ethnic variations are not provided by a largely atheoretical research literature that often only compares broad ethnic categories (such as "Asian" or "Latin American") with the Euro-American majority. There also is not enough known about how presumed ethnic influences on women's and men's drinking change over time. Men from Latin America and the Pacific Rim can often continue traditional drinking patterns in the United States, but women's drinking may change by generations, with U.S.-born daughters or granddaughters of immigrants using alcohol more like women of the Euro-American majority. Gilbert and Collins suggest that gender differences in alcohol use are greatest in ethnic groups whose social activities are gender-segregated. If women become increasingly active in public and mixed-gender settings (such as by acculturation to contemporary U.S. lifestyles), ethnicity-based gender differences in alcohol use may diminish.

Gender influences on drinking may also depend on another poorly understood context: the workplace. Blum and Roman note that many studies have described how gender affects both employment and drinking, but it has been much harder to untangle the connections between employment and drinking, and to learn how the connections may differ for men and women. Oversimplified research may have allowed ideological assumptions about gender, work, and alcohol to remain inadequately tested (e.g., that women who work outside the home increase their alcohol consumption but keep their alcohol-related problems hidden). To show why more thorough research is needed, Blum and Roman use data from surveys of a national employee sample and of clients in over 80 employee assistance programs (EAPs). The employee survey shows that neither job stress nor the combined demands of job and family roles can adequately explain the complexity of relationships between women's and men's employment and alcohol use. One way that jobs may particularly affect women's drinking is through opportunities to drink with co-workers, opportunities that may depend partly on the gender composition of women's occupations. If employees develop drinking-related behavior problems, men's use of EAPs depends more on family pressures and formal referrals than does women's, suggesting that seeking help for drinking problems is affected by gender differences in the perceived need for help. A major lesson of the chapter is that relationships among gender, work, and drinking can be understood only by viewing those terms as general headings for multiple variables interwoven in complex ways.

Alcohol use is imbedded not only in legitimate activities (e.g., work) but also in illegitimate activities (crime). Unfortunately, as Streifel explains, relationships among gender, crime, and drinking are usually studied in terms of only two variables at a time. As a result, we know that crimes are associated with drinking, and that men drink and commit crimes more than do women, but we know little about how gender modifies the alcohol-crime connections. Streifel uses data from a survey of state prison inmates, and data on homicides in eight U.S. cities, to reveal some interactions of gender, crime, and alcohol use that need better explanation. For example, evidence suggests that drinking at the time of criminal activity is more prevalent among male than among female offenders, and is associated more closely with violent crime than with property crime, patterns suggesting that alcohol may release or seem to excuse male hostility and/or aggression. However, a simple connection between alcohol and anger does not explain why associations of violent crime with alcohol use decrease as men get older but increase as women get older. Homicide associated with drinking is also a function of social settings: it is more likely to result from contacts with nonfamily members in public places, a drinking context more normative for men than for women. The drinking that precedes crimes is also predominantly group drinking, for which men may have more opportunities than do women. Such evidence is consistent with the idea that violence is particularly likely to erupt among young men drinking together in bars, and provides further illustration of how gender-differentiated social behavior may affect the outcomes and risks of alcohol use.

CHAPTER 14

Ethnic Variation in Women's and Men's Drinking

M. Jean Gilbert and R. Lorraine Collins

The existence of clear cultural differences in drinking patterns and practices is well documented (Greeley et al., 1980). Cultural prescriptions to a large degree determine who has access to alcohol as well as when, where, and in what circumstances people are allowed or expected to consume alcohol. Cultural beliefs and norms governing the use of alcohol are embedded in and shaped by a broader framework of cultural elements. These elements include religious orientations, affective styles, social roles, social group identifications, social class and occupational structures, status and power differences, and mechanisms of social control. All societies have gender role norms, although the content of rules for male and female behavior varies among cultures. The patterns of alcohol use in a society or ethnic group are typically integrated into the rules prescribed for gender role behavior.

In the United States, most population growth is taking place among groups of non-European background. Such a demographic change will make it more and more important to understand ethnic variations in women's and men's drinking. This chapter discusses issues of gender and alcohol use in four broad population groupings: Asians, Latinos, African-Americans, and Native Americans.

Ethnicity in Alcohol Research

Any discussion of ethnicity raises definitional and conceptual issues. The first of these involves the concept of ethnicity. Ethnicity as discussed here is defined by culture: a shared identity and ideological, normative, and behavioral framework. Though this shared cultural frame may overlap with race or national origin, the fit is usually imperfect. The common cultural perspective and shared identity that distinguishes a group may have evolved in any number of ways: through geographical separation, social or religious affinity, or political and structural oppression, to name just a few.

The categories "Asian," "Latino," "African-American," and "Native American" do not denote ethnic groups or homogeneous populations. They are "ethnic glosses" (Trimble, 1990–91)—convenient census and survey categories that aggregate heterogeneous groups. Thus, "Latino" includes Cubans, Mexican-Americans, Puerto Ricans and other groups. The Asian population includes people from such diverse national backgrounds as China, Japan, Korea, Vietnam, and the Philippines. The U.S. Bureau of Indian Affairs lists 478 Indian tribes, and Alaska Natives are drawn from five different peoples in terms of historical, geographical, and cultural factors (Walker & Kivlahan, 1984). The rubrics "African-American" or "black" used in epidemiological studies mask wide variation: people U.S.-born for many generations and people who have arrived more recently from the Caribbean or from African nations.

Because each ethnic group is heterogeneous, the use of ethnic glosses affects the replication of studies and/or the external validity of findings (see Collins, 1992; Trimble, 1990–91). Sources of heterogeneity within groups include physical characteristics, gender, education, age, socioeconomic status, and acculturation level. These variables mediate, moderate, and sometimes override the effects of cultural norms for alcohol use, because it is not membership in an ethnic group per se that governs an individual's alcohol use, but the extent to which the individual shares the alcohol-related proscriptions and prescriptions common to the shared culture of the ethnic group. In reviewing research for this chapter, it has become quite apparent that very little alcohol research has attempted to get beyond the ethnic glosses to examine inter- and intragroup heterogeneity in alcohol-related practices. Thus, we are left in the tricky position of calling attention to the limitations of ethnic categorization while discussing research based on such categorization.

In the following discussion, every attempt will be made to distinguish discrete groups within the populations covered, if group-specific data are available. Intragroup variability and the sources of variability will be noted. When possible, groups will be referred to by using the terms currently favored by the groups themselves. Also, to avoid using European-American as a standard from which other ethnic groups are distinguished, comparisons with the general population will be made only to serve theoretical purposes.

Research on adult drinking behavior among groups within the four major population segments is very uneven in depth and quality. Much of what we know about gender-related drinking patterns in U.S. ethnic groups is derived from general population surveys relying on self-reports of drinking behavior, attitudes, and, occasionally, sex-role related norms. Data generated from such surveys are typically cross-sectional and descriptive, and can only tell us that groups differ in their gender-patterned drinking practices. Such data shed little light on *why* groups differ.

Research on alcohol use across and within U.S. ethnic groups also lacks rigorous or well-developed theories. For example, Heath (1990-91) suggests that ethnicity research has emphasized social learning as a basis for various aspects of alcohol use, but few researchers have developed models that explain how cultural characteristics are acquired or relate to specific drinking patterns. Additionally, little extant research is truly cross-cultural, because investigators usually have not systematically examined sources of variation and similarity across groups. When research based upon comparative models becomes more common, we may find that factors other than ethnicity can better account for some of the observed variation in drinking behavior across groups. In this chapter we review, wherever possible, research that has explored sources of within-group variation in drinking practices.

A further complication of studies of different cultural groups is that investigators often use different measures of alcohol use and varying conceptualizations of problem drinking or alcoholism. For this reason, we focus on recent studies (1980 or later) that have used comparable or nearly equivalent measures of these variables. Fortunately, many studies of alcohol use among U.S. ethnic groups have used or adapted the following typology developed by Cahalan, Cisin, and Crossley (1969) to categorize drinking practices:

- *Abstainer:* Drinks less than once a year or has never drunk alcoholic beverages.
- *Infrequent drinker:* Drinks less than once a month, but at least once per year; may or may not have five drinks at a sitting.
- *Less frequent, low quantity drinker:* Drinks one to three times per month, less than five drinks at a sitting.
- *Less frequent, high quantity drinker:* Drinks one to three times per month, and has five or more drinks at a sitting at least once a year.
- *Frequent, low quantity drinker:* Drinks once per week or more often, less than five drinks at a sitting.
- *Frequent, high quantity drinker:* Drinks once per week or more often, and has five or more drinks at a sitting at least once per year.
- *Frequent heavy drinker:* Drinks once per week or more often, and has five or more drinks at a sitting once per week or more often.

Often the infrequent and the less frequent, low quantity drinkers together are referred to as "light" drinkers. The frequent, high quantity drinkers and the frequent heavy drinkers are often called "heavy" or "heaviest" drinkers, and the remaining middle categories are called "moderate" drinkers. We will follow this convention. These distinctions are important, because it has generally been found that alcohol-related problems are not associated with drinking per se or even with frequent light drinking, but are associated with regular consumption of large quantities of alcohol.

Gender Variation in Alcohol Consumption among
Asian-American Groups

Data are available regarding gender differences in alcohol use among five Asian groups living in the United States: Japanese, Chinese, Koreans, Filipinos, and Vietnamese. Information on Asian drinking patterns comes primarily from two studies: a major survey of 1,171 Asian-Americans undertaken in Los Angeles in the mid-1980s (Chi et al., 1989; Kitano et al., 1988; Lubben et al., 1988, 1989) and the Joint Japanese/U.S. Alcohol Epidemiological Study (Parrish et al., 1990, 1992; Towle, 1988; Tsunoda et al., 1992). Despite substantial variation in drinking patterns across Asian groups, men were consistently more likely than women to be drinkers, and among drinkers, men were more likely than women to be heavy drinkers.

The Los Angeles study included adult Koreans (280), Japanese (295), Chinese (298), and Filipinos (230). The sample was drawn from Los Angeles phone directories by randomizing ethnically identifiable surnames. It was comprised primarily of adult immigrants to the United States, with the exception of the Japanese subsample, which was predominantly U.S.-born. As Chi and associates (1989) note, the sample characteristics made it likely that drinking patterns found in all groups except the Japanese were heavily influenced by drinking norms and practices in the Asian countries of origin.

Gender differences in alcohol use vary greatly across Asian-American groups. In the Los Angeles study, gender differences in abstention were greatest among Filipinos, where 55% of the women did not drink, but only 18% of the men were abstainers. Similarly, 51% of Chinese women were abstainers, but only 22% of Chinese men abstained. Among Koreans, however, rates of abstention were high among both men and women: 75% of the women and 44% of the men did not drink. The Japanese had the lowest rates of abstention and the smallest gender differences: 27% of the women and 17% of the men did not drink. To compare with these figures, a recent study of Vietnamese in Santa Clara County, California, found that 51% of the women were abstainers, while only 6% of the men did not drink—the widest gender difference measured (Padilla et al., 1993).

In most of these groups, few women were heavy or even moderate drinkers, in contrast to men. Among the Chinese, 10% of the women and 37% of the men were moderate drinkers. No Chinese women were heavy drinkers, though 14% of the Chinese men were. Over one-fourth of Korean and Filipino men were heavy drinkers (26% and 29%), while Korean and Filipino women were barely represented in this category (1% and 3%). In the Santa Clara Vietnamese sample, 39% of the men and 6% of the women were moderate to heavy drinkers (Padilla et al., 1993). Women were somewhat more likely to be heavy drinkers among the Japanese-Americans (12% vs 29% of the men), but being born in Japan was associated with heavy drinking among men but not among women. Kitano et al. (1992) point out that heavy drinking among Japanese and Korean men in Los Angeles is as prevalent as it is among men in the general U.S. population, but women in all Asian groups typically drink less than women in the general population.

Chi and colleagues (1989) used logistic regression with data from the Los Angeles study to identify what predicted whether Asian men and women would drink. Friends' use of alcohol predicted drinking and drinking levels among Japanese, Chinese, and Filipino men. Socializing at nightclubs and bars predicted men's drinking among the Japanese and Koreans, but not among the Chinese or Filipinos; the authors note that among Asians, unlike other groups in the U.S. population, it is common for nondrinkers to frequent bars and nightclubs. Participation in sports and attendance at religious services predicted men's abstention from alcohol only among the Japanese. Parents' drinking attitudes and patterns were the primary influences on drinking among Korean men. It is noteworthy that neither income nor marital status was a strong predictor of abstention among Asian men.

Somewhat different factors predicted whether Asian women drank. Japanese and Korean women who played table games together as a pastime (Mah Jongg or Hana) were less likely to drink. Among Chinese, Korean, and Filipino women, regular church attendance made it less likely that they would drink. Among Japanese women, going to bars and nightclubs increased the likelihood that they would drink. It appears that drinking or abstention among Asian men and women depends not only on ethnic background but also on social activities and reference groups.

The Joint Japan/U.S. Epidemiological Project (Kitano et al., 1992) gathered comparative data on Japanese and Japanese-American drinking practices. This study interviewed 1,225 Japanese from four locales in Japan, 514 Japanese-Americans in Oahu, Hawaii, and 516 Japanese-Americans in Santa Clara, California, using the same questionnaire. The Santa Clara sample included both *Nisei* (second generation) and *Sansei* (third generation) Japanese-Americans, while the Hawaiian sample consisted primarily of Sansei.

Drinking patterns of the three groups showed intriguing differences. In Japan, just 9% of the men were abstainers, but 36% of the women did not drink. In Santa Clara, 18% of the men and 26% of the women were abstainers. In Hawaii, the percentage of abstainers among men and women was the same (21%). Heavy drinking was rare among women in all three locations, reported by only 4% in Japan, 4% in Santa Clara, and 9% in Hawaii. Heavy drinking was more common among men in all three places, reported by 32% in Japan, 29% in Hawaii, but only 13% in Santa Clara (perhaps because of effects of aging among the Nisei).

These data, combined with findings from the Los Angeles study (Kitano et al., 1988), suggest that among Japanese descendants in the U.S., women move away from abstention into light or moderate drinking. Men, on the other hand, show a slight tendency to adopt abstention and lighter drinking when living in the U.S. In the absence of cross-generational data on other

Asian-Americans, it is hard to know whether these patterns can be generalized to all Asian groups.

Given the very moderate drinking patterns of Asian women, it is not surprising that they report few problems related to alcohol use. It is somewhat more surprising that Asian men in Los Angeles (Kitano and Chi, 1986–87), who were much more likely to be heavy drinkers, also reported few alcohol-related problems, such as job loss or arrest. Unfortunately, there is little other information on the prevalence of alcohol-related problems or disorders among Asian populations in the United States. The Epidemiological Catchment Area (ECA) study (Regier et al., 1984), which estimated the prevalence of mental health disorders including alcohol abuse and dependence in several U.S. locales, did not include an Asian subsample.

However, studies using the ECA's assessment instrument, the Diagnostic Interview Schedule, were conducted in Taipei, Taiwan, and South Korea (Helzer et al., 1990). Findings from these studies may offer clues about levels of alcohol abuse and dependence among Chinese and Korean immigrants in the U.S. In Taiwan, the lifetime prevalence of alcoholism was 18 times greater for men (13%) than for women (0.7%). In Korea, men's extraordinary lifetime prevalence rate (43%) was 14 times higher than women's (3%). In comparison, lifetime prevalence rates for the general population in St. Louis were 29% for men and 4% for women, a 7:1 ratio. There has been little research on why Korean men report such high rates of alcoholism. However, Yamamoto et al. (1988) note that Koreans are known as the "Irish of the Orient" because of men's heavy alcohol use, and emphasize (as do Lubben et al., 1989) that male socializing in the context of jobs and business relations makes it very important to drink and to keep up with the alcohol consumption of friends.

Much has been made of the facial flushing or vasodilation that occurs among Asians as a result of alcohol use; it has been suggested that this tendency may constrain alcohol use among some Asian groups. However, research now suggests that cultural and attitudinal factors are more important influences on Asian drinking behavior than the flushing response (Johnson et al., 1990; Parrish et al., 1990). Even though many Korean and Japanese males experience flushing, this does not seem to constrain their levels of alcohol use. No evidence of gender differences in the flushing response have been documented, but Parrish et al. found that Japanese and Japanese-American women were more embarrassed by the flushing response than were men.

Gender Variation in Alcohol Consumption among Latinos in the United States

Research among Latinos in the United States has given considerably more attention to Mexican-Americans than to Cuban-Americans and Puerto Ricans (Burnam, 1989; Caetano, 1988a,b; Caetano & Medina-Mora, 1988; Gilbert,

1987, 1989, 1991). However, a 1984 epidemiological survey conducted by Caetano (1988a,b) provides information about all three Latino groups. Subjects were selected through a multistage probability procedure from the U.S. Latino population 18 years and older living in households in the 48 contiguous states. Respondents included 949 Mexican-Americans, 216 Puerto Ricans, and 170 Cuban-Americans.

All three groups showed the familiar pattern that men were more likely than women to drink and to drink heavily. Gender differences in abstention were greatest among Cuban-Americans (males = 12%, females = 42%). Among Puerto Ricans, 19% of the men and 33% of the women did not drink. Mexican-American men and women had bimodal drinking patterns. Mexican-Americans had the highest abstention rates (men = 27%, women = 46%), but they were also the most likely to be in the two heaviest drinking categories (frequent high maximum and frequent heavy drinker) (men = 44%, women = 14%). Fewer Puerto Ricans (men = 24%, women = 5%) and Cuban-Americans (men = 6%, women = 7%) were in these heavy drinking categories. Respondents were also asked to report social, personal, and symptomatic drinking problems in the year prior to the interview. Mexican-Americans were more likely to report experiencing such problems (men = 22%, women = 7%) than were Puerto Ricans (men = 8%, women = 3%) or Cuban-Americans (men = 4%, women = 2%).

Other studies conducted in the United States (Gilbert, 1989) and Mexico (Medina-Mora et al., 1988) generally support the findings from the 1984 U.S. national survey. Gonzalez (1983), studying drinking practices among men and women in Puerto Rico, found that 89% of the heavy drinkers were men. The ECA survey in Los Angeles (Burnam, 1989) found that 32% of Mexican-American men had a lifetime diagnosis of alcohol abuse/dependence, compared with 4.5% of Mexican-American women, a ratio of 7:1. A similar study in Puerto Rico found lifetime prevalence rates of 24.6% for men and 2% for women, a ratio of 12:1 (Canino et al., 1989).

Predictors of drinking, heavy drinking, and alcohol-related problems have been evaluated only for Mexican-Americans in the 1984 U.S. survey (Caetano, 1988b). Among Mexican-American males, the only significant predictor of drinking versus abstaining and of heavier drinking was age: younger men were more likely to be drinkers and heavy drinkers. Drinking problems were more prevalent among Mexican-American men who were aged 18–29 and who had less than a high school education. Mexican-American women were more likely to drink if they were divorced or single and had higher incomes and education. Being divorced or single was the only predictor of heavier drinking and drinking-related problems among women.

Caetano (1988b) has called attention to an unusual drinking pattern among Mexican-American men and women: heavy drinking among the middle-aged. Unlike men in the general population, Mexican-American men of all economic

and educational levels and from all regions in the U.S. continue heavy drinking into their mid-life years. However, heavy drinking among middle-aged
Mexican-American women occurred only among Californians born in the U.S.
who had relatively high levels of income and education. Subsequent longitudinal research (Caetano, 1993) has found that Latino men and women are
more likely to increase their levels of drinking in middle age (40–59) than are
whites or African-Americans. Furthermore, heavy drinking among Latino
males aged 18–29 in 1984 was likely to persist into middle age, in contrast to
white males, who tended to reduce their drinking levels after age 30. Higher
levels of acculturation predicted increased drinking over time among both
male and female Latinos.

Gender Variation in Alcohol Consumption among Native Americans

Much of the research on drinking behavior among Native Americans has focused on drinking-related problems, including high rates of alcohol-related
mortality and morbidity (May, 1989), and fetal alcohol syndrome (May, 1991;
NIAAA, 1990). The lack of general population surveys of drinking among Native Americans may be related to their cultural heterogeneity, their small representation in the U.S. population (less than 1%), and some difficulties in
gaining access to Native American communities. As in other ethnic groups,
variation in the drinking behavior of Native Americans is related to education,
income, age, and gender. Unique sources of variation in drinking behavior include cultural practices related to tribal affiliation, residence in rural areas or
on reservations, and the availability of alcohol on reservations. For example,
May (1989) has suggested that a history of prohibiting drinking by native
peoples, and current prohibition practices on many reservations, may have
contributed to the development of drinking patterns involving rapid drinking
and binge drinking. Over time these patterns may have been adopted as normative drinking among certain subgroups of Native Americans, particularly
in reservation settings (cf., Weibel-Orlando, 1989).

Studies of Native American drinking, and particularly of public drinking, often focus on men's drinking behavior (Leland, 1984). However, information
on drinking among Native American women can be gleaned from a few
sources. May and Smith (1988) administered a questionnaire to 174 Navajo
on the Navajo reservation in northeastern Arizona. The sample ranged in age
from 16 years to 60+ years, and 51% of the participants were female. More
men than women reported ever drinking (64% vs. 40%) and ever having had
an alcohol-related problem (25% vs. 3%). Rates of drinking varied with age,
peaking in the 20–29 year age group (80% of men, 52% of women) and decreasing to relatively low levels by age 60 years (22% of men, and none of the
women). Although drinking varied with age, alcohol-related problems were
said to affect both young and old Navajo.

—

Weisner and colleagues (1984) gathered data on drinking patterns of 155 Native Americans living in Los Angeles, California, in 1978-79. The sample included Sioux, Navajo, indigenous California tribes, and five tribes from eastern Oklahoma (e.g., Cherokee, Seminole). The sample was recruited via network and snowball sampling to include roughly equal numbers of heavy and moderate drinkers as well as nondrinkers. Men and women were represented equally, and the mean age was 35.5 years. Findings indicated that men drank more than women, and the younger and middle-aged drank more than older participants. Lifetime abstainers tended to be older, middle-class women from the eastern Oklahoma tribes. Participants who reported moderate social drinking styles tended to be of higher socioeconomic status (SES) and middle aged or older, and a slight majority were women. Heavy drinking was most likely to be reported by younger, unmarried persons of lower SES, who were less likely to participate in Native American cultural activities.

Weibel-Orlando (1989) compared this sample of urban Native Americans with a sample of Native Americans from the same tribes living on reservations. The sample living on reservations was older, less educated, and more socially stable (e.g., married). The two samples also differed in employment; 37.4% of the urban sample and 51.2% of the reservation sample were unemployed. There was a tendency for urban men to drink more (frequency and quantity) than men on the reservations, but this was due in part to a subgroup of "skid row" urban participants. Men drank significantly more than women in both samples, but there was some tribal variation. Among the Sioux, women in both the urban and reservation samples reported drinking almost as much as their male counterparts.

Generally, however, Native American women tend to drink at lower levels than men (May, 1989; Weibel-Orlando, 1989), and report somewhat fewer social problems related to alcohol use (Leland, 1984). These patterns may vary as a function of tribal affiliation and setting (Weibel-Orlando, 1989). Because there are so few studies and so little information about gender differences in drinking among Native Americans, more research is clearly needed before any firm conclusions about gender differences are possible.

Gender Variation in Alcohol Consumption among African-Americans

The largest studies of alcohol use among African-American men and women have been general population surveys conducted by the Alcohol Research Group (Berkeley, Calif.). In 1984 the Alcohol Research Group conducted a national household survey about alcohol use among 1,947 African-Americans over age 18 (1,224 women, 723 men) (Herd, 1988, 1989, 1990). Women were more likely than men to be abstainers (45% vs. 29%), or to be infrequent or less frequent drinkers (36% vs. 26%). In contrast, only 8% of the women but 33% of the men were in the two heaviest drinking categories.

As in other groups, drinking behavior among African-Americans varies with age, marital status, and income. Among both men and women in the 1984 sample, abstention increased and heavy drinking decreased in older age groups. From ages 18 to 39, about one-third of the women were abstainers, but a majority of women over 40 did not drink. Men in their 30s were less likely to be abstainers (15%) than younger men (23%), but over one-third of men in their 40s abstained from alcohol, as did 60% of men over age 60. The few women who were heavier drinkers became rarer with increasing age (18–29 years = 12%; 40–49 = 10%; 50–59 = 6%). Among men, however, the heavy drinking categories included one-third of the men under age 30 but just over half (51%) of the men in their 30s; after age 40, only about one-fourth (27%) of the men drank this heavily. Herd (1989) points out that the unusual increase in heavier drinking among men in their 30s, discovered in this survey and in an earlier study in the San Francisco area (Caetano & Herd, 1984), may be one of the reasons why middle-aged African-American men experience high rates of alcohol-related health problems (cirrhosis, esophageal cancer) in middle age.

In the 1984 national survey, marital status of African-Americans was unrelated to men's drinking practices. Rates of abstention were similar among single and married women (43% and 44%, respectively), but highest among widows (70%). Women who were middle-aged (40–59) and unmarried were most likely to engage in heavy drinking (Herd, 1988, 1989).

Income variation affected men's and women's drinking differently. Among women, greater family income was related to less abstention ($6,000 or less = 53%, $30,000 or more = 34%). Women's rates of heavy drinking varied little across income categories, although women with the highest family incomes were least likely to be heavy drinkers (5%). Men, on the other hand, had relatively stable rates of abstention across income levels ($6,000 or less = 34%, $30,000 or more = 30%), but income had a curvilinear relationship to heavier drinking, reported by 33% of men at the lowest income level, 28% of men at the highest income level, and 43–45% of men with family incomes between $6,000 and $15,000. Among women, rates of heavier drinking were not related to level of employment (full time = 8%; part time = 10%; homemaker = 8%), but the highest rates of heavy drinking were found among the unemployed (14%). As with Asian-Americans and Latinos, little theory exists to explain why socioeconomic factors affect African-American men's and women's drinking practices differently.

Among African-Americans who drink, men report much higher rates of alcohol-related problems than do women (Herd, 1989). For example, in the 1984 survey, 15% of male drinkers versus 8% of female drinkers reported health problems associated with drinking. Symptoms of physical dependence were reported by 29% of the men but by just 4% of the women. Drunk-driving problems and "people problems" were reported, respectively, by 10% and 14% of the men, but by only 2% and 4% of female drinkers.

Epidemiological Catchment Area studies in three locales (Baltimore, St. Louis, and rural and urban North Carolina) obtained information on alcohol abuse/dependence from a sample of 4,026 African-Americans (Robins, 1989). Five times more males (24%) than females (5%) reported lifetime prevalence of alcohol abuse/dependence. Among both men and women, rates for lifetime prevalence of alcohol disorders were highest in middle-age. Herd (1994) has suggested that sociocultural factors, including unemployment and urban living conditions, may contribute to negative consequences of drinking experienced by African-American men (see also Barr et al., 1993).

The long history of African-Americans in the United States allows historical analysis of how alcohol has been viewed and used over time in African-American culture (Herd, 1985). Such analysis cannot explain gender differences, but does reveal opposing influences on drinking in African-American society. On the one hand, the antislavery and temperance movements were closely linked in the mid-1800s, and opposition to alcohol use has been a consistent tenet of the fundamentalist religious groups that have strongly shaped African-American values. The strength of such religious influences is reflected in surveys of African-Americans (Caetano & Herd, 1984; Herd, 1988), where abstention among men and women is linked to participation in fundamentalist religion. On the other hand, the migration of African-Americans to northern cities in the 1920s and 1930s, coupled with the white supremacist sentiments frequently espoused by prohibitionists, did much to erode temperance norms among African-Americans. These years gave rise to the urban black "nightclub" scene, involving both men and women, which flourished in Harlem, Chicago, and San Francisco, linking alcohol use to sophistication and the good life. Herd (1985) notes that alcohol-related problems grew within the African-American population after this era.

Ethnic Attitudinal Contexts for Gender Differences in the Use of Alcohol

Norms for alcohol use, attitudes about alcohol, expectancies about the positive or negative effects of alcohol use, and rationalizations for drinking are the product of social learning. These cognitions may powerfully influence drinking behavior. Therefore, researchers have tried to learn how gender-related "thinking about drinking" may influence the alcohol practices of ethnic groups.

Possibly the most influential cognitions are the cultural rules that regulate who can drink, how much, when, and where. For example, there are nearly universal norms restricting the use of alcohol by children. Almost as ubiquitous are norms that limit women's use of alcohol more than men's.

For example, the Joint Japan/U.S. study of Japanese and Japanese-Americans (Parrish et al., 1992) showed that people of Japanese heritage in

Santa Clara, in Hawaii, and in Japan all perceived more permissive norms for men's drinking than for women's (in terms of drinking age, quantity consumed, and acceptance of inebriation). In Hawaii and Santa Clara, men and women alike thought that women of most ages should drink "only a small amount." In contrast, in Korea and in Japan men are expected to drink heavily when socializing together (Yamamoto et al., 1988). In Japan, especially, male work group drinking is highly regarded, there is tolerance for men getting drunk, and men can express emotions and opinions while drinking that would be unacceptable when sober. Among Japanese-Americans, Towle (1988) found that men were much more likely than women to report that they used alcohol to gain confidence, to forget worries, and to relieve tension.

Caetano's (1988a) data on three Latino groups (Cuban-American, Mexican-American, and Puerto Rican) show that men in all three groups were more permissive of both male and female drinking than women were, but that both men and women had more permissive norms for male drinking than for female drinking. Most men and women in all three groups did not approve of teenagers of either gender drinking alcohol, but believed that men and women could drink some alcohol once they were 21 and older. However, Cuban-American men and women did not endorse female drinking at any age as strongly as respondents in the other two groups did. Mexican-American men and women were by far the most likely to support both male and female "drinking to feel the effects," and more men than women were supportive of women drinking in this manner.

Expectations about alcohol's effects may have a major influence on drinking behavior, but such expectations have rarely been evaluated in U.S. ethnic groups. An exception is a study by Cervantes and associates (1990–91), who measured expected alcohol effects among young adult Mexican- and Central-Americans. An eight-item scale covered expectations about enhanced social acceptance, physical relaxation, freedom from inhibition, social assertiveness, social pleasure, sexual pleasure, mood elevation, and tension reduction. Expectancy scores correlated positively with drinking levels for both men and women, though the association was much stronger among men. The findings also indicated that men were significantly more likely than women to expect positive effects on all eight variables from "a drink or two."

Native American tribal groups also have gender-related drinking norms. May (1989) summarizes the general pattern for women in the following way:

Among the Navajo and Pueblo tribes of the Southwest . . . it is rare and quite unacceptable for any women to drink at all once they have passed their mid-twenties and have done some experimentation. In other tribes, such as the Plains and Basin tribes, more women are drinkers at all ages and drinking is somewhat more acceptable. (p. 119)

Norms for Native American men seem to vary with tribal affiliation and history. For example, Weisner et al. (1984) reported that eastern Oklahoma Native Americans had more fundamentalist Christian affiliations with long histories of prohibition, which translated into less tolerance of heavy drinking. Sioux respondents had often been exposed to heavy drinking in their youth, were more tolerant of heavy drinking, and tended to consume more heavily than other groups.

There are few sources of data on African-American gender differences in alcohol norms. In Caetano and Herd's (1984) sample from Northern California, women gave less approval than men did for drinking as a way to have fun and/or to enhance social activities. Women were also less tolerant of drunkenness in a woman or man than men were. However, these women disapproved of drunkenness less in men than in women. A different perspective was reported by Connors et al. (1988) from a small sample of African-American college students. In this sample, women more than men tended to view alcohol as more useful for "feeling in charge" and for "relieving emotional distress."

In most studies of ethnic groups, men and women have different views about drinking, and both sexes evaluate men's and women's drinking differently. In general, men have more liberal views than women about everyone's drinking, and both men and women are more permissive about drinking by men. Men are also generally more enthusiastic than women about the benefits of alcohol, and seem to endorse more reasons for using it than women do. These patterns seem to transcend ethnic differences.

Issues of Acculturation in Men's and Women's Drinking Behavior

In ethnic groups that have immigrated to the United States, studies of alcohol use across generations may lead to theories about how acculturation affects men's and women's drinking. Models of acculturative change assume that over time an immigrant population will develop behavior patterns, attitudes, and beliefs more like the population they have entered and less like the population they have left behind. The acculturative processes of dropping, modifying, and adopting cultural traits usually occur at different rates over several generations. Because drinking is in most cultures a social activity, changes in social circumstances, settings, interactive opportunities, and reference groups might be expected to shape new drinking norms and practices. And because men's and women's social roles are likely to differ in both donor and recipient cultures, acculturative changes in drinking behavior may vary across genders.

To place acculturative change in an appropriate context, it is necessary to have a sense of drinking patterns in the U.S. general population. Hilton (1987) reports on general population patterns in a 1984 national sample of adults. Twenty-four percent of the men sampled were abstainers, as were 36% of the women. Twenty-one percent of the men and 33% of the women were infrequent, light drinkers; 18% of both men and women were moderate drinkers. Thirty-six percent of the men and 13% of the women were in the two heaviest drinking categories (frequent high maximum and frequent heavy drinking). Clearly, men in the general population are heavier drinkers than women, with over two-thirds of women either abstainers or light drinkers. However, women in the U.S. are less likely to be nondrinkers and more likely to be moderate or heavy drinkers than women in Latin American and Asian donor countries other than Japan.

As we have seen, recent immigrants to the United States come largely from countries where men are moderate (China, Vietnam) or moderate to heavy (Japan, Korea, Mexico) drinkers, and women are primarily abstainers or very light, infrequent drinkers. In general, men from other countries do not have to change their drinking habits much to match the drinking habits of men in the United States. Japanese men appear to shift somewhat toward more abstention when they come to the U.S. (Kitano et al., 1988), and Mexican men appear to increase the frequency of the modal male Mexican pattern of less frequent/higher quantity per occasion drinking (Caetano & Medina-Mora, 1988). Women in immigrant groups, however, would have to abandon abstention in fairly great numbers and develop a higher prevalence of moderate to heavy drinking to match the drinking patterns of women in the general population. That is precisely what seems to be happening among those Asian and Latino groups for whom we have multigenerational data.

Comparisons of data from Japan and from U.S. studies of Japanese-Americans (Kitano et al., 1988) show that abstention among women drops from a high of 45% in Japan to about 26% among Japanese-American women. Light to moderate drinking increases from 20% among women in Japan to 27% among Japanese-American women in Santa Clara and 45% among their counterparts in Los Angeles.

In studies of Mexican-American women, it is easy to trace progressive changes in drinking practices toward greater conformity with the larger society, when samples are analyzed by generation (Gilbert, 1989; Holck et al., 1984) or when acculturation is measured by an acculturation index (Caetano, 1987; Caetano and Medina-Mora, 1988). Most Mexican women who migrate to the U.S. do not change their abstemious patterns to any great degree; in fact, they are more likely to be abstainers than the women they left behind in Mexico. However, their daughters born in the U.S. and their granddaughters are increasingly less likely to be abstainers and increasingly more likely to be light to moderate drinkers. By the third generation, Mexican-American women's patterns are quite similar to those of women in the general population, including a sizable proportion of heavier drinkers. For example, Caetano and Medina-Mora (1988) report heavier drinking women among 4% of immigrant women, 7% of the first U.S.-born generation, and 32% of women in later generations. Gilbert (1987) documents a similar though less dramatic change from 3% heavy drinkers among immigrant women to 12% in later generations. These changes are positively linked to income and education in a much clearer way than they are for Mexican-American men.

Changes in drinking practices appear to be accompanied by changes in drinking norms, reasons for drinking, and alcohol expectancies. Caetano and Medina-Mora (1988) report that among the Mexican-American women they studied, acculturation was positively correlated with more liberal age and sex norms for drinking. Cervantes and colleagues (1990–91) found that U.S.-born Latinas, compared with those born outside the U.S., had significantly higher expectations that alcohol consumption would aid in social assertiveness, social enjoyment, mood elevation, and tension reduction. The same study found that while immigrant women were much less likely to expect benefits from drinking than their male counterparts, U.S.-born women and men were very similar in the rather high expectations they had about the benefits of alcohol consumption.

A recent study of Mexican-American women (Gilbert, 1991; Gilbert et al., 1994) investigated drinking in a Los Angeles sample stratified into professionals (101), blue-collar workers (92), and homemakers (76). As in other studies (Holck et al., 1984), being professional, being U.S.-born, having higher incomes and educations, and being more acculturated (as measured by an acculturation index) were intercorrelated. Women in the more acculturated professional group used alcohol more frequently and in greater quantities per occasion than blue-collar or homemaking women. The more acculturated professional women also reported significantly higher levels of positive expectations about the benefits of alcohol use, particularly higher expectations of enhanced social pleasure and social assertiveness, as measured by the Alcohol Expectancy Scale (Brown et al., 1987).

The three groups of women were also asked about their participation in 31 types of social events during the prior 30 days, and whether they had consumed alcohol at these events. Women in all three groups attended about the same number of events (mean = 13), but professional women attended many more types of events than nonprofessional women. Nonprofessional women participated primarily in family-based events, while professional women participated in both family-based social events *and* numerous work and civic activities. Professional women consumed alcohol at 43% of the events they attended, but women in the other two groups had alcohol at only 10% of their social events. Almost all of the events attended by nonprofessional women included an even mix of Latino men and women; for professional women, on the other hand, social events tended to be ethnically mixed and included predominantly female and predominantly male occasions (20% of each) as well as mixed-gender events (60%). Professionals reported observing intoxicated persons at one-fourth of the social events they attended; blue-collar women and homemakers saw intoxication at only one in 10 events.

From these data, it appears that as Mexican-American women enter the workforce at higher occupational levels, there is a change in the social context for drinking. There are more frequent and varied opportunities to consume alcohol, and a shift in drinking reference groups from predominantly Latino to more ethnically mixed. Drinking among professional women is more public and is something they do with each other as well as with men. Such changes suggest an increase in actual and normative accessibility of alcohol similar to that found among employed as opposed to unemployed women in the larger population (Parker et al., 1980). However, among these Mexican-American women, the shift to greater accessibility does not seem to occur just with workforce entry but with entry into professional work and its increased contact with people and lifestyles of the larger society. The findings of this study indicate that acculturative changes affecting alcohol use occur at both the behavioral and cognitive levels. Whether similar processes are at work among other immigrant groups remains an issue to be explored in future research.

Conclusions and a Suggested Research Agenda

This overview of research on the predominant non-European ethnic groups in the United States gives just a glimpse of the complexity of gender-related drinking patterns, attitudes, and changes across and within ethnic groups. Although there are some common patterns across groups, such as stronger sanctions against women's drinking than against men's, and lower levels of consumption and alcohol-related problems among women, there are also many unexplained differences. Sources of heterogeneity within groups include education and socioeconomic status, age, religiosity, and level of acculturation. These influences operate inconsistently across and within groups. For example, although income is not an important predictor of drinking overall, in some groups income is related to heavy drinking (Filipino men, some Native Americans, Mexican-American women, and African-American men and women), but not necessarily in the same way. Educational level appears to be positively associated with drinking among women, but not necessarily associated with heavy drinking, and it has much less influence on drinking habits of men.

Drinking among men and women diminishes with aging, and people in all groups studied drink relatively little in their sixties. However, the rate of reduction in consumption between ages 20 and 60 varies considerably across groups. Changes in drinking patterns and attitudes accompany immigration and acculturation, but the pattern of changes appears to vary by ethnicity and gender, and is highly dependent on the interactions of practices from the culture of national origin and the U.S. majority culture. Clearly, drinking behavior in each ethnic group is influenced by historical factors (e.g., colonization, immigration, and acculturation) and by sociocultural variables (e.g., social norms and values, and economic resources). Just how these and other variables interact to produce specific patterns of alcohol use is not well understood, and little theory exists to guide research. Given the dearth of theory, the following suggestions are offered for future research.

Research on U.S. alcohol use and abuse has often included comparisons between European-Americans (as the numerical and cultural majority) and other, numerically smaller non-European ethnic groups. The utility of such comparisons has been limited, because they often rely on the untested assumption that each of the compared groups is internally homogeneous. These are erroneous assumptions, since differences within ethnic categories or groups are often as large or larger than the differences between them. Most importantly, research that shows comparisons between ethnic groups rarely provide explanations for the differences seen within groups (Collins, in press; Heath, 1990–91). In research agendas for future studies of gender issues in ethnic alcohol research, an important question is whether to focus on within-group differences or on between-group comparisons. The focus should depend on the purpose for which the research is undertaken.

Much alcohol-related research is applied research. It is funded because excessive use of alcohol is seen as unhealthy and a contributor to a variety of social ills. The research is undertaken with the hope that the data obtained can be used to set policy, allocate resources, or inform the design of prevention and treatment interventions. Most of such practical applications of research data occur within specific regions, localities, or communities. For these purposes, research attention to local drinking patterns and to micronorms among people who wear the same ethnic label (e.g., Cuban-Americans, Mexican-Americans, or Puerto Ricans) would be far more useful than generalized comparisons across broad ethnic categories. For example, in allocating resources and designing services for the large Mexican-American population in Los Angeles, it is very helpful to know that (1) the men are much more likely to have alcohol dependence problems than the women, and (2) Mexican-American women of higher socioeconomic status are more likely to have alcohol-related problems than their lower income sisters.

To answer broader theoretical questions of how alcohol use is (or is not) related to gender, rigorous comparisons between ethnic groups can shed a great deal of light. Such research can help distinguish what are universal processes in all groups and what are group-specific phenomena (Betancourt & Lopez, 1993; Rogler, 1989). To date, little theory-driven research has been designed to identify specific cultural features that influence drinking patterns among men and women. Instead, as in many of the studies discussed here, the drinking patterns of men and women in different ethnic groups are compared, sometimes controlling for demographic and socioeconomic factors, and residual differences are attributed to "culture," often with some reference to hypothesized variation in an unmeasured subjective cultural norm or value believed to be characteristic of the ethnic groups.

To improve such comparative research, investigators need to construct theoretical frameworks that not only take into account social-structural variables, but also specify and measure gender-related cultural elements believed to influence drinking behavior. Elements such as sex role norms and gender-related affective and interactional styles could be operationalized and tested for their relationships to drinking practices within and across groups.

For example, there is considerable ethnographic data to indicate that greater gender differences in drinking levels and styles occur in cultural groups whose social activities are often sex-segregated, such as in Korea, Japan, and Mexico. In these nations, men and women do most of their socializing in same-sex groups, with men tending to drink large quantities and women tending to abstain from alcohol. In such societies alcohol use symbolizes or is embedded in highly differentiated role configurations for men and women, configurations that also include wider public and economic roles for men than for women, and greater access for men to social power and economic resources. After coming to the U.S., where sex roles are becoming less differentiated and women have greater access to educational and economic resources, women from such societies begin to take on more visible public roles, and their social and normative access to alcohol increases. This is clearly what has happened among Mexican-Americans, and may also be the reason why Japanese women increase their alcohol use across American-born generations. This general pattern deserves further study in cross-cultural research.

Methodological critiques of research on ethnic differences in substance use (e.g., Collins, 1992, 1993) have outlined the limitations of research to date and have recommended improvements. The recommendations would include (1) studying variables that are sources of heterogeneity within groups; (2) developing culturally sensitive measures relevant to the populations being studied; (3) using multimethod assessment and/or observational methods for validating self-reports; and (4) using ethnographic methods to gain more in-depth understanding of drinking behavior and contexts in various groups. Alcohol researchers need to avoid preconceptions about the ethnic groups they plan to study, and they need to learn more about the historical and social contexts in which each ethnic group and its patterns of gender differentiation exist. Also, research on ethnicity and drinking needs to modify its sometimes narrow focus on the negative effects of alcohol use, such as mortality, morbidity, and social problems. In many ethnic groups alcohol use is an integral part of culturally important activities, and much of the social use of alcohol does not produce untoward consequences. Only by studying and understanding such normative drinking, as well as the more costly patterns of alcohol use, will it be possible to understand how ethnicity and gender interact to influence men's and women's drinking.

References

Barr, K.E.M., Farrell, M.P., Barnes, G.M., & Welte, J.W. (1993). Race, class, and gender differences in substance abuse: Evidence of middle-class/underclass polarization among black males. *Social Problems, 40,* 314-327.

Betancourt, H., & Lopez, S.R. (1993). The study of culture, ethnicity, and race in American psychology. *American Psychologist, 48,* 629-637.

Brown, S.A., Christiansen, B.A., & Goldman, M.S. (1987). The Alcohol Expectancy Questionnaire: An instrument for the assessment of adolescent and adult alcohol expectancies. *Journal of Studies on Alcohol, 48,* 483-491.

Burnam, M.A. (1989). Prevalence of alcohol abuse and dependence among Mexican Americans and non-Hispanic whites in the community. In D. Spiegler, D. Tate, S. Aitken, & C. Christian (Eds.), *Alcohol use among U.S. ethnic minorities* (DHHS Publication No. ADM 89-1435). Washington, DC: U.S. Government Printing Office.

Caetano, R. (1987). Acculturation and drinking patterns among U.S. Hispanics. *British Journal of Addiction, 82,* 789-799.

Caetano, R. (1988a). Alcohol use among Hispanic groups in the United States. *American Journal of Drug and Alcohol Abuse, 14,* 293-308.

Caetano, R. (1988b). Alcohol use among Mexican Americans and in the U.S. population. In M.J. Gilbert (Ed.), *Alcohol consumption among Mexicans and Mexican Americans: A binational perspective* (pp. 53-84). Los Angeles: Spanish Speaking Mental Health Research Center, University of California.

Caetano, R. (1993, June 19-24). Longitudinal changes in drinking patterns among whites, blacks, and Hispanics, 1984-1992. Presented at the annual meeting of the Research Society on Alcoholism, San Antonio, Texas.

Caetano, R., & Herd, D. (1984). Black drinking practices in northern California. *American Journal of Drug and Alcohol Abuse, 10,* 571-587.

Caetano, R., & Medina-Mora, M.E. (1988). Acculturation and drinking among people of Mexican descent in Mexico and the United States. *Journal of Studies on Alcohol, 49,* 462-471.

Cahalan, D., Cisin, I.H., & Crossley, H.M. (1969). *American drinking practices: A national study of drinking behavior and attitudes.* New Brunswick, NJ: Rutgers Center of Alcohol Studies.

Canino, G.J., Bird, H., Rubio, M., Geil, K.P., Bravo, M., & Shrout, P. (1989). Prevalence of alcohol abuse and dependence in Puerto Rico. In D. Spiegler, D. Tate, S. Aitken, & C. Christian (Eds.), *Alcohol use among U.S. ethnic minorities* (DHHS Publication No. ADM 89-1435). Washington, DC: U.S. Government Printing Office.

Cervantes, R.C., Gilbert, M.J., Salgado de Snyder, N., & Padilla, A.M. (1990-91). Psychosocial and cognitive correlates of alcohol use in younger adult immigrant and U.S.-born Hispanics. *International Journal of the Addictions, 25,* 687-708.

Chi, I., Lubben, J.E., & Kitano, H.H.L. (1989). Differences in drinking behavior among three Asian-American groups. *Journal of Studies on Alcohol, 50,* 15-23.

Collins, R.L. (1992). Methodological issues in conducting substance abuse research on ethnic minority populations. *Drugs & Society, 6,* 59-77.

Collins, R.L. (1993). Women's issues in alcohol use and cigarette smoking. In J.S. Baer, G.A. Marlatt, & R.J. McMahon (Eds.), *Addictive behaviors across the lifespan: Prevention, treatment, and policy issues.* Newbury Park, CA: Sage.

Collins, R.L. (in press). Issues of ethnicity in research on the prevention of substance abuse. In G.J. Botvin, S. Schinke, & M. Orlandi (Eds.), *Drug abuse prevention with multi-ethnic youth.* Newbury Park, CA: Sage.

Connors, G.J., Maisto, S.A., & Watson, D.W. (1988). Racial factors influencing college students' ratings of alcohol's usefulness. *Drug and Alcohol Dependence, 21,* 247-252.

Gilbert, M.J. (1987). Alcohol consumption patterns in immigrant and later generation Mexican American women. *Hispanic Journal of the Behavioral Sciences, 9,* 299-313.

Gilbert, M.J. (1989). Alcohol-related practices, problems, and norms among Mexican Americans: An overview. In D.L. Spiegler, D.A. Tate, S.S. Aitken, & C.M. Christian (Eds.), *Alcohol use among U.S. ethnic minorities* (pp. 115-134) (NIAAA Monograph No. 18; DHHS Publication No. ADM 89-1435). Washington, DC: U.S. Government Printing Office.

Gilbert, M.J. (1991). Acculturation and changes in drinking patterns among Mexican-American women: Implications for prevention. *Alcohol Health & Research World, 15,* 234-238.

Gilbert, M.J., Mora, J., & Ferguson, L.R. (1994). Alcohol expectations among Mexican American women. *International Journal of the Addictions, 29,* 1127-1147.

Gonzalez, E. (1983). *Magnitud y patrones de consumo de alcohol en Puerto Rico.* San Juan: Estado Libre Asociado de Puerto Rico, Departamento de Servicos Contra la Adiccion, Secretaria Auxiliar del Instituto y Servicios Especiales.

Greeley, A.M., McCready, W.C., & Theisen, G. (1980). *Ethnic drinking subcultures.* Brooklyn, NY: J.F. Bergin Publishers.

Heath, D.B. (1990-91). Uses and misuses of the concept of ethnicity in alcohol studies: An essay in deconstruction. *International Journal of the Addictions, 25,* 607-628.

Helzer, J.E., Canino, G.J., Yeh, E.-K., Bland, R.C., Lee, C.K., Hwu, H.-G., & Newman, S. (1990). Alcoholism—North America and Asia: A comparison of population surveys with the Diagnostic Interview Schedule. *Archives of General Psychiatry, 47,* 313-319.

Herd, D. (1985). Ambiguity in black drinking norms: An ethnohistorical interpretation. In L.A. Bennett & G.M. Ames (Eds.), *The American experience with alcohol: Contrasting cultural perspectives.* New York: Plenum.

Herd, D. (1988). Drinking by black and white women: Results from a national survey. *Social Problems, 35,* 493-505.

Herd, D. (1989). The epidemiology of drinking patterns and alcohol-related problems among U.S. blacks. In D. Spiegler, D. Tate, S. Aitken, & C. Christian (Eds.), *Alcohol use among U.S. ethnic minorities* (pp. 3-50) (DHHS Publication No ADM 89-1435). Washington, DC: U.S. Government Printing Office.

Herd, D. (1990). Subgroup differences in drinking patterns among black and white men: Results from a national survey. *Journal of Studies on Alcohol, 51,* 221-232.

Herd, D. (1994). Predicting drinking problems among black and white men: Results from a national survey. *Journal of Studies on Alcohol, 55,* 61-71.

Hilton, M.E. (1987). Drinking patterns and drinking problems in 1984: Results from a general population survey. *Alcoholism: Clinical and Experimental Research, 11,* 167-175.

Holck, S.E., Warren, C.W., Smith, J.C., & Rochat, R.W. (1984). Alcohol consumption among Mexican American and Anglo women: Results of a survey along the U.S.-Mexico border. *Journal of Studies on Alcohol, 45,* 149-154.

Johnson, R.C., Nagoshi, C.T., Danko, G.P., Honbo, K.A.M., & Chau, L.L. (1990). Familial transmission of alcohol use norms and expectancies and reported alcohol use. *Alcoholism: Clinical and Experimental Research, 14,* 216-220.

Kitano, H.H.L., & Chi, I. (1986-87). Asian Americans and alcohol use: Exploring cultural differences in Los Angeles. *Alcohol Health & Research World, 11,* 42-47.

Kitano, H.H.L., Lubben, J.E., & Chi, I. (1988). Predicting Japanese American drinking behavior. *International Journal of the Addictions, 23,* 417-428.

Kitano, H.H.L, Chi, I., Rhee, S., Law, C.K., & Lubben, J.E. (1992). Norms and alcohol consumption: Japanese in Japan, Hawaii and California. *Journal of Studies on Alcohol, 53,* 33-39.

Leland, J. (1984). Alcohol use and abuse in ethnic minority women: "Different strokes for different folks." In S.C. Wilsnack & L.J. Beckman (Eds.), *Alcohol problems in women: Antecedents, consequences, and intervention* (pp. 66-96). New York: Guilford.

Lubben, J.E., Chi, I., & Kitano, H.H.L. (1988). Exploring Filipino American drinking behavior. *Journal of Studies on Alcohol, 49,* 26-29.

Lubben, J.E., Chi, I., & Kitano, H.H.L. (1989). The relative influence of selected social factors on Korean drinking behavior in Los Angeles. *Advances in Alcohol and Substance Abuse, 8,* 1-17.

May, P.A. (1989). Alcohol abuse and alcoholism among American Indians: An overview. In T.D. Watts and R. Wright, Jr. (Eds.), *Alcoholism in minority populations* (pp. 95-119). Springfield, IL: Charles C Thomas.

May, P.A. (1991). Fetal alcohol effects among North American Indians: Evidence and implications for society. *Alcohol Health & Research World, 15,* 239-248.

May, P.A., & Smith, M.B. (1988). Some Navajo Indian opinions about alcohol abuse and prohibition: A survey and recommendations for policy. *Journal of Studies on Alcohol, 49,* 324-334.

Medina-Mora, M.E., Rascon, M.L., Otero, B.R., & Gutierrez, E. (1988). Patrones de consumo de alcohol de Mexico. In M.J. Gilbert (Ed.), *Alcohol consumption among Mexicans and Mexican Americans: A binational perspective* (pp. 27-52). Los Angeles: Spanish Speaking Mental Health Research Center, University of California.

National Institute on Alcohol Abuse and Alcoholism (NIAAA). (1990). *Seventh special report to the U.S. Congress on alcohol and health* (DHHS Publication No. ADM 90-1656). Washington, DC: U.S. Government Printing Office.

Padilla, A.M., Sung, H., & Nam, T.V. (1993). Attitudes toward alcohol and drinking practices in two Vietnamese samples in Santa Clara County. *Horizons of Vietnamese Thought and Expression, 2,* 53-71.

Parker, D.A., Parker, E.S., Wolz, M.W., & Harford, T.C. (1980). Sex roles and alcohol consumption: A research note. *Journal of Health and Social Behavior, 21,* 43-48.

Parrish, K.M., Higuchi, S., Stinson, F.S., Dufour, M.C., Towle, L.H., & Harford, T.C. (1990). Genetic or cultural determinants of drinking: A study of embarrassment at facial flushing among Japanese and Japanese-Americans. *Journal of Substance Abuse, 2,* 439-447.

Parrish, K.M., Higuchi, S., Stinson, F.S., Towle, L.H., Dufour, M.C., & Harford, T.C. (1992). The association of drinking levels and drinking attitudes among Japanese in Japan and Japanese-Americans in Hawaii and California. *Journal of Substance Abuse, 4,* 165-177.

Regier, D.A., Merse, J.K., Kramer, M., Robins, L.N., Blazer, D.G., Hough, R.L., Eaton, W.W., & Locke, B.Z. (1984). The NIMH Epidemiologic Catchment Area Program. *Archives of General Psychiatry, 41,* 934-941.

Robins, L.N. (1989). Alcohol abuse in blacks and whites as indicated in the Epidemiological Catchment Area Program. In D.L. Spiegler, D.A. Tate, S.S. Aitken, & C.M.

Christian (Eds.), *Alcohol use among U.S. ethnic minorities* (pp. 63–73) (NIAAA Monograph No. 18; DHHS Publication No. ADM 89-1435). Washington, DC: U.S. Government Printing Office.

Rogler, L.N. (1989). The meaning of culturally sensitive research in mental health. *American Journal of Psychiatry, 146,* 296–303.

Towle, L.H. (1988). Japanese-American drinking: Some results from the joint Japanese—U.S. alcohol epidemiology project. *Alcohol Health & Research World, 12,* 216–223.

Trimble, J.E. (1990–91). Ethnic specification, validation prospects, and the future of drug use research. *International Journal of the Addictions, 25,* 149–170.

Tsunoda, T., Parrish, K.M., Higuchi, S., Stinson, F.S., Kono, H., Ogata, M., & Harford, T.C. (1992). The effect of acculturation on drinking attitudes among Japanese in Japan and Japanese Americans in Hawaii and California. *Journal of Studies on Alcohol, 53,* 369–377.

Walker, R.D., & Kivlahan, D.R. (1984). Definitions, models, and methods in research on sociocultural factors in American Indian alcohol use. *Substance and Alcohol Actions/Misuse, 5,* 9–19.

Weibel-Orlando, J.C. (1989). Pass the bottle, bro!: A comparison of urban and rural Indian drinking patterns. In D. Spiegler, D. Tate, S. Aitken, & C. Christian (Eds.), *Alcohol use among U.S. ethnic minorities* (pp. 269–289) (DHHS Publication No. ADM 89-1435). Washington, DC: U.S. Government Printing Office.

Weisner, T.S., Weibel-Orlando, J.C., & Long, J. (1984). "Serious drinking," "White man's drinking" and "tetotaling": Drinking levels and styles in an urban American Indian population. *Journal of Studies on Alcohol, 45,* 237–250.

Yamamoto, J., Yeh, E.-K., Lee, C.-K., & Lin, K.-M. (1988). Alcohol abuse among Koreans and Japanese. In L.H. Towle & T.C. Harford (Eds.), *Cultural influences and drinking patterns: A focus on Hispanic and Japanese populations* (pp. 135–175) (NIAAA Research Monograph No. 19; DHHS Publication No. ADM 88-1563). Washington, DC: U.S. Government Printing Office.

CHAPTER 15

Employment and Drinking

TERRY C. BLUM AND PAUL M. ROMAN

The interrelations among gender, work, and drinking behavior are compelling targets for the development of social theory. Each of these concepts is at "center stage" in contemporary social science, and in evaluations of social policy development and impact. Each of the linkages among these three concepts suggests potential insights of substantial significance.

Theoretical ideas may be initially organized around bivariate relationships: relationships between gender and work, between gender and drinking, and between work and drinking. Given that gender is an ascribed characteristic, only work and drinking behavior can be dependent variables in explanatory models, but all three may serve as independent variables. The range of theoretical questions about these three concepts includes: (1) the impact of gender on the characteristics of work statuses and roles, (2) the impact of gender on patterns of drinking behavior, (3) the impact of work characteristics on drinking behavior, and (4) the impact of drinking behavior on work behaviors, performance, opportunities, and careers.

Data on Gender, Work, and Drinking Relationships

The research literature provides robust findings about the first two relationships. There is a massive literature on the variations in work roles and characteristics associated with gender in the United States (see, for example, England & Farkas, 1986; Reskin & Roos, 1990). This literature reflects the complex variety of forces involved in (1) women's recent large-scale entry into the labor force, (2) public and private social policies that inhibit or enhance such labor force participation, and (3) the generalized status and perception of women as minority group members within the labor force.

A substantial amount of research supports the conclusion that women are subordinated in the workplace. Relative to men, women occupy lower status jobs, have less stable employment, tend to receive lower pay than men for similar work, are limited in their promotional and upward mobility opportunities in the workplace, and are the targets (and victims) of an amorphous set of cultural features of workplaces that support generalized gender discrimination and sexual harassment (Bielby & Baron, 1986; Jacobs, 1992). Women do monopolize a relatively small and limited set of occupations and semi-professions, but top echelon positions in these occupations are often dominated by men (Powell, 1988).

There is also consistency across datasets in the relationships between gender and drinking behavior. Compared with men, women in the U.S. are more frequently abstainers and drink less when they are drinkers (Clark & Hilton, 1991). Furthermore, women are less likely to be problem drinkers, whether problem drinking is defined by alcohol dependence, frequency and quantity of consumption, violation of legal statutes, documented job performance decrements, or generalized role impairments (Harford et al., 1992; Hilton, 1988; Parker & Harford, 1992; Shore, 1992). On the other hand, a smaller body of literature suggests (with somewhat less consistency) that women are more likely to be afflicted by a range of social and psychological problems when they enter treatment for chemical dependency (Roman, 1988).

The work-drinking connection is much less developed in the research literature. The vast majority of relevant studies have hypothesized that features of work are independent variables affecting drinking behavior (e.g., Martin, 1990; Sonnenstuhl & Trice, 1990). The findings in these studies are equivocal, sometimes showing no relationships between the two sets of variables, and otherwise indicating statistically significant but very modest associations when multivariate analyses are employed to isolate the impacts on drinking from a variety of "work stressors" (Martin, 1990).

The idea that work experiences influence women's drinking patterns and problems needs further exploration, because the patterns of influence are unclear in research thus far. Among employed women, Parker and Harford (1992) found that women in higher status occupations (managerial and professional) had a higher prevalence of drinking but not of alcohol dependence. Some research on employee assistance programs (EAPs) indicates that women with alcohol problems are greatly underrepresented (Young et al., 1987), but other data indicate that women with alcohol-related problems are adequately represented in EAPs, if one standardizes for gender differences in alcohol problem prevalence as well as workplace representation of women in the organizations that provide EAPs (Blum & Bennett, 1990). Shore (1992) suggests that employment may influence women's drinking through the gender composition of the workplace and work-related access to alcohol, rather than through the work-related stress focused on in past studies.

However, any fruitful research on such issues will require more complex theories and models (Wilsnack & Wilsnack, 1992), and large longitudinal surveys that oversample women with alcohol-related problems. A problem that faces many analyses of women, work, and drinking is an inadequate number of cases to yield adequate statistical power. This precludes adequate testing of hypotheses, even when datasets include appropriate measures of both objective and perceived work characteristics. Even in very large datasets, the cell sizes tend to be inadequate for analyses powerful enough to detect significant relationships between women's drinking and work. While primary data collection can insure adequate statistical power, the widespread use of secondary datasets often leads, albeit reluctantly, to testing hypotheses on exclusively male samples (Martin et al., 1992).

Investigation of the impact of drinking on work roles and careers has been minimal. This lacuna persists despite consistent findings of higher rates of drinking and problem drinking among unemployed and marginally employed persons in the U.S. (Clark & Hilton, 1991). Furthermore, the clinical literature is full of descriptions of the downward mobility and career deterioration experienced by chronic alcoholics (cf., Mullahy & Sindelar, 1989). Contentions that drinking has such impacts on work serve in large part as the foundation for employee assistance programs, which are targeted at the early identification of workplace alcohol problems, with the goal of employment conservation (Sonnenstuhl & Trice, 1986; Trice & Roman, 1978). Nonetheless, there is little survey research that links drinking behavior with work outcomes across time in representative samples of employed people.

One secondary analysis, limited to men because of inadequate numbers of employed women in the sample, found that the association between alcohol consumption and job performance depended on whether the drinker or his significant others in the workplace reported about his job performance (Blum et al., 1993). Levels of alcohol consumption were unrelated to the employee's self-reports about performance at work. However, co-worker reports about this same individual's work performance revealed an overall negative relationship between levels of alcohol consumption and technical aspects of performance, in addition to negative effects of alcohol consumption on self-direction at work, conflict avoidance at work, and interpersonal relations at work. Research has generally found an association between alcohol-related problems and absenteeism, and that alcoholic employees receive lower supervisory ratings on job performance. However, in studies of on-the-job accidents and turnover, associations with employee alcohol problems have been less consistent (cf., Blum et al., 1993b).

Ideological Underpinnings

While offering rich theoretical opportunities, the three-way relationships among gender, work, and drinking carry a significant load of ideological baggage. For example, the pattern of greater abstinence and lighter drinking among women than among men, and the norms that support this pattern, are imbedded in traditional concepts of gender inequality. The image of women as appropriately abstaining or drinking lightly has a subtle pre-feminist or even anti-feminist bias. In this Victorian and early 20th-century image, it is not

women's "place" to drink, especially to drink heavily. Frequently women's sobriety was essential to support and defend the family against the chronically
heavy drinking or occasionally drunk husband or father. It is not without
irony that women's leadership of the Temperance Movement in the U.S. simultaneously supported this characterization of women's avoidance of alcohol while providing women with fundamental training in political and
organizational leadership.

The linkage of women's abstinence or light drinking to traditional differences between women's and men's roles leads to a rather simple hypothesis:
as gender equality increases, the gender gap in drinking should diminish.
Such an hypothesis is easily linked with women's growing participation in
the workforce, leading to the notion that as women and men achieve parity
in work and family roles, such parity will be matched by similarity in drinking behavior.

This hypothesis has negative implications because of a statistical association. The greater the amount and regularity of alcohol consumption in a population or social segment, the greater the prevalence of drinking-related
problems and consequences in the population or segment. Although this is
by no means a perfect correlation, it suggests that "drinking equality" for
women entails substantial personal and social costs.

The belief that drinking equality between the genders has been enhanced
in recent decades has also reinforced the idea that because of social inequality, there are significant numbers of "hidden alcoholics" among women, both
employed and not employed (Sandmeier, 1980). The minimal or delayed effort to help these "hidden" individuals is viewed as evidence of gender inequality and discrimination. This logic is supported by the lower rates of
women in alcoholism treatment, taken as evidence of bias in diagnostic, referral, and treatment intake processes. Such reasoning in the mid-1970s led
to specific efforts by the National Institute on Alcohol Abuse and Alcoholism
(NIAAA) to fund demonstration projects that provided special alcohol programs for employed women, on the assumption that the programs in place
were designed and implemented for men and thus were inappropriate for
women (Reichman et al., 1988).

Finally, what might be seen as a disproportionate emphasis on drinking as
a consequence rather than as a cause of work experiences has a distinct ideological emphasis. Sociologists have long been attracted to Marxist and neo-
Marxist orientations in conceptualizing the organization of work in American
society, with employees viewed as exploited and/or coopted victims of the
owners of capital. In this framework, drinking is seen as a way to cope with
the stresses and strains produced by work-based forces that exploit the
worker. Drinking may also be seen as a means of ignoring the realities of the
essentially negative relationship between employer and employee. Although
rarely stated, the broad underlying vision is that the availability of alcohol

through legal channels, as a means for psychological escapism and coping, ultimately helps to preserve the socioeconomic status quo. The drinking behavior of victimized women employees fits neatly into this hypothetical schema. With this orientation dominant in sociology, the opposite vision of workers becoming victimized by their own drinking behavior is likely to be neglected.

Thus, interpretation of the three-way relationships among gender, work, and drinking has been based as much or more on ideology as on data. In this chapter we attempt to shed some new light on these linkages through examination of two new datasets.

The Data

This chapter examines two datasets. One dataset is from a U.S. national sample of 3,001 men and women who were employed full time, working in only one job, and employed by others (i.e., not self-employed). Data were collected initially during the summer of 1991, and 60% of the respondents were re-interviewed during the summer of 1992. The data include information about respondent demographics, drinking behavior, and work characteristics.

The second dataset includes information collected from 6,400 clients of employee assistance programs. Over 80 EAPs participated in the data collection between 1990 and 1992 (Blum & Roman, 1992). In addition to the data collected from the EAP clients themselves, EAP coordinators also provided information about each client. The dataset includes information about client demographics, relationships at work, work characteristics, work performance outcomes, and routes of referral to the EAPs. In addition, alcohol-related problems were measured through a self-administered questionnaire, the Alcohol Dependence Scale (ADS; Horn et al., 1985). Depressive symptoms were measured through the self-administered short form of the Beck Depression Inventory (BDI; Beck & Beck, 1972).

The National Employment Survey (NES)

This relatively large dataset was collected by the present authors to deal with a broad range of questions about alcohol-work interfaces. The survey revealed the difficulty of obtaining a sample of employed women drinkers that includes enough problem drinkers to allow gender-specific analyses of problem drinking, as assessed by scores of 2 or more on the CAGE (Ewing, 1984). While it is clearly possible to analyze women's drinking patterns within this dataset, it is more difficult to analyze problem drinking because this was relatively rare among working women in contrast to working men. The women were 0.33 times as likely as men to score 2 or higher on the CAGE, when occupational type and occupational gender mix were held constant (Kraft et al., 1993).

Despite increasing paid employment of women, and increased drinking in some age groups of women (Fillmore, 1984; Wilsnack et al., 1984/85), overall patterns of women's alcohol use have changed little over the past several decades (Shore, 1992). However, women employees are less likely to be abstinent, and are likely to consume more alcohol and to drink more frequently, than women who are not employed outside the home (Parker et al., 1980; Shore, 1992), although employed women still consume less alcohol and have fewer alcohol-related problems than employed men.

At least three explanations have been offered for the apparent effects of employment on women's drinking behavior. These are (1) the effects of stressors on women in the labor force, (2) the effects of greater accessibility of alcohol for working women, and (3) the gender composition of occupations or work groups, which may expose women in different working environments to different drinking norms and opportunities (Shore, 1992). Our data do not allow us to compare women in full-time paid employment with homemakers or part-time employees, but the data do allow us to evaluate both women and men employed full time in a wide range of occupations and in diverse industrial settings.

Stress and Role Demands

Work stress and role conflict explanations did not appear to explain women's drinking patterns in our data. Variables indicative of job characteristics and job stress were not associated with women's problem drinking as measured by the CAGE or as indexed by reports of escapist rather than social reasons for drinking. Women's job characteristics and job stress were also not associated with the number of drinks women consumed per month, or with their frequencies of consuming three or more drinks or five or more drinks on one occasion. These findings are consistent with the results of other studies (Cooper et al., 1990; LaRosa, 1990; Mensch & Kandel, 1988; Parker et al., 1980; Shore, 1990).

There are some indications from other studies of men (see Martin et al., 1992) that job conditions might be part of more complex explanations of drinking. Some of these studies indicate that role overload is significantly related to perceptions about the use of alcohol to relax, which in turn is positively related to alcohol consumption. Lennon's (1987) analysis of employed men and women found a different pattern: in occupations with greater substantive complexity (how much an occupation requires skill, training, and an aptitude for intellectual, verbal, and mathematical tasks), women's average number of drinks per day increased slightly, but men drank less than in other jobs. However, the same study found also that the substantive complexity of an occupation was associated with increased psychological well-being in women but had no relationship to psychological well-being in men. Thus, more complex models (Wilsnack & Wilsnack, 1992) and/or more appropriate measures of job characteristics may be necessary to determine how work roles influence drinking patterns among women.

The need for more complex models is demonstrated by the different ways that combined work and family conditions were associated with employee drinking behavior in the NES (Kraft et al., 1994). Different work and family variables predicted drinking patterns of single women, married women, and married men. For example, combined demands at work and at home (indicated by the presence of children) were positively associated with the average number of drinks per month only among single women. Most job and family variables were not associated with drinks per month for married women or for married men. However, more drinks per month were reported by those married men who contributed half or less of their family's income (and by those single women who received some household support from others). Married women's contributions to household income were unrelated to their average alcohol consumption.

The complexity of job and family influences was also illustrated by subgroup differences in what predicted drinking for escapist reasons (drinking to relax after work, to relieve tensions from the job, or to forget about problems at work). Among single women, job demands were associated with reporting escapist reasons for drinking. Among married women, escapist drinking was associated with work-family conflict, but also with greater autonomy or decision latitude on the job. Among married men, escapist drinking was associated with having no children at home.

Apparently, understanding how combinations of work, family, and gender affect drinking behavior will require more complex theories, datasets, and data analyses than are presently available. However, the findings summarized here suggest that it may be premature to conclude that employee substance use results from characteristics of the workforce rather than from work conditions (cf., Mensch & Kandel, 1988). The effort to decipher the relationships of work (and family) roles with drinking could have an important benefit: it will be easier to prevent drinking problems among employed women and men if there are contributing factors (such as work roles and conditions) that can be changed more readily than personal attributes can.

It is possible that the stresses, complexities, and demands of work roles cannot adequately or consistently explain differences in drinking patterns between women who are employed outside the home and those who are not. As an alternative explanation, could drinking patterns among working women result from opportunities to drink with co-workers, and from drinking norms in occupations or workgroups related to their gender composition?

A review of the NES data (Kraft et al., 1993) found patterns consistent with this alternative hypothesis.

When we analyzed all employees (men and women combined), those in male-dominated occupations (>80% male) had 1.4 times as many opportunities to drink with their co-workers as those in female-dominated occupations (>80% female), and 1.2 times as many opportunities to drink with co-workers as those in mixed gender occupations (20–80% female). Women were less likely than men to have opportunities to drink with co-workers, but even when independent effects of gender and occupational type were controlled for, male-dominated occupations had a large positive effect on such drinking opportunities. However, when men and women were analyzed separately (in effect, examining interaction effects), the gender mix of occupations affected only women, with women having more opportunities to drink with co-workers if they worked in mixed gender occupations (1.3 times more opportunities) or in male-dominated occupations (2 times more opportunities) than if they worked in female-dominated occupations. Also, women in white-collar occupations had more of such drinking opportunities (2.3 times more) than those in service occupations. These data indicate that drinking opportunities were related to occupational situations as we might expect. However, neither gender nor the gender mix of occupations was related to *actual* drinking with co-workers, among all employees, women only, or men only.

An analysis of whether the respondent abstained from alcohol revealed patterns different from those associated with opportunities to drink with co-workers. When only gender mix was used as a predictor, employees in mixed-gender occupations were more likely to drink than those in female-dominated occupations, but rates of abstinence in male-dominated and female-dominated occupations did not differ significantly. When gender was controlled for, women were more likely to be abstainers (1.3×), and employees were more likely to drink in mixed-gender (1.4×) and in male-dominated (1.5×) occupations than in female-dominated occupations. When frequency of access to alcohol in social situations was controlled for, effects of gender and male-dominated occupations on abstinence disappeared. Gender composition of occupations did not predict abstinence among men, and only the comparison of mixed-gender occupations with female-dominated occupations significantly differentiated rates of abstinence among women. Among both men and women, those in white-collar occupations were more likely to drink than those in service occupations.

In other analyses, where drinks per month was the dependent variable, we found a large gender effect, with men consuming more alcohol on average. However, gender composition of occupations was not related to drinks consumed per month in the total sample, among the men, or among the women. Both men and women consumed more drinks per month if they said that alcohol was served more than half the time when they socialized with co-workers.

Research by others has shown that models to explain average alcohol consumption differ from models to explain problem drinking (e.g., Wilsnack et al., 1986). Therefore, we examined effects of gender, gender composition of occupation, opportunities to drink with co-workers, and average drinks per month on two indicators of potential problem drinking. One indicator of problem drinking was self-reported drinking to escape from the effects of one's job. Such drinking was not related to gender, nor was it related to the gender mix of respondents' occupations. Significant predictors of escapist drinking were the amount of alcohol an employee consumed per month, and whether alcohol was supplied when the employee socialized with co-workers. The more that employees drank, and the more opportunities they had to drink with co-workers, the more that employees drank to escape. This pattern held for men and for women, with the effects on escapist drinking being significantly greater for women than for men.

Another indicator of problem drinking was a "yes" answer to two or more of the four items in the CAGE screener for alcoholism (Ewing, 1984; Smart et al., 1991). Women were generally less likely to have CAGE scores indicating problem drinking. High scores on the CAGE were positively associated with the frequency with which alcohol was served when co-workers socialized, and with the number of drinks consumed per month (particularly among women). The data indicate that the availability of alcohol, through association with work peers who are more likely to drink and to engage the employee in drinking off the job, influences an employee's drinking patterns and (to a lesser extent) problem drinking. This raises questions about how much drinkers select themselves into drinking groups at work, and how much work environments structure drinking opportunities.

The gender composition of respondents' occupations was not a significant predictor of high CAGE scores when gender was controlled for as an independent variable. However, when analyses were performed for men and women separately, CAGE scores of 2 or higher were more likely in female-dominated occupations than in male-dominated occupations, for both men (2.1× more likely) and women (3.2× more likely), after controlling for effects of occupation type, drinking with co-workers, and number of drinks consumed per month. This pattern differs from findings of other research (Wilsnack & Wilsnack, 1992) that associated predominantly male occupations with risks of problem drinking among women. Variations in measurement of drinking problems and gender composition of occupations may affect the observed relationships between the two variables. Specifically, one can speculate that CAGE scores, which are likely to be affected by social disapproval, may go up for relatively heavy drinkers in occupational contexts (such as predominantly female occupations) where such drinking appears more deviant and is less likely to be socially supported.

EAP Client Data

While the NES dataset was obtained from a national sample of employed people, the second dataset was derived only from employees who had utilized employee assistance programs. What are EAPs? They include a variety of worksite-based programs designed to assist in identifying and resolving problems that adversely affect an employee's job performance or well-being (Blum & Roman, 1992; Erfurt et al., 1992; Trice, 1992). These problems can involve alcohol or other drug abuse, health, family, marital relations, emotional issues, or other personal concerns. EAPs function most effectively when designed and implemented to provide comprehensive services, including performance-based problem identification, supervisory consultation, confrontation, appropriate treatment linkages, and integration with both the organizational culture and the functions of human resource management (Roman & Blum, 1985).

Thus, in EAPs, alcohol-related problems are identified and assessed along with a range of other problems that may bring an employee to an EAP. Alcohol problems in EAP caseloads vary over time in their prominence and severity, but tend to be early stage problems. In order to deal effectively with alcohol-related problems, EAP services must achieve the right balance between the client's workplace activities and treatment (Sonnenstuhl, 1992).

The clients in the EAP sample may not be representative of all the comparably troubled people in the same workplaces. There are employees with alcohol and other personal problems who seek help on their own, without using an EAP. There are also employees with alcohol or other problems who are not identified as such, or who are still employed but not seeking help even though their problems are known by supervisors and work associates. In addition, it is possible for EAP clients with alcohol problems to be misdiagnosed. Clients who actually have alcohol problems may not be identified as such, and those who are identified as having alcohol-related problems may actually belong in other diagnostic categories.

The EAP clients may also differ in important ways from employees of companies without EAPs. Drinking problems are less prevalent among employees of organizations that provide EAPs. This lower prevalence may be the result of effective EAP prevention efforts or reduction of risk factors internal to the workplace (Trice, 1992); normative workplace cultures that are less conducive to problem drinking (Ames, 1993); or selective employment, by companies with EAPs, of people who are less likely to develop alcohol problems (through either self-selection or specific employer selection procedures). The point to remember is that patterns of alcohol-related problems in the EAP sample may not parallel patterns in the general population, such as in the NES.

In this section we examine possible correlates of drinking problems in EAP caseloads. Possible correlates included demographic characteristics; characteristics of family demands, work, and social relationships; job performance outcomes; and symptoms of depression. These variables were analyzed in three ways: (1) to predict which EAP clients were assessed as having alcohol problems (with gender as a separate predictor); (2) to predict which *women* who were EAP clients were assessed as having alcohol problems; and (3) to predict which EAP clients assessed as having alcohol problems were women.

In our analyses, employees were classified as having an alcohol problem if they scored 9 or above on the Alcohol Dependence Scale (Ross et al., 1990). When the dependent variable was whether or not an EAP client had an alcohol problem, the analyses indicated that women, African-Americans, married people, those with higher levels of education, and those with preschool age or school age children were less likely to have alcohol problems than other employees who used EAPs. Clients with alcohol-related problems were more likely than other clients to have been referred to the EAP by family members. Clients with alcohol problems were also more likely than other clients to have documented job performance problems and attendance problems.

EAP clients with alcohol problems were more likely to have work roles structured in ways that weakened direct supervision and social control of their work. They tended to report more satisfactory relationships at work, but less satisfactory relationships with friends outside of work. They also scored higher on the Beck Depression Inventory, suggesting comorbidity of problems with alcohol and depression. However, the strongest predictor of whether an EAP client had an alcohol problem was gender. Only 11% of the women in the EAP caseloads were assessed as having an alcohol-related problem, compared with 36% of the men (Blum & Roman, 1992).

The patterns described above were based on analyses of all EAP clients. Analyses of only female EAP clients indicate that African-American women, married women, and women with preschool age children were less likely to have alcohol problems than other female clients. Compared to other female EAP clients, women with alcohol problems were more likely to have had family members involved in their referrals, and were more likely to have been referred to EAPs because of documented job performance difficulties and attendance problems. Female clients with alcohol problems also scored higher than other female clients on the Beck Depression Inventory.

Thus, the analyses of female clients and of all clients are similar in several important ways. Both analyses find that demographics, depression, job impairment, and family influence increased the likelihood that employees going to EAPs would have recognizable alcohol problems. In both analyses, job categories, perceived job stress, and most work characteristics (e.g., job autonomy, physical work, and work away from a central setting) did not predict whether EAP clients would have alcohol problems. One exception was that working with little supervision or social control made alcohol problems more likely among male EAP clients than among female clients.

The same set of personal and job characteristics was used to try to predict whether an EAP client with alcohol problems was a man or a woman. Among the clients with alcohol-related problems, women had lower incomes from their jobs than did men. The women were less likely than the men to be blue-collar or supervisory workers, and more likely to be clerical workers. Compared with male clients, women were less likely to work away from supervision, but more likely to perceive their work as including decision latitude or autonomy. Women with alcohol problems were also less likely than men to have their families involved in their referrals to EAPs. Job performance problems, more common among those EAP clients who had alcohol problems, did not differentiate the male and female clients.

The preceding analyses indicate that the variables that distinguish male and female EAP clients with alcohol problems are the same variables that distinguish men and women in the general population. That is, the men earn higher incomes, and are more likely to perform physical work, blue-collar jobs, and jobs that have supervisory responsibility or that are performed without supervisors present. Women earn less, are more likely to have clerical jobs, and are more likely to feel that they have autonomy or decision latitude in their work. Similarities of gender patterns between the EAP clients with alcohol problems and employees in the general population suggest that these employment patterns do not differentiate men's and women's use of EAPs.

Because social processes may powerfully influence whether problem drinkers seek help for their problems, it is important to know whether there are factors that do differentiate how women and men gain access to EAPs. Therefore, the EAP sample was examined to assess whether there were differences in how men and women were referred to EAPs (Blum et al., 1993a). Women were less likely than men to be referred to EAPs through a bureaucratic supervisory process involving formal documentation of job performance problems. This pattern persisted even when demographic characteristics, job type, work characteristics, job performance, depression, and problem severity were controlled for.

On the other hand, it appears that women are more likely than men to have informal referrals to EAPs. That is, women are more likely to report that their supervisors influenced them to use an EAP, even though the EAP administrators do not have any records of supervisors referring these cases on the basis of documented poor job performance. However, gender differences in reports of informal supervisor referrals disappeared when we controlled for employee income, education, job performance criteria, and symptom severity, which were associated both with gender and with informal referrals.

Supervisors may be reluctant to refer employees (particularly women) to EAPs by formal procedures, perhaps because of concerns about adverse effects on working relationships. In our sample, however, the vast majority of EAP clients said they were at least somewhat satisfied with their relationships with their supervisors at the time that they entered the EAP. Employees who reported that their supervisors influenced their decisions to use EAPs were even more likely to be at least somewhat satisfied with their supervisors (86%). Even among those employees referred to EAPs bureaucratically through formally documented performance problems, 68% said they were at least somewhat satisfied with their supervisors. Therefore, concerns about EAP referrals damaging supervisory work relationships may be more myth than reality.

From the data, there is little doubt that supervisors and co-workers have a larger informal influence on getting employees into EAPs than an examination of EAP records might indicate. While such "nudging" may be desirable in many respects, it may also encourage denial and manipulation by employees because informal referrals lack the leverage of formal documented procedures. However, spouses also have an important role in informal EAP referrals, and can motivate employees to seek help for their alcohol problems or other problems through an EAP. Furthermore, it seems clear that improving the process of informal referral, from supervisors and co-workers, or from spouses and other family members, can be an important strategy for helping employed women gain greater benefits from EAPs.

Conclusion

This review of past research and report of new data analyses demonstrates the complexity of issues linking gender, work, and drinking. A multitude of relatively limited findings indicate that perhaps the research on relationships among gender, work, and drinking has been too "generic," paying too little attention to the details, and doing too little to make studies connected and comparable. There is an obvious need to accumulate, integrate, and replicate studies in this area, but progress to meet this need has been slow.

The current literature shows a severe scarcity of intensive case studies and qualitative analyses of how gender, work, and drinking interlock (see, e.g., Ames & Delaney, 1992; Richman, 1992). Theory is also underdeveloped, and in many ways consists largely of common-sense or well-worn ideas borrowed from other gender-related analyses and discourses. At the same time, women's workforce participation is growing and diversifying both nationally and globally, with largely unknown and unexamined social consequences. To learn how women's and men's use and abuse of alcohol is related to their jobs is a research agenda for which there is a great need and great opportunities; it is an agenda whose time is not just right but overdue.

References

Ames, G. (1993). Research and strategies for the primary prevention of workplace alcohol problems. *Alcohol Health & Research World, 17,* 19-27.

Ames, G., & Delaney, W. (1992). Minimization of workplace alcohol problems: The supervisor's role. *Alcoholism: Clinical and Experimental Research, 16,* 180-189.

Beck, A.T., & Beck R.W. (1972). Screening depressed patients in family practice: A rapid technique. *Postgraduate Medicine, 52* (6), 81-85.

Bielby, W.T., & Baron, J.N. (1986). Men and women at work: Sex segregation and statistical discrimination. *American Journal of Sociology, 91,* 759-799.

Blum, T.C., & Bennett, N. (1990). Employee assistance programs: Utilization and referral data, performance management, and prevention concepts. In P.M. Roman (Ed.), *Alcohol problem intervention in the workplace* (pp. 143-163). Westport, CT: Quorum Press.

Blum, T.C., Harwood, E.M., & Roman, P.M. (1993a) Employee assistance referral process: The effects of race, gender, and work characteristics. Presented at the annual meetings of the Southern Sociological Society, Chattanooga, TN.

Blum, T.C., Martin, J.K., & Roman, P.M. (1992). A research note on EAP prevalence, components, and utilization. *Journal of Employee Assistance Research, 1*(1), 209-229.

Blum, T.C. & Roman, P.M. (1992). A description of clients using employee assistance programs. *Alcohol Health & Research World, 16,* 120-128.

Blum, T.C., Roman, P.M., & Martin, J.K. (1993b). Alcohol consumption and work performance. *Journal of Studies on Alcohol, 54,* 61-70.

Clark, W.B., & Hilton, M.E. (Eds.). (1991). *Alcohol in America: Drinking practices and problems.* Albany, NY: SUNY Press.

Cooper, M.L., Russell, M., & Frone, M.R. (1990). Work stress and alcohol effects: A test of stress-induced drinking. *Journal of Health and Social Behavior, 31,* 260-276.

England, P., & Farkas, G. (1986). *Households, employment, and gender: A social, economic, and demographic view.* New York: Aldine.

Erfurt, J.C., Foote, A., & Heirich, M.A. (1992). Integrating employee assistance and wellness: Current and future core technologies of a megabrush program. *Journal of Employee Assistance Research, 1*(1), 1-31.

Ewing, J.A. (1984). Detecting alcoholism: The CAGE questionnaire. *Journal of the American Medical Association, 252,* 1905-1907.

Fillmore, K.M. (1984). "When angels fall": Women's drinking as cultural preoccupation and as reality. In S.C. Wilsnack & L.J. Beckman (Eds.), *Alcohol problems in women: Antecedents, consequences, and intervention* (pp. 7-36). New York: Guilford.

Harford, T.C., Parker, D.A., Grant, B.F., & Dawson, D.A. (1992). Alcohol use and dependence among employed men and women in the United States in 1988. *Alcoholism: Clinical and Experimental Research, 16,* 146-148.

Hilton, M.E. (1988). Trends in U.S. drinking patterns: Further evidence from the past 20 years. *British Journal of Addiction, 83,* 269-278.

Horn, J.L., Skinner, H.A., Wanberg, K.W., & Foster, F.M. (1985). *Alcohol Dependence Scale.* Toronto, Ontario: Addiction Research Foundation.

Jacobs, J.A. (1992). Women's entry into management: Trends in earnings, authority, and values among salaried managers. *Administrative Science Quarterly, 37,* 282-301.

Kraft, J.M., Blum, T.C., Martin, J.K., & Roman, P.M. (1993). Drinking patterns and the gender mix of occupations: Evidence from a national survey of American workers. *Journal of Substance Abuse, 5,* 157-174.

Kraft, J.M., Blum, T.C., Martin, J.K., & Roman, P.M. (1994). Work, family and drinking patterns. Presented at the annual meetings of the Southern Sociological Society, Chattanooga, TN.

LaRosa, J.H. (1990). Executive women and health: Perceptions and practices. *American Journal of Public Health, 80,* 1450-1454.

Lennon, M.C. (1987). Sex differences in distress: The impact of gender and work roles. *Journal of Health and Social Behavior, 28* (3), 290-305.

Martin, J.K. (1990). Jobs, occupations, and patterns of alcohol consumption: A review of the literature. In P.M. Roman (Ed.), *Alcohol problem intervention in the workplace: Employee assistance programs and strategic alternatives* (pp. 45-65). New York: Quorum.

Martin, J.K., Blum, T.C., & Roman, P.M. (1992). Drinking to cope and self-medication: Characteristics of jobs in relation to workers' drinking behavior. *Journal of Organizational Behavior, 13,* 55-71.

Mensch, B.S., & Kandel, D.B. (1988). Do job conditions influence the use of drugs? *Journal of Health and Social Behavior, 29,* 169-184.

Mullahy, J., & Sindelar, J. (1989). Life-cycle effects of alcoholism on education, earnings, and occupation. *Inquiry, 26,* 272-282.

Parker, D.A., & Harford, T.C. (1992). The epidemiology of alcohol consumption and dependence across occupations in the United States. *Alcohol Health & Research World, 16,* 97-105.

Parker, D.A., Parker, E.S., Wolz, M.W., & Harford, T.C. (1980). Sex roles and alcohol consumption: A research note. *Journal of Health and Social Behavior, 21,* 43-48.

Powell, G.N. (1988). *Women and men in management.* Newbury Park, CA: Sage.

Reichman, W., Young, D.W., & Gracin, L. (1988). Identification of alcoholics in the workplace. In M. Galanter (Ed.), *Recent developments in alcoholism: Vol. 6* (pp. 172-181). New York: Plenum.

Reskin, B.F., & Roos, P.A. (1990). *Job queues, gender queues: Explaining women's inroads into male occupations.* Philadelphia: Temple University Press.

Richman, J.A. (1992). Occupational stress, psychological vulnerability and alcohol-related problems over time in future physicians. *Alcoholism: Clinical and Experimental Research, 16,* 166-171.

Roman, P.M. (1988). Growth and transformation in workplace alcoholism programming. In M. Galanter (Ed.), *Recent developments in alcoholism: Vol. 6* (pp. 131-158). New York: Plenum.

Roman, P.M., & Blum, T.C. (1985). The core technology of employee assistance programs. *The Almacan, 15* (3), 8-12.

Ross, H.E., Gavin, D.R., & Skinner, H.A. (1990). Diagnostic validity of the MAST and the Alcohol Dependence Scale in the assessment of DSM-III alcohol disorders. *Journal of Studies on Alcohol, 51,* 506-513.

Sandmeier, M. (1980). *The Invisible alcoholics: Women and alcohol abuse in America.* New York: McGraw-Hill.

Shore, E.R. (1990). Business and professional women: Primary prevention for new role incumbents. In P.M. Roman (Ed.), *Alcohol problem intervention in the workplace: Employee assistance programs and strategic alternatives* (pp. 113-124). New York: Quorum.

Shore, E.R. (1992). Drinking patterns and problems among women in paid employment. *Alcohol Health & Research World, 16,* 160-164.

Smart, R.G., Adlaf, E.M., & Knoke, D. (1991). Use of the CAGE scale in a population survey of drinking. *Journal of Studies on Alcohol, 52,* 593-596.

Sonnenstuhl, W.J. (1992). The job-treatment balance in employee assistance programs. *Alcohol Health & Research World, 16,* 129-133.

Sonnenstuhl, W.J., & Trice, H.M. (1986). *Strategies for employee assistance: The crucial balance.* Ithaca, NY: ILR Press of Cornell University.

Sonnenstuhl, W.J., & Trice, H.M. (1990). *Strategies for employee assistance programs: The crucial balance* (2nd ed.). Ithaca, NY: ILR Press of Cornell University.

Trice, H.M. (1992). Work-related risk factors associated with alcohol abuse. *Alcohol Health & Research World, 16,* 106-111.

Trice, H.M., & Roman, P.M. (1978). *Spirits and demons at work: Alcohol and other drugs on the job.* Ithaca, NY: ILR Press of Cornell University.

Wilsnack, R.W., & Wilsnack, S.C. (1992). Women, work, and alcohol: Failures of simple theories. *Alcoholism: Clinical and Experimental Research, 16,* 172-179.

Wilsnack, S.C., Wilsnack, R.W., & Klassen, A.D. (1984/85). Drinking and drinking problems among women in a U.S. national survey. *Alcohol Health & Research World, 9,* 3-13.

Wilsnack, S.C., Wilsnack, R.W., & Klassen, A.D. (1986). Epidemiological research on women's drinking, 1978-1984. In *Women and alcohol: Health related issues* (pp. 1-68) (NIAAA Research Monograph No. 16; DHHS Publication No. ADM 86-1139). Washington, DC: U.S. Government Printing Office.

Young, D.W., Reichman, W.R., & Levy, M.F. (1987). Differential referral of women and men to employee assistance programs: The role of supervisory attitudes. *Journal of Studies on Alcohol, 48,* 22-28.

CHAPTER 16

Gender, Alcohol Use, and Crime

CATHY STREIFEL

Recent criminological research has drawn attention to how violence pro-voked or accompanied by alcohol use has become a major social prob-lem (Miller et al., 1993; Reid, 1991; Rouse & Unnithan, 1993; U.S. Department of Health and Human Services, 1992). Studies have consistently found a high association between alcohol use and violent crime (Hollis, 1974; Murdoch et al., 1990; Pernanen, 1976; Room, 1982; Welte & Miller, 1987; Wolfgang, 1958). Alcohol use has also been associated with the commission of property crime (Collins, 1981; Ladouceur & Temple, 1985; Welte & Miller, 1987). Some research has reported that alcohol use is more prevalent in violent crimes than in property crimes (Collins, 1981; Room, 1982; Wolfgang & Strohm, 1956), whereas other research has found little to no difference between vio-lent and property offenders in alcohol use (Ladouceur & Temple, 1985; Welte & Miller, 1987).

Violent crime may be facilitated by victim's drinking as well as by offender's drinking. Studies have reported a high prevalence of both offender and vic-tim intoxication (Abel & Zeidenberg, 1985; Mayfield, 1976; Murdoch et al., 1990; Wolfgang & Strohm, 1956); the precipitator of an altercation is the most likely to be intoxicated (Murdoch et al., 1990). Other research has found that individuals with alcohol problems or diagnosed alcoholism are more likely to be involved in alcohol-related violence than are other individuals (Leonard et al., 1985; Mayfield, 1976; Pincock, 1962).

Although research has clearly established that alcohol use is associated with crime, we still know little about *how* the use of alcohol is linked to the commission of criminal acts. Moreover, research to date has failed to exam-ine whether the nature of the relationship between alcohol and crime varies across gender. Research and theory about alcohol-crime connections have fo-cused only on male populations; we do not know whether the processes and mechanisms connecting alcohol and crime are the same for women as they are for men.

The purpose of this chapter is to examine the alcohol-crime relationship across gender. After a review of theory and research on how alcohol use is re-lated to crime, the chapter analyzes the best available data on how gender affects patterns of alcohol-crime connections. Patterns evaluated include (1) the presence of alcohol during or preceding the criminal situation; (2) contexts in which drinking and crime occur together; (3) variations in alcohol-crime relationships by age, race, and socioeconomic status of offenders; (4) victim-offender relationships in alcohol-related violent crimes; and (5) characteristics of victims in alcohol-related vs. non-alcohol-related violent crimes.

Theoretical Perspectives and Explanatory Models

Alcohol and Crime

Pernanen (1981) outlines several theories that have been advanced to explain the association of alcohol use with crime. Disinhibition theory argues that alcohol use serves as a "disinhibitor" or "catalyst" of aggression, in that alcohol may reduce inhibitions and trigger law-violating behavior in some people. Situational theories claim that there may be situational factors that serve as intervening variables—i.e., alcohol use produces some situational factor (e.g., feelings of power, risk taking), which in turn produces criminal behavior. Frustration-aggression theory argues that one's threshold for aggression is lowered by alcohol use; therefore, less frustration is needed to elicit aggression, or cues which would not be perceived as frustrating in a sober state may be so interpreted in an intoxicated state. Common cause explanations propose that there may be a third variable (e.g., stress, emotional instability, low frustration tolerance) which explains the increased probability that both alcohol use and crime will occur. Other models argue that alcohol use and crime may be spuriously related by occurring in the same social contexts; e.g., there may be a higher probability of hostile interactions in places where alcohol is used, or criminal contacts and the planning of crimes may be more likely to take place in public drinking establishments. Unfortunately, none of these theories explain why there might be gender differences in the alcohol-crime relationship.

Gender and Crime

Men commit crimes more frequently than women, and the crimes men commit are more serious. Approximately 85% of all recorded crimes are committed by males. Women commit less than 15% of violent crimes recorded by the police and less than 10% of the recorded serious property crimes (Steffensmeier and Allan, 1991).

Theorists have argued that traditional sex roles may inhibit criminality among women in a number of ways. Young women may be under more powerful direct social control, supervised more closely by parents and other adults, and threatened by greater potential costs if they do deviate (Hirschi, 1969;

Jensen & Eve, 1976). Gilligan (1982) suggests that men and women differ significantly in their moral development, and that women's moral choices are more likely to constrain them from criminal behavior than are men's.

Others have argued that traditional sex roles may inhibit female crime by not creating for women the opportunities and motivations that produce much male crime (Chesney-Lind, 1986; Schur, 1969; Steffensmeier, 1983). When women commit crimes they are most likely to commit unorganized, nonlucrative crimes such as prostitution, shoplifting, check forgery, and credit card fraud—crimes that are associated with traditional female roles (Steffensmeier, 1983). Men, on the other hand, are more likely than women to be involved in serious property crime (e.g., robbery, burglary) and in crimes of violence—acts that are more consistent with traditionally assertive and aggressive male roles.

Past Research on the Alcohol-Crime Relationship

Prevalence of Alcohol by Type of Crime

Discussion of the alcohol-crime link often has an underlying assumption that crimes against property are utilitarian and "rational," while crimes of violence are the result of loss of self-control. Therefore, alcohol should play a much more important role in the commission of crimes of violence because of its disinhibiting effects. However, research findings are mixed with respect to the types of crime most strongly associated with alcohol use. Some researchers have found that alcohol use is more prevalent in violent than in property crime (Collins, 1981; Room, 1983; Wolfgang & Strohm, 1956), whereas others have reported little or no difference in the association of alcohol use with violent versus property crime (Ladouceur & Temple, 1985; Welte & Miller, 1987).

Research has also found that when perpetrators of property crime such as robbery and burglary drink heavily, crimes are unskilled, poorly planned, and not very profitable (Bacon, 1963; Cordilia, 1985). Cordilia (1985) concluded that alcohol facilitates the escalation to casual property crime in a group drinking context, where such unplanned crime serves to keep the group united.

Drinking by the Victim

Risks of violent crime may be increased by the victim's drinking, not just by the offender's drinking. Gerson (1978) reported that in nonmarital assaults, the victim or both the offender and victim had been drinking in 75% of the cases. Hollis (1974) found that 75% of homicide victims in Tennessee had been drinking when they died, and in 80% of these cases, both the offender and victim had been drinking. One way that drinking may put victims at risk is by making them more likely to act in ways that precipitate violence. Victims who precipitate deadly encounters, by being the first to display a weapon or use physical force, are more likely to have been drinking than offenders who initiate violence (Welte & Abel, 1989; Wolfgang & Strohm, 1956).

The Social Context of Alcohol-Related Violence

Alcohol-related violence increases dramatically on the weekends. Analysis of homicide data has consistently found that the proportion of homicides that are alcohol-related is much higher on the weekends than during the week (Abel et al., 1985; Gelfand, 1971; Gerson & Preston, 1979; Wolfgang & Strohm, 1956). Alcohol-related assault has followed a similar pattern (Gerson & Preston, 1979; Wolfgang & Strohm, 1956). Welte and Abel (1989) found that homicides in which the victim had been drinking were more likely than other homicides to occur in the evening or at night, in the warmer months, and in bars or restaurants. These homicides were also less likely to be related to other crimes. Such evidence suggests that alcohol-related homicide may occur more readily as a result of spontaneous hostile interaction in social or public drinking environments. Indeed, Murdoch and colleagues (1990) suggest that it is the drinking environment and not the effects of alcohol per se that increases risks of violent crimes.

However, other research has reported that very few homicides occur on licensed premises (Voss and Hepburn, 1968; Wolfgang, 1958), and that 90% of marital assaults occur in private residences rather than in public drinking settings (Gerson, 1978). Ladouceur and Temple (1985) found that violent offenders were much more likely to drink alone than were other types of offenders. A majority of violent sex offenders reported drinking alone at the time of the offense, compared to 22% of burglars. Such findings suggest that if social drinking environments increase risks for violent crimes, such environments are only a small part of the settings where alcohol-related violence occurs, and effects of alcohol on individual acts of violence do not depend on the company of other drinkers. A major unanswered question is how much the crimes committed by groups of individuals acting together (against persons or property) are facilitated by prior group drinking by the offenders.

The Alcohol-Crime Relationship by Race, Socioeconomic Status, and Age of Offenders and Victims

Much of the alcohol-crime literature has been devoted to examining if and how the alcohol-crime relationship varies by race, socioeconomic status (SES), and age of offenders and victims.

Race. A review of research up to the 1980s concluded that both homicides and alcohol abuse are more prevalent in urban communities, but that this is true especially for African-American males (Gary, 1986). The data indicated that African-American men, especially those under the age of 30, are more likely to be victims of alcohol-related homicides than were either white men or women or African-American women of the same ages. Studies of prison inmates have shown that drinking involvement among African-Americans and whites incarcerated for murder does not differ significantly, although white male prisoners (55%) were more likely to have been drinking than were African-American male prisoners (50%) at the time of the homicidal event (Aarens et al., 1977; Gary, 1986).

Collins (1981) reported that among adult violent offenders, whites were more likely to drink in connection with the commission of crimes than were African-Americans. However, Dawkins and Dawkins (1983), examining the relationship between drinking and criminal behavior among adolescent offenders, found that the relationship between drinking and serious offenses was strong among both whites and African-Americans, but not among Hispanics. Multiple regression analyses further revealed that relative to other background variables and behavioral factors, drinking was the strongest single predictor of criminal offenses among African-Americans, with less importance for whites, and little importance for Hispanics.

These limited findings suggest that alcohol may psychologically or socially facilitate crime more in some racial categories than in others. However, such race differences apparently vary for different age groups of drinkers, and research has said nothing about gender similarities or differences in the influence of race on the connections between drinking and crime.

Socioeconomic status. The few available studies that discuss how socioeconomic status may affect the alcohol-crime connection suggest that the connection is stronger among lower SES individuals. Welte and Miller (1987) found that the proportion of offenders who drank immediately before the commission of a property crime declined rapidly as education and income increased. Greene and Wakefield (1979) examined the patterns of homicide among middle and upper class persons and discovered that alcohol consumption was very seldom involved in these cases. However, homicides among middle and upper income groups are committed mainly by white males, so effects of SES and race on alcohol-crime relationships may overlap in ways that are hard to disentangle.

Age. For both men and women the prevalence of drinking and problems associated with drinking decrease with age (Blane & Hewitt, 1977; Cahalan & Cisin, 1980; Robbins, 1991), although the prevalence is higher for men and women at all ages. Criminal behavior is also systematically related to age. Most serious crime in the United States is committed by youths and young adults, with criminal activity reaching a peak between the ages of 16 and 18 and then decreasing steadily with age (Greenberg, 1985; Greenwood et al., 1980; Petersilia, 1980; Steffensmeier & Allan, 1991; Steffensmeier & Streifel, 1991).

Research also finds that the age-crime relationship is remarkably similar among male and female offenders (Steffensmeier & Streifel, 1991). These patterns suggest that age is important for understanding the relationship between alcohol use and crime, and may be a cause or context for that relationship. However, research to date has not clarified what happens to the connection between alcohol use and criminal involvement as young people grow older.

Temple and Ladouceur (1986) conducted a longitudinal analysis of the drinking and delinquent behavior of a group of young men in an attempt to understand how the relationship between criminal careers and patterns of alcohol use varies as a function of age. They reported that while crime and alcohol use appeared to be related in adolescence, the relationship between these two behaviors diminished with age, until, by age 31, no significant relationship was found. They concluded that "the relationship between alcohol use and crime is the result of 'social circumstances,' not the result of a causal relationship. That is, alcohol and crime are only strongly related at a certain point in the life cycle, suggesting there is something unique to that time in the life cycle that increases a person's chances for involvement in these behaviors" (p. 105). Unfortunately, the study did not examine the age-alcohol-crime relationship among women.

Summary of Past Research

Research has found that alcohol use is often a factor in criminal activity, and in violent crime in particular. Studies show that not only violent offenders but also victims of violent crime have often been drinking beforehand, and that drinking victims often precipitate their own deaths. Among criminal offenders who were drinking at the time of their crimes, violent offenders are likely to have been drinking alone, while property offenders are more likely to have been drinking in a group setting. The alcohol-crime relationship is apparently stronger among people with low levels of income and education, and may be stronger among the young. The alcohol-crime relationship also may vary across racial groups, but the patterns of findings thus far have been inconsistent.

As stated earlier, the research to date has paid little attention to gender differences in how alcohol use is linked to crime. The following section analyzes two large datasets to learn whether there are such gender differences.

New Analyses of Relationships Between Gender, Alcohol, and Crime

Data

The best available data for evaluating gender differences in the alcohol-crime relationship come from surveys of prison inmates and homicide cases.

The *Survey of Inmates of State Correctional Facilities, 1991* (U.S. Department of Justice, 1991) contains information on male and female inmates of state correctional facilities, including information on each inmate's current offense, criminal history, and drug and alcohol use, and demographic characteristics of the inmate population and information on the victim(s) of each inmate's most recent offense.

The *Nature and Patterns of Homicide in Eight American Cities* (Zahn & Riedel, 1978) contains detailed information on 1,748 homicides in eight U.S. cities. Detailed characteristics for each homicide victim include the time and date of the homicide; the victim's age, gender, race, marital status, and SES; and the method of assault, victim-offender relationship, criminal history of the victim and offender, and whether or not the victim and/or offender were drinking at the time of the incident.

Measures

Offense categories. For ease of presentation, the numerous offense categories identified in the prison data were condensed into two categories: violent offenses and property offenses. The violent offenses included homicide, manslaughter, kidnapping, rape, sex offenses other than rape, aggravated assault, simple assault, child abuse, weapons violations, and offenses against the family other than child abuse. The property offenses included robbery, burglary, arson, auto theft, forgery, fraud, embezzlement, grand larceny, petty larceny, stolen property, and vandalism. Condensing the offense categories in this way simplifies the presentation of findings, but could obscure important details. Therefore, individual offense categories were examined separately as well.

Alcohol consumption. The analyses that follow focus mainly on whether or not offenders had been drinking when they committed their crimes. This focus is consistent with most prior research on the alcohol-crime relationship. Unfortunately, the data used here do not include information on the offender's drinking behavior over more extended time periods.

Analyses

The results of the analyses are presented in two parts. First, data from the inmate survey show how gender affects the association of alcohol use with the full range of criminal activity. Second, data from the homicide cases show how gender influences the connections between alcohol use and homicide. For ease of interpretation, all prevalences and comparisons are given in percentages. Wherever percentages are said to differ, the differences are significant at $p < .05$ or better.

Prison Inmates: Results

Gender, Alcohol Use, and Type of Crime

The prevalence of drinking at the time of the offense was much higher for men than women. Forty-five percent of the male prisoners, but only 29% of the female prisoners, were drinking at the time they committed the offenses for which they were serving time. For both male and female prisoners, the percent who were drinking at the time of the offense was higher for violent crimes than for property crimes, but this difference was considerably larger for women than for men. Among male prisoners, 51% of the violent offenders were drinking at the time of the crime, compared to 45% of the property offenders. Among female prisoners, 42% of the violent offenders were drinking at the time of the crime, compared to just 23% of the property offenders. An examination of separate offense categories showed that the gender difference was quite consistent across the offense categories, and was larger for property crimes than for violent crimes.

Analysis by Race, SES, and Age of Offender

Race. Analyses were limited to African-American and white offenders, the two categories for which there was an adequate number of cases to allow analyses by type of crime and drinking status. Among male offenders, whites were more likely than African-Americans to have been drinking at the time of the crime, for both violent crime (55% vs. 44%) and property crime (50% vs. 39%). Among female offenders, there was little difference between African-Americans and whites in the prevalence of drinking at the time of criminal activity; whites drank slightly more often than African-Americans prior to property crimes, but this difference was not statistically significant.

Socioeconomic status. The SES of offenders was measured by income obtained by legal means in the year prior to imprisonment and level of education prior to imprisonment. Income was collapsed into four categories (consistent with prior research): less than $4,000, $4,000 to $9,999, $10,000 to $24,999, and $25,000 or more. Education level was divided into three categories (consistent with prior research): less than the 8th grade, high school graduate, and some college.

For both men and women, the percentages of offenders who were drinking at the time of their crimes decreased as offenders' levels of education and income increased. This is true for both violent and property crimes. However, the effect of income level is smaller for women, especially for property crime. Among male property offenders, 48% of those making less than $4,000 had been drinking at the time they committed their crimes, compared with only

30% of those making $25,000 or more. Among female property offenders, the percentages are 25% and 20%, respectively.

Age. The offender's age, at the time of the arrest for the offense resulting in imprisonment, was categorized as under age 30, 30 to 49, and 50 or older. Among violent male offenders, younger offenders were more likely to have been drinking at the time of the offense. Fifty-three percent of offenders under the age of 30 had been drinking compared to 39% of offenders over the age of 50. Among violent female offenders, on the other hand, the percent drinking at the time of the offense increased with age. Forty-one percent of female offenders under the age of 30 had been drinking at the time of the offense, compared to 51% of those aged 50 or older.

Among female property offenders the prevalence of drinking did not differ significantly across age groups. Twenty-three percent of female property offenders under age 30 had been drinking at the time of the crime, compared with 24% of those aged 31 to 49 and 24% of those over 50. Among male property offenders the relationship between age and drinking was curvilinear. Men 50 or older were most likely to have been drinking (53%), followed by those under the age of 30 (47%), with offenders aged 31 to 49 least likely to have been drinking (40%).

Gender, Drinking Context, and Type of Crime

Inmates who had been drinking when they committed their crimes were asked whether they had been drinking alone or with others, and where they had been drinking. A large majority of both male and female inmates had been drinking with companions prior to committing their crimes, and group drinking had been slightly more prevalent among the violent women (85%) than among the violent men (75%) or the property criminals of both sexes (77%). These findings contradict any previous research stating that violent crime is likely to be preceded by solitary drinking (see, e.g., Gerson & Preston, 1979; Ladouceur & Temple, 1985). However, the prevalence of group drinking varied among different types of violent offenders: men and women convicted of homicide were most likely to have been drinking with companions, while men and women convicted of child abuse and sex offenses were most likely to have been drinking alone.

When violent offenders were asked where they drank prior to their crimes, women were more likely than men to have been drinking at home (36% vs. 24%, respectively), while men were more likely than women to be drinking in a vehicle (13% vs. 6%, respectively). Drinking in a bar, tavern, or club occurred almost as often among the female offenders (25%) as among the male offenders (30%). Similar patterns were found for specific violent offenses.

Among inmates who had been drinking before committing property crimes, there were only minor gender differences in drinking settings. Men were most likely to have been drinking in a bar, tavern, or club (25%), at a friend's house (24%), or at home (20%). Women were most likely to have been drinking at home (28%), in a bar, tavern, or club (23%), or at a friend's house (19%).

Analysis Across Race, Socioeconomic Status, and Age

Race. Among violent offenders who drank before their crimes, African-American and white inmates had the same tendency to drink with companions rather than alone. There were differences, however, in where the offenders had been drinking. Among male violent offenders, African-Americans were more likely than whites to have been drinking at a friend's house (25% vs. 15%) or on the street (10% vs. 4%), but were less likely than whites to have been drinking in a bar, tavern, or club (22% vs. 35%). Among female violent offenders, African-Americans were more likely than whites to have done their drinking at home (42% vs. 31%), and less likely to have been drinking in a bar, tavern, or club (20% vs. 37%).

Drinking alone before property crimes did not vary by gender or race. Among property offenders, such solitary drinking was reported by 22% of the white men, 25% of the African-American men, 25% of the white women and 20% of the African-American women. Female property offenders did not differ by race in their drinking locations, but compared to white male property offenders the African-American male offenders were more likely to have been drinking on the street (17% vs. 7%) and less likely to have been drinking in a bar/tavern/club (15% vs. 24%).

Socioeconomic status. Education did not affect solitary drinking by male and female violent offenders. However, among property offenders, the better-educated male offenders were less likely to drink alone before their crimes (38% of men with less than an eighth grade education compared to 22% percent of men who had attended some college), whereas the better-educated female offenders were more likely to drink alone (10% of women with an eighth grade education or less compared to 38% percent of women who had attended some college). The patterns observed with levels of income parallel the patterns found with levels of education.

In general, higher socioeconomic status is associated with offenders being more likely to do their pre-crime drinking at home or in bars, taverns, or clubs. Higher income male offenders were more likely to drink both at home and in drinking establishments than lower income male offenders. Better educated female property offenders were more likely to drink at home but less likely to drink in bars, taverns, or clubs. Female violent offenders with higher incomes were more likely to drink in drinking establishments before the commission of their crimes.

Age. Among both male and female offenders who drank before their crimes, group drinking was most common among the youngest offenders, while solitary drinking became more common with advancing age. Among the drinking violent offenders, solitary drinking was reported by only 21% of the men and 13% of the women under age 30, but by 38% of the men and 24% of the women aged 50 or older. Among offenders who drank before property crimes, 20% of the men and 18% of the women under age 30 drank alone, but 55% of the men and 50% of the women aged 50 or older drank alone.

Comparisons of where the youngest (<30) and oldest (≥50) offenders drank before their crimes showed that aging led to more drinking at home, among male violent offenders (18% vs. 51%), female violent offenders (23% vs. 62%), and female property offenders (23% vs. 75%). Only the drinking sites of male property offenders were not influenced by aging.

Homicide Cases: Results

The data on 1,748 homicides in eight U.S. cities (Zahn & Riedel, 1978) do not allow all the analyses of gender differences which were presented for the prison survey. The case records show how alcohol use affected where, when, and how men and women committed homicides, and how alcohol use affected men's and women's risks of becoming a homicide victim.

Where Homicides Occur

In general, men were most likely to commit homicide on the street (36% of their cases), while women were most likely to commit homicide in a residence they shared with the victim (34%). However, alcohol consumption increased the likelihood that both men and women would murder in public rather than in private places. In comparisons of male homicide offenders who had been drinking or not drinking before the crime, drinking made the homicide more likely to occur in a bar, tavern, or club (16% vs. 3%) or on the street (36% vs. 28%), and less likely to occur where the victim or the murderer lived (21% vs. 39%). Among female homicide offenders, the pattern was similar. Drinking made the location of homicide more likely to be in a drinking establishment (20% vs. 1%) or on the street (25% vs. 10%), and less likely to be in the victim's or murderer's home (44% vs. 76%).

When Homicides Occur

Alcohol-related homicides by men or women were particularly likely to occur during weekends (Friday through Sunday). In cases where offenders had not been drinking, 48% of homicides by both male and female offenders occurred on weekends. In contrast, in cases where offenders had been drinking, 70% of homicides by women and 58% of homicides by men occurred on weekends. Among offenders who had not been drinking, both men and women were most likely to commit homicide during the earlier part of the evening, between 6 PM and midnight (30% of male-offender homicides and 31% of female-offender homicides). Offenders who had been drinking prior to the crime were more likely to commit homicides late at night or in the early morning hours, between midnight and 6 AM (45% of male-offender homicides and 47% of female-offender homicides).

Victims of Homicide

Consistent with previous research, the case records show that female homicide offenders were most likely to kill a spouse or ex-spouse (33%), other sexual partner (18%), or family member (15%), while males were most likely to kill a friend or acquaintance (36%) and were considerably more likely than females to kill a stranger (18%).

When alcohol is included in the analysis, the distribution of victims changes somewhat. Male homicide offenders who were sober were less likely than those under the influence of alcohol to kill a friend or acquaintance (31% vs. 56%), and more likely to kill a spouse or ex-spouse (9% vs. 3%). Female offenders not drinking at the time of the homicide were less likely than those who were drinking to kill a friend or acquaintance (13% vs. 27%) but considerably more likely to kill a parent or child (11% vs. 0%); drinking did not affect the likelihood that a female homicide offender would kill a spouse or ex-spouse (as 32–33% did).

Among homicides not involving alcohol, 41% of homicides by male offenders and 46% of homicides by female offenders were precipitated by the victims. However, in those homicides where the offender had been drinking, 35% of male-offender homicides and 46% of female-offender homicides were precipitated by the victims. In other words, when alcohol is not involved, male and female offender homicides are about equally likely to have been victim-precipitated. However, when offenders drank before committing homicide, male offenders were much less likely to require provocation by their victims.

The victims of homicides were predominantly male, whether killed by men (82% male) or killed by women (88% male). Among female homicide offenders, the likelihood of killing women increased, but not significantly, if the offenders had been drinking (17% of drinking female offenders killed women compared to 11% of offenders who had not been drinking). In contrast, the victims of male homicide offenders were significantly less likely to be women if the offenders had been drinking (14% of male homicide offenders who had been drinking killed women compared to 21% of nondrinking male homicide offenders). The race of victims was not related to the offenders' drinking. Regardless of whether or not the offender had consumed alcohol prior to the killing, about 60% of the victims of male homicide offenders were African-American, and about 80% of the victims of female offenders were African-American.

Homicides and the Use of a Weapon

Consistent with previous studies, the case data showed that the vast majority of homicides involved use of a weapon (most commonly a firearm). Men were more likely than women to kill with firearms (71% vs. 51%), while women were more likely than men to kill with sharp objects (41% vs. 23%). Among women committing homicide, alcohol consumption was unrelated to the methods used. Fifty-one percent of the women used handguns, and smaller percentages used sharp objects, whether or not they had been drinking. Alcohol use did influence men's methods of committing homicide, however. Men who drank before committing homicide were less likely to use a handgun (50% vs. 61%) and more likely to use a sharp object (21% vs. 14%).

Circumstances Surrounding Homicide

Among both male and female offender homicides, the most common circumstance immediately preceding the homicide was an argument of some sort. Arguments were more likely to precede homicides by both men and women if alcohol was involved. However, there were gender differences in the nature of the arguments that led to homicides. Domestic quarrels often preceded homicides by women, whether the women had been drinking (41% of their homicides) or not (38% of their homicides). Male-offender homicides more often were precipitated by other types of arguments, such as arguments over drugs, gambling, or money; these nondomestic lethal quarrels were more common in cases where offenders had been drinking (63%) than when offenders had not been drinking (41%). In homicides committed by men, the victims were more likely to be killed as a result of armed robbery if the offenders had not been drinking (19%) than if the offenders had been drinking (9%), evidence that some forms of lethal violence are not facilitated by alcohol.

Summary and Discussion of Findings

The current analysis has revealed significant gender differences in the alcohol-crime relationship. These differences suggest that lumping male and female offenders together, or ignoring female offenders altogether, will impede our understanding of how alcohol influences crime and how to improve crime prevention strategies.

First, the alcohol-crime relationship is much stronger among men than among women, suggesting that alcohol may play a different and more important role in male criminality than in female criminality. One reason for the gender difference may be that alcohol facilitates the aggression in violent crime, a form of crime more likely to be committed by males. Among the prison inmates who had committed violent crimes, 51% of the men and 42% of the women had used alcohol beforehand. Among inmates who had committed property crimes, 45% of the men but only 23% of the women had been drinking before their crimes.

Alcohol use is more prevalent not only in male crime, but among certain subgroups of male criminals. White men were more likely than African-American men to have consumed alcohol before committing either violent or property crimes. Female offenders did not show much racial difference in alcohol use. Male offenders were also more likely to drink prior to their crimes if they had low levels of income and education; income did not make as much of a difference for female offenders. Perhaps there is a subculture of drinking norms and expectations among lower-SES white males that increases risks of impulsive or disinhibited criminal behavior (such as through fights and challenges). However, any cultural or social-structural explanation of male subgroup differences in the alcohol-crime relationship must be based on better research than is currently available.

The data reveal an age by gender interaction effect on the alcohol-crime relationship. Among men, the association between violent crime and alcohol use decreases with age, whereas among women the association between violent crime and alcohol use increases with age. One possibility is that alcohol use is an excuse or context for violence among young men (or accompanies antisocial behavior disorder, more common among young men than among young women). In contrast, violence for women is such unusual and abnormal behavior that it may depend on powerful disinhibition such as from alcohol intoxication, and as women age it may become increasingly difficult for them to behave violently unless they are intoxicated. An alternative hypothesis would be that men's and women's violence may depend on different kinds of stressful social relationships (with male acquaintances for men, with spouses for women) that are most likely to provoke violent behavior at different stages of the life cycle. Again, evaluating such possibilities will require much more detailed research.

The prison data show that a clear majority of male and female offenders who drank before committing crimes (violent or property) drank with companions, not alone. Earlier research suggesting that violent criminals drink alone may be relevant only for certain types of violent crime, such as child abuse and sex offenses. Locations of men's and women's pre-crime drinking differed more for violent offenses than for property crimes. Women were more likely to have violent confrontations with drinking partners at home, whereas men were more likely to commit alcohol-related crimes outside the home. This contrast may reflect normal differences in where men and women are likely to drink.

The settings for men's and women's alcohol-related violence also showed racial differences. African-American male offenders were more likely to have been drinking at a friend's house or on the street, and were less likely to have been drinking at a drinking establishment than were the white male offenders. Among women committing violence, African-American women were more likely than white women to have been drinking at home. It is unclear whether these comparisons merely reflect racial differences in normal drinking patterns, or whether the data show racial differences in where violent alcohol-related conflicts are likely to erupt.

Among both male and female violent offenders, younger offenders were more likely to have done their drinking with companions, while older offenders more often drank alone before their crimes. This suggests that violence by younger people, both male and female, results more often from a group drinking context than violent crimes of older offenders. Among both male and female property offenders, the proportion of offenders who drank alone before their crimes greatly increased with age, and older female offenders were much more likely than younger offenders to do their pre-crime drinking at home. The age differences in drinking contexts may reflect differences in the types of property crimes committed by younger versus older offenders. Crimes such as burglary and robbery, which may depend on group cooperation enhanced by social drinking, are committed mainly by younger offenders. Older property offenders are more likely to engage in crimes such as forgery, fraud, and embezzlement, offenses which are less likely to be group activities.

Alcohol may help explain gender differences not only in a variety of violent and property crimes, but also specifically in homicides. In the homicide cases, men were more likely than women to kill people who were not family members in places away from home, while women were more likely than men to kill family members or living companions at home. These gender differences may show the effects of the greater prevalence of heavy drinking among men than among women, because among both men and women, homicides without alcohol consumption are largely domestic, whereas higher percentages of homicides after drinking are nonfamilial murders in public places. As data on violent crimes by women show, alcohol does not reduce risks of domestic violence, but alcohol may increase the risks of deadly public quarrels even more powerfully than it increases the risks of murder at home.

Conclusions

Neither past research nor the findings presented here have demonstrated that alcohol and crime are causally related. However, there is sufficient evidence that crimes would not occur to the same extent or in the same patterns if alcohol were absent, and that men and women show different connections between drinking and crime. It is obvious that further research is needed to understand these gender-specific connections. The question is, in what directions should that research proceed?

To begin with, further research should be designed to detect contingencies and interaction effects. The findings from the prison survey and homicide cases show that the connections between gender, alcohol, and crime are rarely simple. How alcohol modifies the criminal behavior of men and women will depend on the contexts of drinking behavior and the demographic characteristics of the drinkers.

It is also imperative to study more than convicted criminals and people who have committed no crimes. What is missing is information on drinking among those individuals who commit crimes for which they are not arrested, convicted, or imprisoned. Without that information, inferences about how drinking contributes to crime may be based selectively on individuals whose behavior control is most impaired by drinking.

It is equally urgent to study the gender-alcohol-crime relationship longitudinally, across the lifespan. We need to know about the individual's history of involvement in previous criminal events, history of alcohol use, and the relationships between these. If alcohol use was involved in a particular crime, was alcohol also involved in past crimes by the same offender? How often has the person who committed an alcohol-related crime used alcohol similarly in the past without criminal activity? To what extent does alcohol consumption develop as a response to criminal involvement, not just as a cause of crime? Such questions cannot be answered by research that examines only the immediate contexts of crimes as separate cases.

Finally, research on gender, alcohol, and crime needs to take into account the use of other psychoactive substances as well as alcohol. Although much alcohol use before crimes occurs without other substance use, it is also well established that users of other psychoactive substances are exceptionally likely to use and abuse alcohol. Thus, alcohol may be part of a broader pattern of multiple and illicit substance use that increases the likelihood of involvement in criminal activity.

These research proposals are not gender specific, even though the goal would be to obtain enough information about both women and men for gender comparisons. The basic reason for the lack of a gender-specific research agenda is the lack of theory. There is no well-articulated theory or set of hypotheses to explain why the relationships between drinking and crime among women differ in complex ways from the relationships between drinking and crime among men. It is hoped that some of the patterns of gender differences described here will help to stimulate or provoke explanations, which can then move us beyond a genderless view of crime and how alcohol affects it.

References

Aarens, M., Cameron, T., Roizen, J., Roizen, R., Room, R., Schneberk, D., & Wingard, D. (1978). *Alcohol, casualties and crime* (Report C-18). Berkeley, CA: Alcohol Research Group.

Abel, E.L., Strasburger, E.L., & Zeidenberg, P. (1985). Seasonal, monthly, and day-of-week trends in homicide as affected by alcohol and race. *Alcoholism: Clinical and Experimental Research, 9,* 281-283.

Abel, E.L., & Zeidenberg, P. (1985). Age, alcohol and violent death: A postmortem study. *Journal of Studies on Alcohol, 46,* 228-231.

Bacon, S.D. (1963). Alcohol, alcoholism, and crime. *Crime and Delinquency, 9,* 1-14.

Blane, H.T., & Hewitt, L.E. (1977). *Alcohol and youth: An analysis of the literature, 1960-1975* (NTIS No. PB-268-698). Springfield, VA: National Technical Information Service.

Cahalan, D., & Cisin, I.H. (1980). American drinking practices: Summary of findings from a national probability sample: I. Extent of drinking by population subgroups. In D.A. Ward (Ed.), *Alcoholism: Introduction to theory and treatment.* Dubuque, IA: Kendall/Hunt.

Chesney-Lind, M. (1986). Women and crime: The female offender. *Signs: Journal of Women in Culture and Society, 12,* 78-96.

Collins, J.J. (1981). *Alcohol use and criminal behavior: An executive summary.* Washington, DC: National Institute of Justice.

Cordilia, A. (1985). Alcohol and property crime: Exploring the causal nexus. *Journal of Studies on Alcohol, 46,* 161-171.

Dawkins, R.L., & Dawkins, M.P. (1983). Alcohol use and delinquency among black, white, and Hispanic adolescent offenders. *Adolescence, 18,* 799-809.

Gary, L.E. (1986). Drinking, homicide, and the black male. *Journal of Black Studies, 17,* 15-31.

Gelfand, M. (1971). The extent of alcohol consumption by Africans: The significance of the weapon at beer drinks. *Journal of Forensic Medicine, 18,* 53-64.

Gerson, L.W. (1978). Alcohol-related acts of violence: Who was drinking and where the acts occurred. *Journal of Studies on Alcohol, 39,* 1294-1296.

Gerson, L.W. & Preston, D.A. (1979). Alcohol consumption and the incidence of violent crime. *Journal of Studies on Alcohol, 40,* 307-312.

Gilligan, C. (1982). *In a Different Voice: Psychological theory and women's development.* Cambridge, MA: Harvard University Press.

Greenberg, D.F. (1985). Age, crime, and social explanation. *American Journal of Sociology, 91,* 1-21.

Greene, E., & Wakefield, R. (1979). Patterns of middle and upper class homicide. *Journal of Criminal Law and Criminology, 70,* 172-181.

Greenwood, O., Petersilia, J., & Zimring, F. (1980). *Age, crime, and sanctions: The transformation from juvenile to adult court.* Santa Monica, CA: Rand Corporation.

Hirschi, T. (1969). *Causes of delinquency.* Berkeley: University of California Press.

Hollis, W.S. (1974). On the etiology of criminal homicides: The alcohol factor. *Journal of Police Science and Administration, 2,* 50-53.

Jensen, G.J., & Eve, R. (1976). Sex differences in delinquency: An examination of popular sociological explanations. *Criminology, 13,* 427-448.

Ladouceur, P., & Temple, M. (1985). Substance abuse among rapists: A comparison with other serious felons. *Crime and Delinquency, 31,* 269-94.

Leonard, K.E., Bromet, E.J., Parkinson, D.K., Day, N.L., & Ryan, C.M. (1985). Patterns of alcohol use and physically aggressive behavior in men. *Journal of Studies on Alcohol, 46,* 279-282.

Mayfield, D. (1976). Alcoholism, alcohol, intoxication and assaultive behavior. *Diseases of the Nervous System, 37,* 288-291.

Miller, T.R., Cohen, M.A., & Rossman, S.B. (1993). Victim costs of violent crime and resulting injuries. *Health Affairs, 12*(4), 186-197.

Murdoch, D., Pihl, R.O., & Ross, D. (1990). Alcohol and crimes of violence. *International Journal of the Addictions, 25,* 1065-1081.

Pernanen, K. (1976). Alcohol and crimes of violence. In B. Kissin & H. Begleiter (Eds.), *Social aspects of alcoholism* (pp. 351-444). New York: Plenum.

Pernanen, K. (1981). Theoretical aspects of the relationship between alcohol use and crime. In J.J. Collins (Ed.), *Drinking and crime: Perspectives on the relationship between alcohol use and criminal behavior.* New York: Guilford Press.

Petersilia, J. (1980). Criminal career research: A review of recent evidence. In N. Morris & M. Tonry (Eds.), *Crime and justice: An annual review of research: Vol. 2.* Chicago: University of Chicago Press.

Pincock, T.A. (1962). The frequency of alcoholism among self-referred persons and those referred by the courts for psychiatric examination. *Canadian Medical Association Journal, 87,* 282-286.

Reid, S.T. (1991). *Crime and criminology (6th ed.).* Fort Worth, TX: Harcourt Brace Jovanovich College Pubs.

Robbins, C.A. (1991). Social roles and alcohol abuse among older men and women. *Family and Community Health, 13,* 37-48.

Room, R. (1983). Alcohol and crime: Alcohol and criminal behavior and events. In S.H. Kadish et al. (Eds.). *Encyclopedia of crime and justice.* New York: Free Press.

Rouse, T.P., & Unnithan, N.P. (1993). Comparative ideologies and alcoholism: The Protestant and proletarian ethics. *Social Problems, 40,* 213-227.

Schur, E.M. (1969). *Our criminal society: The social and legal sources of crime in America.* Englewood Cliffs, NJ: Prentice-Hall.

Steffensmeier, D.J. (1983). Organizational properties and sex-segregation in the underworld: Building a sociological theory of sex differences in crime. *Social Forces, 61,* 1010-1032.

Steffensmeier, D., & Allan, E. (1991). Gender, age, and crime. In J.F. Sheley (Ed.), *Criminology: A contemporary handbook.* Belmont, CA: Wadsworth.

Steffensmeier, D., & Streifel, C. (1991). Age, gender, and crime across three historical periods: 1935, 1960, and 1985. *Social Forces, 69,* 869-94.

Temple, M., & Ladouceur, P. (1986). The alcohol-crime relationship as an age-specific phenomenon: A longitudinal study. *Contemporary Drug Problems, 13,* 89-115.

U.S. Department of Health and Human Services. Public Health Service. (1991). *Healthy People 2000: National Health Promotion and Disease Prevention Objectives* (DHHS Publication No. PHS 91-50212). Full report, with commentary. Washington, DC: U.S. Government Printing Office.

U.S. Department of Justice. (1991). *Survey of inmates of state correctional facilities, 1991* (ICPSR 8711). Washington, DC: Bureau of Justice Statistics.

Voss, H.L., & Hepburn, J.R. (1968). Patterns in criminal homicide in Chicago. *Journal of Criminal Law, Criminology, and Police Science, 59,* 499-508.

Welte, J.W., & Abel, E.L. (1989). Homicide: Drinking by the victim. *Journal of Studies on Alcohol, 50,* 197-201.

Welte, J.W., & Miller, B.A. (1987). Alcohol use by violent and property offenders. *Drug and Alcohol Dependence, 19,* 313-324.

Wolfgang, M.E. (1958). *Patterns in criminal homicide.* Philadelphia: University of Pennsylvania.

Wolfgang, M.E., & Strohm, R.B. (1956). The relationship between alcohol and criminal homicide. *Quarterly Journal of Studies on Alcohol, 17,* 411-425.

Zahn, M.A., & Riedel, M. (1978). *Nature and patterns of homicide in eight American cities, 1978* (ICPSR 8936). Washington, DC: Bureau of Justice Statistics.

Gender and Social Intervention in Drinking-Related Problems

Introductory Note

A ll of the preceding chapters have been concerned with explaining how gender affects alcohol consumption and its consequences. If men and women differ in how they develop harmful drinking patterns, it might seem logical to develop gender-differentiated approaches for intervening in drinking problems. However, the social responses to women's and men's drinking problems have not been that logical. On the one hand, because problem drinking has been socially stereotyped as a male problem, women's problem drinking has often been neglected or assumed to follow the same patterns as men's. As a result, relatively little is known about how well the methods for detecting and treating men's alcohol-related problems work for women, and about whether gender-specific methods would help women more; and people and programs that try to help men with drinking problems may not be prepared to offer help to women. On the other hand, women who are publicly identified as problem drinkers may be regarded as deviating so far from traditional gender roles and responsibilities that they deserve to be condemned rather than helped. As a result, alcohol-abusing women may be punished for drinking problems that men would be treated for. Each of the chapters in this section examines ways in which assumptions that only men have (or should have) drinking problems may penalize women who need help with problem drinking.

Methods for detecting alcohol-related problems have some characteristics that may limit their usefulness for women, as revealed by Russell, Chan, and Mudar. One limitation is that most of the available screening methods detect advanced stages of alcohol abuse or dependence better than they do early stages. Poor early detection of alcohol problems is detrimental particularly for women because other social practices and policies are likely to deter women from seeking early help for drinking problems (as discussed in the other two chapters of this section). A second limitation of most current screening methods is that they were developed for use with male problem drinkers, and have not been adequately evaluated for how well they detect women's alcohol problems. Some screening instruments are based in part on acting-out behavior and legal problems that are more typical of male than female problem drinkers. Also, any confrontational screening tactics used to break through male denial of drinking problems may backfire with women, particularly if their drinking problems are more easily concealed than men's. Russell, Chan, and Mudar suggest research strategies and screening measures (such as the TWEAK) that may help to reduce some of the problems of insensitivity in detection of women's drinking problems.

Even when women recognize that they need help with drinking-related problems, they may be discouraged from getting the help they need. Walitzer and Connors suggest that treatment professionals may be less likely to offer their services to women than to men, because they regard women's drinking problems as less severe than men's, or because they assume that treatment will help women less than men (an assumption not supported by the evidence summarized in the chapter). Women with alcohol problems may also be unwelcome or uncomfortable in treatment programs designed for men and serving mostly male clients. That may be one reason why alcohol-abusing women tend to seek help from general mental health services instead of from alcohol treatment programs. The need for treatment programs oriented specifically to women was a major reason for developing the Women and Health Program in Buffalo, N.Y. This program aims to help women in the early stages of problem drinking to moderate their alcohol consumption, through training in behavioral self-control strategies, self-monitoring of drinking behavior, and individualized incremental goals for reducing alcohol consumption. Because clients in the program have tended to be older, Euro-American, and well-educated, it is unclear yet whether this approach can be a model for early intervention with all women who have drinking problems, or whether early intervention should be further differentiated for different subgroups of women drinkers.

Women with drinking problems will not have the same chances for treatment that men do unless social policies support such a change. Blume describes how state governments and law enforcement agencies have not supported the same interventions for women's drinking problems as for men's. In a society where women are increasingly encouraged to buy alcoholic beverages, states have found it hard to make federally mandated increases in women's alcohol treatment services. Instead, women have been punished for alcohol impairment in ways that men would not be. A man whose drinking impairs his work and earning power and endangers clients and fellow employees may be referred to an employee assistance program or some other treatment service. A woman whose drinking creates risks for her pregnancy or for her care of her children may be jailed or involuntarily committed and have her children taken away. What matters is not the severity of drinking hazards or the efficacy of measures to control drinking, but the degree to which traditional gender roles have been violated. Men may be treated for problems that arise because they behaved as they were expected to; women may be punished for problems that arise because they behaved as they were expected *not* to. Gender divides not only alcohol use and its effects, but also how we try to control or counteract those effects.

CHAPTER 17

Gender and Screening for Alcohol-Related Problems

MARCIA RUSSELL, ARTHUR W.K. CHAN, AND PAMELA MUDAR

Until recently, instruments for screening and assessment of alcohol-related problems have been developed and validated predominantly on male populations. In this chapter, screening principles and methods used to evaluate screening instruments are reviewed, and gender differences that may influence alcohol screening procedures are discussed. New alcohol screening measures developed especially for use with women are described.

Screening: Principles of Early Detection

Although the terms *screening* and *case-finding* are often used interchangeably, screening refers to the mass-administration of a test among individuals not identified as being at risk. In contrast, case-finding refers to the administration of a test among individuals who have been singled out as already at risk in some way. Research on early detection of alcohol-related problems often pertains to case-finding; however, this work is usually discussed in terms of screening, a practice that will be followed here.

The purpose of screening for a health problem is to identify it in its early stages, so that intervention can take place before serious long-term consequences have occurred. Key factors that determine whether a condition is appropriate for screening are: (1) a recognizable latent or early symptomatic stage and (2) a screening test or examination, acceptable to the population, capable of detecting the condition in its latent or early symptomatic stage (Russell, 1982). Other factors must also be present to justify screening. For example, intervention at the latent or early symptomatic stage must be cost-effective, available, accessible, and acceptable. These issues as they relate to early intervention for alcohol problems in women are discussed elsewhere in this book by Passaro and Little (chapter 4) and by Walitzer and Connors (chapter 18).

The goal of both screening and diagnostic procedures is to identify individuals having a particular disease or condition. However, by definition, screening procedures are less accurate than diagnostic procedures in establishing an individual's "true status" with respect to the condition in question. The usefulness of screening, given that it is less accurate, lies in the fact that its implementation is less time-consuming, less costly, less invasive, or less risky, than alternative diagnostic procedures.

Trends toward Earlier Intervention in Alcohol Disorders

Currently, there is a great deal of support in the alcohol treatment community for early intervention. Prior to the 1970s, the number of alcoholics in treatment was relatively small; patients were typically middle-aged males with multiple, long-standing problems who had exhausted their social and economic resources (Weisner, 1990). Epidemiologic surveys conducted in the 1970s revealed that problem drinkers in the general population were also likely to be male, but they tended to be younger and less disadvantaged than the treatment population, and they had fewer, more isolated drinking problems. These studies alerted policymakers to the fact that, although problem drinkers have fewer problems per capita than alcoholics, they account for a greater proportion of the alcohol-related problems in the United States because of their larger numbers (Institute of Medicine, 1990; Kreitman, 1986). There is currently no reliable method of determining which problem drinkers will progress to end-stage alcoholism. However, early intervention efforts are based on the premise that all drinkers experiencing problems could benefit from assistance in changing their lifestyles so as to decrease their involvement with alcohol. To meet this perceived need, a major expansion in the definition of the population considered appropriate for alcohol treatment took place in the 1980s (Institute of Medicine, 1990; Weisner, 1987). The new target population includes large numbers of alcoholics and problem drinkers who experience serious difficulties related to their alcohol use, but who are more functional than the severe, end-stage alcoholics who most often entered treatment in the past (Institute of Medicine, 1990; Room, 1977; Weisner, 1987). Although recognition of the costs and suffering involved has stimulated research on effective methods to intervene at earlier stages in alcoholism, much less is known about how to identify individuals in the population in need of such intervention. Screening has an important role to play in this regard.

Criteria Used to Evaluate Screening Methods

Before reviewing methods of screening for alcohol disorders, it will be useful to define criteria used to evaluate the effectiveness of screeners and to discuss factors that influence this effectiveness.

Evaluating Screening Methods

A diagnostic procedure that is used in the evaluation of screening tests is referred to as a "gold standard," against which the effectiveness of a screener in predicting a subject's "true" status is assessed. In Table 1, screening and diagnostic results for a hypothetical alcohol disorder are summarized in a 2 × 2 table. Measures of merit useful in evaluating screening procedures are derived from data in such tables, as illustrated: *sensitivity* (the probability that a diagnosed case is positive on the test); *specificity* (the probability that a person not diagnosed as a case is negative on the test); *positive predictive value* (the probability that a person with a positive screening score is diagnosed as a case); and *efficiency* (the overall percent correctly identified) (Hennekens & Buring, 1987).

Although the basic paradigm used to evaluate a screening procedure is straightforward, findings are influenced by: (1) the "gold standard" employed in the study, (2) the population studied, (3) the cut-point used to define a positive screen, (4) the prevalence of the condition for which screening is being

TABLE 1
Evaluating an Alcohol Screening Test

	Alcohol Diagnosis (Gold Standard)		
	Positive	Negative	Total
Results of alcohol screening test:			
Positive	a (4)	b (10)	a + b (14)
Negative	c (1)	d (85)	c + d (86)
Total	a + c (5)	b + d (95)	(100)

Sensitivity $= \dfrac{a}{a + c}$ 4/5 = 80.0%.

Specificity $= \dfrac{d}{b + d}$ 85/95 = 89.5%.

Positive Predictive Value $= \dfrac{a}{a + b}$ 4/14 = 28.6%.

Efficiency $= \dfrac{a + d}{a + b + c + d}$ 89/100 = 89.0%.

a = Positive on both screener and gold standard (true positive).
b = Positive on screener, but not on gold standard (false positive).
c = Negative on screener, but positive on gold standard (false negative).
d = Negative on both screener and gold standard (true negative).

done, and (5) factors that may influence the validity of responses either to the screener or the diagnostic test.

Gold Standards

Careful attention to "gold standards" in published studies reveals that many are poorly defined, subject to unreliability themselves, and not as independent of the screener as one might wish. It is not uncommon, particularly in the earlier studies, for one screener to have been used to validate another. More recent screening evaluations have been much improved by adoption of state-of-the-art methods to assess alcohol disorders.

Epidemiologic research on alcohol disorders was revolutionized in the early 1980s by development of the Diagnostic Interview Schedule (DIS; Robins et al., 1981), a structured interview which could be administered by lay interviewers to assess criteria for the diagnosis of alcohol abuse and dependence. Despite the availability of this new technology, some variability in the assessment of alcohol disorders still exists. One source of variability lies in the criteria used to establish diagnoses (Grant & Towle, 1991). A second source of variability lies in the choice of the interview selected to assess diagnostic criteria (Cottler & Compton, 1993; Hasin, 1991).

Just as the use of standardized diagnostic criteria and structured interviews has begun to bring order to gold standards employed in the evaluation of screening for alcohol disorders, the focus of screening has begun to shift from alcohol disorders to problem drinking. To date, no comparable attempts to develop standardized methods of assessing problem drinking have been made, and this remains a difficulty in evaluating methods proposed to screen for problem drinkers.

When the issue is screening for harmful drinking or risk drinking during pregnancy, the question of a gold standard becomes even more problematical. Questions on alcohol consumption are often used as a gold standard to estimate alcohol intake; however, a rationale for screening is that alcohol consumption may not be reported accurately. Investigators employing this study design are, thus, in the untenable position of evaluating a screener using a gold standard that is thought to be less valid than the screening measure itself. There is a clear need for studies employing more rigorous assessments of alcohol consumption in such evaluations.

The validity of self-report consumption data may be increased by techniques such as the use of a bogus pipeline (Lowe et al., 1986; Wagenaar et al., 1993), collateral sources of data, or contracts with subjects to provide accurate information. When applying the bogus pipeline method, respondents are led to believe that investigators have an independent measure of their alcohol consumption, for example, from a urine, blood, or hair sample. This belief encourages accurate reporting. Collateral sources of data may include medical or legal records providing evidence of alcohol use, or information on a respondent's drinking provided by family members or friends. However, it should be recognized that collateral sources of data may also be inaccurate. For example, a wife may know little of her husband's drinking outside the home, and a husband may be unaware that his wife drinks during the day while he is at work.

Populations Studied

The cost of obtaining follow-up diagnoses has prompted some researchers to validate screening instruments in alcohol treatment settings. A limitation of this approach is that alcoholics in treatment tend to have severe disorders and many symptoms. Accordingly, they score high on screeners, which may overestimate sensitivity and specificity rates. When the same screeners are applied to populations in which the majority of alcohol disorders are mild or moderate, they yield intermediate test scores, which differentiate less effectively between people with and without disorders. This problem is compounded when the goal is early intervention, as is often the case, and problem drinkers are included in the target population to be identified.

The development of structured diagnostic interviews has greatly reduced the cost of determining who in a given population meets criteria for a standardized diagnosis of an alcohol disorder. Lowered diagnostic costs make it feasible to validate screening instruments in populations like the ones in which they will ultimately be used; however, this potential remains to be fully exploited.

Cut-Points

The ideal screening test would be both highly sensitive and highly specific, but in actuality there is usually a tradeoff between sensitivity and specificity for any given test. Most tests yield a range of scores, with some clearly normal, others clearly abnormal, and the remainder somewhere in between. In such situations, the cut-point used to define a positive screening score is arbitrary. If a lenient criterion is used, more individuals with alcohol disorders will be identified (high sensitivity, low false negative rates), but more people without disorders will also screen positive (low specificity, high false positive rates). Conversely, employing a stringent screening criterion will reduce the number of individuals without disorders who screen positive (high specificity, low false positive rate), but more people who have disorders will be missed by the screening test (low sensitivity, high false negative rates). Given the importance of identifying people with alcohol disorders and problem drinkers, greater attention should be given to sensitivity whenever possible.

However, specificity takes on added significance in situations where adequate resources are not available to follow up all individuals who screen positive.

Prevalence

It should be noted that positive predictive values and efficiency scores are influenced by the prevalence of the condition for which one is screening. As illustrated in Table 1, when the prevalence of an alcohol disorder is 5%, a rate which may be even lower among some groups of women, positive predictive values tend to be low even though sensitivity and specificity rates are fairly high. In contrast, a prevalence rate of 5% could yield a high efficiency score even if sensitivity were low, as long as specificity is reasonably high. For example, 95% of the population in Table 1 could be correctly identified simply by assuming there were no alcoholics, an assumption that would yield a sensitivity of 0% and a specificity of 100%.

Factors That May Influence the Validity of Responses Either to the Screener or the Diagnostic Test

Validity is a major concern for screeners and diagnostic tests that depend on accurate reports of alcohol consumption or problems related to alcohol. Alcohol consumption is difficult to remember and summarize accurately, and fear of stigmatization may inhibit disclosure of heavy drinking and alcohol problems. Evidence that respondents underestimate their consumption in alcohol surveys has been provided by studies comparing the amount of alcohol sold in a given region with the consumption estimated from survey data. Typically, self-reported alcohol consumption accounts for only 40-60% of the alcohol sold (for reviews, see Midanik, 1982, 1988), although reporting error is not the only reason for this discrepancy. If all drinkers underestimated their intakes to the same extent, the cut-points of screening instruments could be adjusted to identify the heaviest drinkers; however, investigation of this point has yielded inconclusive results. Some researchers have reported fairly good agreement between self-reports and independent assessments of alcohol intake, whereas others found that heavier drinkers and drinkers with problems underestimated their intakes more than light drinkers (Midanik, 1988).

Despite these limitations, survey researchers have continued to rely on self-reports of alcohol-related behavior. They have been forced to do so by the lack of practical alternatives, but they have been encouraged also by studies demonstrating that the validity of self-report data can be maximized by employing good assessment techniques (Babor et al., 1987; Room, 1990; Skinner, 1984). These techniques, which include such things as putting respondents at ease and clearly stating the questions, should be employed in screening situations to the fullest extent possible.

Self-report data are not the only types of screening information for which the validity of responses is an important issue. The sensitivity and specificity of biologically based tests, discussed later in this chapter, can be influenced by factors such as age, illness, and procedures employed in obtaining, storing, and processing specimens.

The Ultimate Evaluation

Ultimately, the test of any screening program is to demonstrate that it has a favorable long-term impact on health relative to its cost. Establishing the sensitivity and specificity of a screening test is just the first step. It must also be demonstrated that having identified a patient with a drinking problem, the patient can be induced to participate in an intervention, and that the intervention produces long-term health benefits, offsetting the cost of screening and intervention.

Methods of Screening for Alcohol Disorders and Harmful Drinking Patterns

There are several approaches to identifying individuals with alcohol-related problems: brief questionnaires, laboratory tests, physical examinations, and composites of two or more of these methods.

Brief Questionnaires

One of the earliest screening questionnaires to be developed was the Michigan Alcoholism Screening Test (MAST; Selzer, 1971). It consists of 25 questions, many used in previous alcoholism surveys, and was intended to provide a quantitative, structured interview for the detection of alcoholism, an interview that could be rapidly administered by professional as well as nonprofessional personnel. Items that are highly discriminating receive 2 points, and the rest receive 1 point each, except for the following three questions which are considered diagnostic and score 5 each: "Have you ever attended a meeting of Alcoholics Anonymous?" "Have you ever gone to anyone for help about your drinking?" "Have you ever been in a hospital because of drinking?" Scores range from 0 to 53. Originally, scores of 3 or less were considered nonalcoholic, scores of 4 were suggestive of alcoholism, and 5 or more indicated alcoholism. In a subsequent study of males renewing their drivers' licenses, 17% to 19% scored 5 or more on the MAST (Selzer et al., 1975). The authors thought that these rates were too high for alcoholism and stated that cutpoints could be increased to 4 or less, 5 or 6, and 7 or more, respectively, to reduce the number of false positives.

The introduction of the MAST was followed by numerous modifications: the brief MAST (BMAST), based on the 10 most discriminating questions (Pokorny et al., 1972); a self-administered version (Selzer et al., 1975); a short version (SMAST) having 13 items (Selzer et al., 1975); a family form (McAuley et al., 1978); a self-administered (SAAST) expanded form (Hurt et al., 1980; Swenson & Morse, 1975); and the Veteran's Administration Alcoholism Screening Test (VAST), a form that included a time reference (Magruder-Habib et al., 1982).

The MAST has been the object of considerable critical research. As will be discussed later, it was thought that the MAST may not represent the universe of alcoholics because it was developed and tested in hospitalized male alcoholics. In addition, it was hypothesized that it would work better among alcoholics in treatment who have overcome denial and have admitted their dependence on alcohol than among alcoholics who have not been so identified (Kaplan et al., 1974, 1975). Another problem is MAST items that contribute to false positive scores among people who report attending an Alcoholics Anonymous (AA) meeting (but who did not attend because they themselves had a drinking problem), among people who report that drinking caused a problem between them and a family member (but it was the family member's drinking, not theirs, that caused the problem), and among abstainers who report that they do not consider themselves normal drinkers (Fleming & Barry, 1989; Martin et al., 1990).

Finally, factor analyses have revealed that, in addition to items sensitive to problem drinking, the MAST contains two major components that are directed toward the identification of severely affected alcoholics who may have a treatment history (Friedrich et al., 1978; Skinner, 1979). These components, retained even in brief versions of the MAST, may be redundant and counterproductive given the current emphasis on earlier intervention. It seems likely that alcoholics with multiple, long-standing problems would acknowledge having experienced early signs of problem drinking. Therefore, it can be argued that items on alcoholism treatment and serious, late-stage consequences of drinking simply add to the length of the screener and make its goal of identifying an alcohol disorder very obvious, without identifying disorders that would otherwise be missed. Screening instruments that employ items sensitive to the earlier stages of alcohol abuse, many of which are derived from the MAST, are the Malmo-MAST, CAGE, AUDIT, T-ACE, and TWEAK, discussed below. They are all considerably shorter than the MAST and easier to score, increasing their clinical utility. Indeed, for diagnosing alcohol disorders, the development of interview schedules that are shorter and easier to score than the full-length version of the MAST should make its use as an alcohol screening instrument obsolete. A Swedish version of the brief MAST, the Malmo-MAST (Mm-MAST; Kristenson & Trell, 1982), was developed to screen apparently healthy middle-aged men in Malmo. This questionnaire differs from other brief versions of the MAST in that it excludes potentially upsetting items on serious, end-stage alcohol problems.

The CAGE employs four questions designed to be incorporated into a clinical interview to screen for alcoholism (Ewing, 1984; Ewing & Rouse, 1970): "Have you ever felt you ought to *c*ut down on your drinking?" "Have people *a*nnoyed you by criticizing your drinking?" "Have you ever felt bad or *g*uilty about your drinking?" "Have you ever had a drink first thing in the morning to steady your nerves or get rid of a hangover (*e*yeopener)?" Positive responses score 1 point. Ewing and Rouse (1970) had recommended further investigation of patients who scored 1 or more points, but a cut-point of 2 or more has been used more often (e.g., Mayfield et al., 1974).

One limitation of screening instruments such as the MAST and CAGE is that their items assess lifetime experiences related to alcohol abuse. Middle-aged and elderly individuals who may have drunk heavily in their youth are likely to endorse enough items to score positively (Kent, 1991). This can lead to false positives in situations where one is screening for people who have a current drinking problem. Another limitation of screening instruments such as these is that they may not identify heavy drinkers who have not experienced alcohol-related problems (Heck & Lichtenberg, 1990). The Alcohol Use Disorders Identification Test (AUDIT) addresses this shortcoming (Saunders et al., 1993).

The AUDIT is a 10-item screening questionnaire developed in 1982 by an international group of alcohol researchers under the auspices of the World Health Organization (Babor et al., 1989; Saunders et al., 1993). The complete assessment from which AUDIT was derived included a 150-item structured interview, a clinical examination which focused on physical signs of harmful alcohol consumption, and blood sampling for biochemical and hematological tests (Saunders et al., 1993). AUDIT's purpose was the early identification of harmful drinking rather than alcoholism. Therefore, items were selected that best distinguished light drinkers from harmful drinkers, although it can also detect alcoholism with a high degree of accuracy (Babor et al., 1989). Items selected tapped three domains: (1) hazardous alcohol consumption (three questions on the amount and frequency of drinking); (2) dependence symptoms (three questions); and (3) harmful alcohol consumption (four questions on problems caused by alcohol, including adverse psychological reactions). Responses are multiple choice, with item scores ranging from 0 to 4 and totals ranging from 0 to 40; scores over 8 indicate a strong likelihood of hazardous or harmful alcohol consumption.

Another approach to detecting heavy drinking was taken by Sokol and his colleagues, who hypothesized that direct questions about drinking may trigger denial (Sokol et al., 1985). They assessed heavy alcohol use indirectly by asking subjects about their tolerance to alcohol's inebriating effects. They tested the MAST, CAGE, and a tolerance question ("How many drinks does it take to make you feel *high*?") on 971 African-American obstetric patients attending an inner-city clinic in Detroit (Sokol et al., 1989). A discriminant function analysis that included the CAGE and tolerance items revealed that having ever felt bad or guilty about drinking did not contribute significantly to the prediction of risk drinking (more than two drinks/day) near the time of conception. Based on these data, a new, four-item screening instrument, the T-ACE, was proposed (see Appendix). The "tolerance" question scores 2 points if women need more than two drinks to get high, and the three CAGE questions, "annoyed/cut down/eyeopener," each score 1 point; scores of 2 or more are considered positive. T-ACE was as sensitive to periconceptional risk drinking as the much longer MAST, and more sensitive than the CAGE (Sokol et al., 1989). T-ACE was subsequently found to be even more sensitive when an alternative form of the tolerance question was tested: "How many drinks can you hold?" (Martier et al., 1990). This item scores 2 points if women report being able to hold six drinks or more before passing out or falling asleep.

Tolerance is also a key item in the TWEAK questionnaire developed by Russell (1994) (see Appendix). Russell and Bigler (1979) adapted an extended, self-administered form of the MAST for use in a female population. Questions were eliminated that asked about behavior that is more typical of male than female alcohol abuse, such as having fist fights after drinking, and items indicative of an advanced alcohol disorder, such as attendance at AA meetings. Their studies of screening for alcohol abuse among obstetric patients revealed that three questions identified 70% of the women reporting two or more indications of problem drinking: having close friends or relatives *w*orry or complain about their drinking during the past year, blackouts (*a*mnesia), and feeling the need to cut down (*k*ut down) on drinking (Russell & Skinner, 1988). These questions, plus *t*olerance and a question on morning drinking (*e*yeopener), were combined to form the TWEAK test. To score the TWEAK, a seven-point scale is used. Positive responses to the tolerance and worry questions score 2 points each, and each of the last three questions scores 1 point for a positive response. A total score of 2 or more points indicates the woman is likely to be a risk/problem drinker.

The ability of T-ACE, TWEAK, and CAGE to detect periconceptional risk drinking has been studied in African-American inner-city obstetric patients (Russell et al., 1994). The utility of these screens in detecting problem drinking has also been examined (Table 2). Questionnaires were administered by trained interviewers to women on their first visit to a Detroit core city prenatal clinic. The MAST was administered first, followed by the CAGE, questions on periconceptional drinking, and the tolerance question (the number of drinks needed to feel high). The TWEAK and T-ACE were not administered as separate screening instruments; they were constructed using the tolerance question and items embedded in the MAST and CAGE. Periconceptional drinking was based on drinking during a typical week before women became

TABLE 2
Sensitivity and Specificity of T-ACE, TWEAK, and CAGE in Screening for
Periconceptional Risk Drinking and Problem Drinking in African-
American, Inner-City Obstetric Patients

Screener (cut-point)	N	Periconceptional Risk Drinking*		Problem Drinking**	
		Sensitivity (%)	Specificity (%)	Sensitivity (%)	Specificity (%)
T-ACE (2+)	4,743	70	85	74	85
TWEAK (2+)	4,743	79	83	85	82
CAGE (1+)	4,743	68	82	87	82
CAGE (2+)	4,743	49	93	75	94

* One ounce of absolute alcohol (about two standard drinks) per day, or about 14 drinks or more per week.
**A score of 7 or more on the MAST; MAST items that overlapped with screening items were not scored.

pregnant, which was assessed using cognitive interviewing techniques to elicit reports of the amounts and types of alcoholic beverages drunk during each day of the week. Periconceptional risk drinking was defined as 14 or more drinks per week. Women were considered problem drinkers if they scored 7 or more on the MAST; items common to the screens were not scored. Analyses were based on 4,743 consecutive patients who admitted having consumed alcohol at some time.

Results summarized in Table 2 indicate that TWEAK was more sensitive to periconceptional risk drinking and problem drinking than T-ACE. The sensitivity of CAGE to problem drinking was markedly improved by using a cut-point of 1 or more instead of 2 or more. However, even with a cut-point of 1 or more, CAGE was relatively insensitive to risk drinking. These findings are consistent with the origin and goals of the screening instruments. T-ACE, with its tolerance question, was specifically designed to detect risk drinking during pregnancy (Sokol et al., 1989). CAGE was intended to be sensitive to alcoholism (Ewing, 1984). TWEAK combined items on alcohol-related problems common in obstetric and gynecologic patients with the tolerance item shown to be useful in assessing alcohol consumption indirectly. Preliminary findings in samples of the general population, patients in two outpatient clinics of a county hospital, and alcoholic inpatients suggest that the TWEAK can detect heavy drinking and alcohol disorders in both men and women in all these populations (Chan et al., 1993).

TWEAK and AUDIT were more sensitive than CAGE or the Brief MAST in detecting harmful drinking and alcohol dependence among male and female, African-American and white, and injured and noninjured emergency room patients (Cherpitel, 1995a), especially using a cut-point of 2 for TWEAK (Cherpitel, 1995b). Cherpitel (1995c) has proposed a new five-item screen, Rapid Alcohol Problems Screen (RAPS), based on her emergency room data, which performed well across gender, race, and injury subgroups among current drinkers who reported ever having three or more drinks at one time.

There are those in the field who, frustrated by the burgeoning number of screening questionnaires, have said, "Why don't you simply ask people if they are alcoholics?" This is close to the screening approach proposed by Cyr and Wartman (1988), which consists of the following two questions: "Have you ever had a drinking problem?" and "When was your last drink?" Having had a drinking problem and drinking alcohol within the past 24 hours correctly identified 91.5% of 47 patients in an ambulatory medical clinic who scored 5 or more on the MAST, and having neither experience correctly identified 89.7% of 185 patients who scored less than 5. However, no confirmatory studies of this approach have been conducted.

Laboratory Tests

It is well established that alcohol is a highly toxic substance and that repeated exposure to high doses can damage many organ systems (Lieber, 1992). Biochemical changes resulting from this damage have been proposed as indicators or biological markers of alcoholism (Chan, 1990). The two most often used conventional markers of alcoholism are gamma-glutamyltransferase (GGT) and mean corpuscular volume (MCV), which tend to be elevated in alcoholics. Increases in serum GGT levels are the result of alcohol-induced damage to the liver that causes the enzyme to be released into the blood stream. Elevation in MCV levels reflects swollen red blood cells (macrocytosis) caused by excessive alcohol consumption (Lieber, 1992). However, most conventional markers, when used alone, are not specific in detecting hazardous drinking/alcoholism, because elevated levels are also associated with many diseases or drug therapies unrelated to alcohol intake (Chan, 1990).

These limitations prompted some investigators to use a battery of conventional laboratory tests and a statistical technique called discriminant analysis to try to distinguish between alcoholics and nonalcoholics (Chan, 1990; Lieber, 1992). The laboratory tests (e.g., SMA23 series) are those commonly ordered by doctors during routine physical examinations. Although this method provides better sensitivity than single conventional tests, and it is useful in corroborating a clinical diagnosis, it is not sufficiently sensitive or specific to be used as a screening test (Lieber, 1992).

In reviews of research on newer biochemical markers of alcoholism (Chan, 1993; Lieber, 1992), one proposed marker is carbohydrate-deficient transferrin (CDT), levels of which tend to be elevated in alcoholics. Transferrin is a plasma protein that is produced in the liver and is involved in the transport of iron. Most studies comparing alcoholics and nonalcoholics have reported sensitivities of the CDT test to be in the range of 65-95% (Stibler, 1991). However, much lower sensitivities (22-29% in two studies) have been reported in detecting nondependent hazardous or heavy drinkers (Chan, 1993). These data exemplify a common limitation of research on biochemical markers: most investigations have compared known alcoholics with control groups of light drinkers or abstainers. Far less information is available on the sensitivities of biochemical markers in detecting people who drink at hazardous levels, but have not developed symptoms of alcohol dependence. Many people in this category can have normal blood biochemistry, particularly young adults (Chan, 1990).

Biochemical indicators are more objective than tests based on self-report. Accordingly, objective physical findings such as abnormal biochemical tests are valuable adjuncts to clinical interviews. Although research to date has indicated that questionnaire data generally have better sensitivity than biochemical markers in detecting alcoholics or problem drinkers, an abnormal biochemical test can be used effectively by doctors to overcome a patient's denial, and to serve as a catalyst for brief intervention.

Physical Examinations

A clinical examination can reveal subtle abnormalities in problem drinkers that reflect the tissue toxicity of alcohol, the effects of alcohol-related trauma, and/or the signs of alcohol withdrawal (Saunders & Conigrave, 1990). This approach to screening is most widely used in Europe, where a French physician, Le Go, developed a grid which serves as a guide for a brief clinical screening procedure (Babor et al., 1985). Examples of key features are abnormal vascularization of the facial skin (reddening due to enlarged blood vessels); coating of the tongue; hepatomegaly (enlarged liver); and tremor of the mouth, tongue, or hands. A screening instrument based on a history of trauma since the age of 18 has been proposed by Skinner and his colleagues (1984). Their Trauma Scale includes the following items: fractures or dislocations to bones or joints, injury in a road traffic accident, head injury, injury in an assault or fight (not during sports), and injury after drinking.

With the exception of scars and bruises, physical signs of alcohol abuse reflect prolonged and unremitting daily drinking more indicative of late than early stages of alcoholism (Saunders & Conigrave, 1990). Rather than serving as the basis for formal screening procedures, such findings are more useful to alert clinicians to a potential alcohol problem that might otherwise have been missed, either because routine alcohol screening was not done or patients denied drinking problems.

Composite Screening Instruments

The purpose of a composite screening instrument is to increase the sensitivity with which individuals with alcohol-related problems are identified by including measures of both physical and psychological consequences of excessive alcohol use. Examples are the Munich Alcoholism Test (MALT; Feuerlein et al., 1980) and the Alcohol Clinical Index (Skinner et al., 1986).

The Impact of Gender on Screening

Brief Questionnaires

Many of the barriers to identification of alcohol disorders in women have the potential to influence the effectiveness of brief questionnaires used to screen for alcohol-related problems. Cultural beliefs that heavy use of alcohol is more acceptable among men than women may lead to greater denial on screening instruments by women and their families (Lane et al., 1992).

A number of the criteria for a diagnosis of alcohol abuse or dependence are based on a history of acting out behaviors, legal problems, tolerance, and withdrawal symptoms, which are more typical of men than women with alcohol disorders (Dawson & Grant, 1993; Klee et al., 1991; Robbins, 1989). Traditional screening instruments, such as the MAST and its derivatives, that reflect these diagnostic criteria are likely to be less effective among women than men seen in primary care settings because women in such settings are less likely to have experienced social and legal consequences of prolonged alcohol use. Women are rarely arrested for DWI, although this may be changing among young women (Popkin, 1991), and they are less likely than men to get into physical fights while using alcohol. Women are more likely to exhibit passive symptoms, such as depression, and more often enter the mental health treatment system than the alcohol treatment system (Davis & Morse, 1987).

The Mm-MAST was revised in 1983 to make it more appropriate for screening women (Österling et al., 1993). Malmo residents born in 1941 were screened in 1983, and response style to the revised Mm-MAST was examined in 911 male and 911 female screenees, a portion of whom were interviewed by physicians to determine their problem drinking status (Österling et al., 1993). The revised Mm-MAST included all four CAGE items. Compared to positive CAGE responses, women were four times more likely and men were two and one half times more likely to be positive on the Mm-MAST. Among those with positive Mm-MAST/CAGE scores, rates of problem drinking were similar for both men and women. However, false negative rates were lower among Mm-MAST than CAGE negative screenees, suggesting that Mm-MAST was the better screening instrument. Reliability of the Mm-MAST was lower for women than men; Cronbach's alphas were 0.58 and 0.69, respectively, and studies are underway to develop a more female-oriented problem drinking screening questionnaire (Österling et al., 1993).

Even in alcohol treatment populations, women have been found to endorse certain MAST items significantly less often than men (Selzer et al., 1979): "Do you ever feel guilty about your drinking?" "Have you ever gotten into physical fights when drinking?" "Have you ever lost friends [or boyfriends] because of your drinking?" "Have you ever lost a job because of drinking?" "Have you ever been arrested for drunken driving, driving while intoxicated or driving under the influence of alcoholic beverages?" Despite these differences, 92% of the women and 97% of the men in Selzer et al.'s (1979) sample scored over 10, leading the authors to conclude that the MAST was equally effective in detecting alcoholism in the two sexes. This conclusion would not apply to early detection of alcohol problems because total scores may have been very different. As has been discussed earlier, problem drinkers in general population samples would be expected to score lower than alcoholics in treatment. Under such circumstances, the fact that MAST has items more typical of male than female alcoholics would make it less sensitive to problem drinking in women. As illustrated by CAGE data in obstetric patients (Table 2), it may be necessary to lower cut-points of screeners developed in male populations to effectively detect alcohol-related problems in women.

Available findings relevant to this point are contradictory. A study conducted in an Australian alcohol treatment population found that females were more likely to score under 20 on the MAST, whereas males, matched on age and date of admission, were more likely to score over 34 (Blankfield & Maritz, 1990). In contrast, in another treatment population, no gender differences in total scores were found on the SAAST, a self-administered, expanded version of the MAST (Davis & Morse, 1987). Whereas Selzer et al. (1979) reported that alcoholic women were less likely than alcoholic men to report ever feeling guilty about their drinking, Davis and Morse (1987) found the opposite.

It may be that these differences are related to characteristics of the treatment populations studied, or that they reflect temporal changes in attitudes toward drinking. A trend toward less permissive drinking norms in the United States has been reported (Room, 1991). In Britain, safe levels of consumption were reduced as information became available documenting physical harm associated with levels of drinking that were not necessarily addictive. Campaigns to inform people of these lowered safe levels could lead to more individuals reporting the need to cut down and having ever felt guilty about their drinking (Waterson & Murray-Lyon, 1988). Such trends may have implications for the interpretation of alcohol screening questionnaires, most of which include one or both of these items, and women may be more influenced than men by such health messages. Indeed, many women experience guilt about their drinking, whether or not they have alcohol-related problems (Lane et al., 1992). This tendency is likely to be especially marked in obstetric populations that have been exposed to campaigns urging them to abstain during pregnancy, and it may account for the failure of guilty feelings to discriminate between risk and nonrisk drinking around the time of conception in the studies of Sokol and colleagues (1989).

The importance of maintaining a nonthreatening environment when asking women about their alcohol consumption has been documented repeatedly in research conducted on the fetal alcohol syndrome (FAS) (for a review, see Russell, 1988). In one prenatal care setting, nurses who saw the patients before they were recruited into an FAS study started warning them about the dangers of drinking during pregnancy (Nadler et al., 1987). This practice was discovered when the reported prevalence of heavy drinking and alcohol problems decreased precipitously. When intervention efforts were rescheduled to take place after patients had participated in the FAS study, prevalence rates went back up. In another study, higher rates of heavy drinking were reported to sympathetic lay interviewers in prenatal settings than to medical personnel postnatally (Hingson et al., 1982). It was hypothesized that establishing rapport with the interviewers and concern for the health of their children influenced women to report their alcohol consumption more accurately in the prenatal clinic. Postnatally, women may have been concerned about retaining custody of their children if they reported heavy drinking. In the case of children who were not completely well, mothers may have been motivated by feelings of guilt or fear of disapproval to minimize their alcohol use during pregnancy.

Babor et al. (1989) investigated the ability of the AUDIT to discriminate between alcoholics in treatment and hospitalized patients with high and low MAST scores. Hospitalized patients with high MAST scores represent a population often considered a prime target for screening and early intervention efforts. The AUDIT discriminated well between patients with low MAST scores and alcoholics, regardless of sex. However, discrimination between patients with high and low MAST scores was substantial only for males. In the larger assessment, the only measure that discriminated between females with high and low MAST scores was lifetime alcohol problems, probably because of its similarity to MAST items. Another factor assessed that differentiated well between high and low MAST scores among women was a family history of alcoholism (Babor et al., 1989).

The finding that family history is associated with alcoholism more strongly in women than men has been reported previously (Cotton, 1979; Lewis & Bucholz, 1991; Russell et al., 1990). The consistency of these findings suggests that an item on alcoholism or problem drinking in the family might be useful in increasing the sensitivity of alcohol screening in women. Indeed, the 4-Ps, a screening questionnaire developed for use in prenatal clinics, asks about alcohol problems in the *p*ast, in the *p*resent, in your *p*arents, and in your *p*artner (Ewing, 1993). However, in a community survey, only about 9% of the women who reported having alcoholism or problem drinking in their mothers or fathers met criteria for a lifetime diagnosis of alcohol abuse or dependence (Russell, 1990). Therefore, the potential for false positives using this criterion alone would be very high.

Laboratory Tests

Sex differences in some blood variables have been documented (U.S. Department of Health and Human Services & National Center for Health Statistics, 1982): e.g., males have significantly higher serum levels of iron, hemoglobin, and hematocrit, but lower mean corpuscular volume (MCV) levels than females. It has been demonstrated that elevated values of MCV and/or GGT predicted levels of drinking and alcohol-related birth defects in problem drinking obstetric patients (Ylikorkala et al., 1987). Furthermore, it has been suggested that MCV is a better indicator of excessive alcohol consumption in women than in men, and that women are more susceptible to the hematological toxicity of ethanol (Chalmers et al., 1980). Weidner et al. (1991) reported that the association of alcohol and higher levels of high-density lipoprotein cholesterol may occur at lower intakes of alcohol in women than in men. Discriminant analysis of several blood chemistry items yielded better sensitivity and specificity for detecting female than male heavy drinkers (Chalmers et al., 1981).

It may be useful to develop screening algorithms that take both sex and age into account. For example, MCV and mean corpuscular hemoglobin (MCH) increase with age regardless of sex and race (U.S. Department of Health and Human Services & National Center for Health Statistics, 1982). Discriminant analyses of blood chemistry items are not very useful for subjects older than 65 because elderly nonalcoholics are often (50%) classified as alcoholics (Ryback et al., 1980). The inappropriateness of several biochemical tests to screen young heavy drinkers has been reported (Bliding, et al., 1982). Tests such as carbohydrate-deficient transferrin (CDT) and mitochondrial ASAT, which have been found to have high sensitivity and specificity in identifying adult alcoholics over 35 years old (Salaspuro, 1986), were found to have poor sensitivity in identifying young adult (18-25 years old) alcoholics (Chan et al., 1989).

Women have higher baseline values of CDT than men (Anton & Moak, 1994; La Grange et al., 1994, 1995; Stibler et al., 1988a,b). The female CDT levels are not elevated during pregnancy, but conflicting reports have documented higher (La Grange et al., 1995) or unchanged (Anton & Moak, 1994; Stibler et al., 1988a,b) CDT levels when oral contraceptives are used. Although CDT levels were elevated in both male and female alcohol abusers, the CDT test had a much higher sensitivity (79% vs. 44%) in detecting male alcohol abusers than female alcohol abusers (Anton & Moak, 1994). In contrast, Stibler et al. (1988a,b, 1991) reported the sensitivity of elevated CDT in detecting female alcohol abusers to be about 85%. Other studies (Nilssen et al., 1992; Nyström et al., 1992) have also reported gender differences in the sensitivity of the CDT test in detecting heavy drinking, but it should be noted that even the sensitivity of CDT for detecting male heavy drinkers was poor in the populations studied, namely young university students and an unselected Norwegian population. It remains to be determined whether there is a gender difference in the ability of the CDT test to detect relapse in alcoholic patients (Rosman et al., 1995).

Physical Examinations

Few validation studies of the Le Go Grid have been conducted, and all but seven of the patients in studies reviewed by Babor et al. (1985) were men. Although women were included in evaluations of the Trauma Scale, gender differences in its effectiveness as a screening instrument for alcohol-related problems have not been investigated. It is thought that the Trauma Scale probably works better for males than females because it picks up the "active" risk-taking aspects of male alcoholism that tend to result in injury (H. Skinner, personal communication, February 26, 1993).

Composite Screening Instruments

Women appear to develop organic damage related to alcohol after consuming smaller amounts of alcohol or after shorter periods of exposure (e.g., see chapter by Lieber in this book). In recognition of gender differences in vulnerability to the toxic effects of alcohol, the Alcohol Clinical Index employs sex-specific cut-offs to define harmful drinking, 40 grams per day (about 3 or 4 drinks) for women and 60 grams per day (about 5 or 6 drinks) for men, but sex-specific evaluations of its specificity and sensitivity have not been published.

Gender Differences in Screening Targets

Drinking during Pregnancy

As illustrated by the brief review of alcohol screening methods, screeners have been developed for a wide array of targets: risk drinking during pregnancy, harmful or hazardous drinking, problem drinking, and alcohol disorders, abuse, and dependence. The shift of emphasis from screeners aimed at identifying end-stage alcohol disorders to those targeting harmful or hazardous drinking reflects increased interest in early intervention with problem drinkers. The shift also reflects awareness that heavy drinkers may suffer serious somatic effects of alcohol use without ever demonstrating signs of dependence or any of the social and legal consequences that contribute to the diagnosis of an alcohol disorder. Screening for problem drinking and harmful or hazardous drinking is equally valid for men and women, but risk drinking during pregnancy is a unique focus of women's screening.

Recognition of the fetal alcohol syndrome in 1973 added a whole new dimension to the concept of hazardous drinking among women. Levels of drinking unlikely to harm a woman herself have been identified as potentially harmful to her children if consumed while she is pregnant. A recent prospective study of prenatal alcohol exposure indicated that the threshold for clinically significant developmental deficits is an average of more than one drink a day (Jacobson et al., 1993). Few women in the study drank daily; therefore, average intake does not represent a typical dose. Indeed, the median exposure was six drinks per occasion among infants born to women who drank more than an average of one drink a day (Jacobson et al., 1993). However, most of these women were negative on the MAST.

Primate studies suggest that patterns of alcohol exposure comparable to weekend binges early in pregnancy are associated with neurological and cognitive deficits in offspring, even in the absence of effects on dysmorphology and growth, and even if there is no further alcohol exposure in the later months of pregnancy (Clarren et al., 1988). Because women usually do not recognize that they are pregnant until some weeks after conception, it would seem prudent for fertile, sexually active women to avoid ever becoming intoxicated, and for women who think they might be pregnant to restrict their alcohol intake even more (U.S. Surgeon General, 1981). Given that women may be fertile from their teens through their early forties, the potential screening target for risk drinking during pregnancy is broad indeed, providing a rationale for increased attention to contraception among women who drink heavily during their child-bearing years. Despite preliminary evidence that paternal drinking may also have a negative impact on pregnancy outcome (Cicero, 1994), men have no comparable restrictions on their drinking. If these early indications are substantiated, men would have to share with women responsibility for the effect of their alcohol consumption on the development of their children.

There has been little public debate on how to bridge realistically the gap between women's current drinking practices and the surgeon general's recommendations. Risk drinking during pregnancy is clearly a potential target for alcohol screening in women, and preliminary prevention studies are being funded, but programs in this area are notable for their absence (cf., Schorling, 1993).

Alcohol Screening in Drunk Driving and Employee Assistance Programs

Drunk driving and employee assistance programs represent major components of the new emphasis on screening and early intervention (Weisner, 1990), yet these programs may not reach women who abuse alcohol as effectively as they reach men. There are a number of factors contributing to the fact that women are underrepresented in drunk driving programs. To the extent that women are more likely than men to drink at home (Wanberg & Knapp, 1970), they are less likely to drive while intoxicated. If women go out drinking with a male companion, the man is more likely to drive, and if police stop a woman who is driving while intoxicated, they are less likely to arrest her than a man—although this may be changing (Popkin, 1991). No one would wish for women to increase their rates of drunk driving; however, the fact that their arrest rates are relatively low means that screening and early intervention programs that target drunk drivers are likely to be less effective for women than men.

Employee assistance programs also may reach men more effectively than women. Some women do not work outside the home, and many women who do work outside the home have occupations that are poorly served by employee assistance programs. Women may be better able to convince supervisors that tardiness and absenteeism are caused by family rather than alcohol-related problems. Male supervisors may be less suspicious of drinking problems in women or more reluctant to confront a woman about her alcohol use. Finally, women, particularly those in low-level jobs, may be more likely to quit in response to job pressure than to stop drinking.

Summary

The following general conclusions may be drawn regarding screening for alcohol disorders. Brief questionnaires represent the easiest to implement, least expensive, and most effective method of screening for alcohol-related problems currently available. A limitation of questionnaires is that they rely on self-report, and it is important to employ techniques and procedures that maximize the validity of responses, to both screening and diagnostic tests. The utility of objective indicators, such as laboratory tests and physical signs of heavy drinking, is limited because they tend to develop after years of abuse, making them relatively insensitive to early problem drinking. In addition, the assessment of biological markers is usually costly and available only in medical settings. However, in these settings biological markers may be useful indicators of problem drinking among individuals who deny abusing alcohol and those who have no other indications of a problem related to their heavy alcohol use.

It is also worth remembering that asking about alcohol-related problems is important even if some individuals with alcohol problems deny them. It is a way of reaching out to those who are willing to report honestly, but who may not recognize that they have a problem or may be unwilling to bring it up themselves. Furthermore, asking about alcohol problems sends a message acknowledging their importance and indicating the availability of help if and when it may be needed. If this is done consistently, in a nonjudgmental manner, it may be useful in overcoming denial.

It is clear from this review that gender influences screening for alcohol-related problems in a number of ways. The limited evidence available suggests that gender differences in the signs and symptoms of alcohol abuse warrant differences in the screening methods used, in the way screeners are scored and interpreted, or both. Screening and early intervention in drunk driving and employee assistance programs seem likely to reach men more effectively than women. Screening programs targeted at early intervention in female alcohol abuse are in their infancy.

A number of important unresolved issues related to screening have been discussed in this chapter: the shift in focus from screening for alcohol disorders to screening for problem drinking; the need for standardized, improved methods of assessing "gold standards" used to evaluate screeners for alcohol disorders, problem drinking, and harmful or hazardous drinking; the need to evaluate screeners in the populations where they will be used; the choice of cut-points; and the need to take prevalence into account when evaluating the effectiveness of screening procedures.

These unresolved issues related to alcohol screening form the basis for an ambitious research agenda. The need to consider gender issues in addressing these questions doubles the agenda. Many screening studies are conducted in populations which include women, but sex-specific analyses cannot be done because too few women were positive on screening. In the absence of adequate information on the influence of gender on screening, it is not clear whether women are negative on screening because they truly have few alcohol problems or because the screening methods employed are not sensitive to their problems. Focused research and adequate funding are necessary to effectively investigate gender issues in alcohol screening. The importance of early intervention for problem drinking in women more than justifies any added cost of research or screening related to their lower prevalence of alcohol-related problems.

Appendix

CAGE

The CAGE consists of four items:

1. Have you ever felt you ought to *c*ut down on your drinking?
2. Have people *a*nnoyed you by criticizing your drinking?
3. Have you ever felt bad or *g*uilty about your drinking?
4. Have you ever had a drink first thing in the morning to steady your nerves or get rid of a hangover (*e*yeopener)?

Each item receives a score of 1 for a positive response, for a possible total of 4 points.

T-ACE

The T-ACE consists of four items:

1. *T*olerance question.*
2. Have people *a*nnoyed you by criticizing your drinking?
3. Have you ever felt you ought to *c*ut down on your drinking?
4. Have you ever had a drink first thing in the morning to steady your nerves or get rid of a hangover (*e*yeopener)?

Two points are scored for the tolerance question, and 1 point is scored for positive responses to each of the other three questions, for a possible total of 5 points.

TWEAK

The TWEAK consists of five items:

1. *T*olerance question.*
2. Have close friends or relatives *w*orried or complained about your drinking in the past year?
3. *E*ye-opener: Do you sometimes take a drink in the morning when you first get up?
4. *A*mnesia (blackouts): Has a friend or family member ever told you about things you said or did while you were drinking that you could not remember?
5. Do you sometimes feel the need to c/*k*ut down on your drinking?

To score the test, a 7-point scale is used. The first two questions, Tolerance and Worry, each score two points, and each of the last three questions scores 1 point for positive responses.

*Two tolerance questions have been proposed for use, and readers may select the one they think most useful and acceptable for their purposes. One tolerance question is: How many drinks does it take to make you feel *high*? If further clarification is requested, respondents are told, "This is how much it takes before you start to feel different than you usually do." Responses of three or more drinks are considered positive. An alternative tolerance question is: How many drinks can you *hold*? (The number of drinks one can hold before passing out or falling asleep.) An answer of six or more drinks is considered positive.

References

Anton, R.F., & Moak, D.H. (1994). Carbohydrate-deficient transferrin and γ-glutamyl-transferase as markers of heavy alcohol consumption: Gender differences. *Alcoholism: Clinical and Experimental Research, 18,* 747-754.

Babor, T.F., Kranzler, H.R., & Lauerman, R.J. (1989). Early detection of harmful alcohol consumption: Comparison of clinical, laboratory, and self-report screening procedures. *Addictive Behaviors, 14,* 139-157.

Babor, T.F., Stephens, R.S., & Marlatt, G.A. (1987). Verbal report methods in clinical research on alcoholism: Response bias and its minimization. *Journal of Studies on Alcohol, 48,* 410-424.

Babor, T.F., Weill, J., Treffardier, M., & Benard, J.Y. (1985). Detection and diagnosis of alcohol dependence using the Le Go grid method. In N.C. Chang & H.M. Chao (Eds.), *NIAAA research monograph 17: Early identification of alcohol abuse* (pp. 321-338) (DHHS Publication No. ADM 85-1258). Washington, DC: U.S. Government Printing Office.

Blankfield, A., & Maritz, J.S. (1990). Female alcoholics. III. Some clinical associations of the Michigan Alcoholism Screening Test and diagnostic implications. *Acta Psychiatrica Scandinavica, 81,* 483-487.

Bliding, G., Bliding, A., Fex, G., & Törnqvist, C. (1982). The appropriateness of laboratory tests in tracing young heavy drinkers. *Drug and Alcohol Dependence, 10,* 153-158.

Chalmers, D.M., Chanarin, I., MacDermott, S., & Levi, A.J. (1980). Sex-related differences in the haematological effects of excessive alcohol consumption. *Journal of Clinical Pathology, 33,* 3-7.

Chalmers, D.M., Rinsler, M.G., MacDermott, S., Spicer, C.C., & Levi, A.J. (1981). Biochemical and haematological indicators of excessive alcohol consumption. *Gut, 22,* 992-996.

Chan, A.W.K. (1990). Biochemical markers for alcoholism. In M. Windle, & J.S. Searles (Eds.), *Children of alcoholics: Critical perspectives* (pp. 39-72). New York: Guilford.

Chan, A.W.K. (1993). Recent developments in detection and biological indicators of alcoholism. *Drugs & Society, 8,* 31-67.

Chan, A.W.K., Leong, F.W., Schanley, D.L., Welte, J.W., Wieczorek, W., Rej, R., & Whitney, R.B. (1989). Transferrin and mitochondrial aspartate aminotransferase in young adult alcoholics. *Drug and Alcohol Dependence, 23,* 13-18.

Chan, A.W.K., Pristach, E.A., Welte, J.W., & Russell, M. (1993). Use of the TWEAK test in screening for alcoholism/heavy drinking in three populations. *Alcoholism: Clinical and Experimental Research, 17,* 1188-1192.

Cherpitel, C.J. (1995a). Screening for alcohol problems in the emergency department. *Annals of Emergency Medicine, 26,* 158-166.

Cherpitel, C.J. (1995b). Analysis of cut points for screening instruments for alcohol problems in the emergency room. *Journal of Studies on Alcohol, 56,* 695-700.

Cherpitel, C.J. (1995c). Screening for alcohol problems in the emergency room: A rapid alcohol problems screen. *Drug and Alcohol Dependence, 40,* 133-137.

Cicero, T.J. (1994). Effects of paternal exposure to alcohol on offspring development. *Alcohol Health & Research World, 18,* 37-41.

Clarren, S.K., Astley, S.J., & Bowden, D.M. (1988). Physical anomalies and developmental delays in nonhuman primate infants exposed to weekly doses of ethanol during gestation. *Teratology, 37,* 561-569.

Cottler, L.B., & Compton, W.M., III. (1993). Advantages of the CIDI family of instruments in epidemiological research of substance use disorders. *International Journal of Methods in Psychiatric Research, 3,* 109-119.

Cotton N.S. (1979). The familial incidence of alcoholism: A review. *Journal of Studies on Alcohol, 40,* 89-116.

Cyr, M.G., & Wartman, S.A. (1988). The effectiveness of routine screening questions in the detection of alcoholism. *Journal of the American Medical Association, 259,* 51-54.

Davis, L.J., & Morse, R.M. (1987). Age and sex differences in the responses of alcoholics to the Self Administered Alcoholism Screening Test. *Journal of Clinical Psychology, 43,* 423-430.

Dawson, D.A., & Grant, B.F. (1993). Gender effects in diagnosing alcohol abuse and dependence. *Journal of Clinical Psychology, 49*(2), 298-307.

Ewing, H. (1993, July). 4Ps. In N. Burke & D. Caldwell (Eds.), *Maternal substance use assessment methods reference manual. A review of screening and clinical as-*

sessment: Alcohol, tobacco, and other drugs (p. 27). Rockville, MD: CSAP National Resource Center for the Prevention of Perinatal Abuse of Alcohol and Other Drugs.

Ewing, J.A. (1984). Detecting alcoholism: The CAGE questionnaire. *Journal of the American Medical Association, 252,* 1905-1907.

Ewing, J.A., & Rouse, B.A. (1970, February). *Identifying the "hidden alcoholic."* Paper presented at the 29th International Congress on Alcohol and Drug Dependence, Sydney, Australia.

Feuerlein, W., Ringer, C., Küfner, H., & Antons, K. (1980). Diagnosis of alcoholism: The Munich Alcoholism Test (MALT). In M. Galanter (Ed.), *Currents in alcoholism:Vol. VII. Recent advances in research and treatment* (pp. 137-147). New York: Grune & Stratton.

Fleming, M.F., & Barry, K.L. (1989). A study examining the psychometric properties of the SMAST-13. *Journal of Substance Abuse, 1,* 173-182.

Friedrich, W.N., Boriskin, J.A., & Nelson, O. (1978). A factor analytic study of the Michigan Alcoholism Screening Test. *Psychological Reports, 42,* 865-866.

Grant, B.F., & Towle, L.H. (1991). A comparison of diagnostic criteria: DSM-III-R, proposed DSM-IV, and proposed ICD-10. *Alcohol Health & ResearchWorld, 15,* 284-292.

Hasin, D.S. (1991). Diagnostic interviews for assessment: Background, reliability, validity. *Alcohol Health & Research World, 15,* 293-302.

Heck, E.J., & Lichtenberg, J.W. (1990). Validity of the CAGE in screening for problem drinking in college students. *Journal of College Student Development, 31,* 359-364.

Hennekens, C.H., & Buring, J.E. (1987). Screening. In S.L. Mayrent (Ed.), *Epidemiology in medicine* (pp. 327-347). Boston, MA: Little, Brown & Company.

Hingson, R., Alpert, J.J., Day, N., Dooling, E., Kayne, H., Morelock, S., Oppenheimer, E., & Zuckerman, B. (1982). Effects of maternal drinking and marijuana use on fetal growth and development. *Pediatrics, 70,* 539-546.

Hurt, R.D., Morse, R.M., & Swenson, W.M. (1980). Diagnosis of alcoholism with a self-administered alcoholism screening test: Results with 1,002 consecutive patients receiving general examinations. *Mayo Clinic Proceedings, 55,* 365-370.

Institute of Medicine. (1990). *Broadening the base of treatment for alcohol problems.* Washington, DC: National Academy Press.

Jacobson, J.L., Jacobson, S.W., Sokol, R.J., Martier, S.S., Ager, J.W., & Kaplan-Estrin, M.G. (1993). Teratogenic effects of alcohol on infant development. *Alcoholism: Clinical and Experimental Research, 17,* 174-183.

Kaplan, H.B., Kanas, T., Pokorny, A.D., & Lively, G. (1974). Screening tests and self-identification in the detection of alcoholism. *Journal of Health and Social Behavior, 15,* 51-56.

Kaplan, H.B., Pokorny, A.D., Kanas T., & Lively, G. (1975). Self-identification and the underdetection of alcoholism. *Diseases of the Nervous System, 36,* 133-136.

Kent, A. (1991). Measures of alcohol dependence. *Lancet, 338,* 889 (Letter).

Klee, L., Schmidt, C., & Ames, G. (1991). Indicators of women's alcohol problems: What women themselves report. *International Journal of the Addictions, 26,* 879-895.

Kreitman, N. (1986). Alcohol consumption and the preventive paradox. *British Journal of Addiction, 81,* 353-363.

Kristenson, H., & Trell, E. (1982). Indicators of alcohol consumption: Comparisons between a questionnaire (Mm-MAST), interviews and serum gamma-glutamyl transferase (GGT) in a health survey of middle-aged males. *British Journal of Addiction, 77,* 297-304.

La Grange, L., Anton, R.F., Crown, H., & Garcia, S. (1994). A correlational study of carbohydrate-deficient transferrin values and alcohol consumption among Hispanic college students. *Alcoholism: Clinical and Experimental Research, 18,* 653-656.

La Grange, L., Anton, R.F., Garcia, S., & Herrbold, C. (1995). Carbohydrate-deficient transferrin levels in a female population. *Alcoholism: Clinical and Experimental Research, 19,* 100-103.

Lane, P.A., Burge, S., & Graham, A.V. (1992). Management of addictive disorders in women. In M.F. Fleming & K.L. Barry (Eds.), *Addictive disorders* (pp. 260-269). St. Louis, MO: Mosby Year Book.

Lewis, C.E., & Bucholz, K.K. (1991). Alcoholism, antisocial behavior and family history. *British Journal of Addiction, 86,* 177-194.

Lieber, C.S. (1992). *Medical and nutritional complications of alcoholism: Mechanisms and management.* New York: Plenum Medical Book Co.

Lowe, J.B., Windsor, R.A., Adams, B., Morris, J., & Reese, Y. (1986). Use of a bogus pipeline method to increase accuracy of self-reported alcohol consumption among pregnant women. *Journal of Studies on Alcohol, 47,* 173-175.

Magruder-Habib, K., Harris, K.E., & Fraker, G.G. (1982). Validation of the Veterans Alcoholism Screen Test. *Journal of Studies on Alcohol, 43,* 910-926.

Martier, S.S., Sokol, R.J., Bottoms, S., & Ager, J.W. (1990). Optimized screening for risk drinking: Tolerance reconsidered. *Alcoholism: Clinical and Experimental Research, 14,* 315 (Abstract).

Martin, C.S., Liepman, M.R., & Young, C.M. (1990). The Michigan Alcoholism Screening Test: False positives in a college student sample. *Alcoholism: Clinical and Experimental Research, 14,* 853-855.

Mayfield, D., McLeod, G., & Hall, P. (1974). The CAGE questionnaire: Validation of a new alcoholism screening instrument. *American Journal of Psychiatry, 131,* 1121-1123.

McAuley, T., Longabaugh, R., & Gross, H. (1978). Comparative effectiveness of self and family forms of the Michigan Alcoholism Screening Test. *Journal of Studies on Alcohol, 39,* 1622-1627.

Midanik, L. (1982). The validity of self-reported alcohol consumption and alcohol problems: A literature review. *British Journal of Addiction, 77,* 357-382.

Midanik, L.T. (1988). Validity of self-reported alcohol use: A literature review and assessment. *British Journal of Addiction, 83,* 1019-1030.

Nadler, D., Martier, S., Ager, J., & Sokol, R.J. (1987). Triggering denial interferes with obtaining an alcohol history. *Alcoholism: Clinical and Experimental Research, 11,* 212 (Abstract).

Nilssen, O., Huseby, N.E., Høyer, G., Brenn, T., Schirmer, H., & Førde, O.H. (1992). New alcohol markers—How useful are they in population studies: The Svalbard Study 1988-89. *Alcoholism: Clinical and Experimental Research, 16,* 82-86.

Nyström, M., Peräsalo, J., & Salaspuro, M. (1992). Carbohydrate-deficient transferrin (CDT) in serum as a possible indicator of heavy drinking in young university students. *Alcoholism: Clinical and Experimental Research, 16,* 93-97.

Österling, A., Berglund, M., Nilsson, L.-H., & Kristenson, H. (1993). Sex differences in response style to two self-report screening tests on alcoholism. *Scandinavian Journal of Social Medicine, 21,* 83-89.

Pokorny, A.D., Miller, B.A., & Kaplan, H.B. (1972). The brief MAST: A shortened version of the Michigan Alcoholism Screening test. *American Journal of Psychiatry, 129,* 342-345.

Popkin, C.L. (1991). Drinking and driving by young females. *Accident Analysis and Prevention, 23,* 37-44.

Robbins, C. (1989). Sex differences in psychosocial consequences of alcohol and drug abuse. *Journal of Health and Social Behavior, 30,* 117-130.

Robins, L.N., Helzer, J.E., Croughan, J., & Ratcliff, K.S. (1981). National Institute of Mental Health Diagnostic Interview Schedule: Its history, characteristics, and validity. *Archives of General Psychiatry, 38,* 381-389.

Room, R. (1977). Measurement and distribution of drinking patterns and problems in general populations. In G. Edwards, M.M. Gross, M. Keller, J. Moser, & R. Room (Eds.), *Alcohol-related disabilities* (pp. 61-87). Geneva: World Health Organization.

Room, R. (1990). Measuring alcohol consumption in the United States. In L.T. Kozlowski, H.M. Annis, H.D. Cappell, F.B. Glaser, M.S. Goodstadt, Y. Israel, H. Kalant, E.M. Sellers, & E.R. Vingilis (Eds.), *Research advances in alcohol and drug problems:Vol. 10* (pp. 39-80). New York: Plenum.

Room, R. (1991). Cultural changes in drinking and trends in alcohol problems indicators: Recent U.S. experience. In W.B. Clark & M.E. Hilton (Eds.), *Alcohol in America: Drinking practices and problems* (pp. 149-162). Albany, NY: State University of New York Press.

Rosman, A.S., Basu, P., Galvin, K., & Lieber, C.S. (1995). Utility of carbohydrate-deficient transferrin as a marker of relapse in alcoholic patients. *Alcoholism: Clinical and Experimental Research, 19,* 611-616.

Russell, M. (1982). Screening for alcohol-related problems in obstetric and gynecologic patients. In E.L. Abel (Ed.), *Fetal alcohol syndrome:Vol. II. Human studies* (pp. 1-19). Boca Raton, FL: CRC Press.

Russell, M. (1988). Growing up with fetal alcohol syndrome. In L.S. Harris (Ed.), *NIDA research monograph 81. Problems of drug dependence, 1987* (pp. 368-378)(DHHS Publication No. ADM 88-1564). Rockville, MD: National Institute on Drug Abuse.

Russell, M. (1990). Prevalence of alcoholism among children of alcoholics. In M. Windle & J.S. Searles (Eds.), *Children of alcoholics: Critical perspectives* (pp. 9-38). New York: Guilford.

Russell, M. (1993). TWEAK. In N. Burke & D. Caldwell (Eds.), *Maternal substance use assessment methods reference manual. A review of screening and clinical assessment: Alcohol, tobacco, and other drugs* (pp. 41). Rockville, MD: CSAP National Resource Center for the Prevention of Perinatal Abuse of Alcohol and Other Drugs.

Russell, M. (1994). New assessment tools for risk drinking during pregnancy: T-ACE, TWEAK, and others. *Alcohol Health & Research World, 18,* 55-61.

Russell, M., & Bigler, L. (1979). Screening for alcohol-related problems in an outpatient obstetric-gynecologic clinic. *American Journal of Obstetrics and Gynecology, 134,* 4-12.

Russell, M., Cooper, M.L., & Frone, M.R. (1990). The influence of sociodemographic characteristics on familial alcohol problems: Data from a community sample. *Alcoholism: Clinical and Experimental Research, 14,* 221-226.

Russell, M., Martier, S.S., Sokol, R.J., Mudar, P., Bottoms, S., Jacobson, S., & Jacobson, J. (1994). Screening for pregnancy risk-drinking. *Alcoholism: Clinical and Experimental Research, 18,* 1156-1161.

Russell, M., & Skinner, J.B. (1988). Early measures of maternal alcohol misuse as predictors of adverse pregnancy outcomes. *Alcoholism: Clinical and Experimental Research, 12,* 824-830.

Ryback. R.S., Eckardt, M.J., & Pautler, C.P. (1980). Biochemical and hematological correlates of alcoholism. *Research Communications in Chemical Pathology and Pharmacology, 27,* 533-550.

Salaspuro, M. (1986). Conventional and coming laboratory markers of alcoholism and heavy drinking. *Alcoholism: Clinical and Experimental Research, 10,* 5S-12S.

Saunders, J.B., Aasland, O.G., Babor, T.F., de la Fuente, J.R., & Grant, M. (1993). Development of the Alcohol Use Disorders Identification Test (AUDIT): WHO collaborative project on early detection of persons with harmful alcohol consumption-II. *Addiction, 88,* 791-804.

Saunders, J.B., & Conigrave, K.M. (1990). Early identification of alcohol problems. *Canadian Medical Association Journal, 143,* 1060-1069.

Schorling, J.B. (1993). The prevention of prenatal alcohol use: A critical analysis of intervention studies. *Journal of Studies on Alcohol, 54,* 261-267.

Selzer, M.L. (1971). The Michigan Alcoholism Screening Test: The quest for a new diagnostic instrument. *American Journal of Psychiatry, 127,* 1653-1658.

Selzer, M.L., Gomberg, E.S., & Nordhoff, J.A. (1979). Men and women's responses to the Michigan Alcoholism Screening Test. *Journal of Studies on Alcohol, 40,* 502-504

Selzer, M.L., Vinokur, A., & van Rooijen, L. (1975). A self-administered Short Michigan Alcoholism Screening Test (SMAST). *Journal of Studies on Alcohol, 36,* 117-126.

Skinner, H.A. (1979). A multivariate evaluation of the MAST. *Journal of Studies on Alcohol, 40,* 831-844.

Skinner, H.A. (1984). Assessing alcohol use by patients in treatment. In R.G. Smart, H.D. Cappell, F.B. Glaser, Y. Israel, H. Kalant, R.E. Popham, W. Schmidt, & E.M. Sellers (Eds.), *Research advances in alcohol and drug problems:Vol. 8* (pp. 183-207). New York: Plenum.

Skinner, H.A., Holt, S., Schuller, R., Roy, J., & Israel, Y. (1984). Identification of alcohol abuse using laboratory tests and a history of trauma. *Annals of Internal Medicine, 101,* 847-851.

Skinner, H.A., Holt, S., Sheu, W.J., & Israel, Y. (1986). Clinical versus laboratory detection of alcohol abuse: The alcohol clinical index. *British Medical Journal [Clinical Research Ed.], 292,* 1703-1708.

Sokol, R.J., Martier, S.S., & Ager, J.W. (1989). The T-ACE questions: Practical prenatal detection of risk-drinking. *American Journal of Obstetrics and Gynecology, 160,* 863-870.

Sokol, R.J., Martier, S., & Ernhart, C. (1985). Identification of alcohol abuse in the prenatal clinic. In N.C. Chang & H.M. Chao (Eds.), *NIAAA research monograph 17: Early identification of alcohol abuse* (pp. 209-227) (DHHS Publication No. ADM 85-1258). Washington, DC: U.S. Government Printing Office.

Stibler, H. (1991). Carbohydrate-deficient transferrin in serum: A new marker of potentially harmful alcohol consumption reviewed. *Clinical Chemistry, 37,* 2029-2037.

Stibler, H., Borg, S., & Beckman, G. (1988a). Transferrin phenotype and level of carbohydrate-deficient transferrin in healthy individuals. *Alcoholism: Clinical and Experimental Research, 12,* 450-453.

Stibler, H., Borg, S., & Joustra, M. (1991). A modified method for the assay of carbohydrate-deficient transferrin (CDT) in serum. *Alcohol and Alcoholism* (Suppl. 1), 451-454.

Stibler, H., Dahlgren, L., & Borg, S. (1988b). Carbohydrate-deficient transferrin (CDT) in serum in women with early alcohol addiction. *Alcohol, 5,* 393-398.

Swenson, W.M., & Morse, R.M. (1975). The use of a Self-Administered Alcoholism Screening Test (SAAST) in a medical center. *Mayo Clinic Proceedings, 50,* 204-208.

U.S. Department of Health and Human Services & National Center for Health Statistics. (1982). *Hematological and nutritional biochemistry reference data for persons 6 months-74 years of age: United States, 1976-80 (Vital and Health Statistics, Series 11, No. 232).* Washington, DC: U.S. Government Printing Office.

U.S. Surgeon General. (1981). Surgeon General's advisory on alcohol and pregnancy. *FDA Drug Bulletin, 11,* 9-10.

Wagenaar, A.C., Komro, K.A., McGovern, P., Williams, C.L., & Perry, C.L. (1993). Effects of a saliva test pipeline procedure on adolescent self-reported alcohol use. *Addiction, 88,* 199–208.

Wanberg, K.W., & Knapp, J. (1970). Differences in drinking symptoms and behavior of men and women alcoholics. *British Journal of Addiction, 64,* 347–355.

Waterson, E.J., & Murray-Lyon, I.M. (1988). Are the CAGE questions outdated? *British Journal of Addiction, 83,* 1113–1115 (Letter).

Weidner, G., Connor, S.J., Chesney, M.A., Burns, J.W., Connor, W.E., Matarazzo, J.D., & Mendell, N.R. (1991). Sex differences in high density lipoprotein cholesterol among low-level alcohol consumers. *Circulation, 83,* 176–180.

Weisner, C. (1987). The social ecology of alcohol treatment in the United States. In M. Galanter (Ed.), *Recent developments in alcoholism: Vol. 5* (pp. 203–243). New York: Plenum.

Weisner, C. (1990). Coercion in alcohol treatment: Appendix D. In Institute of Medicine (Ed.), *Broadening the base of treatment for alcohol problems* (pp. 579–609). Washington, DC: National Academy of Sciences Press.

Ylikorkala, O., Stenman, U.-H., & Halmesmäki, E. (1987). Gammaglutamyl transferase and mean cell volume reveal maternal alcohol abuse and fetal alcohol effects. *American Journal of Obstetrics and Gynecology, 157,* 344–348.

CHAPTER 18

Gender and Treatment of Alcohol-Related Problems

KIMBERLY S. WALITZER AND GERARD J. CONNORS

While surveys of the general population indicate that alcohol consumption rates in the United States have remained relatively stable during the last several decades (e.g., Hilton, 1988; Hilton & Clark, 1987; Wilsnack & Wilsnack, 1995), alcohol consumption and subclinical problems with alcohol remain relatively prevalent among male and female drinkers. Survey data collected in 1984 indicated that 76% of men and 64% of women over 18 years old were drinkers (i.e., had consumed alcohol during the previous year) and that 48% of men and 25% of women consumed alcohol at least once per week (Hilton, 1987). In terms of tangible negative consequences from alcohol consumption (e.g., heated argument while drinking, drinking had a harmful effect on relationships, lost or nearly lost a job because of drinking), 14% of men and 6% of women reported at least a "moderate" level of alcohol-related problems in the past year.

The Epidemiological Catchment Area (ECA) study has documented the prevalence of clinical alcohol problems in the general population through in-person interviews with over 20,000 respondents (Regier et al., 1984). Across the study survey sites, these data revealed lifetime prevalence rates of 19.1–28.9% for men and 4.2–4.8% for women (Robins et al., 1984) for an alcohol diagnosis (alcohol abuse and dependence as assessed by the Diagnostic and Statistical Manual of Mental Disorders [DSM-III; American Psychiatric Association, 1980]). One-month prevalence rates were lower—5% for men and 0.9% for women (Regier et al., 1988).

Alcoholism has been viewed primarily as a "male" disorder. Diagnostic criteria for alcohol use disorders historically have been based on the known characteristics of male alcoholics, as the majority of research has focused on men. As a result, alcohol use disorders appear to be more readily diagnosed in men, as the diagnostic criteria have been more applicable to them. Women diagnosed with alcohol use problems traditionally have been seen as evidencing greater pathology and poorer outcomes relative to their male counterparts (see Vannicelli, 1984a). This combination of male-oriented diagnostic criteria and negative stereotypes of female alcoholics has contributed to an underdetection of alcohol-related problems in women, a stigmatization of women alcoholics, and an underutilization of alcohol treatment services by women (see National Council on Alcoholism, 1987).

Gender Issues in Treatment Utilization

Gender has been shown to influence markedly the extent to which treatment services are utilized (e.g., see Beckman, 1994; Schober & Annis, 1996). It long has been observed that women underuse treatment opportunities for alcohol-related problems, relative to men. In reviewing this literature, Beckman and Amaro (1984, 1984/85) have documented this difference even when taking into account gender differences in the prevalence of alcohol problems. Women's underutilization of alcoholism treatment services is particularly notable in public facilities (Furst et al., 1981). Such underutilization is apparent not only in traditional alcoholism treatment services, but also in evaluation and secondary prevention arenas as well. Blume (1990) has noted that three types of case finding/early-intervention programs—programs for persons arrested for driving under the influence, public intoxication interventions, and employee assistance programs—reach fewer female than male problem drinkers.

More recently, however, data from the National Drug and Alcoholism Treatment Unit Survey (NDATUS) suggest that women are becoming more equally represented in alcoholism treatment (Substance Abuse and Mental Health Services Administration, 1993). This survey indicates that in the early 1990s, higher proportions of men were in treatment for alcoholism, but higher proportions of women were in treatment for drug abuse and equal proportions of men and women were in treatment for both alcohol and drug abuse. Thus, the tendency for women to underutilize alcohol-specific treatment services may be decreasing relative to the underutilization documented in previous decades.

Many of the studies of gender issues in treatment utilization have included relatively small numbers of subjects, so it has been difficult to investigate other factors that may contribute to underutilization of treatment services by alcohol abusing women. Some dimensions that may offer further insights into treatment utilization among women include ethnicity, socioeconomic status, culture, and religion. Ethnicity, as an example, has been studied by Amaro and colleagues (1987). In their study, African-American and white women entering an alcoholism treatment facility were interviewed about various beliefs and attitudes. The African-American women were found to be younger than the white women in this sample and to have fewer financial resources. The African-American women in the sample were more likely to subscribe to the view that health professionals are central to health maintenance. The African-

American women also were more likely to report feelings of social isolation. Finally, the African-American women were less likely to have third-party insurance coverage for alcoholism treatment services, leaving them with fewer options in terms of obtaining clinical care for their alcohol abuse. To the extent that these variables may represent barriers to treatment (e.g., fewer financial resources and lack of insurance coverage), African-American women may have even more significant barriers to alcohol treatment services compared to white women.

A few cautions regarding generalization of the above findings are worthy of note. First, as noted earlier, these studies frequently have included relatively small groups of subjects, and it therefore is difficult to generalize findings. Second, the data gathered to date have been collected from women who were entering treatment. Few data are available on the characteristics of women who do not seek and/or actually contact a treatment-providing agency. It is not known to what extent the above findings generalize to female alcohol abusers not seeking treatment.

The ECA study (Reiger et al., 1984) avoids the shortcomings of small sample size and use of a treatment sample. While the ECA study does not comment directly on gender and barriers to treatment, it has provided interesting data concerning the comorbidity of other psychiatric disorders with alcohol diagnoses and treatment utilization in a general population sample. Helzer and Pryzbeck (1988) report that psychiatric cormorbidity (i.e., a second psychiatric diagnosis) is more prevalent among female alcohol abusers relative to male alcohol abusers. Specifically, female alcohol abusers were more likely to have a second diagnosis of drug abuse or dependence, phobic disorder, major depression, panic disorder, somatization, or mania (Helzer & Pryzbeck, 1988). For both male and female alcohol abusers, the presence of nonsubstance psychiatric comorbidity increased the probability of general mental health treatment utilization. Interestingly, these analyses indicated that after controlling for both the severity of alcohol symptoms and the total number of psychiatric diagnoses, female alcohol abusers were *more likely* to utilize general mental health treatment services. These findings raise the question of whether the underutilization of alcohol services by women is countered by increased utilization of more general mental health services. Perhaps women are more likely to take their alcohol-related problems to mental health treatment facilities as mental health problems as opposed to alcohol problems per se. Alternatively, perhaps when women's mental health problems include alcohol abuse, they are likely to be treated within the mental health facility rather than to be referred for formal alcohol-specific treatment.

Finally, women's tendencies toward underutilization of clinical services have been discussed more generally in the broader context of mental health care utilization by Russo and Sobel (1981), who note that women's utilization of health care services varies as a function of gender biases and sex role stereotyping regarding particular disorders. They note that for disorders that are congruent with idealized sex role stereotypes, women show increased rates of treatment service utilization relative to men. An example of such a disorder would be depression. However, for disorders that are incongruent with society's view of idealized feminine behavior—such as alcohol use disorders—women show lower rates of service utilization.

Barriers to Treatment Utilization

Having asserted that women tend to underutilize alcoholism treatment services relative to men, it becomes important to begin to identify the barriers to such treatment utilization. A number of such barriers have been identified (see Beckman, 1994; Collins, 1993; Schober & Annis, 1996). One core barrier to treatment utilization by women is that alcoholism treatment services frequently have been structured to reflect and meet the needs of male clients, both in terms of services provided and in the "ambience" of the treatment environment (Thom, 1984). For example, some programs have been male-only due to available inpatient facilities and treatment groups, and programs with a significant male majority may tend to focus on men's alcohol problems, issues, and situations which may or may not overlap with women's issues. Beckman (1984, 1994) has noted that some women do not enter treatment programs because treatment services are not structured in ways that appeal to them or their sense of their needs.

Vannicelli (1984b) has identified three domains of obstacles that also may contribute to the underutilization of services by women. The first domain includes a variety of negative myths regarding women's alcohol abuse. Predominant among these negative myths is the belief that women benefit less from treatment than men. A second domain of obstacles includes stereotyped sex-role expectancies. Examples of these expectancies are the tendencies for some treatment personnel to view female clients as dependent and childlike and to view women's drinking problems as less severe than those of men. Finally, a third obstacle identified by Vannicelli (1984b) is a limited knowledge base in the treatment field about women who abuse alcohol.

Not surprising given the above constellation of obstacles to treatment utilization, women perceive more negative consequences (e.g., loss of job, loss of friends, disrupted family relations) of seeking treatment for an alcohol use disorder than do men (Beckman, 1984, 1994). This is particularly unfortunate when one considers that women usually perceive treatment for alcohol problems as a more potentially effective and helpful opportunity for them than do men (Beckman & Kocel, 1982).

In an effort to influence specific factors associated with treatment utilization and to stimulate research on this topic, clinical researchers have been focusing on the development of models of treatment utilization. Noteworthy examples include the work of Beckman and Kocel (1982) and Thom (1984). The Beckman and Kocel (1982; see also Beckman, 1984) model of alcoholism services utilization draws upon previous research on social and individual determinants of medical care facility utilization and on health beliefs. In applying their model, they have found that women migrate toward treatment programs that have more professionals, that provide treatment services for children, and that provide aftercare services. In her work on women's use of alcoholism treatment services, Thom (1984) has developed a process model. Specifically, Thom subdivides the process of treatment seeking into four related stages: defining the problem, seeking help from others, choosing a treatment-providing agency to contact, and initiating contact with that agency. These models may fruitfully serve as templates for identifying the variables most relevant to understanding the seeking of alcoholism treatment services by women.

Gender Issues in Treatment Effectiveness

The traditional belief regarding gender and alcohol treatment is that women are more difficult to treat and have poorer treatment outcomes relative to men. This belief is difficult to assess because there have been relatively few women included in previous alcoholism treatment outcome research. Vannicelli (1984a) reviewed 23 studies (from a total of 259) that included women and gender-specific treatment outcome data and found that the majority of studies (18) showed no difference in outcomes for female alcoholics and male alcoholics. In the remaining five studies, four indicated superior outcomes for women and one indicated superior outcomes for men. While there have been no meta-analyses of gender differences in treatment outcomes, initial examination of these data does not support the belief that women who present to treatment fare worse than men.

Despite an apparent similarity of treatment efficacy for men and women in alcohol treatment programs, a caveat must be considered. It is not clear whether the women who participate in treatment are representative of all female alcohol abusers. A greater number of barriers to treatment exist for women than for men with alcohol-related problems. The women who seek treatment have, at least partially, overcome barriers such as the "female alcoholic" stigma, family and child care responsibilities, and the possible unattractive aspects of predominantly male treatment programs. Thus, it is possible that the alcoholic woman who seeks treatment may have more severe alcohol impairment or greater distress that motivates her past these barriers relative to women who do not seek treatment. A plausible inference is that only a minority of women with alcohol problems successfully overcome the extant barriers to treatment, and those that do may be more distressed or alcohol impaired.

The existing literature identifies few consistent predictors of treatment outcome for women, including demographics and drinking history variables

(Annis & Liban, 1980; Macdonald, 1987; Vannicelli, 1984a). Demographic variables have been found to predict alcohol outcome in male samples. Younger, married, and employed male alcoholics with a briefer history of alcohol abuse and lower physical dependence appear to have better outcomes (see Nathan & Skinstad, 1987), but it is not clear whether these predictors are valid in female samples. Macdonald (1987) examined personal and social relationships as predictors of outcome in women and reported that a greater number of close and supportive relationships and the lack of dysfunctional (i.e., pro-drinking) relationships were associated with more positive outcomes. Depression also has been examined as a predictor of treatment outcome because of its well-established association with alcohol-related problems. While depressed alcoholic women exhibited a small tendency towards more severe and chronic course (Turnbull & Gomberg, 1988), the presence of depression has been shown to predict better alcohol outcome following treatment (Rounsaville et al., 1987). One interpretation of these findings is that depression and alcohol-related problems may be synergistic in women and, when either or both of the problems receive treatment, alcohol outcome is more likely to be improved and stable.

The belief that male and female alcoholics differ on important dimensions regarding symptoms and treatment needs has led to the development of female-specific treatment programs. Duckert's (1987) literature review of such programs indicated that they include a wide variety of services and orientations, including traditional Alcoholics Anonymous programs, feminist programs, programs emphasizing family therapy and behavioral therapy, and programs for pregnant alcoholic women and alcoholic mothers. While research has not systematically addressed whether women have better outcomes when treated in an all-women setting relative to being treated in a mixed-gender setting, Duckert's (1987) review did indicate that the majority of women-specific programs reported favorable outcomes (e.g., 20% to 60% improvement rates). Dahlgren and Willander (1989), for example, compared women treated in traditional Swedish mixed-sex alcohol treatment facilities with women treated in a specialized women's unit. At two-year follow-up, the women in the specialized all-women's unit had better treatment outcome relative to the control group on a variety of measures. Copeland and Hall (1992) compared women in a women-specific program to women in mixed-sex alcoholism treatment programs. The women in the specialized program were more likely to have dependent children, to be lesbian, and to have histories of childhood sexual abuse and maternal alcoholism. They concluded that women-specialized programs may be more likely to attract women who would not otherwise seek treatment.

Expanding the Scope of Treatment Services for Women

The information presented throughout this chapter converges in support of at least two important observations. The first is that alcohol-related problems are being experienced by a significant number of women. The second observation is that barriers frequently exist that make difficult or preclude the seeking of clinical services by women with alcohol use disorders.

These observations have been highlighted in the Institute of Medicine report on broadening the base of treatment for persons with alcohol use problems (Institute of Medicine, 1990). Among the findings reported by the IOM in their review of available research on treatment for women were the following:

- The number of women seeking treatment for problems with alcohol has increased over the past decade.
- Little is known about treatment interventions that may enhance the likelihood of successful outcomes for alcohol abusing women.
- It is likely that clinical interventions that devote attention to issues particularly relevant to women's concerns will be most effective.

These findings suggest the need to develop and implement a variety of clinical services and opportunities for women with alcohol problems—the range of this variety to be dictated by the extent of heterogeneity in alcohol-related problems among women—and the necessity of conducting methodologically sound process and outcome research on treatment interventions for women.

It was within these contexts that the Women and Health Program was developed and implemented at the Research Institute on Addictions in Buffalo, New York. The Women and Health Program is a secondary prevention intervention directed toward the needs of problem drinking women who do not present with histories of severe dependence on alcohol. The goal of the program is drinking moderation. Previous research has shown that problem drinkers not severely dependent on alcohol are particularly well-suited for such a treatment approach (e.g., Heather & Robertson, 1981; Miller & Hester, 1980; Rosenberg, 1993). These drinkers have not experienced major losses because of their drinking and have not exhibited severe withdrawal symptoms (e.g., convulsions, seizures, delirium tremens) upon cessation of past drinking. Successful responders tend to report fewer than 10 years of problem drinking. The usual treatment is a package of behavioral self-control strategies (e.g., Miller & Munoz, 1982; Sanchez-Craig, 1984; Vogler & Bartz, 1985) that include self-monitoring, functional analysis of drinking behavior, stimulus control training (i.e., limiting or prohibiting drinking in the presence of former stimuli for drinking), and strategies for modifying drinking behavior. These behavioral self-control packages consistently have yielded high improvement rates, frequently exceeding 60% (with success generally defined as abstinence or at least a 30% reduction in drinking from baseline). Such outcomes have been reported by a number of investigators (e.g., Alden, 1988; Brown, 1980; Connors et al., 1992; Miller, 1978; Sanchez-Craig et al., 1984).

Each study provided 12-month follow-up data. Taken together, the studies support the proposition that moderate drinking may be a useful and effective treatment objective with this population of problem drinkers.

The results from two drinking moderation studies are particularly pertinent to the present discussion. In one study, Miller and Joyce (1979) reported data on subjects from several previous treatment outcome studies conducted by Miller and his colleagues. In addition to confirming previous studies' identification of predictors of successful moderation (essentially less severe drinking problems), it was found that female problem drinkers were more successful in attaining moderated drinking than were men. In a second study, Sanchez-Craig et al. (1989) found that women at a 12-month follow-up showed significantly greater reductions in heavy drinking days than did men, regardless of the modality of treatment administration. Thus, there are indications that training in drinking moderation may be a treatment of choice for this population of problem drinking women.

The Women and Health Program

The remainder of this chapter will focus on the Women and Health Program. As noted above, the program was designed to attract an underserved and generally undetected population—women with mild to moderate alcohol-related problems. The program was designed as a drinking moderation treatment program *especially for and specializing in women.* All program notices indicated that the drinking moderation program was for women only and for "early-stage problem drinkers" as opposed to alcoholic women. The free program consisted of an intake appointment and medical screening, followed by 10 weekly small-group meetings (three to six female participants and two female therapists). Over the course of the treatment, alcohol education material and 14 behavioral self-control strategies designed to help the women reduce their alcohol consumption were presented. During treatment, the women monitored daily alcohol consumption using drinking record cards. Each woman set individualized drinking goals for herself, based on her current drinking and how able she felt she was to reduce her drinking in the upcoming weeks. The women recorded their weekly use of drinking reduction strategies, such as goal setting, spacing drinks, sipping instead of gulping, alternating nonalcoholic and alcoholic beverages, identifying nonalcoholic beverage substitutes, and preplanning drinking. Internal strategies included the use of "self-talk" to coach moderated drinking and "self-rewards" to reinforce positive changes. Educational material included information on alcohol effects, metabolism of alcohol, tolerance, physical intoxication and blood alcohol content, and relapse prevention. In addition to the structured component of the treatment protocol, unstructured time was used during each session for the women to discuss their progress toward drinking moderation and the support and opposition present in their environments toward drinking reduction. The group leaders encouraged the women to support and provide feedback to other group members.

The atmosphere of the treatment group sessions was relaxed and nonjudgmental. Each woman's involvement and participation in treatment was left to her own discretion. For example, individualized drinking goals (minimum number of abstinent days per week, maximum drinks in a day, maximum drinks during the week) were set by each member during the first and second sessions, based on current drinking levels and the group leaders' and other participants' feedback. While the group leaders presented general guidelines for goal setting, specific goal decisions were made by the participant. Frequently, the group leaders had to advise participants not to set goals too stringently so that failures to reach very strict drinking goals could be avoided. Instead, small incremental goal-setting was encouraged so that gradual and repeated success experiences would bolster confidence and esteem. A similar approach was used with the drinking reduction strategies. These strategies were presented as techniques that others had found helpful in reducing drinking and were encouraged by the group leaders, but the decision to use or not to use any strategy—and to what extent—was left to each participant. During the portion of the session when the participants described their previous week, the group leaders focused on and reinforced positive efforts and successes. Thus, the center of therapeutic control rested within each participant. The other group members as well as the group leaders were seen as "expert advisors." Similarly, the women in the program were referred to as "participants" rather than "clients." The pervasive attitude of competence and respect was appreciated by the participants, many of whom had concerns about being negatively labeled, lectured to, or punished for their drinking. By the end of the 10 treatment sessions, the women reported substantially reduced alcohol consumption.

Recruitment for the Women and Health Program occurred through newspaper advertisements, and was supplemented by television and radio advertisements, flyers, brochures, and (to a much lesser extent) community referrals. Advertisements briefly described the program and invited interested women to call for more information and a determination regarding their eligibility for the program.

During the first two years of recruitment, the program received 532 calls from interested women. Callers were given a description of the program and asked a series of questions to determine eligibility. Inclusion criteria included drinking 12 standard drinks or more per week, desire to reduce alcohol use (not abstain), and being 21 years of age or older. Exclusion criteria included previous hospitalization for alcohol or drugs, current alcohol-related legal charges, multiple lifetime alcohol-related legal charges, current psychiatric

TABLE 1
Descriptive Information on Women (N = 532) Responding to
Advertisements for the Women and Health Program

	Phone Eligible, Intake Complete (n = 192)	Phone Eligible, Intake Refused (n = 108)	Phone Ineligible (n = 232)
Age	38.7 (9.8)	39.6 (11.9)	39.7 (11.8)
Years of education	14.3[a] (2.1)	13.5[b] (1.9)	13.7 (2.1)
Age drinking regularly	20.4 (6.2)	20.8 (7.8)	21.4 (8.1)
Years heavy drinking	5.6 (5.8)	5.8 (8.0)	4.4 (6.0)
Years problem drinking	3.8 (5.2)	3.2 (3.9)	3.7 (5.9)
Drinking days per week	4.6 (1.8)	4.5 (1.8)	4.1 (2.2)
Drinks per drinking day	6.2 (4.8)	6.4 (3.3)	5.7 (4.1)
Drinks per week	24.0 (10.4)	26.9 (15.0)	23.9 (32.1)
History of DWI	6.8%	3.7%	12.1%
Psychological treatment	21.9%	22.2%	39.7%
Employment (%)			
Full/part-time	74.0	63.9	67.7
Student	7.3	1.9	3.0
Retired	2.1	5.6	3.4
Unemployed	10.4	17.6	15.9
Homemaker	6.3	11.1	9.9
Marital status* (%)			
Single	24.5	26.9	30.6
Married	42.2	48.1	42.2
Separated	6.8	13.0	5.2
Divorced	20.8	10.2	18.1
Widowed	5.7	1.9	3.9

Notes: Values in parentheses are standard deviations. Significance tests (t tests and chi-square tests) were used to compare women who completed the intake appointment (n = 192) with women who refused intake (n = 108). (Women ineligible for treatment were not included in analyses.) Means with different superscripts (a,b) differ significantly at $p < .05$.

*Chi-square test significant at $p < .005$.

treatment or medications, psychiatrically hospitalized in the previous five years, medical condition contraindicating alcohol use, and pregnancy. Of 532 callers, 300 (56%) were eligible and were offered an appointment for an intake assessment.

One hundred ninety-two (64%) of the phone eligible women attended an initial assessment appointment; another 108 chose not to participate in the program. Table 1 displays information on the women who were ineligible based on the telephone interview, those eligible who chose not to participate, and those eligible who completed the intake appointment. In order to identify characteristics that might predict initial treatment involvement, women who completed the intake appointment ($n = 192$) were compared to the women who chose not to participate ($n = 108$). The only statistical differences (based on t tests and chi-square tests) indicated that the participating women reported higher levels of education and differences in marital status (less likely to be single, married, or separated; more likely to be divorced or widowed).

Among the 187 women who completed the intake assessment, 120 (64%) completed the 10-week treatment program. (The five women who completed an intake assessment and participated in pilot treatment groups are not included in Table 2.) Table 2 presents data on these women, the women who did not complete treatment ($n = 51$), and the women who were deemed ineligible based on the medical screen or intake interview ($n = 16$). In order to identify characteristics that might predict treatment completion, women who completed treatment ($n = 120$) were compared to women who did not complete treatment (i.e., the 27 who completed no sessions and the 24 who completed only a few treatment sessions; total $n = 51$). These analyses revealed that the women who did not complete treatment were significantly younger, more likely to have a racial or ethnic background other than Caucasian, more likely to be single or divorced, had fewer years of education, and reported more standard drinks per drinking day at pretreatment. Women completing treatment were less likely to receive DSM-III-R (American Psychiatric Association, 1987) alcohol diagnoses indicating more severe impairment, as assessed by the Diagnostic Interview Schedule, Version 3 (revised) (Robins et al., 1989).

The Women and Health Program has succeeded in attracting public interest in a program to help women moderate their drinking. Conversations with many of the Women and Health Program participants has revealed that the program being designed specifically for women and "early-stage problem drinkers" increased their comfort in calling and becoming involved in the treatment program. It appeared to be critical to the women that the program "fit" them and was developed specifically for them. Had the program recruited for mixed-gender participants or for traditional alcohol treatment, many of them reported that they would not have responded.

In terms of treatment utilization, few differences were noted between women who completed the initial intake appointment and those who were eligible for this appointment but chose not to participate. The participating women reported slightly higher levels of education and were more likely to be divorced and less likely to be single. Several additional differences were noted at the second stage of program recruitment. The women who completed the 10-session treatment program were older, more educated, less likely to be single, and reported fewer standard drinks per drinking day and less severe alcohol diagnoses relative to women who did not attend any treatment sessions or dropped out after several sessions. Women with racial

TABLE 2
Demographic Drinking History and Diagnostic Data on Women ($N = 187$)
Attending a Women and Health Program Intake

	Treatment Completed ($n = 120$)		Treatment Not Completed ($n = 51$)		Ineligible for Treatment ($n = 16$)	
Demographic and Drinking History						
Age	39.8[a]	(10.0)	35.1[b]	(8.2)	41.1	(10.5)
Years of education	14.7[a]	(2.0)	13.3[b]	(2.1)	14.2	(1.5)
Age drinking regularly	20.8	(6.5)	20.0	(5.9)	20.2	(5.9)
Years heavy drinking	5.2	(5.1)	5.7	(4.8)	5.6	(6.0)
Years problem drinking	3.6	(4.4)	3.5	(3.7)	4.8	(4.7)
Drinking days per week	4.7	(1.8)	4.2	(1.7)	4.0	(1.9)
Drinks per drinking day	5.5[a]	(3.3)	7.1[b]	(3.7)	9.8	(11.4)
Drinks per week	22.9	(8.7)	25.2	(11.1)	31.5	(16.5)
History of DWI	5.0%		7.8%		12.5%	
Psychological treatment	25.0%		13.7%		25.0%	
Employment (%)						
Full/part-time	73.3		74.5		75.1	
Student	6.7		9.8		6.3	
Retired	1.7		0.0		6.3	
Unemployed	11.7		9.8		6.3	
Homemaker	6.7		5.9		6.3	
Marital status* (%)						
Single	20.8		33.3		31.3	
Married	45.0		39.2		37.5	
Separated	7.5		0.0		18.8	
Divorced	18.3		25.5		12.3	
Widowed	8.3		2.0		0.0	
Race/ethnicity* (%)						
Caucasian	92.5		74.5		93.8	
African-American	5.0		19.6		6.3	
Hispanic	0.8		5.9		0.0	
Native American	1.7		0.0		0.0	
DSM-III-R Lifetime Diagnoses						
Alcoholic diagnosis* (%)						
None	8.3		10.9		18.8	
Abuse	0.8		0.0		0.0	
Mild dependence	20.8		4.3		0.0	
Moderate dependence	63.3		69.6		50.0	
Severe dependence	6.7		15.2		31.3	
Drug diagnosis (%)						
None	90.8		87.0		81.3	
Abuse	0.0		2.2		6.3	
Mild dependence	0.0		0.0		0.0	
Moderate dependence	9.2		6.5		12.5	
Severe dependence	0.0		4.3		0.0	

TABLE 2 (continued)

	Treatment Completed (*n* = 120)	Treatment Not Completed (*n* = 51)	Ineligible for Treatment (*n* = 16)
Depression diagnosis (%)			
None	64.0	67.4	60.0
Uncomplicated bereavement	2.0	4.3	6.7
Major depressive episode	34.0	28.3	33.3
Generalized anxiety disorder (%)	10.0	0.0	0.0
Panic disorder (%)	5.8	4.3	6.3

Notes: Table does not include five eligible women who participated in pilot treatment groups. Values in parentheses are standard deviations. Significance tests (*t* tests and chi-square tests) were used to compare women who completed treatment (*n* = 120) with women who did not (*n* = 51). (Women ineligible for treatment were not included in analyses.) Means with different superscripts (a,b) differ significantly at $p < .01$.

*Chi-square test significant at $p < .005$.

or ethnic backgrounds other than Caucasian were less likely to complete treatment.

Relative to individuals who present to traditional alcohol treatment programs, the participants of the Women and Health Program probably were higher functioning generally and presented with a variety of resources. The majority of women were educated, employed, and of middle socioeconomic status. Clinically, the women were intelligent, verbal, insightful, and motivated. The program was not as successful in recruiting lower income, unemployed, and/or racial or ethnic minority women, despite varied efforts to enhance visibility of the Women and Health Program for these women. One caveat to be considered is that the initial positive outcomes noted thus far in the Women and Health Program may be partially contingent on the resources of the women attracted to the program. It will be important to replicate these findings on a less advantaged sample of women.

Summary

Historically, women alcohol abusers have occupied a minority status in the field of alcoholism treatment. Alcohol use disorder diagnostic criteria have been based on male alcoholics and treatment programs have been developed for and utilized by predominantly male clientele, while female alcoholics have been viewed as atypical, more difficult to treat, and more pathological. These factors have contributed to a longstanding underrepresentation of women in alcohol treatment programs and, subsequently, in alcohol treatment outcome research. Because female alcohol abusers have been excluded or only present in small numbers in treatment research, knowledge of gender differences regarding treatment effectiveness and treatment outcomes has developed slowly. The available data, however, appear to indicate that female alcohol abusers perceive different barriers to treatment than do their male counterparts. Furthermore, female alcohol abusers respond positively, and in some cases more positively, to treatment efforts relative to men. In an effort to increase the attractiveness of alcohol treatment, programs have been specifically developed and implemented for female alcohol abusers. The Women and Health Program is an example of a program that has been developed to meet the needs of women with mild to moderate alcohol-related problems. The Women and Health Program has successfully reached and involved women who had not previously been involved in any type of alcohol treatment. The women who completed the treatment program were more likely to be Caucasian and older, and to report higher levels of education. The program was not as successful in attracting and involving in treatment women who were of other racial and ethnic backgrounds, younger, and less educated. Although the Women and Health Program has been successful in expanding the scope of treatment to include women with mild to moderate alcohol problems, continued efforts and research are needed to reach women with both mild and severe alcohol-related problems who are currently not represented in treatment.

Acknowledgment

Preparation of this chapter was supported in part by National Institute on Alcohol Abuse and Alcoholism grant AA08076.

References

Alden, L.E. (1988). Behavioral self-management controlled-drinking strategies in a context of secondary prevention. *Journal of Consulting and Clinical Psychology, 56,* 280-286.

Amaro, H., Beckman, L.J., & Mays, V.M. (1987). A comparison of black and white women entering alcoholism treatment. *Journal of Studies on Alcohol, 48,* 220-228.

American Psychiatric Association. (1980). *Diagnostic and statistical manual of mental disorders* (3rd ed.). Washington, DC: Author.

American Psychiatric Association. (1987). *Diagnostic and statistical manual of mental disorders* (3rd ed., rev.). Washington, DC: Author.

Annis, H.M., & Liban, C.B. (1980). Alcoholism in women: Treatment modalities and outcomes. In O.J. Kalant (Ed.), *Research advances in alcohol and drug problems: Vol. 5. Alcohol and drug problems in women* (pp. 385-422). New York: Plenum Press.

Beckman, L.J. (1984). Analysis of the suitability of alcohol treatment resources for women. *Substance and Alcohol Actions/Misuse, 5,* 21-27.

Beckman, L.J. (1994). Treatment needs of women with alcohol problems. *Alcohol Health & Research World, 18,* 206-211.

Beckman, L.J., & Amaro, H. (1984). Patterns of women's use of alcohol treatment agencies. In S.C. Wilsnack & L.J. Beckman (Eds.), *Alcohol problems in women: Antecedents, consequences, and intervention* (pp. 319-348). New York: Guilford Press.

Beckman, L.J., & Amaro, H. (1984/1985). Patterns of women's use of alcohol treatment agencies. *Alcohol Health & Research World, 9* (2), 14-25.

Beckman, L.J., & Kocel, K.M. (1982). The treatment-delivery system and alcohol abuse in women: Social policy implications. *Journal of Social Issues, 38,* 139-151.

Blume, S.B. (1990). Alcohol and drug problems in women: Old attitudes, new knowledge. In H.B. Milkman & L.I. Sederer (Eds.), *Treatment choices for alcoholism and substance abuse* (pp. 183-200). Lexington, MA: Lexington Books.

Brown, R.A. (1980). Conventional education and controlled drinking education courses with convicted drunken drivers. *Behavior Therapy, 11,* 632-642.

Collins, R.L. (1993). Women's issues in alcohol use and cigarette smoking. In J.S. Baer, G.A. Marlatt & R.J. McMahan (Eds.), *Addictive behaviors across the life span: Prevention, treatment, and policy issues* (pp. 274-306). Newbury Park, CA: Sage.

Connors, G.J., Tarbox, A.R., & Faillace, L.A. (1992). Achieving and maintaining gains among problem drinkers: Process and outcome results. *Behavior Therapy, 23,* 449-474.

Copeland, J., & Hall, W. (1992). A comparison of women seeking drug and alcohol treatment in a specialist women's program and two traditional mixed-sex treatment services. *British Journal of Addiction, 87,* 1293-1302.

Dahlgren, L., & Willander, A. (1989). Are specialized treatment facilities for female alcoholics needed? A controlled 2-year follow-up study from a specialized female unit (EWA) versus a mixed male/female treatment facility. *Alcoholism: Clinical and Experimental Research, 13,* 499-504.

Duckert, F. (1987). Recruitment into treatment and effects of treatment for female problem drinkers. *Addictive Behaviors, 12,* 137-150.

Furst, C.J., Beckman, L.J., Nakamura, C.Y., & Weiss, M. (1981). *Utilization of alcoholism treatment services* (Report prepared for the State of California Department of Alcohol and Drug Programs). Los Angeles: University of California at Los Angeles Alcohol Research Center. (Cited in Beckman & Amaro, 1984)

Heather, N., & Robertson, I. (1981). *Controlled drinking.* New York: Methuen.

Helzer, J.E., & Pryzbeck, T.R. (1988). The co-occurrence of alcoholism with other psychiatric disorders in the general population and its impact on treatment. *Journal of Studies on Alcohol, 49,* 219-224.

Hilton, M.E. (1987). Drinking patterns and drinking problems in 1984: Results from a general population survey. *Alcoholism: Clinical and Experimental Research, 11,* 167-175.

Hilton, M.E. (1988). Trends in U.S. drinking patterns: Further evidence from the past 20 years. *British Journal of Addiction, 83,* 269-278.

Hilton, M.E., & Clark, W.B. (1987). Changes in American drinking patterns and problems, 1967-1984. *Journal of Studies on Alcohol, 48,* 515-552.

Institute of Medicine. (1990). *Broadening the base of treatment for alcohol problems.* Washington, DC: National Academy Press.

Macdonald, J.G. (1987). Predictors of treatment outcome for alcoholic women. *International Journal of the Addictions, 22,* 235-248.

Miller, W.R. (1978). Behavioral treatment of problem drinkers: A comparative outcome study of three controlled drinking therapies. *Journal of Consulting and
Clinical Psychology, 46,* 74–86.

Miller, W.R., & Hester, R.K. (1980). Treating the problem drinker: Modern approaches.
In W.R. Miller (Ed.), *The addictive behaviors: Treatment of alcoholism, drug
abuse, smoking and obesity.* Elmsford, NY: Pergamon.

Miller, W.R., & Joyce, M.A. (1979). Prediction of abstinence, controlled drinking, and
heavy drinking outcomes following behavioral self-control training. *Journal of
Consulting & Clinical Psychology, 47,* 773–775.

Miller, W.R., & Munoz, R.F. (1982). *How to control your drinking* (rev. ed.). Albu-
querque, NM: University of New Mexico Press.

Nathan, P.E., & Skinstad, A.-H. (1987). Outcomes of treatment for alcohol problems:
Current methods, problems, and results. *Journal of Consulting and Clinical Psychology, 55,* 332–340.

National Council on Alcoholism (NCA). (1987). *A federal response to a hidden epidemic: Alcohol and other drug problems among women.* New York: Author.

Regier, D.A., Boyd, H.H., Burke, J.D., Jr., Rae, D.S., Myers, J.K., Kramer, M., Robins,
L.N., George, L.K., Karno, M., & Locke, B.Z. (1988). One-month prevalence of mental disorders in the United States: Based on five Epidemiologic Catchment Area
sites. *Archives of General Psychiatry, 45,* 977–986.

Regier, D.A., Myers, J.K., Kramer, M., Robins, L.N., Blazer, D.G., Hough, R.L., Eaton,
W.W. & Locke, B.Z. (1984). The NIMH Epidemiologic Catchment Area program:
Historical context, major objectives and study population characteristics. *Archives
of General Psychiatry, 41,* 934–941.

Robins, L.N., Helzer, J.E., Cottler, L., & Goldring, E. (1989). Diagnostic interview schedule (version 3, rev.). St. Louis, MO: Washington University.

Robins, L.N., Helzer, J.E., Weissman, M.M., Orvaschel, H., Gruenberg, E., Burke, J.D.,
Jr., & Regier, D.A. (1984). Lifetime prevalence of specific psychiatric disorders in
three sites. *Archives of General Psychiatry, 41,* 949–958.

Rosenberg, H. (1993). Prediction of controlled drinking by alcoholics and problem
drinkers. *Psychological Bulletin, 113,* 129–139.

Rounsaville, B.J., Dolinsky, Z.S., Babor, T.F., & Meyer, R.E. (1987). Psychopathology as
a predictor of treatment outcome in alcoholics. *Archives of General Psychiatry,
44,* 505–513.

Russo, N.F., & Sobel, S.B. (1981). Sex differences in the utilization of mental health facilities. *Professional Psychology, 12,* 7–19.

Sanchez-Craig, M. (1984). *A therapist's manual for secondary prevention of alcohol
problems: Procedures for teaching moderate drinking and abstinence.* Toronto:
Addiction Research Foundation.

Sanchez-Craig, M., Annis, H.M., Bornet, A.R., & MacDonald, K.R. (1984). Random
assignment to abstinence and controlled drinking: Evaluation of a cognitive-
behavioral program for problem drinkers. *Journal of Consulting and Clinical Psychology, 52,* 390–403.

Sanchez-Craig, M., Leigh, G., Spivak, K., & Lei, H. (1989). Superior outcome of females
over males after brief treatment for the reduction of heavy drinking. *British Journal of Addiction, 84,* 395–404.

Schober, R., & Annis, H.M. (1996). Barriers to help-seeking for change in drinking: A
gender-focused review of the literature. *Addictive Behaviors, 21,* 81–92.

Substance Abuse and Mental Health Services Administration. (1993). National Drug and
Alcoholism Treatment Unit Survey (NDATUS): 1991 main findings report (DHHS
Publication No. SMA 93-2007). Washington, DC: U.S. Government Printing Office.

Thom, B. (1984). A process approach to women's use of alcohol services. *British Journal of Addiction, 79,* 377-382.

Turnbull, J.E., & Gomberg, E.S.L. (1988). Impact of depressive symptomatology on alcohol problems in women. *Alcoholism: Clinical and Experimental Research, 12,* 374-381.

Vannicelli, M. (1984a). Treatment outcome of alcoholic women: The state of the art in relation to sex bias and expectancy effects. In S.C. Wilsnack & L.J. Beckman (Eds.) *Alcohol problems in women: Antecedents, consequences, and intervention* (pp. 369-412). New York: Guilford Press.

Vannicelli, M. (1984b). Barriers to treatment of alcoholic women. *Substance and Alcohol Actions/Misuse, 5,* 29-37.

Vogler, R.E., & Bartz, W.R. (1985). *The better way to drink: Moderation and control of problem drinking.* Oakland, CA: New Harbinger.

Wilsnack, S.C., & Wilsnack, R.W. (1995). Drinking and problem drinking in US women: Patterns and recent trends. In M. Galanter (Ed.), *Recent developments in alcoholism: Vol. 12. Alcoholism and women* (pp. 29-60). New York: Plenum.

CHAPTER 19

Women and Alcohol: Issues in Social Policy

SHEILA B. BLUME

Throughout history, human societies that have permitted the use of alcohol or other mind-altering drugs have developed separate rules for their use by men and women. An early example is the Code of Hammurabi, dating back 4,000 years, which forbade priestesses (but not male priests) from entering a wine shop to drink and from owning such a shop (Edwards, 1971). The Ancient Romans' Law of Romulus made any use of alcohol by women illegal, and prescribed a capital penalty (McKinlay, 1959). Roman historical records document several instances in which women were put to death by stoning or starvation for this offense. However, rules for acceptable drinking are not primarily expressed in law. Rather, they are founded in social attitudes, customs, and values, which are then expressed in policies that cover a wide range of activities: how high school prom nights are structured, how police handle intoxicated people, how juries decide rape cases, what health insurance benefits are offered to industry, how cigarette and alcoholic beverage manufacturers advertise, and in many other ways.

American history in relation to alcohol and other drugs has been a stormy one, characterized by many broad swings of the policy pendulum between tolerance and prohibition (Lender & Martin, 1987; Musto, 1992). When European settlers arrived in North America, they encountered indigenous cultures that had not developed their own alcoholic beverages. Thus, these groups had no established rules about appropriate drinking. The Europeans brought not only their alcoholic beverages, but also their traditional alcohol-related problems. In addition, as American society evolved, we developed a range of new problems peculiar to the Western Hemisphere. Any look at current alcohol policy should therefore include a historical perspective.

Ideas Governing Alcohol Policy in America

Moore and Gerstein (1981) have identified three "dominant conceptions" or governing ideas concerning alcohol-related problems that have prevailed in American history, and two additional "minority conceptions" that have also had an influence. The first of the dominant ideas, the "colonial view," held sway through the revolutionary period. Alcohol was seen as a valuable food and commodity, a "gift of God." Overindulgence was seen as a personal immoral act, and punishment the appropriate response. Our current statutes related to public intoxication, the first of which was passed in 1619 in the Jamestown (Virginia) Colony, are a legacy of the dominant moralistic thinking of the colonial view.

The second governing idea was the "temperance view," which saw alcohol as a dangerous drug, intoxicating and addicting in itself and, therefore, hazardous for anyone using alcoholic beverages at all. This idea gathered strength from the time of the American Revolution and culminated in the passage of the Eighteenth Amendment to the Constitution in 1919. There was a great deal of debate over whether or not "intoxicating liquors," outlawed by the prohibition amendment, should include only distilled spirits or extend to wine, beer, and cider (considered by some the "beverages of moderation"). The broader interpretation of prohibition prevailed. Although the Twenty-first Amendment repealed prohibition in 1933, the temperance view also left a considerable legacy. On one hand, this conception led to our current differential rate of taxation between distilled spirits, which are taxed at a much higher rate in proportion to alcohol content, and beer and wine, which are taxed far less. On the other hand, following the perceived failure of prohibition, there has been a pervasive opinion among policymakers that any effort to use control of alcoholic beverage availability as a strategy to reduce alcohol-related problems is a foolish and wasted effort.

The third governing idea, the "alcoholism view," has dominated U.S. thinking since the second quarter of the twentieth century. This view focuses on alcoholism as the major problem to be addressed. Alcoholism is understood as a complex disease with biological, psychological, and social features and causes, but neither the chemical substance (alcohol) nor the victim of the illness is seen as evil or to be blamed. From this governing idea have come policies promoting alcoholism treatment, education and prevention, the decriminalization of public intoxication, and protection for the rights of recovering people, as exemplified by the Americans with Disabilities Act.

The two minority conceptions discussed by Moore and Gerstein (1981) are the "control of commerce emphasis" and the "public health perspective." The former conceptualizes alcohol as a commodity. The latter view, promoted by the World Health Organization, focuses on alcoholism as only one of a range of negative health consequences related to alcohol use. Because alcoholics are not the only people who suffer alcohol's adverse effects, this conception dictates that prevention policies must be aimed at a far wider target group than alcoholics alone, namely, the entire population.

An additional important trend in American thinking has been the rising public consciousness about health promotion, with emphasis on such measures as diet, exercise, avoidance of smoking, and stress management. Wilsnack and Wilsnack (1995) have recently reported evidence for a decline in both drinking and heavy drinking by American women since the early 1980s. This trend may be due in part to an increasing level of health concern. To public health educators this awareness affords a valuable opportunity to improve public education concerning alcohol. (For a general summary of alcohol policy issues, see Blume, 1984.)

Attitudes about Women and Alcohol

Society's separate norms for drinking by men and women are based on deeply held cultural beliefs about the differential effects of alcohol on each sex. In the case of women, Western thought dating back at least to the Talmud (Gomberg, 1986) has held that alcohol is a sexual stimulant for women that leads them to promiscuity. The Roman prohibition against drinking by women mentioned above was combined with the law against adultery and justified by writers of the time on the grounds that wine causes women to be lustful and leads them to debauchery (McKinlay, 1959). As Chaucer's 14th Century Wife of Bath remarks, "A woman in her cups has no defense, as lechers known from long experience" (Chaucer, translated by Coghill, 1951). Ogden Nash put it this way: "Candy is dandy but liquor is quicker" (Nash, 1952).

Although careful studies of American women have not substantiated the idea that alcohol makes women promiscuous (Klassen & Wilsnack, 1986), the stereotype is widely accepted and has led to a destructive stigma applied to alcoholic women. This stigma characterizes them as both generally and sexually immoral (i.e., "fallen women"), and in turn simultaneously enhances denial and leads to underrecognition of chemical dependence, especially in middle-class and professional women. The less an alcoholic woman resembles the stereotype of a fallen woman, the less likely she is to be correctly diagnosed in an early stage. The sexual aspect of the stigma further results in the social acceptance of physical and sexual victimization of women who drink. For example, a U.S. study of attitudes toward rape found that a rapist who is intoxicated is considered less responsible for the crime, whereas a victim who is intoxicated is held more to blame (Richardson & Campbell, 1982). This negative stereotype of drinking women should be borne in mind in relation to the current social policy issues discussed below. (For a fuller discussion of the destructive stigma applied to women who drink, see Blume, 1991a.)

Alcohol Availability: Sales, Marketing, Taxation

Policies on pricing, taxation, numbers and locations of sales outlets, and advertising and other marketing practices are meant to influence the drinking practices of both sexes. However, there are a number of issues that apply particularly to women.

Although women consume, on the average, only about half as much beverage alcohol as men, market research has established that women often purchase the alcoholic beverages for their households. Both as a way to increase alcohol consumption by women and to promote specific brands, the alcoholic beverage industry has made women a marketing target in recent years (Jacobson et al., 1983). Advertisements aimed at women link alcoholic beverages with sexiness, power, and freedom (Kilbourne, 1991). Drinking is associated with the nontraditional, exciting, "liberated" lifestyles of attractive modern women. This focus represents an immense change in marketing strategy, which for many years targeted only men. For example, between 1936 and 1958 the Distilled Spirits Council of the United States (DISCUS), the distillers' trade association, had a code prohibiting the use of women in advertising (Marsteller & Karnchanapee, 1980). When this code was revised, women appeared chiefly as decorative appendages, or as evidence of the power and good taste of the male in the ad, much like his fashionable clothing or his expensive car. Advertising directly to women is a recent development, related to the progressive decrease in per capita alcohol consumption in the United States (see below).

Other marketing methods that impact on women include allowing the sale of alcoholic beverages in grocery stores, permitting in-room bars in hotels, and the use of special female promotions such as "ladies' nights" in bars, offering low-priced drinks to women. Grocery stores and supermarkets, heavily patronized by women, are not permitted to sell spirits in 30 states, wine in 16 states, and beer in 5 states. These policies are regularly challenged in many state legislatures. The justification for change often includes the argument that the measure would be a convenience for women. An industry representative is quoted as stating that "sales have more than doubled in the first several years following opening supermarkets to wine sales" in various states (Scott, 1983). Hotel room bars selling alcoholic beverages are permitted in many states. One of the arguments advanced in favor of such facilities is that women guests would be saved the necessity of patronizing the hotel cocktail lounge in order to drink. The desirability of encouraging women to drink alone in their hotel rooms is not considered.

"Ladies' night" promotions have two purposes. The first aim is to attract more women to bars (which are still widely looked upon as male gathering places, particularly during the middle of the week). This also makes the bars more attractive to men looking for female company. The second goal is to promote increased drinking by women. For this purpose, "two for the price of one" is more effective than "drinks half price" for women. Many communities have banned the custom of "ladies' nights," either on the grounds of sex discrimination (against men) or because of public interest in limiting measures aimed at motivating women to drink.

Finally, alcohol producers are developing beverages meant to appeal to women, such as sweetened "wine coolers," a new fruit-flavored malt beverage introduced by Coors, and "Seagram's Spritzers," a carbonated drink in fruit flavors. With unintended irony, industry commentators state that these drinks are meant to appeal to women's interest in good health (California Women's Commission, 1992).

Why this emphasis on women? The average per capita alcohol consumption has been falling in the United States since 1980. Moreover, the nation's demographics are changing, with a steady decrease in the proportion of men aged 20–35 in the population projected over the next 15 years (Eigen, 1992). These young men are in the age-sex group that consumes the most alcohol (especially beer). To maintain sales, the industry must attempt to increase the drinking of other groups. This marketing effort may create a problem for women, who are presently somewhat protected from alcohol-related problems by social customs that discourage heavy drinking by women (see, for example, Klee and Ames, 1987). Concentrated marketing to women can erode these protections. Beverage advertising budgets are high, in the billions of dollars per year. Kilbourne (1991) reports that the annual budget for advertising just one brand of beer (Budweiser) is greater than the entire federal budget for the National Institute on Alcohol Abuse and Alcoholism. Unfortunately, most Americans derive their alcohol education from advertisements. A conscientious effort to break down differences between male and female patterns through advertising could break down women's social protections.

Public policies to counteract this trend include controls on advertising, for example, Bureau of Alcohol, Tobacco, and Firearms rules that ban health claims and the use of young people in alcohol advertisements. Proposals to ban all forms of alcoholic beverage advertising have also been made from time to time. Other efforts have taken the form of public education campaigns and informing the public about the health consequences of drinking, through health warning labels and posters.

The struggle over health warning labels on beverage containers has been a bitter battle that pitted the beverage industry against public health advocates. Although a labeling bill was passed in the U.S. Senate in 1979, it took nearly another 10 years to achieve passage of a labeling act by both houses of Congress. This act went into effect in November of 1989. The effort to establish health warning labels and posters is of special interest to women because information about the potentially damaging effects of drinking during pregnancy has been included in every proposed health warning. This emphasis on pregnancy drew objections from some feminist groups in the early 1980s. Feminist critics feared that women would be singled out for public shame or disapproval of their drinking, while the fact that alcohol also damages the male reproductive system (and is a common cause of impotence) was not featured in the warnings. Illustrating this concern was a case of two servers in Seattle who questioned a drink order by an obviously pregnant woman and showed her a warning label (*Palm Beach Post,* 1991). The patron complained and the two servers were fired. In spite of this possibility, most health advocates feel that on balance the health information conveyed is valuable enough to support label and poster laws.

Another effort to balance the glamorous image of alcohol portrayed in advertising with facts about its adverse health consequences is embodied in a currently proposed federal legislative initiative requiring the inclusion of health warnings on all printed and broadcast beverage alcohol advertisements. This measure would require that every advertisement carry one of five messages in rotation:

- SURGEON GENERAL'S WARNING: Drinking during pregnancy may cause mental retardation and other birth defects. Avoid alcohol during pregnancy.
- WARNING: Alcohol impairs your ability to drive a car or operate machinery.
- WARNING: Alcohol may be hazardous if you are using any other drugs such as over-the-counter, prescription, or illicit drugs.
- WARNING: Drinking alcohol may become addictive.
- WARNING: It's against the law to purchase alcohol for persons under the age of 21.

The bill is enthusiastically endorsed by the nation's major health organizations and being fought by the beverage industry, advertisers, and broadcasters.

A final aspect of policy that influences alcohol availability is the rate and structure of taxation. Increases in alcoholic beverage taxes are associated with a reduction in alcohol-related problems such as deaths from hepatic cirrhosis and highway crashes (see Cook, 1984, for a review of the subject). Although taxation issues affect both sexes, there is some evidence that among the general public, women are more supportive than men of public policy measures to prevent alcohol problems, including those related to alcohol availability (Luks, 1983). American women can become a powerful political force for improved social policy relating to alcohol.

Highway Safety Issues

Policy efforts to prevent alcohol-related highway crashes are generally assumed to apply chiefly to males, since males arrested or convicted for driving while alcohol impaired (DWAI) or driving while intoxicated (DWI) tend to outnumber females 8 or 9 to 1. During the late 1970s and early 80s, those states with a minimum purchase age for alcoholic beverages of 18, 19, or 20 raised the minimum to 21. One of the chief arguments in favor of the change was the expected drop in alcohol-related crashes, deaths, and injuries among drivers aged 18 to 20, whose crash rates far exceeded those of other age groups. Figure 1 illustrates alcohol-related crash rates in New York State in 1980, when the purchase age was 18 (Lillis et al., 1982). Opponents of efforts to raise the legal purchase age argued that such a measure would unfairly penalize young women, because only young men were unsafe drivers. However, Lillis et al. showed that in comparison to other females, 18 to 20 year olds were also overrepresented among alcohol-related crashes, so that the change in purchase age would benefit both sexes.

Raising the alcohol purchase age, along with other policy measures to prevent, detect, and deter DWI, an overall decrease in average per capita alcohol consumption, and shifting population demographics, have all combined to produce a progressive decrease in alcohol-related highway deaths, especially for the 15–24 year age group (see Figure 2; U.S. Public Health Service, 1992). This is certainly a positive accomplishment. However, some changes in women's rates have not been so reassuring. On the national level, between 1982 and 1990 fatal automobile crashes after drinking declined 15% for men but only 4% for women (partly because fatal crashes by all women drivers rose 28% while men's fatal crashes remained stable) (Vegega and Klein, 1992). In New York State between 1978 and 1988, the percentage of convicted DWI/DWAI drivers who were men under age 20 went down, but the percentage who were women age 21 and over went up (Yu et al., 1992). In 1980, 8.8% of all convicted drivers were female. The proportion grew to 13.9% by 1986 and stabilized at about 13% thereafter. Furthermore, although recidivism rates for alcohol-related driving offenses have generally been lower for women than for men (Peck et al., 1994; Waller & Blow, 1995; Yu & Williford, 1995), women's recidivism rates may be catching up with men's as women's driving increases (Yu et al., 1992). Increased opportunities for women to drink and to drive may combine to increase women's risk of alcohol-related driving offenses and accidents. Such changes in women's behavior signal a need for better prevention policies designed specifically for women. In order to advance this goal, more research on drinking and driving among women will be required.

In addition to measures aimed directly at preventing DWI, mandatory safety restraint and mandatory airbag laws have been promoted as a means of reducing the morbidity and mortality of alcohol-related crashes. These laws are of special interest to women in light of the fact that females are twice as likely to be killed or injured as passengers riding with a male drinking driver than as drinking drivers themselves (N.Y. State Division of Alcoholism and Alcohol Abuse, 1982).

FIGURE 1
Drinking Crash Rates per 10,000 Licensed Drivers by Gender, New York
State, 1980 (Source: Lillis et al., 1982)

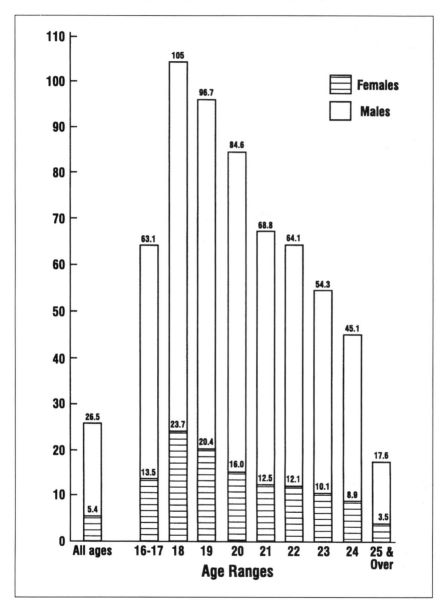

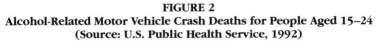

FIGURE 2
Alcohol-Related Motor Vehicle Crash Deaths for People Aged 15–24
(Source: U.S. Public Health Service, 1992)

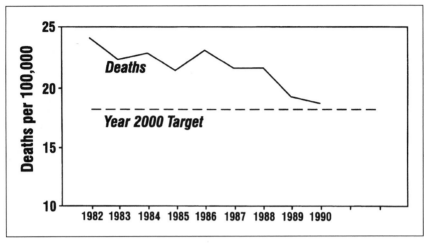

Gender-Related Disparities in the Identification and Treatment of Alcoholism

Although public policies are most often assumed to be aimed at the prevention of alcohol-related problems, many are also important determinants of the availability, appropriateness, and effectiveness of alcoholism treatment. There is reason to believe that women are underrepresented in alcoholism treatment in the United States. While there is some uncertainty about the true male to female ratio of alcohol-related problems severe enough to require treatment, estimates from direct interview studies yield a ratio of roughly 2 to 1 (Williams et al., 1989). A national survey of treatment units in the United States found that on September 30, 1989, women made up only 21.7% of the approximately 50,000 inpatients and 25.9% of the 330,000 outpatients in treatment for alcoholism (NIDA & NIAAA, 1991). Similarly, in New York State in 1989 and 1990, women made up only 20.4% and 21.7%, respectively, of the 30,000 to 33,000 patients treated (NYSDAAA, 1992). Although women tend to seek medical help more readily than do men in general, the alcoholism treatment system seems to be an exception to the rule.

Casefinding Systems

The reasons for this underrepresentation are several. One factor is that the dominant organized casefinding systems in place today (employee assistance programs, drinking driver programs, and other criminal justice alternative sentencing programs) are mainly male-oriented (Blume, 1980). Women alcoholics are more likely to be found by systematic screening in medical practice (Blume, 1991b). However, few such systems are currently in place. Efforts to encourage casefinding in general medical and obstetric/gynecological practice have depended mainly on physician education and persuasion. To date, these educational approaches have not been very successful. An alternative approach might be tried, involving such quasi-public institutions as the Joint Commission on Accreditation of Healthcare Organizations, the American Board of Medical Specialties, and the Accreditation Council for Graduate Medical Education. These organizations could require in-place systems to identify and refer patients suffering from alcoholism and other drug dependencies in order to attain hospital accreditation or approval for residency training. Such a policy could greatly improve the currently inadequate situation. Likewise, the U.S. Department of Health and Human Services and health departments at the state level could require that hospitals establish such screening systems to qualify for Medicare or Medicaid reimbursement. Neither of these approaches has been seriously considered or tried. On the other hand, several states have legislated mandatory urine drug testing and/or reporting for pregnant women or newborns (American Hospital Association, no date). These policies will be discussed further in the "Child Abuse, Neglect, and Custody" section below. Unfortunately, many of the state-mandated testing/reporting systems are used in a coercive, punitive way to remove infants from their mothers, rather than as efforts to improve casefinding, intervention, and referral.

Barriers to Treatment

In addition to a lack of systematic casefinding, women in need of alcoholism treatment encounter multiple sex-specific barriers. These include personal and family denial (Wilsnack, 1991), negative attitudes of significant others (Beckman & Amaro, 1986), lack of special programming for women, lack of child care for women entering treatment, concerns about confidentiality and possible loss of child custody, lack of adequate insurance coverage, and general underfunding and underavailability of public programs. One especially bizarre case illustrates this last point. An article in the *New York Times* (Feb. 1, 1987) reported that in Massachusetts, "alcoholic women who were legally entitled to receive care from the state have instead been jailed as criminals." In 1973, Massachusetts enacted a civil commitment law that allowed a judge to order 30 days of involuntary alcoholism treatment even though no crime had been committed. Men sent for treatment under this law went to an alcoholism program at Bridgewater, a men's prison. However, no women's alcoholism facility was ever established, so the 60 women committed under this law were sent to a women's prison with no program, locked up with criminals, and even denied, through a quirk in the wording of the law, participation in the prison's substance abuse education program. The *Times* article described the case of a 34-year-old woman who was hospitalized for an alcohol-related physical disorder but lacked insurance for alcoholism treatment. She was brought to the attention of the court on the advice of hospital social workers when they could not find an alcoholism program able to accept her. Her court-appointed lawyer at first agreed to the commitment, but brought the woman's case to public attention when she discovered the complete lack of treatment for her client. The practice was then stopped. The *New York Times* (June 14, 1987) later reported the opening of a program for alcoholic women in Boston to serve this population, but stated that the jailing of alcoholic women could be resumed if there is insufficient space at the treatment facility. According to Chavkin (1991), this overcrowding did occur and women were once again being imprisoned.

Lack of Special Programming

The 1989 national treatment unit survey cited previously asked each agency about specialized programming. Only a third of the 2,500 units reporting had programming for women (NIDA & NIAAA, 1991). Since the present alcoholism treatment system is based on a program model originally designed for men, special programming for women is an important ingredient in making the system effective in attracting and helping women. Following a series of hearings on the needs of alcoholic women, Congress enacted an amendment to the Alcohol, Drug and Mental Health Block Grant reauthorization legislation of 1984 (PL 98-509), creating a 5% women's set-aside (Lubinski, 1991). This measure required that each state devote 5% of the annual federal grant that supports alcoholism and drug abuse treatment (the "block grant") to "new and expanded services for women." Unfortunately, the 1984 set-aside requirement was not accompanied by an increase in funding. The National Council on Alcoholism and Drug Dependence subsequently conducted a study of the implementation of the set-aside (NCADD, 1987). The survey found the outcome mixed, with the best results in states that consolidated their resources and used the federal money to establish direct grants to fund new programs. In states that simply asked current programs to spend 5% of their federal funds on programming for women there was little change. The 1988 reauthorization (PL 100-690) increased the women's set-aside to 10% and added a stress on "pregnant women and women with dependent children." It also authorized, for the first time, direct federal grants to develop model programs for drug-affected pregnant and postpartum women and their children. These grants were administered through the Office of Substance Abuse Prevention (OSAP) of the Alcohol, Drug Abuse, and Mental Health Administration (ADAMHA). In addition, a National Resource Center for Perinatal Addiction was established.

In 1991, the federal General Accounting Office (GAO) conducted a study of the efficacy of the 1988 women's set-aside in meeting the needs of pregnant addicts and those with young children. The study concluded that states were unable to estimate the need for such services and that there was little information available on how effectively block grant funds were being used to meet this need (GAO, 1991). The 1992 reauthorization of the block grant returned the women's set-aside to 5%. However, the law now requires states to report to the federal government on the use of these funds. In addition, the legislation requires that pregnant women be given priority in placement into treatment.

The 1992 reauthorization also required a major reorganization of the federal agencies responsible for support of prevention, treatment, and research efforts in alcoholism and other addictions. Established in 1974, ADAMHA had been the lead agency in this federal effort. ADAMHA was originally an umbrella agency for the National Institute of Mental Health (NIMH), the National Institute on Alcohol Abuse and Alcoholism (NIAAA), and the National Institute on Drug Abuse (NIDA). Until 1980, NIAAA and NIDA provided funding for direct service demonstration projects as well as "formula grants" of funds to the states for program development. In 1980 the direct project funds and block grant were merged into a larger, more comprehensive, "block grant" that also included funds for various mental health programs. The 1992 reorganization split the three research institutes from the service delivery component. NIAAA, NIDA, and NIMH became components of the National Institutes of Health (NIH), the federal government's overall health research agency. ADAMHA's other functions became part of the new Substance Abuse and Mental Health Services Administration (SAMHSA), which oversees the Center for Substance Abuse Prevention (CSAP), the Center for Substance Abuse Treatment (CSAT), and the Center for Mental Health Services (CMHS). Both the block grant, which now separates alcoholism and drug abuse funds entirely from those for mental health, and the programs for pregnant and postpartum women remain under SAMHSA's administration. It is now the responsibility of CSAT to assure the appropriate use of the women's set-aside.

Exclusion of Pregnant Women from Treatment

The GAO study (1991) cited above reported that pregnant addicts often experienced negative attitudes during their encounters with health professionals. They felt unwelcome and often were. In a survey of 78 New York City alcohol and drug programs, Chavkin (1990) found that 54% refused to accept pregnant women. Thus, a general lack of treatment availability is compounded by the exclusion of women who are pregnant from many existing facilities. In response to this situation, suit was brought by a pregnant addict against four publicly funded New York alcohol and drug programs which, by policy, excluded pregnant women (*Elaine W v. North General Hospital*) (see *Alcoholism and Drug Abuse Weekly*, 1993). The programs' rationale for excluding pregnant women was the lack of obstetric services in their parent institutions. Arguing that the state's civil rights law forbids sex discrimination in public accommodations (which includes hospitals), the plaintiff settled with two of the programs who agreed to change their admission rules. The other two cases are still in the courts with one finding for the plaintiff having been reversed on appeal (Bertin, 1992).

Lack of Child Care

Many women in need of alcoholism treatment are single parents who feel unable to avail themselves of these services because of lack of adequate child care. A nationwide study conducted by the Association of Junior Leagues between 1985 and 1988 surveyed 463 public alcoholism authorities, 596 treatment programs, and 1,487 gatekeepers in 39 communities (Association of Junior Leagues, 1988; Wilsnack, 1991). All groups reported that the most important barriers to treatment for women include personal denial, family denial, and responsibility for care of dependent children. The greatest program need identified was child care. In spite of this agreement and the existence of viable program models (e.g., Reckman et al., 1984), there are still very few alcoholism facilities providing such care, either in a residential or in an outpatient setting.

The only alternative for women without financial resources who need residential treatment is to look for help with child care from public agencies. Such women often fear losing custody of their children if they do so (see child abuse and neglect issues, below). They also may risk losing financial support from public assistance programs for families with dependent children while they are in residential treatment, and therefore risk being unable to maintain a place for the family to live. These formidable barriers cry out for changes in child abuse law, program design, and public funding policies if we are to bring help to alcoholic women and their families.

Lack of Adequate Insurance Coverage

Third-party payer coverage does not, in the vast majority of cases, cover alcoholism treatment on the same basis as other illnesses. This is true of both public and private insurance. Some policies cover only hospital detoxification, others only outpatient services, and many include high deductibles and copayments, unrealistically low caps on total payment, or rigid limits on inpatient treatment. Utilization review or case management systems may further limit access to benefits by limiting inpatient stays or refusing to approve levels of care recommended by the treating clinician. Although these insurance problems affect both sexes, women are more likely than men to be underemployed and to be generally underinsured. In addition, millions of Americans have no health insurance coverage at all. Again, this is a special problem for young women, who are often in low-paid jobs without benefits (Sternberger & Drew, 1981). A recent study by the Older Womens League, for example, focused on men and women between the ages of 45 and 61 (Older Womens League, 1992). More men (72%) were provided health insurance by their employers than were women (55%). Thirteen percent of the women, compared to 7% of the men, lacked any kind of coverage, public or private. In addition, race seems to be a factor in access to coverage. A study comparing 25 African-American and 67 white women entering alcoholism treatment in California found a great disparity in the proportion who had insurance coverage. White women were 10 times more likely to have such coverage (Amaro et al., 1987).

Calls for reform of the American health care system have proliferated in the 1990s and a variety of state and federal proposals are under consideration. The inclusion of coverage for a continuum of alcoholism services, including provision for child care, and the extension of coverage to all Americans are critical public policy issues for women.

Child Abuse, Neglect, and Custody

Policies on child abuse, neglect, custody, and child care are of special relevance to alcoholic women. Legal definitions of abuse and neglect can act as important treatment barriers. In some jurisdictions child abuse and/or neglect is defined to include the abuse of alcohol or the use or abuse of drugs by the parent. If this is the case, a disadvantaged single parent (almost always female) who requires inpatient treatment for addictive disease will be deterred from seeking the help she needs. By applying to the child protective agency in her community for assistance with temporary child placement, she risks being adjudicated a child abuser or neglector and being unable to resume custody of her children when she leaves the inpatient unit. This was the case in New York State before 1981. In that year the state's Family Court Act was amended to add the following to the definition of a neglected child.

> . . . provided, however, that where the respondent is voluntarily and regularly participating in a rehabilitative program, evidence that the respondent has repeatedly misused a drug or drugs or alcoholic beverages to the extent that he loses self-control of his actions shall not establish that the child is a neglected child in the absence of evidence establishing that the child's physical, mental or emotional condition has been impaired or is in imminent danger of becoming impaired as set forth in paragraph (i) of this subdivision. (New York State Family Court Act, 1981)

This addition to the law converted a definition that was previously perceived as a barrier to treatment into a protection and motivator for treatment for the alcohol- or drug-dependent woman. Of course, the availability of a facility that provides care for both mother and children would be preferable to any form of foster care, even if custody is not at risk.

In a number of states, the definition of child abuse or neglect includes prenatal drug exposure, as reflected in the status of a newborn. For example, in Florida the definition includes "physical dependency of a newborn infant upon any [controlled] drug." In Illinois, the definition of a neglected child includes "any newborn infant whose blood or urine contains any amount of a controlled substance." Such definitions, along with the mandatory child abuse/neglect reporting laws in effect in every state, have led to policies of reporting and automatically removing newborn infants from their mothers on the basis of a positive urine screen in the newborn, or, in some cases, of a diagnosis of fetal alcohol syndrome or effects. This removal and placement into foster care is done independently of any finding that the mother is incapable of caring for the infant, independently of any finding that the mother is in fact alcohol or drug dependent, and independently of any offer of treatment for the mother.

These policies have faced court challenges in several states. A recent example is a Connecticut case, that of Valerie D. This apparently healthy 3-year-old child was taken from her mother at birth because of her mother's cocaine use in the hours before delivery, which led to a finding of cocaine metabolites in the infant's urine. An appeal of a lower court decision to terminate parental rights reached Connecticut's highest court. In an August 1992 decision, the court reversed the termination, holding that parental rights cannot be terminated on the basis of prenatal conduct since the fetus is not a "child" and the pregnant women not yet a "parent" under the child abuse and neglect law of the state (*Connecticut Law Journal,* 1992).

A similar principle was raised in 1990 in a New York lawsuit that challenged the Department of Social Services and several New York City hospitals. At issue was the policy of reporting positive urine drug tests on newborns, automatically resulting in a petition for a family court neglect hearing. About 5,000 such petitions were brought in 1989, with three-quarters resulting in removal of parental custody (Hoffman, 1990). In this case, the mother, Ana R, was tested four times for drugs. The first test was positive, but she denied taking drugs and three subsequent tests were negative. She lost custody. Her attorney pointed out that another woman with the same last name delivered at the same time in the hospital, and that the urine reports may have been mixed up. Although the suit is not settled, New York State subsequently delineated a policy that should stop this practice. In August of 1990 the general counsel of the New York Department of Social Services wrote:

It is the Department's position that the child protective statutes were not intended to apply, nor can they constitutionally be applied, to prenatal conduct by a woman in relation to a fetus. Consequently, a child abuse or maltreatment report may not be indicated solely on an alleged impairment to a newborn's condition resulting from a woman's action while she was pregnant because, although there was a fetus, there was no child in existence at the time the woman committed the acts. Furthermore, such prenatal conduct falls within the woman's constitutional right to privacy and to bodily integrity. For a report to be indicated, there must be some credible evidence that the woman currently is unable to care for the born infant or that her past behavior places the born infant at risk of abuse or maltreatment in the future.

The general counsel continued:

Evidence that an infant was born with positive toxicology, dependent on or with withdrawal symptoms from drugs, with fetal alcohol effect or fetal alcohol syndrome, or with a medical condition attributable to in utero drug or alcohol exposure is not sufficient, by itself, to indicate a report or to take the newborn into protective custody. Such evidence, by itself, does not indicate the extent of a woman's drug or alcohol use, how such use may affect her ability to care for her newborn in the future or whether the child's life or health would be placed in imminent danger if the infant were released to the woman. . . . As mere use of a drug or alcohol by a person legally responsible for a child's care is not sufficient to indicate a report against that person, the social services district cannot indicate such a report unless it has some other evidence, in addition to the newborn's condition, which shows that the woman misuses drugs or alcohol to such an extent that she will be unable to care for the newborn in the future. (see Letter, 1990)

This statement shows the need for a review of the policies and procedures of the state and local child protective systems in other jurisdictions. An automatic mindless removal of a child from its mother on the basis of a breath or urine test, without fair investigation and an effort to provide help to both mother and infant, is not humane public policy.

Questions of confidentiality also arise in these cases. Since 1975, the privacy of alcohol and drug abuse treatment records has been protected by special federal regulations (42 CFR Part 2). Currently all states require the reporting of incidents of suspected child abuse and neglect. In their original form, the federal alcohol and drug confidentiality regulations did not allow the reporting of child abuse or neglect without the signed consent of the patient, a specific court order issued under Subpart E of the regulations, or a legal contract called a qualified service agreement. Each of these options created significant problems (Blume, 1986). In 1987, the confidentiality regulations were revised to allow an initial child abuse or neglect report in accordance with state law, without patient consent. To date, state child abuse reporting laws have not been interpreted to require the reporting of all parents who come for addiction treatment. Only suspected incidents of abuse or neglect are customarily reported. By redefining child abuse or neglect to include alcohol and/or drug use during pregnancy, systems requiring the reporting of all pregnant addicts without their consent have been established in several states. Instead of depending on the clinical judgment exercised by program staff in deciding to report a male parent or a nonpregnant woman, these systems require reporting of all pregnant women in the established category. Such a reporting system appears to contradict the purpose of the federal confidentiality protection, which, in the words of the regulations, "are intended to insure that an alcohol or drug abuse patient in a federally assisted alcohol or drug abuse program is not made more vulnerable by reason of the availability of his or her patient record than an individual who has an alcohol or drug problem and who does not seek treatment." Even where the state reporting mandates are accompanied by laws that prohibit prosecution on the basis of a reported positive urine drug test in pregnancy (e.g., Oregon), this reporting will act as a deterrent to pregnant women who need both obstetric care and addiction treatment.

Policies Related to Alcohol and Other Drug Use in Pregnancy

Mandated Treatment for Pregnant Addicts

Curiously, in light of the critical lack of treatment programs for pregnant alcohol and drug dependent women, serious proposals have been made to mandate such treatment for women unable or unwilling to seek treatment voluntarily (American Medical Association, 1990; Chavkin, 1991; Nelson & Milliken, 1988). This involuntary treatment is *not* proposed as an alternative to criminal sanction for a woman convicted of a crime, but rather for women who have come to the attention of a public authority of some kind solely because they are both pregnant and using some kind of drug (including alcohol). The arguments for and against such treatment are many: Proponents argue that mandatory treatment of pregnant women who are addicted to alcohol and/or other drugs will improve the health and welfare of both mother and fetus. By ordering treatment, civil authorities can overcome reluctance, ambivalence, denial, or just plain refusal to seek help. Furthermore, through a system to monitor the progress of the pregnant addict in treatment, the common problems of dropping out or lack of cooperation can be avoided. In addition, they argue that a woman who elects to carry a pregnancy (rather than have an abortion) has both a moral and legal duty to do whatever is necessary to assure the well-being of her fetus. By establishing mandatory treatment through a civil commitment, the criminalization of addiction in pregnancy can be avoided.

The arguments against mandatory treatment of pregnant addicts are serious enough to warrant close examination. In some respects, these objections are similar to those raised against using the criminal justice system to intervene in alcohol or drug use in pregnancy. In other respects, they are similar to the objections raised against other court-ordered medical treatment during pregnancy (AMA, 1990). Both are considered below.

Moral and legal responsibilities of a woman towards her fetus. In *Roe v. Wade* the U.S. Supreme Court established a woman's right to terminate pregnancy before the fetus is viable outside the uterus. By making a decision to carry the pregnancy, the pregnant woman assumes a moral duty toward the fetus. However, this responsibility is quite different from an established legal duty, for example that of a parent towards a child (AMA, 1990). Legislating a special legal responsibility to enforce a pregnant woman's moral duty would be establishing a penalty on the state of pregnancy itself (AMA, 1990). It should also be remembered that, more than in many other aspects of medical care, socioeconomic factors restrict access to abortion, since law prohibits the use of federal funds to counsel or perform this procedure.

The vast majority of women deciding to carry a pregnancy, including those with addictive disease, want to produce a healthy child. In fact, pregnancy is an excellent motivator for chemically dependent women, but treatment must be available, accessible, and appropriate. The lack of child care, lack of facilities, and all of the other barriers described above apply to pregnant women as well as others. Existing programs often exclude these patients. Program models designed specifically for pregnant women are largely unavailable. In such circumstances, public policy that would establish a legal mandate for treatment seems grossly misplaced.

Controlling the behavior of pregnant women. A major criticism of mandated treatment in pregnancy is that it would introduce into the law the principle of societal control of the behavior of a woman based solely on her state of pregnancy. Although the proposal for mandated treatment is framed in terms of treating women who are addicted, harm to the fetus can be caused by a wide variety of maternal behaviors. Tobacco, a drug not included in mandated treatment models, causes reduced birth weight and increased risk for sudden infant death syndrome. Diet, exercise, stress, and exposure to toxoplasmosis through cat litter all make a contribution to fetal health or damage. For that matter, consumption of alcohol and other drugs by both mother and father before pregnancy is established may have adverse effects on the fetus. As Paltrow (1990) points out, any public policy that treats pregnancy as a conflict between maternal and fetal rights "leads inevitably down a slippery slope."

Mandated reporting. In order for a mandatory treatment system to operate, some kind of reporting procedure would have to be established, as indeed currently exists in 11 states (AHA, 1991). Reporting systems for pregnant women tend to be applied inconsistently, with poor women and women of color overrepresented. For example, a study in Pinellas County, Florida, found a roughly equivalent prevalence of positive urine toxicologies in pregnant women seen in private practice (13.1%) and those cared for in public clinics (16.3%). The prevalence was similar among white (15.4%) and African-American women (14.1%). However, during the six-month period of the study poor women were more likely to be reported to authorities under Florida law than others, and African-American women were 10 times more likely to be reported than white women (Chasnoff et al., 1990).

Another consideration is the timing of reporting. Many women do not know they are pregnant until a few months after conception. This is especially true of chemically dependent women, because heavy drinking and other drug use often disrupt the normal menstrual cycle. Furthermore, many addicted women, particularly disadvantaged ones, do not seek obstetric care until late in pregnancy. Current knowledge about birth defects indicates that much alcohol- and drug-related harm may occur relatively early in pregnancy, as well as later on. Mandated treatment would be likely to be applied late in pregnancy, missing the opportunity to prevent early damage.

Although it could be argued that mandated treatment in late pregnancy would at least be helpful in decreasing postnatal drinking (with positive effects on family well-being), this argument could as easily be applied to justify mandated treatment of fathers-to-be, and thus exposes the gender prejudice inherent in the proposal. Furthermore, if women knew that they would be reported to public authorities, forced into treatment, and perhaps forced to leave (or even risk losing) their homes and families, this would surely deter many from seeking help, either obstetric care or chemical dependency treatment, on their own.

Theoretical basis for mandated treatment. Civil commitment for mental illness is usually justified by the fact that the involuntary patient is found to be dangerous to him/herself or others. Can this theory be applied to pregnant addicts?

If the purpose of involuntary treatment for the pregnant addict is to improve the woman's health because she is a danger to herself, then her sex and condition of pregnancy should not single her out for mandated treatment. All addicts should be treated alike because all put their own health and welfare in peril.

If the purpose of mandated treatment is to prevent danger to another (the fetus), this would elevate the fetus to personhood, while U.S. law has never considered the fetus a person with the full rights of an individual human being. Only a live-born child has that status. Even *Roe v. Wade,* which held that the state has an interest in the welfare of a potentially viable fetus, allowed that late pregnancy abortion was permissible under circumstances determined by public policy (AMA, 1990; Paltrow, 1990). If the fetus is not a separate person, the pregnant woman cannot be said to be "dangerous to others" in the same sense as the mentally ill person subject to involuntary commitment.

Limits to public resources. Public resources are limited. Devoting available funds to education and to improving the accessibility of both prenatal care and addiction treatment makes more sense than devoting these funds to constructing a system to mandate care. As the events in Massachusetts described earlier illustrate, civil commitment does not guarantee adequate care.

Criminal Sanctions

In addition to civil actions taken against pregnant women who suffer from alcoholism or other addictions, the 1980s saw a growing tendency to employ the resources of the criminal justice system (arrest, prosecution, conviction, sentencing to probation with conditions, or imprisonment). In some cases, the women were charged with criminal offenses related to alcohol/drug use during pregnancy. In others, the sentence given for an unrelated offense was more severe than would ordinarily have been the case because the defendant was pregnant (American Civil Liberties Union, 1992). Penalties have included jailing, confinement to a treatment center under 24-hour guard, and house arrest, among others.

Perhaps the first such case was brought in Wyoming (*State of Wyoming v. Osmus,* 1954), where the state supreme court eventually reversed both the manslaughter and criminal neglect convictions of a woman charged with endangering the life of her fetus. In a subsequent California case, a heroin addict who gave birth to twins was convicted of felony child endangerment. The conviction was also reversed on appeal in 1977. In spite of these two precedents, between 1985 and 1992 more than 150 women in 24 states were arrested on criminal charges because of their alcohol and/or drug use during pregnancy (ACLU, 1992). Many more have been coerced by being threatened with arrest or have been pressured to enter a guilty plea to a reduced charge, serving jail terms or probation for crimes they did not commit. This is true in spite of the fact that, as of 1992, no state had enacted a specific criminal statute relating to alcohol or drug use in pregnancy. Instead, charges are brought under criminal child support laws and for abuse and neglect, child endangerment, delivery of drugs to a minor, manslaughter, homicide, and other offenses.

The majority of women arrested have come from poverty backgrounds and minority groups (ACLU, 1992). Most of the cases involve controlled drugs, but, in others, no illegal activity or substance is involved. An example of the latter is the case of Pamela Rae Stewart, a pregnant battered woman who was arrested for "failing to follow her doctor's advice to stay off her feet, to refrain from sexual intercourse, refrain from taking street drugs and seek immediate medical attention if she experienced difficulties with the pregnancy." (The "street drugs" aspect of the charge was not proven.) She was prosecuted under California criminal child support statutes in 1987, but not convicted (see *People v. Stewart,* 1987). In 1990 in Laramie, Wyoming, a 29-year-old pregnant woman went to a police station to file a complaint after being beaten by her husband. She was concerned that the physical abuse would harm her pregnancy. When she was found to have alcohol in her system she was arrested in the emergency room of the hospital to which she had gone for treatment. She was jailed and charged with criminal child abuse for endangering her fetus. The case was subsequently dropped (see *State v. Pfannenstiel,* 1990).

Even in cases where an illegal drug is involved, the pregnant woman is not charged with drug possession, but with far more serious crimes. A well-publicized case was that of Jennifer Johnson. This 23-year-old Florida woman was convicted of two counts of delivery of a controlled substance to a minor in 1989 (*State v. Johnson,* 1989). The substance was benzoylecognine, a cocaine metabolite. She was convicted of delivering it via the umbilical cord to her two newborns, each of whom had a positive urine test for cocaine, during the few seconds between the delivery of the infant and the severing of the cord. She was sentenced to a year of treatment, 14 years of probation, 200 hours of community service, payment of $30 a month to the probation department, and court supervision of prenatal care for any subsequent pregnancy. When she relapsed into drug use she spent three months in jail. This woman had called a helpline during her pregnancy asking for referral to a source of help, but none was available. She confided to her physician her fears that her cocaine use could harm her fetus during each pregnancy. The response she received was her arrest and prosecution. She was only able to enroll in a drug program after she was no longer pregnant. This case was appealed with supporting amicus briefs from a long list of public health and legal rights advocacy organizations. Although the Florida Court of Appeals upheld her conviction, the Florida Supreme Court later reversed the conviction, stating that it refused the "State's invitation to walk down a path that law, public policy, reason and common sense forbid it to tread" (Paltrow, 1992).

What is the basis for this assault on pregnant women? The arguments of prosecutors and others who favor a criminal justice response to pregnant alcohol and drug users are similar to those advanced in favor of mandatory treatment (Beck, 1990; Shaver, 1989). They argue that these policies promote the health of mother and child, get women into treatment, keep them alcohol and drug-free, or at the very least "send a message to drug abusers that they should seek treatment before the criminal justice system has to become involved" (Paltrow, 1990). They argue that voluntary treatment is less effective than involuntary treatment, an opinion that is not supported by what little research exists (Chavkin, 1991).

To understand the motivation behind these measures, one must consider the frustration felt by our society at its failure to win the "war on drugs," its fear of the appearance of a generation of drug-affected, neuropsychologically impaired children, and the intense stigma applied to chemically dependent women. A former secretary of the Department of Health and Human Services has been quoted as saying that "substance abuse by a pregnant woman is tantamount to child abuse, pure and simple" (see *Alcoholism and Drug Abuse Weekly*, 1990). But there is nothing simple about it.

Even if states enacted legislation making alcohol and/or drug use during pregnancy a specific crime, such laws would be likely to be found unconstitutional (Paltrow, 1990). Paltrow observes that "a law which interferes with a fundamental privacy right must withstand searching judicial examination. For the law to survive, the state must establish that it has a compelling interest and must demonstrate that the law is narrowly tailored and furthers the asserted interest." A law criminalizing alcohol or drug use in pregnancy would be unlikely to pass this test. The goal of preventing harm would have to be based on the *certainty* of fetal damage rather than the possibility or potential to cause harm. Yet the factors that determine which fetus will develop fetal alcohol syndrome or complications due to other drug exposure are not established. Given equivalent alcohol use by a large number of women, only a fraction of their progeny will show fetal alcohol effects. The potential for harm with prenatal cocaine exposure is also uncertain (Mayes et al., 1992). In the absence of demonstrated harm, Mariner et al. (1990) point out that "singling out pregnant women highlights the fact that they are being punished not for any act harming the fetus but because they are pregnant and use drugs."

One effort was made to introduce a federal law that would criminalize drug use during pregnancy (the Child Abuse During Pregnancy Prevention Act of 1989). This bill, introduced into the Senate, would have made five $10 million grants to states for the support of services to pregnant addicted women and their infants. To qualify, a state would have to certify that its laws make it a crime to give birth to an infant who is "addicted or otherwise injured or impaired by the substance abuse of the mother during pregnancy." The state must also certify that a conviction for violation of this criminal statute would carry a sentence of three years of mandatory rehabilitation in a custodial setting or certification by medical authorities that the woman was unlikely to engage in substance abuse if released. The bill also required a state reporting plan mandating that health care providers identify "substance abused" infants to the "appropriate authorities" (Lubinski, 1991). This bill was strongly opposed by health advocates, and was never enacted.

Jailing women will not assure that they are in a health-promoting atmosphere in which adequate amounts of food, exercise, rest, and prenatal care are provided. Most jails are overcrowded and lacking in all of the above. In Charleston, South Carolina, in the early 1990s, women who delivered in the public hospital underwent urine testing for drugs. Positive results were reported to the police who arrested the women after delivery, handcuffed them and took them to jail. One woman who arrived still bleeding vaginally was told to sit on a towel (quoted by Paltrow, 1990). Jailing women does not even assure that they do not have access to alcohol or other drugs, since these are present in many jails and prisons (Paltrow, 1990).

Perhaps the clearest statement about the criminalization of addiction in pregnancy may be found in a 1989 policy statement of the American Society of Addiction Medicine, which reads in part: "The imposition of criminal penalties solely because a person suffers from an illness is inappropriate and counterproductive. Criminal prosecution of chemically dependent women will have the overall result of deterring such women from seeking both prenatal care and chemical dependency treatment, thereby increasing, rather than preventing, harm to children and to society as a whole" (see ASAM, 1995).

Policies Related to Research

Alcoholism has traditionally been thought of as a disease of men, in spite of the large numbers of women affected. Research on alcoholism has concentrated on males, leaving significant gaps in knowledge about the disease in females. In short, the history of the alcoholism field is that the classical studies that have informed thinking, such as Snyder's *Alcohol and the Jews* and Vaillant's *The Natural History of Alcoholism*, should have been called "Alcohol and Jewish Men" and "The Natural History of Alcoholism in Men." Instead, the findings of these studies were generalized to what Carpenter and Armenti (1972, p. 515) referred to as "that great invisible half of the animal kingdom, to judge by experiments on alcohol."

The National Institute on Alcohol Abuse and Alcoholism has funded special studies on women and alcohol since the early 1970s. National research conferences (1978, 1984, 1993) and NIAAA research monographs (NIAAA, 1980, 1986, 1993) assembled current findings on women's drinking and recommended directions for future research, including the need for research relevant to policy issues and to primary and secondary prevention of alcohol-related problems in women. These conferences and reports reflected a growing realization from the 1980s on that many aspects of women's health have received insufficient research attention. In 1991, the Alcohol, Drug Abuse, and Mental Health Administration established the Office of Women's Health, which helped to draft guidelines for including women in research. Developed in cooperation with the National Institutes of Health (NIH), this policy requires that all health research studies funded by these agencies either include women in the study population or justify their exclusion on scientific grounds (Institute of Medicine, 1991). Through the Office of Women's Health, ADAMHA sponsored an Institute of Medicine conference reviewing research needs in mental and addictive disorders in women (Institute of Medicine, 1991).

With the reorganization of ADAMHA and the transfer of NIAAA and NIDA to the NIH in 1992, this policy and emphasis will remain in effect. However, it will take many years for scientific knowledge about women to catch up to knowledge about men in relation to alcohol.

Until more is understood, it is important that current knowledge be disseminated to clinicians, program administrators, and policymakers, since many are unaware of the findings of research already reported, such as the close association between a history of physical and sexual abuse in childhood and adulthood with alcohol and drug problems in women (e.g., Miller et al., 1989; Winfield et al., 1990).

Conclusion

This chapter has reviewed some of the more important and more controversial social issues related to women and alcohol, including marketing, taxation, drinking and driving, access to treatment, confidentiality, child abuse, custody, research, mandated treatment, and the criminalization of chemical dependency in pregnancy. On the whole, policymakers are not well informed on these matters. Assumptions about the nature of alcohol as a drug and its effects on society in general and on women in particular are still based on traditional beliefs and stereotypes rather than on the results of scholarly investigation. Moralism often competes with compassion in policy formation. Images of glamour and degradation exist side by side. Thus, the education of policymakers is an important responsibility of professionals concerned with alcohol-related problems.

It is also important to educate the general public in order to promote the disease concept of addictive disorders and to combat stigma. Only then will rational and humane policies govern society's response to its problems with alcohol and other addictive drugs. Only then will women with alcoholism and other addictions be treated with dignity and fairness, as human beings suffering from a treatable disease, rather than as fallen women, as targets for abuse, or as criminals.

References

Alcoholism and Drug Abuse Weekly. (1990). Sullivan calls drug abuse by pregnant women "child abuse." Vol. 2, No. 23, p. 2.

Alcoholism and Drug Abuse Weekly. (1993). Treatment programs cannot bar pregnant women says court. Vol. 5, No. 20, pp. 1–2.

Amaro, H., Beckman, L.J., & Mays, V.M. (1987). A comparison of black and white women entering alcoholism treatment. *Journal of Studies on Alcohol, 48,* 220–228.

American Civil Liberties Union. (1992). *Criminal prosecutions against pregnant women: National update and overview.* New York: Author.

American Hospital Association. (1991). *The role of hospitals in caring for pregnant substance-abusing women.* Chicago: Author.

American Medical Association, Board of Trustees. (1990). Legal interventions during pregnancy: Court-ordered medical treatment and legal penalties for potentially harmful behavior by pregnant women. *Journal of the American Medical Association, 264,* 2663-2670.

American Society of Addiction Medicine, Inc. (1995, May). Public policy statement on chemically dependent women and pregnancy (pp. 41-42). Chevy Chase, MD: Author.

Association of Junior Leagues, Inc. (1988). *Woman to Woman Community Services Survey.* New York: Author.

Beck, J. (1990). Drinking for two—There ought to be a law. *U.S. Journal of Drug and Alcohol Dependence, 34* (4), 5.

Beckman, L.J., & Amaro, H. (1986). Personal and social difficulties faced by women and men entering alcoholism treatment. *Journal of Studies on Alcohol, 47,* 135-145.

Bertin, J. (1992). American Civil Liberties Union, New York Chapter, personal communication.

Blume, S.B. (1980). Clinical research: Casefinding, diagnosis, treatment, and rehabilitation. In *Alcoholism and alcohol abuse among women: Research issues. Proceedings of a workshop* (pp. 119-159) (NIAAA Research Monograph No. 1; DHEW Publication No. ADM-80-835). Washington, DC: U.S. Government Printing Office.

Blume, S.B. (1984). Public policy issues: A summary. In L.J. West (Ed.), *Alcoholism and related problems: Issues for the American public* (pp. 176-191). Upper Saddle River, NJ: Prentice-Hall.

Blume, S.B. (1986). Women and alcohol: Public policy issues. *In Women and alcohol: Health-related issues* (pp. 294-311) (NIAAA Research Monograph No. 16; DHHS Publication No. ADM 86-1139). Washington, DC: U.S. Government Printing Office.

Blume, S.B. (1991a). Sexuality and stigma: The alcoholic woman. *Alcohol Health & Research World, 15,* 139-146.

Blume, S.B. (1991b). Women, alcohol and drugs. In N.S. Miller (Ed.), *Comprehensive handbook of drug and alcohol addiction* (pp. 147-177). New York: Marcel Dekker.

California Women's Commission on Alcohol and Drug Dependencies (1992, Spring). The good, the bad, and the ugly: Current issues in alcohol advertising and women. CWCADD *Newsletter,* pp. 1-3.

Carpenter, J.A., & Armenti, N.P. (1972). Some effects of ethanol on human sexual and aggressive behavior. In B. Kissin & H. Begleiter (Eds.), *The biology of alcoholism,* Vol. II (pp. 509-543). New York: Plenum Press.

Centers for Disease Control. (1992). Trends in alcohol-related traffic facilities, by sex— United States. *Journal of the American Medical Association, 268* (3), 313-314.

Chasnoff, I.J., Landress, H.J., & Barrett, M.E. (1990). The prevalence of illicit-drug or alcohol use during pregnancy and discrepancies in mandatory reporting in Pinellas County, Florida. *New England Journal of Medicine, 322,* 1202-1206.

Chaucer, G. (1951). *The Canterbury Tales* (trans. by Nevill Coghill). Harmondsworth, England: Penguin Classics.

Chavkin, W. (1990). Drug addiction and pregnancy: Policy crossroads. *American Journal of Public Health, 80,* 483-487.

Chavkin, W. (1991). Mandatory treatment for drug use during pregnancy. *Journal of the American Medical Association, 266* (11), 1556-1561.

Connecticut Law Journal. (1992, Aug. 18). In re Valerie D 223, pp. 34-77.

Cook, P.J. (1984). The economics of alcohol consumption and abuse. In L.J. West (Ed.), *Alcoholism and related problems: Issues for the American public* (pp. 56-77). Upper Saddle River, NJ: Prentice Hall.

Edwards, C. (1971). *The Hammurabi Code, and Sinaitic legislation* (p. 43). Port Washington, NY: Kennikat Press.

Eigen, L. (1992). Alcohol advertising trends: The feminization of beer drinking. *Prevention Pipeline, 5*(1), 3-4.

General Accounting Office. (1991). *Women's set-aside does not assure drug treatment for pregnant women.* Washington, DC: Author.

Gomberg, E.S.L. (1986). Women: Alcohol and other drugs. *Drugs and Society, 1,* 75-109.

Hoffman, J. (1990). Challenge drug tests. *Village Voice.*

Institute of Medicine. (1991). *Assessing future research needs: Mental and addictive disorders in women.* Washington, DC: Institute of Medicine of the National Academy of Science.

Jacobson, M., Atkins, R., & Hacker, G. (1983). *The booze merchants: The inebriating of America.* Washington, DC: CSPI Books.

Kilbourne, J. (1991). The spirit of the czar: Selling addictions to women. In P. Roth (Ed.), *Alcohol and drugs are women's issues: Vol. 1. A review of the issues* (pp. 10-22). Metuchen, NJ: Women's Action Alliance & Scarecrow Press.

Klassen, A.D., & Wilsnack, S.C. (1986). Sexual experience and drinking among women in a U.S. national survey. *Archives of Sexual Behavior, 15,* 363-392.

Klee, L., & Ames, G. (1987). Reevaluating risk factors for women's drinking: A study of blue-collar wives. *American Journal of Preventive Medicine, 3,* 31-41.

Lender, M.E., & Martin, J.K. (1987). *Drinking in America: A history.* New York: Free Press.

Letter from Susan Demers (deputy commissioner, New York State Dept. of Social Services) to Barbara Gil (American Enterprise Institute), August 21, 1990. (The deputy commissioner quoted the general counsel's opinion in this letter.)

Lillis, R.P., Williams, T.P., & Williford, W.R. (1982). *The role of 18 year old female drinking drivers in the highway safety problem in New York State* (Research Report Series, No. 17). Albany, NY: Bureau of Alcohol and Highway Safety, New York Division of Alcoholism and Alcohol Abuse.

Lubinski, C. (1991). *Pregnant alcoholic and drug dependent women and drug exposed infants: The evolution of a national policy.* Unpublished manuscript.

Luks, A. (1983). *Will America sober up?* Boston: Beacon.

Mariner, W.K., Glantz, L.H., & Annas, G.J. (1990). Pregnancy, drugs and the perils of prosecution. *Criminal Justice Ethics,* Winter/Spring, 30-41.

Marsteller, P., & Karnchanapee, K. (1980). The use of women in the advertising of distilled spirits, 1956-1979. *Journal of Psychedelic Drugs, 12,* 1-12.

Mayes, L.C., Granger, R.H., Bornstein, M.H., & Zuckerman, B. (1992). The problem of prenatal cocaine exposure: A rush to judgment. *Journal of the American Medical Association, 267* (3), 406-408.

McKinlay, A.P. (1959). The Roman attitude toward women's drinking. In R.G. McCarthy (Ed.), *Drinking and intoxication* (pp. 58-61). New Haven, CT: Yale Center of Alcohol Studies.

Miller, B.A., Downs, W.R., & Gondoli, D.M. (1989). Spousal violence among alcoholic women as compared to a random household sample of women. *Journal of Studies on Alcohol, 50,* 533-540.

Moore, M.H., & Gerstein, D.R. (Eds.) (1981). *Alcohol and public policy: Beyond the shadow of prohibition.* Washington, DC: National Academy Press.

Musto, D.F. (1992). Historical perspectives on alcohol and drug abuse. In: J.H. Lowinson, P. Ruiz, & R.B. Millman (Eds). *Substance abuse: A comprehensive textbook* (pp. 2-14). Baltimore: Williams and Wilkins.

Nash, O. (1952). *Verses from 1929 on.* Boston: Little, Brown.

National Council on Alcoholism and Drug Dependence. (1987). *A federal response to a hidden epidemic: Alcohol and other drug problems among women.* New York: Author.

National Institute on Alcohol Abuse and Alcoholism. (1980). *Alcoholism and alcohol abuse among women: Research issues.* Proceedings of a Workshop, April 2-5, 1978, Jekyll Island, Georgia (NIAAA Research Monograph No. 1; DHEW Publication No. ADM 80-835). Washington, DC: U.S. Government Printing Office.

National Institute on Alcohol Abuse and Alcoholism. (1986). *Women and alcohol: Health related issues* (pp. 294-311). NIAAA Research Monograph No. 16; DHHS Publication No. ADM 86-1139). Washington, DC: U.S. Government Printing Office.

National Institute on Alcohol Abuse and Alcoholism. (1993). Working Group for Prevention Research on Women and Alcohol, Prevention Research Branch, NIAAA, Bethesda, MD, September 1993. Conference proceedings in preparation.

National Institute on Drug Abuse & National Institute on Alcohol Abuse and Alcoholism. (1991). *National Drug and Alcoholism Treatment Unit Survey (NDATUS): 1989 Main findings report* (DHHS Publication No. ADM 91-1729). Washington, DC: U.S. Government Printing Office.

Nelson, L.J., & Milliken, N. (1988). Compelled medical treatment of pregnant women. *Journal of the American Medical Association, 259* (7), 1060-1066.

New York State Division of Alcoholism and Alcohol Abuse. (1982). *Role of women in alcohol and highway safety: Alcoholism backgrounder.* Albany, NY: Author.

New York State Division of Alcoholism and Alcohol Abuse. (1992). *1991 report on special programming for women.* Albany, NY: Author.

New York State Family Court Act, Section 1012, 1981.

Older Women's League. (1992). *Critical condition: Midlife and older women in America's health care system.* Washington, DC: Author.

Palm Beach Post. (1991, March 30). Two fired over warning pregnant customer about alcohol, p. 12A.

Paltrow, L.M. (1990). When becoming pregnant is a crime. *Criminal Justice Ethics,* Winter/Spring, 41-47.

Paltrow, L.M. (1992, July 27). Memorandum to friends of Jennifer Johnson.

Peck, R.C., Arstein-Kerslake, G.W., & Helander, C.J. (1994). Psychometric and biographical correlates of drunk-driving recidivism and treatment program compliance. *Journal of Studies on Alcohol, 55,* 667-678.

People v. Stewart, No. M508197, San Diego Mun. Ct., February 26, 1987.

Reckman, L.W., Babcock, P., & O'Bryan, T. (1984). Meeting the child care needs of the female alcoholic. *Child Welfare 63,* 541-546.

Reyes v. Superior Court, 75 Cal. App. 3d 214, 1977.

Richardson, D., & Campbell, J.L. (1982). Alcohol and rape: The effect of alcohol on attributions of blame for rape. *Personality and Social Psychology Bulletin, 8,* 468-476.

Scott, D.C. (1983, July 29.). How spirits industry takes advantage of changing taste. *Christian Science Monitor.*

Shaver, D. (1989). Prosecute mothers of addiction. *National Center for Prosecution of Child Abuse Update, Special Issue, 3,* December 1989.

State of Wyoming v. Osmus, 276 Psd 469, 1954.

State v. Johnson, No. E89-890-CFA, Florida Circuit Ct., July 13, 1989.

State v. Pfannenstiel, No. 1-9-8 CR County Ct. of Laramie, WY, January 5, 1990.

Sternberger, S.S., & Drew, H. (1981). Women, health insurance and alcoholism. *Alcohol Health & Research World, 5,* 37-38.

U.S. Public Health Service. (1992). *A Public Health Service progress report on healthy people 2000: Alcohol and other drugs.* Washington, DC: Author.

Vegega, M.E., & Klein, T.M. (1992). Trends in alcohol related traffic fatalities, by sex: United States, 1982-1990. *Morbidity and Mortality Weekly Report, 41* (11): 195-197. Reprinted in *Journal of the American Medical Association, 268* (3), 313-314.

Waller, P.F., & Blow, F.C. (1995). Women, alcohol, and driving. In M. Galanter (Ed.), *Recent developments in alcoholism:Vol. 12.Alcoholism and women* (pp. 103-123). New York: Plenum.

Williams, G.D., Grant, B.F., Harford, T.C., & Noble, J. (1989). Population projections using DSM-III criteria: Alcohol abuse and dependence, 1990-2000. *Alcohol Health & Research World, 13,* 366-370.

Wilsnack, S.C. (1991). Barriers to treatment for alcoholic women. *Addiction and Recovery, 11,* 10-12.

Wilsnack, S.C., & Wilsnack, R.W. (1995). Drinking and problem drinking in US women: Patterns and recent trends. In M. Galanter (Ed.), *Recent developments in alcoholism: Vol. 12. Alcoholism and women* (pp. 29-60). New York: Plenum.

Winfield, I., George, L.K., Swartz, M., & Blazer, D.G. (1990). Sexual assault and psychiatric disorders among a community sample of women. *American Journal of Psychiatry, 147* (3), 335-341.

Yu, J., & Williford, W.R. (1995). Drunk-driving recidivism: Predicting factors from arrest context and case disposition. *Journal of Studies on Alcohol, 56,* 60-66.

Yu, J., Essex, D.T., & Williford, W.R. (1992). DWI/DWAI offenders and recidivism by gender in the eighties: A changing trend? *International Journal of the Addictions, 27,* 637-647.

Contributors

Catherine R. Ager, B.A., Institute for Health & Aging, Department of Social and Behavioral Sciences, University of California, San Francisco, California.

Nancy L. Asdigian, Ph.D., Family Research Laboratory, University of New Hampshire, Durham, New Hampshire.

Grace M. Barnes, Ph.D., Research Institute on Addictions, New York State Office of Alcoholism and Substance Abuse Services, and Department of Sociology, University at Buffalo, Buffalo, New York.

Terry C. Blum, Ph.D., DuPree School of Management, Ivan Allen College of Management, Policy and International Affairs, Georgia Institute of Technology, Atlanta, Georgia.

Sheila B. Blume, M.D., C.A.C., Alcoholism, Chemical Dependency and Compulsive Gambling Programs, South Oaks Hospital, Amityville, New York, and Department of Psychiatry, State University of New York at Stony Brook.

Arthur W.K. Chan, Research Institute on Addictions, New York State Office of Alcoholism and Substance Abuse Services, Buffalo, New York.

R. Lorraine Collins, Ph.D., Research Institute on Addictions, New York State Office of Alcoholism and Substance Abuse Services, Buffalo, New York.

Gerard J. Connors, Ph.D., Research Institute on Addictions, New York State Office of Alcoholism and Substance Abuse Services, Buffalo, New York.

M. Lynne Cooper, Ph.D., Department of Psychology, University of Missouri–Columbia, Columbia, Missouri.

Stephanie S. Covington, Ph.D., L.C.S.W., Institute for Relational Development, La Jolla, California.

Barbara A. Dintcheff, M.S., Research Institute on Addictions, New York State Office of Alcoholism and Substance Abuse Services, Buffalo, New York.

Michael P. Farrell, Ph.D., Department of Sociology, University at Buffalo, and Research Institute on Addictions, New York State Office of Alcoholism and Substance Abuse Services, Buffalo, New York.

Heidi P. Ferrer, B.S., Institute for Health & Aging, Department of Social and Behavioral Sciences, University of California, San Francisco, California.

Kaye Middleton Fillmore, Ph.D., Institute for Health & Aging, Department of Social and Behavioral Sciences, University of California, San Francisco, California.

Michael R. Frone, Ph.D., Research Institute on Addictions, New York State Office of Alcoholism and Substance Abuse Services, Buffalo, New York.

M. Jean Gilbert, Ph.D., Kaiser Permanente, Pasadena, California.

Jacqueline M. Golding, Ph.D., Institute for Health & Aging, Department of Social and Behavioral Sciences, University of California, San Francisco, California.

Edith S. Lisansky Gomberg, Ph.D., Department of Psychiatry, University of Michigan, Ann Arbor, Michigan.

Andrew C. Heath, D. Phil., Department of Psychiatry, Washington University School of Medicine, St. Louis, Missouri.

Michie N. Hesselbrock, Ph.D., School of Social Work, University of Connecticut, West Hartford, Connecticut.

Victor M. Hesselbrock, Ph.D., Department of Psychiatry, University of Connecticut Health Center, Farmington, Connecticut.

Rebecca Farmer Huselid, Ph.D., Department of Psychology, Hunter College of the City University of New York, New York, N.Y.

Glenda Kaufman Kantor, Ph.D., Family Research Laboratory, University of New Hampshire, Durham, New Hampshire.

Albert D. Klassen, M.A. (Retired), Department of Neuroscience, University of North Dakota School of Medicine and Health Sciences, Grand Forks, North Dakota.

E. Victor Leino, Ph.D., Division of Complementary Medicine, School of Medicine, University of Maryland at Baltimore, Baltimore, Maryland.

Kenneth E. Leonard, Ph.D., Research Institute on Addictions, New York State Office of Alcoholism and Substance Abuse Services, Buffalo, New York.

Charles S. Lieber, M.D., Alcohol Research and Treatment Center and G.I.-Liver and Nutritional Program, Bronx Veterans Affairs Medical Center, and Mt. Sinai School of Medicine, New York, New York.

Ruth E. Little, Sc.D., National Institute of Environmental Health Sciences, Epidemiology Branch, Research Triangle Park, North Carolina.

Pamela A.F. Madden, Ph.D., Department of Psychiatry, Washington University School of Medicine, St. Louis, Missouri.

Michelle Motoyoshi, M.A., Institute for Health & Aging, Department of Social and Behavioral Sciences, University of California, San Francisco, California.

Pamela Mudar, M.P.H., Research Institute on Addictions, New York State Office of Alcoholism and Substance Abuse Services, Buffalo, New York.

Kristi-Anne Tolo Passaro, Ph.D., Department of Epidemiology, School of Public Health, University of North Carolina, Chapel Hill, North Carolina.

Robert S. Peirce, Ph.D., Research Institute on Addictions, New York State Office of Alcoholism and Substance Abuse Services, Buffalo, New York.

Joseph J. Plaud, Ph.D., Department of Psychology, University of North Dakota, Grand Forks, North Dakota.

Linda J. Roberts, Ph.D., Department of Child and Family Studies, University of Wisconsin, Madison, Wisconsin.

Paul M. Roman, Ph.D., Center for Research on Deviance and Behavioral Health, University of Georgia, Athens, Georgia.

Marcia Russell, Ph.D., Research Institute on Addictions, New York State Office of Alcoholism and Substance Abuse Services, and Department of Social and Preventative Medicine, School of Medicine, University at Buffalo, Buffalo, New York.

Carlisle Shoemaker, M.A., Institute for Health & Aging, Department of Social and Behavioral Sciences, University of California, San Francisco, California.

Wendy S. Slutske, Ph.D., Department of Psychiatry, Washington University School of Medicine, St. Louis, Missouri.

Cathy Streifel, Ph.D., Department of Sociology, Purdue University, West Lafayette, Indiana.

Janet L. Surrey, Ph.D., Harvard Medical School and The Stone Center, Wellesley College, Wellesley, Massachusetts.

Howard Terry, M.A., Institute for Health & Aging, Department of Social and Behavioral Sciences, University of California, San Francisco, California.

Kimberly S. Walitzer, Ph.D., Research Institute on Addictions, New York State Office of Alcoholism and Substance Abuse Services, Buffalo, New York.

Helene Raskin White, Ph.D., Center of Alcohol Studies, Rutgers University, Piscataway, New Jersey.

Richard W. Wilsnack, Ph.D., Department of Neuroscience, University of North Dakota School of Medicine and Health Sciences, Grand Forks, North Dakota.

Sharon C. Wilsnack, Ph.D., Department of Neuroscience, University of North Dakota School of Medicine and Health Sciences, Grand Forks, North Dakota.

Index